D1541675

Recreating Hopewell

Florida A&M University, Tallahassee
Florida Atlantic University, Boca Raton
Florida Gulf Coast University, Ft. Myers
Florida International University, Miami
Florida State University, Tallahassee
University of Central Florida, Orlando
University of Florida, Gainesville
University of North Florida, Jacksonville
University of South Florida, Tampa
University of West Florida, Pensacola

Recreating Hopewell

Edited by Douglas K. Charles and Jane E. Buikstra

University Press of Florida
Gainesville/Tallahassee/Tampa/Boca Raton
Pensacola/Orlando/Miami/Jacksonville/Ft. Myers

Copyright 2006 by Douglas K. Charles and Jane E. Buikstra
Printed in the United States of America on acid-free, recycled paper
All rights reserved

11 10 09 08 07 06   6 5 4 3 2 1

A record of cataloging-in-publication data is available from
the Library of Congress.
ISBN 0-8130-2898-1

Chapter 4, "The Earthwork/Habitation Dichotomy: A Central
Problem of Ohio Hopewell" has been adapted from A. M. Byers'
The Hopewell Episode and is reprinted here with permission of the
Akron Press, copyright 2004 University of Akron. All rights reserved.

The University Press of Florida is the scholarly publishing agency
for the State University System of Florida, comprising Florida A&M
University, Florida Atlantic University, Florida Gulf Coast University,
Florida International University, Florida State University, University
of Central Florida, University of Florida, University of North Florida,
University of South Florida, and University of West Florida.

University Press of Florida
15 Northwest 15th Street
Gainesville, FL 32611-2079
http://www.upf.com

Contents

Figures

Tables

Preface

A primary stimulus for the conference "Perspectives on Middle Woodland at the Millennium" that preceded this volume was the one held in Ohio in 1977, which led to the compilation *Hopewell Archaeology: The Chillicothe Conference* (Brose and Greber 1979). Though more than two decades old at the time of the Center for American Archeology (CAA) conference in July 2000, that volume continues to exert an influence and is the most-cited book in the bibliography of the present work. Clearly, however, the time is ripe to revisit Middle Woodland and Hopewell in the Eastern Woodlands of North America. The lower Illinois Valley was a latecomer to Hopewellian studies, when compared with the Ohio and central Illinois valleys, but intense investigations by CAA researchers have amply documented the significance of this region during the Middle Woodland period (for example, Asch 1976; Asch and Asch 1978, 1985c; Brown 1979, 1981; Buikstra 1976, 1977, 1984, 1988; Buikstra and Charles 1999; Buikstra, Charles, and Rakita 1998; Charles 1992, 1995; Charles and Buikstra 2002; Charles, Leigh, and Buikstra 1988; Charles, Van Nest, and Buikstra 2005; Farnsworth 1973, 2004; Farnsworth and Asch 1986; Farnsworth and Koski 1985; Stafford and Sant 1985b; Struever 1960, 1964, 1965, 1968a, 1968b; Struever and Houart 1972; Van Nest et al. 2001; Wiant and McGimsey 1986b). Thus, it seemed entirely appropriate that the CAA host a conference on Hopewell in a location well known for Middle Woodland studies.

History of the Conference and Volume

The initial inspiration and fund-raising for the conference should be credited to Ken Farnsworth, then director of contract archaeology for the CAA. Ken had originally envisioned a conference patterned after the earlier, highly successful Early Woodland Conference that led to a definitive publication (Farnsworth and Emerson 1986). Ken actively pursued funding, with the able assistance of CAA board member Nick Maggos. As the result of a presentation by Ken at the Lockhaven Country Club in Alton, Illinois, a number of donors were inspired to help with this initiative: Drs. Dale and Linda Chapman; Jim Goodwin; Mr. and Mrs. Paul B. Hanks; Mr. and Mrs. John Helmkamp; Robert L. Higgins; Karl K. Hoagland Jr.; Mr. and Mrs. Tom K. Hutchinson; Paul R. Lauschke Jr.; J. Thomas Long; Nick G. Maggos; Rod A. St. Clair; and Harold J. Thomeczek. The CAA gratefully acknowledges this support, along with funding from the Howard Winters Fund of the CAA.

As plans proceeded, it became clear, however, that funding was not forthcoming both to hold the planned conference and publish the proceedings. At this point, the CAA decided to proceed with the conference, and organizational responsibility shifted to CAA president Jane Buikstra, assisted by Jodie O'Gorman, then director of research for the CAA.

The theme of the conference was altered at this juncture. The focus was shifted from generating a summary compendium anchoring the effort, as was originally envisioned, to planning a conference where those working on Middle Woodland issues could come together to share their newest ideas, including those that were not necessarily ready for publication. The conference, entitled "Perspectives on Middle Woodland at the Millennium," was therefore designed to share ideas and stimulate discussion.

In addition, the organizers decided to invite discussants whose theoretical, regional, and/or topical foci complemented those presenting Middle Woodland research. The rationale was that by adding these scholars to the mix, participants might be stimulated to think "outside the Middle Woodland box" of conventional wisdom. Thus, Lynne Goldstein was invited to consider the session entitled "Sacred Landscapes and Symbolism," and Bruce Smith was asked to discuss papers dealing with "Middle Woodland Settlements and Social Organization" (see Smith, this volume). Bonnie Styles presented a very entertaining reflection on the session entitled "Plants and Animals: Good to Eat . . . Good to Think." A special accent was added to the proceedings through the presence of the plenary speaker, Bob Chapman, from the University of Reading (UK). Bob has contributed to the literature on trade, mortuary monumentalism, and the rise of complexity for continental Europe and thus has an informed perspective from which to reflect on Middle Woodland. Bob also graciously agreed to serve as a discussant for the session entitled "Hopewell Trade and the Interaction Sphere Revisited." The final session, "Perspectives on Middle Woodland beyond Ohio and Illinois," did not have a discussant.

The conference spanned three days, July 19–21, 2000. The first session was held on Wednesday evening, followed by the second and third sessions on Thursday morning. Thursday afternoon included site tours of the Mound House and Golden Eagle sites, led by Julieann Van Nest, Doug Charles, and Jane Buikstra. As the result of the tour, there was consensus that Van Nest's interpretation of sod as a key structural element of Mound House Mound 1 was convincing and that the Golden Eagle earthwork does indeed exist (see Van Nest, this volume). Thursday evening, cocktails and dinner were followed by Bob Chapman's plenary lecture, entitled "Middle Woodland/Hopewell: A View from beyond the Periphery" (see Chapman, this volume). The final two sessions were held on Friday.

Plans to publish a volume from the conference were developed, with Jodie O'Gorman and Jane Buikstra as editors. In 1991 Jodie O'Gorman left her position at the CAA to become assistant professor of anthropology at Michigan State University and assistant curator of anthropology at the MSU Museum. Doug Charles arranged a partial leave from Wesleyan University to take over as part-time CAA director of research for a two-year period, and in that capacity he took over Jodie's role as editor.

Structure of the Volume

Not all of the participants in the conference opted to develop publishable versions of their papers, and some of the contributions have been substantially altered from their original form. Thus, during the review of the final submissions, a somewhat different structure than that of the original conference manifested itself, including a clear emphasis on the Hopewellian phenomenon of the Middle Woodland period. Chapters were grouped in terms of Hopewell in Ohio, Hopewell/Middle Woodland outside of Ohio, and new approaches to Hopewell material culture. In all three sections one message is clear: there is much research to be done in the realm of Hopewell/Middle Woodland archaeology. In many cases the authors of these chapters point out potentially profitable avenues. In the final section of the volume, Bruce Smith and Robert Chapman offer commentary and further suggestions for future research.

This volume is conceived as an update of and a companion to *Hopewell Archaeology: The Chillicothe Conference*. The latter book is very deep in historical scholarship, and those discussions have not been supplanted in the last quarter of a century. In that sense, deep historical documentation in this volume would be redundant. Furthermore, as the title *Recreating Hopewell* is meant to suggest, we see this volume as an outline for new directions for research. The literature being cited is that which the authors are using as their springboards. For example, Stuart Struever's (1968a, 1968b) seminal work on subsistence and settlement does in fact appear importantly in the chapters on the areas west of Ohio. In Ohio, archaeologists have recognized that his model is not particularly applicable in that region and that Olaf Prufer's (1964a, 1965) conception for Ohio is a more relevant starting point. At the same time, the specifics of Struever's mechanistic economic model for the operation of the Hopewell Interaction Sphere (Struever and Houart 1972) are now generally considered misguided, and various authors offer updated conceptions of the workings of the interaction sphere. In general, rather than employing a model of extensive citation (for a bibliography that is quite long as it stands), authors have tended toward referencing specifically relevant works. For example (and chosen as representative of the volume), in chapter 1, Paul Pacheco and William Dancey cite only two works in support of their approach to evolutionary archaeology, despite the existence of a vast literature on the topic. A case can be made, however, that Dunnell 1980 is the seminal work on this subject and that O'Brien and Lyman 2000 represents a current standard. Similarly, only three works are cited in regard to the "hearth of plant domestication," but Smith 1989 and 1992b and Cowan and Watson 1992 embody the primary statements of that notion.

For a variety of reasons this volume has been some time in seeing the light of day, and the editors would like to thank the contributors for their patience. We hope that they, and the other readers of this volume, will find that the wait was worthwhile. We think the contributors have produced a body of work that should readily find a place on bookshelves alongside *Hopewell Archaeology: The Chillicothe Conference*.

Section 1

Hopewell in Ohio

As is invariably the case in any comprehensive coverage of Hopewell, Ohio takes center stage. The intensity of material culture production we define as Hopewell—the earthworks and the exotic items—was seemingly an order of magnitude greater in Ohio than elsewhere during the Middle Woodland period. At present, two issues seem to dominate research into Ohio Hopewell: one revolves around the nature of Hopewellian communities, including their size and mobility and the related question of Hopewellian subsistence; the other involves the nature of, and the activities associated with, the numerous mounds and geometric earthworks. As a number of these chapters demonstrate, these two issues are often seen as intertwined.

Also reflected in these chapters is the historical condition in Ohio—that whereas much is known about the distribution and form of the earthworks, much less has been learned about either the internal structure and contents of the earthworks or the density, size, composition, and distribution of the domestic sites. It is clear, however, that this situation is changing.

Much of the recent debate on Hopewellian communities in Ohio was stimulated by William Dancey and Paul Pacheco's (1997a) dispersed sedentary community model, and their chapter appropriately leads off this section. Chapters 2–4 (Cowan; Yerkes; Byers) take that model as a starting point and offer alternative interpretations. All four of these chapters examine both occupation and earthwork sites. Chapters 5–9 (Greber; Seeman and Branch; Lepper; Sunderhaus and Blosser; Riordan) primarily focus on the distribution, dating, construction, and use of the earthworks, with each chapter bringing important new data or perspectives to bear on these fascinating sites.

1

Integrating Mortuary and Settlement Data on Ohio Hopewell Society

Paul J. Pacheco and William S. Dancey

In this chapter we evaluate and synthesize current understandings of Ohio Hopewell, taking into consideration the growing body of available settlement data. Our goal is to integrate the mortuary-ceremonial aspect of Ohio Hopewell, embodied in mound-earthwork research, with settlement pattern research. In a sense, we hope to bridge the dichotomy between the ceremonial and domestic spheres, which represents the central mystery of Hopewell archaeology (Smith 1992b). We adopt an evolutionary archaeology paradigm (Dunnell 1980; O'Brien and Lyman 2000) and a panregional perspective to address a series of five questions about Ohio Hopewell populations. For this approach we assume that regional-scale settlement data are strongly related to the size, food-getting strategy, and complexity of the populations producing them (Binford 1964, 1980). Since mortuary practices are embedded in the social group, they should bear some relationship to other properties of a group, especially since settlement distributions provide the context in which they originated and were maintained.

The evolutionary archaeology approach is reflected in our synthesis by the emphasis we place on both documenting and explaining variation. It was with this in mind that one of us raised questions about the utility of time-honored cultural historical units for exploring issues concerning prehistoric social variation and cultural change (Dancey 1996b). The standard practice of summarizing archaeological data within a fabric of typologies of sites, artifacts, phases, and cultures leads to such constructs as Hopewell, Adena, Newtown, Peters, and Intrusive Mound. Such an approach risks suppressing variation and breaking the flow of time (Plog 1974). In the case of Hopewell, there are numerous independent lines of evidence that indicate significant temporal and spatial cultural variation within the middle Ohio Valley. The presence and probable meaning of this variation at the scale of tangible cultural groups suggests that the concept of a far-reaching Hopewell culture or phase has no inherent meaning beyond perhaps the highest levels of the Hopewell Interaction Sphere (Caldwell 1964; Greber 1991; Pacheco 1996a; Prufer 1964a, 1997b; Seeman 1979b, 1996).

Evolutionary archaeology, by contrast, attempts to look at the record directly by treating each case on its own, with the hope that temporal estimates can be precise and accurate as well as provide representative spatial data (Dunnell 1989, 1992). Precise temporal control is preferred in testing evolutionary hypotheses, although even crude order can depict the basic outline of population change. The spatial data potentially include measures of population distribution, density, and internal variation. Available regional-scale survey data show that knowledge of how subregional or local Ohio Hopewell populations evolve can be acquired through close examination and systematic research of local areas (see Carskadden and Morton 1996, 1997; Genheimer 1997; Pacheco 1996a, 1997; Prufer and McKenzie 1967). An evolutionary theme is also reflected in viewing this problem as part of a larger one involving the origin and spread of agriculture (Dancey and Pederson 1999; Rindos 1980, 1984), a question that has been central to anthropological research since the beginning.

The middle Ohio Valley, the focus of this study, lies at the northern and eastern edge of the midwestern region that has been well documented as an independent hearth of plant domestication and agriculture (Cowan and Watson 1992; Smith 1989, 1992b). The Ohio River runs from east to west through the region, and the escarpment of the Appalachian Plateau cuts through it from northeast to southwest. Pleistocene glaciers expanded over much of the northern part of the region, providing the clearest geomorphologic feature on the Middle Woodland landscape. The Ohio River originates in the plateau but exits it to flow across the Low Interior Plateau. Several secondary stream systems on the northern part of the region originate on the Till Plain. Two of the river systems cut through the plateau, following a preglacial drainage, to get to the Ohio. Two others drain Till Plain deposits exclusively. Climate in the region is continental. During Middle Woodland times there existed a diverse Carolinian fauna in a rich deciduous forest broken by pockets of prairie that increase in size and frequency to the west.

What Was the Prevailing Subsistence System?

Possibly the easiest question to answer concerns the nature of the prevailing subsistence system, because the verdict appears final that Eastern Woodland peoples, including Hopewellians, regularly consumed the seeds of domesticated plants (Cowan 1978; Ford 1979; Gremillion 1993; Smith 1989, 1992b; Wymer 1996). It is not clear, however, what percentage of their diet came from cultigens. Our own preferred perspective is derived from Rindos (1980, 1984) and his differentiation between incipient, domesticatory, and agricultural societies. The coevolution of domesticated plants with Eastern Woodland peoples appears to have stabilized settlement systems, facilitating sedentism, but not to have freed the human group from dependence on natural reproductive cycles, particularly in terms of hunting. We concur with Diamond's (1999) argument that from an evolutionary (that is, historical) standpoint, the lack of domesticatable animals in eastern North America placed obvious constraints on the niche opportunities of Native American societies residing here, affecting, for example, the evolution, distribution, and function of settlements on the landscape.

Most misunderstandings about the Hopewellian niche revolve around terminology. An important example of such confusion is the issue of whether or not the Ohio Hopewell were farmers. Wymer (1992, 1996, 1997) argues convincingly that available evidence confirms that Ohio Hopewell populations cultivated domesticated varieties of plants such as chenopodium, marsh elder, maygrass, erect knotweed, sunflower, and squash. Given the life cycles of these plants, Wymer posits that Hopewellian people cut small garden plots out of the mature deciduous forests. These gardens were tended and maintained until productivity decreased, at which time they were allowed to go fallow. She also argues that local biomass improved as a result of this gardening system (that is, berries and hazelnuts would have thrived along the edge of gardens, improving forage for deer and other animals). The overall effect is a coevolved symbiotic relationship between the Hopewellians and their landscape, not just their plant complex (see also N. Asch and D. Asch 1985; Crites 1987). Thus Wymer, like Smith (1992b), sees the Hopewellians as farmers.

Nevertheless, these Hopewellians were not farmers in the classic model of Neolithic society established by Old World archaeologists (for example, Braidwood 1963; Childe 1952). Similarly, they were not farmers in the sense of the later North American Mississippian societies either. The concomitant changes in settlement hierarchy and labor organization associated with the transition to full-fledged agricultural societies that occurred in Neolithic and Mississippian populations is not reflected in Ohio Hopewell. Obviously the ecology and energy potential of the domesticated Hopewellian plants is at the heart of the issue, regardless of where one's bias lies.

From our perspective, the widespread distribution of natural food waste at known settlements like Murphy (Dancey 1991), McGraw (Prufer 1965), or Jennison Guard (Blosser 1996; Kozarek 1997) suggests that the Hopewellian subsistence quest is largely tied to cycles of naturally reproducing plants and animals. If that is true, Ohio Hopewell would represent a domesticatory society (Rindos 1980): one that possesses domesticates but is not dependent upon them. This viewpoint makes moot the question of whether or not the Hopewell were farmers but clearly demarcates them from hunter-gatherers. We find Rindos' perspective on the problem to be thought provoking and see a strong correspondence between it and Caldwell's (1958) classic argument that Hopewell represents a culmination of primary forest efficiency, a symbiotic subsistence technology evolving in the post-Pleistocene Eastern Woodlands. Coevolving interrelationships between humans and species of seed plants selected from the forest flora would be the expected outcome of this process. We view the vast majority of Middle Woodland data as representative of populations broken up into regionally homogeneous groups. These groups aggregated at socially prescribed central places at certain times during the year, but in general they were dispersed across the landscape in a complex coevolved relationship between themselves and the plants and animals upon which they depended.

What Is the Prevailing Settlement Pattern
for Ohio Hopewell Populations?

Most of the controversies within Hopewellian studies in the middle Ohio Valley concern the interpretation of settlement data, which have slowly become more abundant over the past few decades. Increased reporting and study beginning in the 1960s has led to a number of competing hypotheses as to what the record means. We support and formalize the model first described by Olaf Prufer (Prufer 1964a, 1965, 1997b; Prufer and McKenzie 1967), which we refer to as the dispersed sedentary community model (Dancey and Pacheco 1997a; see also Pacheco 1988, 1996a). According to this model, Hopewellian communities consisted of single or multiple sedentary household units dispersed across the landscape and sharing centrally located corporate space. While not necessarily including permanent facilities or monuments, in the Hopewellian case the corporate spaces came to be filled to varying degrees by such features as mounded and unmounded mortuary facilities, nonmortuary wooden architecture, and ritual earthen architecture. The mound and earthwork centers, as they are commonly referred to, provided the setting for institutionalized, routinized, recurring communitywide social interaction of many types.

On the basis of our research in the central Muskingum–Licking region and a review of the literature, known Hopewell habitation sites located away from earthworks and mounds fall into two broadly defined categories (Dancey and Pacheco 1997a). The first group represents small, short-term extraction camps (Pacheco 1988). This group includes a few upland rockshelters, although in general, use of the uplands appears to have been limited (Seeman 1996). These camps are interpreted to be the product of logistical mobility, a strategy in which resources are moved to the people by work groups, as opposed to a residential mobility strategy in which the entire group seasonally moves to the resources (Binford 1980, 1982; Kozarek 1997).

The second category of occupation sites represents dispersed sedentary households. In a sample of more than ninety cases, we have documented a high degree of functional and structural redundancy suggestive of broadly equivalent sedentary households, which follows closely upon Prufer's interpretation of the McGraw site (Dancey and Pacheco 1997a; Pacheco 1988; Prufer 1965). Limited available research suggests that contemporaneous household sites are spaced 300–500 meters apart (Genheimer 1997; Pacheco 1997). Variation among documented households is best explained as the product of duration as opposed to seasonality (Dancey 1992a). The internal organization of several well-documented Middle Woodland settlements is shown in figure 1.1. Households were reproductive and economic units, typically consisting of a single, possibly extended family. Documented structures, when excavated, are relatively large. In some cases, individual households appear to have grown through time to include several generations of the reproductive unit. This growth produces a complex archaeological record (fig. 1.2).

At a slightly larger scale, subregional settlement patterns can be revealing,

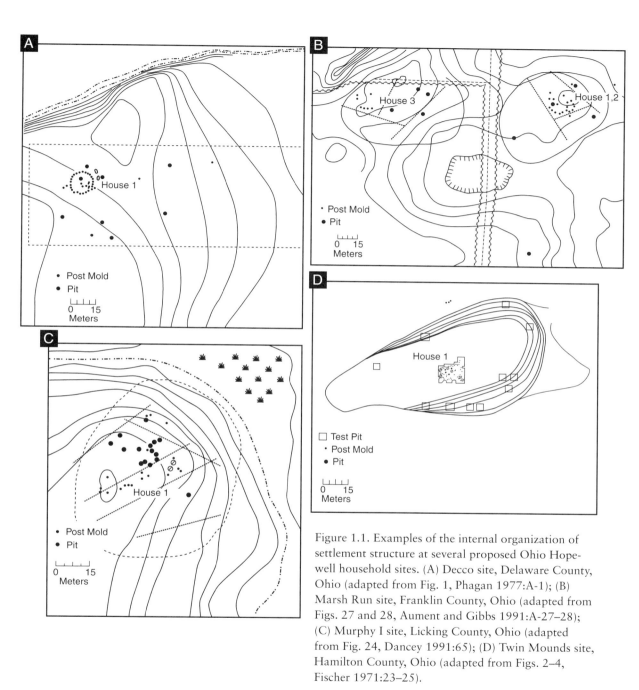

Figure 1.1. Examples of the internal organization of settlement structure at several proposed Ohio Hopewell household sites. (A) Decco site, Delaware County, Ohio (adapted from Fig. 1, Phagan 1977:A-1); (B) Marsh Run site, Franklin County, Ohio (adapted from Figs. 27 and 28, Aument and Gibbs 1991:A-27–28); (C) Murphy I site, Licking County, Ohio (adapted from Fig. 24, Dancey 1991:65); (D) Twin Mounds site, Hamilton County, Ohio (adapted from Figs. 2–4, Fischer 1971:23–25).

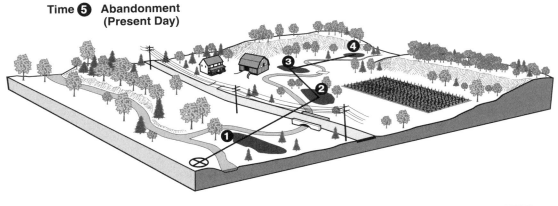

Time ⑤ Abandonment (Present Day)

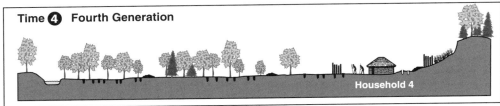

Time ④ Fourth Generation

Household 4

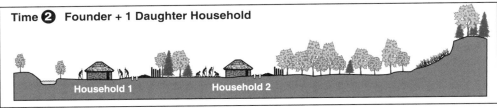

Time ③ Founder Offspring + Daughter

Household 2   Household 3

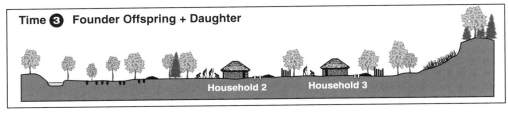

Time ② Founder + 1 Daughter Household

Household 1   Household 2

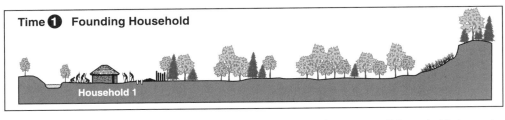

Time ① Founding Household

Household 1

Figure 1.2. Interpretation of the developmental history of the Ohio Hopewell households located within the Murphy Tract, Licking County, Ohio (Pacheco 1997:57–59).

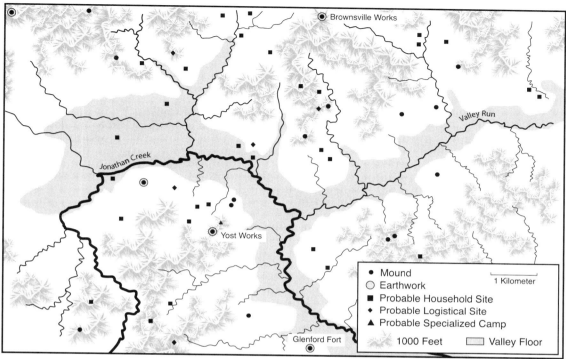

Figure 1.3. Map of all known mounds, earthworks, and Ohio Hopewell settlements within the upper Jonathan Creek subregion, Licking and Perry counties, Ohio. Figure adapted from Fig. 2:11, Pacheco 1996a:30–31. With permission from The Ohio Archaeological Council.

too, as seen in figure 1.3, which shows the locations of probable Middle Woodland settlements along a portion of upper Jonathan Creek in east-central Ohio. This case illustrates the nature of household dispersion. Significantly, some of the settlements cluster in small groups that appear to represent the evolution of household units, as in figure 1.2. Using our model, we can predict in general what the internal organization of sites and regional distributions will look like.

In contrast, the alternative models that have been proposed do not fit available data. The nucleated sedentary model (Converse 1993, 1994; Griffin 1996) requires that all members of a community lived together throughout most, if not all, of a year. As of yet, this evidence has not been found for the early and middle periods of Middle Woodland (circa 100 B.C.–A.D. 300). Cases of incipient or nucleated settlements appear in the late Middle Woodland period, especially during the fifth century, and logically represent the precursors of the nucleated pattern that came to characterize Late Woodland (Burks and Dancey 1999; Carskadden and Morton 1996; Dancey 1992b, 1996b, 1998). Most data point toward community dispersion until at least A.D. 400 in the Ohio Hopewell core area.

The central-place chiefdom model (Lazazzera 2000) similarly has little support. This model posits a social division between elites and commoners, who are tied together via economic redistribution. The evidence for the model is said to be the presence at central places (that is, the earthworks) of large houses, high-quality materials, large storage units, and artifacts obtained from members of the community and from adjacent communities. This explanation proposes that the elites lived adjacent to or within the earthworks and that the earthwork complexes functioned as redistribution points in panregional exchange. Lazazzera (2000) has proposed this interpretation for the Fort Ancient Works, where a cluster of seven structural post-mold patterns was recently discovered during salvage excavations. She views these structures as the village of elite members of the society who deliberately chose to live in the shadows of the dead.

A more conservative explanation for these structural remains is that the Fort Ancient structures are similar to those found with increasing frequency in and among other earthworks (Baby and Langlois 1979; Brown 1982; Cowan, Sunderhaus, and Genheimer 2000). Domestic debris is virtually absent in the majority of these cases, and evidence of rebuilding is rare. While the earthworks and burial mound centers clearly were the loci of single or infrequent constructions of pole structures, they were not elite residences. These structures may have served a variety of different functions, including but not limited to guest/dignitary housing, craft workshops (as Baby and Langlois [1979] argued), or perhaps even exclusive spaces like men's or women's clubs.

In proposing a monolithic construct like the dispersed sedentary community model, our intent is not to suppress variation. Rather, we see the model as describing the parameters of a dynamic process of cultural variation and community evolution (Dancey 1992b, 1996b, 1998). Each region or subregion of Ohio Hopewell would have had its own history of success and failure resulting in cultural variation at the community and household scale. The model only provides an explanation of why the Hopewell communities were dispersed and provides the general parameters of their settlement systems. It does not predict or describe the independent trajectories of each community. This type of variation has been documented at a number of localities: Fort Ancient (Connolly 1996a, 1997); Granville (Pacheco 1997); Harness (Coughlin and Seeman 1997); Philo, Rix Mills, and Dresden (Carskadden and Morton 1996, 1997); Pollock (Riordan 1995, 1996); Salt Creek (Church and Ericksen 1997); Seip and Baum (Greber 1997); Stubbs (Genheimer 1997); Twin-Creek (Keener and Biehl 1999); and Cowan, Sunderhaus, and Genheimer 2000.

We feel that the dispersed sedentary community model applies in general outline to the central Scioto, central Muskingum–Licking, and the Great and Little Miami regions of Ohio Hopewell and probably to other nearby large clusters as well (for example, Marietta and Portsmouth). Variation in settlement patterns along the periphery of the Ohio Hopewell core, in places like eastern Indiana (Cochran 1996), the Hocking River valley (Greber 1991; Murphy 1989), and the southern part of the central Muskingum Valley (Carskadden and Morton 1996) are of great interest. Such variations provide the source for cultural changes that potentially came to affect the entire middle Ohio Valley (Dancey 1998). At various sites throughout the middle Ohio Valley (for example, Lichliter [Allman 1957], Pyles [Railey 1984], Rogers [Kreinbrink 1992], and Hansen [Ahler 1992]), there is evidence as early as the fourth century A.D. of a shift in the organization of human society. Ultimately this shift led people away from rituals and interactions that artificially bound together their dispersed groups (Fuller 1981; Railey 1991).

Smith (1992b) views dispersed farming as the basic pattern for all Middle Woodland communities. It is significant to point out that while his sample includes Ohio, he draws largely on data from Tennessee and Illinois, where the bias against settlement research is not as ingrained. The spectacular mounds and earthworks in the Ohio area drew attention away from settlement archaeology, whereas in areas with few or no earthworks and modest burial mounds, documentation of the settlement pattern is vastly more robust. Now that settlement data are accumulating on Ohio Hopewell, it appears that Smith's model requires modification. As has been done before us, we picture the Middle Woodland landscape across the Midwest, and even beyond, as including different levels of investment in mortuary-related earthen architecture. In the middle Ohio Valley, community investment in this practice extended over several hundred years in some cases. Coexisting with these earthwork-building communities were those practicing mound burial. These more conservative communities predominate in Illinois and Tennessee, although there is evidence of earthworks at sites like Pinson and Mann. This would appear to be a significant regional distinction probably indicative in some way of sociocultural complexity (Seeman 1979b: 390–407). It also suggests that there are qualitative differences between regional expressions of the Hopewellian leitmotif.

Why Are the Ohio Hopewell Dispersed and Sedentary?

There are occasional upland and hinterland sites throughout the region that contain Hopewell components, but, as Seeman (1996) has documented for rockshelters, these were utilized sparingly and sporadically. Jonah's Run (Brose and White 1979) is a well-documented example of an excavated hinterland hunting site (fig. 1.4). Assemblage composition at Jonah's Run contrasts directly with proposed household sites: there is little debitage, and tools are common. As explained before, this site would be considered a logistical site from the standpoint of our model.

The rest of the well-documented Hopewell sites are dispersed, are relatively small, and tend to cluster in regions with mounds and earthworks. The problem becomes one of interpretation. Are sites like McGraw, Overly, Decco, Dow #2, Murphy, Murphy III, Cox B, Twin Mounds, Jennison Guard, Marsh Run, and Madiera Brown the remains of sedentary households, as we contend, or seasonal camps (Church and Ericksen 1997; Cowan, this volume; Lepper and Yerkes 1997; Yerkes 1988, 1990, 1994, this volume)? We would argue that this seasonal mobility model is not supported by the preponderance of available

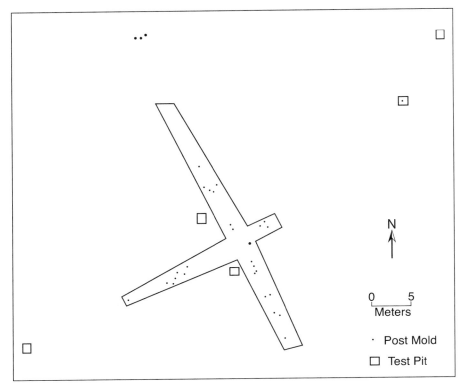

Figure 1.4. Settlement structure of Jonah's Run site, a proposed upland Ohio Hope-well logistical site, showing excavated trench and test units. Figure adapted from Fig. 9, Brose and White 1979:216.

evidence. Our reasons are varied and have been presented in detail elsewhere (Dancey 1992a; Dancey and Pacheco 1997a; Pacheco 1993, 1996a). Here we will try to synthesize the argument for sedentism and then address why sedentism and dispersion describe the Ohio Hopewell case.

Sedentary and mobile settlement systems produce qualitatively different ar-chaeological deposits (table 1.1). The underlying principle is that the continual relocation of the settlement, whether on a seasonal or an annual basis, entails a very different group-place relationship than that found among stationary groups. A sedentary group stays put on the plot marked out, with anticipated use of space in mind when the settlement was founded, whereas a mobile group potentially changes activity locations with every return to the same place (Kent 1992). Because of this, sedentary settlements can be expected to have main-tained space and a clear archaeological signature of settlement layout, while nonsedentary settlements have low maintenance and clarity (Murray 1980).

Relatively small Hopewell refuse deposits are easily recognized during survey and excavations, and all of the proposed sedentary household sites listed above contain such deposits (Dancey 1991, 1992a, 1998; Pacheco 1988, 1993, 1996a, 1997). This includes the famous McGraw site, where excavations were con-

Table 1.1. Some Contrastive Properties of the Archaeological Deposits of Sedentary and Mobile Settlement Types

Deposit Property	Settlement Type	
	Sedentary	Mobile
Maintenance of settlement space	High	Low
Degree of layout clarity	High	Low
Incidence of artifact fragmentation	High	Low
Incidence of recycled tools	High	Low
Distribution of historical types	Aggregated	Dispersed

Source: Rafferty 1985.

ducted exclusively in a sealed refuse deposit (Prufer 1965). Furthermore, Kozarek has elegantly applied this line of reasoning to her interpretation of a year-round sedentary occupation at the Jennison Guard site, while Dancey (1991) has done similarly for the Murphy site.

Notable differences between sites are best explained as the product of site duration (Dancey 1992a). The effect of differential duration can be seen in variations among settlements, with deposits losing clarity the longer they are continuously occupied (fig. 1.1). The only exceptions are refuse deposits, which become denser and clearer as time goes on. Some sites consist of only one or two structures with a few cooking pits, various basin-shaped facilities, and small low-density refuse dumps (for example, Decco and Madiera Brown). At the other end of the scale are those sites with dozens of pit features, rebuilt structures, and dense refuse deposits (for example, Murphy and Twin Mounds). The other cases are intermediate between these two extremes (for example, Marsh Run, Cox B, Murphy III, and Jennison Guard).

The proponents of seasonal mobility for Hopewell cite different data sets as evidence that these sites were not continuously occupied: seasonality of plant remains (Church and Ericksen 1997), edge wear patterns (Yerkes 1988, 1990, 1994), biface-dominated lithic assemblages (Cowan this volume), and the existence of semipermanent structures within and around the earthworks (Cowan, this volume; Lepper and Yerkes 1997). Similarly, the wide ranges of radiocarbon dates for McGraw and Murphy have been interpreted as evidence for palimpsests of repeated occupation at widely different times (Carr and Haas 1996; Clay 1998). We do not view these observations as inconsistent with our position that the households are sedentary. It is more of a quibble about the number of, and length of, occupations at each site. Importantly, none of the positions taken by these various authors provides explanations for the maintained living spaces at these sites. As a whole, they tend to say little about the overall structure of the archaeological record.

Yet the reason for sedentary dispersion remains poorly explained. Why did the Ohio Hopewell distribute themselves in this pattern? From our perspective, the answer to this question is an evolutionary one involving the creation, use, and maintenance of the Hopewellian niche. Once again we would mention

Caldwell's (1958) concept of primary forest efficiency, because it is important to recognize that the accumulation of knowledge about seasonal scheduling of subsistence labor evolved as part of a long-term process of human-land interaction beginning in the Late Pleistocene. It was within this context that the coevolutionary relationships between humans and plants evolved and led to domestication and gardening by dispersed sedentary groups.

Put simply, the Hopewell were dispersed and sedentary because this was part of a long-term trajectory of evolving human-land relationships in which local Woodland peoples utilized their environment through a pattern of dispersion arranged at the scale of households (Wymer 1996). As households decreased the size of their catchments, and thus their mobility, while at the same time increasing the dependability of their harvests, maintenance of social boundaries and human relationships provided a social stimulus for the mound and earthwork phenomenon. Thus, even though concepts like sedentism and dispersion are poorly defined concepts of what are no doubt complex continuums of mobility and group organizational structure, the essence of the evolutionary argument is clear. Ohio Hopewell people built mounds and earthworks and engaged in the many-faceted forms of symbolic display and exchange because people were spread across favorable landscapes in a network of stable household-scale catchments.

Middle Woodland populations throughout the Eastern Woodlands were classic generalists who utilized a wide variety of resources, including cultigens (Crites 1987; Kozarek 1997; Wymer 1992). Subsistence data from widely varying environments are overall quite similar, indicating a broad pattern of small-scale artificial ecosystems dependent on the garden patches cut into the mature deciduous forests (Wymer 1996). In addition to the high-yielding cultivated plants that Smith (1989, 1992b) documents, nuts from hickory and hazelnut trees in particular were of primary importance, but nuts from black walnut and butternut trees as well as acorns were also collected (Wymer 1987a). These nut trees prefer different habitats and would have produced inconsistent yields from year to year, adding another level of patchiness to the niche (Ford 1979:236). Nonetheless, net combined yields within a catchment area of 26 square kilometers are staggering; estimates vary between 250,000 and 1,000,000 bushels of harvestable mast (Munson, Parmalee, and Yarnell 1971:414–415). Presumably, dense patches of berries, tubers, and greens would also have been seasonally available in mature deciduous woodlands, especially in disturbed areas (Kozarek 1997).

Human disturbance was crucial to the character of the local Hopewellian niche in the Licking Valley:

> Middle Woodland populations were creating, in the immediate vicinity of their living spaces, limited, but deliberately induced open environments by cutting and maintaining clearings in the dense forest. These clearings in the local ecosystem resulted in artificial patchy environment and enhancement of local resource diversity. Abandoned and overgrown

gardens would have increased the diversity of both floral and faunal resources, hence making them more attractive to humans. Thus, although the horticultural activities at each individual hamlet were relatively small-scale (certainly when compared to the later and larger Late Woodland settlements), the cumulative effects of a dispersed series of hamlets throughout the valley may have created a significant impact on the resource base of the Licking Valley. (Wymer 1997:161)

For example, berries and hazelnuts do best in secondary growth contexts (Wymer 1987a). N. B. Asch and D. L. Asch (1985:53) have proposed that controlled burning was used to stimulate the growth of hazelnut and other selected nut trees, such as hickory and oak, that are fire resistant. Palynological research at Cliff Palace Pond in Kentucky has demonstrated that fire was a tool in the human utilization of the landscape as early as the Late Archaic (Delcourt et al. 1998). Open edges promote foraging by forest mammals, especially white-tailed deer and raccoon. Thus, Hopewell forest clearance would have improved the local resource base beyond promoting the propagation of the cultigens.

While faunal remains generally tend to be poorly preserved at Ohio Hopewell habitation sites, there are good records from McGraw (Prufer 1965) and Jennison Guard (Blosser 1996; Kozarek 1997). Faunal remains are better known from Illinois Hopewell domestic sites (Munson, Parmalee, and Yarnell 1971), providing a baseline for comparison. The pattern of faunal use that emerges is clear: not surprisingly, white-tailed deer were by far the most important animal resource (Ford 1979). Estimates of consumable proportions of meat utilized at these sites range from 70 percent to 92 percent. Over three dozen other species round out the animal resource base (Reidhead 1981).

Deer densities in Eastern Woodland temperate forest biomes have been estimated at between 10 and 85 individuals per 2.59 square kilometers, with an average of 15.4 deer per square kilometer (Shelford 1963:26–28). While some have cautioned against overextending this density figure (for example, Starna and Relethford 1985:826–828), it should be clear from the above discussion that Hopewellian land clearance practices would improve, rather than reduce, deer forage and thus would increase deer densities. Deer herds can sustain predation rates nearing 50 percent without an appreciable decline in numbers, especially with preferential culling of males and the ability of female deer to spontaneously twin when conditions are favorable (Shelford 1963; Shriver 1987).

Single-hunter stalking techniques, including tree stands, produce the highest success rates for hunters of white-tailed deer (Reidhead 1981:129). Group drives actually decrease the overall ratio of meat kilocalories to labor by over half (Reidhead 1981:128). The relative efficiencies of different white-tailed deer hunting strategies appear to result from several factors, including a lack of significant herding behavior, habitual use of trails, a regimented daily cycle, and restricted home foraging ranges. Hoekstra (1972:188–192) estimates the mean home range of white-tailed deer to vary between 1.6 and 3.2 kilometers from a

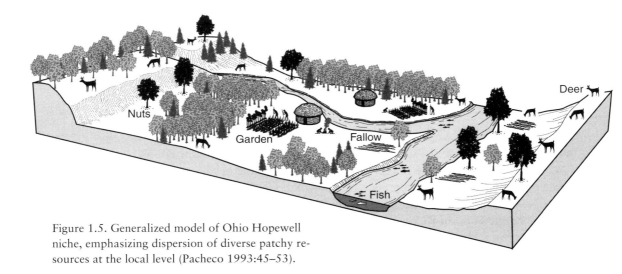

Figure 1.5. Generalized model of Ohio Hopewell niche, emphasizing dispersion of diverse patchy resources at the local level (Pacheco 1993:45–53).

central location (like the birthing spot). Therefore, deer represent a fairly evenly dispersed but mobile resource, best exploited by skilled individual hunters.

As an ecological response to the availability and predictability of food resources, group dispersion is favored by organisms when resources are evenly dispersed, stable, and homogeneous (Horn 1968). A similar response has been shown to be applicable to human foraging/collecting populations (Harpending and Davis 1977). In contrast, coarse-grained patchy resource distributions favor group aggregation, while mobile clumped resource distributions are most successfully exploited by mobile foragers (MacArthur and Pianka 1966).

As outlined above, the niche of Ohio Hopewell populations can be considered stable, with generalized exploitation of relatively predictable but independently patchy resources. When considered from the standpoint of the aggregate 10-square-kilometer catchment, however, the patchiness of the resource base is evened out into a dispersed homogeneous pattern. Therefore, paradoxically, the Hopewell pattern of a generalized use of diverse species, each possessing underlying patchy distributions, in combination with dispersed land clearance for gardens, produces a net pattern of evenly distributed and predictable resources (fig. 1.5). Therefore, within local regions or communities, dispersed households should show broadly similar catchments. Kozarek's (1997) analysis of adjacent catchments near the Jennison Guard site confirms this pattern.

Ohio Hopewell populations were dispersed and sedentary because of their niche. Small reliable catchments favored sedentism, and the set of resources in them—especially the all-important deer—was best exploited by small, dispersed groups organized at the scale of households. Use of mounds and earthworks by these populations implies that community-level catchments were corporately owned by lineage-based descent groups (Railey 1991). Such corporate identity is reflected in territorial behavior that is marked by the distribution of mounds and earthworks. Thus, dispersion, territoriality, and use of earthwork mound centers by lineage-based descent groups evolved as an ecological relationship involving people, their environment, and resource distributions.

How Well Does the Distribution and Variation of Mortuary (Mound and Earthwork) Sites and Symbolic Traits Fit the Proposed Settlement Model?

Figure 1.6 shows a map of earthworks in Ohio excluding only sites consisting of a defensive moat and/or embankment of a type that is known to occur in the Late Woodland (Dancey 1992b). All other recorded cases are included, without

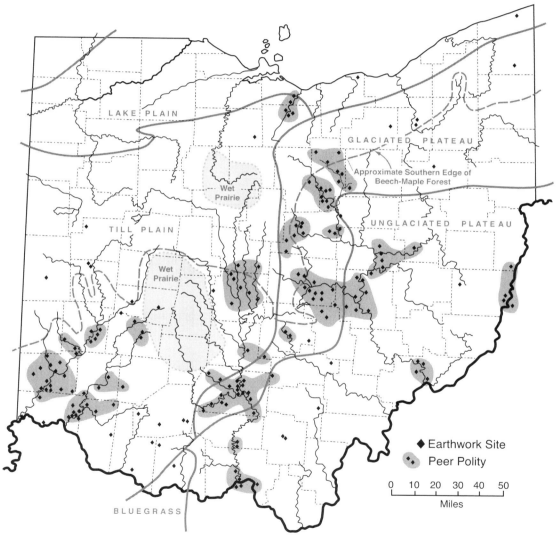

Figure 1.6. Distribution of earthworks and proposed Ohio Hopewell polities. All known earthworks are included on this map except those affiliated with Late Woodland villages. Polities represent contiguous groups of two or more earthworks affiliated with mounds of known Ohio Hopewell origin within the same or related drainages. Figure adapted from Fig. 1, Pacheco 1993:14.

an attempt to distinguish between Hopewell and Adena constructions. Fragmentary figures are included because a formation process approach would assume that construction terminates at the abandonment of the practice. This also allows for the inclusion of the sites that have been more recently damaged.

Not taking into account differential lengths of occupation and construction, it would appear that the area was widely inhabited by earthwork builders, although with strong avoidance of marsh and prairie. We see also differing densities corresponding to the regional terrain and to the width of valley systems. The map appears to be a map of real Middle Woodland communities. Evidence suggests that there were changes in preferred earthwork shapes through time, probably beginning with circles and ending with circle-square combinations and causeways (DeBoer 1997). If this is true, the distribution was widest early and had shrunk to locations along the interface between the Till Plain and the Glaciated Plateau when the practice of constructing earthworks was in decline around A.D. 400.

Early maps of mound distributions on a state level corroborate this pattern, providing strong evidence for regional and subregional clustering (Dancey 1984; Mills 1914). Even if one doubts some of the information in Mills' *Archaeological Atlas of Ohio,* the obvious barren areas, the high densities corresponding to the complexity of associated earthworks, and the relationship of the distribution to terrain ruggedness are striking. If nothing else, such a map probably points to the general character of population size, history, and composition. A nearest-neighbor analysis of mound spacing along the Licking and Muskingum rivers in Ohio showed that mounds formed regularly spaced (that is, dispersed) clusters and that the individual clusters contained a mix of mound sizes with larger mounds tending to cluster within larger groups (Pacheco 1989). Not surprisingly, it is mostly the largest mounds that have survived modern development.

Earthwork shapes and construction history vary greatly, as do burial mound construction and burial practice. Recent research has clarified two aspects of Hopewell mound and earthwork sizes and shapes. Regarding size, it is clear that few burial mounds or earthwork complexes were single-event constructions (DeBoer 1997; Greber 1997; Riordan 1995, 1996; Wymer, Lepper, and Pickard 1992). Although Connolly (1996a) argues for predetermined, long-range design for Fort Ancient, we suspect that in most cases choices were situational. This means, of course, that the archaeological presence of earthworks is the way they looked at the end of their use-life. By extension, the symbolic "message" that structural archaeologists derive from the earthwork only existed as the coherent symbol of interest after its abandonment.

Hopewellian portable art was richly varied and only partially preserved. A wide variety of mineral and biological materials are known archaeologically, and it seems likely that perishable materials such as wood were also used extensively, as has been documented for Middle Woodland societies in Florida (Purdy 1991). All glittery materials were prized, especially mica, copper, and shell. Musical instruments, mythical beings, figurines—Hopewell has it all. Symbols were limited to a standard set of themes. It would seem hard to believe that Hopewellian art is not an expression of social, cultural, and psychological properties of Middle Woodland populations. In the present case we are, of course, interested in the covariation between population density, settlement pattern, and environment at a variety of social scales: intrahousehold, interhousehold (that is, community), regional or intercommunity (that is, polity), interregional, and supraregional.

One of the most definitive interregional studies is Seeman's (1979b) test of Struever and Houart's (1972) model. Seeman examined distribution maps of the major Hopewell Interaction Sphere artifacts to see if the model could be sustained. He found no evidence to support a functional hierarchy of central-place distribution, as argued by Struever and Houart, but found instead that the greatest concentration of Hopewellian traits occurred in southern Ohio. He also found striking differences between local traditions across eastern North America. Subsequently he has commented (Seeman 1995) on the localized nature of style zones during the Middle Woodland and the apparent correlation of artifact types (for example, ear spools, mica, and Ross Barbed obsidian points) with their degree of visibility, from personal objects to community symbols, and beyond. Seeman argues that symbolic messages contained in Hopewellian artifact styles were meant to be understood in different ways on a variety of social scales.

In another study, Cowan (1996) analyzed Hopewellian portable art (pipes, cutouts, necklaces, and so forth) using Wobst's (1977) information transmission model. Cowan concluded that there were three levels of symboling: the personal, in which the symbol has meaning only among the owner's immediate household (for example, zoomorphic platform pipes); the cultural, in which the symbol reflects the common values of the total community (for example, caches of artifacts made of nonlocal materials); and the social, in which the symbol communicates the owner's social position (for example, ear spools). This latter message could function both within a community and between different communities.

The significance of these studies from our perspective lies in their apparent correspondence with our settlement model. The portable art reflects the social order of small-scale societies lacking dependent relationships between neighboring communities. As with the individuality of burial treatment described by Braun (1979; Braun, Griffin, and Titterington 1982), there is little evidence of social iconography above the scale of the local group. No universal Hopewellian banner exists.

What Is the Scale of Human Organization and What Are the Corresponding Population Densities?

As organized by the dispersed sedentary community model, we read the record of Ohio Hopewell as exhibiting clustering at six scales. These clusters represent proxies to the scales of human organization utilized by Hopewellian groups.

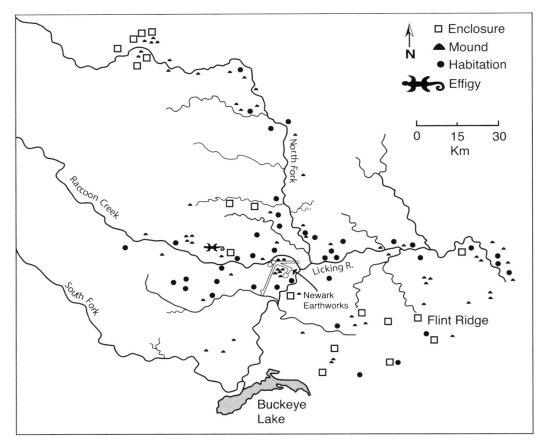

Figure 1.7. Distribution of known Ohio Hopewell habitation sites, earthworks, and mounds in the upper Licking River valley, Licking County, Ohio. Figure adapted from Fig. 2.1, Pacheco 1997:61. With permission from Kent State University Press.

The smallest scale is at the level of within-settlement variation. This scale would proxy individual labor. Since sedentary households maintained space, identification of activity areas within household space is possible (Dancey 1991, 1992b). Likewise, spatially distinct areas of bladelets have been identified in sites thought to be specialized camps in which ritual or craft artifacts were produced (Baby and Langlois 1979; Genheimer 1997; Greber, Davis, and Du-Fresne 1981; Pacheco 1993, 1997; Prufer and McKenzie 1967). In a recent article, Spielmann (2002:202) suggests that the small-scale craft production observed in Ohio Hopewell is best understood as attached to or embedded in the ritual context itself, rather than as a product of a particular segment of the society whose members operate as craft specialists. The next highest scale is the level of the settlement, with households as the principal units of production within Hopewell society. At the local or intracommunity scale, the dwellings and activity areas of several generations of families are distributed along short runs on valley bottoms or around upland springs (fig. 1.2). At the scale of the community, household groups cluster around earthwork and burial mound locations (fig. 1.3). Communities are spaced along major drainage systems (figs. 1.6 and 1.7) and would have interacted at earthwork and mound centers to create alliances and obligations with one another (Railey 1991) as peer-polities (Braun 1986).

Each community was the principal economic unit of the tradition, and when a community was linked with its neighbors to form a polity, intercommunity relationships would have been equitable (Renfrew and Cherry 1986). Burial status and wealth appear to have been related to individual achievement (Braun, Griffin, and Titterington 1982; Greber 1979a, 1979b). There was no institutionalized social differentiation, and leaders emerged in specific situations rather than existing as a matter of ascribed rank. Exchange relations facilitating the movement of artifacts, foods, and raw materials endured among these polities for more than four hundred years. The monumental architecture shows sharp regional differences, within limits, and variable life spans. From this perspective, Ohio Hopewell represents an egalitarian society with a sequential hierarchy (Braun 1991a; Johnson 1982).

An additional scale exists at the level of regional groups of peer-polities. This scale transcends regional drainage systems, linking the groups into a broader tradition. Distant groups probably rarely interacted directly; when they did, meetings probably occurred at places like Newark and Hopewell works. This final scale bears close resemblance to the concept of the Hopewell Interaction Sphere (Caldwell 1964; Prufer 1964a; Seeman 1979b). Yet earthwork and mound sizes and distributions within these two key settlement systems of Ohio Hopewell are surprisingly different. The Newark Earthworks are centrally located within the Licking Valley (fig. 1.7) and have no equal in terms of size and quantity of remains (Lepper 1988; Pacheco 1993, 1996a, 1997). In the central Scioto, the Hopewell Earthworks are clearly unsurpassed in importance, yet there are five other large earthwork-mound centers within 30 kilometers (Greber 1979a, 1991; Seeman 1979b). It is unlikely that the Hopewell Earthworks functioned at a purely local scale. Instead, the site's importance appears to be more likely that of a regional polity center and an interregional transaction center, perhaps even of the kind envisioned by Struever and Houart (1972).

One expression of the organizational differences in scale and integration between the Licking and central Scioto regions can be expressed by use of the rank-size rule (Johnson 1977, 1980, 1982; Paynter 1983), which plots the log of a settlement rank against the log of its size. The rule predicts a log-linear rank-size relationship as a settlement system becomes fully integrated or centralized (Johnson 1977). For archaeological cases of developing cultural complexity, deviations from the expected pattern are the norm. In this instance, the deviations form the basis of the comparison for the Licking and central Scioto examples.

A plot of the rank-size relationships between the known and suspected

Middle Woodland earthworks in the central Scioto Valley is shown in figure 1.8. The rank-size relationships deviate significantly from the expected pattern. They can be described as convex (Johnson 1977, 1980). While the Hopewell Earthworks occupies the position of top rank, as expected for a regional polity center, either the size of local community centers (like Seip and Harness) is larger than expected or the size of the largest place (Hopewell) is smaller than expected. Johnson (1980:151) argues that system convexity "is attributed to significant interactional boundaries within an area of analysis, or more generally to the pooling of independent or relatively independent systems in the analysis."

Thus, the rank-size distribution for the central Scioto region suggests the pooling of independent social systems, which probably are in direct competition with one another. The five tripartite earthworks (see Greber 1979a) in the region occupy a secondary plateau, metaphorically speaking, beneath the Hopewell earthworks in figure 1.8. These probably represent the centers of the independent social systems in the region. Directly below this group of five are earthworks from the Hopeton–Mound City cluster, which may in itself represent yet another independent social group. The weakly integrated settlement system of the central Scioto region appears to include as many as six independent social units, which were loosely integrated through the Hopewell Earthworks.

A much different perspective is gained from examination of the rank-size plot for the Licking Valley earthworks (fig. 1.8). The rank-size relationships also deviate significantly from the expected in this case, but this time they are in the direction of concavity. The Licking Hopewell distribution can be described as primo-convex, which is a variation of the classic primate distribution (Johnson 1987; Pacheco 1996a). Primate distributions reflect the situation in which the principal center is significantly larger than expected or the lower-ranking centers are smaller than expected (Johnson 1977:496). Primate distributions are attributed to either minimization of competition within the system or boundary maintenance by the primate center between it and an equal or larger system (that is, the central Scioto region). Both of these situations would lead to suppression of the midlevel or secondary centers (Johnson 1980:173). Both explanations may have some validity in the Licking case. The slight convexity shown by figure 1.8 is created by the presence of three to four midlevel or second-tier centers. Like the Scioto example, these may reflect a degree of relatively independent social units, which are ultimately articulated through Newark (see Johnson 1987 for a general discussion of primo-convexity). The smaller centers on the tail of the Licking rank-size plot may actually be Early Woodland centers. However, their removal would not change the overall primo-convexity of the plot.

Thus, rank-size analysis suggests significant differences between the organization and integration of the central Scioto and Licking regions. The central Scioto region reflects a lack of overall integration, with significant competition between autonomous and independent social units (that is, sequential hierarchy in the sense of Braun 1991a). While the Hopewell Earthworks is clearly the highest-order center in this region with possibly widespread interregional con-

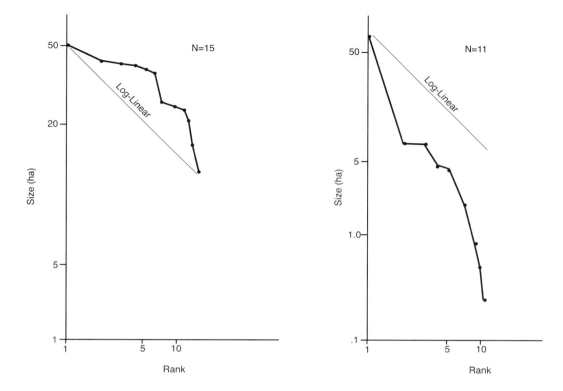

Figure 1.8. Comparison of rank-size plots for (left) central Scioto region (unpublished notes in possession of authors based on classic surveys) and (right) Licking region (from Table 2:1, Pacheco 1996a:25).

nections (see also Seeman 1979b), as a polity center for the central Scioto it was only marginally successful in integrating the independent Hopewell groups occupying the region. The Licking Valley, by contrast, possesses a dominant primate center, which suppressed competition among the relatively autonomous social units within the region. Most likely, the large size of Newark Earthworks represents a centuries-long "united front" of the Licking Hopewell peer-polity in their interactions with the "powerful" peer-polity located 90 kilometers to the southwest in the central Scioto Valley. Here large earthwork size and complexity reflect the demands of symbolically and architecturally defining and maintaining the system's identity and boundaries (both territorial and ideological) against encroachment by the other group.

Finally, it is important to put corresponding population densities into perspective with the suggested settlement patterns. A broad consensus exists that Hopewell populations were neither large nor densely packed. Yet population estimates or demographic studies are rare. Two of the best estimates to date are Asch's (1976) study of Illinois Hopewell burial data and Greber's (1997) reconstruction of the Paint Creek community in Ross County, Ohio. Both studies

Table 1.2. Estimates of Newark-area Hopewell Population

Household Size	Percentage of All Households Identified				
	100%	75%	50%	25%	10%
5 people	170	225	340	680	1,700
10 people	340	450	680	1,360	3,400
15 people	510	675	1,020	2,040	5,100
20 people	680	900	1,360	2,720	6,800
25 people	850	1,125	1,700	3,400	8,500

Source: Pacheco 1988, 1996a.
Note: Based on 34 known settlements.

estimate overall Hopewell population densities at no more than one to two people per square kilometer, although certain social/environmental conditions produced higher relative population densities. We concur with their view but would like to put a settlement perspective on the issue.

Examination of the Licking Valley surrounding the Newark Earthworks (fig. 1.7) indicates that at least relatively speaking, Newark was a population magnet for dispersed households. After about 1 kilometer, dispersed households are packed into the area up to about 20 kilometers from the earthworks. Households in the Licking Valley favored well-drained outwash terraces and upland wetlands. This pattern is repeated around other earthwork sites in Ohio where regional settlement patterns are known (Genheimer 1997; Pacheco 1996a). Asch (1976) noted that packing in the Illinois Valley occurs along the river frontage, where densities might reach more than twenty individuals per linear kilometer, with upland densities much lower. Similarly, at the aggregate scale, settlement systems like Newark included upwards of 1,500 square kilometers (Pacheco 1988), most of which is fairly empty (of households) hinterland. This additional territory would serve to bring overall population densities back down into the range of one to two persons per square kilometer. It probably also served as both a social buffer zone and a hunting reserve.

Preliminary research in the Licking Valley confirms this view of population density. Currently we have identified thirty-four probable household sites within 20 kilometers of Newark (Pacheco 1988, 1996a). By constructing a matrix that varies household size for the rows and the percentage of identified households for the columns, we can estimate population within this area (following the method outlined by Sumner [1989]). Five rows were created for average household size and five columns were created for the percentage of all identified contemporaneous households in the system (table 1.2). The midpoint of the matrix is 1,020 people, with a range from a minimum estimate of 170 to a maximum estimate of 8,500. While this method is undoubtedly crude, it does support the general consensus that Ohio Hopewell settlement systems had relatively low population densities, especially as compared to expectations derived from ethnographic concepts of chiefdom-level societies. Our own guess is that the entire Newark system, including all of the outlying subcommunities like Dresden and Upper Jonathan Creek, included at most between 4,000 and 5,000 people at any one time. These people were spread over an area of approximately 3,000 square kilometers. Thus overall population density is less than two people per square kilometer. In closing, we would note that such an estimate is entirely consistent with population densities recorded in ethnographically documented New World dispersed sedentary societies like the Mapuche (Dillehay 1990, 1992) and the Chachi (DeBoer and Blitz 1991).

Summary

In this chapter we have attempted to integrate Ohio Hopewell settlement and mortuary data into a comprehensive understanding of Ohio Hopewell society by addressing a series of questions. Standing on the intellectual shoulders of Prufer (1964a, 1997b) and utilizing an evolutionary archaeology perspective, we outline our model of Ohio Hopewell community organization. In our view, Ohio Hopewell communities are composed of dispersed sedentary households that cluster in the vicinity of sacred precincts containing earthen architecture. While lacking permanent residences, the centers are periodically visited in culturally determined annual cycles by the local community and on occasion by representatives from neighboring communities and regional polities. Ohio Hopewell communities are anchored to their centers by corporate ownership of stable territories or socially bounded regions. Community members are dispersed in sedentary households that utilize small catchments, which include both active and fallow gardens where small starchy and oily seed plants are cultivated. The distribution of the people and their land disturbance activities produced a synergistic effect on local biomass. Hopewell dispersion in Ohio evolved as a result of a long-term process of human-land interactions, which in our opinion is at the heart of the issue of why Ohio Hopewell communities built and used mounds and earthworks. We hope we have successfully shown that available data favor this interpretation of Ohio Hopewell society.

2

A Mobile Hopewell?

Questioning Assumptions of Ohio Hopewell Sedentism

Frank L. Cowan

For nearly four decades, many Ohio archaeologists have held that Hopewell populations lived in small, dispersed, semisedentary hamlets near corporate ceremonial centers (Prufer 1964a, 1965). Within the past decade or so, some researchers have dropped the qualifier "semi-," arguing that Ohio Hopewell populations were completely sedentary and that many of the hamlets surrounding earthwork complexes were occupied nearly continuously for long periods of time (Dancey 1991; Dancey and Pacheco 1997a; Pacheco 1996a, 1997). The Prufer-Dancey-Pacheco model (fig. 2.1) is, at present, the only well-articulated model of Ohio Hopewell subsistence-settlement systems, and it is certainly the most influential.

However, for several reasons it seems unlikely that many of the small sites championed as examples of sedentary hamlets represent true sedentism. This chapter will address two of the issues that make sedentism implausible. First, the stone tool assemblages recovered from Ohio Hopewell sites make no organizational sense for sedentary or semisedentary residences, and many of the tool forms we recognize as diagnostic of "Hopewell" were probably designed for use primarily within ceremonial settings. Second, the abundance and nature of the housing now known to exist adjacent to earthwork complexes have implications for the distances that congregants traveled to convene at such community gathering places.

It is likely that we have not yet recognized the full functional range of Ohio Middle Woodland sites. We have come a long way from viewing Ohio Hopewell only in terms of the great mounds and earthworks that once dotted southern Ohio and in terms of the artifacts found within those earthen structures. I suspect that we still have a long way to go to have a full understanding of Ohio's Middle Woodland cultures.

Lithic Tool Assemblage Implications for Settlement Organization

The differences between the recognized lithic technologies of Ohio Hopewell and those of all other periods of Ohio prehistory are profound and puzzling. In

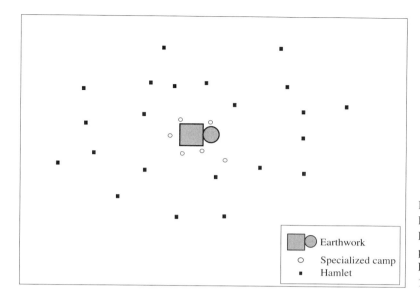

Figure 2.1. Dancey-Pacheco model of Ohio Hopewell settlement pattern. Redrawn from Dancey and Pacheco 1997a:Fig. 1.2.

Ohio, as throughout North America, the dominant tool-making trajectories were the production of unretouched and edge-retouched flakes from simple flake cores and the production of extensively shaped bifaces. Lithic technologies based on blades or bladelets are extraordinarily rare in the Americas (Parry 1994), and where they do occur, they are always ancillary to other tool-production strategies. Yet bladelets absolutely dominate the assemblages of Ohio Hopewell sites (Genheimer 1996; Greber, Davis, and DuFresne 1981). Bifacial tools are much less abundant, and simple core flaking as a tool-production method appears to be nearly absent at most Ohio Hopewell sites.

Throughout the Americas, bifacially flaked stone tool production strategies predominated among mobile populations (Parry and Kelly 1987). Conservative in the consumption of raw materials, long lived, and multifunctional, bifacial tools had several distinct advantages (table 2.1) for people who needed portable toolkits (Cowan 1999). Those advantages outweighed the significant costs of bifacial tool production: the need for raw materials of reasonably high quality, advanced flintknapping skills, and appreciable time investments for the production of individual tools.

Although the basic functional requirements of sedentary populations were generally the same as those of mobile peoples (Odell 1998), the organizational requirements were quite different, as the lithic technologies of sedentary peoples were not constrained by the need for toolkit portability. For the most part, sedentary populations relied on much simpler and less costly tool designs and production methods than did mobile peoples (Cowan 1999; Parry and Kelly 1987). The percussion detachment of flake tools from simple cores involved minimal production costs in that it took little time and was a skill available to all members of society; it did not require the intercession of advanced flintknappers. Because there are few technical constraints for such tool production, sed-

Table 2.1. Comparisons of Costs and Benefits for Chipped Stone Tool Production Methods

Costs and Benefits	Bifacial Tools	Flake Tools from Cores	Ohio Hopewell Bladelet Tools
Raw Material Constraints	High	Low	Very high
Production Skill Costs	High	Low	Very high
Production Time Costs	High	Low	Moderate
Multifunctional Utility of Individual Tools	High	Low	Very low
Tool Use-Life	Long	Short	Very short
Toolkit Portability	High	Low	Low

entary populations usually made considerable use of locally available raw materials, regardless of that material's knapping qualities.

Figure 2.2 illustrates how such technological decision making plays out in assemblages representing distinctly different kinds and levels of mobility (Cowan 1994, 1999). Bifacial tools dominate sites used by highly mobile logistical parties, while sites occupied by sedentary families are dominated by simple flake core technology. Sites used by moderately mobile groups exhibit a mixed technological strategy. These data (fig. 2.2) are from sites of three culture-historical periods in western New York rather than Ohio, and they do not include Hopewellian assemblages; nevertheless, the patterns are very strong, and the principles are not regionally or temporally limited.

Base camps were places where a very wide range of activities took place and where tool use was nearly constant and tool needs diverse (table 2.2). Base camps were residences for whole social groups, including young and old, men and women, adept craftspeople and novices. We should expect almost all members of a co-residential group to have produced and used stone tools. Residential

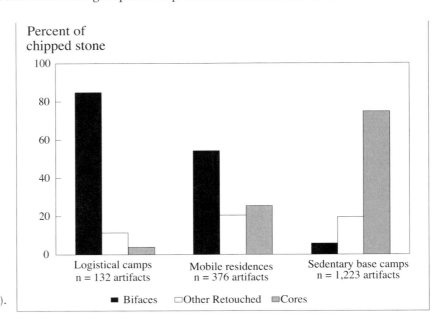

Figure 2.2. Assemblage content and mobility (data from Cowan 1994).

Table 2.2. Expectations for Lithic Assemblages at Sedentary Base Camps

Parameter	Characteristic
Economic Necessity	Functionally complete toolkits
	Diverse range of tool forms
Social Composition	Tool use by all members of co-residential group
	Tool production by all members of co-residential group
	Considerable evidence for novice tool makers
Functional Expediency	Opportunistic use of local raw materials
	Extensive retouch, resharpening, reuse, recycling
	Considerable use wear on discarded tools
Tool Designs	Diverse: Wide range of unretouched and retouched flake tools
	Secondary emphasis on robust bifaces
Production Methods	Diverse: Emphasis on simple core-flaking
	Secondary emphasis on robust bifaces

base camps were not places where everyday economic needs would routinely have been addressed with highly stylized toolkits if those toolkits were costly to produce and/or energetically inefficient.

What about Ohio Bladelets?

Ohio Hopewell bladelets have properties and characteristics quite different from bifacial or core-flaking technologies (table 2.1). Ohio Hopewell bladelets are also distinct from most other blade technologies around the world. World-wide, blades and bladelets were often "blanks" to be retouched into a wide variety of specific edge and shape characteristics (for example, De Sonneville-Bordes and Perrot 1954, 1955, 1956a, 1956b; Tixier 1974). Many blade technologies produced products large enough to be conveniently handheld or products that were retouched to fit existing hafting mechanisms. Retouch was also used to alter fragile blade/bladelet edges to enhance functional performance and tool longevity.

Ohio Hopewell bladelets, by contrast, are very small and delicate, averaging roughly 35–40 millimeters in length, about 12 millimeters in width, and 3 millimeters in thickness (Greber, Davis, and DuFresne 1981). Only rarely are they retouched. Small, highly standardized bladelets were costly to produce. Production demanded very high quality raw materials and considerable technical skill. Shaping and maintaining the cores to ensure well-controlled bladelet removals was time-consuming. Ohio Hopewell bladelets are inconvenient to hold and difficult to manipulate. Because of their small size, they were not well suited for intensive use without hafting, yet seldom do they exhibit the kinds of retouch that would have facilitated hafting (Keeley 1982). They also do not show the intensive use wear or repetitive resharpening that would be evident had they been placed into hafting mechanisms.

Small bladelets could and did perform a variety of functional tasks (Odell 1994; Yerkes 1990, 1994), but their design characteristics are simply not well suited to the full range of everyday functional needs that would be facilitated by

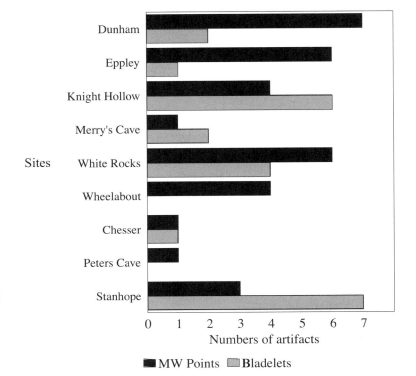

Figure 2.3. Middle Woodland (MW) points and bladelets in Ohio rockshelter sites (from Seeman 1996).

tools of varied mass, shapes, and edge characteristics. Use-wear analyses of bladelets recovered from excavated contexts where they were not subject to the abuses of agricultural tillage (for example, Cowan 1987; Mallouf 1982; Odell 1985a) indicate that most were little-used prior to discard (Yerkes 1990, 1994).

Bladelets are indeed tools (Genheimer 1996), but a bladelet-based toolkit is not an effective or functionally complete toolkit. It is hard to imagine a sedentary stone-tool-using society in which most members of that society could not have produced most tools. It is even harder to imagine the utility, much less the selective advantage, of a technology in which the dominant tool forms would have been difficult to pick up and use during those parts of the year when outdoors work might have required mittens. In contexts where high mobility and toolkit portability can be assumed, bladelets are relatively incidental in assemblages. In a sample of Middle Woodland rockshelters (Seeman 1996), formally diagnostic Middle Woodland projectile points outnumber bladelets by a ratio of 1.4 to 1 (fig. 2.3). If temporally nondiagnostic bifaces had been included in these figures, the biface-to-bladelet ratio would undoubtedly be much higher. Bladelets were thus not a fundamental part of the transported toolkit, while bifacial tools were.

Highly specialized production areas imply some specialization of use. Bladelet production seems to have been generally limited to areas clustered immediately around earthworks and at workshops adjacent to quarries (Lepper, Yerkes, and Pickard 2001). In southwestern Ohio, specialized bladelet and biface production areas are located outside the earthwork walls of Fort Ancient (Connolly and Sullivan 1998; Cowan, Genheimer, and Sunderhaus 1997; Cowan, Sunderhaus, and Genheimer 2004) and at Stubbs Earthworks (Cowan, Sunderhaus, and Genheimer 1999a), as well as at Turner. Evidence for specialized production areas are also known at Baum and at Harness Sites 6, 18, and 25 (Coughlin and Seeman 1997:237–238; Greber, Davis, and DuFresne 1981), as well as at other sites in central Ohio. These "core patches" appear to be locations where expert flintknappers produced specialized tools for use in ceremonial contexts.

Excavations near the parallel walls of the Fort Ancient site (Cowan, Genheimer, and Sunderhaus 1997; Cowan, Sunderhaus, and Genheimer 2004) demonstrate that some specialized bladelet production areas were used long enough or often enough to warrant investment in substantial wooden architecture (fig. 2.4). The remnants of at least two irregular square structures coincide with the densest surface concentration of bladelet production debris. Feature 8, presumably associated with one of the two structures, contained scores of bladelet

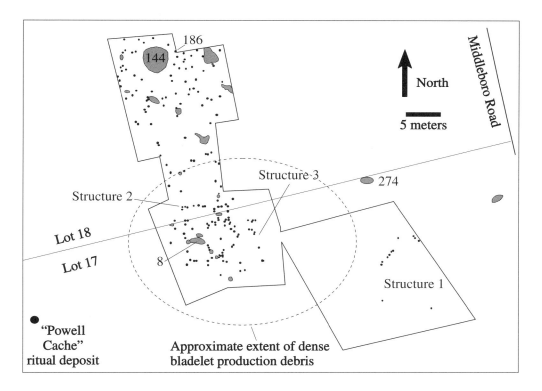

Figure 2.4. Post molds, pits, and bladelet production area near the eastern end of the parallel walls, Gregory's Field Tract, Fort Ancient site, Warren County, Ohio (1996 excavations).

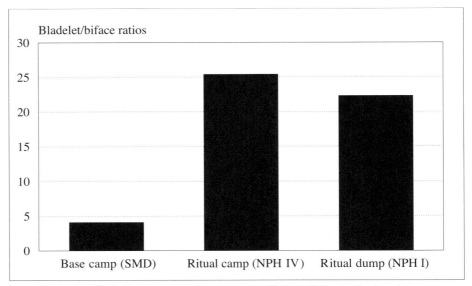

Figure 2.5. Bladelet/biface ratios in Illinois Hopewell sites (from Stafford and Sant 1985a; Wiant and McGimsey 1986a). SMD=Smiling Dan, NPH=Napoleon Hollow.

fragments and thousands of small chert flakes. Several other wooden structures were located nearby, although flake densities within the plow zone diminished markedly away from the mapped flake concentration. However, Feature 144, near the northern end of the excavation, contained hundreds of bladelet fragments, thousands of flakes, four exhausted bladelet cores, and wood charcoal that dated to 1830 ±100 B.P.

Not all the post molds in this portion of the Fort Ancient site necessarily relate to specialized tool production. One post mold, Feature 186, and a hearth, Feature 274, yielded Early Woodland radiocarbon dates, which suggest a long nonresidential use of this portion of the Fort Ancient site. The proximity of the "Powell Cache," a small pit that contained a ritual deposit of scores of Hopewellian bifaces, bladelets, and flakes of obsidian, crystal quartz, and other exotic raw materials (Essenpreis and Moseley 1984; Gramly 2003), suggests that other kinds of ritual behaviors were carried out in this area. What is abundantly clear, however, is that the associated artifacts and debris do not represent residential activities; this area was used for a very limited array of specialized tool production activities and other ritual functions (Cowan, Sunderhaus, and Genheimer 2004).

In summary, Ohio Hopewell bladelets were highly specialized tool forms. While not task-specific in function, they were tools that were designed for use within particular social-ceremonial contexts. Within and immediately around ceremonial centers, Ohio Hopewell bladelets may have served mundane purposes, but they are not simply a stylistic variant of flake tools. Rather, they replaced mundane flake tools within specific, ritually charged contexts. A somewhat similar contextual specialization is found in Illinois (fig. 2.5), where bladelets dominate the assemblages of ritually oriented sites (Wiant and Mc-

Gimsey 1986b) and occur in much lower proportions in residential locations (Stafford and Sant 1985b). In Illinois, they also appear to have been used for a much narrower range of uses in ritual sites than in residential contexts (Odell 1994).

The Strange Case of Ohio Hopewell Lithic Technology

Ohio Hopewell lithic assemblages exhibit unusual technological specialization. In most assemblages (for example, Genheimer 1996; Coughlin and Seeman 1997), the reported ratios of bladelets to bifaces range from about 6:1 to well over 30:1 (fig. 2.6). Reported ratios are generally from surface collections, which are subject to numerous preservation biases, including the preferential removal of bifacial tools from plowed surfaces by generations of artifact collectors. Most Hopewell sites do, however, show evidence of use during other culture-historical periods. Since most biface fragments are not temporally diagnostic, multicomponent sites tend to exhibit deflated bladelet-biface ratios. Nonetheless, simple flake cores are nearly absent in most Ohio Hopewell assemblages, and edge-retouched tools—such as scrapers, drills, borers, burins, and backed flake tools—are also extraordinarily rare. Unretouched flakes, for the most part, are limited to the byproducts of bladelet core shaping and maintenance and, secondarily, to the small-scale by-products of final bifacial retouch. Few unretouched flakes are large enough to have been used effectively as handheld tools.

The paucity of evidence for hafting and intensive use indicates that most bladelets had very short use-lives—that is, they were used only briefly prior to

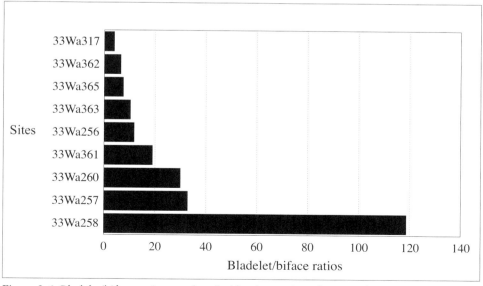

Figure 2.6. Bladelet/biface ratios at select Stubbs cluster sites (from Genheimer 1996).

discard. The discard rates of bladelets were very high relative to other tools, especially compared to bifacial or other large, heavily retouched tools. Bladelets would quickly come to dominate discard assemblages even if they did not dominate actual use assemblages. This fact alone greatly diminishes the argument for occupation longevity and intensity of activity at many of the small sites that surround earthworks. If we "filter out" the large numbers of bladelets and their by-products from Ohio Hopewell lithic assemblages, we are left with assemblages that are absolutely dominated by bifaces and by the by-products of biface production. Reliance on bifacial tool technologies is a hallmark of highly mobile populations.

Lithic raw material studies of Ohio Hopewell sites also point to major anomalies in the interpretation of some Ohio Hopewell sites as sedentary base camps (Vickery 1996). Energetic considerations of lithic tool production and use behaviors suggest that simple tools produced for everyday subsistence and maintenance purposes in sedentary residential sites would be composed primarily of locally available raw materials, even if those raw materials were of lesser quality than potentially available nonlocal or exotic lithic materials. Yet presumed Middle Woodland residential sites (Dancey and Pacheco 1997a:Table 1.1), such as Twin Mounds Village (Fischer 1974; Hawkins 1996; Kaltenthaler 1992), Jennison Guard (Blosser 1996; Kozarek 1997; Whitacre and Whitacre 1986), and Smith (Sunderhaus, Riggs, and Cowan 2001), are dominated by nonlocal raw materials, despite relative proximity to technologically useful cherts in local gravel deposits and the Brassfield, Cedarville-Guelph, and Laurel formation outcrops (Vickery 1996:Figure 7.1). Lithic raw materials from Harrison County/Wyandotte and Flint Ridge source areas alone account for 99 percent and 94 percent of the presently sourced lithic raw materials (Vickery 1996:Table 7.1) at Jennison Guard and Twin Mounds Village, respectively, both located at the mouth of the Great Miami River valley. The Harrison County/Wyandotte chert resource area, which accounts for the vast majority of the lithic materials at those sites, is approximately 160 kilometers from those sites, and the Flint Ridge deposits are 180 kilometers distant. Similarly, locally available raw materials are very scant in the assemblage from the Smith site in the Little Miami River valley (Sunderhaus, Riggs, and Cowan 2001). The frequencies of exotic cherts at these sites rival or exceed the frequencies noted at nearby earthwork complexes, where Harrison County/Wyandotte, Flint Ridge, Haney/Paoli (northeastern Kentucky), and Knox (eastern Tennessee) cherts comprise 94 percent and 96 percent of the Fort Ancient and Stubbs Earthworks assemblages, respectively (Vickery 1996:Table 7.1). Such lithic resource specialization and a steadfast avoidance of locally available and technologically useful raw materials are in stark contrast with behaviors normally associated with sedentary residential sites.

Murphy Site Complex

The Murphy site complex, located within 3 kilometers of the Newark Earthworks, figures importantly in this discussion since the Murphy complex forms the core of the argument for Ohio Hopewell sedentism. One of the most intensively investigated and comprehensively reported sets of Hopewell artifact concentrations outside earthworks in Ohio, the Murphy site complex is argued to be a series of long-term, year-round residences (Dancey 1991; Dancey and Pacheco 1997a; Pacheco 1996a, 1997).

The excavated feature assemblage of the Murphy site yields a 2:1 bladelet/ biface ratio, and flake cores and retouched tools are extremely rare. Use-wear polishes were poorly developed (Yerkes 1990, 1994), indicating very little use prior to discard. Factor out the bladelets, and we see two interpretive signatures: very sparse artifact densities and a biface-dominated assemblage characteristic of highly mobile logistical parties. What we do not see is an assemblage characteristic of a long-term residential base camp.

Pacheco (1996a, 1997; Dancey and Pacheco 1997a) has extended the investigations of the Murphy site complex to include surface collections from nine concentrations of Hopewell artifacts in an area of 30 hectares. Most of the artifact concentrations are interpreted as residential hamlets. The surface data include artifacts from both earlier and later time periods, but Pacheco (1997) recommends that most artifacts of nonlocal Wyandotte chert can reasonably be assumed to be of Middle Woodland origin. Those data indicate that there is a 14:1 ratio of bladelets to bifaces (fig. 2.7). There are very few flake cores and very few retouched tools other than bifaces. The ratio of bladelets to bifaces among Vanport chert artifacts (3.4:1) is much lower (fig. 2.8) than the Wyandotte ratio. However, the Murphy complex lies only about 20 kilometers from the Flint Ridge chert quarries, and most of the recovered Vanport chert projectile points are diagnostic of other time periods (Pacheco 1997:Table 2.1). It is

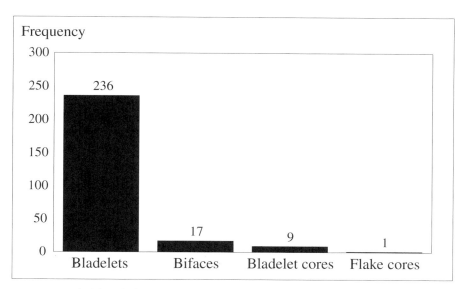

Figure 2.7. Bladelets, bifaces, and cores of Wyandotte chert at the Murphy complex (from Pacheco 1997:73).

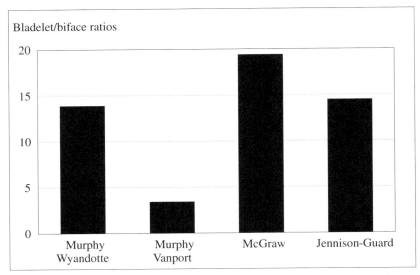

Figure 2.8. Bladelet/biface ratios at select Ohio Hopewell "residential hamlets" (from Pacheco 1997; see also Coughlin and Seeman 1997).

not certain how many of the nondiagnostic bifaces of Vanport chert may relate to the Middle Woodland or to other culture-historical periods.

If the Murphy site complex does represent a series of residences, the technology bears no resemblance to that typical of sedentary residential sites. The lithic assemblage is dominated by bladelet production and secondarily by bifacial tool production. Tools and production residues characteristic of long-term residences of whole family groups are very sparse. Similar observations can be made about the lithic assemblages from other Hopewell sites that are often argued to have been sedentary residential sites (fig. 2.8), such as McGraw (Prufer 1965) and Jennison Guard (Blosser 1996; Kozarek 1997; Whitacre and Whitacre 1986).

Evidence for Housing at Ohio Hopewell Sites

An entirely different line of reasoning can be brought to bear on the settlement systems of Ohio Hopewellian populations. Prufer, Dancey, Pacheco, and others have interpreted Hopewell artifact scatters on the immediate peripheries of Ohio Hopewell earthworks as "specialized camps" (fig. 2.1) used by community members during periodic community gatherings.

Stubbs Earthwork Complex

Recent salvage excavations (Cowan and Clay 1998; Cowan and Sunderhaus 2002; Cowan, Sunderhaus, and Genheimer 1998, 1999a, 1999b, 2000; Sunderhaus, Riggs, and Cowan 2001) at remnants of the Stubbs Earthwork site complex (fig. 2.9) give us a glimpse of what these "specialized camps" look like. Although not detailed here, other recent excavations outside the earthwork walls of the Hopewellian Fort Ancient site (Cowan, Genheimer, and Sunderhaus 1997; Cowan, Sunderhaus, and Genheimer 2004) also serve to bolster our understanding of near-earthwork site use patterns.

The Stubbs Earthworks investigations of 1998 and 1999 included 3,800 square meters of systematic excavation (fig. 2.10). Most of the excavations were conducted outside the earthwork enclosure, and evidence for wooden Hopewell architecture was found in several areas. At distances of approximately 20 meters to well over 300 meters from the presumed location of the earthen walls, four separate excavations revealed evidence for at least fifteen houselike, wooden Hopewell structures. These Hopewell structures were found in nearly every major excavation block that was situated on relatively well drained ground near terrace margins or adjacent to potential water sources (fig. 2.10: Transects 2, 10,

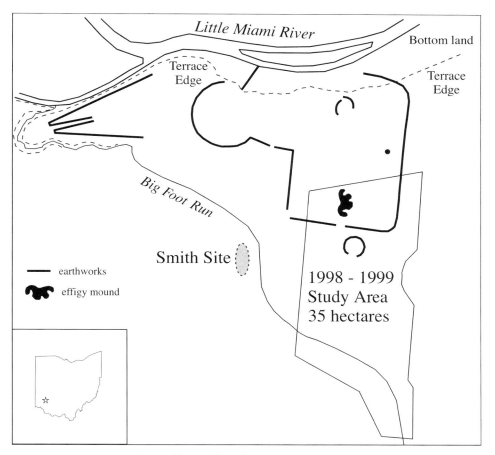

Figure 2.9. Project areas for Stubbs Earthworks (33WA1) 1998–1999 and Smith site (33WA362) 2001 project areas (adapted from Whittlesey 1851).

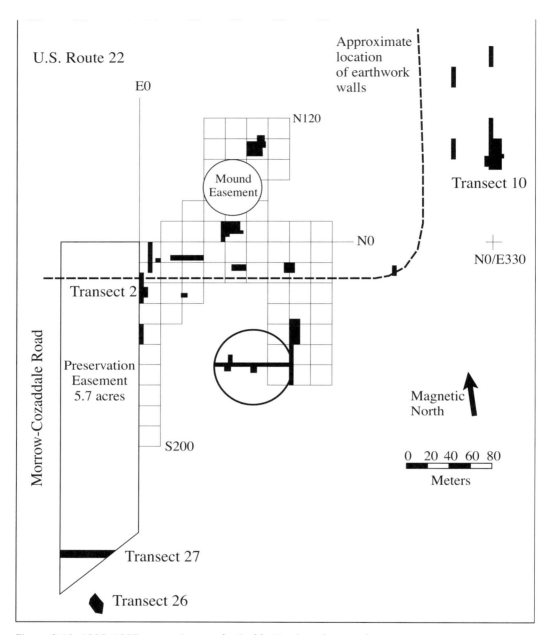

Figure 2.10. 1998–1999 excavations at the Stubbs Earthworks site, showing preservation easements, magnetometer survey areas, and excavations (May–November 1998 and June–October 1999). The numbered excavation transects contained coherent evidence for the wooden architecture discussed in this chapter.

Table 2.3. Radiocarbon Age Estimates for Hopewell Houselike Structures, Stubbs Earthworks Site (33WA1) and Smith Site (33WA362)

Structure Number	Feature Number (post molds and pits)	Lab Number	Radiocarbon Age B.P. (corrected for $^{12}C/^{13}C$ ratio)	Weighted Average Radiocarbon Age B.P. by Structure
1	42	Beta-166639	1750 ±40	1785 ±30
	48	Beta-166641	1820 ±40	
2[a]	119	Beta-156234	1640 ±60	1595 ±40
	150	Beta-156235	1890 ±70	
	158	Beta-156236	1550 ±60	
3	80	Beta-166642	1730 ±40	1785 ±30
	202	Beta-166640	1840 ±40	
4	191	Beta-156237	1770 ±60	1820 ±40
	223	Beta-156238	1850 ±70	
	376	Beta-156239	1850 ±70	
5	256	Beta-156240	1820 ±70	1810 ±40
	294	Beta-156241	1800 ±60	
	332	Beta-156527	1810 ±70	
6	142	Beta-156528	1890 ±60	1810 ±40
	321	Beta-156526	1730 ±60	
19 and 21	951[b]	Beta-156531	1920 ±60	1920 ±60
Smith 1	14	ISGS-5438	1890 ±70	not averaged
	23[c]	ISGS-5437	1690 ±70	
Smith pit	37 (wood)	ISGS-5440	1820 ±70	not averaged
	37 (nutshell)[c]	ISGS-5441	1420 ±70	

a. Weighted average does not include Feature 150.
b. Pit intrusive into wall trenches.
c. Improbably late radiocarbon age estimates.

26, and 27). The houselike structures that were sufficiently exposed to permit measurement ranged from 30 to 100 square meters of interior floor space. Most were single-posted, rectangular structures with rounded corners, although considerable architectural variability is evident.

Structure 1, probably located less than 20 meters outside the major Stubbs Earthwork enclosure, is a single-posted, rectangular structure with rounded corners and interior support posts (fig. 2.11). The weighted average of two AMS dates on charcoal from the fills of two post molds indicates that the structure dates to approximately 1785 ±30 B.P. (table 2.3).

Many (perhaps all) of the rectangular structures at Stubbs Earthworks were built within shallow house basins using the wall-trench construction technique (fig. 2.12), a building technique not previously documented for Ohio Hopewell. Several excavated areas are very crowded with the remains of houselike structures. Transect 27, a 400-square-meter excavation located approximately 330 meters south of the earthwork, included at least eight well-documented wall-trench "houses" (Structures 14–21) and perhaps at least three others. Many structures overlapped one another, and several structures were directly superimposed over the imprint of previously dismantled structures. Dashed lines in figure 2.12 indicate three additional unlabeled structures that were not recognized

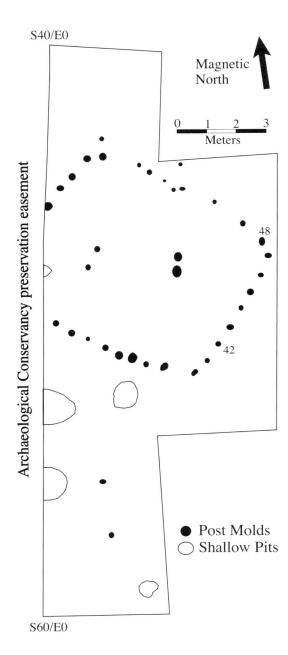

Figure 2.11. Hopewellian Structure 1 in Transect 2, Stubbs Earthworks site. The numbered post molds are radiocarbon dated and listed in table 2.3.

during the fieldwork but became apparent after investigators studied maps of "residual" post molds. None of the Transect 27 structures are yet directly dated, but a pit feature that intruded into the overlap of the earlier wall trenches of Structures 19 and 21 dates to 1920 ±60 B.P. (Beta-156531).

In Transect 10, approximately 60 meters east of the earthwork enclosure, a cluster of at least five post structures was exposed (fig. 2.13). This cluster included two quadrilateral structures (Structures 4 and 5), two circular structures

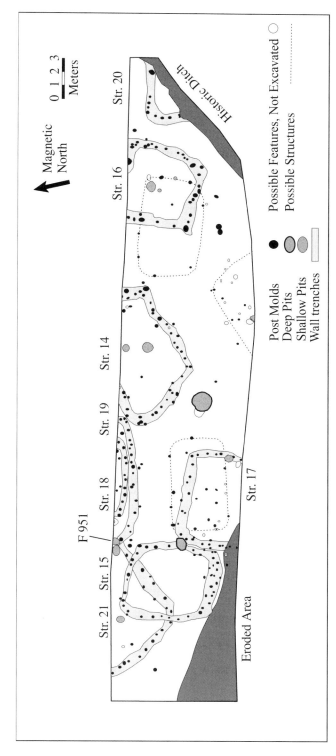

Figure 2.12. Structures 14–21 in Transect 27, Stubbs Earthworks site (excavated June–October 1999). Dashed lines indicate probable additional structures not recognized during excavation. Pit feature 951 is radiocarbon dated and listed in table 2.3.

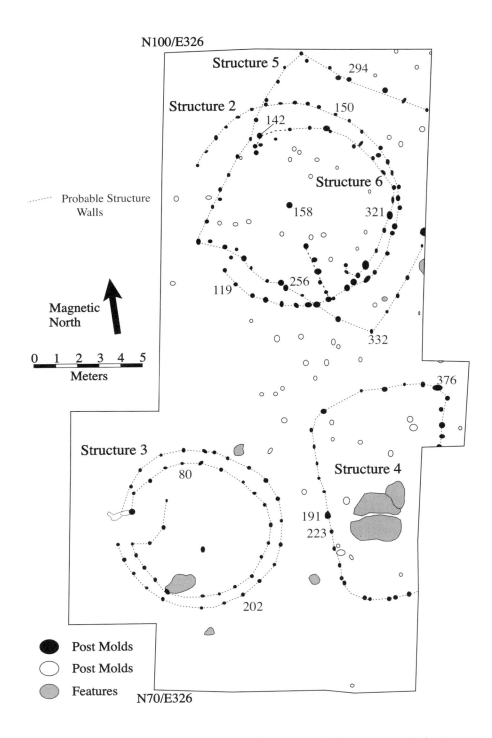

Figure 2.13. Structures 2–6 in Transect 10, Stubbs Earthworks site (excavated July–August 1998). The numbered post molds are radiocarbon dated and listed in table 2.3.

(Structures 2 and 3), and one C-shaped structure (Structure 6). Four of the five structures (Structures 3, 4, 5, and 6) are more or less contemporary within the precision afforded by radiocarbon dating and date to the second century A.D. (table 2.3). Structure 2 probably dates to the fourth century A.D., although one post mold was refilled with soil bearing charcoal dated a couple of centuries earlier (Cowan and Sunderhaus 2002). It is possible that some of these different structural forms had different functional uses. There are many "residual" post molds in Transect 10, some of which probably represent portions of structures we did not recognize during excavation. Sequential rebuilding over previously

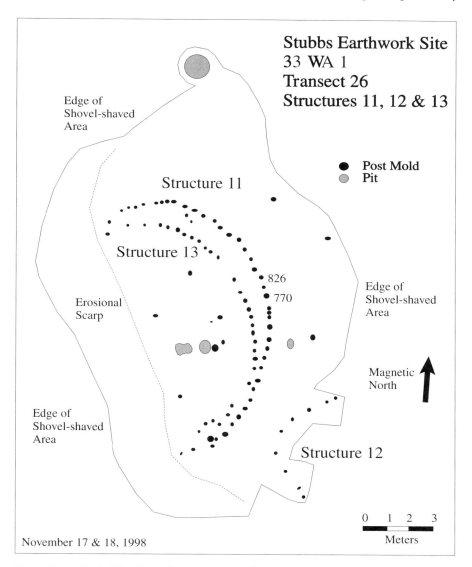

Figure 2.14. Early Woodland Structures 11 and 13 and Hopewellian Structure 12, Transect 26, Stubbs Earthworks site (excavated November 17 and 18, 1998). Post molds 770 and 826 produced Early Wooland dates (Cowan and Sunderhaus 2002).

used spaces suggests that favorable locations adjacent to the earthworks were in high demand.

In an area where earthmoving equipment exposed a series of post molds that we had only the briefest opportunity to investigate (fig. 2.14), we documented fragments of three structures. Two superimposed circular structures measuring 10 meters in diameter are now understood to be of Early Woodland age, based on two radiocarbon-dated post molds from Structure 11 (Cowan and Sunderhaus 2002). However, the corner of a third structure, Structure 12, is also visible. Rectangular with rounded corners, Structure 12 is undoubtedly Hopewellian.

Fragmentary evidence for many other house-sized and houselike structures was observed in several other portions of the site, although time constraints and ongoing construction prevented their full exposure and documentation. Along the terrace edge of Bigfoot Run, a small tributary creek, heavy construction equipment revealed scores of post molds, including several discrete lines of post molds to the east of Transects 26 and 27 (see fig. 2.10). Opportunistic examination of the profiles of water-line and sewer-line construction trenches along the highway to the east and west of the northern edge of the project area (see fig. 2.9) revealed clusters of post molds and pit features that probably also reflect the locations of additional houselike structures. It is very clear that houselike structures were extraordinarily common in many portions of the site outside the earthwork walls.

While the appearance of crowding at the Stubbs Earthworks is, of course, largely the result of long-term site use, it also suggests that suitable housing space in favorable locations adjacent to the earthworks was at a premium. Numerous houselike structures must have been in place at any given time throughout the site's period of use.

Perhaps counterintuitively, the more evidence I see for housing at Stubbs Earthworks, the more I am convinced that these sites may indeed be "vacant ceremonial centers," as initially suggested by Prufer (1964a) and championed by Dancey and Pacheco. I have used the term *houselike* to describe these wooden structures because they very clearly were not places of everyday domestic abode. The accumulations of lithic artifacts and tool-production debris, pottery, fire-cracked rock, charcoal, burnt soil, food remains, and other consequences of prolonged human habitation are notably sparse in subsurface features. Below-ground storage capacity is much too low to have sufficed for long-term residential purposes. Where storage pits were found, they had not been subsequently reused for the disposal of household refuse. These houselike structures were clearly used for a much more limited range of activities than would be expected at residential households, and only episodic use is indicated. Similar evidence has been found at the Fort Ancient site (Cowan, Genheimer, and Sunderhaus 1997; Cowan, Sunderhaus, and Genheimer 1999a, 2004), and there are hints of similar patterns in some central Ohio Hopewell sites as well.

The Smith Site: A Stubbs Cluster Residential Hamlet?

The nearby Smith site (33WA362), part of the Stubbs cluster (Genheimer 1996, 1997), is located on a high, blufflike terrace remnant overlooking the Stubbs Earthworks (see fig. 2.9). On the basis of analysis of surface collections, Genheimer (1997:294) tentatively suggested that the Smith site might fit the general parameters of Pacheco's (1988) hamlet hypothesis, and Dancey and Pacheco (1997a:Table 1.1) list the Smith site as an example of a long-term residential hamlet associated with the Stubbs Earthworks.

Excavations in 2001 (Sunderhaus, Riggs, and Cowan 2001) offered the rare opportunity to examine a purported Hopewell "hamlet" and to compare its subsurface remains with those of nearby "specialized camps" immediately adjacent to an earthwork complex. The emergency salvage excavations of three widely separated areas, albeit very limited in scale, revealed that the Smith site was indeed a locality with numerous houselike Hopewellian structures and subsurface features.

Figure 2.15 illustrates the Smith site's Structure 1, a completely exposed Hopewellian structure with interior dimensions of about 64 square meters. Like many of the structures immediately surrounding the earthwork on the lower terrace, it was roughly square with rounded corners and interior supports. The distinctive form of the structure, mica in the fills of some post molds, and radiocarbon dating (Cowan, Sunderhaus, and Genheimer 2003) substantiate its Hopewellian age. Radiocarbon age estimates from charcoal in two post molds yield diverse results (Table 2.3), but the earlier date of 1890 +/-70 B.P. is more likely to be accurate. An unusual feature is the very wide (3.16 meters) entryway on the south side of the structure along with what appears to be a second, smaller (1.5 meters) entryway near the northeast corner. Although the floor of the structure had been lost to plowing, there was no subsoil indication of an interior hearth. The absence of a hearth, the unusually wide entryways, and the exposed ridge-top location all suggest that this structure was not designed or located for cold weather use. One small pit was located in the interior, and two others were located immediately outside the structure; however, none of these pits contained substantial amounts of refuse.

Thirty meters north of Structure 1, the opportunistic excavation of a sandy ridge crest overlooking the valley revealed a compact cluster of nearly a hundred features (fig. 2.16). Most of the features were post molds, although there were also many deep pits. Construction damage and schedules precluded sufficiently wide exposures to make sense of the post-mold patterns, but clearly at least four or more overlapping post structures were represented. Despite the extraordinary density of features and the presence of many deep pits, there were remarkably few artifacts (a very few small flakes, small bladelet fragments, sherds, and some fire-cracked rocks). Charcoal, burnt soil, and other expected consequences of long-term residential use were notably sparse.

What is remarkable about the Smith site is the general absence of artifacts, charcoal, or burnt soil in the pits and post molds. Such accumulations are characteristic results of long-term residential occupations. The only feature at this

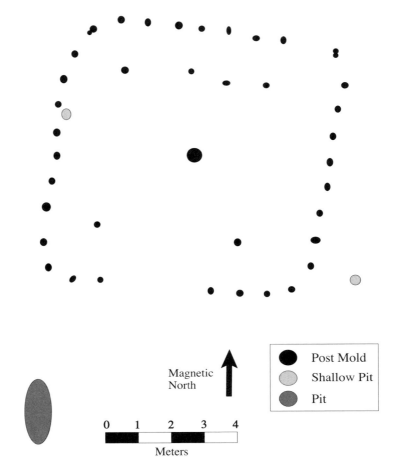

Figure 2.15. Hopewellian Structure 1 (excavated June–July 2001) of the Smith site (33WA362).

site to exhibit significant quantities of cultural debris was a very large, deep pit fortuitously exposed at the very northern end of the site, at a considerable distance from our other excavations. That pit contained a remarkable number of artifacts, including about seventy bladelet fragments, much mica, and sherds from at least twenty-three vessels, 43 percent of which were fine wares of the Hopewell or Southeastern series. The stone tools and the assemblage as a whole, however, cannot be considered characteristic of normal residential activities, and the pit is interpreted as having been filled with debris from nearby special-purpose activities. Two radiocarbon age estimates from Feature 37 (Cowan, Sunderhaus, and Genheimer 2003) yielded inexplicably disparate results (Table 2.3); the earlier date of 1820 +/-70 B.P. falls within the Hopewellian time period, while the younger date is much too young for the pit's cultural contents. Available evidence thus indicates that the Smith site was used frequently during the Middle Woodland period but only for relatively brief periods of time and

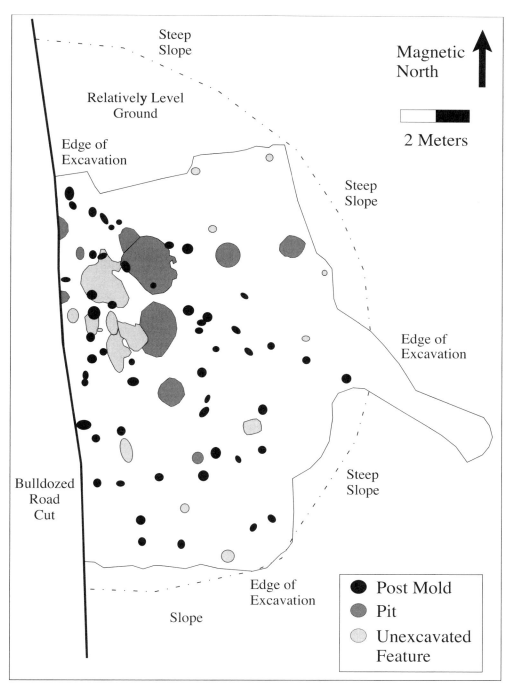

Figure 2.16. Post molds and pits in the Sandy Knoll transect, Smith site (33WA362).

only for a limited range of purposes. All evidence to date suggests that the site was used for the same kinds of restricted purposes exhibited by the structures immediately surrounding the Stubbs Earthworks.

Were Ohio Middle Woodland Populations Mobile?

The most clearly articulated model of Ohio Hopewell settlement (Dancey and Pacheco 1997a) views each community as consisting of numerous sedentary hamlets closely clustered around a ceremonial center (fig. 2.1). The geographic scales of such communities are not specified in the proposed model, but the most commonly cited examples of sedentary hamlets, such as Murphy, McGraw (Prufer 1965), and Jennison Guard (Blosser 1996; Kozarek 1997), are all located within easy walking distance of the nearest earthwork complex.

It is not clear why a sedentary community would need an abundance of well-built, special-purpose housing facilities on the immediate fringes of a ceremonial gathering place if its year-round residences were located no more than an hour's walk away from the community center. The geographic scale of these communities is so limited that formal, highly visible community gathering places would not have been necessary to promote intracommunity communication and social solidarity. Everyday foraging and informal household visitation would easily have brought the members of such a community into daily, face-to-face contact without the necessity of constructing monumental architecture.

The imposing grandeur of Ohio Hopewell ceremonial sites suggests that they were gathering places for much more widespread and, probably, much more mobile communities than is suggested by the Prufer-Dancey-Pacheco sedentary hamlet model. Monumental architecture implies a strong need for social integration, and the scale of the architecture implies the geographic scale of the attractive force. The abundance of what seem to be "guest houses" further implies a highly dispersed population whose members periodically traveled relatively great distances to attend community gatherings.

The commonly cited candidates for sedentary hamlets have none of the technological characteristics of long-term residential sites occupied by whole social groups and a full range of tool-making, tool-using inhabitants. The bladelet tools that dominate their assemblages were a symbolic substitute for mundane tools for use within ritually important places. When one strips away the overlying veneer of bladelet tools, one is left with a biface-dominated assemblage suggestive of high mobility, not of sedentism.

Finally, it remains unclear what really distinguishes the purported sedentary hamlets from the specialized camps located only a few hundred meters away. The hamlets of the model would just as easily represent other short-term camps used during socially integrative events. Rigorous comparisons have yet to be conducted to determine what similarities and differences exist in assemblage and feature content and internal spatial structure between Hopewellian activity areas presently interpreted as having fulfilled fundamentally different functions within an individual earthwork-centered community.

We are still left with the problem of where and how Ohio Middle Woodland people lived when not attending a ritually focused communitywide event. The lines of reasoning expressed here imply that Hopewell people may not have looked particularly "Hopewell" at home. A significantly different suite of technological strategies would have been used for everyday living than were used at large-scale public functions. My suspicion is that those strategies would have consisted of a technological mix that combined bifacial tools with simple flake-core technology. Many of the bifacial tools associated with actual residential sites and other subsistence-related activity areas would probably be more robust than those typically thought of as Hopewellian, and they might well be typologically different from what we recognize as Hopewellian. The delicate bladelets and distinctively shaped, very thin bifacial tools we see as diagnostic of Hopewell were paraphernalia reserved for use in ritual activities, especially at socially special places within a much larger regional landscape of habitual use.

This chapter questions whether many of the small sites presently interpreted as sedentary Hopewell hamlets were indeed long-term residential base camps occupied by complete social groups. If they are not, then we still have not identified key components of a complete settlement system for Ohio's Middle Woodland populations. Ultimately, we have not resolved the issue of whether Middle Woodland populations were sedentary and logistically mobile or whether they were residentially mobile, but there is reason to suspect that Ohio Hopewellian subsistence-settlement systems extended over larger areas and involved higher levels of residential mobility than the presently popular sedentary hamlet model indicates. Somewhere out there, there must be an Ohio Middle Woodland that doesn't look particularly "Hopewell."

3

Middle Woodland Settlements and Social Organization in the Central Ohio Valley

Were the Hopewell Really Farmers?

Richard W. Yerkes

The people we call the Hopewell are one of the best-known but least-understood prehistoric cultures in the world. Their artifacts, burials, mounds, and earthworks are spectacular and are the most elaborate built environment in the prehistoric United States (Clay 1998). For many, the magnitude of Hopewell earthwork construction and the abundance of exotic artifacts is difficult to explain in the absence of well-developed agriculture, a hierarchical social structure, craft specialization, and centralized redistribution (Hall 1997:156). However, there is no empirical evidence for any of these features in Ohio Hopewell societies.

Several archaeologists believe that the Ohio Hopewell were sedentary swidden farmers occupying dispersed hamlets near large, vacant, ceremonial centers (fig. 3.1). These archaeologists suggest that the Archaic and Early Woodland ancestors of the Hopewell were complex hunter-gatherers who lived in areas where wild food was abundant. They argue that by 100 B.C., the Hopewell had domesticated several native weedy plants (Dancey and Pacheco 1997b; Pacheco 1996a, 1997; Wymer 1993). It is assumed that domesticates were added to a broad spectrum of wild foods, but eventually they became the main food source of the Hopewell.

A different view of Ohio Hopewell is more appropriate. For years, Hall (1980, 1997) and Griffin (1964, 1997) described Hopewell societies as egalitarian and decentralized. No Hopewell merchant princes were sustained by agricultural surpluses. Like most American Indians, the Hopewell gained prestige not by accumulating wealth but by giving gifts to others (Hall 1997:156). Consumption of domesticated plants does not transform the Ohio Hopewell societies into sedentary farmers, and the construction of elaborate ceremonial and mortuary features does not turn them into chiefdoms. Hopewell societies were examples of complex but mobile tribes.

The few small domestic Hopewell sites that have been excavated have not produced any evidence that they were occupied for long periods of time (figs. 3.2–3.4). The social organization of the Ohio Hopewell allowed them to be

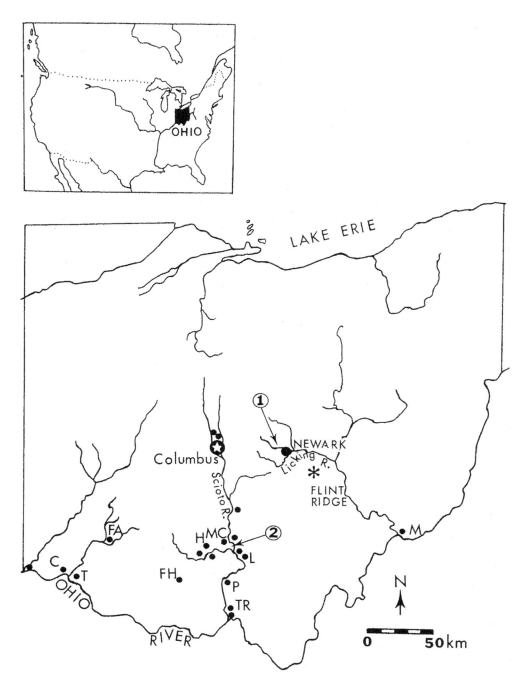

Figure 3.1. The location of (1) the Murphy site (33LI212) and (2) the McGraw site in relation to the major Ohio Hopewell earthworks (black dots). The Newark Earthworks, which includes the Hale's House site (33LI252), is shown by the larger black dot. C = Cincinnati, FA = Fort Ancient, FH = Fort Hill, H = Hopewell, L = Liberty (Edwin Harness), M = Marietta, MC = Mound City, P = Piketon, T = Turner, TR = Tremper.

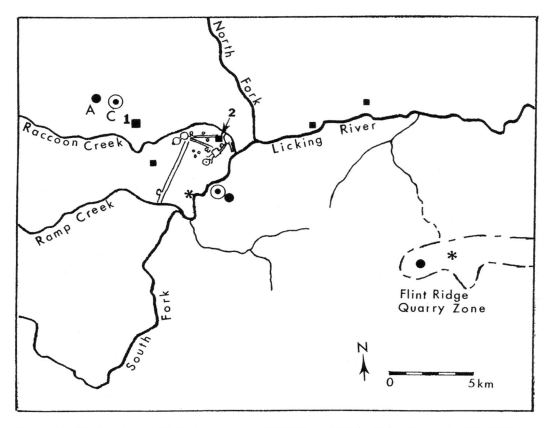

Figure 3.2. The location of (1) the Murphy site (33LI212) and (2) the Hale's House site (33LI252) in and near the Newark Earthworks. Some of the other recorded Hopewell sites are also shown, including small habitation sites (black squares), mounds (black dots), and small earthworks (black dots in circles), as well as biface, bladelet core, and bladelet caches (asterisks). A = Alligator Mound, C = Crescent Mound.

mobile and dispersed, yet well integrated. The organization needed for the construction of monumental earthworks, the production and distribution of exotic goods, and the emergence of some status differentiation is known to have developed within segmentary societies or complex tribes (Fowles 2002; Sahlins 1968; Service 1962). The flexibility of tribal models provides a more useful framework for understanding Hopewell social organization. The Hopewell do not reveal their secrets easily, and there are aspects of their behavior that we may never understand. However, their elaborate cultural landscape testifies to their ability to maintain local and individual autonomy within an extensive tribal network for several centuries. The Ohio Hopewell earthworks and the elaborate goods that are found within them were not products of emerging Middle Woodland chiefdoms that were competing with each other for political and social territories. In this regard they stand in stark contrast to the later Mississippian societies of the Southeast. An elaborate ceremonial complex may have been necessary to bind the small mobile populations that still sought wild foods to meet most of their subsistence needs (Hall 1997). The Hopewell show us the degree of cultural complexity that can be achieved with the organizational flexibility of tribal networks, even if the Hopewell lacked food surpluses, specialized production, and permanent residences.

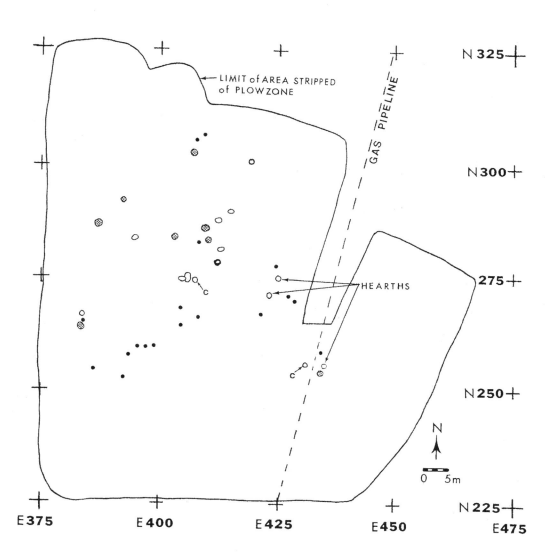

Figure 3.3. The distribution of the 43 excavated features in the 6,500–square-meter area where the plow zone was removed at the Murphy site (33LI212). Note the dispersed pattern of postholes (black dots), earth ovens (shaded), shallow cylindrical pits (marked with "c"), shallow basins (unshaded), and burned areas (marked as hearths).

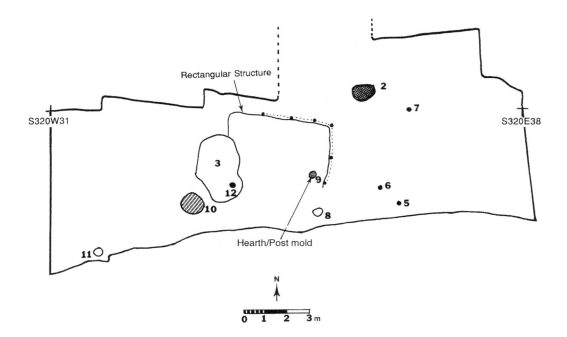

Figure 3.4. The excavated features at the Hale's House site (33LI252), which is located within the Newark Earthworks complex. Note the L-shaped arrangement of postholes (linked by dashed line) that the excavator (E. E. Hale Jr.) believed were part of a rectangular structure. Feature 2 is a shallow basin. Feature 3 is a large, shallow refuse pit. Features 8 and 11 are shallow basins. Features 5, 6, 7, and 12 are postholes. The excavator called Feature 9 a burned area or posthole. Feature 10 is an earth oven. Redrawn from Hale 1980; also see Lepper and Yerkes 1997.

Hopewell Agriculture and Settlement Systems

Archaeologists assumed the existence of Woodland agriculture in the Ohio Valley long before any empirical evidence for farming had been recovered from archaeological contexts (Clay and Niquette 1989:17). It was once thought that the Ohio Hopewell were maize farmers who lived in sedentary villages near their mounds and earthworks. It was believed that the construction of the earthworks and the presentation of the elaborate Hopewell mortuary rituals required a food surplus and an agricultural economy (Thomas 1894:614–620; Willey and Phillips 1958:157–158). There is no convincing evidence to support this view. A recent model has them living in dispersed farmsteads or hamlets near "vacant" earthwork complexes and growing native weedy crops using a system of shifting slash-and-burn cultivation (Dancey and Pacheco 1997b; Prufer 1965; Wymer 1993). There is not much support for this model either.

Hall (1997:156) suggests that the elaborate ceremonial complex of the Ohio Hopewell developed as part of an organizational solution for tribal societies whose subsistence was based on hunting, fishing, gathering nuts and wild plants, and sowing and harvesting some native domesticated plants. To obtain food and fiber, Ohio Hopewell societies seem to have traveled to locations where food was abundant during different seasons of the year. Their seasonal mobility created a dispersed settlement system. To avoid becoming isolated, these groups needed some means of social integration. Constructing earthworks and participating in elaborate rituals may have been a way of maintaining ties between the dispersed members of these mobile societies.

Exotic goods and foodstuffs were exchanged at Hopewell ceremonial centers, but the primary function of the earthworks may have been social, rather than economic. Too often we see the earthworks described only in economic terms. They are called transaction or redistribution centers for Interaction Sphere artifacts and food supplies. For some archaeologists, the rationale for Hopewell exchange and the investment of labor in earthwork and mound construction is that by doing these things, dispersed groups would maintain ties that allowed them to share food during times of scarcity (Brose 1979; Ford 1979; Wymer 1993). However, the Hopewell may have had other reasons to travel to the earthworks. Fortier (1998:357) suggests that Hopewell earthworks were rendezvous centers that operated like the Great Basin Shoshone fandangos. Steward (1938:237) observed that the feasting, dancing, and visiting at the fandangos promoted social intercourse without economic motivation (also see Clay 1998 for similar ideas about Adena ceremonial centers).

The Hopewell concern with food shortages and fluctuating resources may have led to the adoption of a mobile, dispersed subsistence system. Small groups may have spread out and traveled to locations where certain resources were abundant during certain seasons of the year. This solution to the problem of unpredictable and uneven food resources would have led to a situation where the small groups were becoming isolated from each other. Scheduled feasts, adoption ceremonies, and burial rituals held at the earthworks would have allowed the dispersed groups to maintain ties. This would have kept the Hopewell tribes integrated (Hall 1997; Seeman 1995).

Small Hopewell Settlements

The contrast between the large Ohio Hopewell ceremonial complexes and the tiny Middle Woodland sites that are spread over the floodplains, terraces, and uplands of the central Ohio Valley is striking (Aument 1992; Baker 1993; Cowan, this volume; Cowan, Sunderhaus, and Genheimer 1999b, 2000; Yerkes 1990, 1994, 2002a, 2002b). There are no large, nucleated Hopewell villages located near the earthworks. Why did the people who built these earthen monuments disperse into such small and widely scattered habitation sites when they left the ceremonial sites? To account for this disparity, in one model of Ohio Hopewell settlement systems the small sites are called "sedentary hamlets" (Dancey 1991; Dancey and Pacheco 1997a; Pacheco 1996a, 1997). However, several archaeologists have questioned the assumption that these small Ohio Hopewell domestic sites were occupied nearly continuously for long periods of time (Clay and Creasman 1999; Cowan, this volume; Weller von Molsdorff, Burks, and Burcham 1999; Yerkes 1990, 1994, 2002a, 2002b). If sedentary sites are stable, formally organized, year-round settlements (Holley 1993:279; Murdock 1967:159), then excavations at such sites should reveal substantial domestic dwellings (which may have evidence of rebuilding) and numerous storage pits. There should be a diverse artifact assemblage including discarded tools that show evidence of both short-term and long-term use, and the remains of plants and animals that were obtained during different seasons of the year. Ethnographic studies have shown that sedentary groups construct larger and more complex structures and facilities than do mobile groups (Binford 1983; Clay and Creasman 1999; Cowan, this volume; Fortier 1998; Holley 1993; Kent 1991, 1992; Sanders 1990).

Analysis of radiocarbon dates from two small Hopewell sites located near major earthworks (the Murphy and McGraw sites) revealed that there were several brief occupation episodes at each site, not the single long-term occupations proposed in the dispersed hamlet model (Carr and Haas 1996). No substantial domestic structures, thick middens, or other evidence for long-term occupation were found at these sites (Lepper and Yerkes 1997; Yerkes 1990, 2002a, 2002b). The deep bell-shaped or flat-bottomed storage pits that are so common at villages inhabited by Late Prehistoric (A.D. 1000–1670) agricultural groups like the Fort Ancient tribes (Nass 1987; Nass and Yerkes 1995; Wagner 1996) are not found at the small Hopewell sites (figs. 3.3 and 3.4). The features found at these small Ohio Valley Hopewell sites include shallow basins, hearths, and earth ovens, types that are quite common at sites occupied by mobile Archaic foragers (Kozarek 1997; McElrath et al. 1984; Yerkes 1986).

Wagner (1996:267–268) has examined the use of underground storage pits by Fort Ancient groups. She argues that the pits provided "concealed storage" for foods and other goods during the winter season, when the villages were abandoned and the Fort Ancient populations dispersed to hunting camps. The concealed storage pits indicate that the Fort Ancient groups planned on coming back to the villages in the spring. The absence of concealed storage pits or cache pits at the small Ohio Hopewell sites suggests that these Middle Woodland groups may not have intended to return to those sites in the near future. The mobile settlement-subsistence system employed by the Ohio Hopewell seems to have included regular trips to the earthworks for feasting, adoption, mortuary rituals, exchange, and social interaction. Following these visits, small groups dispersed to different locations during different seasons to hunt, fish, gather nuts and wild plants, and harvest the native domesticated plants that they had sown earlier.

The Starchy, Oily, Weedy Plants

The three most common weedy plants found at the small Ohio Hopewell sites near the Newark Earthworks in Licking County, Ohio, are erect knotweed (*Polygonum erectum*), goosefoot (*Chenopodium* spp.), and maygrass (*Phalaris caroliniana*) (Wymer 1993, 1997). Sumpweed (*Iva annua* var. *macrocarpa*) and sunflower (*Helianthus annuus*) are present but less common. These starchy and oily weeds are classified as native domesticated plants by virtue of the observed changes in the morphology of their seeds or by their presence at archaeological sites that are believed to lie beyond the natural range of the weed. Wymer (1996, 1997) assumed that forests were cleared and gardens were maintained to grow these cultigens, since charcoal from "second-growth" taxa was recovered at some small Ohio Hopewell sites. However, foragers are known to burn and clear forests to improve the habitat of wild plants and animals, and this may account for the presence of the charcoal from "second growth" taxa at the small Hopewell sites (Harlan 1994; Stewart 1956:118–121; Styles and Klippel 1996:118–120). No one has demonstrated that these native weedy plants depended on humans for their propagation. Paleoethnobotanists suggest that sunflower, sumpweed, and *Chenopodium* were domesticated between 2500 and 1000 B.C. in eastern North America. Mobile Late Archaic foragers probably domesticated knotweed and maygrass during the same interval (Fritz 1990; Watson 1996:162). These plants were domesticated at least 900 years before the Hopewell cultural climax, and yet the attainment of this cultural zenith has been attributed to an agricultural "revolution" that led to increased sedentism, food production, and the concentration of dispersed populations (Seeman 1992b:35; Wymer 1997).

Hopewell Farmers?

Wymer (1997:161) describes the Ohio Hopewell as farmers, but if farming is defined as a system of agricultural crop production that employs systematic soil preparation and tillage (Harris 1997), and if agriculture is reserved for contexts in which human groups depend on plants for most of their subsistence needs (Bronson 1977:26), then the Hopewell were certainly not farmers. The Hopewell may have practiced a form of cultivation by sowing (with or without tilling the soil) and harvesting useful species of wild and/or domesticated plants (Bronson 1977; Harris 1997; Murdock 1967:159; Stoltman and Baerreis 1983:257), but it is misleading to view these starchy, oily weeds as agricultural plants that depended on humans for their reproduction. The weedy cultigens were supplements to the wild nuts, plants, fish, and game that supported the Hopewell, as they had supported their ancestors (Dunne and Green 1998; Watson 1988, 1989; Yarnell 1993). Ohio Valley Hopewell populations do not exhibit the patterns of caries and dental wear that are associated with agricultural societies and high-carbohydrate diets (Sciulli 1997).

There is no evidence for increased cultivation of these native weedy plants by the Hopewell either. In fact, increased use of these starchy and oily plants takes place after the Hopewell "collapse" during the Late Woodland period. Braun (1988:21) noted that charred weedy plant seeds increase from less than 10 percent in Middle Woodland floral assemblages to over 80 percent in Late Woodland samples in Missouri and Illinois, while Wymer (1987b:254, 1993) similarly

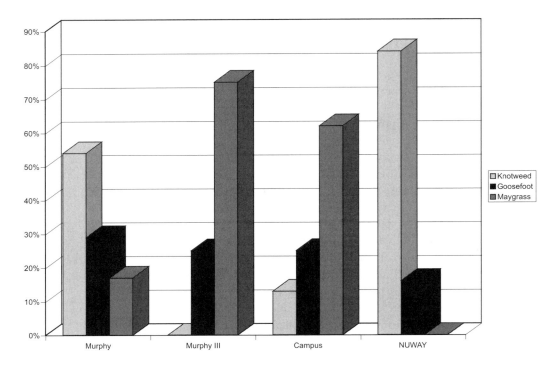

Figure 3.5. Percentages of native weedy domesticates at small Ohio Hopewell sites in Licking County, Ohio. Data from Wymer 1987b, 1993, 1997.

observed that starchy and oily plant remains were more prominent in Late Woodland floral assemblages in central Ohio (also see Dancey 1996b). It is better to view the Middle Woodland cultigens as favored species whose propagation was encouraged by mobile Hopewell foragers than as domesticated field crops or agricultural staples.

Planting seeds was not uncommon among hunter-gatherers (Harlan 1994:13). In North America, the usual pattern was to burn a patch of vegetation in the fall and sow some seeds in the spring. There was no need to remain at the location where the seeds were sown. The foragers needed to return only when the seeds had ripened. These Middle Woodland domesticated weedy seed plants were probably secondary in importance to forest plant foods like hickory nuts, acorns, and wild berries (Watson 1988:42–43).

There was great variability in the kinds and proportions of plants utilized by different groups of Ohio Hopewell. They were probably quite sophisticated in their use of plants, but they did not have to live in sedentary farmsteads or hamlets to sow and harvest the plants they found useful. The relative abundance of the three starchy weeds recovered at the four small Ohio Hopewell sites studied by Wymer (1997) was quite variable (fig. 3.5). These sites were located

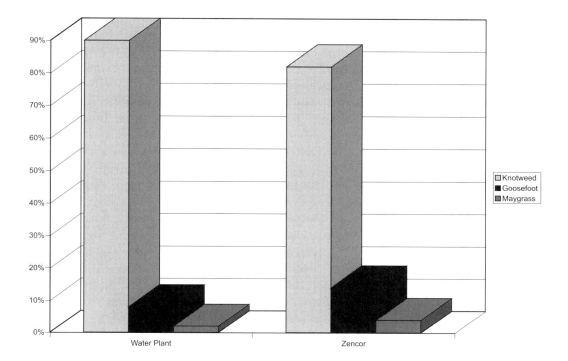

Figure 3.6. Percentages of native weedy domesticates at two Late Woodland sites in Franklin County, Ohio. Data from Wymer 1987b, 1993, 1997.

in different microenvironmental zones, and the small floral samples from the four sites may contain the plants that were most common at each location during the season that they were occupied. When Wymer (1987b, 1993) studied the plant remains from two larger Late Woodland (A.D. 400–1000) sites near Columbus, Ohio, she found a similar pattern of plant species abundance at both sites (fig. 3.6). This may be due to the fact that the Late Woodland samples represent the seeds collected over several seasons rather than a single season. These data reveal that patterns of Ohio Hopewell plant utilization are consistent with the methods employed by hunter-gatherers (summarized in Harlan 1994).

There is also evidence that the Hopewell obtained food from different locations during different seasons of the year. More seeds of the starchy, oily native domesticates were found in hearths, earth ovens, and shallow pits at the small sites located on floodplains and terraces near the major earthworks. Small Ohio Hopewell sites located in the uplands usually have more carbonized hickory nut, black walnut, and hazelnut husks and wild berry seeds in their features (Aument 1992; Baker 1978; Weller von Molsdorff, Burks, and Burcham 1999). The lowland sites seem to have been revisited during the warmer months, while the upland sites were occupied during the colder months of the year.

Sedentary Farmsteads?

Sedentary populations were extremely rare in the Ohio Valley during prehistoric and early historic times. For example, Fort Ancient groups are considered to be "consummate maize agriculturists" (Wagner 1996:256), and yet they spent only the warmer months of the year in their circular villages. Family groups dispersed to hunting camps during the winter (Essenpreis 1978; Wagner 1996). This pattern of seasonal nucleation and dispersal was practiced by many of the historic agricultural tribes of the Ohio Valley–Great Lakes region, such as the Shawnee, Miami, and Potawatomi (Callender 1978b; Fitting and Cleland 1969; Mason 1981:32–36; Murdock 1967).

The development of Late Prehistoric native agricultural systems that included clearing some of the forest, tilling the soil with hoes, and cultivating maize, squash, beans, sunflower, tobacco, and several other plants did not lead to year-round residence at permanent villages (Hall 1980; Stoltman and Baerreis 1983:259–262; Wagner 1996). There is no evidence to support the idea that the sowing and harvesting of native weedy plants forced the prehistoric foragers of the Ohio Valley to become sedentary farmers during the Middle Woodland period. The relationship between subsistence practices and sedentism is complex. All foragers are not mobile, and all farmers are not sedentary (Baker 1993; Becker 1999:22; Phillips 1998:217). Consuming native domesticated plants does not make the Ohio Hopewell farmers. The presence of domesticated weedy plants at the small settlements is not an archaeological correlate of sedentism.

Mobility patterns are often reconstructed from seasonal patterns in the faunal and floral remains recovered at prehistoric sites (Cross 1988; Monks 1981; Yerkes 1987). However, interpretations of the degree of sedentism at small Ohio Hopewell sites are not based on seasonal proxy data. Kozarek (1997:133) claims that evidence of "multiseasonal" exploitation of animals and the presence of seasonally available species indicate that the small Jennison Guard Hopewell site (located on the Ohio River floodplain near Cincinnati) was a permanent settlement. However, she presented no empirical data in support of her claim. Repeated occupations by Hopewell groups returning to the site at different seasons of the year may give the illusion of a permanent occupation (Becker 1999:2), and it is difficult to distinguish multiple occupations from continuous ones in the archaeological record (Rocek and Bar-Yosef 1998; Yerkes 1986).

Instead, a number of untested assumptions are made to estimate how long people resided at these small sites. Wymer (1997:160–161) assumes that the only way the Hopewell could have obtained weedy native plants and hazelnuts is if they stayed in the same location all year long (however, she finds the lack of any remains of house structures at small settlements like the Murphy site to be "puzzling"). Others cite the "structure" of activities at a site—as reflected in the distribution of artifacts and features—as archaeological correlates for sedentism (Dancey 1991; Kozarek 1997; Wymer 1997). This approach is based on the untested assumption that discrete activity areas, few overlapping features, and systematic refuse disposal would characterize sedentary settlements. It is assumed that these sites were permanently occupied for extended and uninterrupted periods of time. However, if this were the case, why are there no permanent structures, storage pits, or substantial middens at these sites?

In fact, the assumed correlates for sedentism (discrete activity areas, few overlapping features, and systematic refuse disposal) may actually indicate very brief occupation episodes at the Murphy site and the excavated portions of the Jennison Guard site (Dancey 1991; Kozarek 1997). Refitting, microwear, and spatial analysis studies at Old World sites occupied by mobile foragers revealed similar patterns of discrete activity areas, few overlapping features, and systematic refuse disposal (Becker 1999; Becker and Wendorf 1993; Cahen, Keeley, and van Noten 1979). These Old World sites were shown to be short-term occupations, not permanent settlements.

Pacheco (1988:92–93) listed the following archaeological correlates for sedentary Hopewell farmsteads along Raccoon Creek near the Newark Earthworks: the sites are small, functionally similar, structurally identical, and linearly dispersed. However, Baker (1993:32) noted that these features are also characteristics of sites that were part of mobile hunting-and-gathering settlement/subsistence systems.

There is no evidence that domesticated plants were staples in the diets of the Ohio Hopewell societies or that the Ohio Hopewell invested substantial amounts of labor in food production activities. No prehistoric agricultural tools are associated with the Ohio Hopewell. While later Fort Ancient and Mississippian societies made and used hoes made of chipped stone, shell, and bone (scapulae) and deer-jaw sickles, no comparable farming tools have been found at Ohio Hopewell sites (Brown 1964a; Cobb 1989; Wagner 1996). The toolkit of the Ohio Hopewell is a hunting-and-gathering toolkit (Yerkes 1994, 2002b; see also Cowan, this volume).

Conclusion

There is no need to invent a "unique" system of swidden agriculture with no ethnographic analog to explain Ohio Hopewell subsistence practices. For more than thirty years, Robert L. Hall has argued that there is nothing about Ohio Hopewell societies that could not be explained by the workings of cultural processes that were known from eyewitness accounts of historic Woodland tribal societies (Hall 1980:408, 1997:156). Hall's doctrine of cultural uniformitarianism can help us understand Ohio Hopewell subsistence and learn why they devoted so much time and energy to the construction of mounds and earthworks and to the exchange of elaborate artifacts. Rather than indulging in a form of cultural catastrophism that views the Ohio Hopewell as a society with no analogs, we should affirm their connection with their Native American descendants (Hall 1997). An examination of the ethnohistorical record can provide us with hypotheses about Hopewell behavior that can be tested with archaeological data.

The Earthwork/Habitation Dichotomy

A Central Problem of Ohio Hopewell

A. Martin Byers

The central and largely underdebated issue in Ohio Hopewell studies is the social nature of the relationship that is expressed in the earthwork/habitation settlement dichotomy. This dichotomy is characterized by an almost complete lack of overlap between the material cultural assemblages and the features of these two types of locales. Of course, this is not to deny that there is considerable debate about the Ohio Hopewell settlement system. But this debate does not address the nature of the relation manifested in this dichotomy. Instead, it has focused on the occupational statuses of both earthwork and habitation locales. Were the dispersed habitation locales permanently occupied hamlets (Dancey and Pacheco 1997a; Pacheco and Dancey, this volume), or were they occupied only as seasonal gardening camps (Cowan 1999, this volume; Yerkes 1990, this volume)? Were the earthworks occupied permanently, or were they effectively vacant throughout most of the year, serving as the context of large ritual gatherings only for brief periods from one year to the next (Dancey and Pacheco 1997a; Pacheco and Dancey, this volume)? Or were the earthworks being constantly used by variably sized aggregations of those living in the surrounding habitation locales (Greber 1997)?

As in all debates, there is usually a core that none of the debaters disputes. In this case, there seems to be general agreement that a local embankment earthwork and its associated structures were built, used, and owned by the population that occupied the surrounding dispersed habitation locales, regardless of whether earthworks were occupied permanently or temporarily, or whether habitations were occupied year-round or seasonally (Connolly 1997; Cowan, this volume; Dancey 1988a, 1991, 1992b, 1996b; Dancey and Pacheco 1997a; Greber 1997; Lepper 1988, 1996, 1998b; Pacheco 1988, 1993, 1996a, 1997; Pacheco and Dancey, this volume; Prufer 1964a, 1965, 1997b; Yerkes 1990, this volume). This core agreement even allows for the flexibility of collective ownership, recognizing that some of the larger earthworks might have been built and used by alliances of those groups responsible for the smaller earthworks (Dancey and Pacheco 1997a).

In short, despite the debate over occupancy status, all parties generally assume that the earthwork-habitation relation as manifested in this dichotomy is appropriately characterized in corporate (kinship-based) proprietorship terms. By general agreement, the social dimension is usually elaborated by treating the earthworks as the symbolic center of the proprietorial corporation or alliance that also acted as a monumental symbolic claim of exclusive control or ownership of all the surrounding territory. This generally accepted view will be termed here the exclusive territorial account of the Ohio Hopewell dichotomy.

This chapter will not address the occupational status debate. Rather, it focuses on the presupposition of the debate, namely, the exclusive territorial account. This account will be critiqued and an alternative, termed the dual clan-cult account, will be presented. This chapter will argue that the dichotomy manifests two different and mutually exclusive social organizations—the habitation locales being the domestic residences of kin groups, probably organized as nested lineage-clan systems, and the earthworks being the sacred places of autonomous world-renewal sodalities or cults (Byers 2004). Two open-ended and mutually exclusive social networks of clans and cults, then, constituted the social system of southern and south-central Ohio during the Middle Woodland period. Hence, active adults occupied two social worlds, clan and cult, and quite literally and regularly passed back and forth from one to the other as they fulfilled the social duties and obligations appropriate and specific to each social sphere.

If the domestic habitation locales are linked together into open-ended networks by kinship descent and alliance, then it makes intuitive sense to postulate that the world-renewal cults would be based on some common social principle that was nonkinship in nature. I have argued elsewhere and empirically grounded the claim that these cults would most likely be based on the social-structural principles of same-gender (probably male)/same-generation companionship (Byers 1996). To be more specific, I have postulated that a cult was constituted by the integration of at least one senior age-grade with at least one junior age-grade with attached shamanic priests. I have termed these ecclesiastic-communal cults, and the earthworks served as the sacred contexts of world-renewal ritual (see also Byers 2004 for a fuller discussion of this organization).

In terms of the dual clan-cult account, therefore, the dichotomy manifests a kinship/companionship duality. A careful interpretive analysis of the material cultural distribution between these two site types is the basis for this claim.

Symbolism and Material Cultural Style

To address the social nature of the earthwork-habitation relation, a short discussion of the symbolic meaning of material culture is called for. I have found that the way we meaningfully use the court warrant is a useful analogy for understanding material culture (Byers 1999). Warrants are critical documentary artifacts by which their legitimate bearers are constituted as officers of the court (for example, bailiffs or sheriffs). With the appropriate warrant a sheriff's physically seizing and handcuffing a party is constituted as a legal act of arrest. In the absence of the warrant, this same behavior might be better characterized as an assault. I have claimed that warranting, in this sense, is not limited to literate society. Rather, it is a basic part of all human social life. Therefore, it would be as critically necessary for nonliterate as for literate societies. Since nonliterate societies lack any forms of authoritative documentation, it is intuitively reasonable to assume that material cultural items would serve this purpose.

Warrants (or more properly, the instruments of warranting) are always symbolic in nature. The symbolic aspect of material culture is recognized by archaeologists to be carried by style. It is postulated that material cultural style has symbolic powers equivalent to those mediated in modern societies by warrants and other authoritative documentation: licenses, money, stamps, passports, and visas, as well as nondocumentary symbols such as military and police badges, insignias, uniforms, and so on (Douglas 1982). This means that warranting is a symbolic material process that is built into the use of the artifacts by virtue of their stylistics, which constitute them as symbolic pragmatic devices.

All this would mean, for example, that in a typical foraging society, anyone who is expected to carry out regular predatory behaviors on animals would quite matter-of-factly use tools displaying the local hunting styles. In this way he ensures being perceived as a hunter. Implicit in this, of course, is the opposite: those who use hunting gear bearing unfamiliar styles will be treated as strangers. To be perceived as a stranger, in this case, may be tantamount to being perceived as an actual or potential poacher by the local population, even though the predatory behaviors these strangers might perform would be no different objectively from those performed by local men using tools bearing recognized hunting styles. Thus, by bearing appropriate styles, ordinary and not-so-ordinary artifacts serve as different types of symbolic warrants, by which the "raw" behaviors they typically mediate are constituted as the appropriate types of social activities their doers intend.

Dual Ritual Spheres or Unitary Ritual Sphere?

It is suggested here that while the mutually exclusive social networks of clans and cults, as postulated by the dual clan-cult account, would differ in terms of interests (the lineage/clans having domestic and kinship alliance concerns and the cults having world-renewal and cult alliance concerns), this does not mean that only the cult networks, and not the lineage/clan networks, would have ritual concerns and practices. As illustrated in the above hunting example, symbolic pragmatics in preindustrial societies always take on a strong ritual dimension so that even domestic subsistence and settlement practices would incorporate ritual (Ingold 1987). In the same way, the world-renewal ritual sphere of the cults had cosmological-ecological interests as part of its core world-renewal concerns. Therefore, in accordance with the autonomy of clan and cult, it is postulated that these two mutually autonomous organizations would also constitute two mutually autonomous ritual spheres.

Typically, autonomous ritual spheres maintain their separate identifications through mutual symbolic contrast. Separation of socio-sacred locales is maintained by explicit proscriptions that safeguard the sanctity of the two separate groups (Douglas 1966). This is not to claim that one ritual sphere has greater or lesser sanctity than the other. It simply argues that the operation of two distinct ritual spheres based on different structural axes (for example, kinship and companionship) should lead to their maintaining respective purity by promoting a general avoidance of mixing the resources, objects, and activities across the spheres. Therefore, it is logical to postulate under the dual clan-cult account that the earthwork/habitation dichotomy not only manifested a companionship/kinship contrast, but also grounded a duality of ritual spheres. The sanctity of these two spheres was maintained by strong proscriptions by which to avoid the mixing of ritual resources, objects, and activities across the spheres. I will call this the dual ritual spheres account, and it is treated as a key ancillary to the dual clan-cult account. This means that demonstration of the dual ritual spheres account is direct support of the dual clan-cult account under which it is subsumed.

Because the exclusive territorial account treats the earthwork/habitation dichotomy as manifesting a modular territorial polity in which the earthwork locale is the ancestral mortuary center of the dispersed domestic habitations, it follows that only one ritual sphere would be expected to exist. While it would be expected that some immediate-family rituals might be held in the separate habitation locales, the earthwork was the community center of the corporate kin group, and collective ceremonial activity would have been performed there. This can be called the unitary ritual sphere account, and it can be treated as ancillary to the exclusive territorial account.

Under the dual ritual spheres account, while there are strong proscriptions separating these two spheres, the membership would not be mutually exclusive. Individuals are members of both a clan and typically at least one cult and are expected to move regularly and freely from their lineage/clan locales to their cult locales in accordance with their duties in each. Under these conditions, a basic practical problem would be ensuring that in moving between these two ritually contrasting locales, individuals would not mix the ritual materials of one sphere with those of the other. This problem would not exist in the social world postulated under the unitary ritual sphere account, since there would be no proscription between moving ritual resources from habitation to earthwork or from earthwork to habitation. Instead, the proscriptions would apply between different ritual locales—since, of course, each earthwork locale defines an exclusive corporate polity. Individuals would be full members of only their natal ritual earthwork and "adopted" members of their affinal ritual earthwork (or earthworks). Therefore, they would not have free access to the earthworks of neighboring groups to which they had no descent or affinal affiliations.

If the earthwork-habitation relation was unitary in nature, as postulated under the unitary ritual sphere account, then the earthworks would act as the front stage of major ritual performances and the nearby (although dispersed) habitation locales would serve as the backstage, where much of the preritual preparation would be carried out. The exclusive territorial account, under which the unitary ritual sphere account is subsumed, in general recognizes that the embankment locales would be effectively "vacant" for some or much of the year, while the "hamlets" would be occupied year-round or at least seasonally. It would be reasonable to postulate that much of the ritual paraphernalia so richly associated with mortuary deposits on the floors of the embankment earthwork mounds would have been produced and possibly even stored at the domestic habitation locales. Therefore, not only should there be some lost and misplaced artifacts of the type found at the earthwork sites in the habitation locales, but also much of the production debitage of this regalia should be found in the habitations.

In fact, the distribution of these ritual materials is well known to Ohio Hopewell archaeologists, and it is a critical part of identifying the earthwork/habitation dichotomy. That is, the contrast characterizing the earthwork/habitation dichotomy is not simply a matter of massive earthworks, on the one hand, and dispersed habitation locales, on the other. This contrast is underscored by the effective absence from the habitation locales of any of the classic Ohio Hopewell ritual paraphernalia.

One very important artifact category, however, would appear to work against this conclusion and in support of the unitary ritual sphere account: the Hopewell bladelet is ubiquitous and prolific across the earthwork/habitation dichotomy (Connolly 1996a:262; Dancey 1991:55–60; Fortier 2000b:191–194; Genheimer 1996:94; Greber, Davis, and DuFresne 1981:490; Morrow 1987:146–147; Odell 1994:102–104; Pacheco 1988:45–52; Yerkes 1990:171). Furthermore, analyses have demonstrated that it displays the same range of wear and damage across both spheres, suggesting that objectively it was used in an equivalent manner, no matter in which locale.

All this clearly would seem to counter the claim of the dual ritual spheres account, namely, that proscriptions would be in place to prevent mixing ritual resources and artifacts across spheres. This suggests that, despite the absence of most of the categories of ritual paraphernalia from the habitation locales, the earthwork/habitation dichotomy in fact manifests a unitary ritual sphere. Of course, since the proscriptions apply only to ritual materials, it could be argued that the bladelet is exempted because it was an expedient, practical tool and therefore was not specialized as a ritual tool (Fortier 2000b:204–206).

Ritual or Expedient Tool?

Much would seem to hinge on whether the bladelet is more appropriately characterized in ritual or in utilitarian terms. As humble as it is in appearance, the bladelet is generally recognized to be no less important in demarcating the

Hopewell phenomenon in the Eastern Woodlands than are the well-known and very elaborate items constituting the Hopewellian artifact assemblage (Fortier 2000b; Genheimer 1996; Greber, Davis, and DuFresne 1981; Morrow 1987; Odell 1994; Pacheco 1993; Yerkes 1990). Indeed, in keeping with this critical role of marking the Hopewell sphere, in general, Odell (1994) has recently argued that the bladelet was directly innovated to be a critical Hopewell ritual tool. He also reiterated the view accepted by most archaeologists that its appearance, use, and disappearance marked the Hopewell/Middle Woodland period. "It is probable . . . that prismatic-blade [bladelet] technology developed with Hopewell ritual. When these practices died out at the end of the Middle Woodland period, the blade technology died with them" (Odell 1994:117).

All this would certainly favor the unitary ritual sphere model, suggesting that as a ritual tool, the bladelet's use in both locales marks its users as having participated in a unitary ritual sphere. However, Odell (1994:117) went on to claim that in fact the bladelet had a dual function, being used as both a ritual and a standard, expedient tool. He argued that "when blades were either manufactured or introduced in a residential situation, they lost all ritual connotations and became, in the minds of the tool users, indistinguishable from ordinary flakes. In a very real sense, then, blades served different functions in different contexts."

Odell's claim for the mixed ritual/utilitarian nature of the bladelet is based on his comparative analysis of wear and usage patterns of bladelets found in four Illinois Middle Woodland settings: the Smiling Dan habitation site, the Napoleon Hollow floodplain site, the nearby Napoleon Hollow hillslope locality, and the Elizabeth Mound Group. While the bladelets from each of these sites display the same range of usage, the proportion of type of usage varies. The bladelets found in the Elizabeth mounds and the hillslope feature reflect a focus on slicing and cutting of soft materials, as in hide preparing, flesh cutting, and some woodworking. The bladelet collection from the adjoining Napoleon Hollow floodplain site has a more varied mix, with a greater tendency toward cutting, scraping, and engraving of medium-to-hard materials, notably "wood working, graving, projectile use, and probably some . . . butchery and manipulation of soft materials" (Odell 1994:116). Odell accounted for this difference by interpreting the Napoleon Hollow floodplain site as probably having been occupied by elites during times when they were conducting Hopewell ceremonies at the Elizabeth mounds. This mound site is on the bluff top immediately above the Napoleon Hollow site, and the hillslope feature is between the two. This latter location, in contrast, may have resulted from the deposition of ritual wastage from the mounds or from use of the location preparatory to rituals being held at the floodplain site.

The bladelet usage, along with the very prolific use of flake tools, at the Smiling Dan site, which Odell pointed out would be broadly similar to the Murphy Tract site near Newark, Ohio, displays the same broad range of tasks as is apparent in the other three sites. The bladelets found at the Smiling Dan site, however, would have been used for the most varied range of tasks of the four and moreover indicate that the favored tasks employing these bladelets required cutting, drilling, and engraving of medium and hard materials, including wood, bone, and shell. Odell also pointed out that the same range of usage applies to the flake tools, which are twice as common as bladelet tools. He argued that this range of variation across the sites, particularly with greater focus or specialization in the range of soft-to-medium working for the assumed ritual locales (Odell 1994:113–114), supports the conclusion that when found in ritual or ritual-related sites, the bladelet was primarily used as a ritual tool, and when found in a residential locale, it was used as an ordinary practical implement, in much the same way as the even more prolific flake implement. "When the mortuary influence became negligible, as at Smiling Dan, it is no longer possible to detect functional specificity within the blade component. When brought back to ordinary residences, blades became dissociated from their raison d'être within the society and were used for the same mundane functions as flakes or bifaces" (Odell 1994:114).

He admits to finding it puzzling, however, that both flake implements and bladelets, equally "expedient," would be used in the same habitation locales to mediate the same interventions, noting that "it is difficult to understand why tool users would employ blades at all in a residential situation, when flake technologies had sufficed for these purposes for millennia" (Odell 1994:117).

Critique

If Odell is right—namely, that the context determines the nature of the action that the bladelet mediates—then the distribution of the bladelet across earthwork and habitation locales would still support the unitary ritual sphere account, since the bladelet would serve as a ritual tool only in the former context. However, as Odell recognized, this explanation also leaves an unresolved puzzle. Why should the older tradition of expedient flake tools continue to be used in the habitation zone along with the introduced Hopewell bladelet if both could be and were used for precisely the same purposes? This is particularly puzzling since the two implements were produced using different core techniques. The flake tool was tied to the bifacial tool tradition and its discoid core technique; as Odell pointed out, this technique had been used for millennia. This is also a very flexible technique, since the same core can be used to produce the whole range of bifacial tools along with flake tools. In contrast, the bladelet was made using the prismatic core technique, and this is largely restricted to bladelet production, since—as Morrow argued (1987:144–145; also see Montet-White, 1968)—once initiated, the core cannot be modified to produce bifacial blanks.

This is not a minor puzzle. Failing to resolve it, in fact, actually undermines Odell's argument that the bladelet served as a ritual tool. This is because if the ritual function of the bladelet could be transformed into a straightforward utilitarian function simply by being used in the domestic habitation, then there would be no point to introducing it as a ritual tool in the first place. The flake tool could be recruited directly to this purpose, deriving its ritual meaning and function by being used in the Hopewell earthwork locale. This puzzle can be resolved, however, and in favor of the dual ritual spheres account, by rearticulating it in symbolic pragmatic terms.

First, I fully support Odell's claim that the bladelet was a critical ritual tool (but not for the same reasons as he presents, that is, the apparent specialized use of the bladelet in Illinois Hopewell ceremonial locales). Second, both the bladelet and the flake tools must be understood as having action warranting power, except that their use would constitute different types of material actions. Therefore, since, as Odell argues, the objective interventions that both tools were used to mediate were the same, it follows that the tangible differences that mark the bladelet/flake duality are stylistic in nature, thereby manifesting a critical symbolic pragmatic contrast. If it is accepted that the bladelet had ritual symbolic warranting meaning, then the prolific use of the flake tools in the same domestic locale as the Hopewell bladelet suggests that the bladelet was introduced (along with its contrasting core technology) specifically because, whatever the symbolic pragmatic meaning of the flake tools, it was understood as being incompatible with the action nature of the behaviors that the bladelets were intended to mediate. Therefore, the bladelet/flake contrast ensured that the flake tools were seen as *not* being ritual tools. In short, and contra Odell, this means that the bladelet was used as a ritual tool across both earthwork and habitation locales. If this is the case, then the empirical support for the ritual nature of the bladelet comes not from the variation in the uses of the bladelet between the Elizabeth Mound Group, the hillslope feature, and the Napoleon Hollow site, on the one hand, and the Smiling Dan site, on the other (as noted by Odell [1994]), but from the continuity of the older flake tool tradition after the bladelet was introduced in both locales. The specialized focus of the bladelet use in the ceremonial locales and its more generalized use in the domestic habitation locales would manifest the different types of rituals appropriate to each.

Would support for the ritual nature of the bladelet be diminished if it turns out that the same bladelet/flake tool duality also occurs in the ceremonial locales? Not really. As I stated earlier, the proscription against mixing materials across the two ritual spheres would probably apply only to ritual artifacts and resources. If flake tools were not used for ritual purposes, then their presence in the earthworks could be attributed to their having been used to fulfill mundane needs, such as everyday subsistence tasks. Odell presented little data on the presence of flake tools in the ceremonial locales of the Illinois River valley, pointing out only that the excavators of the Napoleon Hollow site commented "on the relative abundance of blades and flakes of exotic raw materials, particularly obsidian" (Odell 1994:108). He then focused on the bladelets. Thus, it is possible that these flakes of exotic materials may not have been tools but simply the by-product of production using these exotic materials. Furthermore, in my reading of the literature on the Ohio earthworks, I have noted many references to bladelets, but I do not recall any references to flake tools, as such. Further research in flake tool distribution is called for, therefore, not to confirm the claim that the Hopewell bladelet is a ritual tool but to clarify the nature of the differences in the two ritual spheres postulated under the dual ritual spheres account. The presence of flake tools in the earthwork locales would neither confirm nor disconfirm the dual ritual spheres account. However, their general absence would suggest that the earthwork locales constituted even such "mundane" tasks as the preparing and consuming of foods and other materials to have a ritual import. If so, this distribution pattern would reinforce the nature of Hopewell ritual as different from the nature of the ritual that occurred in the habitation locale.

Does all this mean that Odell's claim that "context" determines action is wrong? No. In this case, his general thesis about context is quite correct. Pragmatics is very much a study of how mutual recognition of the meaning of place, locale, or situation determines the action nature of the behaviors being performed (Levinson 1983; Searle 1983:4–13, 1995:59–78). The implication, however, is that the term *context* should be recognized as a symbolic pragmatic term. It is not simply another term for place or locale or situation. It is the place, locale, or situation in terms of its symbolic pragmatic nature, that is, its action-constitutive moment. Therefore, one would be correct in saying that the Hopewell earthwork locale was a ritual context and that according to the dual clan-cult account, the type of ritual it mediated was world renewal in nature. Of course, the corollary that follows from this premise is that the regular use of both the bladelet and the flake tool in the habitation locales suggests an internal structuring of the habitation locales into mundane/ritual contextual spheres.

In short, just as the styles of artifacts conventionally bear the symbolic pragmatic or warranting moment by which the behaviors they mediate counted as the social actions intended, so do the stylistics of locales conventionally bear the pragmatic or context moment by which the behaviors performed within them count as the social actions intended. Therefore, as humble as it was, the bladelet was as much a part of the symbolic pragmatics by which the context nature of the earthwork locale was constituted as was the rest of the material assemblage of this locale: the embankment earthworks themselves, the great houses, the mortuary facilities, and so on.

While this symbolic pragmatic approach resolves the bladelet/flake puzzle, it only partly rescues or preserves Odell's overall claim that the bladelet was tied to Hopewell as a ritual tool. This must be modified by deleting the term "Hopewell" as the operative word. This leaves in place the rest of the claim, namely, that the bladelet was a ritual tool set up to constitute the behaviors it mediated as ritual. This modification also allows extending Odell's claim to include habitation locales, where bladelets are also not uncommonly found. The bladelet, in short, would be part of constituting the habitation zone (or parts of it at certain times) as also having a ritual context nature, but one that is in direct contrast to the types of ritual performed in the earthwork context, as postulated under the dual ritual spheres account. That this ritual nature would contrast with the ritual nature of the Hopewellian earthworks is supported by the effective absence from the habitation locales of all the other materials that are associated with the Hopewellian earthwork locales.

Critical Analogy

To illustrate how "purely" practical tools can serve to constitute ritual spheres, a particularly apt example would be the symbolic pragmatics of everyday food preparation and consumption in Orthodox and Conservative Jewish households. The context nature of the residential locale of such a family entails the possession and use of two easily distinguishable, parallel and complementary sets of kitchen tools and facilities for everyday food storage, preparation, and consumption, with one set exclusively used with meat-based meals and the other exclusively used with meals based on milk and related products. This separation is not to privilege one type of meal over the other. Both "meat meals" and "milk meals" are equally valued. However, mixing "milk" and "meat," or any related components, is strictly proscribed by the religious Kosher protocols, and to allow this mixing to happen, even if done inadvertently, is to commit a serious transgression requiring ritual cleansing of both the implements and those who transgressed and possibly the total household (depending on the degree of orthodoxy, disposal of the polluted implements may be required). Above all, the spiritual status of the whole household is critically constituted through fulfilling these rules in the patterning of the kitchen. Therefore, this stylistic distinction not only manifests two complementary food spheres, but also is partly constitutive of these as ritual spheres. By sustaining their purity, the spiritual harmony and balance of the household is sustained.

The Ohio Hopewell bladelet complex, of course, implicates a similar proscriptive ritual strategy for the Middle Woodland period of this region. However, it was realized quite differently from that outlined above for the Orthodox Jewish home. This is probably because of certain critically different conditions of the two ways of life. In the case of the Orthodox Jewish household, a single, permanent locale is occupied, and avoiding mixing across spheres is accomplished by installing permanent but separate facilities and using hardware that is tangibly different and kept separate. In contrast, the Ohio Hopewell strategy was developed by mobile participants moving from one to the other ritual locale. Thus, as pointed out above, the "expedient" nature of the bladelet tool— as well as its distinctiveness with regard both to (equally) expedient flake and curated tools—would constitute its unique value as a ritual tool that was quickly produced when needed, used, and discarded, making it an essential medium constituting two ritual spheres having two separate locales being maintained as two separate and different ritual contexts.

As indicated in table 4.1, however, there may be another patterning of the bladelet complex that can be used to develop the dual ritual spheres account. This is the apparent duality of the chert types, thereby suggesting that the ritual sphere of each locale was structured into two complementary sets of rituals. Characteristically, across both habitation and earthwork locales, the bladelet is predominantly made of two select and contrasting cherts. In Ohio Hopewell, the preferred cherts were often Wyandotte chert and Flint Ridge (Vanport) chert. A similar pattern has been noted for other regions (for instance, Cobden-

Table 4.1. Dual Ritual Spheres of Ohio Hopewell

| | Type of Locale | |
Main Chert Type	Earthwork	Habitation
Flint Ridge (Vanport)	Ritual Sphere E-FR	Ritual Sphere H-FR
Wyandotte	Ritual Sphere E-W	Ritual Sphere H-W

Note: E = Earthwork, H = Habitation, FR = Flint Ridge (Vanport), W = Wyandotte.

Dongola and Burlington Crescent Quarries cherts in the central Mississippi Valley region; see Morrow 1987). However, the symbolic pragmatic force of the chert duality would have been different from that of the bladelet. The latter would have been proscriptive in nature, serving to prevent the inadvertent reuse of a ritual tool. Since the Wyandotte/Flint Ridge duality is realized in the bladelet form in both habitation and earthwork locales, the chert duality would not have been needed to serve this proscriptive purpose. Therefore, the consequences of transgressing the Wyandotte/Flint Ridge duality (or its equivalent) would not have had the same implications that transgressing the reuse prohibition would have had. This would have given some flexibility to the emergence and sustaining of this chert dichotomy. Circumstances (such as temporary unavailability of one of the preferred cherts) could have served to justify using some "at hand" substitute. The passing of circumstantial constraints would be marked by the rapid return to the preferred cherts for mediating the complementary rituals. Experimentation would also have been more permissible. For example, Genheimer (1996:97) noted that, of the bladelets he found at the Stubbs cluster sites, the majority was made of Wyandotte and Flint Ridge (Vanport) cherts, while the minority was made of Knox chert from eastern Tennessee (about 40 percent, 20 percent, and 10 percent, respectively; $n = 374$). A notable exception to this chert duality might be Liberty Works. According to Greber, Davis, and DuFresne (1981:494), "thousands of pieces of debitage (largely Flint Ridge materials) have come from the site, as have numerous cores." I take this to mean that essentially only Flint Ridge (Vanport) chert was used for bladelet production at this site, a point confirmed by Vickery's analysis (1983:80). While the Flint Ridge (Vanport) quarries are more than 160 kilometers northeast of Chillicothe, there was a great deal of bladelet-quality chert within the local region. In sum, as indicated in table 4.1, the dual ritual spheres account postulates a double ritual duality.

Even though the dual ritual spheres account can be used to argue that it would be highly improbable for the bladelet complex to have emerged in a unitary ritual sphere as postulated by the exclusive territorial account, it does not follow that a dual clan-cult social system postulated above would necessarily entail the development of the bladelet complex. The Adena archaeological record also probably manifests a dual clan-cult social system (Clay 1991, 1992, 1998). However, it did not manifest the bladelet complex, although some regional Late Adena manifestations apparently did pick up this complex (for example, those in the Hocking and middle Muskingum drainages), suggesting that these may have been emulating neighboring Ohio Hopewell (Carskadden and Morton 1997:371). It is also possible, of course, that the Adena had some preexisting, currently unrecognized, symbolic pragmatic equivalent to the Ohio Hopewell bladelet complex. What the dual ritual spheres account does claim is that for a phenomenon like the bladelet complex to emerge, a necessary but not a sufficient condition for it would be a dual clan-cult system (or its equivalent).

Conclusion

By resolving a number of puzzles (for example, the context/locale duality, the bladelet/flake duality, the effective absence of standard Hopewell ritual material from the habitation locales, and the ubiquitous distribution of the bladelet), the dual ritual spheres account has demonstrated that it can more coherently explain the distribution of Hopewellian materials, including the distribution of the Hopewell bladelet, than can the unitary ritual sphere account. Since the former is an essential ancillary of the dual clan-cult account, this establishes reasons for accepting the latter account over the exclusive territorial account. Moreover, the dual clan-cult account recognizes that considerable variation in earthwork magnitude, form, and siting can and will occur independently of any equivalent variation in the habitation zones. This is because, by postulating the autonomous nature of the clans and cults, it uncouples the Hopewell earthworks and their distribution from the habitation locales and their distribution. It also justifies exploring the cultic dimension in its own right, thereby expanding our understanding of Ohio Hopewell.

5

Enclosures and Communities in Ohio Hopewell

An Essay

N'omi B. Greber

The numerous earthworks, walls, and mounds that existed in the Ohio River valley prior to A.D. 1800 became a focus of speculation and study tied to the origins of professional archaeology in North America. These are some of the "ancient monuments of the Mississippi Valley"—earthen and stone constructions found in widespread, but not necessarily contiguous, groupings in eastern North America (Squier and Davis 1848). During more than three millennia, peoples with strikingly different subsistence bases constructed walls and enclosures (for example, Mainfort and Sullivan 1998a:2). Plan forms, internal strata, and apparent usage show considerable temporal, geographic, and cultural variation. Some of this variability was concentrated along the several southerly flowing tributaries of the central Ohio River that formed the homeland of peoples we call Ohio Hopewell: the Great Miami, Little Miami, Scioto, and Muskingum rivers and Brush Creek (fig. 5.1).

Since the eighteenth century, ground plans have generally been the major database for interpretations and speculations on the purpose of earthen and stone walls (Byers 1987, 1996; DeBoer 1997; Fowke 1902; Squier and Davis 1848). Early fieldwork included the mapping of wall and mound sites (for example, Heart 1789). The maps are still useful today. Only limited information on the internal structure of many of the earthworks is available, however, since excavations tended to concentrate on mounds rather than on walls (for example, Atwater 1820; Mills 1907; Moorehead 1892; Shetrone 1926; Squier and Davis 1848; Thomas 1894). Although the database is still relatively slim, discussions about the functions of enclosures have made their way into print in recent times (Mainfort and Sullivan 1998b; Pacheco 1996b; Saunders et al. 1997). A major hindrance for interpretation is the lack of chronological control. For a few Ohio sites we have physical evidence of construction materials; for fewer we know building sequence; and for even fewer we can estimate the time of construction and use.

Considering the Ohio enclosures as artifacts writ large, we can determine that the raw materials are apparently relatively local and that walls were made where we find them (or, more accurately, where we find their remnants). All sites

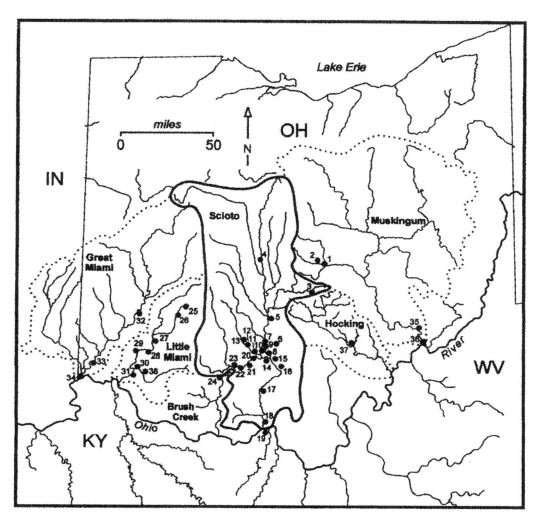

Figure 5.1. Sites mentioned in text. 1 = Newark, 2 = Grandville, 3 = Rock Mill, 4 = Worthington, 5 = Circleville, 6 = Blackwater, 7 = Dunlap, 8 = Hopeton, 9 = Mound City, 10 = Junction, 11 = Anderson, 12 = Hopewell, 13 = Frankfort (Old Town Works), 14 = Works East, 15 = Highbank, 16 = Liberty, 17 = Seal, 18 = Tremper, 19 = Portsmouth, 20 = Spruce Hill, 21 = Baum, 22 = Seip, 23 = Bainbridge, 24 = Fort Hill, 25 = Pollock, 26 = Ancient Work, 27 = Fort Ancient, 28 = Stubbs, 29 = Foster, 30 = Milford, 31 = Turner, 32 = Alexander, 33 = Hamilton, 34 = Miami Fort, 35 = Lowell, 36 = Marietta, 37 = The Plains, 38 = East Fork.

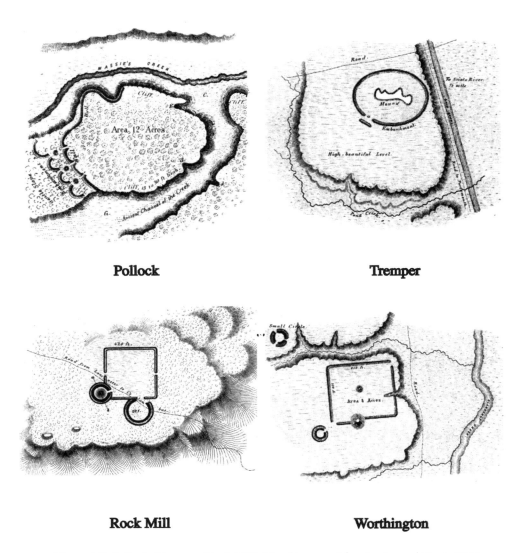

Pollock   **Tremper**

Rock Mill   **Worthington**

Figure 5.2. Pollock, Tremper, Rock Mill, Worthington. After Squier and Davis 1848.

have been affected by modern land use. The addition of geophysical remote sensing techniques to field surveys has aided in the relocation of eroded or lost walls and enabled the identification of previously unknown ones (Greber 1999a; Lynott and Weymouth 2002; Pederson and Burks 2002; Pederson, Burks, and Dancey 2002). In this essay, to make comparisons of enclosure sites across and within the Hopewell valleys, I use various combinations of attributes to define study units that group sites. These attributes include architectural details such as size, strata, and ground plan; geographic and topographic location; assumed cultural context based on local archaeological finds; and chronological relationships that must often be assumed. Our questions concern the place of these monuments within the lives of those who built them. The walls formed a context for sets of important and varied activities and events, including the building of the walls themselves. Individuals and groups who planned, supported, and participated in these endeavors formed the community associated with a given enclosure at each given point in time. Recognizing the apparent time depth of at least one millennium for the construction of enclosures in the central Ohio Valley (for example, Clay 1988; Dancey 1988a) and five to six centuries of Hopewell manifestations within a portion of the area, one expects changes in the scale and composition of the associated communities. Chronological relationships in terms of human generations among the enclosure sites are not yet clearly defined (Greber 2003). Thus, the details and pace of change can only be approximated as we seek to understand the geographic bounds and settlement pattern; economic, political, and social aspects; and the cultural worldview of possible communities. Patterns in the spatial distributions of enclosures at both local and regional scales may offer suggestions for definitions of associated communities, as may patterns in other attributes of design and construction. Some examples of patterns and the communities they suggest follow.

General Distribution

In the central Ohio Valley, from eastern Indiana to the western edge of West Virginia, enclosure sites fall singly and in clusters along large and small streams. Records based on published and archived data for more than 170 sites are on file in the Department of Archaeology, Cleveland Museum of Natural History. Limited field checks have verified the location and condition of some of the 103 sites found in southern Ohio, particularly those in Ross County. Across southern Ohio, enclosures are more frequent in the glaciated regions, avoiding the area of bogs, swamps, and wet prairie that lies between the upper Scioto and Little Miami valleys (for example, Atwater 1820:frontispiece; Dancey 1996b:Figure 23.2). Traditionally sites have been classified as hilltop versus those of geometric form found on the secondary terraces that are above the active floodplain and below the surrounding hills (for example, Dancey 1996b; Prufer 1964a; Squier and Davis 1848). The plan forms of Hopewell hilltop enclosures include cut-off walls, full enclosures, and conjoined enclosures. Sites on lower terraces include single-wall geometric plan forms, groups of such forms, and complex geometric shapes of conjoined enclosures. For the vast majority, the time of construction and use are not known.

In the Little Miami Valley, a hilltop area is partially enclosed at Pollock (fig. 5.2). A single wall follows a hilltop edge above Brush Creek at Fort Hill (fig. 5.3). Two similarly shaped enclosures are joined together at the Fort Ancient site on the Little Miami (fig. 5.3). A simple wall surrounds smaller earthworks at Granville on the Licking, a tributary of the Muskingum (fig. 5.4). Hilltop enclosures occur but infrequently outside of Ohio. A good example is in Old Stone Fort State Archaeological Park, Tennessee.

Single geometric shapes—for example, circular, elliptical, or variously rounded or angled walls—occur on secondary terraces, as at Mound City (fig.

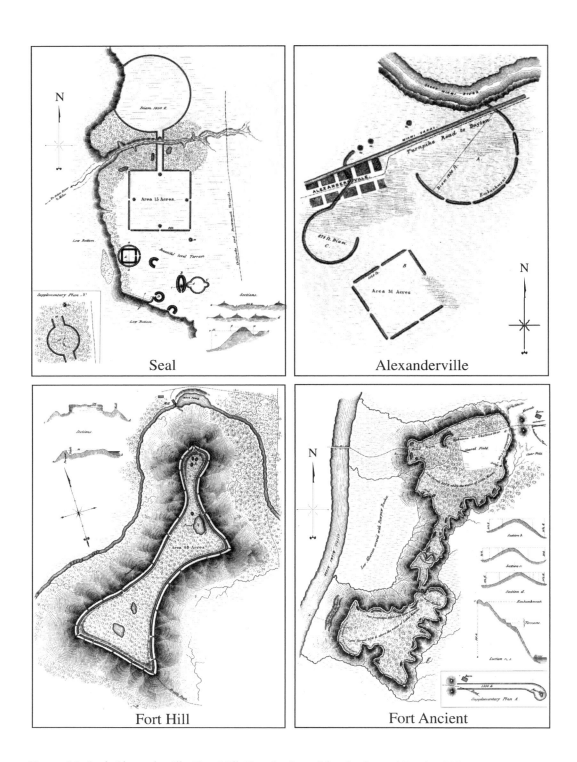

Figure 5.3. Seal, Alexanderville, Fort Hill, Fort Ancient. After Squier and Davis 1848.

5.5) and Tremper (fig. 5.2) in the central and lower Scioto valleys, respectively. Multiple simple geometric forms, usually sets of circles, are found at sites traditionally placed in pre-Hopewell Early Woodland times (for example, The Plains; fig. 5.6). While this is likely true for some sites, hard data are scarce. Thus, consideration should be given to possible later occurrences, particularly in areas outside Hopewell valleys, such as the Hocking River Valley (Greber 1991,

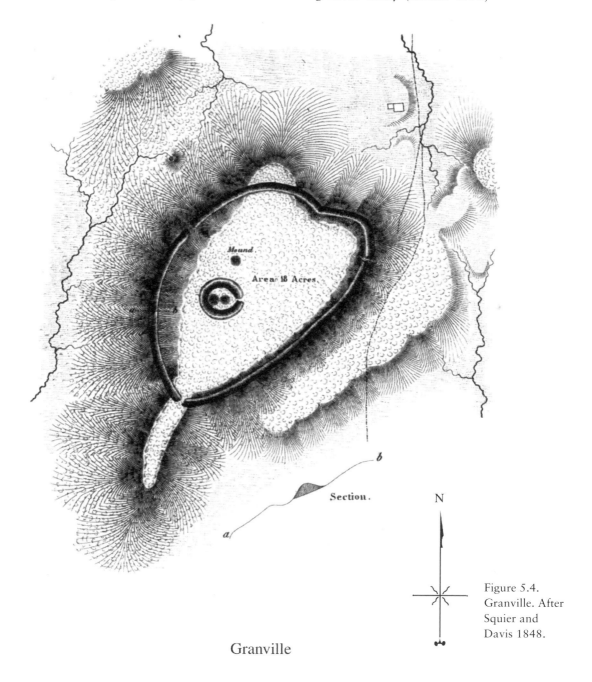

Granville

Figure 5.4. Granville. After Squier and Davis 1848.

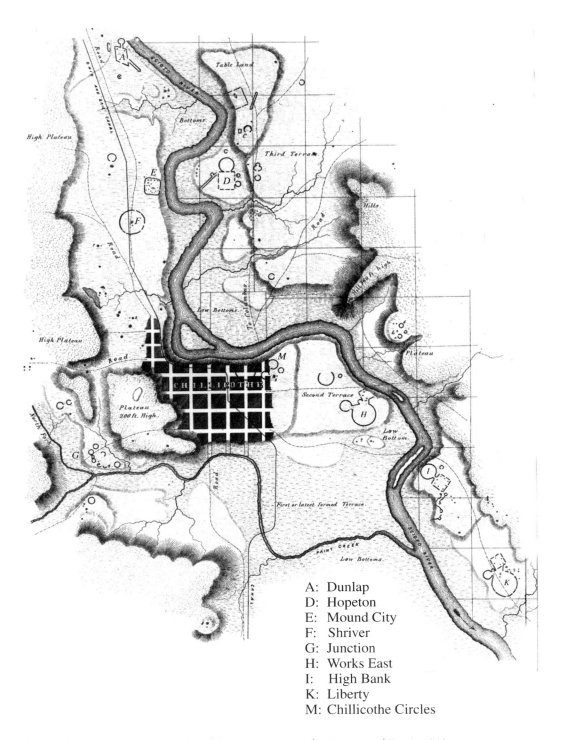

A: Dunlap
D: Hopeton
E: Mound City
F: Shriver
G: Junction
H: Works East
I: High Bank
K: Liberty
M: Chillicothe Circles

Figure 5.5. Sites along twelve miles of the Scioto River. After Squier and Davis 1848.

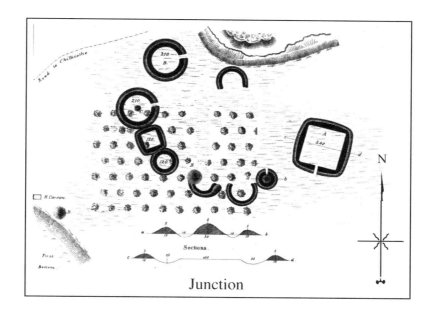

Junction

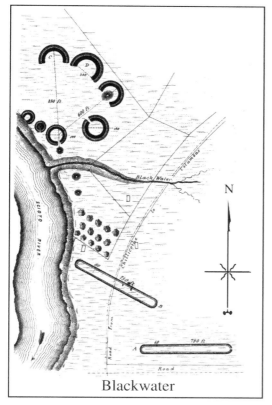

Blackwater

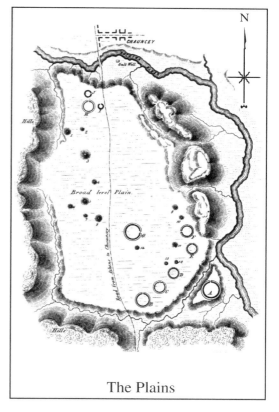

The Plains

Figure 5.6. Junction, Blackwater, The Plains. After Squier and Davis 1848.

Table 5.1. Enclosure Types by River Drainage

Enclosure Type	Great Miami	Little Miami	Brush Creek	Scioto	Muskingum
Effigy	0	0	1	0	1
Hilltop	12	3	3	4	8
Simple	11	6	3	8	12
Multiple	2	2	2	8	0
Complex	2	6	0	16	2

2005). Complex geometric constructions formed by joining together simple forms also occur on lower terraces, as at the Alexanderville Group on the Great Miami (fig. 5.3), Stubbs on the Little Miami (Cowan and Sunderhaus 2002), and High Bank in the central Scioto Valley (fig. 5.5). Such complex constructions are virtually unknown at Middle Woodland sites outside Ohio. Simple geometric forms are more widespread.

While noting that we cannot place the majority in time, we can determine patterning in the distribution of earthworks classified in this traditional manner (table 5.1). Not surprisingly, the largest number of hilltop enclosures occurs along the Great Miami, and the most complex enclosures are found along the Scioto. Simple forms are the predominant type along the Muskingum, although the largest complex geometric construction in Ohio is found at Newark. The cumulative frequencies of classes within each valley are shown in figure 5.7. This format compensates somewhat for the difference in size of the drainage areas. The patterns for the Great Miami and Muskingum rivers and Brush Creek tend to group together, as do the Scioto and Little Miami distributions. This dichotomy is consistent with patterns seen among these valleys in other aspects of material culture, including designs of ritual spaces and deposits of artifacts (Greber 1996). The similarity of patterns found in Brush Creek and the Great Miami and Muskingum valleys suggests a possible sharing of the appropriate manner by which to define special spaces set aside for social uses. This patterning highlights the anomalous nature of the great Newark Earthworks.

Hilltop enclosures are found in all regions, ranging from 44 percent of the total number in the Great Miami Valley to 11 percent in the Scioto Valley. An early interpretation of the function of the hilltop enclosures is evident in the name "Fort" given to them in the nineteenth century (for example, Squier and Davis 1848). In publications resulting from a resurgence of fieldwork in the 1960s, they were interpreted specifically as forts or refuges for local populations at the end of the Hopewell era (Prufer 1964a:64). Radiocarbon dates provided by more recent excavations of walls demonstrate that construction of hilltop enclosures began early in the Hopewell era at Pollock and Fort Ancient and continued for many generations (Connolly 1996b; Greber 2003; Riordan 1995). Riordan (1996:250) notes that "we have evidence that Pollock, and in all likelihood Fort Ancient, were both in use by the first century A.D. . . . their use probably persisted as long as other Hopewellian phenomena." The complex arrangements of ponds, walkways, and other special features built about the

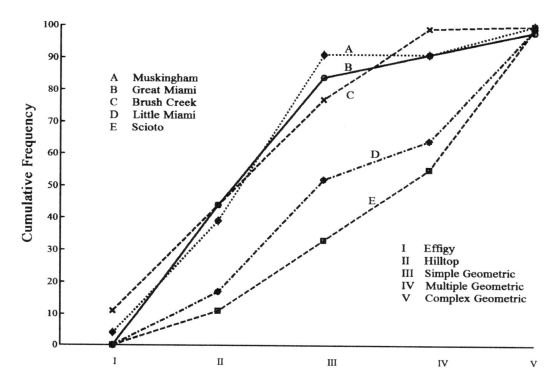

Figure 5.7. Cumulative frequency of enclosure types by river drainage.

openings in the walls at Fort Ancient indicate ceremonial, ritual, political, and other related uses of the enclosures that would have inhibited the practical use of the walls as a European-style fort (Connolly 1996b; Essenpreis and Moseley 1984). A possible change in function over time has been suggested as an interpretation of the five periods of wall construction at Pollock: the first and last uses as a socially set-aside space with a period of possible use as a refuge area in between (Riordan 1996:250–253, this volume). The fourth construction phase consisted of a line of substantial wooden posts placed on the lower strata. There was no sign of rebuilding, and the posts were covered by the final stratum immediately after they were burned down. The lower ends of the posts had been mud-plastered. Riordan considers the substantial nature of the construction, and the occurrence of burned posts at Foster's and Miami Fort in the Little Miami Valley, as indicating possible use of these areas as refuges. However, he also notes that the covering of the burned posts was likely done not by raiders but by the users of the space. The burning and then mantling of structures that required considerable effort to build and maintain was not unusual in the Hopewell era. Frequently, fires marked the end of active use of single- or multiroomed wooden structures (special places) just before they were covered by layers of earth and stones.

Classifying without Using Topography

If topography is ignored, different arbitrary classes can be defined by size (horizontal space) and ground plan. The most numerous class includes generally circular, relatively small-walled structures (diameters about 30–75 meters), usually with one break (called a "gateway" or "opening"). References often cite the break as "towards the east," but such a statement has not to my knowledge been quantified. Other orientations clearly occur (fig. 5.6). Frequently there is an internal ditch adjacent to the wall, suggesting a single stratum that would have been relatively easy to build using soils from the ditch. Such enclosures occur singly, in clusters, and mixed in with more complex enclosures. As is true for all plan form classes, some enclosures have one or more mounds inside or adjacent, while some do not.

The small size and simple construction of each enclosure is consistent with an assumption of a relatively small number of builders, perhaps equivalent to the size of an extended family. Multiple occurrences could represent different groups sharing an area or the same group reusing an area. This design is the most geographically widespread in the central Ohio Valley and possibly the most long-lived. The wide distribution and longevity of this form suggest that there was an underlying cultural unity shared by the groups who built these structures, though the associated activities certainly could have varied. It is frequently assumed, but not proven, that these are Early Woodland affairs. There is little associated settlement data, but Early Woodland "ritual" sites appear to be separate from domestic locations (Seeman 1986). Scattered mound sites have been interpreted as representing focal points for a single autonomous social group or for several similarly organized groups, but they are not necessarily found at a central location in the settlement pattern (Clay 1986). Perhaps the small enclosures had similar associations. The small circles found amidst complex designs, such as at Newark or High Bank, may have been built before, after, or at the same time as other parts of the walls (fig. 5.5). If they are ancestral in the sequence of wall building, did their meaning change as the site plan grew? If they are later additions to the plan, what was their function? Chronological relationships can significantly affect interpretations of the size and/or type of associated social units.

Larger simple enclosures (100 meters or more across) form a second class that is found across southern Ohio. Both simple walled enclosures built on mesalike hilltops and those built on secondary terraces are included in this class. The major shape of the former is largely determined by the bluff edge; the latter have various geometric plan forms (for example, fig. 5.8). Like the smaller circular enclosures, the larger geometric enclosures occur singly, occasionally in clusters, or as separate parts of complex designs. Clusters of simple hilltop enclosures are not known and are unlikely due to the topographic constraints. Some of the large enclosures surround mounds; some do not. Most cannot be confidently assigned to any era. The large size and changes in plan form suggest that the cultural canons responsible for the construction and use of these enclo-

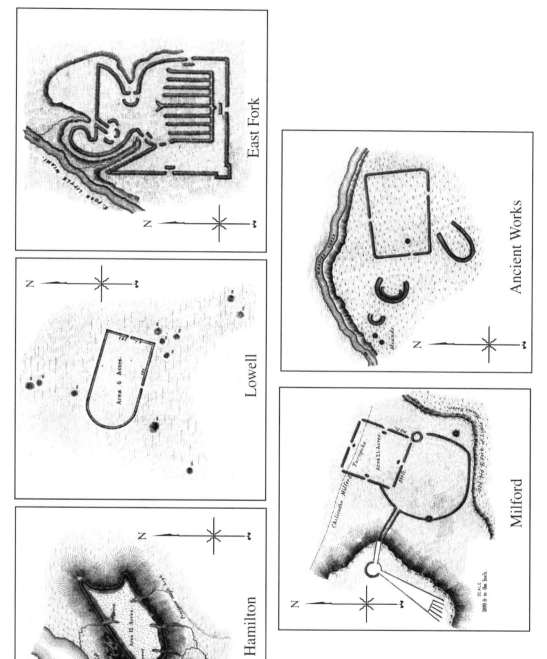

Figure 5.8. Hamilton, Lowell, Milford, East Fork, Ancient Works. After Squier and Davis 1848.

sures differ from those associated with the first class of smaller circular embankments. Despite the difference in topographic setting, the social and physical
commitment needed for the construction of a single simple walled hilltop enclosure such as Fort Hill could have approximated that required to build one of the
large circles formerly within Chillicothe. Neither of these enclosures had interior mounds. Similarly, near Hamilton in the Great Miami Valley, a hilltop wall
that surrounded two mounds could have required construction resources similar to those used for the large Shriver "circle" and its interior mound on the
secondary terrace south of Mound City (fig. 5.5).

It is likely that different meanings were associated with the subclasses of
larger geometric enclosures defined by similar plan forms. Some (but again, not
all) surround a single large mound or multiple smaller mounds. The low oval
wall around the Tremper Mound and the similar one about Seip-Pricer Mound
may represent an extension of the use of a small circle to define a special space.
The size and likely (but assumed) association with the large mounds does suggest a larger available pool of builders than was needed for the smaller enclosures. The simple Mound City wall sets apart a relatively small area containing
a set of densely packed mounds. This combination suggests a unique place
within the central Scioto region. Another subclass recorded across southern
Ohio contains relatively isolated large single-walled simple enclosures with
sharp angles (fig. 5.8). I view their designs as intentional but difficult to interpret
in isolation.

If size alone is considered to be the major attribute defining the class, one
possible interpretation is that all large simple enclosures represent corporate
effort and purposes greater than those of one family. Using embankments to
mark a space is a basic shared social concept whether the space was on a hilltop
or on a lower terrace. The resources needed to build large simple walled enclosures were likely of the same general magnitude in all the Hopewell valleys, with
the caveat that length (or height) cannot alone predict the time and effort needed
to build a wall. Construction materials and strata design are also important.

The last major class includes complex and/or conjoined combinations of
forms. These also fall into large and small size classes, but due to space constraints I cannot emphasize that aspect here. Within the large size class, there is
a single hilltop enclosure: Fort Ancient on the Little Miami (fig. 5.3). The complex design, construction effort, time commitment, and features associated with
the walls and adjacent areas at Fort Ancient reflect social values equivalent to
those that formed sites such as the Liberty or Seip earthworks in the central
Scioto Valley (figs. 5.5, 5.9). The major difference is that there is only one Fort
Ancient. In the central Scioto the Hopewell Site itself is also unique, but it com-
bines a wider range of Ohio Hopewell characteristics than does Fort Ancient,
including both hilltop and geometric wall designs.

If examples from across the Hopewell valleys are considered, unusual complex geometric forms may be partly surveyor interpretation, partly degradation,
and possibly original design (fig. 5.8). Forms incomplete to our eyes, such as at
Alexanderville and Stubbs, may be works left in progress (fig. 5.3). Conjoined

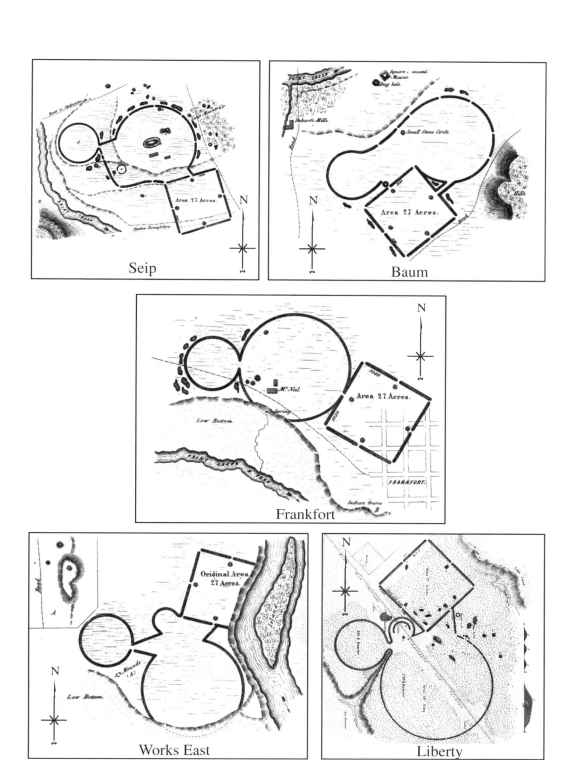

Figure 5.9. Seip, Baum, Frankfort, Works East, Liberty. After Squier and Davis 1848.

enclosures do not necessarily indicate an increase in the size of the associated communities, compared to those that built single large enclosures, if additions to the earthwork complex represent construction over time. This appears to be the case, for example, at Fort Ancient and Newark. Is there a time difference between the construction of hilltop and geometric enclosures? The cheek-by-jowl existence of such sites in the Paint Creek valley (Seip, Baum, and Spruce Hill) and relative closeness along the Little Miami (Fort Ancient, Foster, and Stubbs) makes temporal differences an obvious interpretation in a particular given area. Yet, the coexistence today of synagogue, mosque, Byzantine cathedral, and evangelical church—as urban neighbors that all trace their heritage back to a common ancient root—gives anthropological pause. Our sparse chronological framework cannot yet resolve this issue.

In sum, using only enclosure size and plan form suggests some interregional commonalties. The process of defining space by building an earthen/stone wall is a basic shared cultural element. The ground plan designs seen in the conjoined "polygon-circle" enclosures found across regions likely reflect local interpretations of a shared idea. In southern Ohio the occurrence of larger enclosures is more widespread than major concentrations of artifacts. The Great Miami Valley, like the Muskingum, contains more walls than remarkable artifacts. The Muskingum contains a remarkable suite of walls. Local communities used economic and social resources that produced different types of cultural remains reflecting the mosaic of selective participation in the Hopewellian worldview. We ask, in sharing this view, what was the "catchment area" for the labor that constructed Newark, Portsmouth, and the Hopewell site? Concomitantly, who provided the thousands of artifacts deposited at Hopewell and the hundreds at Turner?

Internal Strata: A Measure of Resource Commitment

Variations in the soils used to construct embankments have been noted for nearly two hundred years (for example, Atwater 1820; Squier and Davis 1848:4–6, passim). The relatively small number of excavations, past and ongoing, demonstrates a range in wall strata complexity that crosscuts topographic and plan form classes. Excavations at Mound City, Anderson, and Spruce Hill reveal single stratum walls about one meter high. However, at Mound City (simple geometric form), soils were thrown up from adjacent areas (Brown and Baby 1966). The red clayey soil of the Anderson polygon (complex geometric form) and the sandstone rubble on the isthmus at Spruce Hill are from local but not adjacent sources (Pickard and Pahdopony 1995; Ruby 1998). Fort Hill may have a relatively simple internal design: a ditch and adjacent earthen wall shored up with sandstone slabs (Prufer 1997a). In contrast, at Pollock, excavations revealed a complex five-stage construction sequence, spanning 150 years or more, that showed a transformation from a wooden fence, perhaps defensive in nature, to an earthen embankment more important for its symbolic significance (Riordan 1995, 1996, this volume). Fort Ancient, the greatest hilltop enclosure, went through a possibly longer period of construction and transformation. Three construction stages have been identified in its walls. Excavations in and around several gateways also reveal complex internal designs incorporating varied uses of stones, soils, ponds, and wooden posts (Connolly 1996b, 1997; Connolly and Sieg 1996; Lazazzera 2000; Sieg and Connolly 1997; Sunderhaus and Blosser, this volume).

Among the complex geometric enclosures, the design of the large oval wall at Turner is unique. A section of the relatively low wall covered a stone platform set on a low ridge of earth, apparently obtained from the adjacent area. On the pavement were ritual altars, hearths, and interments—the only below-wall interments known in Ohio Hopewell (Greber 1993b, 1996:Figure 4A; Willoughby and Hooton 1922). At other sites, features indicating ritual-ceremonial activities as part of the process of wall construction do occur.

The Hopeton Earthworks, directly across the Scioto from Mound City, include a large circle intersecting an incomplete polygon defined by eleven separate segments, a set of parallel walls, and smaller circular elements (fig. 5.5). Five trenches have been excavated across several separate segments of the polygon (Lynott 2001, 2002, 2004; Lynott and Weymouth 2002; Ruby 1997a). The wall profiles from each trench vary in detail, but there are some overall similarities. The topsoil was removed prior to construction. In three of the trenches, the first stratum placed was composed of yellowish soils topped by a second reddish layer. The lighter color faced the interior of the polygon; the darker formed the outside of the wall. Both strata were covered, apparently soon after they were placed, by loamy soils that raised the wall to its final height. Small fired areas on and near the base appear to be the remains of ritual-ceremonial events. The particular shade of red and/or yellow varies, probably due to natural variations in the soils from the specific areas on the terrace from which each batch was obtained. The spectacular red layer found in 2001 is the darkest red I have seen in such walls. The colors found in the trench placed across the curving wall segment at the northeast corner of the enclosure differ, with a reddish soil on the inner side and grey on the outer. Possibly this is a version of the generalized light-versus-dark contrast found in Hopewell designs, or possibly the difference is due to change through time. Two dates associated with features found beneath and within this segment are some eight hundred years younger than those from other segments (Lynott 2004). Six dates from features found in 1996 and in the other trenches suggest a probable building time between A.D. 150 and A.D. 250 (Lynott 2004).

The High Bank Works, located on the Scioto about 19 river kilometers south of Hopeton, form one of the more complexly designed sets of enclosures found in the region (fig. 5.5). The major sections include a relatively rare octagonal enclosure, small and large circular features, and linear walls. Three trenches excavated across the Great Circle wall document more varied activities preceding the raising of the wall than have been found to date at Hopeton (Greber 1998a, 1999a, 2002). To form a construction base, the builders cleared the ground surface and exposed the clayey subsoil. On this floor near the neck joining the octagonal and circular enclosures, a fence was built using closely spaced and deeply set oak posts. Prior to wall construction the fence was dismantled, partially burned, and covered with alternating light and dark layers of coarse gravels.

Along the wall towards the west, a short distance beyond the end of the fence, is an area of the floor where several posts had briefly stood and then been removed. This area was covered by thin alternating yellow and black layers of soils apparently brought from the nearby floodplain. A reddish clay soil formed the exterior side of the wall; a yellow, silty clay loess formed the interior. Along parts of the wall a single layer of cobbles followed a cambered path between them. The top surfaces of these strata showed no signs of exposure. Less than one-fourth of the original height remained in these sections, but the edges of the upper layers that covered the initial strata and two erosional episodes, apparently before and after A.D. 1800, were seen.

A different construction sequence was found in the third trench, placed directly across the circle from the middle of the neck. The base for the aboriginal construction was the same as previously found: the deliberately exposed clayey B-horizon soils. More than two hundred posts had been placed on this floor and then removed. Within the confines of the 2-x-18-meter excavation trench, no pattern in the post placement was discernable. It is likely that additional postholes exist outside our trench. A layer of heavy gravels in a clayey matrix was placed over the floor and refilled postholes. The first stratum of the wall itself was truncated by the plow zone. It was composed of a reddish sandy clay placed over a portion of the gravel layer. A line of small diameter oak posts extended across the floor near the outer edge of the wall. Radiocarbon dates indicate that this flurry of activities and those that took place across the circle were contemporaneous (circa 1860 ±40 B.P.; Greber 2002:Table 1), within the accuracy of radiocarbon dating.

A two-stage construction sequence including an initial ditch has been documented at Newark's Great Circle. Here again, contrasting soil colors were used to mark the interior and exterior aspects of the circle: bright yellow-brown inside, dark brown outside (Lepper 1996; Wymer, Lepper, and Pickard 1992). The contrast of light and dark was also used in the design of many features found within the enclosures at Turner, including structures, hearths, and artifact deposits, but not in any given element of the embankment. In the total earthwork design, the dark loamy fill of the oval contrasts with the light gravels that formed the wall of the conjoined circle (Greber 1993b, 1996). A similar type of contrast can be seen at the Seip Earthworks, where the darkness of the adjacent midden soils used for the largest generally circular element contrasts with the reddish orange of the culturally sterile soils that formed the conjoined square.

The interior wall designs from several sites that juxtapose two colors from the Hopewell palette of red, black, yellow, and white follow design choices similar to those seen in other types of structural remains and in the design and deposition of portable artifacts. A line oriented southwest to northeast divided the two-tone floor covering in the structure beneath Turner Mound 4

(Willoughby and Hooton 1922:62–64). Side-by-side coverings of black and white mantled the deposit of artifacts placed on the same floor (Greber 1996:Figure 9.9). Red and yellow clays together refilled postholes beneath Hopewell Mound 2 and Capitolium Mound at Marietta. One finds black and red paint on mica cutouts, copper and silver on ear spools. One sees a shared esthetic whether or not one wishes to look for specific interpretations of these patterns.

In some cases, prior to the raising of the wall, activities took place at the site that indicate the importance of the initiation of the building process and perhaps of the planning phase. Differences seen among sites in construction methods clearly indicate differences in the effort needed to design, to obtain, and to place strata. One therefore expects that volume alone cannot best predict the amount of time and/or labor put into wall building.

Radiocarbon Dates: Hints of Relative Chronology

Radiocarbon dates are associated with wall construction at Fort Ancient, Miami Fort, Pollock, Stubbs, and Turner in the Little Miami Valley; Anderson, High Bank, and Hopeton in the central Scioto; and Newark in the Muskingum. These help to define an era, but even the thirteen dates from carefully chosen proveniences cannot yet separate the five construction episodes found by excavation at Pollock. The range of dates does indicate that alterations were accomplished by several generations who used the site for more than a century circa 1950 to 1750 B.P. (Riordan 1995, 1996). Dates from the Fort Ancient walls exhibit a similar time range. A significant number of dates have come from features found within and near the walls (Connolly and Lepper 2004). These have not yet been tied to the actual wall construction stages. At Stubbs, 8 kilometers below Fort Ancient, dates from three large posts—part of the complete circle of 172 posts covered by the Great Circle wall—fall towards the younger end of the range, circa 1770 ±60 B.P. (Cowan and Sunderhaus 2002:Table 1). Farther downstream at Turner, two dates from a ritual feature built on the stone platform beneath a section of the oval wall average to 1750 ±50 B.P. (Greber 2003:Table 6.1). The feature appears to have been covered shortly after its use by the final stratum of the low wall. This date does not necessarily represent the construction time of the entire enclosure. However, it does suggest that Turner and Stubbs were in use at about the same time. Again, we still have only an era, not a specific generation. The single Fort Miami date (1680 ±130 B.P.) is an early Michigan assay on wood charcoal believed to have been associated with initial construction (Maslowski, Niquette, and Wingfield 1995; Riordan 1996:248). It could possibly overlap with the other dates from the valley.

In the central Scioto, the six clustered dates from Hopeton suggest a younger and shorter time range of wall construction than that at Fort Ancient, circa 1800 to 1700 B.P. (Lynott 2004). Some 19 kilometers downstream at High Bank, the burned fence near the neck appears to have been covered shortly after it was decommissioned. It is apparently associated with initial wall construction but does not necessarily date the time when the circular wall was raised to at least twice the height of the walls at Turner and Anderson. The average of a date based on charcoal from an aboveground section of the dismantled fence and three dates from an in situ charred post is 1860 ±40 B.P. Two dates from the line of small posts on the construction floor directly across the circle give the same average (Greber 2002:Table 1). This suggests that the initial construction of the entire wall took place within a short time, possibly several years. It is possible that some walls were being built at both Hopeton and High Bank at the "same" time; the data cannot yet verify this conclusion. An older date comes from a burned post found under the relatively low, single-stratum polygonal wall by the salvage excavation at Anderson (Pickard and Pahdopony 1995), located on the North Fork of Paint Creek, just east of the Hopewell site. It is likely that the post was burned shortly before it was covered by wall construction. Combining the two dates gives a weighted average of 1945 ±65 B.P. This date falls within the Pollock range. Possibly the construction of the Anderson polygon preceded that of the High Bank Great Circle.

The Newark dates are from separate elements of the enclosure. They also cannot be considered as dates for the entire complex, but they are consistent with an assumption of use of the site over several centuries. Within one standard deviation the date from the Great Circle, 2110 ±80 B.P., falls at the older end of the Pollock range, while the two dates from the Octagon are younger and average to the younger end of the Hopeton time range, circa 1680 ±80 B.P. (Maslowski, Niquette, and Wingfield 1995).

In sum, dates directly associated with wall construction indicate that walls were apparently constructed throughout the Hopewell era in the three valleys. Some complex wall strata indicate generations of building episodes at the same wall and possibly different construction designs for individual episodes. It is highly likely that construction was in progress at more than one earthwork at the same time within each valley. The data are not yet sufficient to allow a firm chronology within or across regions.

Land Use within and near Enclosures

Comparisons thus far have been based on data from the walls themselves. Considering information on archaeological features in the neighborhood of enclosures adds a layer of variation. Pairing enclosures and assumed associated domestic localities, Dancey and Pacheco (1997a; see also Dancey 1996b) distilled recorded settlement data and proposed a regularity in the spatial distribution and a common function for each enclosure site. Dancey (1996b:400; emphasis added) concluded "that *regularity characterizes the entire data set*, although the interval between enclosures is different in different places. In Ross County, for example, the average is 7 km, while in the lower Little Miami it is 3 km, and in other segments of the two Miamis it is approximately 10 kilometers." Distances were measured from a given enclosure to its nearest neighbor regardless of differences in plan form. In the extension of this assumed spacing to their proposed

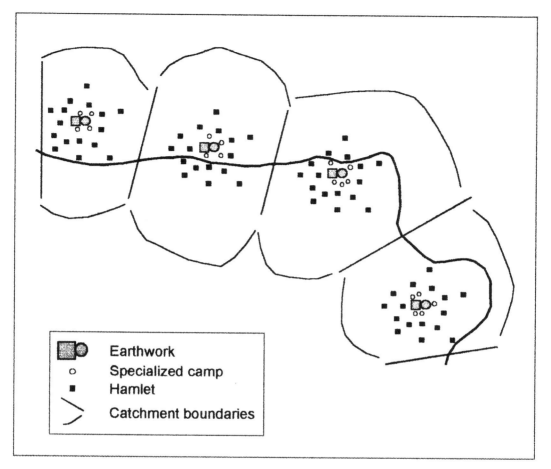

Figure 5.10. Generalized model of Hopewellian community structure. After Dancey and Pacheco 1997a:Fig. 1.2.

settlement pattern, Dancey and Pacheco (1997a:Figure 1.2) present a series of equally spaced adjacent enclosures, each surrounded by a number of domestic localities (fig. 5.10). It was intended by the authors that this diagram show a generalized ground plan rather than the specific circle-square plan (William Dancey, personal communication, 2000). A companion figure (Dancey and Pacheco 1997a:Figure 1.4) shows changes through time in the construction sequence for a generalized enclosure site (see also Greber 1997:Figure 8.3).

The locational pattern of Hopewellian communities assumed to be centered on an earthwork becomes complex as the locations and perhaps the character of domestic quarters at a given site change through time. Thus, the footprint of the assumed associated community also changes through time (for example, Dancey and Pacheco 1997a:Figure 1.3). "Since it is usually impossible to identify contemporaneous sites within a settlement system, the pattern definition is based on an equilibrium assumption. Thus, a settlement pattern represents a period of 'stable' adaptation, and change is marked by the appearance of a new pattern that represents another period of stability. . . . [T]he continuum of spatial and temporal processes is fragmented, creating artificial homogeneity and pattern" (Root 1983:197).

Assuming that one can find a specific time at which a settlement pattern such as shown in figure 5.10 existed, there are still additional assumptions to consider. The first is that earthworks are equally spaced across the landscape. The second assumption is that every earthwork has the same set of archaeological features associated with it and, as a corollary, that each has a similar function in the lives of its users.

Earthwork Spacing

With respect to the first assumption, the use of the word *equal* as depicted in the hypothetical settlement model was intended by the authors to allow for environmental variation (William Dancey, personal communication, 2000). Correlating coordinates plotted on USGS 7.5-minute quadrangle maps with the appropriate Ross County soil charts (Petro, Shumate, and Tabb 1967) helps to clarify the distribution of geometric earthworks. Starting at a given enclosure, the best predictor for the location of the nearest neighbor along the same river appears to be the nearest area of Fox soils large enough for such a construction. For example, from Frankfort along North Fork to Paint Creek we find Old Town Works, Hopewell Group, Anderson, and Junction (fig. 5.1; Petro, Shumate, and Tabb 1967:26–27, 36, 48). As has been noted for some time, geometric earthworks are usually located on the second terrace above the presently active floodplain, where Fox-Oakley soils have developed over calcareous glacial outwash (for example, Squier and Davis 1848:59). These sites are well drained and relatively flat (0–6 percent slope). Dan LeMaster (personal communication, 1997), the Ohio regional soils scientist of the U.S. Department of Agriculture, states that these glacial parent materials, terrace locations, and soils series always cooccur. The choice of such a location along the Scioto or along the Little Miami, such as at Stubbs, may reflect sensible engineering choices that satisfy the need for a large ground area and subsoils that provide good drainage for the wooden-walled structures found in the environs of many enclosures (for example, Baby and Langlois 1979; Cowan, this volume; Cowan, Sunderhaus, and Genheimer 1998, 1999b). The densest concentration of large geometric enclosures occurs within the numerous microenvironmental plots of Ross County, where more such areas occur than in any other region of comparable size in the central Ohio Valley (Greber 1993a; Maslowski and Seeman 1992). The construction of a hilltop enclosure also requires a specific topography. Whether these two sets of conditions or other environmental factors were truly important in site placement needs further study in all the valleys of southern Ohio. Material resources allow but do not necessarily determine human activities in any given area. The level of need, even for food, can be culturally determined. "Processes affecting the regional distribution of settlements occur along a variety of axes, as well as on a variety of scales" (Root 1983:197).

Earthwork Environs

In considering the usefulness of the second assumption and its corollary, one would like to examine sites located in similar environmental settings that also share other comparable attributes to best illustrate possible commonalities or differences in structure or function. Several such sites share a generally similar environment near Chillicothe. Liberty, Works East, Seip, and Baum also share similar ground plans, as do Hopeton and High Bank. The Liberty Works and Works East are on opposite banks of the Scioto about 10 kilometers apart (fig. 5.5). Fortunately, for the environs at Liberty there are both provenienced surface data and excavation data. Coughlin and Seeman (1997:Figures 9.1, 9.4) document archaeological localities near and within the Liberty Works based on the surface material collected for more than twenty-five years by the landowner, Robert Harness. Combining this information with excavation data and radiocarbon dates gives a picture of the use of the area over many generations (Greber 2003; Greber, Davis, and DuFresne 1981; Greber et al. 1983; Mills 1907; Putnam 1884, 1886; Seeman 1998; Seeman and Soday 1980). Probable changes in settlement patterns appear, even during the time of active construction of the Edwin Harness Mound, a classic large Hopewell construction located within the enclosure.

Coughlin and Seeman (1997) have identified several different types of Hopewell occupational remains within and near the enclosure walls. On the basis of surface materials they describe one domestic locale less than 2 kilometers from the enclosure as containing habitation density between that of the isolated "hamlets," considered by many as the predominant Ohio Hopewell settlement pattern (for example, Dancey and Pacheco 1997a; Pacheco and Dancey, this volume), and "villages" (for example, Griffin 1996, 1997): "We interpret Site A as representing an important, *probably late*, variation on the predominant Ohio settlement layout" (Coughlin and Seeman 1997:240; emphasis added).

Radiocarbon dates from Edwin Harness indicate that the use of the Big House and construction of the mound took place over many generations (Greber et al. 1983:Table 3.2). Mound building extended beyond Middle Woodland times and into the Late Woodland when Harness Site 28, a settlement of circular houses just across the modern road from the mound site, was occupied (Coughlin and Seeman 1997:236; Seeman 1998:19–20). Probably while the last additions were being added to the large mound, small mounds were placed over small nearby specialized areas (Greber 2003:107–109, Table 6.1). "We suspect that the sociostructural adjustments promoting these trends toward larger habitation sites played out over a period of *several centuries* may document a shift in central tendency rather than a strict and sudden dichotomous transformation at the Middle Woodland/Late Woodland temporal boundary" (Coughlin and Seeman 1997:240; emphasis added).

Even though specific mound features and off-mound localities have not yet been tied together, the dates from the construction of Edwin Harness agree well with such a sequence. I concur with Coughlin and Seeman that the existence of sites such as Site A should be expected. The end of Ohio Hopewell was a fuzzy process. In painting an overview of total site use we must remember that the chronological relationship between the construction of the large mound and the large enclosure is not known. The apparent sequence of long-term use at Liberty contrasts with what is known of the area about Works East, where there are no large or small mounds and no record of activities beyond wall building. This negative evidence is difficult to evaluate today in the heavily impacted earthwork area now inside Chillicothe (fig. 5.5).

A similar pattern is better documented west of Chillicothe at Seip and Baum earthworks in Paint Creek valley. These enclosures and their environs are on opposite banks of the creek, about 6 kilometers apart. Their ground plans closely resemble those of Liberty and Works East (fig. 5.9). The features and artifacts recorded from Seip indicate a much greater use of the area during Middle Woodland times than use of the corresponding area at Baum. Many mounds at Seip have been found to be Hopewell, while there are no such mounds at Baum (Greber 1995, 1997, 1998b, 1998c; Mills 1906, 1909). Standing at Seip today and looking eastward to the nearby horizon, one sees Spruce Hill with Baum at its foot. The apparent difference in site use and the physical closeness suggest to me that the enclosures at Seip and Baum represent two complementary aspects of one worldview and that one community used both sites. I assume a similar paired functional relationship for Liberty and Works East.

In the central Scioto, another pair of sites that share similar ground plans illustrates a possibly more complex intersite relationship. Hopeton and High Bank are on the east bank of the Scioto about 19 river kilometers apart (fig. 5.5). High Bank is about halfway between Works East and Liberty. Surface collections (professional and avocational) and test excavations at Hopeton have documented scattered Hopewellian debris similar to that used as evidence for isolated hamlets, workshops, or other specialized areas in the Dancey and Pacheco model. Artifacts and features from other time periods are also known and indicate long-term use of the area. Three mounds were within the Hopeton polygon. The upper strata in the Hopeton polygon contain a relatively small number of sherds and flint flakes scattered in the wall fill. These materials were apparently picked up from the surface of nearby areas containing debris similar to that found in other localities at the site. As at Liberty, the users of Hopeton left behind limited evidence of their existence in addition to the walls themselves (Brose 1977; Lynott 2001, 2002; Ruby 1997a; Squier and Davis 1848).

The ground surface on the terrace near and within the High Bank Great Circle and Octagon appears empty of Middle Woodland artifacts. This contrasts with both Hopeton and the nearby Liberty Works. Excavations in the Octagon (Greber and Shane 2003; Shane 1973) showed that the earth used to form the enclosure walls—unlike the large semicircular wall at Seip, the Mound City wall, and the eastern wall of the Great Enclosure at Hopewell—did not contain artifactual debris. Artifacts were not found in the remnants of the loamy soils used for the upper strata seen in the test excavations of the wall remnant at the High Bank Great Circle, nor in the lower culturally sterile strata. High Bank was clearly a site important to its Middle Woodland builders, but any activities they performed within or near the walls appear to have left little physical evidence on the ground. I interpret the plenitude of posts found in 2002 to be directly associated with wall construction; no artifacts have been found on or near the floor (Greber 2002; Greber and Shane 2003). The features found beneath the Great Circle wall strongly suggest that complex rituals took place as the wall was first being built. The internal structure of the Octagon walls differs. To date, no features have been found at the base, and the strata composed of locally available soils and gravels appear to be more simply placed as sheet additions rather than in the more complex arrangements seen in the Great Circle wall. The patterns seen in a limited magnetic survey of two Octagon segments compared with the more extensive maps of the Great Circle corroborate the differences in wall construction.

Comparing the strata seen in the single trench cut across the Hopeton Circle with those of the Polygon, there is some suggestion of a difference in wall design between the Polygon and Circle. If these data reflect the design of the entire embankments, is the contrast in wall strata at both sites intentional, that is, complementary? Circles and polygons were used as complementary elements in the designs of portable artifacts. Two of the copper cutouts from the Copper Deposit, Hopewell Mound 25, are shaped as opposing swastikas, square in outline and "turning" in opposite directions (Greber and Ruhl 1989:119, Figures 4.41, 4.42). A circular variation of the form is found on an effigy pipe from a small deposit in the Harness Big House: a curved swastika is framed within a circle carved on the back of the human head effigy (Greber 1989:81; Greber et al. 1983:Figure 3.5). Pairs of ritual basins at Turner show design contrast both in circular versus rounded "rectangular" shapes and in dark versus light fills (Greber 1996:Figure 9.8).

The design of embankments as "artifacts writ large" appears to share similar architectural canons contrasting shape and fill of polygons and circles at High Bank and apparently Hopeton. What were the relationships among the builders and users of these two complex enclosures? The similarities in ground plan suggest shared views on a symbolic design, perhaps "complementary," with the Hopeton Polygon reflecting the High Bank Great Circle. The contrast in apparent use of the environs appears similar to the contrast suggested for Seip and Baum. However, the probable close association of users of Mound City and Hopeton suggests stronger ties to this local region than to the area of High Bank and Liberty.

Did Hopeton and High Bank have different or similar functions in the lives of their builders? What were the relationships among the builders and users of these six complex enclosures near Chillicothe? In proposing answers to any of these questions we come back again to the original problem we encountered in comparing the physical characteristics of enclosures and their environs: we do not yet know which were in use at the same time. The limited information that is available suggests differences in the uses of the land around some neighboring enclosures, such as High Bank and Liberty. Significant differences in the design and construction methods of neighboring enclosures also occur—again, as at Liberty and High Bank. Symbolic elements found in ground plans and strata are consistent with those found in wooden architecture, mound forms, and the crafting and handling of portable objects. Within a relatively rich environment, contiguous communities along a river are a reasonable model of regional organization (compare Roundtree 1989:frontispiece). It is more difficult to identify the particular enclosures and other archaeological localities associated with such communities. Adjacent communities may not follow the same pattern at a given point in time.

Enclosure Ground Plans: Possible Symbolic Changes

Ohio Hopewell iconography extends across media. Style changes in portable artifacts have been used as a basis for determining relative chronological relationships within the Hopewell era (Greber 2003; Riggs 1998; Ruhl 1996; Ruhl and Seeman 1998; Seeman 1977). Extending this to built landscapes, I use as a basic attribute the iconographic nature of enclosure ground plans and examine their potential reflection of changes through time. To minimize the possible effect of geographic differences, I consider variations in the iconography of enclosures in a restricted geographic area near present-day Chillicothe (fig. 5.5).

The simple geometric wall at Mound City (fig. 5.5), sometimes referred to as a "rounded square," differs in ground plan from sites having true circular or square enclosures in Ross County. The common use of the word *square* in describing ground plans can be misleading. In the central Ohio Valley, less than 10 percent of the recorded complex enclosures include a literally square element. The forming of sharp angles rather than rounded ones was, I believe, a conscious choice by the builders. The occurrence of the Mound City plan form at other area sites points out the deliberate nature of the design. In the early 1800s, a similarly shaped enclosure (but without interior mounds) was located on the Worthington estate between the Adena Mound and Mound City; it is shown on the estate map curated at Adena State Memorial. Probably because of the degradation already caused by farming in the area, it was not included in the 1846 survey by Ephraim Squier and Edwin Davis (Squier and Davis 1848:xxxix). Single and conjoined wooden structures share this plan form, but it is not the only shape for such constructions, even at Mound City (Brown 1979:213; Greber et al. 1983:Figures 2.4, 2.6; Mills 1916, 1922:Figure 17).

Related forms were mapped at the Junction Works that lie near the entrance of North Fork into Paint Creek, less than 9 kilometers south of Mound City. Here a version of the Mound City form encloses a space about one-tenth the size of Mound City (figs. 5.5, 5.6). The Junction wall encloses no mounds. Inside is a square space, a socially special place, that is made by cutting into the ground, rather than a square horizontal area surrounded by a wall built up on the ground. The latter form occurs at the nearby Works East and Liberty (fig. 5.5). The construction contrast, as a positive and negative rendition of a similar design element, is consistent with Ohio Hopewell iconography in portable objects. Filled and blank areas are juxtaposed on engraved bones and incised pottery. Open and filled areas form a complex design on a copper cutout from the Copper Deposit, Hopewell Mound 25. Representations of animals from land, sky, and water are superimposed and interwoven with a quartered circle. The inner design elements portraying a bear face, raptor claws, and crocodilian features are formed by both cutout and intact copper (FMNH Catalogue Number 56165; Greber and Ruhl 1989:Figure 7.2).

Perhaps a different desired contrast was the impetus for the design at Junction. Assuming that many circular walls that surround relatively small circular inner spaces are chronologically earlier, is the Junction variant the beginning of a new style for defining interior space? A transition from a circular to a rectangular space has been interpreted as a sign of an increase in complexity in the use of a defined space (Hunter-Anderson 1977). Following Hunter-Anderson, Brown (1979:212) places the Mound City form in the class of rectangles and attributes the form to "the late period Ohio Hopewell." However, the "rounded rectangle" shape of Mound City and circular forms are conjoined within the Harness Big House (Greber et al. 1983:Figures 2.6, 3.3). In the environs of the Stubbs Earthworks, recent salvage work has recovered portions of twenty single-roomed wooden structures of varying floor plans (Cowan, this volume; Cowan, Sunderhaus, and Genheimer 1999b). Three structures with different floor plans are reported as coeval "within the precision afforded by radiocarbon dating" (Cowan and Sunderhaus 2002:11). Factors other than (or in addition to) time were apparently influencing architectural designs.

At Junction, two circles and a smaller version of the Mound City wall surrounding an intaglio inner square are conjoined. The juxtaposition of three asymmetric units is also a pattern repeated in other types of constructions, and the abstract concept appears to be more important than its use in a given construction. For example, the Seip-Conjoined Big House has a three-part asymmetric floor plan (Greber 1979b:Figure 7). The asymmetry of the final conjoined mounds—each covering one room—might be reflecting the sizes of the rooms they each mantle. However, the final form of the huge Mound 25 at the Hopewell site does not appear to be attributable to the footprint of the initial space. The westerly outer mound had a broader base but was lower than the easterly outer mound. This appears to be a design choice. If we focus on the inner square, the design intent of the conjoined two circles and Mound City form at Junction may be a version of the large-scale pattern seen at Works East and Liberty, where a square wall is joined to rounded elements (fig. 5.9). Another version of this pattern at Junction is seen as a line of two crescent-shaped walls and a circular wall surrounding a conical mound.

Two sets of three asymmetric elements are mapped for the Blackwater Group, about 27 kilometers northeast of Mound City (figs. 5.1, 5.6). Another variation on the asymmetric three-element theme occurs at Anderson, about 7 kilometers west of Mound City, where a large polygon (sometimes referred to as a "square") is joined to two small rounded enclosures (Pickard and Pahdopony

1995). A related version also occurs in the Scioto drainage at Rock Mill in Fairfield County, where the two recorded smaller elements appear to be more nearly circular (fig. 5.2). This is a reverse of the "smaller square, larger circles" motif found at Works East and Liberty (fig. 5.9). Here, "smaller" is a relative term. All the earthworks at Junction could fit into the square enclosure at Liberty with room to spare. Does the change in relative size of element shapes or in the overall size of the earthworks reflect a difference in function or cultural meaning of the whole earthwork? Or is the theme of three asymmetric elements the determining cultural canon regardless of size? In the central Scioto, complicated enclosure designs occur at Hopeton, High Bank, and Dunlap. The similarities in ground plan between Hopeton and High Bank are striking (fig. 5.5). Dunlap, about 5 kilometers north of Mound City, appears to be a mirror image of Hopeton. There are no true square-shaped enclosures at these sites. As verified in aerial photographs, the apparently less clearly constructed "polygon" at Hopeton has the curvature of a Mound City form at one end (northeasterly) and sharper angles that more closely resemble those of the clearer octagon shape at High Bank at the other (southeasterly). The available samples of wall strata also suggest a less refined construction design at Hopeton (Greber 2002; Lynott 2001, 2002, 2004; Ruby 1997a).

Additional replicas and variations of the plan forms already described occur in the county. What attributes might reflect possible differences in function or time that this range represents? If we assume that the cultural canons used to design the asymmetric three-part designs at sites such as Junction are related to those that explode into oversized space at Liberty, Works East, Seip, Baum, and Frankfort (fig. 5.9), how are the sites related in time? As has been pointed out, smaller and simpler plan forms are not necessarily earlier in time (for example, Brown 1986a; Greber 1991). What is the chronological relationship between the simple wall form at Mound City, the variants at Junction, and perhaps an incomplete variant at Hopeton? What was the basis on which a Hopewell architect chose the manner of conjoining three asymmetric elements? What determined the use of a "square" or a "circle" as one of these elements?

Enclosures and Polities

Within the some 60,000 square kilometers of the Ohio Hopewell homeland, the regional cultural divisions based on river drainage were quite likely stable throughout Middle Woodland times, but the relationships among the divisions probably changed. The Scioto River drainage, the second largest in the state, covers nearly 17,000 square kilometers. Within the rich natural environment of the central Scioto, I suggest that there were four polities—North Fork, Paint Creek, Chillicothe North, and Chillicothe South—with a fifth, Lower Scioto, located at the conjunction of the Scioto and the Ohio (fig. 5.11; Greber 1993a). These are defined by geography, the built environment, and uses of portable objects, all of which also reflect their interactions of these polities. The general areal extent of these major divisions was likely stable throughout the Hopewell

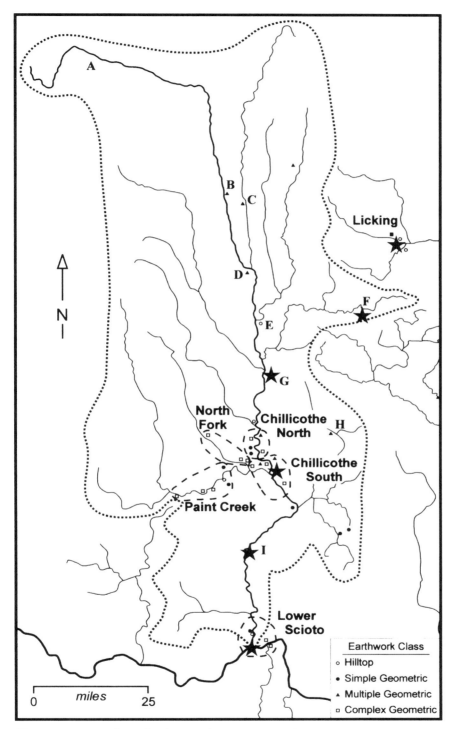

Figure 5.11. Hypothetical polities in the Scioto River drainage at one point in time during the Hopewell era. Areal extent not estimated for unnamed polities A–I. Stars indicate selected true square-shaped enclosures.

era, but the borders were not concrete walls, and hegemony changed. Each polity formed at least part of the community associated with the earthworks built within its borders. I do not have sufficient information to estimate boundaries of other polities in the drainage. Their participation in an interaction sphere is assumed by the building of a symbolically designed enclosure or, in a single instance, the occurrence of a classic interaction sphere token, a copper-covered panpipe found beneath the Robinson Mound at the headwaters in Hardin County (fig. 5.11:A). Caldwell's (1958) interaction sphere concept—a network of interactions founded on a common ideology, worldview, or set of religious beliefs held by groups having differing political, economic, and social organizations—provides a model for this distribution of polities.

I can only briefly indicate the possible tenor of the five major polities. A large multiroomed civic-ceremonial structure at Tremper, an incredible collection of walls and mounds at the Portsmouth Works, and the Ohio pipestone quarries show the active participation of the people living in the Lower Scioto polity. Artifacts from Tremper indicate ties to at least one special place at the Hopewell Site in the North Fork polity. For North Fork, Paint Creek, and Chillicothe South I chose a brief point of time in the Hopewell era when a unique series of earthworks suggests a time of strong social ties among these polities (Greber 1993a, 1997:219). This series unites three asymmetric elements on a large scale: two pairs of enclosures and one single enclosure (fig. 5.9). The overall iconography defines the series; details of the designs define the pairs and the single. The squares at Works East and Liberty in Chillicothe South are on the northern sides, and the smaller loops between the square and the medium circle form similar patterns. The squares at Seip and Baum in Paint Creek are on the south, and the circular elements (although not as well defined) again are patterned in a similar fashion. At Frankfort in North Fork, the two circles and the square are directly conjoined in an east-west fashion and in a more spare overall design.

In the adjoining polity—Chillicothe North—Dunlap and Hopeton are rare mirror images of each other (fig. 5.5). It is almost certain that the walls at Mound City and at Hopeton across the river were both visible at the same time and perhaps in use at the same time. In addition to enclosures, there is a complex suite of other cultural remains to consider while attempting to gain an understanding of the history within each polity. Elsewhere I have discussed some of these, including the designs of civic-ceremonial structures, the contexts of specific artifacts, and the occurrence of large, elongate mounds that are a rare mound form (Greber 1996). Within each central Scioto polity, the earthworks include one large, linear multistage mound: the central mound of Hopewell Mound 25 in North Fork; Seip-Pricer in Paint Creek; Edwin Harness in Chillicothe South; and the poorly documented Carriage Factory–Miller Mound in Chillicothe North (Greber 1991, 2005).

Trails That Join

Among the polities, the locations of enclosures sharing similar relatively rare iconographic elements form an interesting, though possibly accidental, pattern that begins at the mouth of the Scioto and ends in the Muskingum region (see sites noted by stars in fig. 11). A nineteenth-century map curated at the Cincinnati Museum Center shows both a square and an octagon in the southern areas of the Portsmouth Works. This map, attributed to R. Galbraith, has not been field tested to my knowledge. The octagon, the rarest design element, is well documented at High Bank and in the Muskingum drainage at Newark. Designs including a square element, each with a local variant, occur at Seal Township between Portsmouth and Chillicothe (fig. 5.11:I), near present-day Circleville and the entrance of Darby Creek (fig. 5.11:G), northeast of Circleville at Rock Mill near present-day Lancaster (fig. 5.11:F), and finally at Newark on the Licking (fig. 5.11). At Seal, both the aboveground and the intaglio square elements are recorded (fig. 5.3). At Circleville, a circular enclosure approximately 300 meters in diameter was directly conjoined to a square approximately 270 meters on a side. The circle was formed by an unusual double embankment (Atwater 1820; Squier and Davis 1948:Figure 10). Farther upstream on the Scioto, in a more fringe area near the mouth of the Olentangy, a local version of the design has a rectangular element (fig. 5.1:4).

A trail following a path marked by the stars in fig. 11 that would pass by each of the sites where a true square is recorded is documented in the journal of Christopher Gist, a frontier guide, who in 1751 traveled from Logstown, near the present Ohio-Pennsylvania border, to Lower Shawnee Town, near present-day Portsmouth (Hanna 1911:2:279). After reaching the Licking, Gist followed the main trail leading to Maguck, an Indian settlement near present-day Circleville, by way of Hockhocking, near present-day Lancaster. He described the several trails that intersected at Maguck. One led north to the Sandusky, another northwest to the Great Miami (passing close to the headwaters of the Little Miami), and the third south along the eastern bank of the Scioto to Lower Shawnee Town. These are shown on Charles Hanna's map (1911:1:284). Such a set of trails could well have served the social, political, religious, and economic needs of the five major hypothetical Hopewell polities and their neighbors. Historic records cannot verify the existence of these trails eighteen or more centuries before Gist's journey. Yet the custom for travelers on foot to use a river as a map by following ridges generally parallel to the river is undoubtedly old.

Comments

Embankment walls mark a location and also define the types of human activities appropriate for the inner and outer spaces created by the wall. Perhaps, for the builders, some walls formed a barrier to human or suprahuman beings or forces. Others may have represented events or activities associated with culture heroes or mythic cosmologies and thus represent culture history and the cosmos written large on the land. Others may have made political or social statements. Enclosures have a strong symbolic aspect beyond indicating the commitment of physical and social resources to their construction and maintenance. They leave us with questions concerning the relationship of these resources to political-social-religious organizations and domestic settlements.

Many, but not necessarily all, enclosures occur on land that was used for many generations, indicating a long-term commitment to a "place." Through time, the people using these places as local, nearby, or faraway visitors would each be a part of an associated community, though at different levels of social and physical commitment. Artifacts containing heavily symbolic meanings can be carried to local, nearby, or faraway places (compare Seeman 1995), but people themselves must come to or stay at a symbolic place to carry on a meeting, a ritual, or a ceremony, or to build a wall. How far could or would they walk each day? If any locales at Liberty are contemporaneous, perhaps some of the differing domestic categories suggested by Coughlin and Seeman (1997) include remnants of daily domestic activities that might reflect the different levels of association with a special place. Relatively small numbers of people could have been involved in small-scale activities and leave minimal traces of their presence. One would expect a larger number of participants when extensive stretches of walls (or major additions to mound strata) were being constructed. It is unlikely that work progressed a single day at a time on such extensive projects. Large gatherings likely were timed by a shared ritual calendar.

It does appear that, in general, the communities identified as Hopewell lived lightly on the land. Also, the localities identified as having Hopewell domestic debris are often multicomponent. This set of circumstances may suggest that we may not really know what a "Hopewell" settlement looks like in the archaeological record. Smith (1992a:243) discusses "loose concentrations" of one to three households located "in the general proximity of corporate-ceremonial centers." This description is reminiscent of Coughlin and Seeman's (1997) Site A. Smith (1992a:243) concludes that "habitation zones in a number of different regions require extensive excavation in order to establish the level of the social and spatial organization inherent in these poorly known settlements." The history of land use at Liberty and the radiocarbon dates from the Edwin Harness remnant would be consistent with a scenario indicating that all suggested domestic housing patterns could be applicable to Ohio Hopewell. Defining the last strata on Edwin Harness as Hopewell would allow Harness Site 28 to be identified as a "Hopewell" community. This could help to solve the "housing shortage" described by Griffin (1996, 1997), but possibly not at a calendrical date he would have expected or necessarily accepted. As an early description of Liberty states, "the whole work appears to have been but partially finished, or constructed in haste" (Squier and Davis 1848:56). An "unfinished" state would be consistent with construction of the wall at the end of an era. If, like the final additions to the Edwin Harness Mound, the construction of the walls also falls into the Late Woodland time period, we need to rethink the date at which we "end" the Ohio Hopewell era.

In building theories concerning the communities associated with major enclosures, we clearly need to allow for possible changes in the social and physical organizations of these communities. More importantly, we need to be aware that we do not yet know the number of enclosures in use at the same time in each local region or across regions. In defining communities associated with enclosures we need to take into account the possibilities that one polity may have supported more than one earthwork complex and that one earthwork may have had the support of more than one polity. The Hopewell site is an excellent candidate to be an example of the latter case (Greber and Ruhl 1989).

Although in this essay I have emphasized the variations in physical and social aspects of the many earthen and stone enclosures found in southern Ohio, I would not like to leave the impression that this represents a chaotic, or constantly changing, cultural climate. The number of human generations represented in even a conservative estimate of the time extent of Ohio Hopewell indicates an era of basic social stability, likely enlivened by changes in local leadership associated with shifting prestige and reinterpretations of the acceptable manner of being Hopewell.

Acknowledgments

I extend many thanks to Frank Cowan, Brian Redmond, Katharine Ruhl, Bret Ruby, Bruce Smith, and Kathryn Wood, who read various versions as a verbal presentation metamorphosed into an essay. I alone am responsible for any errors and all opinions.

6

The Mounded Landscapes of Ohio

Hopewell Patterns and Placements

Mark F. Seeman and James L. Branch

The concept of a "cultural landscape" has gained increasing favor among archaeologists. In part, this is because it provides for a contextualized assessment of sites and their spatial distributions. A landscape is cultural to the extent that it physically embodies the history, structure, and contents of human behavior in such a way that they are not readily separable from one another (Hood 1996:121). In this view, Western concepts of place or environment may be far different from or even irrelevant to a truly meaningful characterization of people on the land (for example, Basso 1996; Hood 1996; Waselkov 1989). Certainly the "real" landscape for native Australians in a Dreamtime where time, space, and place are connected in nonlinear fashion is very different from that implied by a modern map of the same region made by Western cartographers (Tilley 1994). Native American Woodland societies inhabiting the American Midwest two thousand years ago also lived in worlds of their own creation. They actively constructed these worlds, not only interpreting the landscape in ways that were meaningful to them, but also adding to it a variety of buildings, monuments, pathways, fields, and public spaces.

Our specific interest here is in the cultural landscape of the ancient Midwest as it pertains to the question of Hopewell origins in Ohio. "Hopewell" is a distinctive archaeological construct that has been used to describe certain relatively costly patterns of exchange and public ritual in the Midwest beginning sometime around 2000 B.P. (Griffin 1978; Seeman 1992b). Hopewell has remained a central focus of archaeological inquiry in North America for over a century, and correspondingly, it has proved a source of rich and varied interpretations. Ohio Hopewell populations were among the first farmers in the Midwest, increasingly modifying the land as they planted a variety of grains and at least one vegetable (Smith 1992b). As such, they perceived the world differently than their predecessors (for example, Berry 1976; Bradley 1991a). Hopewell peoples in Ohio made use of a large corpus of material symbols, making and displaying them in diverse and complex ways far different from those of preceding populations (Ruhl and Seeman 1998; Seeman 1995). Ancestral ties, world renewal, and personal connections to animal spirit helpers were all probably important aspects of Hopewell belief. Ohio Hopewell populations also were great builders, utilizing earth, timbers, and poles to create a dizzying array of geometric enclosures, screens, ditches, public buildings, and mounds. Some of these were intended to have transitory importance and were disassembled and/or desanctified on the spot. Others were meant to be enduring elements of the cultural landscape. In this sense, Ohio Hopewell societies lived in worlds of their own creation, where the construction and manipulation of a meaningful geography ensure a spatial reality far different from any early twenty-first century perspective.

In this chapter we interpret one important component of these efforts, Ohio Hopewell mound placement, within a complex and developing Woodland landscape. More specifically, we will focus on the spatial relationships of varying scale that link Hopewell mound building with earlier mound-building efforts in Ohio. Our emphasis on a cultural landscape perspective in this regard stems from the fact that even the best empirically based studies have fallen short in providing rules that explain site distributions, and also from the recognition that multiple perspectives on the past can only enrich our understanding of it.

Many contemporary studies of cultural landscape in archaeology, anthropology, and geography have been able to ground the meaning of the land in history. Thus, for example, the contemporary British landscape is understandable as the cumulative product of land-use practices rooted in Roman and medieval times largely because historical documents dating to these periods exist and can be interpreted (for example, Aston 1985; Aston and Rowley 1974; Reed 1990; Thomas 1996). In the absence of long-term histories of this sort, archaeologists interested in cultural landscapes must construct them using multiple "supporting lines of inference" (Wylie 1992). Supporting lines of inference can itself be interpreted in a variety of ways. Thus, for example, Barnes and Dashun (1996) strengthen their case that the northern Chinese Neolithic ceremonial center of Niuheliang was positioned to take advantage of a vista of a boar-shaped mountain range by finding boar votive offerings at the site, by referencing the long-term importance of boar ceremonialism in this region, and by noting that the modern Chinese place-name for this mountain range is a boar image. Alternately, Richards (1996) builds a landscape context by integrating English physiography, Neolithic farming, standing stones, and passage graves in a world where social practices were shaped more by belief than by the economy. Crumley and Marquardt's (1987; see also Moran 1990) approach, central to our own investigations, is to work between several spatial scales in contextualizing the cultural landscape of medieval Burgundy. A scalar study necessarily provides multiple perspectives on a given problem; as Marquardt and Crumley (1987:5) note, what appears to be homogeneous at one scale can appear quite heterogeneous at another. Similarly, events that occur at a subordinate level can have major effects on superior-level interactions, and we must have an eye on both to see the connection. In this approach, context is built by working back and forth among these scales of action—in real terms, relationships to region, to community, and to household—focusing analytical attention on relationships of emerging continuity and contradiction. Today, the availability of Geographic Information Systems (GIS) techniques makes the sort of multiscale studies that we favor much more feasible now than in the past.

Returning to the Ohio Valley, it must first be said that much of what is seen as a distinct set of "Hopewell" practices is actually strongly rooted in local history and that these practices were performed within a regional landscape that was by no means pristine, unspoiled, or "natural." Palynology and the analysis of wood charcoal indicate that portions of the region had been cleared of heavy timber as early as 3000 B.P. (Delcourt et al. 1998). Mound building itself had begun here well before 2500 B.P., and substantial circular and oval earthen enclosures were constructed and used nearly as early. Certainly the two to three hundred years prior to the origin of Ohio Hopewell saw an accelerated pace of land modification activities, particularly pertaining to the building of the many hundreds (possibly thousands) of mounds and earthworks that dotted southern Ohio in conjunction with Adena ceremonialism (Dragoo 1963:197–198). People participating in the latter were using a broader range of environmental contexts than subsequent Hopewell populations and show a very limited involvement in food production (Seeman 1996; Wymer 1992). Mortuary rites of the period centered on the display of a limited set of symbols made of local raw materials, the construction of elaborate log crypts and circular structures, the use of bark mantles, and, of course, mound building (for example, Clay 1998; Hays 1995). Although the essential elements of belief were probably quite similar, the performance of Adena ceremonialism was fairly variable from site to site and valley to valley. While most archaeologists agree that it began sometime around 2500 B.P., there is considerable disagreement regarding its ending. Estimates for the latter range from 2000 B.P. in some portions of the middle Ohio Valley to as recently as 1500 B.P. in others (compare Seeman 1992b:26–27 with Clay 1998:15). More important than any absolute time frame is the relative relationship between Adena and Hopewell sites. Here we would agree with Carr and Haas (1996:28) that any argument for significant temporal overlap between Adena and Hopewell in the Scioto Valley, the geographic focus of our study, based on the available radiocarbon evidence is a weak one.

Hopewell ritual programs were sufficiently different from Adena programs to suggest a significant reworking of local ideologies around 2000 B.P. in south-central Ohio. Potentially, these processes also carry spatial connotations in the sense that ritual performances, especially those pertaining to mound building, took place within a Woodland landscape that already had been actively constructed, manipulated, and lived in by Early Woodland Adena societies for at least five hundred years. Thus, Hopewell mound placement decisions were made within a context rich in possibilities for building both spatial continuities and discontinuities with the Adena past as new identities were constructed through ritual practice. It is our position that these decisions were originally multiscalar and should be interpreted as such. Following from Crumley and Marquardt, we wish to examine Adena and Hopewell mound placement at several scales but will focus our attention at the confluence of Paint Creek and the Scioto River in Ross County, Ohio, an area considered to be the "core" of both manifestations since the time of Webb and Snow (1945:Map 1). Before such an examination can begin, however, it is necessary to briefly consider the range of purposes that such constructions might have served.

The Meaning of Adena and Hopewell Mounds

Mound building in eastern North America was first seen as an indication of widespread migrations and, somewhat later, as a useful trait for describing local culture histories (for example, Silverberg 1968). In consort with shifting theoretical canons, Woodland mound building is today generally seen as pertaining to two general purposes: the marking of territory and the covering of sacred places. The "territorial marker" interpretation can be traced most directly to the work of British archaeologist Colin Renfrew, who, in a seminal work, interprets Neolithic long barrows as centrally placed, corporate facilities connecting the living, the dead, and the land in highly visible fashion (Renfrew 1973b, 1976). This territorial interpretation subsequently has been expanded and modified, but the notion of mound building as a regional adaptation to situations of increasing competition and social complexity remains (for example, Bradley 1991b; Chapman 1981:80, 1995; Earle 1991). On this side of the Atlantic, the notion that mounds were used as territorial markers is best associated with Charles (1985, 1992) and his interpretations of Hopewell burial mounds along the bluffs of the lower Illinois River valley. The constraining location of the linear bluff edge, however, dictates that the distribution of lineage territory-marking mounds in Illinois was quite different than in Neolithic Wessex, as were the size range and shape of these constructions. It would be difficult to place concentric territories around the linearly distributed Illinois Valley sites, and in fact Charles does not do so. It also should be noted that whereas British long barrows provide very limited information, often existing as little more than crop stains showing former locations, Illinois Hopewell mounds offer better preservation and a corresponding broader range of archaeological cues. The larger question looming here is to what degree a formal correspondence is necessary to make the British territorial analogy applicable to the Illinois case. In the end, and following Johnson (1999:102), we are left not with proof but only with the choice of either agreeing or disagreeing with the argument. Most, we think, find it acceptable to assume that Illinois Hopewell mound building in a specific sense and Woodland mound building in general carried at least some territorial connotation, but we must be open to the probability that the signified "territories" may have been complexly structured and in part disjunctive with the location of the mounds themselves.

Mounds as "sacred places" carry stronger social-practice and ideological connotations. Mounds are constructed out of particular sociocultural practices—practices that take place within the specific cultural and historical conditions they maintain. In this view, burial mound construction can be seen as a context for the living to renegotiate relationships of affinity and obligation.

Sacred places thus represent continuity of space but discontinuity among sets of constantly renegotiated meanings. Similarly, these sacred spaces can be seen to have history through repeated use. Recently, Buikstra, Charles, and Rakita (1998:94) have discussed the long-term, but varying, use of a particular sand ridge in the lower Illinois Valley for ritual. Clay (1998:18) also, in his study of Adena mounds in Kentucky, emphasizes the varying ritual activities that may take place on the successive surfaces of a sacred location, only some of which result in mound construction. Following from the work of Bradley (1993, 1996, 1998), the social meaning of these spatial continuities should be quite varied, ranging from attempts to legitimize through identification with place, to attempts to subordinate or supplant by using old spaces in new ways.

In sum, mounds carry connotations of both territorial identity and the varying social actions that produced them. Both interpretations need to be foregrounded as Hopewell mound building practices are considered within scales of varying spatial scope and history.

Three Views of the Hopewell Landscape

The Regional Landscape: The Scioto Valley

Drainages, to the extent that they represent easy lines of communication and resource continuities, are useful scales of analysis. The Scioto River is a moderately sized stream that drains much of central Ohio, extending approximately 130 miles from its source in the Till Plains of north-central Ohio to its confluence with the Ohio River near the present city of Portsmouth. The Scioto is a modest, underfit stream flanked by a series of well-defined and complex terraces. Valley soils are fertile, and the diversity of terrestrial resources is high. Mound building was a vital component of the Woodland landscape in this valley.

There are two region-level summaries of mound distributional information for the Scioto Valley area: Mills' (1914) *Archaeological Atlas of Ohio* and the Ohio Historic Preservation Office's *Ohio Archaeological Inventory*. The *Atlas* was a priority of the Ohio Archaeological and Historical Society as early as 1894, and its creation involved all three of the main figures in early Ohio archaeology: Warren K. Moorehead, William C. Mills, and Henry C. Shetrone. Together, they documented over 3,500 mounds in Ohio, with over 950 in the Scioto Valley (fig. 6.1). The methods used to document these sites are unclear but did involve verifying locations in the field. While the *Atlas* still has research value, printing errors, the size of the map symbols, and the scale used to plot the sites on county road maps mean that it cannot be used to pinpoint site locations (Dancey 1984).

The *Ohio Archaeological Inventory* was initiated in the 1970s and is the official site registry for Ohio. It records a total of 1,505 mounds for all of Ohio, less than half the total shown in the *Atlas*. However, since much of the data in the *Inventory,* particularly for destroyed or excavated sites, are derived from the old Ohio Historical Society card file (maintained since at least the time of

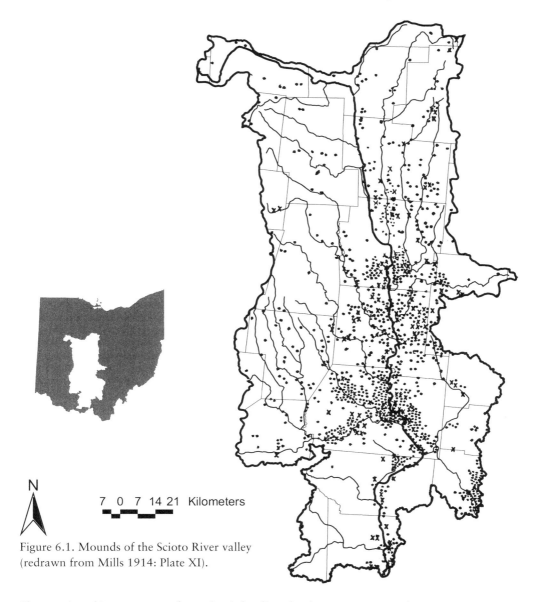

N
7 0 7 14 21 Kilometers

Figure 6.1. Mounds of the Scioto River valley
(redrawn from Mills 1914: Plate XI).

Shetrone) and in some cases from the *Atlas* directly, these two summaries are not
independent of one another. A Pearson product moment correlation of the *Atlas*
and the *Inventory* data show a strong relationship (r = 0.7004). The *Inventory*
has been added to, subtracted from, and revised many times as new generations
of curators and managers reinterpret the available information. The *Atlas* was
done much earlier, was compiled by a small number of collaborators, and provides a larger sample.

For purposes of providing a general view of Hopewell mound building in the
Scioto region, the *Atlas* is especially useful, and it can be used to elucidate three
patterns of interest. First, comparatively large numbers of mounds were constructed along the Scioto, the adjacent Great and Little Miami Valleys to the

west, and the Muskingum Valley to the east, when compared to the number identified in the intervening uplands. Because of the proximity of upland, terrace, and floodplain in these valleys, resources were richer and more varied there than in interdrainage areas (Maslowski and Seeman 1992). A second pattern is the constrained/unconstrained mound distribution along the Scioto that correlates with the glaciated Till Plains and the unglaciated Appalachian Plateau sections of the valley. A similar distribution is found in the Muskingum drainage to the east. Mounds in these two drainages are less frequent in the "constrained" south than in the "unconstrained" north. At this scale, these distributions are analogous to the linear, constrained pattern of the Illinois Valley and the unconstrained patterns of Wessex posited by Charles and Renfrew, respectively, as discussed previously. Each type of network carries different implications for social engagement, and a location that funnels contact between such systems is in a central position to affect regional relations (see Clark and Blake 1996:263). A third pattern is the clustered distribution of Hopewell mounds in the central portion of the Scioto drainage in what is now Ross County, Ohio. This pattern is not observable directly from the *Atlas* but is supported by comparing that distribution with Adena and Hopewell site distributions documented in Webb and Baby 1957, Webb and Snow 1945, Fischer 1974, and Seeman 1979b. A total of about 115 Hopewell mounds can be documented for the valley, a very small percentage of the 952 mapped in the *Atlas*. These numbers indicate a decrease in mound-building efforts from the Early Woodland to the Middle Woodland period and a concentration of the latter efforts in one area of the drainage. This Hopewell concentration corresponds with that portion of the Scioto showing both the greatest ecological diversity and a change in distributional pattern (constrained/unconstrained) for previous mound construction. Hopewell mounds in the Miami and Muskingum valleys also show patterns of increased spatial clustering when compared to Adena constructions, but each valley distribution shows a different relationship to these earlier mounds and to the overall drainage structure than along the Scioto. The reasons for this more focused Hopewell distribution in each of these valleys were probably similar, but the principles affecting the relative size and location of such clusters within each drainage clearly differed. Across all of southern Ohio circa 2000 B.P., Hopewell ideology supported an increased spatial concentration of ritual but at different kinds of places.

As a means of discussing additional aspects of mound building within the Scioto Valley region, we wish to introduce at this point the notion of "mound size" and to focus attention specifically on the distribution of truly big mounds. Large mounds are hard to overlook, and their locations are more accurately reported than those of smaller mounds. More importantly, big mounds can be assumed to approximate the maximum working capabilities of a social group engaged in this sort of activity. Brumfiel (1976), in examining the relationship between carrying capacity and population size, clearly recognized the implications of this principle. Similarly, Naroll and Margolis (1974) focused their attention on only the largest settlements in a given system in developing cross-cultural comparisons of complexity. There is a theoretical maximum mound size that lies beyond the organizational capabilities of a given society, and as that maximum is approached, the organizational parameters of the system are tested. Following Bullington (1988:223, 234), we have defined "big" as more than 28 meters in diameter—or in cases where no basal dimensions are available, more than 6 meters in height. It should be noted that Bullington believes that mounds of this size required the cooperative efforts of at least two local Hopewell groups in the Illinois Valley.

Of the sixty-three big mounds in the Scioto Valley, fifty-one of these are Adena, eleven are Hopewell, and one is Fort Ancient, a much later cultural complex. A comparison of the distribution of these big sites with that of all mounds recorded for the drainage in Mills' *Atlas* suggests that the bigger mounds tended to be built in environmentally productive areas associated with the main valley. The scarcity of big mounds along the small western tributaries and in the most northerly portions of the drainage is notable in this regard.

A bivariate plot of the mean basal diameter against maximum height for large Adena and Hopewell mounds reveals several trends (fig. 6.2). First, with the exception of Hopewell Mound 25, the range of diameters and heights of the Hopewell and earlier Adena mounds are similar. The implication is that for mound building itself, there was little difference in the size of the groups cooperating in their construction. Second, the opportunities to construct mounds of this size occurred less frequently among Hopewell groups, and when it did, activities were narrowly focused in the Ross County area (fig. 6.3). Finally, it should be noted that the "biggest of the big" Adena mounds—the twenty largest—were rank-ordered and evaluated for location. Ten of the top twenty (and nine of the top ten) Adena mounds were located near the Scioto–Paint Creek confluence. This suggests that the Hopewell distribution is in part the continuation of a pattern of concentrated ritual efforts that were already under way in that locality.

The Local Landscape: The Scioto–Paint Creek Confluence

Within the Scioto Valley, the area where Paint Creek enters the main valley has been famous since the 1820s as a center of Woodland mound construction. No other place in eastern North America of similar size saw as many mounds built between 3000 B.P. and 1500 B.P. Some of these were also among the largest Woodland mounds ever built. By narrowing the focus to the Scioto–Paint Creek confluence, we are at a scale where decision-making processes were influenced by circumstances that may have little relevance for interpreting mound-building activities elsewhere. However, because of the strong representation of late Adena (Robbins complex) and early Hopewell (the Mound City complex) ritual programs here, this is an especially important context for considering the question of Hopewell origins.

Owing to a distinctive set of biological and geological circumstances, the Scioto–Paint Creek confluence is the most productive resource area in the drainage, and it compares favorably with other resource-rich areas elsewhere in the

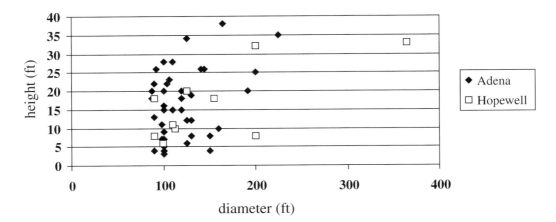

Figure 6.2. A size comparison of the largest Adena and Hopewell mounds in the Scioto Valley.

middle Ohio Valley (Maslowski and Seeman 1992). For precisely the same set of circumstances, it is also an area characterized by bold vistas and rare landforms, prompting, as Moorehead (1892:144) noted, "expressions of admiration from travelers who are familiar with the noted landscapes of the world . . . equal to many that have been celebrated in song and story, or transferred to the canvas of the painter." Copperas Mountain, a 90-meter-high, massive black shale cliff lying immediately southeast of the Seip earthworks, is one such feature, and its physical presence plus associated white florescences of alum (an astringent) pyrites, quartz crystals, and nesting vultures must have made it a significant component of the Woodland landscape. Shetrone (1926:190–191) believed that materials obtained from this locale were used in Hopewell rituals. Other features such as caves, salt springs, kames, eskers, and prairies helped to create a particular and meaningful world for the Woodland populations in this portion of south-central Ohio. Still, it is the change in relief associated with the Till Plains/Appalachian Plateau border that is the most notable feature at this scale. The fact that the glacial margin strikes both the Plateau and the valley of the entrenched Teays system so squarely here causes local relief differences to be especially pronounced (Gordon 1969:82). As a context for interaction, the Scioto–Paint Creek confluence is appropriately sized to have been exploited by a modest number of neighboring communities or lineages at any given time.

What was the mounded landscape of Ross County like? At the end of the nineteenth century, Moorehead (1892:145) wrote, "At the first settlement of this territory by the whites, mounds were to be seen everywhere. They existed on the level lands in almost as great numbers as do the farmhouses at the present day. Scores, even hundreds, have been opened, and at present very few are intact." Although Moorehead had firsthand knowledge of many Ross County mounds, his concept of mound density was based in part on the survey of Concord Township conducted by antiquarian Arthur Coover (Mills 1900:335–

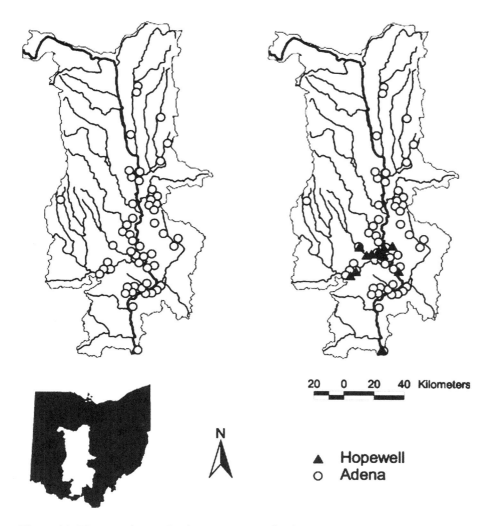

Figure 6.3. Big mounds in a developing Scioto Valley landscape (*left*, Adena mounds circa 2500–2000 B.P.; *right*, Adena and Hopewell mounds circa 2000–1600 B.P.).

342). Coover recorded over 50 mounds from this township alone. Sometime later, Mills (1914:71) reported 370 mounds for the entire county. In 1998, the Ohio Archaeological Inventory (OAI), the official state registry, listed 106 mounds for the county. Differing criteria and, more importantly, increasing urbanization, gravel mining, looting, and farming practices that have destroyed or damaged mounds at a rapid rate probably account for these discrepancies. Nineteenth-century excavation efforts also were focused here, and although we may lament the limitations that result from the field methods and records of that day, we must accept their effects on our own interpretations.

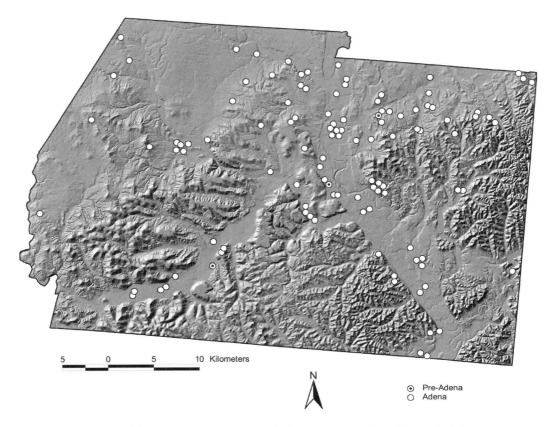

Figure 6.4. Adena and pre-Adena mound placements near the Paint Creek–Scioto River confluence, Ross County, Ohio, circa 3000–2000 B.P.

To investigate landscape construction through mound building at the Scioto–Paint Creek confluence, we made a more intensive effort to document the distribution of Woodland mounds at this scale than we employed for the drainage as a whole. Detailed GIS coverages of topography, streams, slope, and mound locations were developed. Records of the OAI were supplemented with personal interviews, university records, published literature, and contract reports. On this basis, 238 mounds were located and classified to cultural/temporal period. Three mounds pertain to the Red Ochre complex and are presumed to date to the early portion of the Early Woodland period, circa 3000–2500 B.P.; forty-six are Adena and are presumed to date to the second half of the Early Woodland period, circa 2500–2000 B.P.; ninety-eight mounds are Hopewell and are presumed to date to the Middle Woodland period circa 2000–1600 B.P. The remaining ninety-one mounds are of indeterminate temporal affiliation.

Our mapped summaries of the Scioto–Paint Creek area (figs. 6.4 and 6.5) show both similarities to and differences from patterns evident at a smaller scale. In the Scioto–Paint Creek area, mounds were built rarely by pre-Adena groups; with only three cases, no further interpretation is attempted. In com-

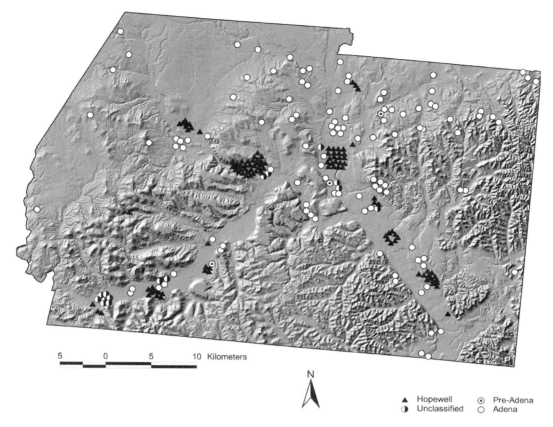

Figure 6.5. The mounded landscape of the Paint Creek–Scioto River confluence, Ross County, Ohio, circa 2000–1600 B.P.

parison, both Adena and Hopewell mounds are frequent, but they display noticeably different patterns of placement: Adena mound building is dispersed, and Hopewell mound building is clustered. Actually, Hopewell mound construction is clustered at two levels. Not only do mounds occur more frequently in proximity to their nearest neighbor, but also the vast majority of Hopewell mounds are concentrated at two localities: Mound City and Hopewell. Hopewell clusters tend toward regular spacing; they do not seem to "map on" to earlier Adena constructions in any consistent fashion.

It should be noted that in addition to being more spatially clustered than Adena mounds, Hopewell mounds in the Scioto–Paint Creek area occur in different kinds of places. A great variety of settings were chosen for Adena mounds, but in general, these are at higher relative elevations above the main watercourses (the Scioto, Paint Creek, and North Fork). Although some of them are sited on highly visible landforms, most are not in hilltop situations. Put differently, mound locations tend to be framed by adjacent hills rather than being on them. These locations do not correlate with catchments of the highest economic potential located along the Scioto. In contrast, Hopewell mounds are located on terrace surfaces in the main valleys. It should be noted that neither Adena nor Hopewell groups showed much interest in the strong "bluff" feature along the western edge of the valley in south-central Ross County, contrary to the Illinois example discussed previously.

To increase the interpretability of Woodland mound building at this scale, a discriminate function analysis using the known Hopewell, the known Adena, and the indeterminate mounds was performed. Using just two variables, relative elevation and average distance to four nearest mounds, only three Adena (7 percent of a total of forty-six) and ten Hopewell (10 percent of a total of ninety-eight) sites were misclassified (Branch 2000). Using these same variables, seventy-nine of the ninety-one indeterminate mounds could be classified as either Adena (sixty-five of ninety-one, or 71 percent) or Hopewell (fourteen of ninety-one, or 15 percent). Although the classification of these indeterminate mounds simply confirms the observed patterning, it does make clearer the dispersed and varying locations of Adena mound locations. More importantly, it supports the interpretation that the numbers of Adena and Hopewell mounds in this area were actually about the same but that the mounds were positioned differently on the land.

Viewshed: Mt. Logan and Vicinity

To make the scale finer yet, we wish to focus on an approximately two-mile section of the Scioto Valley exactly at the Plateau/Till Plain border and in the immediate vicinity of Mount Logan. Mount Logan together with Sugar Loaf and Bald Hill form an isolated complex of named promontories on the extreme northern edge of the Plateau (fig. 6.6), a unique, highly visible feature in south-central Ohio (Gordon 1969:82). The sunrise over Mount Logan figures prominently on the state seal of Ohio, possibly due to a spark of inspiration after a night of carousing on the part of Governor Thomas Worthington and his guests (Hobbs 2000; Knabenshue 1902). The high densities of raptors associated with the thermals coming off this highland would not have been lost on Woodland populations concerned with these birds and their connection to the Upper World (Bildstein 1987:3; Brandy 1976). At this scale, we have reintroduced the large/small mound distinction and examine locational patterning between them for both Adena and Hopewell. There are about forty-five small mounds and ten large mounds here, a considerable number for so small an area (fig. 6.7). Many of these correspond to what Greber (1991:6) called the "Chillicothe Northwest" group. The large mounds orient to Mount Logan, and at the same time they are in line of sight of one another. The Story mound and the Adena mound, two of the latest Adena constructions (based on the presence of "Robbins" diagnostics; see Dragoo 1963), are part of this grouping, as are Mound City Mound 3 and Mound City Mound 7. The latter are presumed to be among the earliest of the large Ohio Hopewell constructions. Ritual staging, the range of symbols, and the choice of raw materials are substantially different between these two groups, which were ostensibly separated by a minimal amount of time. An interesting detail in this regard is the strong reliance on Flint Ridge flint

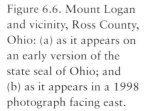

a

b

Figure 6.6. Mount Logan and vicinity, Ross County, Ohio: (a) as it appears on an early version of the state seal of Ohio; and (b) as it appears in a 1998 photograph facing east.

at the Story and Adena mounds, the use of Wyandotte chert at Mound City, and the resurgence of Flint Ridge use at later Hopewell sites in the area. At this scale, the early Hopewell mound builders at Mound City can be seen to have shown continuity in the use of a particularly important setting but to have used it in a calculated and different way.

Conclusion

By moving back and forth between scales, the observer will necessarily see the distribution of Ohio Hopewell mounds from several vantage points. At the drainage scale, the most obvious relationship is the decreased frequency of mound building when compared to earlier periods. A strong secondary trend is the intense focus of Hopewell efforts in the Scioto–Paint Creek confluence area of the valley. This clustered distribution opposes the more generalized pattern-ing of earlier and more numerous Adena mounds, clearly connoting the devel-opment of new principles for locating rituals on the land. At the most complex levels of Adena ceremonialism, as connoted by those mounds with the largest floor space, this concentration already may have been under way.

Within the Scioto–Paint Creek portion of the Scioto drainage, Adena and Hopewell mounds occurred in relatively equal frequency but were located in different types of places. Adena mounds, which at a smaller (drainage) scale relate to constrained/unconstrained distributions, appear to loosely align along the area of most prominent relief, in some cases on hills and in places framed by hills. Hopewell mounds have a much more limited distribution, and most occur in one of two tight clusters less than two miles apart.

At a larger scale, the orientation of big mounds to Mount Logan and the

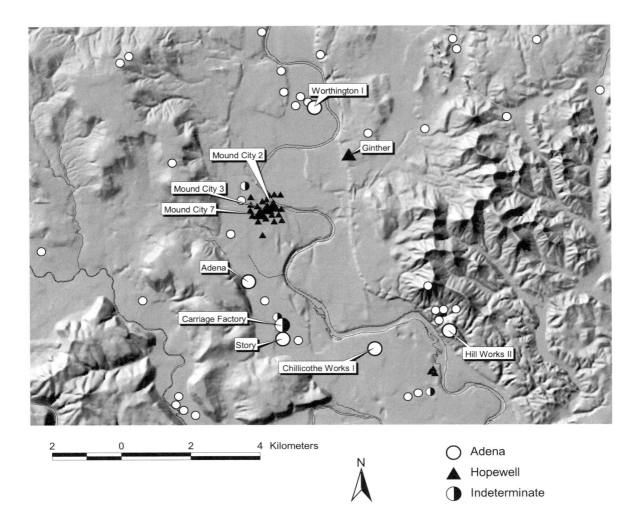

Figure 6.7. The Mount Logan area and Woodland period mounds nearby, Ross County, Ohio.

different settings of ritual activities at Mound City and Hopewell are notable. The mounds at Mound City complement a landscape already dramatically shaped by earlier Adena rituals but with a contrast imposed by way of new ritual programs. Conversely, the mounds at the Hopewell type-site, presumably constructed somewhat later in time than Mound City but showing strong ritual continuities with it, hold a contrasting relationship to the Mount Logan landscape. It is through the manipulation of these kinds of relationships that Hopewell identities were created.

Mound-building efforts did not appreciably escalate after 2000 B.P. in south-central Ohio—mounds were not bigger, nor were they more numerous. Their distribution, however, becomes tremendously constrained. Although it is likely that Hopewell settlement was undergoing a similar spatial concentration (for example, Coughlin and Seeman 1997), one does not necessarily imply the other.

The use of regional-level ritual centers by very dispersed populations is not unprecedented in prehistoric Ohio; for example, both the Williams and the Libben site were large regional centers in northern Ohio where dispersed Early Woodland and Late Woodland populations buried thousands of people (Stothers and Abel 1993:66–73; Stothers et al. 1994:170–175). Regardless, a narrower range of acceptable mound-building choices could easily accentuate inequities among perspective participants, in part, as a function of residential proximity.

We conclude that for Ohio Hopewell, the "sacred place" aspects of mound building became more actively managed, and any "territorial" aspects somewhat less so. Hopewell mounds were symbols, potentially pertaining to both identity and ideology. The changes in the location and pattern of their construction about 2000 B.P. is dramatic and innovative and at the same time consistent with active changes in broader symbolic systems. Borrowing from Garwood (1991), we would posit that conceptually this change marked a shift away from a mounded landscape composed of many places where history took place (cyclical ritual activity) and toward a few places that carried the "weight of history," thereby providing a clearer justification for validating lines of descent and other social-political arrangements.

7

The Great Hopewell Road and the Role of the Pilgrimage in the Hopewell Interaction Sphere

Bradley T. Lepper

Throughout prehistoric America, many societies built networks of roads, the significance of which transcends economic utility (see Trombold 1991 for examples). These sacred roads can be quite long, often stretching dozens of kilometers to connect one special place with another, and they are very straight. The most well documented examples of such roads were built in the Yucatán Peninsula by the Maya between A.D. 300 and 900 and in the southwestern United States by the Anasazi from A.D. 900 to 1150 (for example, Freidel and Sabloff 1984; Saville 1935; Wicklein 1994). In the woodlands of eastern North America, no such monumental roads were believed to have existed, although relatively short avenues, defined by parallel earthen walls, were a common feature of many of the Hopewellian earthworks of the Ohio Valley built between 100 B.C. and A.D. 400.

The purpose of this chapter is to review the evidence for a Hopewell road that began at the Newark Earthworks and extended off the margins of every nineteenth-century map (for example, fig. 7.1) of that "remarkable plain" (Squier and Davis 1848:69). It is not yet known where that road ended, but I have argued elsewhere that it was a monumental construction that stretched for some ninety kilometers across central Ohio (Lepper 1995, 1996, 1998b). This "Great Hopewell Road" would have been longer than the longest known Anasazi road, and it was built as many as five centuries earlier. Using various lines of evidence, including American Indian oral traditions, I also consider how the Hopewell people of central Ohio might have used such a road.

Early Accounts

The earliest documented reference to what I have termed the Great Hopewell Road occurs in Caleb Atwater's 1820 *Description of the Antiquities Discovered in the State of Ohio and Other Western States*. Atwater noted that parallel walls of earth had been observed at various locations southwest of Newark, and he speculated that these were the remains of a prehistoric road that had extended for as much as "thirty miles," connecting the Newark Works with another set of mounds and enclosures (Atwater 1820:129).

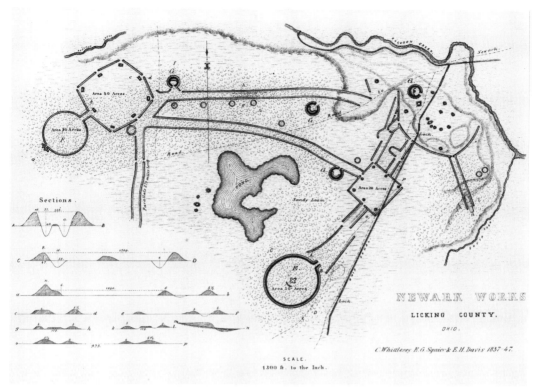

Figure 7.1. The Newark Works (Squier and Davis 1848). The map contains numerous errors (see Thomas 1894:459–468). The walls of the Great Hopewell Road are depicted incorrectly as irregularly sinuous lines trending roughly southward. Although the notation on the map indicates the walls extend only 2.5 miles (4 kilometers), there is no discussion in the text as to whether the surveyors made a serious effort to test Atwater's claim that the road might go as far as 30 miles. Compare the length and orientation of these walls with those in figure 7.2 (for additional comparisons, see also LCAALS 1985; Reeves 1936; and Whittlesey 1836).

In 1862, James Salisbury, a local physician and antiquarian (who somewhat later in his career would achieve culinary immortality by inventing Salisbury steak [Moore 1980]), along with his brother Charles, followed the parallel walls for six miles (fig. 7.2) "over fertile fields, through tangled swamps and across streams, still keeping their undeviating course" (Salisbury and Salisbury 1862:15). The brothers Salisbury did not follow the great "high way" to its end but speculated that if it continued, it would lead "near Circleville & Chillicothe where [there] are extensive ancient ruins" (1862:15).

In 1870, local historian Samuel Park reported the claim of Jesse Thompson, at that time a resident of Hebron, Ohio. Thompson said that "when he first settled on Walnut Creek, in Fairfield county . . . about the beginning of the present century, there was a graded road, easily traced in the timber . . . and he always thought it to be a road leading from the works near Newark to those at Circleville" (Park 1870:41). Park attempted to locate this road without success

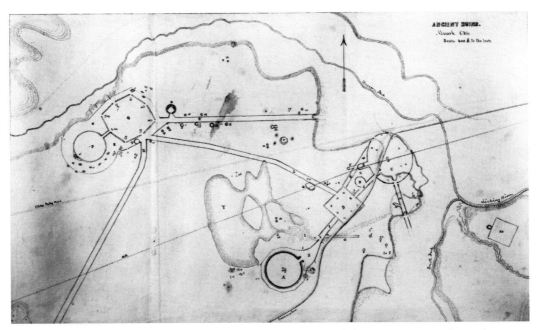

Figure 7.2. Newark Earthworks, drawn by James and Charles Salisbury, circa 1862. This is the most accurate and comprehensive of the several known maps of the Newark Works. After Salisbury and Salisbury 1862: Plate VII. Courtesy, American Antiquarian Society.

and doubted that "in the present improved state of the country it could be found" (1870:41).

In 1930, Warren Weiant Jr., a local Newark businessman and aviation enthusiast, brought aerial reconnaissance to bear on the archaeology of the Moundbuilders and defied Park's pessimism. He observed very straight parallel lines in the soil extending from Newark's octagon "southwestward in a straight line for Millersport" (Weiant 1931). Millersport is located in Fairfield County, 17 kilometers southwest of Newark and barely 2 kilometers south of a parcel of land known to have been owned by Jesse Thompson as late as 1831 (Fairfield County Recorder's Office, Deed Records). If the very straight lines surveyed by the Salisburys and depicted in Weiant's photographs (fig. 7.3; see also Reeves 1936) are extended, they are found to lead directly towards Chillicothe, not Circleville as Thompson incorrectly supposed.

Is Chillicothe a plausible destination for a Hopewell Road beginning in Newark? The Scioto Valley, above and below the site of modern Chillicothe, is filled with dozens of ancient mounds and earthworks (Squier and Davis 1848:Plate II; see also DeBoer 1997), many of which exhibit "extraordinary coincidences" in form and scale (Squier and Davis 1848:71) with elements of the Newark Earthworks. One of these earthworks (see fig. 5.5) demonstrates a particular connection to Newark's ancient geometry (DeBoer 1997:235; Lepper 1996). High Bank Works is a circular embankment connected to an octagonal enclosure (Squier and Davis 1848:Plate XVI). The Ohio Hopewell built only two of these

Figure 7.3. Aerial photograph showing the outline of a small semicircular enclosure attached to the parallel walls of the Great Hopewell Road (see also Reeves 1936; Shetrone 1937). Weiant claimed that such circular enclosures branched off the parallel walls at regular intervals of 1–1.5 miles (1.6–2.4 kilometers). They are reminiscent of the *herraduras* associated with the Anasazi roads (Kincaid 1983; Nials, Stein, and Roney 1987). Kennedy (1994:55) speculated that they might be shrines analogous to the Stations of the Cross in the Christian pilgrimage tradition. An alternative interpretation is that they are the remains of "trail lodges" (Parker 1923:278) built to provide accommodations for travelers along the pilgrimage route. The woodlot at the top of the photograph still exists and preserves the only surviving nearly intact remnant of the Great Hopewell Road. The Van Voorhis Walls (33LI401) are located about 3 kilometers south of Newark's octagon. However, the property is privately owned and is being considered for development (DUCS 1998). Photograph taken by Warren Weiant Jr., circa 1920. Courtesy, Warren Weiant III.

combinations, one in present-day Chillicothe and the other in present-day Newark. The circles are identical in size (320 meters in diameter), and both of these sites encode consistent and complementary information about the 18.6-year lunar cycle (Hively and Horn 1982, 1984; Lepper 1998a). This celestially inspired architecture bespeaks a calendrical function and an emphasis on a lunar clock for the timing of rituals and social gatherings.

Shared architectural geometries and astronomical alignments connected ancient Newark and Chillicothe. Did a formalized and very straight highway also connect these grandest of Hopewellian ceremonial centers?

Searching for the Great Hopewell Road

Extrapolating from the documented trajectory of Newark's parallel walls, I have identified a corridor between Newark and Chillicothe in which I have sought evidence of vestiges of the Great Hopewell Road. So far, I have identified five locations where there is suggestive evidence of road remnants. This evidence consists of parallel linear crop marks observed within the corridor at the predicted compass bearing. Clearly, not all linear markings in the soil represent traces of ancient roads. Conclusions based upon these crop marks must be regarded as tentative. Only future investigations at these localities will establish whether they are earthwork remnants or some unrelated disturbance of the soil. However, the observations of nineteenth-century antiquarians and early-twentieth-century aviators (Reeves 1936; Shetrone 1937; Weiant 1931) combined with the evidence gleaned from modern aerial photography are consistent with what could be expected if a great road of low, parallel walls once extended from Newark to Chillicothe in a remarkably straight line. But why would the Hopewell people have built such a road?

The Hopewell culture ceased to be a going concern by about A.D. 400, so there were no practitioners of Hopewell culture present when inquisitive Europeans arrived in the Ohio Valley. The Mayan people, however, still retained traditions of building monumental roads, similar in many respects to the Great Hopewell Road, when the Spanish arrived in the jungles of the Yucatán (Folan 1991). When asked, they said these long, straight roads were sacred routes of pilgrimage. For example, the Spanish priest Diego Lopez Cogolludo observed in 1688 that "there are enormous paved highways which traverse all this kingdom and they say they ended in the east on the seashore . . . so that they might arrive at Cozumel for the fulfillment of their vows, to offer their sacrifices, to ask for help in their needs, and for the mistaken adoration of their false gods" (quoted in Tozzer 1941:109). The Mayan name for such a highway was *sacbe,* which means "white road" (Freidel and Sabloff 1984:82). *Sacbe* also is a Mayan name for the Milky Way (Freidel, Schele, and Parker 1993:76–78). The Hopewell did not migrate to the Yucatán Peninsula and become the Maya. It is, nevertheless, possible that they shared certain ancient beliefs with their Mesoamerican cousins. And perhaps faint echoes of those beliefs still resonate within the woodlands of eastern North America.

The "Beautiful White Path"

The Delaware Indians, or Lenni Lenape, describe life's journey as the "Beautiful White Path," and this journey was enacted ritually in the Big House ceremony (Speck 1931). Frank Speck (1915:23, 1931:23) believed that the "White Path" of the Delaware also represented the Milky Way, the "Spirit or Ghost Path," over which the souls of the dead would continue their journey into the spirit world.

David Zeisberger, a Moravian missionary among the Delaware Indians of eastern Ohio in the late eighteenth century, wrote about Delaware chiefs building long, straight roads through the wilderness: "[W]hen the chiefs among the Indians lay out a trail several hundred miles through the woods, they cut away thorn and thicket, clear trees, rocks and stones out of the way, cut through the hills, level up the track and strew it with white sand, so they may easily go from one nation to another" (Zeisberger [1780] 1910:35). Zeisberger had never encountered a road like this, so he assumed that his Delaware informants were speaking metaphorically. He seems not to have considered the possibility that such roads might have deteriorated and become overgrown after untold centuries of abandonment.

Daniel Brinton, a nineteenth-century anthropologist, recorded another obscure tradition of the Delaware Indians that may shed some light on the purpose of these long roads strewn with white sand. The Reverend Albert Seqaqknind Anthony, a Delaware Indian, told Brinton that before any European had landed on their shores, the Lenape had "a string of white wampum beads . . . which stretched from the Atlantic to the Pacific, and on this *white road* their envoys traveled from one great ocean to the other, safe from attack" (Brinton 1890:188; emphasis added).

Wampum: The "White Road" of the Eastern Woodlands

According to Nabokov (1996:42–43), among the peoples of the Eastern Woodlands, wampum functioned as a "potent and sacred mnemonic aid" that could operate retrospectively, to aid in historical recollections, as well as "'prospectively,' as a means for organizing the present, and even future, events." Lewis Henry Morgan (1851:73) recorded that "white wampum was the Iroquois emblem of purity and faith [and] it was used before the periodical religious festivals." Hamell (1992:457) observed that the white shells of wampum functioned as "a metaphor for light, and thus for life itself." The many correspondences between Mayan "white roads," the straight and wide Hopewell road, the long roads strewn with white sand of Delaware tradition, and the "white road" of wampum suggest that these all share some symbolic equivalence.

Hopewell Interaction Networks: Trade or Tribute?

The Hopewell are frequently described as participants in an exchange network that spanned much of North America, with diverse peoples from Missouri to

New York and from Michigan to Florida participating in this dynamic web of interactions (for example, Griffin 1952b; Struever and Houart 1972). Although some of Ohio's Flint Ridge flint trickled out of the Newark area to these ends of the Hopewell world, there is considerably more evidence of exotic material coming into Ohio than of Ohio goods going out (for example, Greber 1991:1; Griffin 1978:249). No one has explained satisfactorily how this disparity makes sense in terms of the economics of trade.

I propose that Hopewellian Newark and Chillicothe were pilgrimage centers like Mecca or Santiago de Compostela:

> [A pilgrimage center's] defining characteristic is the attraction of devotees from a large, often multiethnic and/or multinational catchment area. Pilgrims travel to a pilgrimage center in order to carry out religious devotions; they are not resident at the shrine. Whereas a ceremonial center services a local population, is maintained by that population, and has a small to significantly sized socioeconomically diverse *residential* population, the pilgrimage center is noteworthy for its ability to draw a *transient* population of worshippers from across a social, political, economic, cultural and spatial spectrum and, in so doing, to synthesize critical social and cultural elements from wider patterns of belief and practice in a region or regions. (Silverman 1994:2–3; emphasis in original)

Aspects of the dispersed sedentary community model of Ohio Hopewell settlement devised initially by Prufer (1965) and formalized by Dancey and Pacheco (1997a) offer some support for viewing the gigantic Newark Earthworks as a "pilgrimage center"; see also Dancey and Pacheco in chapter 1 of this volume. Regardless of how many people lived more or less permanently in the immediate vicinity of the earthworks, the truly monumental ritual spaces of the Hopewell, such as the Newark Earthworks, clearly were not created to serve only a resident population. Indeed, the Murphy IV site—located 2.5 kilometers west of the Newark Works and identified by Pacheco (1997:52) as an anomalous specialized camp on the basis of a high frequency of bladelets and flakes of Wyandotte chert—might plausibly be interpreted as a seasonal encampment of pilgrims from the Wyandotte chert source area (see also Vickery 1996:123). The evidence for high mobility and transient occupations at earthworks described by Lepper and Yerkes (1997; see also Yerkes, this volume) and Cowan (this volume) also supports the view that large numbers of people came to the large earthwork centers as periodic, short-term visitors.

Pilgrims from across Ohio and eastern North America would have come to places such as Newark and Chillicothe with offerings of rare and precious items (see, for example, Vickery 1996:123). Perhaps these offerings were in payment for the healing of an illness (for example, O'Connor 1997:370–372), for the council of an oracle, or for the acquisition of spiritual power (for example, Townsend 1997:440). The scattered bladelets and leaf-shaped bifaces of Flint

Ridge flint recovered at Hopewell-era sites across the midcontinent may have served as pilgrim's badges or souvenirs of the great hajj (Coleman and Elsner 1995:100; Morinis 1992:6). In this way, the sacred landscape would have become "diffused, permeating even the everyday lives of those who have never been to" Newark or Chillicothe (Coleman and Elsner 1995:6).

The investiture of Flint Ridge flint with sacredness would explain why Hopewellians so intensively utilized it, and why its use was almost totally forsaken by all later peoples (for example, Prufer and Shane 1970:78; see also Lepper, Yerkes, and Pickard 2001). Perhaps the factors involved in the collapse of the Hopewell culture resulted in subsequent groups proscribing as taboo the abandoned machinery of Hopewell ritual, including the geometric enclosures, the Great Hopewell Road, and the quarries of the rainbow-colored rock at Flint Ridge. Some tribes of the Eastern Woodlands did, indeed, regard certain sites as places to be avoided: "Indian tradition still keeps alive the fact that these grounds have been the theatre of blood; and such is their abhorrence of scenes once enacted here, that except in a few very rare instances, they do not visit the regions near the ancient forts and burying grounds. 'Ote-queh-sa-he-eh' is their exclamation—"'Tis the field of blood'" (Clark 1849:2:263).

Hopewell Pilgrimage

In summary, the evidence presented here supports the proposition that there was, indeed, a Great Hopewell Road. It was a set of parallel earthen walls that extended from Newark's octagon for at least 17 kilometers according to the Salisbury survey and Weiant's corroborative aerial observations.

The trajectory established by the documented portions of the Great Hopewell Road aligns it directly towards the largest concentration of contemporary earthworks in North America. Given the demonstrated cultural connections between these centers (for example, Lepper 1998a) and the lack of any obvious "target" of comparable Hopewellian interest along the corridor between Newark and Chillicothe (see Mills 1914), it is reasonable to conclude that this alignment is not coincidental. Whether or not the road consisted of meter-high walls spaced 60 meters apart for the entire 90 kilometers between these centers is a separate proposition that must be tested by investigations at putative road remnants.

Another test of the plausibility of the notion of the Great Hopewell Road consists of what it can contribute to our understanding of Hopewell culture. Does the notion wildly conflict with our present knowledge of the interests and capabilities of tribal societies in general and Ohio's Middle Woodland people in particular? Does it illuminate otherwise obscure aspects of Hopewell culture?

The Hopewell people certainly were capable of conceiving of and building the Great Hopewell Road. Lekson (1999:118) has observed that "no technical equipment or esoteric knowledge" is required to survey and project a straight line across many kilometers of even highly irregular terrain. Judging from the many thousands of cubic meters of earth moved by the Hopewell builders of the

Newark Earthworks and the myriad mounds and enclosures of the Scioto Valley, the construction of the Great Hopewell Road would have been well within the capabilities of the Hopewell.

The Great Hopewell Road was not, therefore, a superhuman achievement, but it was, nonetheless, an impressive accomplishment. Its arrow-straight course was an alien imposition across the forests of Ohio that, prior to this construction, had known only the winding paths of least resistance used by animals and people in their movements through the forest. In building such a monumental road, the Hopewell builders were forging a dramatically new kind of connection between two distant places. The long, straight road would not have been simply a route of commerce and communication; it was a conduit of unifying ritual (see Malville and Malville 2001 for a similar interpretation of the Chaco Canyon roads).

The ritual significance of the straight path for Indians of the Eastern Woodlands is affirmed by a mid-nineteenth-century account of a traditional Onondaga ceremony: "A straight line is pointed out, upon which all good people are directed to walk. . . . They are admonished that there should be no deviation, to the right or left, into the paths of vice, but keep straight forward in the ways of rectitude and virtue" (Clark 1849:1:54). It might be argued that these ideas reflect the recent adoption of Christian imagery, but this particular group of Onondaga was resistant to the imposition of the Christian religion. They had deposed one chief when he converted to Christianity (Pulszky and Pulszky 1853:214), and the small minority of Christianized Indians in this community did not participate in the traditional ceremonies (Pulszky and Pulszky 1853:220).

Turner (1974:166) has written that "pilgrimages are liminal phenomena" and that the pilgrimage center "represents a threshold, a place and moment 'in and out of time'" (Turner 1974:197). Pilgrims traveling on the Great Hopewell Road and gathering at the various earthworks—perhaps to celebrate some rite of passage, perhaps to participate in the construction of a mound—would experience, according to Turner, a sense of *communitas,* or sublime unity with those with whom the mystery was shared (compare Sallnow 1981). The building and use of such roads would have forged a spiritual union among participants that would have solidified the forging of other unions with more down-to-earth concerns, such as the arrangement of marriages or the negotiation of alliances.

The elaborate artistic productions of the Hopewell would have provided a rich and highly visible iconographic vocabulary with which pilgrims and hosts, who may not have shared a common language, could have communicated considerable social information (see Cowan 1996). This would explain the remarkable degree of uniformity in Hopewell symbolic adornments, raw material selection, and monumental architecture (for example, Byers 1996:180; Cowan 1996:143; Marshall 1996:218; Romain 1996:205; and Vickery 1996:117).

The *communitas* experienced by Hopewell pilgrims was embodied in the exchange of gifts: exotic treasures or perhaps several days of labor offered to the caretakers/shamans/chieftains of the pilgrimage centers. In return, the pilgrim would take away a renewed sense of belonging and a feeling of having partici-pated in something larger than oneself; he or she might also have taken away a bladelet or biface crafted from Flint Ridge flint as a token or talisman of the magical experience.

This admittedly speculative scenario provides a context for understanding formerly perplexing features of Hopewell archaeology (compare Greber 1997:209). The earthworks were built to an extraordinary scale because ex-traordinary numbers of pilgrims periodically visited them. The pilgrims did not stay for long and therefore did not require substantial, long-term residential districts. Large amounts of exotica accumulated at the pilgrimage centers, while small but significant amounts of local material were taken away as pilgrim's tokens. Finally, the Great Hopewell Road was the unifying "white road" of "rectitude and virtue" upon which pilgrims might travel to and from these cen-ters "safe from attack."

There are precedents in prehistoric America for long, straight roadways con-necting one special place with another. In fact, such roads have been docu-mented in almost every region of North and South America except, until re-cently, the Eastern Woodlands of North America (Trombold 1991). The Great Hopewell Road is not even the earliest documented expression of this wide-spread cultural phenomenon in the Eastern Woodlands. Gibson (1986:226) describes a "causeway" at the Poverty Point site that extends at least half a kilometer from the interior plaza of the principal enclosure to the southwest, maintaining a straight course across a depression (borrow pit) that may have been a pond (Gibson 1986:225). The near ubiquity of such roads in the Ameri-cas makes their presence in the Ohio Valley less of an anomaly than their ab-sence would be.

Historic Algonquian traditions of long, straight "white roads" equated with the Milky Way and with belts of sacred wampum may reflect cultural recon-figurations of actual, but abandoned, sacred roads functionally equivalent to Mayan long, straight "white roads" also equated with the Milky Way. The monumental sacred landscape of the Hopewell had become too grand for the political realities of the succeeding Late Woodland and Late Prehistoric societies in Ohio. Yet even though pilgrims ceased to ply the Great Hopewell Road, civil and religious leaders still looked to selected aspects of the Hopewellian sacred vocabulary, such as the shells of white wampum, to validate political alliances and sanctify the journey through this world and into the next along the "Beau-tiful White Path."

Epilogue

In his commentary on the version of this chapter presented at the "Perspectives on Middle Woodland at the Millennium" conference, Robert Chapman sug-gested that the analogy I have drawn between Newark and known pilgrimage sites such as Mecca is flawed. Mecca, for example, is a point of convergence for many roads drawing pilgrims from all points of the compass. Newark, by contrast, appears to be a node linked by a single conduit to another locus (or set of loci) of related activity. There is some validity to this observation. I was initially led to emphasize the sociopolitical implications of the connection between these places rather than the religious (Lepper 1998b:133–134). However, I have been drawn increasingly, and perhaps naively, to the pilgrimage analogy based on a conviction that we should take seriously the few statements made by Native Americans plausibly related to such phenomena (Echo-Hawk 2000; compare Mason 2000). Moreover, I think the analogy offers compelling insights into our understanding of the Hopewell Interaction Sphere in general and, in particular, the role of Flint Ridge flint in this network of interaction. I recognize that the analogy with Mecca is not perfect, but it is strengthened by tantalizing evidence for other Hopewell roads.

According to Squier and Davis (1848:20), at the Fort Ancient hilltop enclosure, in southern Ohio, there was a parallel walled road extending 1,350 feet before it ended in a small, irregularly shaped enclosure surrounding a mound. Brine (1894:91) reported a claim of some local farmers that "there once existed other parallel banks connected with the fort which could be traced for several miles, but that these had been destroyed."

Drake (1815:211) described an ancient road associated with earthworks in the vicinity of Milford on the Little Miami River about 30 kilometers southwest of Fort Ancient. This road consisted of a raised "causeway" 1 to 2 feet (0.3 to 0.6 meters) high and 20 to 30 feet (6 to 9 meters) wide, and it was "discernable for two miles" (3.2 kilometers).

Metz evidently believed that there was a prehistoric road of some sort leading "from the Mariemont area to a point near Chillicothe" (Starr 1960:80). The evidence for this claim is anecdotal, but Starr's (1960:80) call for further investigation of "Metz's papers, and a reexamination of the route" would seem to be warranted.

These few suggestive reports, taken together with the evidence for the Great Hopewell Road, call for a reevaluation of the nature of formalized interaction between Hopewell centers. Perhaps a network of roads once connected many of the earthworks, and pilgrims visited them in a ritualized sequence. It also should not be overlooked that at Newark there were two other avenues framed by straight, parallel walls that allowed entrance to the earthwork complex from alternative directions (fig. 7.2; see also Lepper 1998b:119). Although relatively short, these ceremonial roads would have served to channel the movement of people into and through this labyrinthine earthwork.

I have one final point to make in regard to my use of Native American oral traditions. My references to the oral traditions of the Lenni Lenape and the Onondaga should in no way be read as a claim that these particular tribes are the modern heirs to the legacy of the Hopewell. It may not be possible to single out any particular modern group as the certain descendants of the Hopewell. Even the apocryphal *Walam Olum*, accepted by some tribal leaders as an authentic history of the Lenni Lenape (for example, Poolaw 1993), explicitly identifies the builders of the mounds as a people unaffiliated with either the Lenape or the

Iroquois (see also Heckewelder 1881:48–50; Voegelin 1954:132). But the influence of the Hopewell was widespread. It is possible that any group living in the Eastern Woodlands could have been touched by the Hopewell and that their descendants might preserve oral traditions that relate to or derive from that sudden florescence of art, ritual, and architecture. I do not pretend to have isolated elements of veritable Hopewell ideology in snippets of Lenape and Onondaga oral traditions, but such connections may be present and may offer us special insights that we can test against the archaeological record (for example, Hall 1997:169; compare Mason 2000).

Acknowledgments

My thanks to Jodie O'Gorman and Jane Buikstra for organizing and hosting the "Perspectives on Middle Woodland at the Millennium" conference and for inviting me to participate. I thank the following individuals for their help at various points along the (not-so-straight) way: Jonathan Bowen (Ohio Historical Society), Martin Byers (Vanier College), Robert Connolly (Northeast Louisiana University), Warren DeBoer (Queens College/State University of New York), Robert Fletcher, Tod Frolking (Denison University), Jeff Gill, Jim Givens (Ohio Department of Natural Resources), N'omi Greber (Cleveland Museum of Natural History), Paul Hooge (Licking County Archaeology and Landmarks Society), Jay Johnson (University of Mississippi), Roger Kennedy, Tom Law, Stephen Lekson (University of Colorado), Michael Mickelson (Denison University), Douglas Payne, Robert Petersen (National Park Service), William Pickard, William Romain, Priscilla Steele (Fairfield County Regional Planning Commission), Daniel Young (Environmental Research Institute of Michigan [ERIM]), Warren Weiant III, and Dee Anne Wymer (Bloomsburg University). My acknowledgment of the debt I owe these various colleagues should in no way be construed to mean that any of them necessarily agree with all the conclusions I report herein.

Funding or technical support for this research was provided by the Ohio Archaeological Council, the Ohio Department of Transportation, National Aeronautics and Space Administration (NASA), ERIM, Denison University, Columbus Academy, Daveda Bundy, Mady Noble, Vicki Ross, Elaine Sekerak, and Jennifer West.

I extend special thanks to my wife, Karen Lepper, and our sons, Benjamin and Peter. Their sacrifices have made this work possible.

8

Water and Mud and the Recreation of the World

Ted S. Sunderhaus and Jack K. Blosser

Fort Ancient (33WA2), a Hopewell hilltop enclosure located along the Little Miami River in southwestern Ohio (fig. 8.1), is the largest and, arguably, most complex of the hilltop enclosures in this portion of the Midwest (Connolly 1996b; Prufer 1996; Riordan 1996). Excluding the now-destroyed parallel walls formerly located northeast of the enclosure, more than 5.5 kilometers of embankment walls enclose 51 hectares (126 acres) of social space.

Water

From 1996 through 1999, the authors undertook a pedestrian survey of the Fort Ancient State Memorial. One goal of the survey was to record the presence, size, and location of extant architectural features (Sunderhaus and Blosser 2001). As a result, 131 discrete water features, typically referred to as borrow pits, were recorded (fig. 8.2). Lewis M. Hosea (1874:292), the earliest antiquarian to actually excavate at the site and publish his findings, when discussing these fea-

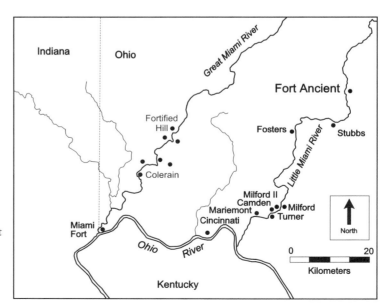

Figure 8.1. Map of southwestern Ohio showing most of the Hopewell earthwork sites in the Great and Little Miami drainages.

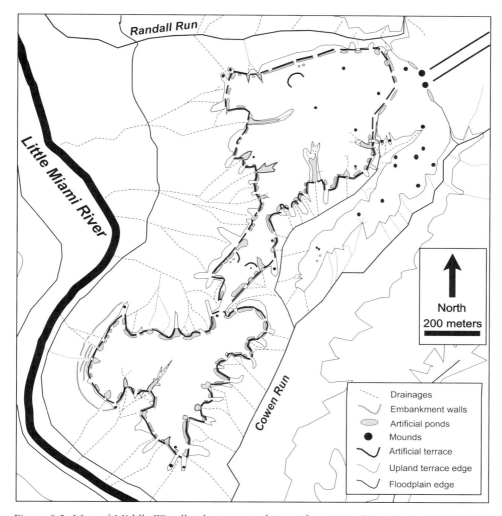

Figure 8.2. Map of Middle Woodland constructed water features at Fort Ancient.

tures wrote that the "excavations are frequently so considerable as to suggest a special design in their construction." Assertions that such features simply represent expedient sources of earth for the construction of adjacent walls and associated mounds (for example, Prufer 1997a) are countered by Connolly's (1996b, 1998) argument that, while the earth from them was often so used, their construction was intentional and followed specific rules and trends for their placement. We further agree with Connolly's contention that the features served multiple functions. The features were designed to create readily accessible sources of potable water while providing drainage for higher elevated portions of the earthwork's interior. In limiting access to and egress from the enclosure, these water features played a role in the human activities that took place inside the earthwork. Beyond this, the water features appear to have been designed to

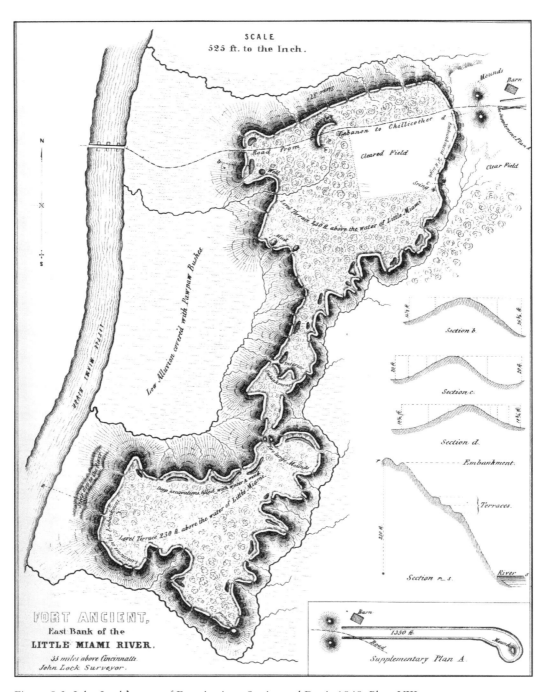

Figure 8.3. John Lock's map of Fort Ancient. Squier and Davis 1848: Plate VIII.

influence the form and meanings of the social activity that occurred within the enclosure (Wesson 1998).

Examination of the geology, hydrology, and present-day land use in the vicinity of Fort Ancient confirms the assumption that shallow depressions such as those at Fort Ancient will indeed hold water. Bypassed by the most recent (Wisconsin) glacial advance, the highly weathered Illinoian till that blankets the area includes a water-impermeable fragipan (Garner, Reeder, and Ernst 1973). Today sizable depressions can be excavated to serve as farm ponds, with virtually the only water loss being due to evaporation.

John Lock's map of Fort Ancient, used by Squier and Davis (1848:Plate VIII), illustrates twenty-four bodies of standing water associated with the earthworks (fig. 8.3). Both Moorehead (1890, 1895) and William C. Mills (1908) mention these and other ponds, some of which they excavated. More recent evidence of the ability of these features to hold water is represented by the Civilian Conservation Corps' (CCC) efforts to drain them in the 1930s by digging shallow surface trenches or by inserting ceramic drain tiles into deeper trenches and subsequently backfilling and constructing mortared brick and stone drain heads and headwalls (fig. 8.4). No detailed records were kept of all CCC projects undertaken at Fort Ancient; these features were discovered only through recent archaeological survey and testing (Connolly 1996b; Sunderhaus and Blosser 2001).

While the CCC drainage project was largely successful, a few ponds inside the enclosure failed to drain (for reasons unknown) and today retain water throughout much of the year. One and possibly two ponds with CCC drainage apparatus appear to have been designed only to limit the amount of water contained within them rather than to completely drain them. One of these ponds, located in the South Fort of the earthwork, had a mortared stone retaining wall and overflow drain and was intentionally designed to be a lily pond by the CCC. A second may also represent an attempt to regulate the amount of water contained therein, or alternatively its flawed design and construction failed to achieve total drainage.

Soil cores extracted from these two features to obtain pollen samples and stratigraphically associated samples for radiocarbon assays reveal a continuous column of undisturbed stratified gleyed soils that developed in a nonoxygenated environment from the Middle Woodland period, when the earthwork was constructed, to the present day (McLauchlan 2000b). Both radiocarbon samples from the earliest depositional episodes in these two pond features date to the Middle Woodland period (McLauchlan 2000b).

Connolly's (1996b) detection of a pattern in the placement of constructed water features or ponds prompted him to regard them as the product of an "architectural grammar." He noted that they tend to be clustered near primary gateways and constricted areas of the site, either flanking a gateway inside the earthwork or designed to bar access through certain gateways. It also appears that natural water features were intentionally incorporated into the architec-

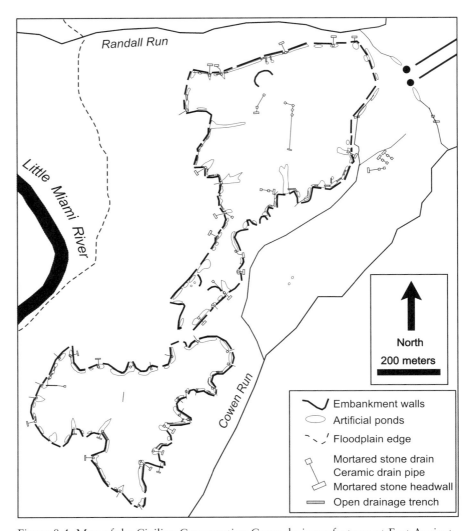

Figure 8.4. Map of the Civilian Conservation Corps drainage features at Fort Ancient.

tural design of the enclosure in an unaltered form (Sunderhaus and Blosser 2001).

There are four distinct architectural combinations in the so-called Twin Mounds complex in the northeastern portion of the Fort Ancient site (fig. 8.2): paired ("twin") mounds, parallel walls, and two intentionally constructed ponds flanking the twin mounds to the north and south, each of which is connected to a natural water source adjacent to it. All of these architectural features have until now been considered to have been on the exterior of the enclosure. The northernmost pond flanking the twin mounds drains into a tributary of Randall Run, while the southernmost one drains into a tributary of Cowen Run (fig. 8.2). This set of conjoined water features and natural tributaries segregates the plateau east of the earthwork from surrounding landforms, thereby creating the effect of the eastern plateau either being part of the site, as a part of the axis mundi, or being some type of liminal space, neither inside nor outside. This cluster of architectural features described here as the Twin Mounds complex forms the border of this enclosure. This effect explains certain architectural elements that do not seem to conform to the "grammar" observed by Connolly elsewhere at Fort Ancient. For example, several water features in the northeast quadrant of the site are located outside, rather than within, the embankment walls. These ponds achieve conformity when the Twin Mounds complex with its associated constructed and natural water features is viewed as having been the actual boundary of the corporate space. The same reasoning can be applied to the location of the thirteen mounds on this eastern plateau that would also then be included within the boundaries of the site's corporate space.

Casting doubt on these interpretations is the fact that a few of the early maps of Fort Ancient (Atwater 1820; Moorehead 1890 [Cowen]; and Squier and Davis 1848 [Lock]) show the southern Twin Mounds pond draining into a different tributary of Cowen Run than that which our investigation indicates. If correct, this would have effectively isolated the eastern plateau from the rest of the enclosure. There are, however, two maps (Morgan 1946; USGS 1916) that agree with our observations. This prompted investigation of the possibility that the CCC or earlier work at the site had altered the drainage by filling in the northern portion of the tributary recorded on the earlier set of maps.

Accordingly, a series of twenty-five cores was extracted in an arc around the current headwaters of the hypothesized tributary into which Atwater, Clinton Cowen (in Moorehead 1890), and Lock (in Squier and Davis 1848) indicated the southernmost pond of the Twin Mound complex drained. The pattern of soil core placement ensured that meanders of the tributary would not go undetected. Coring began 10 meters southwest of the present-day headwaters, with all but one penetrating the surface to at least a depth of 1 meter. All but one of the series of core samples revealed a relatively undisturbed, natural soil profile. The exception was a sample indicating a cultural feature with charcoal, burned limestone, and flint debitage. Burned limestone encountered in this core sample blocked penetration of the coring tool to the 1-meter target depth. Soil cores taken at 50 centimeters in the four cardinal directions away from this feature revealed undisturbed soil profiles, indicating that the feature was not a filled drainage channel and that its diameter was less than 1 meter. An Illinoian till B-horizon with well-developed ped structure occurred in all the other core samples, demonstrating that the horizon was both ancient and undisturbed.

Based on the results of the soil coring tests described above, it may be concluded that the earlier maps showing the southern Twin Mounds pond draining into an alternative tributary of Cowen Run are incorrect. Predating any CCC work at Fort Ancient by several decades, the earliest USGS (1916) map of this area agrees with both Morgan's 1946 map (fig. 8.5) and that compiled through the research presented in this chapter with respect to the tributary drainage (fig. 8.2).

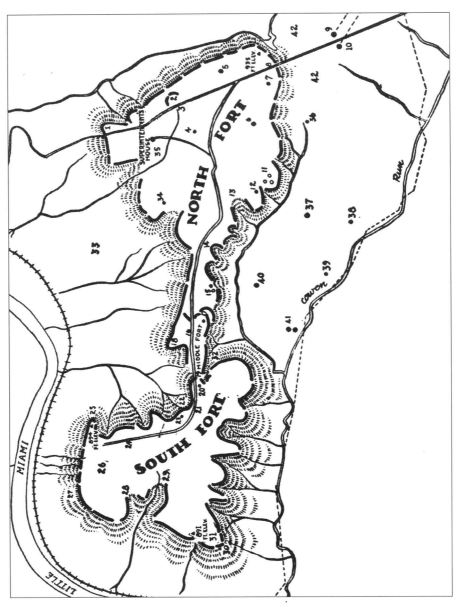

Figure 8.5. Map of Fort Ancient. After Morgan (1946).

The inference that all constructed water features except the two associated with the Twin Mounds complex occur within the site corporate space (here redefined to include the eastern plateau and area west of the Twin Mounds complex) augments Connolly's architectural rules and trends governing the placement of constructed water features. To these rules and trends may be added the following: (1) appropriate entry into the earthwork's interior through primary gateways required one to pass between two constructed water features, perhaps symbolically representing passage through or over water; (2) pedestrian movement from one portion of the site to another also required passage between two bodies of water; and (3) all constructed water features with the exception of the two border elements associated with the Twin Mounds complex are interior to the corporate space.

The prehistoric symbolism suggested in this manner may have persisted into historic times in the Eastern Woodlands, as represented by some ethnographic accounts of migration myths that include passage over a large body of water (Howard 1981). The Fort Ancient water features also may have played a role in ritual purification, the association of water and purification being common in the Eastern Woodlands and worldwide (Campbell 1962; Eliade 1987).

Water is quite commonly associated with the three-tiered Eastern Woodland world, with water typically associated with the lower or underworld (Burland 1968; Howard 1981; Marriott and Rachlin 1968). The enclosed corporate space of the Fort Ancient earthworks was probably considered by its builders and users as an axis mundi—a point where travel or communication was possible to and between all three tiers of the Eastern Woodland world. It is proposed here that the ponds at Fort Ancient were intended in part to symbolically represent the lower world of this three-tiered system.

Fort Ancient probably is not the only Hopewell earthwork complex with intentionally constructed and symbolically meaningful water features. For example, several sites with "borrow pits" that may have functioned in such a manner are illustrated by Squier and Davis (1848), including Newark, Spruce Hill, Fort Hill, Mound City, Seip, and Liberty Earthworks (Squier and Davis 1848: Plates XXV, IV, V, XIX, XXI [no. 2], and XX). Early maps such as these, however, often lack clear-cut indications of patterning in the placement of "borrow pits," probably owing to a disregard of their potential significance on the part of early antiquarians. Atwater's map of Fort Ancient recorded no ponds; Lock's map, only 24; and an unpublished map of Fort Ancient by Cleveland Abbe (fig. 8.6; Abbe 1869) recorded 26 such features. The recent systematic investigations reveal the existence of more than 130 (fig. 8.2). Careful scrutiny of the architectural features of other Hopewell earthworks for possible patterns in their distribution and placement may prove to be a potentially fruitful investigative endeavor. A good example of this type of research is that conducted by James Brown and Raymond Baby at Mound City in 1963–64 (Baby and Brown 1964; Brown and Baby 1966). During these excavations an additional borrow pit was discovered, which was not recorded on any of the earlier maps of the site. This pond or borrow pit makes the distribution of these features at this site more symmetrical than was previously thought.

While water itself is difficult to represent three-dimensionally, Hopewell iconography does include a number of water-related forms with possible symbolic associations. Among several such items—not uncommonly made of exotic raw materials—are alligator and shark teeth, barracuda jaws, and abalone shell, in addition to the carapaces and/or plastrons of marine species of turtles. Water is also associated with many Ohio Hopewell animal effigy pipes and two-dimen-

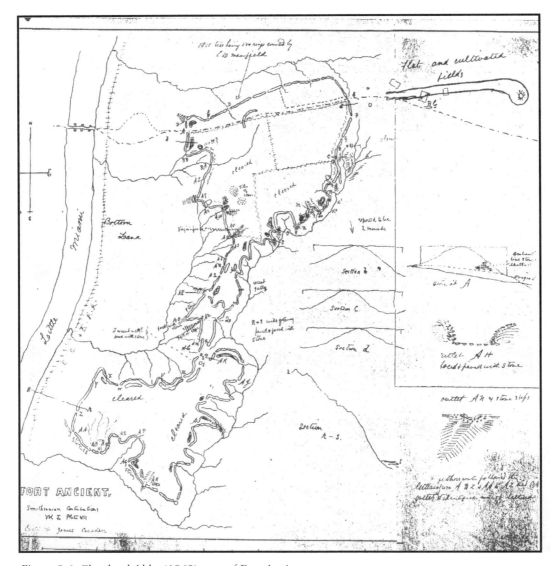

Figure 8.6. Cleveland Abbe (1869) map of Fort Ancient.

sional art in both naturalistic and mythical forms. Represented are such animals as toads, frogs, otters, and beavers, some of which, according to ethnohistoric accounts, played important roles in Eastern Woodland creation myths. Birds in Eastern Woodland mythology were typically associated with the upper world (Hudson 1976). Waterbirds, however, should probably be considered as having special abilities, given their ability to travel between all three tiers of the Eastern Woodland world (Buikstra, Charles, and Rakita 1998).

Mud

During salvage excavations in 1995, a profile trench through Gateway 84 revealed a multistage construction sequence for the earthworks walls (fig. 8.7). The surface on which the embankments were constructed was prepared by removing the overlaying A soil horizon and depositing a thin (2 to 5 centimeters thick) gray clay floor on top of the underlying B horizon. All of the soils used in the next stage were oxygenated B-, A-, and E-horizon soils, in that order of frequency of use. The former soils were loaded on the gray clay floor in an undulating fashion, forming three distinct ridges with two valleys between (fig. 8.7, 1a-d). Two kinds of soil were used for the next stage of embankment wall construction (fig. 8.7, 2a-b): (1) oxygenated B-, A-, and E-horizon soils; and (2) nonoxygenated gleyed soils that were rather uniform in color and consistency, apparently having been obtained from similar hydrologic sources. The latter exhibit apparent basket loading in two vertically stacked columns (gray banding zones) (Sieg and Connolly 1997:Figure 3.4).

These columns were supported by simultaneous deposition of a mixture of Illinoian till and other oxygenated soil types on either side of each gleyed column, also in apparent basket loading (fig. 8.7, 2c, 3a). These gleyed soil columns attained a maximum height of 2.65 meters as this stage of the embankment wall was built higher. The final stage of embankment wall construction was again a mixture of B-, A-, and E-horizon soils, only in this instance they were broadcast rather than deposited in basket loads (fig. 8.7, 3b).

There are only three possible sources of water-laden gleyed soils in and around the Fort Ancient earthworks that could have been used in embankment wall construction. The most likely source available to the builders of this earthwork would have been naturally occurring ponds in the area. These kettle ponds were once widely scattered in this Illinoian till plain (Braun 1916; Nelson 1952), but they are easily destroyed by modern agricultural practices (for example, moldboard plowing and various types of soil drainage technologies). In several areas on this state memorial property and on some of the adjacent properties there are extant kettle ponds with standing water throughout the year, except during periods of extreme drought. The largest source of gleyed soils would have been on the floodplain of the Little Miami River in wetland areas; however, while there are considerable nonoxygenated soils in these wetland environments, the extreme vertical ascent of 75 meters from this source to the embankment walls makes it highly unlikely that the floodplain was the source of the gleyed soils incorporated into the earthwork walls. A third possible source could have been the constructed water features at the site. While they today contain extensive deposits of nonoxygenated gleyed soils, such features are unlikely to have been the source of gleyed soils for two reasons. First is the fact that embankment wall construction was contemporary with and in part dependent upon the construction of the pond features, since the ponds were probably one of the sources of borrow for the embankments. Second, the gleyed soils in these

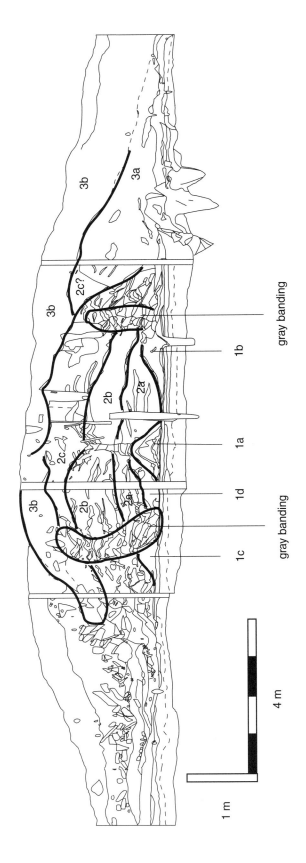

Figure 8.7. Profile of Embankment Wall 1 at Gateway 84. After Sieg and Connolly 1997:Fig. 3.4.

constructed ponds are full of Middle Woodland cultural material, including carbon, burned rock, pottery, lithics, and animal bone. The gleyed soils used in the construction of the embankment walls lacked cultural material. Thus, the kettle ponds appear to be the only viable source of gleyed soils used in the embankment walls.

The initial gray clay floor underlying the embankment was gleyed in origin; therefore, it probably had a symbolic water association. Water associations were not apparent during the next stage of embankment wall construction, but the patterned preparation of this stage suggests that it served as a platform upon which a world recreation ceremony was conducted, perhaps with much later ethnographic representation in the Mud Diver or Earth Diver myth (Blair 1916; Count 1952; Howard 1981; Marriott and Rachlin 1968). This world recreation ceremony is seen in the following stage of embankment wall construction, in the vertically stacked gleyed soils columns. It is suggested here that these water-laden gleyed soils were sought specifically because they were obtained from under the surface of a body of water, thus playing a symbolic role in reenacting the Mud Diver myth, or the creation of dry land. The final stage of the embankment wall again appears to lack water associations. This suggests that reenactment of the recreation myths was either abandoned or shifted to another location at this or other sites. Similar gleyed deposits have been documented in other Ohio and Illinois mounds, often with similar explanations offered for their occurrence in mounds and other settings (Buikstra, Charles, and Rakita 1998; Hall 1979; Thomas 1894).

Conclusion

Admittedly much of the above is speculative and based on analogies with historic Eastern Woodland mythologies and other ethnohistoric accounts. Much is also, however, based on patterned architectural elements. This patterning is demonstrably rule-governed, with even apparently nonconforming features actually controlled by the same set of apparently emic rules. The archaeological investigation of ancient belief systems is undoubtedly one of the most difficult challenges for our science, yet its importance to our understanding of ancient cultural systems is of paramount importance.

9

Altering a Middle Woodland Enclosure

Questions of Design and Environment

Robert V. Riordan

Recent archaeological work at several Middle Woodland enclosures has demonstrated that the architectural designs recorded by such early scholars as Davis, Squier, Whittlesey, and McBride were the end products of the cumulative changes introduced during and after their periods of use. This insight has led to the realization that the ways in which the sites were used may, in at least some instances, have also changed over time (Mainfort and Sullivan 1998a:12). This chapter identifies three kinds of architectural modifications to which enclosures were subjected, illustrated with examples from Ohio.

Architectural Change

Earthen enclosures were subjected to three kinds of architectural modifications: augmentations, additions, and alterations. An *augmentation* is a change that enlarged but did not reconfigure or redefine the results of previous construction efforts. At Hopewellian enclosures, augmentations occurred when embankments were increased in breadth and height, and they can be archaeologically recognized in successive soil deposits that were heaped upon earthwork embankments. Augmentations are known principally from hilltop enclosures, notably Pollock and Fort Ancient, but may have occurred at geometric enclosures as well.

The impetus that drove some Hopewellian groups to raise the vertical height, and necessarily the width, of their earthworks by heaping on successive mantles of soil and sometimes stone is unknown. Imposing the ethic that bigger was better on any particular local Middle Woodland enclosure-building group is fraught with obvious interpretive peril. Perhaps the formal augmentation of an otherwise acceptably designed enclosure was one way for the members of subsequent generations to continue to participate in the active realization of an enclosure's meaning.

An *addition,* the second type of architectural modification, refers to embankment sections or other formal features like mounds and ditches that were appended to an enclosure's original design elements (those existing at the end of an episode of construction) without changing the basic conception of the place. The term encompasses elements that were later tacked onto an original plan, as well as linear extensions of embankments appended in pursuit of the gradual execution of a master design. Large enclosures may have been too ambitiously drawn for their full outlines to have been completed in one working season. In the Midwest there was the further necessity of stopping work when the ground froze, but even in warmer climes work must have periodically ceased owing to the inability of small societies to indefinitely sustain economically nonproductive labor forces.

Additions could be archaeologically recognized if successive sections of embankments yield reliably different radiometric ages. Short breaks of up to several years between construction episodes, however, will generally not be subject to radiometric detection. The linear overlapping of embankment sections may, however, be stratigraphically evident, and the development of A-horizon soils on such buried surfaces can indicate that several seasons or more elapsed between construction episodes. Many of the larger Ohio enclosures were probably built over a period of years, under a consistent conception and direction. Such phased construction is evident at Seip (Greber 1997) and the Pollock hilltop enclosure (Riordan 1995) and has been long suspected at Fort Ancient (Connolly 1996b; Essenpreis and Moseley 1984). Long lapses in construction may have led to the injection of new personalities and ideas, both of which may have been architecturally expressed. These changes would still fall under this definition of addition, so long as an enclosure's raison d'être was unchanged.

The third type of modification, *alteration,* describes a change made to an architectural form that had been achieved at the end of a construction stage, serving to change the symbolism and/or appropriate use of a particular place. An alteration represents the restatement of an architectural composition, involving a shift in either its use, its iconic symbolism, or both. Alterations may or may not have involved a change in the overall function of an enclosure, and changes in symbolic meaning may not have altered the form of the rituals. Alterations may, however, have rendered some previous architectural elements superfluous. Depending upon the extent to which they intruded on the new composition, and perhaps also on the size and availability of labor forces, redundant elements may have been either removed from the landscape or simply left in place and ignored. Byers (1987:296), however, has argued that alterations accomplished by the removal of previous efforts would have violated the special sanctity of the soils utilized for embankment construction (what he has termed the "sacred earth principle") and thus would never have occurred.

Middle Woodland builders routinely revisited landscapes utilized in earlier periods. The small circular and C-shaped elements found at some Hopewellian earthworks, such as Newark and High Bank, echo forms found at Early Woodland sites. If they were survivals from an earlier time they may have been incorporated into the new compositions, or, alternatively, they may have been considered too inconsequential, too much trouble, or too sacred to have been removed. To date, however, no such earthwork has been sufficiently investigated for this question to be conclusively addressed.

The Fort Ancient earthwork is considered to be a pure Middle Woodland product, an enclosure believed by generations of archaeologists to have been developed over some length of time. The parallel embankments at the northeast corner of Fort Ancient's North Fort are thought to have been built very late in the history of the site's development (Connolly 1996b), and they seem to be out of character with the rest of the site's earthen architecture. These embankments would minimally have been an addition as defined here if they were built after some version of the North Fort enclosure already existed. If, however, their construction shifted or refocused the symbolic import of the original composition, then they constituted a site alteration. The difficulty in deciding these kinds of questions is obviously that we usually do not know exactly what messages their builders were intending to convey to their contemporary audiences; enclosures are in this sense emic boxes, and we are currently stuck on the outside looking in.

The fundamental problem for diachronic interpretive schemes of the major Ohio Hopewell earthwork sites is the almost complete absence of archaeological examples of their development. This is due in part to the history of excavations at Ohio enclosures: most of the work was done before sites were considered to have had developmental histories and also before chronometric dating techniques existed. As a result, enclosure construction stages have generally been the subject of speculation rather than interpretation.

Remodeling the Pollock Works

The Pollock Works is a small hilltop enclosure located in southwestern Ohio. Seasonal excavations have been focused on the embankments and gateways since 1981, and the results to date provide some examples of modifications of the sorts noted above. Briefly, the earthworks at Pollock are situated on the west and northwest sides of a limestone plateau that had been isolated from the surrounding terrain due to erosion by Massie's Creek, which today flows only along the plateau's north side (fig. 9.1). The enclosure's embankments have previously been subdivided for purposes of easier reference into two sections (Riordan 1995)—the barrier wall and the perimeter wall. The barrier wall is a north–south set of embankments on the west that runs from the outcropping limestone cliff of the mesa on the south to the edge of the 7-meter-high bluff that overlooks the creek and which is penetrated by three gateways. The perimeter wall runs east from this juncture along the sinuous bluff edge and ends atop the vertical cliff that abruptly outcrops on the mid-north side.

The evidence that architectural modifications were made at the site is largely stratigraphic, with successive soil mantles indicating layered augmentations of the embankments. This was particularly important on the barrier wall segments, where over the course of several decades multiple soil deposits increased

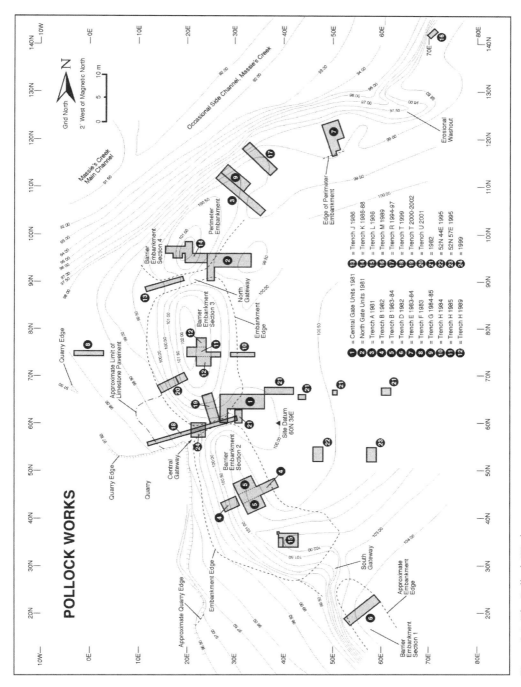

Figure 9.1. The Pollock Works.

their height from about 1.3 meters to 3 meters. These also increased the horizontal spread of the embankment footprints to more than 10 meters. Three stages of this form of construction were previously outlined (Riordan 1995), a scheme that simplified a somewhat more complex picture. At some places along the walls, localized soil deposits were horizontally spread over only a few meters; in one embankment, a limestone deposit was present that was an atypical, and perhaps only opportunistic, use of stone in place of soil. Continued analysis and new excavations have supported the published notion that the barrier embankments were initially developed in three augmented stages of construction. They do not seem to have introduced any fundamental changes to the enclosure but appear only to have reiterated the original design.

Augmentation

The north–south barrier wall is penetrated by three gateways that serve to form four embankment segments. The wall connects a cliff outcropping of exposed bedrock on the south with the Massie's Creek bluff on the north. Trenches excavated in each segment all show evidence of augmentation. The results at Trench B will serve as an example. This excavation was in the barrier wall segment between the central and south gateways. Work began in the enclosure's interior, just beyond the apparent end of the embankment; we learned later that the embankment had originally extended inward a bit farther. At the embankment's summit, a 0.7-meter-wide baulk was left standing, with excavation resumed on the exterior slope (fig. 9.2). The excavation was terminated in the rock piled at the lower end of the exterior slope and did not completely penetrate the wall. Strata are identified in this discussion by their Harris matrix numbers, listed within parentheses.

The results lead us to infer that the first work at the enclosure site was probably the clearing of old-growth trees from at least the portion designated for embankment construction. Work began with the deposition of a thin, approximately 2-centimeter-thick layer (43) of silty clay, followed by a stratum (42) of loaded soils about 8–9 meters wide and 1–1.3 meters high. On one of the trench profiles, a large piece of limestone was found resting on the surface of stratum 42, but it seems to be an isolated case, not part of a consistent covering.

This wide, loaded stratum was followed by several discrete strata (38–41), similarly composed of loaded soils. These added a total of about 80 centimeters at their point of greatest thickness, which occurred below the apical point of the final embankment stage. The exact extent to which these strata added to the width of the embankment is uncertain, owing to incomplete excavation. Embankment expansion was mostly limited to the interior side and probably added only about 1 meter of width. At the exterior end of the trench, the wall's footprint was expanded by a half-meter or less, with deposition having ended at the summit.

These loaded strata, which together are viewed as having constituted the second construction stage (in the scheme advanced in Riordan 1995), were followed by a single more homogeneous stratum of soil (37), which constituted

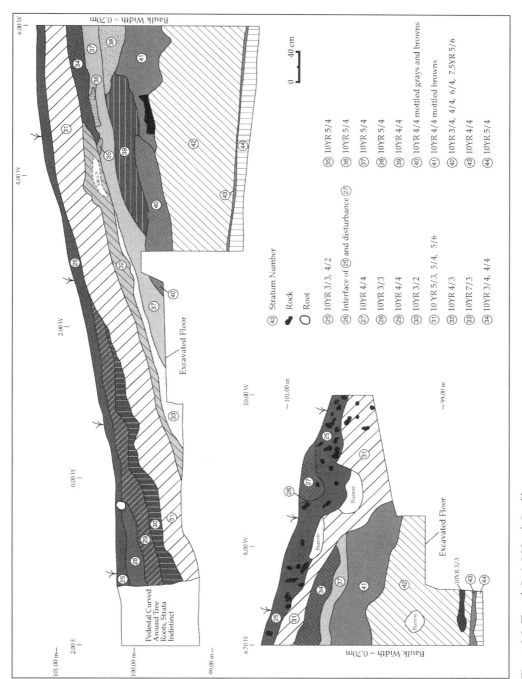

Figure 9.2. Trench B, 0.5 North Profile.

construction stage 3. This measured about 20 centimeters thick near the point of the embankment's vertical apex. Again, the excavation depth that was reached along the relevant portion of the profile was insufficient to provide definite figures, but the footprint probably expanded by about another meter toward the interior. On the exterior side, however, this stratum terminated on top of the loaded strata below, adding to the wall's height but not its width.

An additional thin soil layer (33) was then added only to the interior side of the embankment. It runs about two-thirds of the way up the slope, measuring only a few centimeters thick at the upper end but showing signs of having added more height at the lower end and perhaps 0.5 meters or so of width. It was probably localized along only a few lateral meters of the embankment and does not appear to constitute a true construction stage.

On top of the 4 meters of the broad summit of the embankment was next added a soil deposit 20–30 centimeters thick (34), which was probably also a localized addition. It is overlapped on its interior side by a stratum (32) that extends down the inner slope. This is composed of soil and organic matter from the stockade that was built on top of the stage 3 wall and is described in greater detail below. While its thickness varied, it averaged about 20 centimeters. The stockade itself is identified as the fourth construction stage.

The last soil mantle is a stratum (31) of homogeneous appearance and color that averages 40 centimeters thick. Unlike the strata noted above, this one was distributed evenly to both sides of the embankment, adding as much as 4 meters of width to the wall. At the exterior end it terminates in a considerable deposit of rock. Above this, additional limestone—probably culled from the creek bed or quarried from the cliffs upstream along Massie's Creek—was used to face the exterior side of the embankment all the way up to its summit. The final stratum is a recent humus (25), which, on the exterior side, is mingled with the stone noted above. During historic times, soil eroded from the enclosure's upper plateau and piled up against the interior lower end of the wall, creating several recent strata (28–30).

Addition

While radiocarbon dates from the perimeter embankment generally provide later dates than those from within the barrier wall, we can also point to one instance where stratigraphic data support the existence of an addition. This occurs at the northern end of the barrier wall, where it meets the perimeter wall, which then extends to the east. The embankment gradually descends from a height of about 2 meters adjacent to the north gateway to 1 meter or less only 15 meters to the east, atop the bluff edge.

Fired soils were discovered at Trenches K and A; these soils are believed to have been part of a stockade. At Trench A, fired soil and associated burned timbers occurred on the old ground surface, below the embankment. At Trench K, by contrast, they were found above three soil strata, some 1.5 meters above the original surface. Soil auger cores taken between the two trenches show that the burned elements gradually rise as they surmount embankment soil deposits between A and K. Additionally, one of the north–south profiles in Trench K clearly showed the declination of the surface of the original barrier wall toward the bluff edge.

Alteration

Almost a decade ago, the burned timbers found at several locations underneath the perimeter embankment and on the surface of the third stage of the barrier wall were interpreted as having been the remains of a stockade. It served to complete the enclosing of the plateau, connecting the limestone cliff that out-crops south of the south gateway with the higher cliff on the north. The stockade certainly constituted an addition to the site, but it was probably also an alter-ation. With its appearance, the enclosure would have shifted from being a place of ritual/ceremonial activity to one where a premium was placed on defensive considerations.

I had always been dismissive of notions of fortified Hopewellian hilltops, reasoning—along with many others—that the sites were too large and poorly designed from a military perspective to have been forts or even refuges (for example, Prufer 1964a). However, what quacks like a duck, and figuratively leaves its feather molt behind, may sometimes really be a duck! Traces of the stockade have been found at the base of all eight trenches dug in the perimeter wall and in three of the four that penetrated the barrier wall. It appears to have stood 4–5 meters high on the bluff and 2 meters high on the barrier wall seg-ments, supported in rock-chinked postholes generally spaced a half-meter to a meter apart. Horizontally woven branches filled the spaces between its vertical members, and its lowest 2 meters were probably daubed with clay along most of its length. It is this construction, at such variance with the earlier design, which is viewed as the first alteration at Pollock, something that changed the very nature of the place.

The stockade itself was subsequently destroyed, probably within a decade after its construction. Its traces everywhere indicate that it was burned, which has been previously interpreted as having been done by the people who built it (Riordan 1995:85). This arises from the state of its remains: in many places, while its timbers still smoldered, it was covered by the soil of the perimeter embankment and the final mantle that was added to the barrier wall segments. Getting such a structure to burn so consistently over such a large linear distance was surely no easy task in those preaccelerant days. The event seems unlikely to have been an accident. Since the immediate environment had probably been recently denuded of much of its wood to satisfy the stockade's need for some-thing like six hundred vertical posts, plus all the wood required for the interwo-ven elements, its accidental destruction by a forest fire seems unlikely. Some other natural agent, such as a lightning strike, *might* have caused it, if no one was present to witness and deal with the danger. The enclosure probably stood vacant and untended most of the time, even during its period of use, and such opportunities were probably plentiful. But the rapidity with which embankment construction evidently followed the fire seems to contravene this hypothesis.

The preservation of so many carbonized timbers argues that the stockade's destruction was effected through the concerted efforts of people who also stood by, ready to immediately begin building over it.

Recent fieldwork also permits us to address the question of whether the gateway openings were likewise altered during the period of the stockade's existence. During an early field season, a probe and two small test excavations across the interior sides of the central and north gateways had shown that both were surfaced with stone. Some stone had also been detected on the ground surface outside the central gateway, and more had been used to face the sides of the gateways and the exterior surfaces of the barrier wall. The small mounds depicted outside the gateways by Squier and Davis (1848) were noted by Davis in an 1847 letter to Squier as having been composed of stone. These mounds had already been destroyed, their stones having been burned for lime (Davis 1847).

The edges of the pavement outside the central gateway were sought in 1999 with several small trenches. Stones were found to have been deposited to a maximum of 12 meters to the west of the approximate center of the gateway and about 10 meters to the north of this line. The area just southwest of the gateway had been destroyed by historic quarrying and could not be examined. If, however, the area to the south was symmetrical with the paved area to the north, then approximately 180 square meters outside the gateway had been paved.

A 3-×-3–meter unit aligned with the site grid just outside the gateway was stripped of its topsoil to give a visual sense of the paving. Subsequently, a profile trench was dug from the interior side of the gateway through this unit and out past the western limit of the stone paving. The trench was 80 centimeters wide and ultimately 20 meters long, and it was taken down to sterile subsoil, which was reached at a much shallower depth at the outer, western end than in the middle of the gateway. All the rock, which was uniformly limestone, was weighed, and aggregate weights were kept along each meter of the trench. Artifact recovery was limited to a few stone tools, some discovered in the quarter-inch sifters and some in situ. These included a chert bladelet, a stone maul (located outside the gateway and under the pavement stones), and three Archaic projectile points or point fragments.

Our earlier probing had led us to expect that the trench would reveal the stone as a consistent but somewhat scattered presence. Surprisingly, the stones were found to be quite uniformly embedded two and three deep, in a 30- to 40-centimeter-thick layer over most of the area (fig. 9.3). Much more stone had been employed than we had expected to find: the profile trench contained a total of 3.2 tons of stone. From this, the entire surviving pavement is estimated to contain 30–35 tons of rock. If the destroyed southern portion was symmetrical with the area to the north, then there may have been an additional 27 tons, for an exterior pavement total of some 60 tons.

The stones used ranged in size from small pieces that weighed less than a quarter kilogram to larger stones weighing more than 70 kilograms. The act of paving this area, and probably the deposition of stone on the embankment exteriors and gateway sides, was an activity that could have involved all the

Figure 9.3. Trench T, excavated through stone pavement outside the central gateway.

members of the community, including adults, small children, and the elderly. This aspect of the enclosure's remodeling was therefore a potentially unifying undertaking by the owning group, in which all could literally have taken a hand.

The area just inside (east of) the central gateway was also excavated, revealing an additional 4 meters of pavement. Unlike the paving that surfaced the gateway and the area outside, almost all of this short section was composed of stones that had been carefully selected and fitted together to form a narrow, smooth-surfaced ramp that sloped down into the enclosure. The ramp was only about as wide as the trench, 80 centimeters or a bit less, and horizontal expansion of the trench verified that it disappeared on both sides. It is assumed to be prehistoric and to date to the Middle Woodland period; while most of it was left in place undisturbed, no historic material was found below those portions of it that were temporarily removed. It was too narrow to have been efficiently used by a wagon or tractor and thus seems unlikely to have been built in historic times.

Below the stones that surfaced the central gateway a significant find was made. The stones capped a posthole (#34) that was over 50 centimeters in diameter and 70 centimeters deep. Its presence suggests that the stockade, known to have been present on top of the barrier embankment sections to either side, had also been extended through the gateway. The post itself had apparently been pulled prior to the capping of the posthole by the stones of the pavement. In

2002, a second post (#36) was detected (but not yet excavated) on the north side of the gateway. It has a diameter of 50 centimeters, and its center is about 1.5 meters from the approximate center of post 34. These two posts may have served as the anchors for an actual gate that physically restricted access to the enclosure. If so, this represents a structural difference in "gateway" design, compared with gateways that were simply gaps between embankment segments. This appears to be the first discovery of such a feature at a Hopewell earthwork, but most earthwork gateways have never been examined for this type of construction.

While the appearance of the stockade is viewed as the first alteration of the enclosure, its second alteration involved the stockade's destruction when the apparent need for it had ended. This was followed by the addition of the final soil cap to the embankments, the surfacing of their exteriors with stone, and the construction of the perimeter embankment. The paving of the exterior approach to the central gateway was probably among the last of the acts that served to formally and symbolically reconfigure the enclosure away from the brief but dramatic change in its use that the stockade had represented.

Conclusion

The Pollock Works was augmented, added to, and altered over the course of a century or more. Recent fieldwork demonstrates that the use of many tons of limestone was a particularly important component of the last major construction episode. This added limestone altered the external appearance of the barrier wall and formed a durable surface outside and through the central gateway that may have announced the special nature of that entrance. The construction of the short ramp of fitted stones into the enclosure's interior may have been intended to distinguish that area from the rest of the pavement. It is tempting to think of this section versus the rest in structurally dichotomous terms: smooth versus rough, inside versus outside, organized versus chaotic, and so on. Whether this tells us something of the Middle Woodland population who built and used this structure or the archaeologists who interpret their work is an open question, one with potentially different resolutions depending upon one's theoretical stance.

The archaeological exploration of Middle Woodland earthen architectural sites has been under way now for well over a century. Nevertheless, the recognition that some enclosures were modified and even reconfigured as an inherent aspect of their histories and use is something that is only now being actively recognized. From a diachronic perspective, the recognition of discrete construction stages may yield functional and cognitive information about sites and those who built them; when such data are routinely available, it may be possible to recognize patterns of development across classes of sites. The synchronic counterpoint to this is that each successive version of an enclosure should be understood as having successively met the needs, whatever they may have been, of its owners. This would be true even when the architecture is different from its original formulation and from its end appearance.

The currently unique circumstances within the construction stages documented at Pollock—stockade construction, destruction, and aspects of its subsequent remodeling—have wider implications for our investigation of other portions of the Middle Woodland world. While the Pollock stockade and its replacement features are at present curiosities and anomalies, future work may render them as intelligible responses to environmental conditions that have yet to be fully defined. The detailed regional history of the first three centuries A.D. that will form this context will come from systematic work at other enclosures, from burial sites and the study of skeletal collections, from material culture studies, and from residential remains at the ever-elusive Ohio Hopewell housing developments.

Section 2

Hopewell/Middle Woodland outside Ohio

Chapters 10–19 explore Hopewell and Middle Woodland in regions outside Ohio. The chapters are arranged geographically starting in Georgia (Jefferies; Steinen), then jumping to Indiana (Ruby; Mangold and Schurr) and arcing through Michigan (Garland and DesJardins; Brashler, Martin, Parker, Robertson, and Hambacher), Wisconsin (Jeske; Stoltman), and Illinois (Fortier). Kansas City Hopewell (Logan) represents the westernmost extension of Hopewellian culture. These chapters are not a representative sample of the regional distribution of Hopewellian societies: the Southeast is underrepresented (but see Anderson and Mainfort 2002b), and the lower Mississippi Valley is not covered at all (although this was not the case in the original conference program). Rather, the chapters reflect responses to the original conference invitations and to the call for publishable versions of papers that were presented.

Nevertheless, these chapters do seem to be representative of much of non-Ohio Hopewellian/Middle Woodland research. In contrast to the results of a century and a half of investigation into Ohio Hopewell, clear cultural historical documentation is a goal for many other regions. As such, some of these chapters focus on developing chronological and geographical frameworks. As several authors suggest, years—even decades—of such research may still be necessary before we can adequately address some of the really interesting questions about this period of midwestern prehistory. One question that does appear in a number of chapters is the extent and/or nature of regional participation in what has generally come to be known as the Hopewell Interaction Sphere (following Caldwell 1964). The general answer would seem to be that participation varied a great deal. Similarly, the nature of subsistence is highly variable from region to region. Neither of these conclusions is new, but the increasing amount of relevant information available allows more sophisticated modeling of the social and economic processes involved (for example, chapters by Fortier, Jeske, and Ruby).

10

Death Rituals at the Tunacunnhee Site

Middle Woodland Mortuary Practices in Northwestern Georgia

Richard W. Jefferies

In the summer of 1973, Joseph R. Caldwell directed archaeological investigations at the Tunacunnhee site (9DD25), a Middle Woodland mound and habitation complex in northwestern Georgia (fig. 10.1). Excavation efforts focused on the four earth-and-stone burial mounds and their mortuary features, revealing more than thirty burials containing a variety of exotic artifacts and materials including copper ear spools, panpipes, and breast plates; platform pipes; mica objects; shark teeth; and crystal quartz (Jefferies 1976, 1979). Artifacts like these are traditionally associated with Hopewell sites in the Midwest and Southeast (Brose and Greber 1979; Caldwell 1964; Pacheco 1996b; Seeman 1979b; Struever and Houart 1972). The presence of these artifacts at Tunacunnhee indicates that some Middle Woodland inhabitants of northwestern Georgia interacted with contemporary groups that lived throughout much of eastern North America.

Although the mounds were the primary focus of the 1973 investigations, excavation of a portion of the nearby Lookout Creek floodplain exposed part of what was thought to be an associated habitation area (fig. 10.2). Similar pottery, projectile points, and radiocarbon dates supported the contemporaneity of these two parts of the Tunacunnhee site. Habitation area excavations yielded a variety of features and artifacts attributable to typical Middle Woodland extractive and maintenance tasks. Other excavated materials, such as prismatic blades and copper, mica, and crystal quartz artifacts, are uncommon on south Appalachian Middle Woodland habitation sites. The presence of these materials suggested that while the nearby mounds were the final resting place for some of the deceased, a variety of ceremonial activities preceding final interment had taken place in the habitation area. As suggested by Walthall (1985), at least part of the Tunacunnhee site appears to have served as a "ceremonial encampment" where Middle Woodland inhabitants prepared both the living and the dead for the coming final interment, made implements to process the remains of the deceased, and manufactured objects to accompany them in death. The presence of less exotic domestic refuse suggests that the Middle Woodland mound builders also lived in this part of the site while they went about their ritual activities.

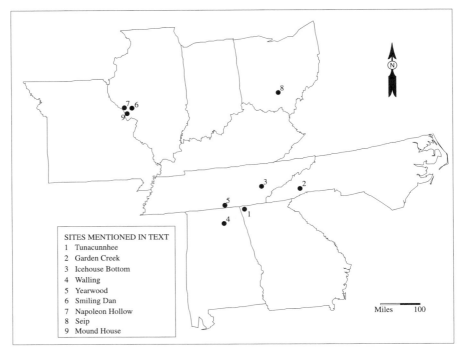

SITES MENTIONED IN TEXT
1 Tunacunnhee
2 Garden Creek
3 Icehouse Bottom
4 Walling
5 Yearwood
6 Smiling Dan
7 Napoleon Hollow
8 Seip
9 Mound House

Miles   100

Figure 10.1. Middle Woodland sites mentioned in text.

A superficial examination of the habitation area artifacts followed the 1973 field season, but other than the brief description in my master's thesis (Jefferies 1975), no systematic analysis was ever conducted. During the spring and summer of 1998, habitation area records and artifacts were reexamined to more thoroughly investigate the range of activities represented. The resulting quantitative and spatial data are used to examine the diversity and distribution of features and artifacts, assess the range of associated activities, and reevaluate Walthall's (1985) model of Hopewellian ceremonial centers in the southern Appalachian region.

Middle Woodland Mounds, Ceremonial Camps, and Mortuary Rituals

The many spectacular Middle Woodland burial mounds of the North American midcontinent have been of interest to antiquarians and archaeologists for nearly two hundred years (McAdams 1881; Mills 1909, 1916, 1922; Moorehead 1922; Putnam 1885; Shetrone 1926; Snyder 1898; Squier and Davis 1848; Thomas 1894). Analyses of these mounds and their contents have yielded abundant information on mortuary practices, economics, and social organization (Braun 1979; Brose 1994; Brose and Greber 1979; Brown 1979; Buikstra 1976; Charles 1992, 1995; Seeman 1979a; Tainter 1977).

Cross-cultural studies of mortuary practices demonstrate that many societies do not view death as instantaneous. Often, considerable time passes between death and final interment. The intervening time is filled with various rituals that enable both the living and the dead to complete this rite of passage successfully (Huntington and Metcalf 1979:13). The end of this "intermediary period" is often marked by ceremonies during which the remains of the deceased are recovered, ritually processed, and moved to a new location (Hertz 1907, cited in Huntington and Metcalf 1979:13). Presumably, many activities associated with preparing the deceased for final disposal would have taken place not at the immediate gravesite but at a nearby location.

Over the past forty years, archaeologists have identified a number of Middle Woodland sites that may represent where the "intermediary" aspects of the mortuary program were carried out. In the 1960s, Struever (1968b) defined a new kind of mortuary site, the mortuary camp, based on his research in the lower Illinois River valley. Mortuary camps, located near Hopewell mound cemeteries, consisted of brief, specialized occupations during which the inhabitants constructed the mounds, performed mortuary rituals, and buried the dead. In addition to mortuary activities, individuals performed tasks, such as food preparation and tool production, to support the mortuary camp's "living" inhabitants (Struever 1968b:308).

In subsequent years, continued study of the region's Middle Woodland settlement patterns and mortuary practices has enabled archaeologists to refine Struever's "mortuary camp" model (see Buikstra, Charles, and Rakita 1998 for a detailed discussion). On the basis of research at the Napoleon Hollow site (fig. 10.1), Wiant and McGimsey (1986b) argued that parts of the site served as a residential area for those who conducted ritual activities at the nearby Elizabeth Mound Group. Evidence for these activities included numerous exotic materials (especially obsidian), a high percentage of Hopewell series ceramics, low fauna species diversity, and proximity to the Elizabeth mounds. The presence of subsistence-related artifacts and certain feature types indicates that Napoleon Hollow also served other functions that did not directly relate to mortuary activities. As a result, McGimsey and Wiant (1986:540) proposed the concept of the "ritual camp" as an alternative to Struever's "mortuary camp" model.

Buikstra, Charles, and Rakita's (1998) recent investigations at the Mound House site (fig. 10.1) have further expanded our understanding of Middle Woodland mortuary complexity and ritual encampments. They suggested that archaeologists must look beyond the boundaries of specific mortuary sites to consider the temporal, spatial, and symbolic dynamics of all of the components that comprise the surrounding sacred landscape (Buikstra, Charles, and Rakita 1998:94). They argued that in the lower Illinois River valley, certain loci—like the Mound House site—served as ceremonial precincts where multicommunity mortuary encampments were established and residents conducted elaborate mortuary ceremonies and other activities that facilitated social cohesion and provided a forum for structuring social, political, and economic relationships (Buikstra, Charles, and Rakita 1998:94).

Middle Woodland ceremonial camps are also known in the South Appalachian Highlands. Walthall (1985) recognized that while the region's highly

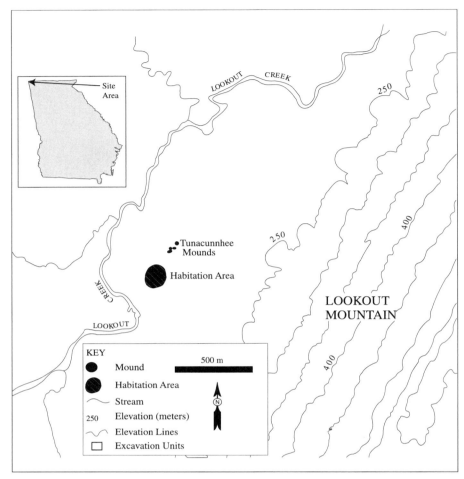

Figure 10.2. Location of Tunacunnhee mounds and habitation area. Excavation units not to scale.

documented burial mounds mark the final resting place of the deceased, other mortuary-related activities involving both the living and the dead were performed at other, often less conspicuous, locations in the surrounding region. Many of these ceremonial loci resemble the mortuary or ceremonial camps described for the Illinois River valley (Buikstra, Charles, and Rakita 1998; Struever 1968b; Wiant and McGimsey 1986b).

Walthall (1985:243) suggested that several Middle Woodland sites dating from A.D. 1 to 200, including Tunacunnhee (Jefferies 1976, 1979) in Georgia, Walling (Knight 1990; Walthall 1973) in Alabama, Yearwood (Butler 1977, 1979) and Icehouse Bottom (Chapman 1973) in Tennessee, and Garden Creek (Keel 1976) in North Carolina (fig. 10.1) functioned as ceremonial encampments resembling, and perhaps affiliated with, some midwestern Hopewell sites. Basing his interpretation on characteristics that distinguished these sites from typical south Appalachian Middle Woodland habitation sites—including their small size, lack of structure superpositioning, proximity to burial mounds, numerous prismatic blades, and small tetrapodal jars (Walthall 1985:250–251)—he interpreted these sites as ceremonial centers where "ritual activities related to mortuary processing and communal feasting" took place (Walthall 1985:261).

Field Investigations

Defined by a dark oval midden stain, the Tunacunnhee habitation area measures approximately 30 × 60 meters (fig. 10.2). Investigation was accomplished through the excavation (fig. 10.3) of twenty-five 10-×-10-foot (approximately

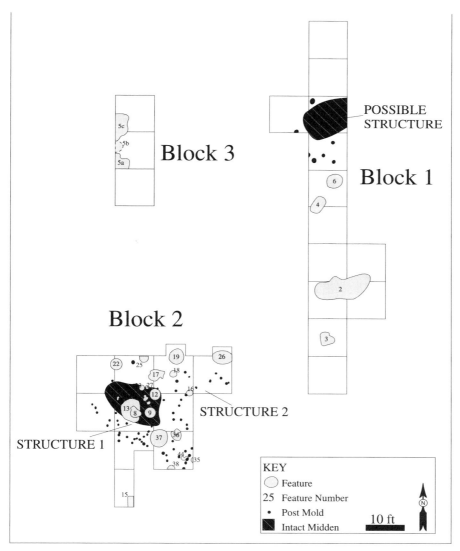

Figure 10.3. Habitation area features, post molds, structures, and midden concentrations.

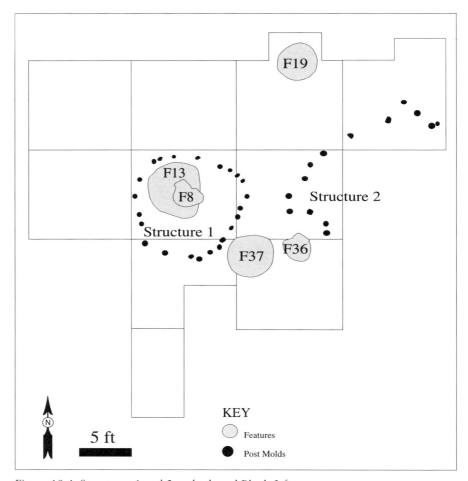

Figure 10.4. Structures 1 and 2 and selected Block 2 features.

3-×-3-meter) units. Initially, a north–south line of thirteen units, designated as Block 1, was opened along the midden's eastern edge. Block 2, consisting of nine units, was then excavated just to the west of Block 1. Finally, the three units comprising Block 3 were excavated north of Block 2. The total area exposed in the three excavation blocks was more than 230 square meters.

Excavation revealed more than eighty post molds, some of which formed parts of at least two structures. Structure 1 consisted of a 3-meter-diameter post-mold pattern containing twenty-four post molds ranging from 7 to 15 centimeters in diameter and spaced from 15 to 60 centimeters apart (fig. 10.4). Two rock-filled hearths (Features 8 and 13) were inside the Structure 1 post-mold pattern, but the contemporaneity of the features and the structure is conjectural. Structure 1's floor area (7.25 square meters) falls in the lower end of Smith's (1992a:Figure 9.8) distribution of eighty-three Middle Woodland habitation and corporate-ceremonial structures in eastern North America. The structure's small size suggests that it was not a typical habitation structure but perhaps served some type of ritual or ceremonial function.

Structure 2 is represented by a larger oval or subrectangular post-mold pattern just to the east of Structure 1 (fig. 10.4). Structure 2 post molds were generally greater in diameter and deeper than those of Structure 1, suggesting a larger, more substantial building. If the post-mold pattern shown in figure 10.4 is an accurate representation of the structure's shape, it would have been over 7 meters in diameter and would have had a floor area of approximately 42 square meters. No Block 2 features appear to be directly associated with Structure 2, although additional features may exist in the unexcavated portion of the post-mold pattern.

Comparison of Structure 2 with structures exposed at contemporary southeastern and midwestern Middle Woodland sites indicates that its 42-square-meter floor area falls near the middle of Smith's size distribution for habitation structures (Smith 1992a:Figure 9.8). Structures of similar size, shape, and method of construction are known for a number of these sites (Kline, Crites, and Faulkner 1982; Stafford and Sant 1985b; Wiant and McGimsey 1986b). Smith (1992a:213, Figure 9.9) has referred to these oval-to-circular, single-wall post structures as one settlement component of the "Hopewell household unit."

Excavation exposed a third cluster of post molds at the north end of Block 1 (fig. 10.3). Post molds were arranged in a roughly circular pattern suggesting a structure diameter of approximately 6 meters. Two pits (Features 4 and 6) were directly south of this possible structure.

In addition to structures, excavation revealed twenty-seven features, consisting of pits, burned areas, and midden and rock concentrations (fig. 10.3). More than one-third ($n = 10$) were classified as "circular, basin-shaped pits" ranging from 30 to 150 centimeters in diameter and from 15 to 85 centimeters deep. Basin-shaped pits contained substantial amounts of cultural material, including chert debitage, sherds, bone, and rock. Two of the basin-shaped pits (Features 19 and 37) contained numerous flakes, sherds, and deer bone, as well as a variety of exotic materials, including crystal quartz flakes and a core, prismatic blades, and portions of small tetrapodal vessels. The proximity of Features 19 and 37 to the two structures raises the possibility that they and their contents are associated with activities that took place in and around the structures. Charcoal collected from the base of one basin-shaped pit (Feature 19) yielded an uncalibrated radiocarbon date of A.D. 280 ±125 (UGA-ML-10). Three "subrectangular pits" contained oxidized clay and rock, indicating that they had been used for cooking or other heat-related activities.

Cultural Materials

The Tunacunnhee habitation area investigations yielded 1,693 sherds, of which 42 percent came from features and 58 percent from general midden contexts. Most of the sherds fit into one of six categories based on temper type (limestone or grit) and surface treatment (plain, cord marked, simple stamped/brushed).

Analysis revealed one check-stamped and one fabric-impressed sherd. Decorated pottery was extremely rare, consisting of a few incised, punctated, and/or burnished sherds.

Fifty-eight percent of the habitation area pottery is limestone-tempered; the remaining 42 percent is grit-tempered. Surface treatment varies considerably between temper types. Approximately 50 percent of the limestone-tempered pottery is cord marked as opposed to only 4 percent of the grit-tempered material. Simple-stamped/brushed exteriors are much more common on grit-tempered sherds than on limestone-tempered pottery (30 percent versus 10 percent).

Limestone-tempered, cordmarked sherds resemble Candy Creek Cordmarked pottery, as defined by Lewis and Kneberg (1946). The grit-tempered sherds are tempered with distinctive angular pieces of crushed granitic rock (Stoltman, personal communication, 1998). Some pieces of grit-tempered pottery resemble Cartersville series ceramics (Caldwell 1958:45) found in northern Georgia. Others have a micaceous paste similar to that found in Connestee ceramics (Keel 1972) from the Appalachian Summit area of western North Carolina and eastern Tennessee.

Most of the habitation area sherds appear to be attributable to Middle Woodland jars used to prepare and store food. Unfortunately, the small size of the sherds hinders the identification of specific vessel forms. The presence of several basal portions and isolated "feet" from small tetrapodal vessels indicates that this vessel form was used for some habitation area activities. Tetrapodal vessels were both limestone- and grit-tempered. Two examples of this vessel form were found in Tunacunnhee Mound C (Jefferies 1976:Plate 21). In addition to tetrapodal vessels, a flat-bottomed, limestone-tempered pan or tub having a plain exterior surface was found in Feature 37. Both vessel types were freestanding, making them suitable for use in various ritual activities (Walthall 1985:258).

Thin-section analysis of a small sample of habitation area sherds, conducted by Jim Stoltman, suggests the presence of nonlocal pottery at the Tunacunnhee habitation area (Stoltman, personal communications, 2003). His assessment of paste and temper attributes suggests that two grit-tempered, simple-stamped sherds from Feature 37 favorably compare with Connestee pottery and were probably manufactured in the Appalachian region. Connestee-like ceramics are also reported from a number of other Middle Woodland sites in the Southeast and Midwest (Seeman 1979b:378; Stoltman, personal communication, 2000; Walthall 1985:252). Additional sherds were identified as nonlocal, but their place of manufacture could not be determined.

Habitation area flaked stone artifacts consist of more than six thousand pieces of debitage and four hundred tools. More than 99 percent of the flaked stone artifacts were made from local Fort Payne or, more commonly, St. Louis cherts. Debitage analysis indicated that a full range of biface production activities had been performed in the habitation area, an inference supported by the abundance of early to late stage bifaces (Jefferies 1982). Artifact diversity indices indicate that a wide range of extractive and maintenance activities had been conducted in the habitation area (Jefferies 1982). The most common flaked stone tools were trianguloid projectile points (Jefferies 1976:Plate 23), most of which resemble Greeneville, Nolichucky, or Copena types (Justice 1987). These points, commonly associated with Middle Woodland occupations in the mid-South, date from A.D. 150 to 500 (Justice 1987:208–211). Other types of flaked stone tools include end and side scrapers, perforators, and notched pieces (Jefferies 1978).

Overall, most of the habitation area ceramics and flaked stone artifacts resemble those found at many other south Appalachian Middle Woodland habitation sites, particularly McFarland phase sites in central Tennessee (Faulkner and McCollough 1973:423–424; Lewis and Kneberg 1957). Site inhabitants used flaked stone tools to perform a variety of extractive and maintenance tasks. Most of the sherds appear to be from "typical" small to medium-sized cooking and storage vessels.

Tunacunnhee Habitation Area Ritual Activity

The more extensive 1998 analysis of the habitation area material identified more than 180 artifacts that either were made of nonlocal materials (largely crystal quartz, mica, or copper) or had been produced using a specialized technology (such as prismatic blades). Materials such as these are not commonly found on south Appalachian Middle Woodland sites. The presence of these exotic items and their association with certain features suggests that individuals conducted other, more esoteric tasks besides those of daily life. The remainder of this chapter focuses on the diversity and spatial distribution of these features and artifacts and their relationships to mound-related activities.

Structures and Features

Structure 1, the small circular structure containing a central hearth, resembled structures found at some Hopewell-affiliated sites in the Midwest. For example, Wray and MacNeish (1961:17) describe a similar structure at the Weaver site in the lower Illinois River valley. The small circular structure, also located in a habitation area adjacent to several Hopewell burial mounds, was approximately 2.5 meters in diameter, slightly smaller than the Tunacunnhee structure. Like the Tunacunnhee structure, a large pit was situated within the Weaver structure. Excavators found Hopewell sherds and a Hopewell celt in the pit. Wray and MacNeish (1961:17) suggest that the Weaver site structure was a partially subterranean sweat house. The Tunacunnhee structure—with its central, rock-filled firepits (Features 8 and 13)—may have had a similar function.

During the Historic period, southeastern Indians, including the Cherokee and the Creeks, used sweating and sweat houses in their curing rituals (Hudson 1976:343–345). The Creeks believed that people who buried the dead commonly suffered from illnesses and were in need of ritual purification (Hudson 1976:343). Driver (1972:133) indicates that Creek sweat houses were usually small, domed-shaped structures with circular ground plans. Water was sprinkled on hot stones to create water vapor (1972:417–418). Although separated by nearly two thousand years, the architectural similarity of Structure 1 and its associated features and the descriptions of some historic southeastern sweat houses is intriguing. Archaeologists working in the American Bottom of west-central Illinois have identified similar small, circular sweat houses or lodges at some Mississippian sites (Emerson 1997b:174–175; Milner 1998:96, 101). The association of these small structures with sites dating to circa A.D. 1100 provides temporal and cultural continuity for the use of sweat houses between the Middle Woodland and Historic periods. Small circular structures containing rare nonutilitarian artifacts were also identified at the Peisker site in the Illinois River valley (Staab 1984:Table 5–1, 136), but since these structures lacked evidence for burning, they probably were not sweat houses. They may have served instead as spirit or conjuring lodges (Staab 1984:138–139).

Features 19, 36, and 37—and their contents, including crystal quartz artifacts, prismatic blades, mica, and fragments of small tetrapodal vessels—resembled features found at a number of Ohio Hopewell sites (Baby and Langlois 1979; Greber 1996; Seeman 1979b). These three features were located immediately adjacent to Structures 1 and 2 (fig. 10.4), raising the possibility that they and their contents were associated with structure activities. At least three other habitation area features contained multiple types of exotic artifacts.

Situations similar to those described for Tunacunnhee have been documented by Seeman (1979a:40–43) at several Ohio Hopewell mortuary sites. Archaeological investigations at many of these sites have uncovered structures and associated features containing bladelets, projectile points, ceramics, mica, and animal bone, suggesting that they were the locations of ritual feasting. Specifically, Baby and Langlois (cited in Seeman 1979a:41) described several off-mound structures at the Seip Mound complex in Ross County, Ohio, that yielded no evidence of mortuary activity but instead contained mica, shells, unusual lithic assemblages, and/or features suggesting that these structures were the sites of specialized workshops. Baby and Langlois (1979:18) proposed that these structures housed the skilled artisans who produced the "elaborate ceremonial and ornamental objects for which Hopewell is noted." These pits are associated with structures inside the earthworks and adjacent to the large mound (Baby and Langlois 1979). Baby and Langlois (1979) suggested that burial artifacts had been produced in these structures for later placement with mound burials. Radiocarbon dates from Seip (A.D. 230 ±80 and A.D. 280 ±55) are coeval with the acceptable Tunacunnhee habitation area date (A.D. 280 ±125) (Jefferies 1976).

McGimsey and Wiant (1986) have documented a similar occurrence at the Napoleon Hollow site, a Middle Woodland mortuary site in the lower Illinois River valley. Like Tunacunnhee, Napoleon Hollow is near a Middle Woodland burial mound complex, the Elizabeth Mound Group, situated on the nearby bluff crest. Excavation of Block IV of the Napoleon Hollow site revealed an 8-meter-diameter structure and fifteen associated surface and pit features. The interpretation of Block IV as a mortuary camp is based on the proximity to the

Elizabeth mounds, the presence of prismatic blades, abundant nonlocal raw material (particularly obsidian), a large quantity of Hopewell series pottery, and abundant remains of deer bone from the "meaty" part of the animal, possibly associated with feasting (McGimsey and Wiant 1986:536–538). Scattered human bone fragments found near the Block IV structure suggest that it had served as a "temporary repository for human remains" (McGimsey and Wiant 1986:538–539). Four radiocarbon dates associated with the structure or features range from 50 ±70 B.C. to A.D. 140 ±70 (Wiant and McGimsey 1986b:73).

The scarcity of direct evidence for mortuary activity and the Block IV artifact assemblage that includes many nonmortuary-related artifacts strongly suggest that Napoleon Hollow served other, more secular functions as well (McGimsey and Wiant 1986:539). McGimsey and Wiant (1986:539–40) argued that Napoleon Hollow had been a ritual camp where (1) higher-status individuals lived and/or conducted activities, (2) ceremonial/ritual activities were frequently performed, and (3) artifacts were commonly prepared for use in those contexts.

Prismatic Blades

Prismatic blades occur at many Ohio and Illinois Hopewell sites, where they are found in both domestic and mortuary contexts (Genheimer 1996; Hofman 1987; Kellar 1979; Lemons and Church 1998; Odell 1994; Yerkes 1990). In some cases, they comprise the majority of formal tool types (Genheimer 1996:94). Edge-wear analyses suggest that prismatic blades functioned as light-duty knives, scrapers, gravers, perforators, and spokeshaves and were used for cutting, shaving, engraving, and scraping tasks involving both plant and animal materials (Genheimer 1996:95; Odell 1985b, 1994; Yerkes 1990, cited in Genheimer 1996). Some Ohio Hopewell blades were hafted; others were used without hafting (Genheimer 1996:101–103). Genheimer (1996:103) maintains that "bladelets may represent either a general purpose or functionally specific utilitarian tool in a highly standardized form."

Odell (1994:117) has recently proposed that prismatic blade technology developed along with Hopewell mortuary ceremonialism. His use-wear analysis of prismatic blades from three Illinois River valley Middle Woodland sites suggests that blades from the habitation site (Smiling Dan) had been used for a variety of tasks performed on many different materials. In contrast, blades were more common at mortuary-related sites (Napoleon Hollow), and they had primarily been used for cutting and scraping soft materials as part of the manufacture of objects to accompany the dead (Odell 1994:102, 117).

Although prismatic blades occur at south Appalachian Middle Woodland ceremonial centers, they are not a common tool form. Some south Appalachian prismatic blades are made of nonlocal materials, particularly Flint Ridge chalcedony (Walthall 1985:251). Others are made from local cherts or, occasionally, other types of stone. In view of their unusual contexts at these sites, Walthall (1985:256–257) suggested that prismatic blades were part of the mortuary pro-

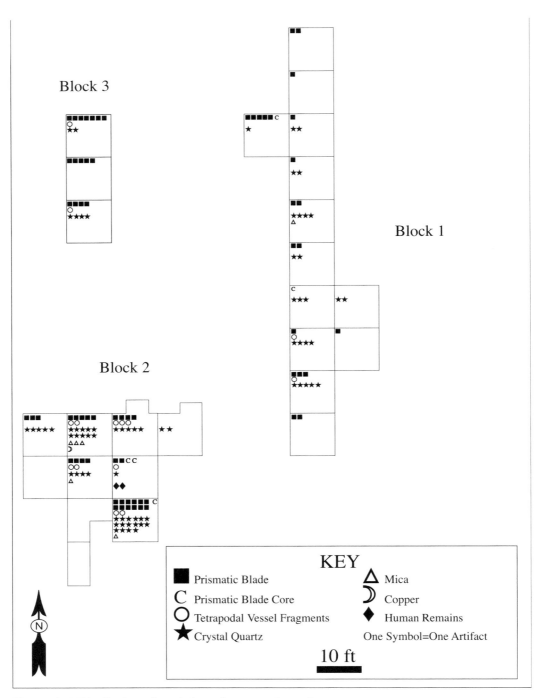

Figure 10.5. Distribution of exotic items by excavation unit.

gram, perhaps having been used for dissecting cadavers, cleaning skeletal remains, or preparing foods consumed during ritual feasting.

Tunacunnhee habitation area excavations yielded at least sixty-five prismatic blades and five blade cores (fig. 10.5). Most of the blades were manufactured from local St. Louis chert; two, however, were made of crystal quartz (Jefferies 1976:Plate 23). A single blade of Ohio Flint Ridge chalcedony was found in one mound (Jefferies 1976:30–31).

Prismatic blades were distributed throughout the habitation area, with approximately one-third coming from feature contexts. Feature 37, a large basin-shaped pit located between Structures 1 and 2, contained eight blades. The presence of thirty blades and three blade cores near Structure 1 suggests that blade production and use occurred in this part of the site. Unlike some Ohio sites, at Tunacunnhee, prismatic blades comprised less than 15 percent of all flaked stone tools, leaving bifacial flaking as the technology of choice for making most flaked stone implements. Nevertheless, blade technology constituted a small, specialized part of the Tunacunnhee lithic industry. Prismatic blades accounted for slightly more than 14 percent of retouched tools at the Smiling Dan site (Odell 1994:105).

Although the Tunacunnhee human skeletal remains were not examined for evidence of dissection, bundle burials and isolated skeletal elements in the mounds suggest that some bodies had been disarticulated prior to interment. Isolated human skeletal elements found in the habitation area midden also support a practice of postmortem manipulation of human remains (see below).

Small Tetrapodal Jars

Small tetrapodal jars, usually with simple- or check-stamped exteriors, are known for many southeastern and midwestern Middle Woodland mortuary sites (Fenton and Jefferies 1991; Knight 1990:162; Mainfort 1996:381; Seeman 1979b:378; Walthall 1985:252). Seeman (1979b:378–379) suggested that they, like copper, marine shell, and mica, were occasionally exchanged through Middle Woodland interregional networks. Grit-tempered specimens found in several midwestern Middle Woodland burial mounds appear to have been manufactured in the Southeast, representing "intrusive elements into the local tradition" (Seeman 1979b:378). Some of these tetrapodal vessels eventually ended up in burial contexts (Jefferies 1976:31).

The small capacity of these jars, averaging about two pints (Walthall 1985:253), made them impractical for preparing or serving food to groups. Instead, Walthall (1985:261) suggested that they, like their more highly decorated midwestern counterparts, had been used to serve food offerings to the dead. The small "feet" on their bases would have made them freestanding, a useful attribute if they were being displayed as part of the mortuary ritual. Portions of two small tetrapodal vessels were found in one of the Tunacunnhee mounds (Jefferies 1976:Plate 21), indicating their use in mortuary activities at this site.

Habitation area excavations yielded fourteen small ceramic feet and several tetrapodal vessel bases from both feature and midden contexts (fig. 10.5). Fifty percent of the feet are grit-tempered, and 43 percent are limestone-tempered. The temper of one foot could not be determined. The surfaces of most of the feet were plain, but one limestone-tempered vessel base was cord marked and one grit-tempered foot was simple stamped. The feet occurred throughout the habitation area. However, more than 70 percent came from the vicinity of Structures 1 and 2.

Crystal Quartz

Crystal quartz artifacts are found at many Hopewell-related sites throughout the East (Seeman 1979b:Table 10). Although this material is not as common as copper, mica, or marine shell, Seeman (1979b:303–304) ranked crystal quartz as "intermediate" in importance along with bear canines, silver, shark teeth, and other commonly recognized Hopewell exchange items.

Large, high-quality quartz crystals do not occur in extreme northwestern Georgia. Some crystal quartz can be found in the Blue Ridge Mountains of northeastern Georgia and eastern Tennessee, roughly one hundred miles east of Tunacunnhee. However, Seeman maintains that most Hopewell crystal quartz probably came from the vicinity of Hot Springs, Arkansas, or the Catskill Mountains of New York (Seeman 1979b:298; also see Gaines et al. 1997). The ceremonial use of crystal quartz at Tunacunnhee is indicated by a biface and a flake associated with Burial 19F in Mound D and a single flake associated with an isolated cranium (Burial 20) in Mound C (Jefferies 1976).

More than seventy crystal quartz flakes, prismatic blades, cores, and bifaces were found in seven habitation area features, as well as in general midden contexts (fig. 10.5). The numerous crystal quartz artifacts suggest that Tunacunnhee inhabitants were processing crystals at the site to make items for the mortuary rituals. More than 60 percent of the crystal quartz artifacts came from the immediate vicinity of Structures 1 and 2. The two crystal quartz prismatic blades represent the unique blending of nonlocal raw materials and a highly specialized lithic technology.

Mica

Mica is one of the most common and widely distributed exotic raw materials associated with Hopewell mortuary activity, exceeded only by copper and shell (Seeman 1979b:Table 10). Mica artifacts occur as zoomorphic and geometric cutouts (Seeman 1979b:316–317) or more commonly as trimmed mica sheets or mirrors (Seeman 1979b:333). Examples ($n = 8$) of both cutouts and mirrors were found with Tunacunnhee mound burials (Jefferies 1976:26).

Six specimens of mica were found in the Tunacunnhee habitation area features and midden (fig. 10.5). The edges of four specimens appear to have been modified by cutting, perhaps during the manufacture of artifacts found with some of the mound burials. Most of the mica came from feature and midden contexts in the vicinity of Structures 1 and 2.

Copper

Copper artifacts constitute the most common and widely distributed category of "exotic" materials exchanged among Middle Woodland groups, occurring in more than 160 sites throughout eastern North America (Seeman 1979b:Table 10). Copper was used to make many different kinds of artifacts, ranging from ear spools to panpipes. Much of the copper exchanged among Middle Woodland groups came from the Lake Superior region (Seeman 1979b:292), but a small amount may have come from local southeastern sources (Goad 1979: 244). The Tunacunnhee mounds contained at least twenty-nine copper artifacts, most of which were associated with burials (Jefferies 1979).

One small piece of copper was found in the habitation area midden adjacent to Structure 1 (fig. 10.5). The fragment may be part of an awl or a similar pointed implement, or it may simply be residue from artifact production. Similar kinds of copper objects from the Smiling Dan site in Illinois are described as single- and double-pointed awls (Stafford 1985b:176).

Human Remains

The postmortem manipulation of human remains at Tunacunnhee was documented by the recovery of an isolated human cranium and two mandibles from Mound C, as well as a nearby bundle burial (Burial 14) containing the remains of at least six individuals (Jefferies 1976:10, 12). The incorporation of single or multiple human skeletal elements in Hopewell mortuary programs is well documented in both Ohio and Illinois (Buikstra 1979:225–226; Webb and Snow 1945:283–287).

Excavation of one habitation area unit in Block 2 yielded portions of two human skeletal elements (fig. 10.5). Both specimens were found in a general midden context. One specimen was the distal portion of a humerus; the other was a midportion of a tibia. The elements were from one or more adults. The proximity of the skeletal remains to Structures 1 and 2 supports the hypothesis that these two structures were associated with habitation area mortuary rituals. Scattered skeletal elements would be expected in areas where human remains were stored and/or processed for future burial in another location such as a mound (Brown 1979:213; Buikstra 1976:17; McGimsey and Wiant 1986:538–539).

Summary and Conclusions

In summary, a small but significant number of the Tunacunnhee habitation area features and artifacts appears to be associated with preparing either the living or the dead for the mortuary ritual. Most of the artifacts were made from nonlocal raw materials that could have been brought to the site by visiting groups or obtained through interregional trade networks. Many of these same exotic items and materials were placed with the dead buried in the nearby mounds. The spatial distribution of these materials suggests that many of these activities occurred in the vicinity of Structures 1 and 2.

In contrast, other habitation area materials are attributable to more secular domestic activities such as plant and animal procurement and processing and tool production and maintenance. Undoubtedly, the people responsible for processing and disposing of the dead also had to carry out the more mundane activities of daily life while they went about their ritual duties. Thus, ritual tasks comprised only part of the Tunacunnhee habitation area activities, much like at the Napoleon Hollow site in Illinois.

Habitation area mortuary activities may have included manufacturing artifacts to be placed with the dead, processing the bodies of the deceased prior to interment, and possibly (as suggested by the number of large-mammal bones found in some features) ritual feasting. At least some of the habitation area features also appear to have been used by the living while preparing the dead for burial—in particular, Structure 1, the possible sweat house. Structure 2 may have served as a residence or work area for the living while preparing for the mortuary ritual.

The ritual significance of Structures 1 and 2, along with their associated features, is supported by the distribution of exotic materials. The greatest number occurred in the vicinity of these structures, suggesting that this had been the focal point of ritual activity. Associated features also contained a diverse assortment of exotic materials. As at Seip in Ohio and Napoleon Hollow in Illinois, the Tunacunnhee structures may represent workshops where ceremonial and ornamental objects were produced. Scattered human bones found in the vicinity of the Tunacunnhee structures may also be attributable to the processing of bodies for eventual mound burial. While habitation area mortuary activities may have been centered around Structures 1 and 2, exotic materials found in features and midden contexts in other parts of the habitation area suggest that these activities may have been more widespread.

In keeping with Walthall's (1985) proposed "ceremonial encampment" model, the results of the 1998 analysis demonstrate that while the Tunacunnhee mounds were the final resting place of the deceased, important ritual activities associated with the mortuary program were also conducted in the nearby habitation area. The recognition that different components of the Tunacunnhee mortuary program were carried out at spatially discrete locations underscores the organizational and symbolic complexity of Middle Woodland cultural landscapes. The locations and functions of some of these ritual spots, like the burial mounds, are well understood. Other ritual locations are much more ephemeral and very difficult to detect and interpret. Nevertheless, as urged by Buikstra, Charles, and Rakita (1998), if we are to understand fully the spatial, temporal, and symbolic dynamics of Middle Woodland sacred landscapes, we must look beyond the immediate boundaries of the burial site.

Acknowledgments

Special thanks are extended to David Hally and Mark Williams (University of Georgia) for making the Tunacunnhee collections available for analysis and for their hospitality while working in Athens. Figures were prepared by Kary Stackelbeck and Victor Thompson (University of Kentucky). Sissel Schroeder, Bruce Smith, and Victor Thompson provided important comments on earlier drafts of this chapter. A preliminary version of this chapter was presented at the 1998 Southeastern Archaeological Conference in Greenville, South Carolina.

11

Kolomoki

Cycling, Settlement Patterns, and Cultural Change in a Late Middle Woodland Society

Karl T. Steinen

Kolomoki is one of the most interesting and least understood archaeological sites in the southeastern United States. Located about 10 kilometers east of the Chattahoochee River on the bank of Little Kolomoki Creek in Early County, Georgia, this large and complex site was the focus for ceremonial and civic activities during the Woodland period from approximately A.D. 300 to A.D. 750 (fig. 11.1).

What makes Kolomoki so interesting is the fact that it has the appearance of a Mississippian period civic center. Like Mississippian centers, Kolomoki is dominated by a large truncated pyramidal mound. This mound fronts on a plaza that is, in turn, surrounded by an extensive village midden. There are two elaborate burial mounds and at least five smaller mounds at the site. Nevertheless, Kolomoki is from 250 to 600 years too early in time to be a Mississippian site.

Chronology and Culture

The cultural sequence at Kolomoki closely follows that developed by Gordon R. Willey for the eastern Gulf Coastal Plain (Willey 1949). Summarized in table 11.1, this sequence is marked by developments and transitions in ceramic styles. For our discussion the two significant ceramic series, and by extension archaeological cultures, are Swift Creek and Weeden Island. Swift Creek pottery and culture are generally divided into two (Early and Late) or three (Early, Middle, and Late) subperiods based on the surface decoration used and the manner in which the rims of the pots were finished (Caldwell 1958; Kelly and Smith 1975). The earliest Swift Creek pottery had rather small, yet complex, stamp designs, very small tetrapods, and rims that looked like pinched piecrusts. As time progressed the designs became larger, the tetrapods disappeared, and the rims changed to plain and eventually to a folded-in form. Swift Creek sites also contain large percentages of plain pottery and small percentages of simple-stamped ceramics.

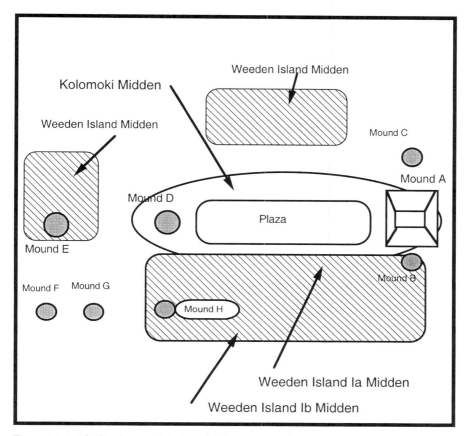

Figure 11.1. Idealized map of Kolomoki showing site features.

At about A.D. 400 a significantly new kind of pottery appeared in southwestern Georgia and adjoining areas of Alabama and Florida. This pottery, called Weeden Island, is decorated with incised and punctated patterns, and it is strikingly similar to the Troyville and Coles Creek pottery of Louisiana (Milanich 2002; Steinen 1976; Willey 1949). Archaeologists have traditionally divided

Table 11.1. Sears and Willey Chronologies

Willey[a]	Sears' Original[b]	Sears' Revised[c]
Lamar	Lamar	Lamar
Weeden Island II	Kolomoki (Swift Creek)	Weeden Island Ib
Weeden Island I	Weeden Island Ib	Weeden Island Ia
Swift Creek	Weeden Island Ia	Kolomoki (Swift Creek)
Deptford	Deptford	Deptford

a. Willey 1949.
b. Sears 1951a, 1956.
c. Sears 1992.

Weeden Island into Early and Late, or I and II. The differences between the two are based on the kinds of pottery found with Weeden Island series ceramics, more than on changes in the Weeden Island series itself. Early Weeden Island (or Weeden Island I) collections have a significant presence of Late Swift Creek and plain pottery, while Late Weeden Island (or Weeden Island II) collections have the complicated-stamped materials replaced by what is called Wakulla Check Stamped. This latter type represents a reappearance of check-stamped materials in southwestern Georgia. Unmarked pottery continues to be found in abundance at Late Weeden Island sites. The use of check stamping seemed to disappear in southwestern Georgia during the Swift Creek and Weeden Island I periods; however, on the Florida Gulf Coast there was never an interruption in its presence, as demonstrated at the Tucker site (Sears 1963).

When William H. Sears conducted his excavations at Kolomoki, he was working during the period of development of ceramic chronologies in the Southeast. He thought that the Swift Creek Complicated Stamped could be divided into additional temporally and spatially sensitive types, including Kolomoki Complicated Stamped, a type that has been used by few other archaeologists. Sears' (1951a, 1956) definition, first presented in his dissertation and later repeated in two monographs, included too many design variations to be reliably used (Steinen 2002). It is possible, however, to identify two stamp designs that are found repeatedly in what are usually considered Weeden Island mounds and in only three village deposits in any number (Steinen 1976). This distribution of two distinctive ceramic motifs, the scroll and the figure eight, as well as their distinctive flat bases, allows us to recognize an important role for this pottery type. I have argued elsewhere that the patterned distribution of Kolomoki Complicated Stamped pottery symbolizes an evolving social/religious elite within the Swift Creek–Weeden Island culture that was focused on the Kolomoki site (Steinen 1976, 1998, 2002).

For close to fifty years Sears disagreed with Willey's sequence and felt that the complicated-stamped materials at Kolomoki were predated by the punctated and incised Weeden Island materials. However, in 1994 he published a retraction and accepted the chronology that everyone else had been using for decades (Sears 1992). His original and revised chronologies are presented in table 11.1.

There is no Deptford at Kolomoki. A few miles to the northwest of Kolomoki, however, is the Mandeville site, a Deptford/Early Swift Creek ceremonial center (Keller, Kelly, and McMichael 1962; B. A. Smith 1975, 1979). This site is important because it predates Kolomoki and is a clear manifestation of Hopewellian ceremonialism on the Chattahoochee River. Sears (1962) has discussed what he terms the Yent and Greenpoint complexes, which are the Hopewell and post-Hopewell ceremonial patterns associated with Deptford and Early Swift Creek cultures, respectively. The Hopewellian inclusion of exotica in burial mounds continues through Weeden Island. Such Hopewell-inspired artifacts as copper ear spools and conch shell dippers are commonly found with Weeden Island burials. The Hopewellian emphasis on certain species of animals, especially waterbirds, is found in the Weeden Island ceramics as well. The classic

Table 11.2. Site Features with Assigned Function and Period of Use

Site Feature	Function	Period
Mound A	Civic/ceremonial	Kolomoki
Mound B	Feasting?	Weeden Island Ia or Ib
Mound C	Unknown	Weeden Island Ia or Ib
Mound D	Burial	Weeden Island Ia
Mound E	Burial	Kolomoki
Mound F	Civic/ceremonial	Weeden Island Ia or Ib
Mound G	Unknown	Unknown
Mound H	Civic/ceremonial	Weeden Island Ia or Ib
Midden	Habitation	Kolomoki/Weeden Island Ia and Ib
Plaza	Civic/ceremonial	Kolomoki
Wall	Ceremonial	Kolomoki/Weeden Island Ia and Ib

Weeden Island effigy vessels are clearly derived from earlier Hopewell styles. Thus, we can think of Swift Creek and Weeden Island ceremonial patterns as linear developments from a Hopewellian foundation.

The final pre-Mississippian occupation of southwestern Georgia is marked by the disappearance of Weeden Island ceramics and a significant increase in Wakulla Check Stamped pottery. Often called the Wakulla period, this is a somewhat odd occurrence: while there are Wakulla middens, there are no pure Wakulla burial mounds. Almost all of what can be considered Late Weeden Island mounds contain Wakulla Check Stamped pots, but there are no mounds that contain this distinctive check stamping to the exclusion of the Weeden Island series materials (Steinen 1976, 2002). This may represent one of several possibilities: the people who were making and using the Wakulla materials in the villages saved Weeden Island pots from earlier times (perhaps hundreds of years) for inclusion in the mounds, they continued to make Weeden Island pots specifically for inclusion in the burial mounds, or there simply were no pure Wakulla mounds constructed.

The Kolomoki Site

Kolomoki was described by nineteenth-century archaeologists (Jones 1873; McKinley 1873; Palmer 1884; Pickett 1851; White 1854), but it was not until the 1940s, when Charles H. Fairbanks (1940a, 1940b, 1941a, 1941b, 1946) conducted some excavations at the site, that it became widely known. Beginning in 1948, Sears (1956) extensively tested the midden and excavated the majority of mounds at the site. More recently, areas of the midden were tested by Johnson (1997) and Pluckhahn (1998, 2000, 2002, 2003). Features of the site are summarized in table 11.2 and shown in figure 11.1.

The total number of mounds at Kolomoki is not certain. It is possible that what is labeled Mound G is not a mound at all. Early investigators report a series of different mounds and an earthen wall surrounding the site that Sears did not relocate. Indications of this wall are clearly visible on aerial photographs, and portions of it were identified by Pluckhahn (2002, 2003). The different mound counts and the probable presence of an earthen wall complicate our understanding of Kolomoki.

The Mounds

Mound A

This imposing earthen structure is 17 meters high and 100 × 60 meters at the base. Its long axis is in a north–south direction, so that it faces west towards Mounds D and E and the oval village area and plaza. The summit of the mound has two distinct surfaces, the southern one being a good 1 meter higher than the northern one.

Sears excavated two test units into Mound A: the first, measuring 10 feet (approximately 3 meters) square, was excavated to a depth of over 2 meters into the southern summit of the mound, and the second, measuring 20 feet by 10 feet (approximately 6 × 3 meters), was placed at the southwest side of the mound at ground level. These units showed that the final cap on the mound was red clay overlaying a white clay layer, the last fully buried layer of the mound. Plain and complicated-stamped pottery in the white layer date that component to the Swift Creek/Kolomoki occupation of the site. The materials in the red clay layer are mixed and represent the full range of occupation of the site. This mixture of materials in the final layer suggests that it was scraped from the midden area.

Mound B

This mound is located about 30 meters south of Mound A and is 15 meters in diameter and 1.5 meters high. Excavations disclosed that the mound included the remains of many large posts, 60 to 75 centimeters in diameter, that had been erected in this area. These posts were set up to 75 to 90 centimeters into the ground, some in V-shaped trenches. This mound does not represent a single construction or ceremony, because there are clear indications of superimposed posts.

Ceramics recovered from this mound include the full range of materials found at the site, as is true for the surrounding areas of midden. This indicates that Mound B was constructed during the last phases of occupation of the site.

Mound C

Mound C is located approximately 90 meters north of Mound A. It is about the same size as Mound B, but its contents are totally different. The eastern half of the mound was completely excavated, a trench was dug through the western half, and the topsoil was stripped off of one of the remaining sections. The interior of the mound consists of basket loads of red and yellow clay, topsoil, midden, and white sand. There were no discernible patterns to this loading, and the fact that there were no developed soils on the interior of the mound demonstrates that it was constructed in a single episode. Most of the pottery recovered from the excavations was plain and complicated stamped, although there were a few sherds from the Weeden Island series present. This demonstrates that Mound C, like Mound B, was constructed during the final occupation of the site.

Mound D

This is an extremely large and complex burial mound that Sears believed was the product of a single continuous ceremony. At the time of excavation in 1950 and 1951, it was 6 meters high and had a diameter of 30 meters. There are four recognizable building stages, numerous burials, cremations, rock slabs, and a deposit of elaborate ceramic vessels, many of which are in the form of stylized animals.

Mound E

Mound E is the second burial mound at Kolomoki. It is located about 275 meters west of Mound A and in almost a direct line with Mound D. About the only structural similarities that Mound D has with Mound E are that both are conical in shape, have east-side ceramic deposits, and contain rock slabs as part of their internal structures.

The most impressive feature of this mound is the central burial pit. Sears described this 2-meter-deep pit as funnel-shaped with vertical walls in its lower half (Sears 1951b). The lower portion of the pit was approximately 2 × 3 meters in size. On the floor of the pit was a thoroughly cremated skeleton. Included in the mound were several other burials, individual skulls, and numerous Hopewell-derived artifacts, including a copper ear spool.

Mound F

This mound is located over 120 meters south of Mound E. At the time of excavations it was 2 meters high and measured 15 × 18 meters. Only a few artifacts, all assignable to the final occupation of the site, were recovered from Mound F. However, the excavations showed that the mound had been constructed in two distinct phases. The first was a 9-meter-square flat-topped white clay mound that was about 1 meter high. Interestingly, this core mound had an interior of soft black humus that was covered by only a thin layer of white clay. The final cap of the mound was red clay that seems to have originated from the area immediately around the primary mound.

Mound G

This mound, just to the east of Mound F, was not excavated. It was used as a cemetery for Mercier Plantation.

Mound H

This mound is approximately 120 meters south of Mound D and is structurally similar to Mound G. In this case the interior mound is made of yellow clay, and the final cap (like that of Mound G) was derived from the midden surrounding the mound. There was, however, no soft humus similar to that in Mound F.

The Midden and Plaza

The midden at Kolomoki has been ravaged by years of plowing and sheet erosion. The plow zone extends to a depth of approximately 15 centimeters below the current ground level. The only undisturbed midden was found in what appear to be shallow dips or depressions in the original ground surface.

Careful surface collection and test trenches show that the midden has three distinct areas. The first is an oval ring that extends from the north and south sides of Mound A to beyond Mound D, the second is a vacant plaza area surrounded by the oval midden, and the third is mixed with the southern and northern sides of the oval midden. The southern portion of the last midden extends outside of the boundaries of the park. The midden is rich with pottery and has remarkably well preserved animal bone in it. Sears' excavations did not uncover any indications of houses or subsurface storage pits. In the late 1990s, Pluckhahn conducted an extensive shovel testing of Kolomoki that was supplemented by formal test excavations. He was able to identify and excavate a house with a central hearth that dated to the earlier stages of the occupation of the site (Pluckhahn 2002:251; Pluckhahn 2003).

Sears' (1956) work provided only a glimpse at the economic patterns at Kolomoki. Results of the more recent excavations suggest that there was little if any significant change in the use of faunal and floral materials through time (Pluckhahn 2002, 2003). I have suggested (Steinen 1998), based on comparative data from the south and north of Kolomoki, that there may have been a form of dispersed maize horticulture practiced at the site, although the only direct evidence for this are a few fragments of maize (Pluckhahn 2002:274, Table 5–7).

The Wall

An analysis of aerial photographs coupled with ground truthing has documented the presence of a low earthen wall surrounding Kolomoki (Pluckhahn 2002, 2003). This wall was mentioned and mapped by earlier archaeologists (for example, Jones 1873), but it was not located by Sears. Similar earthen walls have been found at Hopewell sites in the Midwest and Florida. The embankment at Kolomoki probably served to delineate the entire site as a sacred area, as was apparently the case for the Hopewell enclosures (Sears 1982).

Site Reconstruction

It is possible to reconstruct how and when different parts of the Kolomoki site were occupied and used.

Initial Phase of Occupation: Kolomoki

The Kolomoki occupation of the site is associated with the oval midden, Mound A, and Mound E. The exact function of Mound A is not known. Other than lacking a ramp on its front (west) side, it is similar to truncated pyramidal mounds found at Mississippian civic centers. Historically, these kinds of mounds were the residences of chiefs, the foci of community activities, and, often, the locations of charnel houses. Smaller truncated pyramidal mounds are found at other Woodland sites, the closest being Mandeville (Kellar, Kelly, and McMichael 1962; B. A. Smith 1975). If the people who lived at Kolomoki built Mound A, we can assume that some form of village occupation preceded the mound construction. Whether Mound A was the residence of a ceremonial/political leader or had some other function cannot be determined at this time, but its sheer size and geometric regularity was the product of prodigious coordinated work activities.

The overall community plan—the midden, plaza, and Mound A—indicates that the focus of the everyday lives of the people was inward, toward the community. The size and complexity of Mounds A and E, as well as the regularity of the midden at this time, indicate that the Kolomoki society was well organized (Sears 1968). To construct mounds as large, regular in shape, and with the internal complexity of Mounds D and E, the social leadership must have been able to muster and direct a substantial work force. In the past this kind of social leadership and site plan has been attributed to chiefly or near-chiefly status of the political leadership (Sears 1968; Steinen 1976); in recent years, however, it has been recognized that complex burials and platform mounds can be the product of nonchiefdom societies (Milanich 2002; Milanich et al. 1984; Pluckhahn 2002, 2003).

Second Phase of Occupation: Weeden Island I

There is a significant shift in the use of the site at the conclusion of the Kolomoki phase occupation, as shown by the abandonment of a site plan centered on the plaza. If Sears' test data for Mound A are accurate and it was not used after the Kolomoki phase occupation, and if Mound D represents the ceremonial climax of this phase at the site, then the Weeden Island I occupation represents a significant shift in community organization and the beginning of a decentralization in sociopolitical authority.

The earliest Weeden Island occupation of the site, labeled Weeden Island Ia by Sears, is found along the southern side of the oval midden. There is a second Weeden Island occupation that Sears called Weeden Island Ib, also found to the south of the oval midden, overlapping the Weeden Island Ia materials and continuing south to the earthen wall that surrounded the site. Plain and Weeden Island sherds, and an absence of Swift Creek materials, mark this occupation. This Weeden Island I occupation is found to the north and northwest of the now-abandoned plaza area as well (Johnson 1997; Pluckhahn 2000, 2002, 2003). These Weeden Island midden areas are organized very differently from the Kolomoki midden. The most important difference is that there is not a central plaza that could have served as the focus for community activities.

Site Deconstruction: Three Traditions and Culture Change

How can we understand this transformation in the site plan of Kolomoki? As far as we can tell, except for the change in the community plan, there was little if any discernable change in the everyday lives of the people at Kolomoki. In the past, most archaeologists tended to look at Weeden Island life as a monolithic village/ political/religious tradition. Sears (1973) has, however, presented a model of a sacred/secular dichotomy in Weeden Island ceramics in which there is a distinct difference between the ceramics found in mounds and middens, especially in peninsular Florida. This dichotomy can be thought of as representing two different traditions in the cultural development of Weeden Island, not just a difference in ceramics. I suggest that there is a third, political, tradition that functioned alongside the sacred and secular. This tripartite division of the culture is similar to Binford's (1962) technomic/sociotechnic/ideotechnic distinction, with the village tradition corresponding to the technomic, the political tradition corresponding to the sociotechnic, and the religious tradition corresponding to the ideotechnic system.

Using the idea of three parallel and overlapping social traditions at Kolomoki, one can understand how village life could continue for over half a millennium with little real change, while the sacred and political systems underwent dramatic shifts during the same period. Pre-urban secular traditions are remarkably resistant to change, while their corresponding political and sacred traditions can and do take on significant new patterns within relatively short periods of time (Redfield 1953). The long-standing, and thoroughly documented, village tradition of the Woodland period at Kolomoki and throughout the eastern Gulf Coastal Plain was overlain by a religious tradition with its roots in Hopewell that had a strong pattern of development into the Mississippian period (Anderson 1998:296). This, in turn, was intertwined with a sinuous development of political organization that saw the growth and then decline of chiefdom or chiefdomlike structures at Mandeville, Kolomoki, and other Middle and terminal Middle Woodland societies in the Southeast (Milanich 2002; Steinen 1976, 1998, 2002). The suggested relationships of these three traditions are shown in figure 11.2. The technological overlap, in the form of artifacts and symbols, is clearly seen in the ceramics in both secular and sacred contexts of the Woodland cultures (Sears 1973). While there is a significant difference between midden (secular) and mound (sacred) collections, there are also striking similarities. For instance, Swift Creek and Weeden Island pots and sherds are found in both contexts. Effigy pots are generally confined to the mounds, while sherds from similar vessels are often encountered in middens. This latter example may represent vestiges of burial ceremonies that saw the breaking or "killing" of the pots in the village areas before they were included in the burial mounds.

The relationship of the Kolomoki Complicated Stamped pottery with the secular and religious traditions is clear (Steinen 2002). The scroll and figure-eight motifs associated with Kolomoki Complicated Stamped ceramics (Sears 1956) are found in association with most, if not all, of the east-side deposit

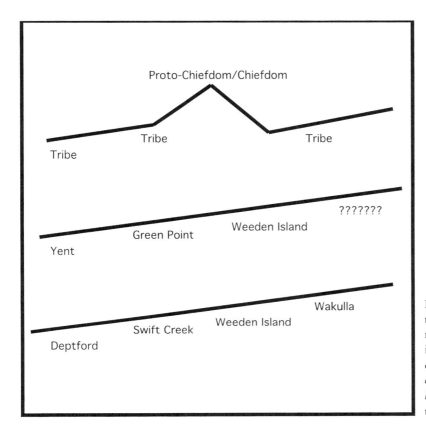

Figure 11.2. Proposed trajectories of development of the three traditions. *Top*: political organization; *middle*: ceremonial traditions; *bottom*: secular village traditions.

mounds found on the panhandle coast of Florida and in southern Georgia and Alabama (Sears 1956, 1992; Steinen 1976, 2002). These mounds present the full range of Late Swift Creek and Weeden Island sacred deposits and far outlive the Late Swift Creek village tradition. As Kolomoki evolved as a spiritual center (and possibly as the focus for chiefly activities) and then declined, the Kolomoki Complicated Stamped vessels served as the visual reference for this religious hegemony at Kolomoki and other locales. After Kolomoki declined, the regional historical and spiritual ties to this site and the sacred tradition that had been centered there were maintained by having the scroll and figure-eight designs present on either whole pots or sherds that were included in the mounds, sometimes in what can be considered symbolic burials at the center of the mounds (Steinen 1987, 2002). Thus the village tradition continued; the political tradition cycled; and the religious tradition developed and changed, not only at Kolomoki, but also across the eastern portion of the Gulf Coastal Plain.

This Kolomoki-dominated religious hegemony that I have suggested did not exist across the Weeden Island world (fig. 11.3). Peninsular Florida has significantly different patterns than those found along the Chattahoochee and the panhandle coast of Florida. This is best shown by the excavations of the McKeithen site in Lake County, Florida (Milanich et al. 1984). McKeithen, like Kolomoki, has a plaza/midden/mound community plan, but complicated-

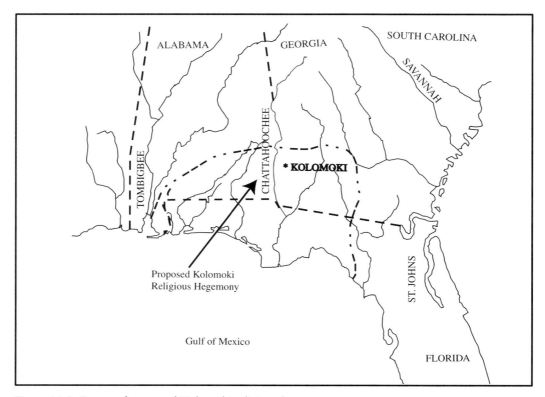

Figure 11.3. Extent of proposed Kolomoki religious hegemony.

stamped ceramics, especially Kolomoki Complicated Stamped, are conspicuously underrepresented in both the mounds and the midden. Indeed, the McKeithen burial mound, Mound C, appears to have burials on its east, south, and southwest sides, and it does not have the distinctive east-side ceramic deposit that is characteristic of the heartland of Weeden Island (Milanich et al. 1984:112–117). Farther south along the coast of Florida, south of the Warrior River, Weeden Island mounds are what Sears calls continuous-use mounds that represent the long-term addition of burials and burial furniture. Complicated-stamped ceramics of any kind are absent from both mound and midden contexts in this area (Milanich 2002; Sears 1973; Steinen 1976). Milanich (2002) presents a more detailed discussion of the regional differences in Weeden Island culture, but he does not emphasize the role of complicated-stamped ceramics.

Summary

We know that the earliest occupation of Kolomoki was also its most complex. We know that Kolomoki and Weeden Island ceremonialism is a development of Hopewell. We know that there are no Late Woodland period ceremonial centers in southwestern Georgia. But we do not know why. Did Kolomoki, and by extension Woodland ceremonialism, have such a marked decline because its preagricultural base was not able to support the large and extensive populations needed for chiefdoms (Kohler 1991)? Was there a substantial flaw in the presumed kin-based social system that did not allow for a continued development of a system that was approaching chiefly status (Milanich 2002; Milanich et al. 1984)? Was there a Late Woodland breakdown in all-important regional exchange systems that provided the exotic materials that were fundamental to Hopewell and post-Hopewell ceremonialism?

Our understanding of the complexities of the Woodland period is really just beginning. The historical relationships between the Midwest and the Southeast are fully documented in the presence of Hopewellian ceremonialism. Unlike the post-Hopewell Midwest, elaborate ceremonialism continued to develop and thrive in southwestern Georgia, where Kolomoki was the focus of continued religious and political development. Kolomoki lasted for perhaps 450 years, but its legacy continued into the development of Mississippian culture. The work by Johnson (1997) and Pluckhahn (1998, 2000, 2002, 2003) in the village area of Kolomoki has added much-needed detail to our understanding of this enigmatic site. Syntheses by Anderson (1998), Anderson and Mainfort (2002a), Bense (1998), Milanich (2002), Percy and Brose (1974), Snow (1998), Steinen (1998), and Stephenson, Bense, and Snow (2002) provide new and exciting interpretative and analytical models to our understanding of the Woodland period in southwestern Georgia and adjacent areas. Yet none of these studies has managed to effectively account for the similarities in ceramic inclusions in the total range of what are recognized as Weeden Island mounds. By recognizing that the figure-eight and scroll designs may be directly linked to a post-Hopewell religious hegemony focused on the Kolomoki site, we can begin to unravel the intricacies of late Middle Woodland life in the eastern reaches of the Gulf Coastal Plain.

Acknowledgments

This chapter resulted from many years of working on problems of Woodland life and politics in Georgia and Florida. It benefited from countless conversations with the late Bill Sears, as well as Jerry Milanich, Lew Larson, Tom Pluckhahn, Tim Kohler, and Pete Provost. Part of this work was supported by the National Science Foundation (NSF Grant #9512651). All errors of fact or interpretation are, naturally, my own.

12

The Mann Phase

Hopewellian Community Organization in the Wabash Lowland

Bret J. Ruby

Over the past thirty years, the horizons of Hopewellian archaeology have expanded from an almost exclusive focus on mound and earthwork centers to a view that includes the domestic activities and habitations of those who built and used the earthworks—a view that encompasses entire Hopewellian communities. This chapter examines the spatial and functional organization of one such community in the Wabash Lowland, a little-known region of the Hopewellian world centered on the confluence of the Wabash and Ohio rivers.

The Wabash Lowland lies at the geographic midpoint between Illinois and Ohio, the centers of two of the most flamboyant expressions of Hopewellian culture in the Eastern Woodlands. Unfortunately, this region has not enjoyed the same focus of Hopewellian research. The examination of this little-known region will contribute to our understanding of interregional variation in Hopewellian settlement, subsistence, ceremonialism, and community organization, a necessary prerequisite to moving beyond simplistic and normative understandings of Woodland period cultural change (Seeman 1992b).

Hopewellian Communities

Bruce Smith (1992a) has developed a general model of Hopewellian communities. Smith's model emphasizes the spatial and functional division of Hopewellian communities into two distinct contexts: the "corporate-ceremonial" and "domestic" spheres of Hopewellian life. The corporate-ceremonial sphere is the theater of corporate action and ceremonial integration—the stage of symbolism, ritual, politics, and status. The domestic sphere is the province of everyday life—the field of subsistence production and consumption. The corporate-ceremonial sphere stands at the literal and figurative core of Hopewellian community life, played out and expressed in a variety of contexts: mounds and mortuary facilities, geometric earthwork centers, and an assortment of nonresidential buildings. By comparison, the domestic sphere is scaled down in size and complexity and is played out in the context of households, hamlets, and short-term extractive camps dispersed around the corporate-ceremonial centers of the community. Smith finds little evidence for domestic occupations exceeding three house-holds in size, though when these are considered together with the monumental corporate-ceremonial centers, it is evident that communities encompassed a much larger, but dispersed, population. Smith argues that these communities were supported by food-production economies based on indigenous domesti-cated and cultivated seed plants.

Smith's model was developed using data drawn primarily from three regions: west-central Illinois, south-central Tennessee, and the American Bottom. This chapter will examine data from the Wabash Lowland as a comparison.

The Mann Phase Occupation of the Lower Wabash–Ohio River Region

Regional Environmental Context

The study area is coterminous with the Wabash Lowland physiographic zone, a region characterized by low, rolling, loess-mantled uplands and broad alluvial valleys traversed by meandering streams (Fidlar 1948). This area marks the beginning of the lower Ohio Valley as a distinct environmental zone. This por-tion of the Ohio Valley is distinguished from the middle Ohio by its meandering course, significantly broader floodplain, well-developed valley-margin terraces, and extensive backwater oxbow lake and slough development. These same characteristics distinguish the lower Wabash Valley from its upstream reaches.

It has often been noted that the ecology of the Wabash Lowland has a south-ern rather than midwestern cast. It represents the northeasternmost extension of a relatively mild climatic and hydrologic regime characteristic of the extreme lower Ohio Valley and the northern portions of the lower Mississippi Valley. That these factors had significant adaptive consequences is borne out by the observation that the range of several plants, animals, and prehistoric cultures reach their northeasternmost extreme here (Adams 1949; Green and Munson 1978; Higgenbotham 1983; Redmond 1990).

Table 12.1 presents some comparative climatic data drawn from stations located near the lower Illinois Valley (White Hall, Illinois), the Cairo Lowlands at the Ohio-Mississippi confluence (Cairo, Illinois), the Wabash Lowland (Evansville, Indiana), the middle Ohio Valley (Portsmouth/Sciotoville, Ohio) and the central Scioto Valley (Circleville, Ohio). In terms of mean annual tem-perature (a crude measure of annual biotic productivity), mean January tem-perature (a measure of cold-season stress), and growing-season rainfall (a mea-sure of agricultural potential), the Wabash Lowland is most similar to the Cairo Lowlands. By contrast, the lower Illinois Valley, mid-Ohio Valley, and central Scioto Valley are less productive, more stressful during the cold season, and drier through the growing season. The median length of the growing season in the Wabash Lowland is again most similar to that of the Cairo Lowlands and exceeds the lower Illinois Valley, mid-Ohio Valley, and central Scioto Valley values by two to four weeks. Differences of these magnitudes could certainly play a role in explaining interregional cultural variability (Maslowski and Seeman 1992; Ruby, Carr, and Charles 2005).

Table 12.1. Comparative Climate Data

Region	Mean Annual Temperature °F	Mean January Temperature °F	Median Growing Season Days (32°F base)	Rainfall, Inches (Apr–Jun)	Rainfall, Inches (Jul–Sep)
White Hall, Ill.	52.0	24.2	185	11.09	10.28
Cairo, Ill.	59.0	33.4	233	14.65	11.70
Evansville, Ind.	57.3	32.3	200	13.74	11.55
Portsmouth/ Sciotoville, Ohio	54.3	30.2	186	11.33	11.69
Circleville, Ohio	51.7	26.6	172	11.62	11.30

Source: Historical archives of the Midwestern Climate Center, Champaign, Illinois, http://mcc.sws.uiuc.edu.

Material Culture

The Mann phase represents the later of two Hopewellian manifestations in the lower Wabash area. Mann phase material culture is best known from assemblages excavated by Kellar (1979) in the 1960s and 1970s at the Mann site, located on the north bank of the Ohio River, about 15 kilometers east of the mouth of the Wabash. Stylistic considerations and a small series of radiocarbon dates place the Mann phase between about A.D. 100 and A.D. 500.

Mann phase ceramics are predominantly thin-walled cordmarked and plain jars, often with restricted necks and notched lips, and tempered with grog, limestone, and fine grit or sand. Braun and others (Braun 1983, 1987; Hargrave 1982) have documented a clear directional trend in the technological evolution of Woodland period ceramics in Illinois toward vessels designed to facilitate efficient long-term boiling and to withstand the associated thermal stresses. Vessel shape, wall thickness, and the type, size, and density of temper particles all converge on attribute states that promote efficient heat transfer and high resistance to thermal shock. This trend is correlated with the rising importance of cultivated and domesticated starchy seeds in midcontinental subsistence strategies (Braun 1987; Smith 1992a). The globular shapes, thin walls, and fine grog and limestone tempers displayed by these Mann phase vessels all reflect a technology that is well adapted to efficient long-term boiling, and it is reasonable to suggest that considerable quantities of starchy seeds were processed through them.

The decorated portion of the assemblage is dominated by a variety of distinctively Hopewellian techniques and motifs. Zoned and stamped ceramics occur at relatively high frequencies, but unzoned rocker stamping applied rather sloppily over the entire vessel surface is the most common decorative technique. This, along with brushed surface treatments, ally the assemblage with other late Hopewellian assemblages represented by the Pike and Baehr series in Illinois and Chillicothe Rocker Stamped and Chillicothe Brushed ceramics in Ohio.

The most distinctive aspect of the Mann phase ceramic assemblage is the frequent occurrence of decorative types more commonly known from the Southeast. These include a variety of carved paddle-stamped and footed vessels usually associated with Caldwell's (1958) Southern Appalachian tradition.

Most of these are complicated stamped, of which the vast majority display curvilinear motifs. Rectilinear designs occur in the minority. Two simple-stamped types are also well represented. The most common variety has fine, shallow, and closely spaced grooves, often resembling brushing. The other variety has wide lands and deep grooves. Tetrapodal supports on plain, cordmarked, and simple-stamped vessels have also been recovered.

Complicated-stamped ceramics occur more frequently in the Mann phase than in any other cultural unit in the Ohio Valley. In fact, complicated-stamped ceramics represent the second most common decorative treatment in the assemblage, after unzoned rocker stamping. Stylistically, these Mann site examples are most similar to the Swift Creek manifestations of central and southern Georgia. Attributes of paste and temper make it clear, however, that these vessels are locally produced and not imports (Rein 1974; Ruby and Shriner 2000).

Simple stamping has a less restricted spatial, temporal, and quantitative distribution in the Ohio Valley. It forms a minor constituent of many Early and Middle Woodland assemblages in Ohio and Kentucky, and it is a major constituent of Middle and Late Woodland assemblages in the central Wabash Valley. While much of this material is undoubtedly locally produced in the Ohio Valley region, one type, Turner Simple Stamped B (characterized by narrow lands and grooves resembling brushing), has been identified in Ohio Hopewell assemblages as an import from the Appalachian Summit (Chapman and Keel 1979; Griffin 1983a; Keel 1976, n.d.; Prufer 1965, 1968). Analyses of attributes of paste and temper in the Mann site simple-stamped assemblage have also identified a similar fine-spaced variety as an import from the same region (Ruby and Shriner 2000). The wide-spaced variety appears to be a local product.

Lowe Cluster and Steuben expanding-stem bifaces are diagnostic of the Mann phase in the lower Wabash area, as are large trianguloid Copena Cluster bifaces. All of these types are characteristic of late Middle Woodland and early Late Woodland assemblages dating after about A.D. 100–200 (Justice 1987).

Lamellar blades are a ubiquitous element of Mann phase lithic technology. In terms of blade width, platform dimensions, and platform preparation techniques, lamellar blades from Mann phase contexts are indistinguishable from the Ohio Hopewell prepared blade and core industry defined by Greber, Davis, and DuFresne (1981). This distinctive tradition is readily distinguishable from Havana tradition "Fulton technique" blade technology in Illinois (Montet-White 1968) and the earlier Middle Woodland Crab Orchard tradition blade industries in the lower Wabash area (Ruby 1997b).

Subsistence

Archaeobotanical assemblages from two sites point to a well-developed pre-maize agricultural system at the core of the Mann phase subsistence economy. In two samples from the Mann site itself, about 80 percent of the identifiable seeds belong to one of four starchy seeded annual plants believed to have been cultivated in midwestern pre-maize agricultural systems: maygrass (*Phalaris caroliniana*), goosefoot (*Chenopodium* sp.), knotweed (*Polygonum* sp.), and

Table 12.2. Middle Woodland Period Seed:Nutshell Ratios

Region Site	Nut:Wood Ratio[a]	Seeds/Gram Nutshell	Source
American Bottom			
Mund[b]	1.30	9.2	Johannessen 1988; Parker 1989
Holding[c]	0.60	135.3	Parker 1989
Truck #7[c,d]	0.40	34.2	Johannessen 1988; Parker 1989
Lower Illinois Valley			
Smiling Dan[d,e]	0.78	24.3	D. Asch and N. Asch 1985b
Massey and Archie[d,e]	0.19	24.1	D. Asch and N. Asch 1985a
Napoleon Hollow[d,e]	0.09	6.7	N. Asch and D. Asch 1986
Wabash Lowland			
Grabert[d,e]	0.06	168.8	Ruby 1993, 1997b
South-Central Illinois			
Consol	na	3.1	Hargrave and Butler 1993
11WM100	na	6.7	Hargrave and Butler 1993
Thomas Fox	na	25.3	Hargrave and Butler 1993
Mollie Baker	na	4.7	Hargrave and Butler 1993
Eleven other Crab Orchard sites	na	<2.0	Hargrave and Butler 1993

a. Ratio of fragments in >2 mm fraction.
b. Total seeds/total nutshell.
c. Total seeds/total nutshell, posthole samples excluded.
d. Nutshell weight for each sample estimated by (% nutshell in >2 mm fraction) × (sample weight).
e. Raw data standardized to equal sediment volumes for each sample prior to making calculation.

little barley (*Hordeum pusillum*). Cucurbit rind fragments are present in both samples as well. A larger and more extensively quantified assemblage is available from the Grabert site, a small Mann phase occupation described below, where more than 80 percent of the identifiable seeds represent cultivated or domesticated plants: sunflower (*Helianthus annuus*), maygrass, goosefoot, knotweed, and little barley.

A common relative measure of the degree to which the subsistence economies of various populations have shifted from a focus on nut resources to the intensive collection and production of seed crops is the ratio of the number of seeds to grams of nutshell in archaeobotanical assemblages. In table 12.2, the Grabert site assemblage is compared to several well-documented Middle Woodland period archaeobotanical assemblages. The Grabert site seed to nutshell ratio is a remarkably high 168.8 seeds per gram of nutshell, the highest value reported for any of the sites in the sample. The density of seeds per liter of fill processed is equal to or greater than all of the contemporary assemblages reported from the American Bottom, west-central and south-central Illinois, and central Ohio (Ruby 1997b:459–464).

A related measure of the importance of nut resources is the ratio of nutshell fragments to wood fragments. Johannessen (1988), using data from forty-eight site components in the American Bottom, has documented a clear decline in mean nut to wood ratios from a high of 6.1:1 in the Late Archaic to a low of 0.1:1 during the Emergent Mississippian. This trend apparently reflects a shift in subsistence focus from nut resources to cultivated seed crops. The nut to wood ratio for the Grabert site assemblage is a remarkably low 0.06:1, which is comparable to values not reached in the American Bottom until the Emergent Mississippian, and lower than any of the Middle Woodland samples reported in table 12.2.

Finally, both fall harvest and spring harvest seeds often co-occur in the same contexts at both Mann and Grabert. This suggests the use of storage as an intensification strategy within the Mann phase subsistence system.

Settlement Variability

Until recently, only a handful of components in the Wabash Lowland were recognized as related to the Mann site, linked by the presence of complicated-stamped ceramics. It has recently been possible to identify a total of fifty-one related components in the Wabash Lowland of southwestern Indiana by focusing on the distinctive attributes of the undecorated ceramic assemblage from the Mann site (Ruby 1993, 1997b). This same study identified an additional sixty components bearing temporally diagnostic Lowe and Copena Cluster bifaces and/or the distinctive "Ohio style" lamellar blades and blade cores characteristic of the Mann site blade assemblage. These 111 components, plus one additional mound site, are now recognized as components of the Mann phase occupation of southwestern Indiana. To date, funding considerations have not permitted a search for Mann phase components beyond the Indiana side of the Wabash and Ohio rivers. This is not a serious limitation, as there is every reason to believe that the Indiana side encompasses the full range of variability in environment and settlement types that would be encountered if the analysis were extended across the rivers into Illinois and Kentucky.

Three site types—households or hamlets, short-term extractive camps, and corporate-ceremonial centers—subsume most of the functional variability in Mann phase settlements. The Mann site stands in a class by itself and cannot be relegated exclusively to either the corporate-ceremonial or the domestic sphere. It is distinguished from the other classes by its size, intensity of occupation, and complexity as measured by investment in mound and earthwork construction, the quantity and diversity of exotica present, and the range of activities evident.

The Mann Site

The Mann site (12PO2) is located on a high flat terrace overlooking an extensive backwater slough and a broad expanse of Ohio River floodplain, about 20 kilometers upstream from the Wabash River confluence. The site consists of a series of geometric earthworks, mounds, and an extensive habitation area (fig. 12.1). The total site complex covers an area of about 175 hectares.

Corporate-Ceremonial Contexts. A series of aerial photographs, limited field observations, and amateur excavations reveal something of the nature and magnitude of corporate-ceremonial sphere contexts at the Mann site. Two rectangular enclosures dominate the western edge of the site. One (IU 2) is a three-sided

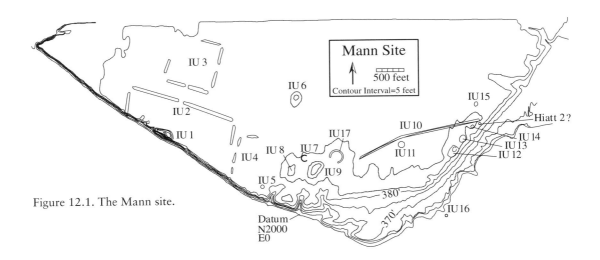

Figure 12.1. The Mann site.

rectangular enclosure 600 meters long and 300 meters wide, opening on Cypress Slough to the south. The other work (IU 3) is a regular square, the maximum length of each side closely approximating 310 meters. The corners of this work and the midpoints of each of the sides are marked by openings or gateways approximately 15 meters wide. The basic design of this square enclosure is duplicated at ten other Hopewellian mound and earthwork complexes (Squier and Davis 1848). With the exception of the enclosure at the Mann site, all such squares are limited to the Ohio region. These squares range in size from 243 to 360 meters on a side and cluster tightly around a mean length of 307 meters (standard deviation = 36 meters). Five of the works in Ross County, Ohio, are identical in size and are integrated within larger tripartite enclosure complexes.

Located within the larger rectangular enclosure is a very large loaf-shaped mound (IU 1). Nothing is known about the contents of this mound. The central portion of the site is dominated by two large rectangular flat-topped mounds (IU 8 and 9), two C-shaped embankments (IU 7 and 17), and another large conical mound (IU 6). The eastern portion of the site contains a linear embankment (IU 10) stretching some 700 meters, as well as five smaller conical mounds (IU 12-15, Hiatt 2). A small circular enclosure is located along an intermittent stream defining the eastern edge of the site complex (IU 16). These structures obviously represent a tremendous investment of corporate labor. In fact, two of the Mann site mounds rank among the five largest Middle Woodland mounds in the Midwest, the others being the Mann phase GE mound in Indiana, and Hopewell Mound 25 and the Seip-Pricer Mound, both in Ross County, Ohio.

None of the Mann site mounds has been explored professionally. We do have two written accounts documenting amateur and antiquarian explorations in the largest of the flat-topped mounds and in several of the smaller conical structures (Hiatt n.d.; Lacer n.d.). The excavations in the large flat-topped mound (IU 9) indicate that this structure served as a stage for ceremonial activities not directly associated with the burial of the dead. There were at least three horizontal sand floors located at intervals well above the base of the mound. These strata were active surfaces, as they are associated with several post molds (though no obvious pattern was documented); middenlike deposits of charcoal, burned bone, lithic debris, and broken pottery; and eight shallow, basin-shaped pit features. These pits contained a variety of exotic raw materials and finished artifacts indicative of nonmortuary ceremonialism (including galena, crystal quartz, obsidian, mica, engraved bone, drilled canines, turtle shell fragments, ceramic vessels, and more), most of which had been subjected to intense fire or mechanical breakage. There is also some evidence that feasting may have been one of the activities associated with the sand floors and pit features located within this mound. Several of these contexts produced evidence of burned and unburned animal bone and charred nuts and seeds. Burned material from one of these pits produced a radiocarbon date of A.D. 420 ±45 (Kellar 1979:DIC-1017, uncalibrated).

Platform mounds are rare in Middle Woodland contexts but not entirely unknown. Similar structures have been reported from at least two sites in south-central Ohio, Ginther and Marietta (N'omi Greber, personal communication 1996; Pickard 1996; Prufer 1968:41–45; Shetrone 1925; Squier and Davis 1848:73–77). Limited testing in one of the Marietta mounds recently yielded a Middle Woodland artifact assemblage in association with charred material radiocarbon dated to the second and third centuries A.D. (Beta-78012: 1670 ±60 rcybp; Beta-78013: 1790 ±50 rcybp; Beta-78014: 1660 ±60 rcybp). The internal structure of this mound revealed a series of prepared horizontal activity floors composed of thin lenses of clays, sands, and gravels similar to those documented in Mann Mound IU 9 (N'omi Greber, personal communication 1996; Pickard 1996). Middle Woodland platform mounds have also been reported from several locations in the mid-South and the lower Mississippi Valley: Johnston in western Tennessee (Kwas and Mainfort 1986), Ingomar in northeastern Mississippi (Rafferty 1983, 1987), Walling in Alabama (Knight 1990), Leist in the Yazoo basin (Phillips 1970:368–369), and Marksville in the lower Mississippi Valley (Toth 1974).

The most extensive and best-documented series of Middle Woodland platform mounds is found at Pinson Mounds in western Tennessee (Mainfort 1986; Mainfort and Walling 1992; Mainfort, Broster, and Johnson 1982). The Pinson Mounds complex contains at least twelve mounds, an ovoid embankment some 350 meters in diameter (one of a very few geometric earthworks outside of Ohio), and several associated Middle Woodland habitation areas. In total, the complex covers some 160 hectares. As such, Pinson and Mann are the largest and most complex Middle Woodland centers outside of Ohio.

At least six of the mounds at Pinson (Mounds 5, 9, 10, 15, 28, and 29) are flat-topped platform mounds (Mainfort 1986). Three of these mounds (Mounds 5, 10, and 28) have been systematically investigated. These platform mounds at Pinson are similar to the large platform mound at Mann in terms of shape (generally rectangular), construction (multiple stages, each surmounted by one or more horizontal sand floors or other activity areas), and the incorporated features (basin-shaped pits and middenlike deposits) and cultural materials (charcoal, burned bone, lithic debris, and broken pottery). Radiocarbon dates from the Pinson mound platforms suggest a period of use and construction in the first three centuries A.D. (Mainfort 1986; Mainfort and Walling 1992).

Importantly, there is little evidence to suggest that the ceremonialism indicated at the large platform mound at Mann or the platform mounds at Pinson was directly related to mortuary activities. This nonmortuary ceremonialism may have promoted integrative functions that crosscut social divisions based on kinship. Rather than burials and associated funerary objects, charcoal, burned soil, fire-cracked rock, animal bone, ceramics, and lithic debris characterize these platform mound deposits at Mann and Pinson. These sorts of deposits are more typical of domestic occupations, suggesting that food processing, consumption, and discard were important elements in the ceremonial activities conducted at the mound.

The smaller conical mounds at the eastern extreme of the Mann site are more clearly associated with mortuary activity. At least one of these mounds contained a central log-lined crypt surrounded by earthen ramparts (Lacer n.d.). This facility apparently served as the focus for a mortuary program involving extended manipulation and processing of the dead. Within and surrounding the facility were at least fifty-seven burials: eighteen extended burials, thirty-two disarticulated reburials, six cremations, and one flexed burial. Both adults and children are represented, and about one-half of the burials were accompanied by grave goods including copper ear spools, marine shell and freshwater pearl beads, cut and drilled bear canines, and a variety of other exotica. Data from the other small conical mounds are more limited but are consistent with this same pattern. The small scale of these facilities and their clear association with mortuary activity suggests a very different sort of ceremonialism than that represented by the geometric earthworks and platform mounds at the site.

In addition to the finished artifacts, debitage resulting from the manufacture of artifacts from exotic raw materials is not at all rare in nonmound contexts at the Mann site. At least twenty-six different Hopewell Interaction Sphere commodities (raw materials and finished artifacts) are represented. Only 5 of the 242 sites reviewed by Seeman (1979b) contained a comparable diversity.

Domestic Contexts. The most unique characteristic of the Mann site, relative to the other major Hopewell centers, is the areal extent and density of midden deposits. Surface surveys and midden stains visible in aerial photographs document dense habitation debris covering an area of at least 40 hectares. Some fraction of this total is attributable to a Late Prehistoric (Caborn-Welborn phase) occupation. However, all observers agree that the vast majority of this debris relates to the Middle Woodland occupation. The debris field is essentially continuous near the southern margin of the site. As one approaches the northern boundary, away from the high terrace edge, the surface debris is entirely attributable to the Mann phase occupation and begins to resolve into a series of discontinuous patches 0.5 hectares or less in size (Kellar 1979:102; Lacer n.d.:1–4).

Kellar's four Indiana University field schools conducted between 1964 and 1977 encountered habitation debris far in excess of what might be expected if the site had been occupied only by ritual specialists (Kellar 1979; Ruby 1997b). Excavations in 1964 encountered a terrace-edge trash dump covering at least 100 square meters and extending almost 1 meter below the ground surface. Widely spaced excavations in 1966 and 1967 encountered clusters of shallow, basin-shaped pits, as well as two very large features approximately 2 meters across and up to 1.5 meters deep with fills suggesting use as earth ovens. In 1966, one trench measuring 5 × 10 feet (1.5 × 3 meters) was excavated through midden deposits to a depth of more than 3 meters, apparently sampling a back-filled borrow pit. Finally, excavations in 1977 documented two large pit features: one was a straight-sided, cylindrical flat-bottomed pit that may have served as a storage facility; the other was a very large (3 × 1.5 meters, or more), shallow basin containing alternating layers of burned limestone and midden debris, suggesting a very large food-processing facility.

In short, each area tested has revealed high densities of food-processing and storage facilities and some very deep midden accumulations. No structures have been identified, but scattered postholes suggest their presence. The internal organization of the site suggests a very weak spatial separation of corporate-ceremonial and domestic sphere activities: mounds, earthworks, and dense habitation debris are not clearly segregated in the most intensively surveyed central portion of the site. While the density of habitation debris is impressive, the few available radiocarbon dates document almost three centuries of occupation during the Mann phase, and additional dates would be more likely to expand than to contract this range. It is not necessary to conclude that a large population was present at any one time or that individual household units were tightly integrated socially, politically, or economically. In fact, the presence of small (less than 0.5 hectare), discrete, and organizationally independent midden patches on the periphery of the most heavily occupied area points to a long series of temporally and spatially shifting occupations by relatively small and autonomous social units.

Corporate-Ceremonial Centers

At least two other sites in the study area served corporate-ceremonial functions during the Mann phase. These differ markedly in scale, one being among the largest Middle Woodland constructions anywhere, the other much more modest in proportion. As is the case with Mann, these sites were located on upland or terrace landforms, suggesting that they may have been occupied during periods when the lowland hamlets were inaccessible.

GE Mound. The GE mound (also known as the Mount Vernon site, 12PO885) is located in an upland setting near the mouth of the Wabash River, about 8 kilometers west of the Mann site (Seeman 1995; Tomak 1990, 1994). The site was discovered in 1988 during earthmoving operations associated with the construction of a county road. The site was subsequently subjected to extensive looting. Several indictments and convictions under the Archaeological Resources Protection Act ensued, and some of the artifacts removed from the mound were recovered. In addition, the Indiana Department of Transportation (IDOT) conducted limited test excavations designed to determine the extent of the damage to the site in 1988 (Tomak 1990, 1994).

The GE mound was an investment of labor on a truly monumental scale. Prior to its disturbance, the GE mound was a loaf-shaped structure approximately 125 meters long, 50 meters wide, and 6 meters high. The site ranks among the five largest Hopewell mounds in the Midwest, comparable in size to the Seip-Pricer Mound in south-central Ohio.

The context of the artifacts recovered is sketchy at best, but the GE site was clearly the focus of a complex ceremonial program: the "main feature of the mound was a central deposit containing several thousand bifaces, and . . . this deposit was surrounded or capped with human burials and artifact deposits" (Seeman 1992a:24). Most, if not all, of the artifacts appear to have been recovered at or near the mound floor, perhaps in formal deposits. No intact burials were recovered, but the presence of both burned and unburned human bone in the IDOT collections from the site suggests that extended processing and manipulation of the dead was an element of the mortuary program.

Many (often spectacular) status and ceremonial artifacts were recovered from the mound, suggesting that Mann phase populations were major players in Hopewellian exchange or procurement systems. Among these artifacts are included more than two thousand large ovate bifaces (most fashioned of Burlington chert from the lower Illinois Valley area), at least three large crystal quartz bifaces, at least ten obsidian bifaces, five mica cutouts, thirteen copper ear spools (eight with silver covers), three copper panpipes (two with silver covers), copper nuggets and beads, and a size-graded series of twenty-three copper celts (see Seeman 1992a:Table 1 for a complete listing). The most temporally sensitive of these are the obsidian and the stylistic attributes of one of the silver-covered ear spools. Both of these should date close to or after A.D. 100 (Griffin 1965; Griffin, Gordus, and Wright 1969; Hatch et al. 1990; Ruhl 1992). Seeman (1992a) estimates that the GE assemblage was deposited between circa A.D. 100 and A.D. 300. On this basis GE is assigned to the Mann phase rather than the earlier Crab Orchard occupation of the region.

Several observations support the notion that this structure represents something more than just a burial ground, that it served as a corporate-ceremonial center, a context for integrative ritual, activity, and symbolism. First there is the imposing size of the structure, which certainly speaks of a considerable investment of labor, and which undoubtedly required the participation of social groups organized at a level far above that of the individual household. Second there is the structure as monument, a structure possessing the attributes of prominence and persistence—an enduring symbol of corporate identity made manifest on the landscape (Charles, Buikstra, and Konigsberg 1986; Wheatley 1996:84–88). It is also apparent that many of the artifacts deposited in the mound had been intentionally destroyed through heating or smashing. It seems reasonable to speculate that the destruction of artifacts so evidently imbued with wealth and symbolism had the potential to serve as the focus of an impressive public spectacle.

Finally, the GE mound appears to have been spatially as well as functionally divorced from the domestic sphere. There is no evidence of any domestic habitation immediately adjacent to the mound or in the nearby lowlands. In fact, the only evidence of activity in the vicinity of the mound comes in the form of chert debitage related to the production or refinement of bifaces for inclusion in the central deposit.

The Martin Site (12VG41). At least one other site in the lower Wabash region appears to belong within the corporate-ceremonial sphere of the Mann phase Hopewellian community. The Martin site consists of three small conical mounds preserved in a nineteenth-century cemetery. The largest stands less than 2 meters high. Because they have not been excavated, their attribution to the Mann phase is based upon debris in the vicinity of the mounds and is consequently less than certain. Surrounding the mounds is a low-density scatter containing lamellar blades and undecorated ceramics similar to those found at the Mann site. The greatest density of materials is contained within a single 40-×-60-meter area.

Households and Hamlets

The third class of sites within the Mann phase community belongs to the domestic sphere and conforms quite closely to the hamlet composed of one to three households identified by Smith (1992a) in other regions of Hopewell occupation. In surface collections, these hamlets are defined by the presence of utilitarian ceramics, rare occurrences of decorated ceramics, and a wide range of lithic tool types and debitage. Fifty-one components conforming to this description have been identified to date in southwestern Indiana.

Test excavations at three of these sites—Hovey Lake (12PO10), Kuester (12VG71), and Ellerbusch (12W56)—reveal a redundant pattern of small-scale occupations represented by loose clusters of shallow basin-shaped pits, thin middens, and scattered postholes (Apfelstadt 1971, 1973; Green 1977; Martin 1958; Ruby 1997b). The basin-shaped pits always contain fire-cracked rock and often display direct evidence of in situ burning, suggesting food processing rather than storage functions. None of these sites has produced evidence of belowground storage facilities.

The Grabert site (12PO248), dating to circa A.D. 150 (Beta-38550: 1780 ±60 rcybp; Beta-38551: 1810 ±60 rcybp), is the largest and most extensively excavated of the Mann phase hamlets (Ruby 1997b). Controlled surface collections documented three discrete midden concentrations within a total scatter covering 1.6 hectares. The individual concentrations ranged in size from 500 to 1,500 square meters. A large earthen mound, unexcavated but probably affiliated, stands within 100 meters of the occupation area.

Block excavations exposed 93 square meters of the central and largest concentration and revealed the remains of at least two overlapping circular or oval single-wall post structures. Although neither of the structures was completely exposed, it is possible to estimate that one of them was no more than 4 meters in diameter. A circular structure of this size (12.56 square meters) would accommodate approximately five individuals. This is toward the low end of the range of Middle Woodland domestic household sizes reported by Smith (1992a:Figure 9.8). In his survey, household floor areas ranged from 4.5 to 130.5 square meters, which would have accommodated an estimated two to eighteen individuals. Only one of the twenty-six corporate-ceremonial structures reported by Smith was smaller than the Grabert structure, and most had floor areas greater than 130.5 square meters.

Two shallow basin-shaped pits and two small bathtub-shaped pits lay to the north and east of the structural postholes. The bathtub-shaped features displayed clear evidence of in situ burning and were probably small earth ovens. No direct evidence of in situ burning was noted within the basin-shaped features, but their shapes argue for food processing rather than storage functions.

As described above, the archaeobotanical assemblage from the Grabert site documents a relatively high dependence on seeds relative to nuts, and more than 80 percent of these seeds represent cultivated or domesticated starchy annuals. The faunal assemblage from Grabert is small in size and restricted in species diversity, emphasizing terrestrial mammals. There is little evidence for exploitation of fish or waterfowl, despite proximity to suitable sources. Mammals comprise almost 90 percent of the identified species. About 49 percent of this total are white-tailed deer; 45 percent are forest or forest-edge species including raccoon, opossum, dog, squirrel, rabbit, and fox; and 6 percent are semiaquatic mammals including rice rat, beaver, and mink. Birds (turkey, swan, and ducks) comprise only about 7 percent of the total identifiable specimens. Only two invertebrate specimens were recovered: both were mussel shells, and one of these had been perforated for suspension or perhaps for use as a hoe. Of the few reptiles represented, 92 percent are turtles, and of these about 75 percent are common box turtles: land species that are best exploited during the warm season. In short, the faunal assemblage is characteristic of a small-scale, short-term, warm-season occupation (Ruby 1997b; Ruby, Kearney, and Adams 1993).

When plotted on a map of regional topography, the distribution of households and hamlets shows the same focus on main valley bottomland settings characteristic of Middle Woodland period settlement elsewhere in the midcontinent. Only three (6 percent) of these occupations occur in interior upland settings. In terms of major soil associations, the household distribution shows a marked preference for highly productive floodplain (38 percent), low terrace (42 percent), and high terrace/lacustrine plain (15 percent) settings. About 80 percent of these households or hamlets are located within the active floodplain or on low terrace landforms. These locations are exposed to significant risk of late winter and spring floods, suggesting that they may have been occupied only during the warm season.

Short-Term Extractive Camps

The final element of the Mann phase community might be described as the short-term extractive camp. Unfortunately, none of these sites has been excavated, so their actual function remains somewhat speculative. Sites identified as short-term extractive camps are characterized by restricted tool assemblages, typically including only diagnostic projectile points, debitage reflecting tool maintenance activities, and lamellar blades or blade cores. Ceramics are absent. Sixty-one components conforming to this description have been identified in southwestern Indiana. These sites are more numerous than the household sites discussed above, have a wider spatial distribution, and occupy a more diverse array of environmental settings. Several sites occupy interior upland and tributary stream settings in addition to the floodplain and terrace settings chosen for the ceramic-bearing household occupations.

Discussion

This chapter began with a consideration of Smith's (1992a) model of Hopewellian communities as networks of small, dispersed, and largely autonomous agricultural households integrated through ritual and ceremony conducted at corporate centers marked by mounds and earthworks. It is appropriate at this point to reconsider this model in the light of the Hopewellian Mann phase components described above. Smith's model is applicable at least in outline to the Wabash Lowland. At the core of Smith's model is the conclusion that Hopewellian populations in the midcontinent were supported by pre-maize agricultural economies focused on a suite of indigenous seed-bearing annual plants. All the available evidence from Mann phase contexts in the Wabash Lowland supports this conclusion and even suggests that Mann phase agricultural practices may have been more intensive than those of some of their contemporaries. The density and relative frequency of the cultivated or domesticated squash, goosefoot, sunflower, knotweed, maygrass, and little barley seeds in Mann phase assemblages are equal to or greater than those of other Middle Woodland assemblages. Furthermore, comparative indices measuring the frequency of seeds to nuts document a significant commitment to seed exploitation, not only in comparison to earlier assemblages, but also in comparison to contemporary midwestern populations.

For Smith, the basic Hopewellian farming settlement consists of one to three largely autonomous household units. The settlements themselves are dispersed along river valley segments, favoring the more productive main valley settings. For the most part, the Wabash Lowland data seem to fit this pattern quite well. Fifty-one small-scale ceramic-bearing occupations have been identified in the area, dispersed in main valley floodplain and terrace settings. Many appear to be short-term, warm-season occupations. More widely distributed small, aceramic sites may have served as short-term extractive camps situated to exploit a wider range of environments and resources.

Another core component of Smith's model is the division of Hopewellian communities into spatially and functionally distinct corporate-ceremonial and domestic spheres. The Wabash Lowland area also displays elements of this pattern. This is most clearly seen in the case of the GE mound: it stands as an obvious result of significant labor investment, and yet it is entirely isolated from any evidence of domestic habitation. In addition, the vast majority of household occupations are isolated and unaccompanied by any apparent corporate-ceremonial facilities. Domestic occupations and corporate-ceremonial facilities do occur in close proximity to one another at the Mann, Grabert, and Martin sites. This suggests that these two spheres may not have been as distinct as portrayed in Smith's model.

The Wabash Lowland data document a number of even more significant departures from Smith's model. This is seen most clearly in the anomalous size and density of the domestic occupation at the Mann site. No other known Middle Woodland site in any region approaches this scale of occupation. This need not be interpreted as a well-integrated village or "urban" center, however. There is no evidence that the domestic occupation at the Mann site conformed to any village plan, and in fact the northern portion of the site is characterized by scattered, individual household-scale occupations. Nonetheless, the aggregate scale of domestic habitation here is apparently unique in the Hopewellian world. This anomaly highlights the notion that the relationships between individual household units are driven by a complex web of economic, ecological, social, and political forces acting both centripetally and centrifugally.

In the case of the lower Wabash area, it is possible that the relatively higher resource potential (as measured by the greater rainfall, longer growing season, and warmer temperatures, as well as the extensive availability of floodplain, backwater, and riverine resources) and the concentration of resources near the Wabash-Ohio confluence may have favored aggregation here on at least a seasonal basis. Others (Coughlin and Seeman 1997; Dancey 1992b; Dancey and Pacheco 1997a) have documented a trend toward larger settlement aggregations that emerged late in the Middle Woodland period in south-central Ohio and culminated in the formation of nucleated villages during the fifth and sixth centuries A.D., perhaps as a defensive response to increased competition. Fine-grained chronological control within the Middle Woodland period is lacking in the Wabash Lowland, but the available dates from the Mann site suggest occupation well into the fifth century. It is possible that the aggregation of settlement at the Mann site reflects a panregional trend toward larger settlements late in the Middle Woodland period. At any rate, this review indicates that despite some broad interregional similarities in the organization of Hopewellian domestic spheres, there is considerable variability in the relationships between the fundamental building blocks of Hopewellian communities.

The Wabash Lowland data also point to dimensions of variability that are not emphasized in Smith's model: in size and complexity among corporate-ceremonial centers; in the nature of ritual and ceremony; and in the size and composition of the social units involved. The geometric earthworks at the Mann site, the very large loaf-shaped mounds at Mann and GE, the Mann site platform mounds, and the small conical mounds at the Mann and Martin sites all represent very different kinds of ceremonial centers.

The construction of monumental geometric earthworks during the Mann phase represents a qualitatively different means of defining and using social space compared to the small conical mounds seen at Mann, Martin, and elsewhere. Mounds embody the principles of architecture as *monument*: prominence, persistence, and directional and rotational focus. Enclosures and embankments add to these the principles of architecture as *boundary*: they are more than just focal points; they define distinct precincts, restrict and direct movement and focus in more complex patterns, and embody more complex symbolizations of order (see Kostof 1995:3–41). Simply on the basis of these formal grounds, it would seem imprudent to treat these varied constructions as equivalent units in a general model of Hopewellian communities. The excavated evidence from the small conical mounds at the Mann site suggests that these served relatively small social groups (one or a few households) as mortuary facilities and perhaps as ancestral monuments. There is little evidence to suggest that the geometric enclosures at the Mann site or elsewhere were directly related to mortuary activity, and their scale suggests construction and use by social groups far in excess of just one household or even a few.

A similar contrast obtains when the very large loaf-shaped mounds such as GE and Mann 1 are compared to the small conical mounds at the Mann and Martin sites. The available data concerning the contents and structure of the GE mound suggest that it served as a context for the ostentatious display and destruction of prodigious quantities of valued objects, accompanied by relatively little evidence of mortuary activity. Both the size of the mound and the size and contents of the artifact deposits placed within suggest a level of suprahousehold participation and integration far in excess of that obtaining at any of the small conical mounds.

Finally, the structure and contents of the multistaged platform mound at the Mann site point to a very different sort of ceremonialism than that expressed in the small conical mounds at the Mann and Martin sites. The midden deposits and pits filled with burned and broken exotica found in this platform mound may be related to integrative activities and displays intended to appeal to a wider range of social groups than mortuary activities focused on deceased relatives and ancestors.

This review highlights the potential of the Wabash Lowland as an underutilized resource in our quest to understand interregional variation in Hopewellian settlement, subsistence, ceremonialism, and community organization. The fundamental unit of community organization and the basic subsistence strategy of the Mann phase appear similar to those documented among contemporary populations in the Midwest, but there are also significant differences in community organization and in the intensity of agricultural commitment. This review further emphasizes the variability in corporate-ceremonial facilities and challenges us to consider how this might reflect variability in Hopewellian community organization (see Ruby, Carr, and Charles 2005).

13

The Goodall Tradition

Recent Research and New Perspectives

William L. Mangold and Mark R. Schurr

The Goodall tradition is a regional variant of Havana Hopewell located in northwestern Indiana and southwestern Lower Michigan. The recognition of a distinctive Goodall tradition, in the sense of a regionally distinctive archaeological culture with continuity over time, has its roots in Quimby's (1941b) definition of the Goodall focus, one of the first (if not the first) formally defined archaeological entities in Indiana. The Goodall focus was constructed using the midwestern taxonomic method. It grouped together ten burial mound sites (components) based on the presence of shared traits, especially shared pottery types. Of the ten sites of the Goodall focus, nine were located in Michigan and only one, the Goodall site itself, was located outside the state, in Indiana (fig. 13.1).

The choice of the Goodall site as the nominal or type site for the Goodall focus is somewhat surprising. The definition of a focus as "a group of components which show a marked similarity in their cultural traits" (Quimby 1941b:136) would suggest that the site closest to the geographic center of the focus is most likely to share the most traits with all other components. Quimby did not explicitly justify naming the focus for the Goodall site, but his nomenclature probably reflects several things. First, the archaeological database was extremely limited at that time, consisting primarily of poorly provenienced collections from uncontrolled excavations, and the Goodall site had produced one of the largest pottery collections available for examination. Second, the Goodall site, with twenty-two mounds, was the largest site in the focus. Third, and perhaps most importantly, it was then thought that the Goodall focus represented a rapid migration of Hopewellian people from Illinois (Quimby 1941b, 1943). From this perspective, the Goodall site would indeed be most representative of the basic cultural pattern.

The Goodall focus has several defects beyond those inherent in the midwestern taxonomic method. The focus spanned a very large geographic area, with a linear distance of over three hundred kilometers between Goodall, at the southern end, and the Brooks component at the northern end. It also crossed five major river valleys (the Kankakee, St. Joseph, Kalamazoo, Grand, and

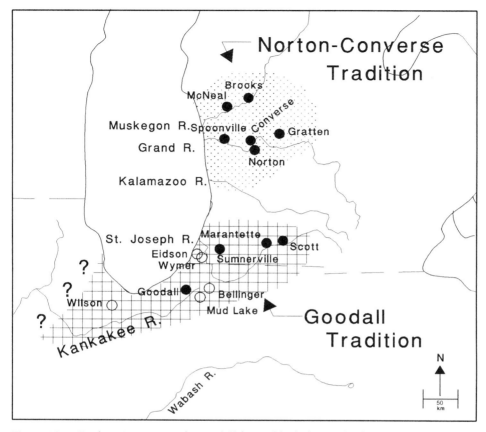

Figure 13.1. Site location map with Goodall focus (black dot) and other (open circle) sites.

Muskegon). From a contemporary phase-based perspective, which generally seeks to define archaeological phases that are more limited in geographic extent (usually confined to a river valley or a segment thereof), this is an uncomfortably large region. The focus definition was also highly selective, ignoring other Hopewellian sites in the same region. For example, in northwestern Indiana, the Upp-Wark Mound Group in Porter County and the Union Mills Group in LaPorte County had both produced artifacts that were clearly Hopewellian (Lilly 1937), as had the Litchfield (or Bellinger) mound in St. Joseph (anonymous 1925; Karst 1969). These sites were not included in the Goodall focus because artifacts from the mounds were collected by looters, were sketchily described in print, and, most likely, were not available for Quimby to study. Sites that had been carefully investigated, such as the mounds in Porter County excavated by McAllister (1932) a decade earlier, were excluded because they had not produced significant amounts of pottery (presumably the ceramics had been destroyed or removed earlier by looters).

The problematic definition of the Goodall focus is best illustrated by the fact that almost every archaeologist who has worked with materials from northwestern Indiana over the past three decades has tried to revise or even eliminate Goodall as a taxonomic entity. Brown (1964b), on the basis of an examination of sherds in the Ernest W. Young collection from northwestern Indiana and site distributions along the Kankakee, redefined northwestern Indiana Middle Woodland as a regionally specific ecological adaptation within the Prairie Peninsula. Brown was the first to note that the Goodall focus as originally defined was based primarily on the distribution of Hopewell ware. Of the ten sites in the Goodall focus, only Goodall was known at that time to have produced Havana-style pottery, and it was therefore the only Havana tradition site. Brown also provided a credible alternative to the migration theory for Goodall origins, pointing out that early Havana styles such as Marion Thick and Neteler Stamped were present in collections from northwestern Indiana and from the Moccasin Bluff site on the St. Joseph River in southwestern Lower Michigan. He also provided the first specific model of the Goodall settlement pattern (see below).

Brown's distinction between the Middle Woodland occupations of northwestern Indiana and those of western Michigan was reinforced by Griffin, Flanders, and Titterington (1970) in their analysis of excavations at the Norton site. They also suggested that the concept of the Goodall focus should be discarded. In their opinion the Goodall site was most closely affiliated with the Utica Mounds in Illinois, and both Goodall and Utica should be placed in a single upper Illinois Havana expression. In regard to the Goodall focus, they noted that "something systematic should be done with it in the near future" (Griffin, Flanders, and Titterington 1970:189).

Pottery was essential to the original definition of the Goodall focus, and analysis of pottery styles still plays the most important role in the definition of the Goodall tradition. The first systematic reexamination of the ceramics from Goodall focus sites since Quimby's definition of the focus was conducted by Mangold (1981b). In addition to ceramics from Goodall focus sites, he also incorporated data from the Bobinski site (20BE282) near New Buffalo, Michigan, and the Mushroom site (20AE88) in the Kalamazoo River basin. The Bobinski site was located near a reported mound group that had been looted in the latter portion of the nineteenth century. Limited excavations in a modern garden produced Naples Dentate sherds as well as other Middle Woodland ceramics. In 1978 and 1980, excavations were conducted by Western Michigan University at the Mushroom site. This site was the first Middle Woodland site found in the Kalamazoo River basin and was radiocarbon dated to A.D. 295.

Mangold's (1981b) thesis focused upon Middle Woodland ceramics from eighteen Middle Woodland sites in western Michigan and northwestern Indiana that were dispersed through many private, university, and museum collections. The material he analyzed included ceramics from the sites Quimby (1941b) had used to establish the Goodall focus. From the data available at that time, it appeared as though two distinct ceramic style zones existed, separating the Kankakee and Saint Joseph rivers from the Grand and Muskegon (fig. 13.1). This provided a formal delineation of the trends noted earlier by Brown (1964b) and Griffin, Flanders, and Titterington (1970). While the concept of differing style zones may no longer be supportable as originally defined, the division of the former Goodall focus into two distinct geographic regions continues to be a viable construct.

Recent Goodall Research

The modern era of Goodall research in northwestern Indiana began in 1992. Since then, the authors have used field surveys, excavations, and geophysical surveys to investigate Middle Woodland sites in northwestern Indiana, especially in St. Joseph and LaPorte counties. Reconnaissance surveys in St. Joseph (Schurr 1992) and LaPorte counties (Schurr 1993) have provided data on site distributions in the upper Kankakee and St. Joseph valleys. Excavations at the Bellinger Mound (12SJ6), along with geophysical surveys and excavations at its associated habitation site (Schurr 1997a, 1997b), have shown that even badly damaged Middle Woodland sites possess significant data recovery potential. Mangold (1997) conducted surface investigations at the Goodall site (12LE9) in 1994, attempting to more tightly delineate numerous small occupational areas in close proximity to the suspected mound locations. From surface surveys, it was possible to determine the approximate positions of four badly deflated mounds out of the suspected total of twenty-two. In 1994, the investigators knew of no maps that showed the positions or total number of mounds at the site. Surface and geophysical surveys supplemented with excavations at Goodall and Mud Lake (12LE14), and additional surface and geophysical surveys at four other Middle Woodland sites (Schurr 1998, 1999), relocated several more mounds at Goodall and provided the first well-provenienced data on Goodall tradition sites in over half a century.

Excavations

The Bellinger Mound

The first intensive investigation of a Middle Woodland mound site in northwestern Indiana in over fifty years was conducted at the Bellinger Mound (12SJ6, also known as the Litchfield Mound, after the unfortunate practice of naming mounds for their looters). The site is located at the edge of a glacial outwash terrace on Pine Creek, a tributary of the Kankakee River, in St. Joseph County, Indiana. The Bellinger Mound is typical of the vast majority (97 percent) of reported Middle Woodland mounds in northwestern Indiana, having been looted decades earlier (anonymous 1925:346) and then plowed and eroded into near invisibility. In 1992, investigations were designed to explore the periphery of the mound to search for features that had been protected from erosion by the mound mantle, to obtain samples of charcoal for radiocarbon dating, and to sample the fill in the looted portion of the mound. The 1992 excavations showed that the center of the mound had been badly disturbed but that the looter's backfill and intact portions of the mound mantle still contained artifacts useful for dating the mound's construction. Two more seasons of excavation determined the internal architecture of the mound and identified two archaeological components representing two distinct occupations (Schurr 1997a). The earlier occupation was characterized by contracting-stemmed points, "Marion Thin" pottery with incised decorations applied over a cordmarked surface, and a small Sister Creeks Punctated vessel. This component was confined to a thin paleosol or midden lens preserved under the northern edge of the mound, predating the mound's construction. The second component is the mound itself. It represents a very late Middle Woodland occupation with expanding-stemmed points; the presence of limestone-tempered plain body sherds (although a minority compared to grit-tempered sherds); and ceramic decorative treatments, including brushing and punctations, similar to those of Havana tradition styles that are known to be late in the Illinois Valley (for example, Steuben Punctated). The assemblage also included a Sumnerville Incised rim and rims with Weaver-like profiles. The later Bellinger component probably dates to around A.D. 350 and suggests that the Bellinger Mound may be one of the last Middle Woodland mounds constructed in the region.

The Goodall Site

In 1993, reconnaissance surveys in LaPorte County, Indiana, delineated Woodland to Historic period settlement patterns in the eastern half of the county and resulted in the "rediscovery" of the Goodall site (Schurr 1993). Written descriptions of the site dating back to 1834, when Government Land Office (GLO) surveyors passed through the area, note two groups of mounds on either side of the section line. Many collectors, both amateur and semiprofessional, visited the site throughout the nineteenth and early twentieth centuries. As looting, erosion, and intensive surface collecting continued, artifacts became rarer, and collectors eventually lost interest in the site (Mangold 1998). The condition of the site in 1993 was very similar to that of the Bellinger site, but the investigations at Bellinger had shown that even badly damaged Middle Woodland sites could contain significant intact archaeological deposits. Subsequent controlled surface surveys, geophysical surveys, and excavations at the site confirmed that intact deposits were present and that even looters' back-dirt could provide important archaeological data. The most intensive investigations have been conducted in the vicinity of a mound remnant near the center of the site.

The Goodall site is located on an outwash terrace where a small creek (officially called Bowman's Creek but known locally by the less appealing sobriquet of "Sewer Creek") would have entered the Kankakee Marsh from the uplands. The GLO surveyors noted twelve mounds at the site, but a total of twenty-two mounds were probably present originally. The mounds are arranged in three clusters or groups, and the GLO surveyors apparently missed part of the central group and the entire eastern group. No single authoritative map of the site exists. Documents with the Ernest W. Young collection, curated at the Illinois State Museum, contain two maps of the site, with slightly different locations for some of the mounds. Given what is now known about the site, the Notre Dame

University field school investigations have focused on Mound 15 or 16 (depending on which of Young's maps is correct), located near the center of the site. Excavations were designed to determine the internal architecture of the mound. As was the case at Bellinger, the central tomb had been virtually destroyed by looting, but it was probably a subsurface pit approximately 1 meter on a side. Instead of being capped with muck and marl, however, the tomb was capped with a sandy marl that was often difficult to distinguish from the sandy midden used to cap the mound. No evidence of flanking trenches was noted. Looting had destroyed much more of the central tomb than was the case at Bellinger. Fortunately, while the looting had been very destructive, it had not been systematic, and various artifacts had been overlooked by the looters. Portions of broken pottery vessels were found in the back-dirt or at the interface between the back-dirt and the intact soils. Hopewell ware rim sherds from four different vessels were found in the looters' backfill in 1996, and additional portions of two of these vessels, along with a third, were collected during later seasons. Additional sherds from the fourth Hopewell ware vessel may still be present in the unexcavated portions of the looter's pit.

The assemblage from the mound is still being analyzed, but pottery styles are characteristic of that portion of the Middle Woodland period when mortuary ceremonialism and participation in the Hopewell Interaction Sphere were at their peak. All of the Hopewell ware sherds from the mound are limestone tempered, with finely crosshatched rims and zoned rocker dentate-stamped decorations. Two vessels were quadrilobate, and one bears an avian motif. A Brangenburg rim was also found. All of these vessels could easily represent imports from the lower Illinois Valley. Paste and temper differ markedly from the grit-tempered plain or Naples stamped sherds found in the mound midden and in Ernest W. Young's surface collections from the site (Mangold 1998). Other Hopewell Interaction Sphere artifacts from the mound include two small copper celts originally wrapped in fabric, a lump of galena, a sheet of mica, and two copper awls. One of the Hopewell vessels was broken by the looters but left in the mound. It contained three spoons made of worked Blanding's turtle carapaces (undecorated), a flint blade of what appears to be Burlington chert, and a single bottle gourd seed (*Langineria siceria*, L. Bush, personal communication 1998). Lithics from the mound are consistent with the rest of the assemblage. Point styles are *affinis* Snyders and made of heat-treated Burlington or of Wyandotte chert. Small lamellar blades are also made of these cherts, along with two examples of what appears to be Flint Ridge.

Geophysical Surveys

In 1995, geophysical surveys and very limited ground-truthing excavations were conducted in the best-preserved portion of the habitation area at the Bellinger site. Only one feature was found in an area of 4,000 square meters: the base of a shallow hearth or pit feature lined with fire-cracked rock, which had been largely destroyed by plowing (Schurr 1997b). The site appeared to have been severely eroded—not surprising, given the sandy soils at the site. Low densities of chert flakes and fire-cracked rock in the former plow zone suggest that the inhabitation of the site was not very intense.

Magnetic and resistivity surveys in the vicinity of Mound 16 at Goodall using a variety of sampling intervals and resistivity-probe spacings over several years had never identified geophysical signals that could be attributed to the mound or nonmound features. Additional surveys covering 5,020 square meters in the vicinity of the mound and to the southwest of it, followed by ground-truthing excavations, revealed why earlier geophysical surveys had been unsuccessful. The geophysical surveys southwest of the mound remnant detected two additional mound remnants, one of which was not associated with a visible topographic elevation. A test of this location showed that the remnants of a mound with a muck-and-marl cap were responsible for the detectable anomaly. Geophysical surveys at Bellinger, Mud Lake (12LE14), and the Williams Mounds (12SJ330) indicated that the techniques used for the geophysical surveys were very effective at detecting mucky caps but could not detect mounds without such features (Schurr 1999).

The Ernest W. Young Collection

In 1997, Mangold (1998) began intensive analyses of the Ernest Young collection housed in the Illinois State Museum. The collection had been gathered by Young, an avocational archaeologist from South Bend, Indiana, over at least a fifty-year period starting in the early twentieth century. It includes material from many Middle Woodland sites in northwestern Indiana, including Goodall, Mud Lake, and Good's Ford. In 1998, the majority of the collection was loaned to the University of Notre Dame. Among Young's notes were several maps detailing the locations of the mounds at Goodall and providing the numbering system that had been in use at that time. From this information it was possible to associate artifacts from Goodall in several other collections that were identified only by mound number to physical locations at the site. As shown below, the large and well-provenienced Young collection provides a remarkable sample of the Goodall tradition material culture from an era when gentler cultivation practices produced surface collections with very large sherds.

Material Culture

Ceramics

The Woodland ceramics found within the region are firmly within the Havana tradition and range from Early Woodland Marion Thick to types similar to Weaver wares in Illinois. Very few sites have the full sequence, and the number of types found at a site is usually quite small. Naples and Hummel dentate-stamped vessels, however, occur at almost every Middle Woodland site in the Kankakee Valley. At the Goodall site, the Young collection (the largest made at the site over the longest period of time) indicates that these Havana styles represent 92.4 percent of the decorated rim sherds. Just over 50 percent have interior beveled lips, with the angle of some of the beveling being quite pronounced. The thickness of the sherds ranges from 0.55 to 1.3 centimeters, with the mean being 0.97 centimeters (Mangold 1998).

There are some stylistic differences among these dentate-stamped sherds, however. Most of those from Goodall were decorated with large toothed stamps (5 millimeters or larger). Sherds with similar-sized dentates have been found at the Kuhne site (Loy 1968) and the Sister Creeks site (Meinkoth et al. 1995), both in the upper Illinois River valley. Sherds with these large-sized dentates do not appear throughout the region, and the Goodall site may represent the eastern-most distribution of that type. As it is the dominant type at the Goodall site, it may also be restricted to that period of time as well.

The size of the dentate appears to decrease over time until, during the late Middle Woodland, the dentate stamping tool probably more closely resembled a modern pocket comb. This type of motif has been found at Mud Lake and Sumnerville and is associated with the LaPorte phase. In most cases, the width of the decoration band on the rim also becomes narrower over time.

Earlier Havana ceramics found in the region, such as Neteler and Naples Barred Ovoid, hint at earlier occupations. Crescent stamping, however, seems to continue into Goodall times. Two vessels recovered from the area of Mound 22 (after its removal) have that motif or vestiges of that decorative motif on their rims.

To date, Hopewell series ceramics seem to be primarily restricted to burial contexts at Goodall. They are limestone tempered, indicating importation from the Illinois River valley, as that material is not known to be available in north-western Indiana. Locally produced Middle Woodland sherds are grit tempered. They can often be easily distinguished by the white feldspar included with the grit. This can occur in heavy proportions and with rather large individual fragments. One quadrilobate vessel with an avian motif has been determined to have been manufactured in the lower Illinois Valley based on style and macroscopic paste appearance (K. Farnsworth, personal communication 1998). A limestone-tempered Brangenberg rim sherd was found in a disturbed context in Mound 16 at Goodall. The Young collection also contained a Brangenberg rim sherd. The nearest site producing similar rims is the Steuben site, which dates to circa A.D. 1–200 (K. Farnsworth, personal communication 1998; Morse 1963).

Goodall Mound 16 has also produced four major rim sections, including two nearly complete vessels, which have the Hopewell series crosshatched pattern. The sections are large enough to permit the observation that the typical cross-hatching is interrupted at regular intervals. This "interrupted crosshatch" motif occurs in the lower Illinois Valley and its tributaries at the Apple Creek, Crane, Loy, Macoupin, Napoleon Hollow, Peisker (K. Farnsworth, personal communication 1998), and Smiling Dan sites (Stafford and Sant 1985b). The motif had not been recognized in the Goodall region prior to this, primarily owing to the small size of the rim sherds recovered.

Lithics

Middle Woodland sites in the region are noted for the presence of exotic cherts, primarily Burlington (both natural and heat treated) and Wyandotte. In Young's Goodall site collection, 79.7 percent of the complete lamellar blades were made of Burlington (23.7 percent natural; 76.3 percent heat treated) and 13 percent were Wyandotte. For bifaces, Wyandotte chert was preferred (52.5 percent). In Mangold's (1997) recent survey of the Goodall area, similar results were noted. At Mud Lake, the percentage of exotic cherts drops while that of the local glacial till cherts increases. This is indicative of the later Middle Woodland. Other cherts that also represent interaction sphere activity include Knife River (three artifacts at Goodall as well as two from other Middle Woodland sites along the Kankakee) and obsidian (one flake at Bellinger village and one at Mud Lake).

Lamellar blades at Goodall are wide, more like those found at Illinois sites, with the complete specimens having a mean width of 1.836 centimeters. Goodall and the small sites around it produced a large number (*n* = 299) of blades or blade fragments. This may indicate specific tasks, possibly burial or ceremonial oriented, occurring at the site. Mangold (1997) has suggested that the blades may have been used in the shaving of ritual participants' heads or in bloodletting or scarring.

The *affinis* Snyders point is the most commonly found projectile point at the Goodall site and most other sites of the period. One Norton point, however, was identified at Goodall, and two other Nortonlike points were collected from excavated contexts at Mud Lake. Others may have been present at Goodall, but the reuse and resharpening of the points make that identification difficult. The points appear to have been curated and used until resharpening was no longer possible. While some reworked points may have been used as hafted scrapers, the majority do not show characteristics of such use. Wyandotte chert predominates in the point assemblage.

Havana scrapers like those described by Cantwell (1980) are fairly common. Sixty-five were found in Young's collection from Goodall. They ranged in shape from round to ovoid to almost square and were primarily unifacial with steep edges.

Other

At least thirty-six copper objects have been documented as coming from the Goodall site. The copper celt was the most common form (*n* = 19), with copper awls being the second most common (*n* = 12). A single fragment of partially worked copper might hint that raw material was being traded along with finished items.

New Perspectives

Recent investigations have provided new information about Goodall tradition site distributions and settlement patterns. Well-provenienced artifacts from excavated contexts can now be used to develop a basic chronological framework and to examine the relationships between Goodall and other contemporary occupations. For the first time, some limited information about subsistence activities is also available. Analysis of field projects and collections is still under way, but these recent investigations have already provided new perspectives on Goodall, along with a host of future research questions.

Goodall Chronology

Earlier Chronological Schemes

The midwestern taxonomic system is atemporal, so Quimby's definition of the Goodall focus did not attempt to determine the span of time represented by the sites. Later, the Goodall focus—as originally defined—was recognized to contain sites that spanned at least several centuries, and the Goodall ceramic complex was subdivided into at least two chronologically distinct phases (Griffin, Flanders, and Titterington 1970): the Utica phase (dated from about A.D. 1 to A.D. 100) and the later LaPorte phase (from about A.D. 100 to A.D. 300). The Utica and LaPorte phases were distinguished from each other by the popularity of various pottery types (fig. 13.2).

One of the most important diagnostic markers for distinguishing LaPorte from Utica phase occupations is the presence of limestone tempering in pottery from the later period (Griffin 1952c; Griffin, Flanders, and Titterington 1970). This diagnostic criterion may not be a good horizon marker in the Kankakee area because of the lack of limestone bedrock in the region. Decorative techniques will probably be of more use in refining Middle Woodland chronologies in northwestern Indiana. Assemblages of late Middle Woodland pottery from the Kankakee Valley can be expected to have lower proportions of limestone-tempered pottery compared to sites in the Illinois Valley and to contain grit-tempered vessels in Hopewell styles. It may be difficult to distinguish Utica phase sites from LaPorte phase sites, because grit temper probably predominated throughout the entire Middle Woodland period in the study area. Relatively thick plain or cordmarked sherds from utilitarian vessels tempered with limestone can be dated to the Frazier phase at the very end of the Middle Woodland period in the central Illinois Valley. In LaPorte County, grit-tempered sherds fitting within the type descriptions of Havana Cordmarked and Havana Plain (Griffin 1952c) can be expected to predominate at all times, and it may be very difficult to assign undecorated sherds to subperiods within the Middle Woodland period.

Faulkner (1972) divided the Middle Woodland period of the Kankakee basin into early and late subperiods (fig. 13.2) that were roughly equivalent to the Utica and LaPorte phases as defined by Griffin, Flanders, and Titterington (1970). Faulkner, however, used different terms, avoiding phase names and preferring instead to simply divide the Middle Woodland period into early and late portions. According to Faulkner, early Middle Woodland occupation of the region could be distinguished by diagnostic pottery types previously described for the late Early Woodland Morton complex in the central Illinois valley (Griffin 1952c; Griffin, Flanders, and Titterington 1970). Morton complex pottery styles found in the Kankakee Valley include Morton Incised and Sister Creeks Punctated. The early Havana tradition pottery styles (Griffin 1952c; Griffin, Flanders, and Titterington 1970) of Havana Cordmarked, Havana Plain, Neteler Stamped, and Fettie Incised were also used by Faulkner as diagnostic of early Middle Woodland occupations in the Kankakee region. Thus, the early Middle Woodland period defined by Faulkner (1972) is contemporary with both the Morton and the Fulton phase in the central Illinois Valley (fig. 13.2), as defined by Griffin, Flanders, and Titterington (1970).

Late Middle Woodland sites were identified by the presence of new styles of pottery that were accompanied by changes in settlement patterns and mortuary behavior. Pottery styles diagnostic of the late Middle Woodland period, as defined by Faulkner (1972), include Havana Zoned, Naples Stamped, and Hopewell wares.

A Provisional Goodall Chronology

After more than eight years of Middle Woodland investigations in northwestern Indiana, the authors feel that the time has come to propose a chronology that appears to more accurately reflect the Middle Woodland period in the region (fig. 13.2). The chronology has its foundations in earlier versions but departs significantly from them. Wolforth (1993) had previously separated the northwestern Indiana Middle Woodland phases from those of the upper Illinois River valley, and the chronology proposed here builds upon the foundation that he provisionally established.

The first step is to do away with Utica as a phase name for the region. The Utica site is a significant distance removed from the core of the Goodall area. While there may have been some interaction between the two, the Utica site cannot be used to represent the Kankakee Middle Woodland. There are also major differences in the cultural manifestations at Utica in comparison with Goodall. For example, the mounds at Utica and nearby sites contained few Hopewell Interaction Sphere items, no *affinis* Snyders points, and few lamellar blades (Henriksen 1965). While Henriksen concludes that the earliest mounds at Utica are early Hopewell, it is possible that they predate Goodall, albeit slightly. Also, a number of the mounds at Utica may not even be of Middle Woodland construction.

The next logical step is to establish a *Goodall phase*, with the Goodall site being the type site. Based upon current analyses, the Goodall phase represents a time period from circa A.D. 1 to 200. At this time, the culture was actively involved in the Hopewell Interaction Sphere, pottery included Havana wares along with imported and locally produced Hopewell wares (fig. 13.3), *affinis* Snyders projectile points and lamellar blades were common, and mound construction was at its height.

It is proposed that the *LaPorte phase* be retained as following Goodall but that its represented time period be shifted slightly to A.D. 200 to 400. This shift more accurately reflects the period of decline in mound building; less involvement with interregional trade, including the cessation of the importation of

Date	Cultural Period	Kankakee Valley			Illinois Valley		
		Mangold/Schurr [a]	Griffin [b]	Faulkner [c]	Central [b]	Central [d]	Upper [e]
AD 700	Late Woodland	Walkerton [f]	Undefined	Walkerton	Weaver	Weaver	Weaver/Swanson
AD 400	Middle Woodland	LaPorte [g]	LaPorte	Late Middle Woodland	Steuben	Frazier	Steuben
AD 200		Goodall [h]	Utica		Ogden	Ogden	Utica
AD 1		Stillwell			Fulton	Fulton	
20 BC	Early Woodland	North Liberty [i]	Undefined	Early Middle Woodland	Morton	Late Morton/ Caldwell	Undefined
						Early/Late Morton	

Figure 13.2. Goodall tradition phases. *Sources*: [a]this volume; [b]Griffin, Flanders, and Titterington 1970; [c]Faulkner 1972; [d]Munson 1986; [e]Wolforth 1993. *Localities*: [f]includes Walkerton, Weise, and Wunderink Mounds sites; [g]includes Bellinger Mound, Sumnerville, Marantette, Scott, and Mud Lake (12LE14) sites; [h]includes Goodall, Union Mills, and Good's Ford sites; [i]includes Bellinger premound and Mud Lake surface.

limestone-tempered ceramic vessels; replacement of *affinis* Snyders points by expanding-stemmed forms (fig. 13.4); and a movement out of the central Kankakee area.

The hypothetical *Stillwell phase* is used for the Kankakee Valley equivalent of the Fulton phase, and therefore it immediately precedes the Goodall phase. It is not possible for us to assign specific sites to the Stillwell phase at this time. Stillwell phase occupations can presumably be distinguished from later Goodall phase components by a Havana ware assemblage that lacks Hopewell ware, just as the Fulton phase is distinguished from the Ogden phase in the central Illinois Valley (Griffin, Flanders, and Titterington 1970; Munson 1986). Havana styles characteristic of the Fulton phase (Naples Stamped, Havana Zoned, and Havana Plain and Cordmarked) are well documented in Kankakee Valley surface collections (fig. 13.5) but have not been found in excavated contexts shown to predate the appearance of Hopewell ware.

It is also proposed that a new North Liberty phase be established to identify the period of still-earlier Havana activities and ceramics in the region, such as those seen on the original ground surface below the Bellinger Mound (Schurr

Figure 13.3. Goodall phase artifacts: (A) and (B) *affinis* Snyders points; (C) and (D) Hopewell ware rims; (E) Hopewell ware vessel with avian motif; (F) Hopewell ware. All artifacts are from the Goodall site.

Figure 13.4. LaPorte phase artifacts: (A) Steuben Expanding Stemmed point; (B) and (C) local variants of Steuben Punctated; (D) Sumnerville Incised rim sherd; (E) and (F) plain rocker-stamped sherds. All artifacts are from the Bellinger site.

Figure 13.5. Stillwell phase artifacts: (A) *affinis* Snyders point (Goodall); (B) Hummel/
Naples Stamped; (C) and (D) Havana Zoned. All sherds are from the Mud Lake site.

1997a) and in the collections from Mud Lake (fig. 13.6). Exact parameters for
the phase are not well defined at this time, but the phase would have existed
prior to 200 B.C. It is hoped that additional research at Mud Lake will help to
verify this position.

Settlement Patterns and Subsistence

Brown's Binary Model

Brown (1964b) presented a relatively simple model of Goodall settlement, based
on what was then known about Middle Woodland site distributions in the
Kankakee Valley of Indiana. In his model, there were two kinds of sites. Mound
groups were located at the edges of the marshes where secondary streams entered. Each mound group site was paired with a large satellite site located in the
marsh near the Kankakee River. The Mud Lake site did not fit the model because
it was not located on the outwash terrace margin. The anomalous location of
this site has long been recognized, including in a typewritten comparison of
mound site locations by Ernest W. Young (1943).

Figure 13.6. North Liberty phase artifacts: (A) and (B) contracting-stem points (Bellinger site); (C) "Marion Thin" incised (Bellinger site); (D) and (E) ovoid barred stamped (Mud Lake and Goodall sites); (F) semicircular stamped; (G) Neteler Stamped variant (Mud Lake site).

Faulkner's Agricultural Nucleation Model

According to Faulkner (1972), sites occupied during the early Middle Woodland period were located on sand islands and ridges in the marsh, on the edge of the moraine-studded uplands, and on sand dunes in the Calumet Lacustrine zone. The wide distribution of sites across many environmental zones suggested a continuation of broad-spectrum hunting-and-gathering economies developed during the Late Archaic. Mortuary activities during the period were reflected in the construction of low, dome-shaped mounds at sites such as Griesmer and, perhaps, Brown Ranch, although the latter site may date to the late Middle Woodland period (Faulkner 1972). Faulkner saw little change in subsistence or mortuary practices from the Early Woodland to the early Middle Woodland in the Kankakee region, except that mound burial was definitely established by the later period.

Site distributions changed significantly during the late Middle Woodland period. The Calumet Lacustrine zone adjacent to Lake Michigan was largely abandoned, and habitation sites associated with large mound groups (up to ten or more mounds) were established on sandy outwash deposits or uplands along the edge of the Kankakee Marsh. Examples of sites dating to this period in the Kankakee Valley include Goodall, La Count, Union Mills, and Upp-Wark (also known as Boone Grove). These sites were located to exploit both upland and marsh resources and are in settings that would not have required abandonment during the wet season. Heavier concentrations of pottery from domestic sites may indicate increased populations or increased duration of occupation. During this period, occupants of the Kankakee Valley participated in Hopewell mortuary ceremonies and constructed some of the larger mounds to cover tombs holding burials with exotic grave goods.

Faulkner (1972) attributed the changes in settlement pattern and mortuary activities during the late Middle Woodland period to the introduction of maize agriculture to the region, an idea we now know to be incorrect. Instead of maize cultivation, the intensive collection, harvesting, and in some cases domestication of small-seeded indigenous annuals was an important element of Middle Woodland subsistence practices in some areas (Ford 1985a). Along the lower Illinois Valley in west-central Illinois, several sites have produced evidence for the intensive collection and in some cases domestication of small-seeded starchy annuals (Asch and Asch 1985c).

Direct information on plant use within the Goodall tradition during the Middle Woodland period is very limited. Three flotation samples from Bellinger Mound contained mainly oak charcoal. Hazelnut shell was the only nutshell present. Two chenopod seeds were identified in one sample, but they appeared to be of a wild variety. Uncarbonized chenopod seeds in the flotation samples suggest that the seed may be a better indication of the local environment than evidence for food collection. A single bottle gourd seed was recovered from the soil contained within a Hopewell ware vessel at the Goodall site. This seed shows that at least one domesticate was present but does not provide support for intensive cultivation. It is possible that the starchy-seeded annuals were cultivated in the region, and perhaps the oily-seeded *Iva* (sumpweed) as well, but habitation sites with intact features that could provide evidence of subsistence activities have yet to be identified or excavated.

New Perspectives on Goodall Settlement and Subsistence

Mound Site Distributions. Available data suggest that Brown's binary model is too simple and that Faulkner's agricultural nucleation model overestimates the role of food production in Goodall subsistence. Many more mound and habitation sites have been identified since these models were developed. In northwestern Indiana, mounds occur both singly and in groups. Sixty-four site numbers have been assigned to mounds or mound groups. At this time, 116 mounds have been documented in the study area, based on sites where estimates of the number of mounds are available.

A minority of mounds in the region (twenty-nine, approximately 25 percent) are single mounds. These are more likely to be reported but unconfirmed mounds, whereas confirmed mounds are more likely to be found within groups. Most mounds are found in mound groups ranging in size from two to twenty-two mounds. The largest mound groups are Knox Mounds, Upp-Wark, and Union Mills, with ten to twelve mounds each; Goodall, with twenty-two mounds; and Mud Lake, with at least eight mounds. With the exception of Goodall, Mud Lake, and Upp-Wark, these larger sites remain largely uninvestigated by professional archaeologists, beyond field checking of potential site locations. The Knox mound group is thought to have been entirely destroyed, and except for Goodall and Mud Lake, none has been excavated in the modern era. The larger mound groups are composed of several subgroups, most containing from two to five mounds. Larger mound groups are thus distinguished from smaller ones because they appear to be aggregations of smaller mound groups. In general, the chronological development within each group remains unknown.

Site distributions (fig. 13.7) suggest that the Goodall phase is primarily an upper Kankakee Valley phenomenon, with most sites located between Porter and St. Joseph counties in Indiana. Major mound groups extend from Upp-Wark on the west to Mud Lake on the east. Most mound sites are located on the northern side of the valley, except for Knox and other mound sites in Starke County and the Bellinger and Williams sites at the upper end of the valley near the confluence of the Kankakee and Pine Creek (a major tributary). Excavations at the Bellinger site (Schurr 1997a) indicate that these outlying sites may be relatively late. The preference for site locations on the northern edge of the valley probably reflects the importance of upland resources that can be found in the forested moraines and open prairies to the north and the use of the uplands as a land transportation corridor. The historic Sauk Trail passed through the uplands, and the Indiana Toll Road still follows the same general path.

Proximity to the Kankakee River may have also been an important determinant of mound group location. The Kankakee River meanders away from the uplands in western LaPorte County, and the absence of mound groups between Upp-Wark and Union Mills may reflect the relatively long distance between the upland margin and the Kankakee River channel in this part of the valley. The Kankakee meanders toward the uplands near Upp-Wark and then meanders to the south in Lake County, perhaps accounting for the absence of marsh-edge sites in Lake County, and ultimately determining the western limit of the Goodall settlement system.

Peripheral mound groups include sites in St. Joseph County, Indiana. The Chain O'Lakes and New Carlisle mound groups are both located within the valley of a northern tributary extension of the Kankakee. The pair of mounds at Baugo Creek are the only documented mounds in the St. Joseph River valley in St. Joseph County. These mounds were apparently destroyed by a housing development in the 1950s. They were located where Baugo Creek, a relatively large creek, enters the St. Joseph. Historic records show that there was a marsh in this area. These peripheral mound sites continue to reflect the Goodall preference for marsh-edge locations, but their small size suggests that they are at the eastern limit of the Goodall settlement system.

The St. Joseph Valley sites have been aptly described as being the "Goodall periphery" (Garland and DesJardins, this volume). Early Woodland occupations of the lower St. Joseph River valley (Garland 1986; Garland and Beld

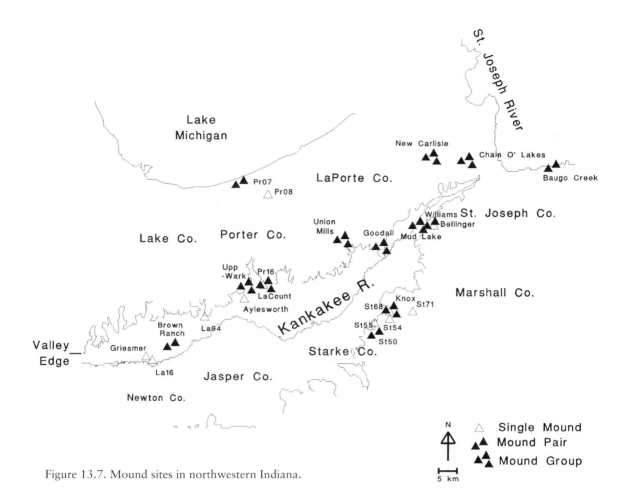

Figure 13.7. Mound sites in northwestern Indiana.

1999) are very similar to the early component at Bellinger Mound in the Kankakee Valley. A Havana occupation has been documented from the middle St. Joseph River valley at the Strobel site (20SJ180), contemporary with the Stillwell phase Goodall occupation of the Kankakee Valley. A copper ear spool from Marantette (Quimby 1944:421) is of the early type (Ruhl 2002; Ruhl and Seeman 1998) and is consistent with an early occupation of the Goodall periphery. Mounds of the periphery, such as the Sumnerville group, Scott, and Marantette, are similar to Bellinger and probably represent outward expansion in all directions from the central Kankakee area of Middle Woodland peoples during the LaPorte phase. While the middle St. Joseph River valley may have been visited during the earlier period, as indicated by a few Havana sherds at Moccasin Bluff (Bettarel and Smith 1973), any substantial presence was probably later. Documents in the Ernest W. Young collection indicate that a reported mound at Moccasin Bluff (Bettarel and Smith 1973:108) was not present at the site in the early twentieth century and only appeared there as a spoil pile after grading had been done for a highway.

Habitation Areas. All mound sites that have been investigated by professional archaeologists are associated with scatters of habitation debris. Earlier reports of collections from the vicinity of the Goodall site (Brown 1964b) clearly indicate that a habitation area was associated with the mound group. In addition to the area containing the mounds, several Middle Woodland habitation sites are located within the vicinity of Goodall. Relatively sparse debris scatters were observed on tightly clustered sites to the south, east, and northeast of the mounds. A manuscript map in the Ernest W. Young collection shows a notation for "lodges" in some of these locations.

Surface surveys at Goodall, Mud Lake, and Upp-Wark have shown that the mound groups at Goodall and Mud Lake are surrounded by extensive but very light debris scatters that produce diagnostic artifacts spanning the entire cultural sequence of the region from Paleoindian to Upper Mississippian. At the Upp-Wark site, habitation debris is confined to a very narrow band adjacent to Wolf Creek, which flows along the northern edge of the site. The sparse artifact scatters characteristic of the habitation areas of Goodall tradition sites suggests that occupations in the Kankakee Valley were shorter-term than was the case for sites in the central and lower Illinois Valley. Kingsley (1999) has proposed that Michigan Hopewell sites represent a subsistence system based on intensive harvest collection of early domesticates with a settlement system centered on large, intensively occupied base camps that may have been inhabited through most of the year. The sparse debris at Goodall tradition sites, however, along with the absence of evidence for substantial architectural construction, storage, or Eastern Agricultural Complex domesticates, suggest that Goodall subsistence was not based on the intensive collecting system envisioned by Kingsley. The failure to identify intensive use of plants or domesticates at relatively large habitation sites in the Grand Valley (Brashler et al., this volume) further weakens an intensive harvest collection model for Michigan Hopewell.

Middle Woodland period diagnostics were also found during field surveys conducted within approximately 1.2 kilometers of the Goodall site. Sites producing Middle Woodland artifacts consisted of small habitations located along the margins of upland marshes, ponds, or bogs. These small sites consisted of sparse scatters of debitage and fire-cracked rock and did not produce pottery. Their close proximity to the Goodall site and relatively ephemeral nature suggest that these sites were used for short periods of time to exploit wetland resources. As these same settings also produce Archaic period artifacts, this is undoubtedly a reflection of a subsistence activity with great time depth.

As Brown (1964b) noted, sites within the Kankakee Marsh are an important part of the Goodall settlement system. These sites are usually located on islands formed by large sandy hills or dunes within the marsh. As was the case for the mound groups, the islands were preferred settlement locations throughout the region's prehistory. Every site that has been examined by reconnaissance survey under good conditions has produced evidence of Middle Woodland occupation. The presence of pottery on these sites suggests that they served as more than special-purpose extractive camps. The islands located within the meander belt immediately adjacent to the Kankakee River were the most intensively occupied. Middle Woodland occupations of islands along the upper Kankakee require further investigation, which should include both surveys and excavations to better define the sizes of these sites and the roles they played in the Goodall tradition settlement-subsistence system. Unfortunately, the sandy, acidic, highly leached and easily eroded soils of the islands are not conducive to site preservation.

Diagnostic Middle Woodland point styles (*affinis* Snyders and Steuben Expanding Stem) also appear to have been widely distributed throughout the uplands, based on reports from artifact collectors and limited field surveys. They are usually found as isolates or are associated with small, sparse scatters of lithic debris and fire-cracked rock. Pottery is absent. These sites appear to suggest brief, seasonal use of the uplands.

In summary, four types of sites appear to have been used during the Middle Woodland period. These consisted of marsh-edge mound groups with associated habitations, small marsh extraction sites presumably oriented toward aquatic resources, large island sites, and small camps in the uplands. Occasionally, these latter sites are also associated with a kettle lake/marsh environment, such as the Pardee site (20BE224) in the Galien River valley, immediately north of the Kankakee Valley (Mangold 1981b). The four site types suggest seasonal movements between the marsh, marsh edge, and uplands. While populations may have briefly aggregated on the marsh margins and islands for up to several months at a time, the idea that mound group sites represent some sort of permanent agricultural settlement severely overestimates the degree of sedentism in the Goodall settlement system.

External Relationships. Based upon current data, the Goodall phase has strong ties to the upper Illinois River valley, especially the "Big Bend" area. Ceramics at Goodall phase sites are similar to types from this region. There was also a lithic "raptor" effigy found at Goodall that closely resembles one from the Steuben site. The presence of large quantities of Burlington chert would reinforce this assessment.

The number of copper items found at Goodall and LaPorte phase sites is almost three times that found in the Grand and Muskegon regions. Only in the latter region have large numbers of copper beads been found (over 250), while only 3 have been reported from northwestern Indiana. It is suggested that the flow of copper from its sources in the Upper Peninsula of Michigan followed a western route through Wisconsin and northern and northeastern Illinois. This same route was preferred during later historic periods.

The Goodall site, with its large number of copper artifacts, may have been a distribution point, and the copper found in southern Michigan may have been obtained in trade with Goodall. Beads may represent a more easily transported item or may be the result of larger or damaged items being recycled.

The occurrence of bottle gourd at Goodall can be roughly compared to Illinois River sites of the same period, such as Smiling Dan, which also produced Knife River chert.

Ties to the north cannot be as well established. Only the presence of turkey-bone awls in Mound 16 and flanking trenches at Bellinger are comparable with those found at Norton.

Conclusion

Recent research has provided new information about the Goodall phase, which can now be seen as a regional subtradition of Havana Hopewell rather than a Middle Woodland migration from Illinois. It is a regionally distinctive subtradition that followed its own distinctive cultural trajectory but was strongly influenced by contacts with the Illinois Valley during the apogee of Hopewellian developments. As is so often the case, new information has answered some old questions while raising many more new ones.

The western limit of Goodall needs to be more clearly defined. Virtually no data on site distributions are available from the lower Kankakee in western Lake County, Indiana, to the river's confluence with the Illinois River. Basic site distribution surveys are needed in this area to determine the western limits of Goodall, along with a modern reassessment of the archaeology of the Utica site.

We have presented a basic model for Goodall chronological development, but the dates are based entirely on comparisons with radiocarbon-dated sites outside of the Goodall tradition. Unfortunately, the sparse habitation debris, along with the heavily leached and easily eroded soils preferred for site locations, contribute to very poor preservation of faunal and botanical remains. Excavations at the Mud Lake site, with its heavier silty soils and long occupation sequence, may provide the best opportunity for obtaining carbon samples suitable for radiocarbon dating and evidence for Goodall subsistence.

The Goodall tradition is known almost exclusively from the excavation of mound sites. The investigation of habitation sites is clearly a high priority for future research if we are to have a more balanced perspective on Goodall occupations.

Artifacts removed from Goodall sites during the nineteenth and early twentieth centuries are still being identified in museum collections scattered over a very large area. No map of the Goodall site was known to exist until 1998, when several were found among the notes of Ernest Young. Other potentially significant data may exist that have not yet come to light.

Future research should also investigate Goodall social organization. Whereas the most complex Hopewellian societies have been characterized as "Big Men" societies (Smith 1986), and some have even been described as chiefdoms (Seeman 1979a), the Goodall tradition was at the lower end of complexity for Middle Woodland societies, and it is not certain if they represent "Big Men" societies or something even less complex. Better reconstructions of mound size and site distributions via geophysical surveys will be necessary to better quantify the complexity of Goodall and its place in the world of Hopewellian interactions.

14

Between Goodall and Norton

Middle Woodland Settlement Patterns and Interaction Networks in Southwestern Michigan

Elizabeth B. Garland and Arthur L. DesJardins

In 1964, James Brown suggested that the Goodall site and related sites in the Kankakee Valley comprise a regional variant of the Havana tradition that is largely coextensive with the Prairie Peninsula. The western Michigan sites in the Grand and Muskegon valleys he found to be stylistically different, forming a distinct cultural unit in a different environmental setting in the major river valleys. Accordingly, it was recommended that the Goodall taxon, as originally formulated by Quimby (1941a, 1941b), be dropped. Brown included the Moccasin Bluff site on the lower St. Joseph River in Goodall-Havana but was equivocal about inclusion of the Sumnerville Mounds (Brown 1964b:108, 121).

Quimby had noted the absence of Hopewell mounds in the Kalamazoo Valley, situated between the St. Joseph and Grand rivers, and little was known about prehistoric occupation of the Kalamazoo Valley until the middle 1960s, when initial surveys and test excavations were conducted by archaeologists from Western Michigan University. Late Woodland sites were located in the lower valley, but evidence of the Middle Woodland was limited to a small number of rocker-stamped sherds at one site. When state funding became available in the 1970s, two major site location surveys were undertaken. Between 1976 and 1981, Cremin directed the Kalamazoo Basin Survey, a systematic survey of a series of transects across the valley from near the outlet at Lake Michigan to the headwaters in Jackson County (Cremin 1980, 1981). Garland directed a more intensive three-year settlement-pattern survey in portions of the lower valley (Garland and Kingsley 1979; Garland and Parachini 1981; Garland and Rhead 1980). Throughout all of this survey work, the recovery of Middle Woodlands cultural material was minimal and limited almost entirely to projectile points, often isolated finds. The settlement-pattern survey identified many Late Woodland sites in the lower Kalamazoo basin, but the near absence of Middle Woodland material prompted initial formulation of Kingsley's environmentally based intensive harvest collecting settlement-system analysis of western Michigan Hopewell (Kingsley 1978, 1981). In Kingsley's model, base camps on or near floodplains were an essential component of the settlement system, and, since the lower Kalamazoo Valley lacks floodplains, the region was avoided by Havana groups entering western Michigan from the south. Following the lead of Flanders and Griffin, Kingsley proposed that the term "Norton tradition," comprising earlier Norton and later Converse phases, be employed for western Michigan Hopewell (Griffin, Flanders, and Titterington 1970; Kingsley 1981).

In 1981, Mangold completed a comprehensive stylistic analysis of Middle Woodland ceramics from western Michigan and the Kankakee Valley. The Mushroom site, a Middle Woodland campsite on the Kalamazoo River, had recently been test excavated. Mangold illustrated ceramics from Mushroom and provided a summary of decorative attributes in his study (Mangold 1981b). Rather than grouping all of western Michigan into the Norton tradition as Kingsley had done, Mangold recognized two broad ceramic style zones: the Goodall Style Zone in the Kankakee and St. Joseph valleys, and the Norton-Converse Style Zone in the northern Grand and Muskegon area (Mangold 1981b; Schurr 1997a). The Mushroom site was included in the Converse phase. Mangold observed that the Goodall Style Zone is characterized by Havana ceramic attributes: linear dentate stamping, straight and vertical rim, beveled lip, and notching of the interior lip. Goodall design elements are relatively larger than in the northern style zone, including larger tooth size of dentate stamps. Following a strong early presence of linear dentate stamping in the Grand and Muskegon sites, the Norton-Converse Style Zone later becomes dominated by Hopewell and Baehr styles: cambered and crosshatched rims and plain and dentate rocker stamping, with plain rocker stamping the dominant attribute. Generally, fine line decoration is typical in contrast with the bolder Havana treatments (Mangold 1981b:271–273). Recent radiocarbon dating (Brashler et al., this volume) has shown that much of the Hopewell series Converse material is in fact contemporary with the Norton phase.

In the two decades since the important early studies by Kingsley and Mangold, many new sites have been identified (fig. 14.1). Excavations have been conducted in the lower St. Joseph area at the US-31 project sites and the Sumnerville Mounds locale. Additional Middle Woodland sites have been identified in excavations and limited testing in the middle St. Joseph basin, and several new sites have been excavated in the Kalamazoo Valley. Results of recent fieldwork and analyses of public and private collections presented here can serve to increase our understanding of cultural dynamics in this region that lies between the major expressions of Goodall Havana in Indiana and the Norton tradition in west-central Michigan.

St. Joseph Valley Sites

When Middle Woodland site locations are plotted on the regional vegetation map compiled from the Government Land Office (GLO) surveys, twelve of fourteen known St. Joseph Valley and Galien River mound and village sites are located in oak and oak-hickory forest settings, with a north-trending distribu-

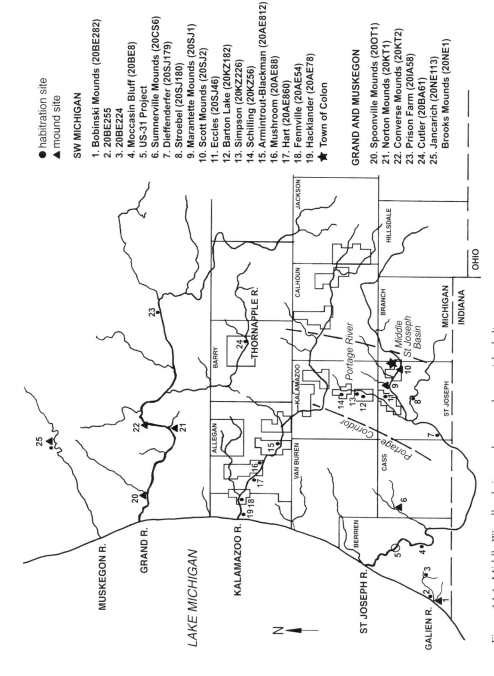

● habitation site
▲ mound site

SW MICHIGAN

1. Bobinski Mounds (20BE282)
2. 20BE255
3. 20BE224
4. Moccasin Bluff (20BE8)
5. US-31 Project
6. Sumnerville Mounds (20CS6)
7. Dieffenderfer (20SJ179)
8. Stroebel (20SJ180)
9. Marantette Mounds (20SJ1)
10. Scott Mounds (20SJ2)
11. Eccles (20SJ46)
12. Barton Lake (20KZ182)
13. Simpson (20KZ226)
14. Schilling (20KZ56)
15. Armintrout-Blackman (20AE812)
16. Mushroom (20AE88)
17. Hart (20AE860)
18. Fennville (20AE54)
19. Hacklander (20AE78)
★ Town of Colon

GRAND AND MUSKEGON

20. Spoonville Mounds (20OT1)
21. Norton Mounds (20KT1)
22. Converse Mounds (20KT2)
23. Prison Farm (20IA58)
24. Cutler (20BA61)
25. Jancarich (20NE113)
    Brooks Mounds (20NE1)

Figure 14.1. Middle Woodland sites and surveyed areas (shaded).

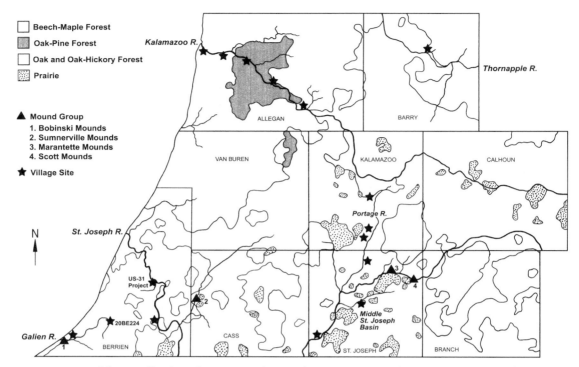

Figure 14.2. Middle Woodland site locations and major forest types in southwestern Michigan. After Brewer 1980.

tion along the Portage River in the prairie/oak savanna region of the middle St. Joseph basin, known as the "Portage Corridor" (fig. 14.2). The three major mound groups—Sumnerville, Marantette, and Scott—are situated on prairie edges; the small Strobel and Dieffenderfer components are close to prairies, and the Portage River sites are in lake and prairie-edge settings. The prairie remnants that dot the landscape of southern Michigan today represent the northeastern extension of the Prairie Peninsula (Brown 1964b). Oak openings around prairie edges would have been highly productive in a hunting-and-collecting strategy, providing browse for deer, acorns, hard-shelled nuts, and a variety of other plant resources.

To the west, the Moccasin Bluff site and lower Galien River sites have oak and oak-hickory forest associations within a much larger area of beech-maple forest in central and western Berrien County. One site in the upper Galien basin (20BE224) and the US-31 project sites are located in the beech-maple area. Beech-maple forests, characterized by extreme shade conditions that exclude other plants, are resource poor in comparison with oak and oak-hickory forests (Ebbers 1990:104). Paleoecological change based on pollen core data (Kapp 1999:56–58) indicates that starting about 2500 B.P., the climate in southern Michigan became moister and cooler. Beech-maple forest expanded as oak-hickory and prairie/oak savanna contracted in areal extent, suggesting that forest composition in Hopewell times was similar to that recorded in the nineteenth-century GLO mapping.

The mitigation phase of the US-31 Berrien County Freeway project (Garland 1990b) included intensive investigation of four sites on the lower St. Joseph River in favorable upland and floodplain locations. A single plain, undecorated pot from the bluff-top Eidson site (20BE122) and sherds from perhaps three Havana Cordmarked vessels from the Rock Hearth site (20BE307) on the floodplain comprise the only clearly Middle Woodland ceramics recovered during intensive site excavation in this project. No rocker-stamped or other Hopewell styles were present, in contrast to the major Havana-Hopewell occupation eight miles to the south at the Moccasin Bluff site (Bettarel and Smith 1973). The near absence of Havana-Hopewell ceramics in the US-31 project sites, located within beech-maple forest, is consistent with a southern-derived Goodall-Havana tradition occupying a continuous oak-hickory forest resource/environmental zone in northeastern Indiana and southwestern Michigan, a distribution that is supported by recently identified middle St. Joseph basin sites.

Quimby (1941b) reported the three major Hopewell mound groups in the St. Joseph Valley, all of them excavated in the nineteenth century. Some materials from these mounds are curated in the Grand Rapids Public Museum (Quimby 1941b). Most of what has survived is from the Sumnerville component, with smaller amounts from Marantette and Scott. Sumnerville is the largest Hopewell mound group south of the Grand River. The site is located on the Dowagiac River in Cass County and is usually described as having nine mounds, based on GLO survey notes. However, the excavator of many of these mounds, E. H. Crane, stated that there were fifteen mounds at Sumnerville within an area of 40 hectares (*Dowagiac Daily News*, 1888). Ceramics from the mounds include a limestone-tempered Hopewell zoned vessel imported from Illinois, as well as grit-tempered types considered to be local copies of Hopewell ware.

The Marantette mounds, also excavated by Crane, were located on the main trench of the river in St. Joseph County. The contents of a single mound were reported by Quimby, but a local informant stated that there were more mounds, possibly as many as five; none is visible today. No ceramics can be definitely associated with the Marantette group, but a distinctive type of copper ear spool links Marantette with the Goodall site (Quimby 1944:421), and copper ear spools are not found in the Grand or Muskegon Valley mounds.

Little is known about the Scott Mound (20SJ2) excavated by Crane near the town of Colon several miles east of Marantette. The single vessel attributed to the Scott mound could be from either Scott or Marantette (Quimby 1941b:117). Local histories record that Crane excavated a total of six mounds in Colon Township (Cutler 1906; Everts 1887). Contents of several Colon-area mounds (20SJ6, 20SJ7) were reported to include "flints" and fire hearths containing animal and fish bone but no human remains and evidently no ceramics. These appear to be similar to the Alberts mounds in Wisconsin that date to the early Middle Woodland period (Jeske, this volume). Similar temporal placement for

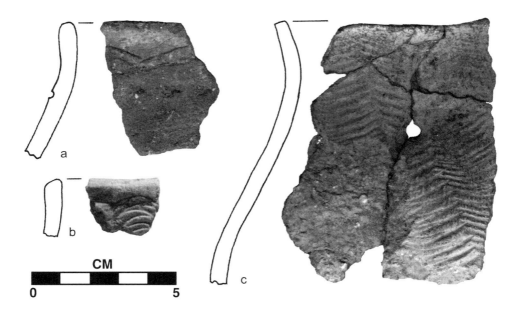

Figure 14.3. Middle St. Joseph basin ceramics: (a) and (b) Dieffenderfer site (20SJ179); (c) Schilling site (20KZ56).

the Colon mounds is suggested by the presence of many large Middle Woodland points in a private collection from the vicinity of the mounds.

The Bobinski site at the mouth of the Galien River in the southwest corner of Michigan is reported to have had three mounds. The presence of Havana ceramics and other Middle Woodland materials at Bobinski and two other sites in the Galien basin are considered to reflect influence from the Goodall area (Mangold 1981a, 1981b).

Previous analysts have agreed that the Middle Woodland ceramics from the Moccasin Bluff site, largely from private collections, include Havana types affiliated with Goodall (Bettarel and Smith 1973; Brown 1964b; Mangold 1981b). Early Neteler and Fettie types—not found (or very rare) elsewhere in Michigan—are present at Moccasin Bluff. A limestone-tempered Hopewell plain bowl and Hopewell dentate rocker-stamped sherds came from a burial group that may have included a small mound at the southern end of the site (Bettarel and Smith 1973:108). Early Middle Woodland Havana and grit-tempered Hopewell-related ceramics at Moccasin Bluff reflect the presence of a fairly intensive occupation.

Five Middle Woodland village components (figs. 14.3, 14.4) have recently been identified in the middle St. Joseph drainage. The Dieffenderfer site on the main river trench is an important Late Woodland site with primary ceramic relationships toward the east (Cremin and DesJardins 2001; Steeby 1997). A handful of Hopewell-related pottery from a small occupation was identified in a restricted area of the site. The collection includes plain rocker-stamped rims from several vessels (fig. 14.3a, b) and two bilaterally thickened rims with flattened lips that are similar to Brangenberg Plain (fig. 14.4a, b). One of the latter has sparse fine-grit temper; the second, with well-mixed paste and no visible temper, has distinctive bright red overall surface color. These Dieffenderfer rims are narrower than classic Brangenberg forms but are clearly related to the type. Brangenberg rims are present at the Goodall site (William Mangold, personal communication 2000) and are found more widely in Illinois and Ohio Hopewell sites. This type has not been reported elsewhere in Michigan.

The Strobel site on the tributary Prairie River produced a small amount of Naples-style zoned dentate stamped pottery, probably representing three vessels (Garland and DesJardins 1995). The site was found by a local collector; test excavation produced very little additional cultural material (fig. 14.4g). The only rim sherd has a steep bevel, suggesting ceramic affiliation with Indiana sites, although the outer edge of the lip is rounded, unlike the sharp profile typical of beveled Kankakee Valley ceramics. The Strobel site represents a small encampment of perhaps one or two families.

The Portage River is a slow, south-flowing stream that rises very close to the Kalamazoo River. It drains south toward the St. Joseph through a broad corridor of lakes and small creeks to its junction with the main trench at the town of Three Rivers in central St. Joseph County. Large private collections with Late

Figure 14.4. Middle St. Joseph basin ceramics: (a) and (b) Dieffenderfer site (20SJ179); (c) and (d) Simpson site (20KZ226); (e) and (f) Eccles site (20SJ46); (g) Strobel site (20SJ180).

Archaic and Middle Woodland points and polished stone artifacts from the Portage River area were observed during initial field and informant surveys in the 1960s. The first site location survey in the lower Portage River area was undertaken in 1980 (Dorothy and Garland 1981). Many large multicomponent sites were identified, although no ceramics were recovered by an experienced field crew. This initial work was followed by numerous surveys and test excavations over large portions of the Portage River drainage under the direction of Cremin; Middle Woodland ceramics have been identified at three of these sites.

The Eccles site is located on the southeastern side of Portage Lake. Sherds from two vessels were recovered in testing. One is a deeply channeled and noded rim (fig. 14.4f), an unusual combination of attributes not observed elsewhere. Body sherds from a second vessel (fig. 14.4e) exhibit bold, dentate-stamped impressions filling a curvilinear zone, similar both to Prison Farm examples and to a cord-wrapped-tool–impressed vessel at Norton Mounds (Brashler, Laidler, and Martin 1998; Griffin, Flanders, and Titterington 1970:173c). Owing to limited testing, this component at Eccles is of unknown size.

Northwest of Eccles in Kalamazoo County is the important Simpson site, situated north of Barton Lake. Simpson may have a substantial Middle Woodland component, based on field records showing test-unit recovery of ceramics spanning a 25-square-meter area and the presence of pit features. A Naples Dentate-like rim with a square lip and narrow (1.5 millimeters) linear stamping at an oblique angle to the lip (fig. 14.4c), and a plain, thick body sherd with a zone line were found in one unit. A second rim, found 5 meters distant, has a square lip and similar narrow stamping and is probably from a different vessel. Three small split rim fragments with fingernail impressions (fig. 14.4d) and thick, cordmarked body sherds were recovered in a pit feature. Similar fingernail decoration on a vessel with a square lip is reported at 20BE255 on the lower Galien River (Mangold 1981a:37). The Simpson site may be relatively large, and the presence of pit features makes it of particular interest for further investigation.

The Schilling site is situated on East Lake in southern Kalamazoo County. Middle Woodland points are included in a donated collection from the site. During test excavations, sherds from more than half of a single Middle Woodland vessel were the only ceramics recovered. The vessel wall is thin (6 millimeters), and the rim, with a drilled hole, flares to a thinned lip (fig. 14.3c). Plain rocker stamping covers the entire vessel from lip to base; there is no zoning. Decoration is carefully applied in vertical columns of tightly spaced stamping, with adjacent columns creating a herringbone pattern across the surface, an effect reminiscent of simple-stamped treatment in Ohio Hopewell wares (compare Prufer 1968:145). The Schilling vessel is a unique Hopewell expression within our study area. Also unique at Schilling and in southwestern Michigan is a fragment of an obsidian biface, evidently a large preform. This material has been determined by x-ray fluorescence to be from Obsidian Cliff in Yellowstone National Park, the source area for most of the obsidian in Ohio and Illinois Hopewell deposits (Griffin, Gordus, and Wright 1969; Hughes 2000a).

The final village site material in the St. Joseph Valley to be considered is from two occupation areas near the Sumnerville mounds. Early avocational archaeologists considered 20CS99 on the Dowagiac River to be *the* village site. We have several surface collections of lithics from 20CS99, but unfortunately, because of potential crop damage, the area was not accessible to the 1989 university field school. We did test the margin of this site, recovering a small number of thin plain and cordmarked body sherds but no rims. An adjacent property held initial promise, but investigators learned that the topsoil had been scraped off many years ago for construction of an earthen dam. In testing, we recovered debitage and two plain rocker-stamped, zoned body sherds; no remnant pit features were identified.

Following Crane's excavation in 1888, two of the Sumnerville mounds, each approximately 10 meters in diameter and 1.5–2 meters high, were preserved in a woodlot and are relatively intact today. In 1989, a systematic sample of 1-x-1-meter units was excavated at 20CS6 in a plowed field east of these mounds; additional testing was done in areas closer to the mounds (Garland 1990a). Included within the fill of a large pit in the plowed area was a deposit of red ocher containing a small undecorated pot, a blade of Burlington chert, and a broken polished stone gorget. Two ossuaries unaccompanied by grave goods were found nearby. A light scatter of thin plain and cordmarked sherds and small amounts of debitage were recovered in the excavated sample, predominantly in units closest to the mounds. There were no fire-cracked rocks or features related to domestic activity. Decorated sherds include two rims: one is rather crudely incised or brushed; the second is a Sumnerville Incised rim with well-executed fine-line incising parallel to the lip. We also recovered a brushed body sherd 1 centimeter in thickness and a zoned body sherd with very fine rocker incising in one area and fine dentate decoration in a second zone. Hopewell and Baehr motifs characterize this small assemblage from 20CS6, which appears to represent one or more short-term occupations related to mortuary ceremonial activity.

The fifteen burial mounds in the Sumnerville area (accepting Crane's figure), reflect use over multiple generations, possibly several hundred years, and perhaps by different cultural groups. A small number of sherds from Sumnerville in the Grand Rapids Museum includes two with relatively thick rims: one is Naples Dentate Stamped and the other is a noded cordmarked rim with tool marks on the interior lip. These sherds are from Walter Mound 1, presumably the largest of a group of three mounds located a half-mile north of 20CS6, and the linear group of six mounds described in the GLO survey (Garland 1990a:191–192). The Walter Mounds are associated with a horseshoe-shaped enclosure that is visible in aerial photos. Walter Mound 1 was reported in a nineteenth-century account to be 15 meters in diameter and 4 meters high, the largest mound in Cass County (Mathews 1882:14).

In our excavated samples and various surface collections from Sumnerville made over a period of several years, we recovered nothing similar to the Havana Walter mounds material. Walter may represent the initial group of mounds con-

Table 14.1. Sumnerville Mounds–Area Points and Debitage Raw Material

Raw Material or Chert Type Site/Type	N	Bayport	Norwood	Burlington	Wyandotte	Flint Ridge	Upper Mercer	Onondaga	Local
Points[a]									
20CS99 (n=9)									
Manker Corner-notched	1								1
Norton Corner-notched	1	1							
Untyped Corner-notched	7	3							4
20CS6 (n=3)									
Untyped Corner-notched	3	1						1	1
Debitage[b]									
20CS99	145	8.9	2.1	12.4	1.4	0	0	0	75.2
20CS6	1,317	11.0	1.0	< 0.1	0.3	0.3	0.5	0	86.9

a. Site values as counts.
b. Site values as percentages.

structed at Sumnerville and the material appears to be Goodall related. The six mounds in a line appear to be associated with Sumnerville Incised and Baehr ceramics more closely related to the Kalamazoo Valley sites and the Norton tradition.

We recovered nine Middle Woodland cultural material projectile points from village contexts at Sumnerville: one Manker, one Norton, and seven untyped corner-notched (table 14.1). Four points (44 percent) are of Bayport chert. Additionally, Sumnerville has the highest percentage of Bayport chert debitage (approximately 10 percent) of all sites analyzed in this study. The high proportion of Burlington chert from surface collection at 20CS99 suggests a Goodall relationship, whereas Burlington is virtually absent at 20CS6, the excavated area with Hopewell ceramics near the two extant mounds. The absence of Snyders points and the prominence of Bayport chert at Sumnerville, along with the low occurrence of Wyandotte chert in the lithic assemblage as a whole, distinguishes Sumnerville from sites farther to the east in the middle St. Joseph and Portage River area, as will be discussed further in the lithics section below.

The foregoing assessment of Middle Woodland in the St. Joseph Valley has shown that for the most part sites are affiliated with Goodall-Havana to the south and west. With the exception of Sumnerville, they exhibit little or no ceramic relationship to the Kalamazoo Valley sites. The Walter group suggests southern affiliation, but other evidence, including Sumnerville Incised ceramics and a high frequency of Bayport chert, attests to interaction with (or integration with) the Norton tradition. Given the ambiguous status of Sumnerville, and because the information from most sites is extremely limited, the term "Goodall periphery," having both stylistic and geographic connotation, seems the most appropriate designation for the St. Joseph Valley sites.

The Kalamazoo Valley Sites

The environmental setting of the Kalamazoo Valley Middle Woodland sites is very different from the oak-hickory forest and prairie locales of the St. Joseph. The five known Kalamazoo village sites with ceramics are all located along the main trench of the river in central Allegan County, an area dominated by oak-pine forest. A beech-maple zone near Lake Michigan has frequent admixture of hemlock, and northern white pine occurs throughout much of the area. Allegan County thus has a mosaic of plant communities, including extensive areas of swamps and swamp forest associations of elm, ash, and maple bordering the river along its lower course.

The lower Kalamazoo Valley begins below the Allegan Dam, the location of the first rapids or riffles, where the river crosses a bedrock sill. Downstream from this point the river floods bank to bank and there is no floodplain development, as extensively discussed by Kingsley (1978, 1981). The two sites that reflect repeated use over an extended period of time, Mushroom and Armintrout-Blackman, are both located above the Allegan Dam in the middle river valley. Information on subsistence is virtually nonexistent from the Kalamazoo sites, since deep intact pit features for cooking or storage that might provide such data have not been identified.

Armintrout-Blackman Site

The Armintrout-Blackman site has produced the longest Middle Woodland sequence and provides important correlations between ceramics and projectile point types. The site is concentrated around a seasonal spring at the edge of the bluff on the north side of the river in an area 40 meters long by about 8 meters wide (fig. 14.5). This upper-terrace occupation has been completely excavated by members of the Michigan Archaeological Society, assisted by one university field school. Results of the first period of fieldwork have been published (Spero et al. 1991). Subsequent work since 1994 on the west side of the upper terrace and on the lower terrace, as yet unpublished, has added significantly to site interpretation.

Armintrout-Blackman was seasonally occupied by Woodland groups from the Early/Middle Woodland transition into the Late Woodland (DesJardins 2001; Spero et al. 1991). No pit features can be reliably assigned to the Middle Woodland period, which remains undated by radiocarbon. Limited Late Woodland activity is represented by Madison points and construction of small storage pits on the upper terrace. Although the site has been plowed to the edge of the bluff, sandy soil minimizes lateral displacement of artifacts, which in turn enhances recognition of spatially defined Middle Woodland ceramic components and lithic associations. Unlike most plow-zone sites, Armintrout-Blackman has fortunately received little attention from past collectors.

The earliest component is represented by interior-exterior cordmarked ceramics; four or five vessels may be present. These are generally thicker than later types, but massive lower wall and basal sherds are not present. One of these

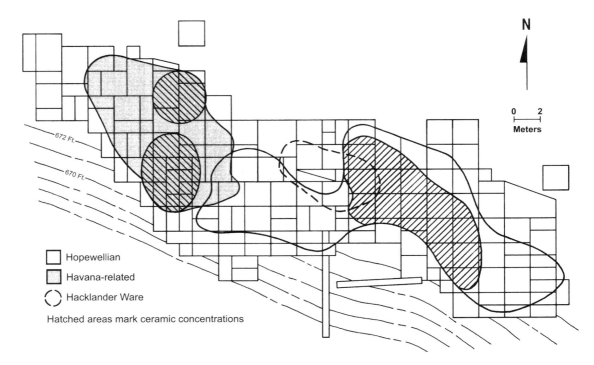

Figure 14.5. Ceramic distributions on the upper terrace at the Armintrout-Blackman site.

vessels has Sister Creeks decoration, five rows of five finger-pinched punctates around the exterior rim and upper wall (fig. 14.6a). A second pot has a small corded-tool impression on the rim. Several additional interior-exterior cord-marked vessels are undecorated. Chronological placement of this occupation is unknown, but various typological expressions of interior-exterior cord marking may persist late in the Kalamazoo Valley (Garland and Beld 1999). Seven stemmed points may be associated with this early component at Armintrout-Blackman.

Ceramic distributions indicate the presence of two principal Middle Woodland components that exhibit clear spatial separation (fig. 14.5). The west side of the site is dominated by Havana-related types, some fifteen to twenty vessels (fig. 14.6b–f). These occur in two concentrations that reflect activity by different small groups. Thick cordmarked and noded pots, cord-wrapped-stick rim treatments, deep circular punctates on the lower rim, and cordmarked vessels with smoothed rims and rounded lips are present. Beveled lips are rare, and linear dentate stamping and zoning are absent. Some of the cordmarked and noded rims are similar to ceramics at the Prison Farm site in the Grand Valley (Brashler, Laidler, and Martin 1998). The smoothed-rim vessels (fig. 14.6f) resemble Middle Woodland Plain ware at the Schultz site in rim and lip morphology (Fischer 1972:179–181). There is variability that probably reflects some time depth within the west-side ceramics; greater thickness sets all of this material apart from the Hopewellian component, however.

Figure 14.6. Armintrout-Blackman site (20AE812), Early Woodland and Havana-related occupation ceramics: (a) Sister Creeks, interior cordmarked; (b), (c), and (e) cordmarked, noded; (d) noded, cord-wrapped-tool lip impressions, punctates on smoothed rim; (f) straight smoothed rim, rounded lip.

The occupation in the central and eastern part of the site is represented by some twenty-five thin-walled vessels with Hopewell and Baehr-related decorative treatments (Morgan 1985; Spero et al. 1991). Ceramics from this component, designated Hopewellian on the map, are illustrated in figure 14.7. Plain rocker-stamped rim treatment predominates, occurring on ten vessels (Spero et al. 1991). Zoned plain rocker-stamped body decoration is very common; combed and brushed surfaces are also well represented. A variant of Sumnerville Incised and Baehr-related brushed and crosshatched rims were identified, along with a number of plain undecorated rims. One of the rocker-stamped rims is from a very small, thin-walled lobed pot (fig. 14.7b). Similarities in this component to Green Point Rocker Stamped ceramics at the Schultz site have been noted (Spero et al. 1991), but dentate rocker stamping, common at Schultz, is very rare in the upper-terrace Hopewellian component at Armintrout-Blackman.

Cordmarked sherds that appear to be Late Woodland were also found on the east side of the site. The rims of several vessels are thickened and exhibit bidirectional cord marking that sets off rim from body (fig. 14.7f), simulating Middle Woodland rim treatments; it is suggested that these vessels are locally transitional to Late Woodland. A small Hacklander ware component of probable

Figure 14.7. Armintrout-Blackman site (20AE812), Hopewellian occupation ceramics: (a), (b), and (c) rocker stamped; (d), (e), and (g) crosshatched (sherd g is from lower terrace); (i) incised; (h) plain; (f) bidirectional cordmarked.

early Middle Woodland age is represented by three vessels in the central area of the site.

The inferred temporal relationship of the Hopewellian component, including generally later wares, is supported by spatial separation between the two major components at Armintrout-Blackman and is not without parallel in Michigan. At the Schultz site in the Saginaw Valley, thick Havana-related ceramics (Tittabawassee ware) were stratified below Green Point ware with plain and dentate rocker-stamped and incised decoration. This stratigraphic relationship at Schultz is not entirely clear-cut, but there is "little evidence of blending or contemporaneity" between the two wares (Fischer 1972:158). However, an AMS date in the second century A.D. on a Green Point vessel at the Fletcher site (Lovis 1990) seems to indicate temporal overlap with earlier Middle Woodland material in the Saginaw Valley, leaving open the same possibility at Armintrout-Blackman. On present evidence, spatial separation representing a time difference is the preferred explanation; early dates from the Converse site (Brashler et al., this volume), however, invite further evaluation of Armintrout-Blackman ceramics.

Two vessels from the lower terrace at Armintrout-Blackman—a cambered and channeled rim with fine-line cross-hatching and bordering punctates (fig.

Figure 14.8. Zoned dentate rocker-stamped vessels: (a) Armintrout-Blackman, lower terrace; (b) Mushroom site.

14.7g), and a zoned dentate rocker-stamped vessel (fig. 14.8a)—are unlike ceramics from the upper-terrace Hopewellian component. The dentate-stamped pot is stylistically similar to a Green Point Dentate Stamped vessel at Schultz (Fischer 1972:172a) and a pot from the Mushroom site (fig. 14.8b). The Armintrout-Blackman vessel has a vertical rim, however, while the other two have flared rims.

A distinction between the Havana and Hopewellian occupations at Armintrout-Blackman is supported by the spatial distribution of projectile point types (DesJardins 2001). Norton (n = 10) and untyped corner-notched points (n = 24) are highly correlated with Havana-like ceramics on the western side of the site, whereas Middle Woodland expanding-stem forms (n = 22) predominate within the Hopewellian occupation. Virtually all the points made from nonlocal cherts, principally Bayport and Norwood, are corner-notched styles (table 14.2), whereas the expanding-stem points are all of local cherts, except for a single example of Norwood.

Mushroom Site

A second large Middle Woodland site in the Kalamazoo Valley, also on the north side of the river, is the Mushroom site, located one mile upriver from the Allegan Dam. In marked contrast to the spatially concentrated Armintrout-Blackman site, Mushroom has a discontinuous occupation that sprawls over 1.5 hectares on the second and third terraces of the river (Mangold 1981a). Plowing has disturbed most of the site, and much of the third-terrace occupation was in a sand blowout that had been heavily collected for many years; previous collections could not be located. The Allegan Dam Road passes directly through the center of the site, creating a major impact. The Mushroom site was identified and surface collected in 1978 and extensively tested by the field school in 1980.

Table 14.2. Armintrout-Blackman and Mushroom Points and Debitage Raw Material

Raw Material or Chert Type Site/Type	N	Bayport	Norwood	Burlington	Wyandotte	Flint Ridge	Upper Mercer	Onondaga	Local
Points[a]									
Armintrout-Blackman (*n*=34)									
Norton Corner-notched	10	2							8
Untyped Corner-notched	24	5	4	1					14
Mushroom (*n*=7)									
Norton Corner-notched	5	3							2
Untyped Corner-notched	2								2
Debitage[b]									
20CS99	27,002	0.6	0.2	0.9	0.1	0.6	<0.1	0	97.5
20CS6	5,618	1.5	1.1	2.1	0.8	<0.1	0.4	0	94.1

a. Site values as counts.
b. Site values as percentages.

We were fortunate to find a small intact hearth near the edge of the sand blowout that produced a calibrated date of A.D. 410 (Uga-2347) in tight association with plain rocker-stamped and thin cordmarked body sherds.

The Mushroom site is predominately Middle Woodland, with a small Late Woodland component in one area. One Dickson point was recovered in addition to corner-notched Middle Woodland types. Meaningful distributional associations between the points and ceramics could not be established. Mangold (1981b) summarized selected stylistic attributes from thirty to forty decorated Middle Woodland vessels. Twenty-five plain Middle Woodland rims and a smaller number of Late Woodland rims were also identified in the collection.

Among the earliest ceramic evidence at the site is a single interior-exterior cordmarked, noded sherd that is 14 millimeters thick (fig. 14.9b); no other sherds approach this thickness. Mushroom Cordmarked (fig. 14.9a) is a relatively thin interior-exterior cordmarked type with distinctive dark mineral temper (Garland 1986; Mangold 1981b). It is represented by three or more vessels, most from a restricted area of the site. Mushroom Cordmarked is well made and undecorated. It may belong in the Early/Middle Woodland transition, or as Mangold believes, it may be a Middle Woodland type (Garland 1986; Mangold 1981b:269). The entire question of late persistence of interior-exterior cord marking in western Michigan poses a major interpretative problem for regional archaeology (Garland 1986; Garland and Beld 1999).

Norton tradition attributes at Mushroom include beveled lips on four vertical rims, one with a sharp-angled profile. A plain body sherd with prominent concentric curvilinear zoning (fig. 14.9d) recalls both the Goodall site (Quimby 1941b:127) and a vessel from the burial pit below Brooks Mound A in the Muskegon Valley (Prahl 1991:86). Narrow linear dentate stamping is present as a minor type of rim and lip decoration (fig. 14.9g). These attributes are not present in the Havana-related component at Armintrout-Blackman, with the exception of one beveled rim.

Figure 14.9. Mushroom site (20AE88) ceramics: (a) Mushroom Cordmarked, interior-exterior cordmarked; (b) cordmarked, noded; (c) plain; (d) curvilinear zoned; (e) crosshatched, noded; (f) tool impressed, noded; (g) linear dentate stamped; (h) incised, noded; (i) interrupted crosshatched.

Closer ceramic comparisons between the two sites are seen with the Baehr types, including the predominance of plain rocker-stamped, incised, brushed, and combed decorative treatments. Dentate rocker stamping may be somewhat more common at Mushroom, although many sherds may be from a single vessel (fig. 14.8b). Punctate rim decoration similar to Steuben Punctated (fig. 14.10a, b) occurs at Mushroom, but it is not clearly present at Armintrout-Blackman.

Sumnerville Incised, with parallel horizontal incising on the rim, is present at both sites. The incising on the Mushroom rim (fig. 14.10d) is a very fine line, carefully executed, and closely resembles a rim from 20CS6 at Sumnerville, whereas the Armintrout-Blackman rim (fig. 14.7i) has deeper and more closely spaced incision. Crosshatched rims also occur at both sites but differ in that several Mushroom rims seem closer to the classic Hopewell type: closely spaced fine-line incising, with small bordering punctates on cambered rims. One of these has an interrupted crosshatched design (fig. 14.10i), a widespread Hopewell motif (William Mangold, personal communication). In comparison, crosshatched rims from the upper terrace at Armintrout-Blackman are wider and the

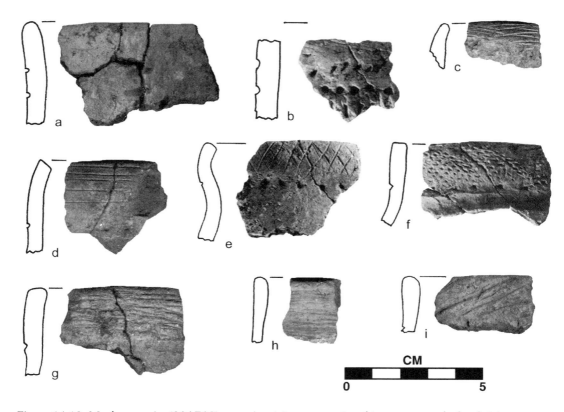

Figure 14.10. Mushroom site (20AE88) ceramics: (a) punctate rim; (b) punctate neck sherd; (c) rocker stamped; (d) Sumnerville Incised; (e) crosshatched; (f) dentate rocker stamped; (g) and (i) incised; (h) brushed.

design is less well executed; an incised line rather than punctates directly borders the rim (fig. 14.7d, e).

Four body sherds of the temporally and culturally enigmatic Hacklander ware, seemingly ever present at western Michigan Middle Woodland sites, were recovered at the Mushroom site. Perhaps the greatest overall contrast between the ceramic assemblages from these two important Middle Woodland campsites is the minimal presence at Mushroom of ceramics similar to the west-side Havana-related occupation or occupations at Armintrout-Blackman.

The information encoded in the elaborate zoned decoration on the dentate rocker-stamped vessels from both sites, the precise expression of the interrupted crosshatched rim motif at Mushroom, and the small lobed pot at Armintrout-Blackman afford intriguing glimpses into the wider Hopewellian symbolic world from the vantage of these Kalamazoo Valley campsites far removed from the major centers of mortuary ceremonialism.

The Mushroom site, heavily collected in the past and not fully excavated, has a much smaller number of lithic diagnostics than does Armintrout-Blackman (table 14.2). Three Norton points made of Bayport chert are the only exotic cherts represented. Both sites have small amounts of southern exotic chert debitage, but the generally higher percentages at Mushroom hint at more diverse interactions with other groups.

Hart Site

The Hart site is on the south bluff of the Kalamazoo River within the oak-pine woodlands of the lower valley. The site is located near the edge of the actively eroding cut bank, and it was discovered in 1999 when large segments of a Middle Woodland pot were found on the erosional slope below the bluff edge. Salvage excavation and testing by the Michigan Archaeological Society followed (Garland and DesJardins 1999; Garland 2000). The salvaged vessel is Naples Dentate Stamped, cordmarked and noded, with two rows of bold, deeply impressed dentate stamps and a rounded lip (fig. 14.11a). No additional Havana sherds were recovered on the site surface in the immediate vicinity of this vessel, but a block excavation 20 meters to the east near the bluff edge revealed a mixed deposit of Middle and Early Woodland materials. A Snyders point of local chert (fig. 14.11c) and rim sherds of a thick, undecorated, smoothed cordmarked vessel with a rounded lip were recovered. This vessel has the massive temper and crudely finished surfaces indicative of Early Woodland ceramics. Body sherds representing two additional vessels, believed to be Middle Woodland, were also present in the block excavation. Charcoal from the base of a deep fire pit has been dated at cal B.P. 2410 ±60 (Beta-145464); a second Snyders point and probable Middle Woodland sherds were recovered in the upper fill zone of this pit.

The Hart site is situated so as to command a long view of the Kalamazoo River in both directions. On its western side the terrain descends to a lower elevation, providing easy access to the river. The presence of Late Woodland and Upper Mississippian ceramics and features in other areas of the site indicates that this was a favored locality throughout much of the Woodland period; the Late Woodland 46th Street site (Rogers 1972) is located approximately 130 meters east of Hart. Hopewell or Baehr-related ceramics are notably absent at Hart and its environs.

The Naples Dentate Stamped vessel suggests a relationship to Illinois valley ceramics in the Big Bend area and could date within the first century B.C. (William Mangold, personal communication, 2000). The Havana occupation at Hart appears to be short term and of small size, although an undetermined portion of the site has been lost to the river. The two Snyders points of local chert from Hart are the only points of this type from the Kalamazoo Valley Middle Woodland as presently known. The presence of at least one contemporary site in this region is indicated by a very similar Naples Dentate Stamped rim with a single row of stamps and a flattened lip (fig. 14.11b) that was received in a donated collection some thirty years ago. We have been unable to establish the location of this site, known only to be in the vicinity of Swan Creek, a north-flowing tributary several miles upstream from Hart.

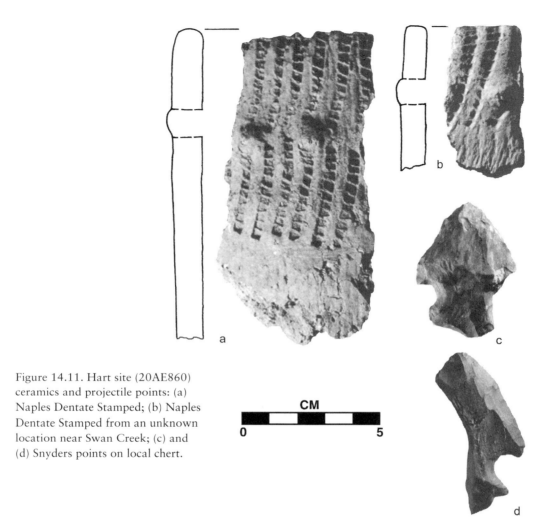

Figure 14.11. Hart site (20AE860) ceramics and projectile points: (a) Naples Dentate Stamped; (b) Naples Dentate Stamped from an unknown location near Swan Creek; (c) and (d) Snyders points on local chert.

Fennville Site

The Fennville site is located on the south side of the river downstream from Hart. A Hopewellian component was identified (Rogers 1972:87) in a disturbed interior location about 90 meters south of the main site, a large early Late Woodland occupation located on the bluff edge above a spring. Surface collection and preliminary testing were carried out in the 1960s, but the extent of the Hopewellian occupation could not be determined. The site was destroyed for a new bridge access before further work could be done. Plain rocker-stamped rims, very fine-line zoned and burnished plain rocker-stamped body sherds, and an incised body sherd were among the ceramics recovered (fig. 14.12). An untyped corner-notched point made of local chert is probably associated with this component.

Hacklander Site

The Hacklander site is located near the mouth of the Kalamazoo River where the river enters Lake Michigan. It is a large site with major components containing Late Woodland Allegan and Hacklander wares (Garland 1976; Kingsley 1977, 1989). The site is on the sloping south bank, with the highest elevation about 1 meter above the present river level. A small Hopewellian component, unmixed with later ceramics, was identified in a restricted area at the lowest elevation on the site. This occupation was contained within a 4-×-8-meter block that was completely excavated. Rim sherds of four vessels were recovered; Baehr rocker stamping and incising characterize the assemblage (fig. 14.12). There was a considerable amount of debitage, but no points were directly associated with this occupation. One Norton point made of local chert and two untyped corner-notched points, one of Bayport and one of local chert, were identified in the collection from this intensively excavated site. These points were not associated with Hacklander ware, nor can we specify a Hacklander point type.

The Hacklander site is situated at a constriction in the river valley and was certainly a crossing point; a historically known trail leads to the site from the

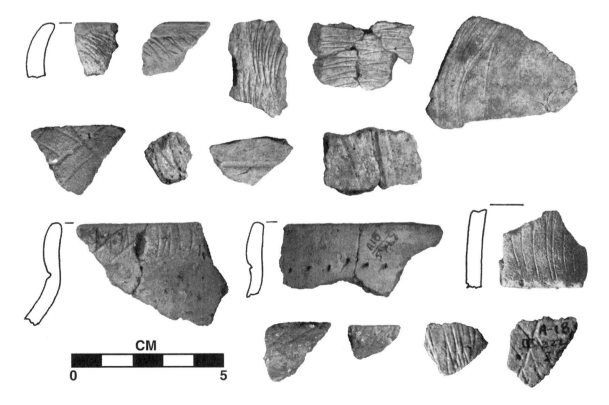

Figure 14.12. *Upper two rows*, Hacklander site (20AE78) ceramics; *lower two rows*, Fennville site (20AE54) ceramics.

south. In this regard, it is interesting to note that ease of river crossing seems to have been a factor in Middle Woodland site location in the Kalamazoo Valley. All five known campsites, large and small, are at or near places where the valley narrows; three are at bridge locations.

External Relationships of the Kalamazoo Sites

Four of the five Kalamazoo sites (fig. 14.13), excluding Hart, have expressions of Hopewell and Baehr ceramics similar to Spoonville and other sites in the Grand Valley. As a group these Hopewellian components stand in contrast to sites in the Goodall periphery, particularly in relation to sites in the Portage Corridor. Specific resemblance was seen between examples of Sumnerville Incised at Mushroom and at Sumnerville; burnished surfaces and very fine-line incising at Fennville, and to a lesser extent at Hacklander, also recall Sumnerville decorative treatments. It is possible that groups affiliated with Sumnerville may have visited the lower Kalamazoo Valley or otherwise interacted with local people. The presence at Sumnerville of Bayport chert in significant quantities, as well as some Norwood chert, strengthens the case for interaction between Sumnerville and the northern Middle Woodland, whereas the spatially separated Walter Mounds appear to be Goodall related.

The Mushroom site exhibits clear relationship with Spoonville in the lower Grand Valley; Mangold (1981b) observed near identity between two Hopewell series vessels from Mushroom and Spoonville, probably made by the same potter. Regional group mobility or exchange of women between groups could explain these close ceramic similarities. In previous studies the Mushroom Cordmarked type has been compared to pottery from the northern Toft Lake site and also to Spoonville, as well as to Kankakee basin sites (Mangold 1981b:45–47; see also Garland 1986; Garland and Beld 1999; Schurr 1997a). The Naples Dentate Stamped vessel and Snyders points at the Hart site present intriguing evidence for early contact with the south.

Armintrout-Blackman has a long Middle Woodland sequence that includes Havana-related or early Norton tradition ceramics that appear similar to cordmarked noded pots from Prison Farm (Brashler, Laidler, and Martin 1998) and to a cordmarked noded variant of Tittabawassee ware at 20GR14 in the Saginaw uplands (Beld 1991). The Hopewellian ceramics at Armintrout-Blackman are generally related to Grand Valley Hopewell series wares.

Projectile points made of Bayport chert predominate among the exotic cherts in the Kalamazoo sites, and five points of Norwood chert at Armintrout-Blackman indicate contacts with Grand Valley groups that procured this material from the north. Norwood debitage is found at the Mushroom site and also in the Middle Woodland area of the Hacklander site. Distinctive ceramic assemblages and the predominance of Norton points and Bayport and Norwood cherts place the Kalamazoo sites in a regional cultural and geographic context north and west of the Portage Corridor. The five Kalamazoo sites collectively reflect varying degrees of ceramic similarity to each other and to the Norton

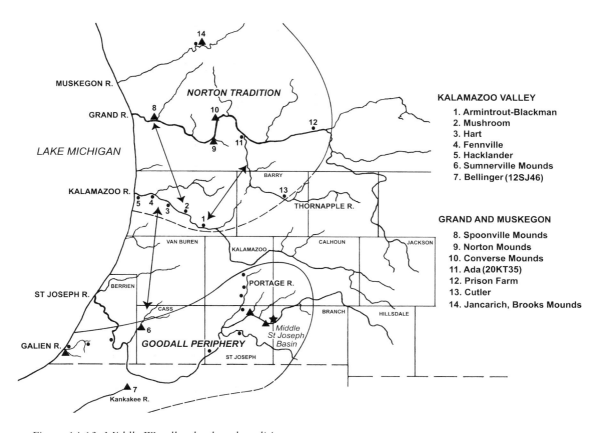

Figure 14.13. Middle Woodland cultural traditions.

tradition. They can best be regarded as Norton-affiliated, pending more detailed comparative studies.

Middle Woodland Projectile Points and Lithic Raw Materials

Analysis of lithic material focused on the distribution of widely recognized Middle Woodland corner-notched point styles and associated raw materials. Data were obtained from site excavations, extensive area survey projects, and provenienced private collections, representing the first attempt to examine all readily available data within an eleven-county study area in southwestern Michigan. In total the lithic data examined comprise 208 Middle Woodland points and over 40,000 pieces of lithic debitage from twenty-five excavated sites, sixty-seven individual survey sites, and three important private collections. The latter include the Drumm collection from the Colon area, in the vicinity of the Scott Mound and others in the middle St. Joseph Valley; a collection from the Schilling site (20KZ56) in the Portage River area; and a third from the Cutler site (20BA61) in the middle reaches of the Thornapple River in the Grand River basin. These collections are very informative because they contain the projectile

Table 14.3. Early Woodland Stemmed Points Raw Material Summary

Raw Material or Chert Type Region/Subarea	N	Bayport	Norwood	Burlington	Wyandotte	Flint Ridge	Upper Mercer	Onondaga	Loca
Kramer (n=35)									
Portage-Thornapple Corridor									
Middle St. Joseph Basin	6								6
Portage River Area	7	3							4
Thornapple River Area	4	3							1
Middle Kalamazoo Valley	6	2							4
Lower Kalamazoo Valley									
Upper Kalamazoo Valley									
Sumnerville Mounds Area									
US-31 Project Area	12								12
Totals (counts)	35	8							27
(percentage of total)		22.9							77.1
Other Early Woodland Stemmed (n=63)									
Portage-Thornapple Corridor									
Middle St. Joseph Basin	22	1		1	13	3		2	2
Portage River Area	9	1			1		1		6
Thornapple River Area	10	2		2	2			2	2
Middle Kalamazoo Valley	6	1			4				1
Lower Kalamazoo Valley	4				1				3
Upper Kalamazoo Valley									
Sumnerville Mounds Area									
US-31 Project Area	12	1		2	1				8
Totals (counts)	63	6		5	22	3	1	4	22
(percentage of total)		9.5		7.9	34.9	4.8	1.7	6.3	34.9

points that have largely disappeared from existing surfaces after a century of collecting. Unfortunately, the important Portage River area has been the focus of especially intensive long-term collecting.

The distribution of different point types associated with distinctive raw materials during the Middle Woodland period in southwestern Michigan has precedence in the Early Woodland period. Square-stemmed Kramer points (Justice 1987:184; Ozker 1982:91–96) represent an important point type in southern Michigan Early Woodland assemblages. Other Early Woodland stemmed points related to Dickson, Adena, and Robbins types (Justice 1987:187–196) also have a wide distribution in southwestern Michigan. These points typically exhibit a contracting stem morphology, although we have identified several with straight to slightly expanding basal configurations, similar to what Justice described for some late Adena and Robbins examples. All of our Early Woodland points occur in highest frequency (59.2 percent) in the middle St. Joseph basin, the Portage River area, and the Thornapple River area (table 14.3). We have previously referred to the middle St. Joseph and Portage River region as the Portage Corridor (fig. 14.1). Early and Middle Woodland lithic evidence however, suggests that this interactive corridor can be extended northward into the Thornapple River area and thus will be hereafter termed the Portage-Thornapple

Corridor, representing an important avenue of material exchange linking the Grand River basin to the region south of our study area.

Kramer points ($n = 35$) are made exclusively from either Bayport chert or locally available glacial till cherts (table 14.3); of those made of Bayport chert, six of eight (75.0 percent) are in the Portage-Thornapple Corridor. Other stemmed points ($n = 63$) in our study area have variable raw material associations; thirty-five (55.6 percent) are made from exotic cherts from distant southern and eastern source areas, predominantly Wyandotte chert from Harrison County, Indiana. Of those made from these distant raw materials, twenty-six (41.3 percent) occur within the Portage-Thornapple Corridor. These distributions indicate that interaction occurred between Michigan Early Woodland people and groups in many distant areas and that the Portage-Thornapple Corridor was an important conduit for material exchange.

Middle Woodland corner-notched points in this study have been divided into four stylistic variants of the Snyders Cluster (Justice 1987:201–204; Montet-White 1968): Snyders, Norton Corner-notched, Manker Corner-notched, and an untyped category of small corner-notched forms. Expanding-stem points related to Manker Stemmed (Montet-White 1968:73) and Lowe Flared Base and Steuben Expanding Stemmed types (Justice 1987:208–214) are associated with the later Middle Woodland component at the Armintrout-Blackman site. However, this expanding-stem category was not monitored elsewhere in our study area owing to a lack of clear ceramic associations and potential typological confusion with Late Archaic expanding-stem types (for summary discussion see Brashler, Garland, and Lovis 1994).

Our sample of thirty-two Snyders points (fig. 14.14a–b) yielded the characteristics of broad-bladed forms with biplano to biconvex profiles, broad flat percussion-flake scars, and deep corner notches produced by indirect percussion and pressure-flake retouch. Blades on most specimens evidence varying degrees of reworking. The deep notching technique on these broad-bladed forms has resulted in points exhibiting a relatively long stem and broad neck width, greater than was observed for all other corner-notched types in our study area.

Norton Corner-notched points (fig. 14.14c) are a common Middle Woodland form in western Michigan, exemplified by a morphologically distinctive group of points from the Norton Mounds in the Grand River basin (Griffin, Flanders, and Titterington 1970). Norton points ($n = 60$) are characterized as relatively long and narrow-bladed forms with notches placed low in the corners of the preform, and notch openings that typically lack the depth and breadth exhibited in Snyders examples (Montet-White 1965, 1968:71). Many of our Norton points also have primary conchoidal flake scars in notch areas that are more readily discernable because of less secondary retouch, in contrast to the more extensively retouched and much deeper notches in Snyders points. Average neck width and stem length is less than in Snyders points, as is illustrated in the scatter plot of these two values in figure 14.15. All but two Snyders points fall well outside the clustering of Norton points from our study area and the Norton Mounds sample.

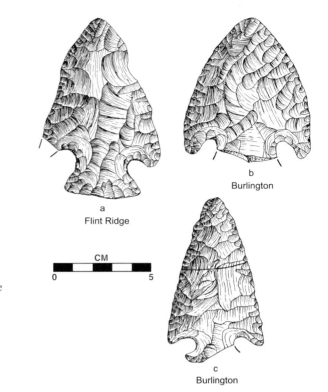

Figure 14.14. Middle
Woodland projectile
points: (a) and (b)
Snyders points from the
Drumm collection, middle
St. Joseph basin; (c)
Norton point from the
Schilling site, Portage
River area.

a
Flint Ridge

b
Burlington

c
Burlington

CM
0   5

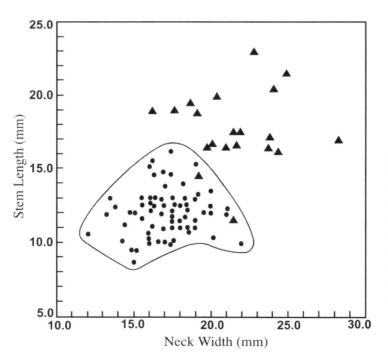

Figure 14.15. Stem
length versus neck width
of measurable specimens
of Snyders points (black
triangle) from study area
($n = 20$) and Norton
points (black dot) from
study area ($n = 39$) and
from Norton Mounds
($n = 27$).

Table 14.4. Snyders and Norton Points Descriptive Statistics

Type Characteristic	Count	Mean	Std Dev	Coef Var	Range	Min	Max
Snyders							
Length	20	65.57	13.58	20.71	51.6	44.4	96.0
Width	28	44.69	7.19	16.09	31.3	33.7	65.0
Thickness	31	10.03	1.66	16.55	8.2	7.8	16.0
Stem Length	20	18.28	3.64	19.91	18.0	11.5	29.5
Neck Width	29	21.25	2.90	13.65	13.2	15.0	28.2
Norton Corner-notched							
Length	31	55.94	10.13	18.11	44.3	39.9	84.2
Width	57	31.72	6.04	19.04	27.5	20.8	48.3
Thickness	53	8.83	1.68	19.03	7.5	5.0	12.5
Stem Length	40	12.29	1.84	14.97	7.5	8.7	16.2
Neck Width	57	16.74	1.92	11.47	10.3	12.1	22.4
Norton Mounds[a]							
Length	28	73.04	8.45	11.57	29.0	58.5	87.5
Width	28	41.93	4.29	10.23	18.0	32.0	50.0
Thickness	28	8.61	1.37	15.91	7.0	7.0	14.0
Stem Length	27	11.48	1.06	9.23	4.0	9.5	13.5
Neck Width	28	18.03	1.82	10.09	8.5	13.5	22.0

Note: Std Dev = standard deviation; Coef Var = coefficient of variation; Min = minimum value; Max = maximum value.
a. From Griffin, Flanders, and Titterington 1970.

Manker Corner-notched points (*n* = 18) are viewed as a smaller broad-bladed variant of the Snyders form (Justice 1987:201; Montet-White 1968:71). All of our Manker points are also broad ovate forms, but cross sections tend to be biconvex and notches are typically smaller and not as broad as the Snyders examples. Additionally, several specimens show direct evidence of manufacture from a flake blank, as opposed to intermediate preform stages, with final shaping being limited to bifacial blade-margin refinement. Stem length is similar to that of Norton points, but neck width averages 19.4 millimeters, falling in between the Snyders and Norton values in table 14.4.

Untyped corner-notched points (*n* = 98) are the most highly variable and typologically problematic Middle Woodland point form in southwestern Michigan. They are also the most ubiquitous point types found within habitation site contexts. Untyped corner-notched points range in size from medium-sized narrow ovate points that probably served as dart tips, to heavily reworked specimens recycled into other tool forms. Many of the latter also have haft element characteristics and metric parameters that are within the range of Norton points. Typologically, untyped corner-notched points can be considered a correlate of *affinis* Snyders (Justice 1987:204; Montet-White 1965).

Point types are unevenly distributed over the study area and are heavily weighted toward private collections and excavated sites. Table 14.5 shows the distribution of point types and raw materials organized by major subareas. Twenty-six of the thirty-two Snyders points occur within the Portage-Thorn-

Table 14.5. Middle Woodland Point Types and Raw Materials by Subareas

Raw Material or Chert Type Area/Subarea	N	Bayport	Norwood	Burlington	Wyandotte	Flint Ridge	Upper Mercer	Onondaga	Local
Snyders (*n*=32)									
Portage-Thornapple Corridor									
Middle St. Joseph Basin	10			5	3	1		1	
Portage River Area	4			1	1	1			1
Thornapple River Area	12			10		1			1
Middle Kalamazoo Valley									
Lower Kalamazoo Valley	3					1			2
Upper Kalamazoo Valley	1			1					
Sumnerville Mounds Area									
US-31 Project Area	2			1	1				
Totals (counts)	32			18	5	4		1	4
(percentage of total)				56.3	15.6	12.5		3.1	12.5
Norton Corner-notched (*n*=60)									
Portage-Thornapple Corridor									
Middle St. Joseph Basin	8	4						1	3
Portage River Area	12	4	1	2					5
Thornapple River Area	12	7				1			4
Middle Kalamazoo Valley	21	11							10
Lower Kalamazoo Valley	2								2
Upper Kalamazoo Valley									
Sumnerville Mounds Area	1	1							
US-31 Project Area	4								4
Totals (counts)	60	27	1	2		1		1	28
(percentage of total)		45.0	1.7	3.3		1.7		1.7	46.6
Manker Corner-notched (*n*=18)									
Portage-Thornapple Corridor									
Middle St. Joseph Basin	2	1		1					
Portage River Area	7			6					1
Thornapple River Area	1				1				
Middle Kalamazoo Valley									
Lower Kalamazoo Valley	4								4
Upper Kalamazoo Valley									
Sumnerville Mounds Area	1								1
US-31 Project Area	3								3
Totals (counts)	18	1		7	1				9
(percentage of total)		5.6		38.9	5.6				49.9
Untyped Corner-notched (*n*=98)									
Portage-Thornapple Corridor									
Middle St. Joseph Basin	15	1		1		1			12
Portage River Area	20	4	6	1			1		8
Thornapple River Area	4	2	1						1
Middle Kalamazoo Valley	36	7	4	1					24
Lower Kalamazoo Valley	5	2		1					2
Upper Kalamazoo Valley	2								2
Sumnerville Mounds Area	10	4						1	5
US-31 Project Area	6								6
Totals (counts)	98	20	11	4		1	1	1	60
(percentage of total)		20.4	11.2	4.1		1.0	1.0	1.0	61.3

apple Corridor, where all but two are made from southern and eastern exotic raw materials, including Burlington (61.5 percent), Wyandotte (15.4 percent), Flint Ridge (11.5 percent), and Onondaga (3.8 percent). In contrast, outside the corridor only two Snyders (7.8 percent) points are made of local cherts, and both of these are at the Hart site. It is significant that we have no Snyders points made of either Bayport or Norwood chert.

Norton points also occur in highest frequency in the Portage-Thornapple Corridor. Some of the largest and best-made Norton points—of Bayport, Burlington, and Flint Ridge cherts—occur in private collections from this area. Importantly, Norton points made from southern exotic cherts are found only in the middle St. Joseph and Portage River region, with the exception of a single point of Flint Ridge in the Thornapple River area. The relatively high number of Norton points in the middle Kalamazoo Valley are the result of intensive investigations at the Armintrout-Blackman and Mushroom sites, which together produced fifteen of twenty-one Norton points in the entire Kalamazoo basin. Of these fifteen, eleven are Bayport chert and the rest are local chert. When all Norton points in our sample are examined, the best-made examples outside of the Portage-Thornapple Corridor are the group of fifteen Norton points of Bayport and high-quality local till cherts from the Armintrout-Blackman and Mushroom sites. In contrast, Norton points from the lower Kalamazoo and US-31 project area in the lower St. Joseph Valley are all made from local till cherts and are smaller than the Mushroom and Armintrout-Blackman specimens.

Manker Corner-notched points ($n = 18$) are widely distributed in our study area. Like Snyders points, Manker Corner-notched points are also most numerous in the middle St. Joseph and Portage River area, where seven of the nine examples are of Burlington chert. In contrast, all but one of the Manker points outside of this region are made from local till cherts, with the exception of one specimen of Wyandotte chert in the Cutler collection from the Thornapple River area.

As stated above, untyped corner-notched points ($n = 98$) are a highly variable class. They are also more evenly distributed throughout our study area, with the highest numbers occurring at the fully excavated Armintrout-Blackman site ($n = 24$) and within the Portage River area ($n = 20$). Within this class of points there is a sharp decline in frequencies of both Bayport and the distant exotic cherts, concomitant with increasing use of Norwood and a wide variety of locally available till cherts.

Debitage was analyzed from most localities that yielded Middle Woodland points. We specifically monitored the occurrence of exotic raw material types because of their very high frequencies at the Prison Farm site in the middle Grand River Valley (Brashler, Laidler, and Martin 1998:175), particularly Wyandotte (15.1 percent) and Burlington and other unidentified white cherts (24.4 percent). In our study area, Wyandotte and Burlington are the most important southern exotic raw materials and occur in highest relative frequencies in the middle St. Joseph and Portage River region (table 14.6), supporting the

Table 14.6. Debitage Raw Material Summary

Region	N	Bayport	Norwood	Burlington	Wyandotte	Flint Ridge	Upper Mercer	Onondaga	Local
Middle St. Joseph Basin	605	2.4		6.1	1.7	1.8	0.5		87.5
Portage River Area	2,448	3.6	0.7	5.5	4.0	0.7	2.9		82.6
Middle Kalamazoo Valley	32,620	0.7	0.3	1.1	0.2	0.5	<0.1		97.1
Lower Kalamazoo Valley	2,355	0.5	0.3	2.9	0.6	0.1	1.0		94.6
Upper Kalamazoo Valley	767	10.6		5.2	0.1	2.1	3.4	0.4	78.2
Sumnerville Mounds Area	1,462	10.8	1.1	1.3	0.4	0.3	0.5		85.6

Note: Site values as percentages.

inference that these materials possibly entered the Grand Valley via this route. Unfortunately we have no meaningful data from the Thornapple River area.

There is some evidence that both Burlington and Wyandotte cherts were entering the Portage River area as preforms or discoidals. Burlington preforms were also observed in the Portage River sites and in the Cutler collection from the Thornapple River area. The single Cutler specimen is a very large ovate preform measuring 16 centimeters in length, 7 centimeters in width, and nearly 1.5 centimeters in thickness. An unfinished Snyders point of Wyandotte chert comes from the Schilling site in the Portage River area, and several other examples in the Drumm collection from the Colon area also appear incompletely finished.

Bayport debitage occurs in high frequency at the Prison Farm site, possibly because the occupants may have had access to the Bayport source areas in the Saginaw region (Brashler, Laidler, and Martin 1998:175). Occasional examples of broken, large ovate preforms made of Bayport chert were encountered as isolated finds within the study area. These occur in higher frequency, along with complete unbroken examples and considerable quantities of large bifacial thinning flakes, in the Portage River area. Norwood chert debitage is also present in this same area but does not extend into the middle St. Joseph.

In the Middle Woodland period we see a pattern of point style/raw material associations analogous to that observed in the Early Woodland period, with the Portage-Thornapple Corridor again providing the most abundant evidence. Thirty-two Norton points in the corridor are highly correlated with Bayport and local till cherts (table 14.5). This contrasts sharply with the southern-affiliated Snyders type (*n* = 26) that was made almost exclusively from distant exotic cherts, principally Burlington, followed by Wyandotte and Flint Ridge. These relative frequencies for Snyders (and Manker) mirror those at the Goodall site, where Burlington is the most common chert, followed by Wyandotte (William Mangold, personal communication, 2000).

It is evident that the distribution of the Snyders type in southern Michigan correlates strongly with the extension of Goodall-related ceramics into the prairie/oak-hickory forest zone in the middle St. Joseph and Portage River region (fig. 14.2). Snyders points of Flint Ridge chert in the corridor also indicate that some Ohio contact occurred. The Snyders point type is not seen in the Grand Valley sites (Janet Brashler, personal communication 2000), so while Burlington and Wyandotte cherts evidently passed through our area in semiprocessed form to the Grand Valley, the culturally associated Snyders point type does not penetrate beyond the Thornapple River area. Exotic cherts, particularly Wyandotte, clearly had significance to Norton people. For example, chert variously described as Dongola or Hornstone (Wyandotte) at the Norton Mounds site had special importance as finished artifacts and as groups of flakes in burial contexts (Griffin, Flanders, and Titterington 1970:179).

While it appears that people of the Norton tradition were present in this southern area, a conclusion based on the large number of identified Norton points, the five Norton points made from cherts from southern sources are not easy to interpret. Two examples made of Burlington chert come from the Schilling site in Kalamazoo County and are of unusual interest. One of these (fig. 14.14c) is a morphological match with points in a burial cache in Mound M at the Norton Mounds site (Griffin, Flanders, and Titterington 1970:Plate 170; Kingsley 1999:Figure 8.7). This point might represent an import or an exchange item in this southern region, or it could have been locally made by a Norton artisan. We lack excavated data from the Thornapple basin; however, the presence of Snyders points and a preform made from southern exotic cherts in the Cutler collection, along with a single Norton point of Flint Ridge chert and several more of Bayport, indicates that this landscape deserves consideration as an important avenue of material exchange between Norton tradition and southern Goodall-related groups in the middle St. Joseph and Portage River region (fig. 14.16). This inference has support in the high frequency of Norton points made from Bayport chert in the middle Kalamazoo Valley sites (to the exclusion of any other nonlocal raw materials) and in the occurrence of ovate Bayport preforms at (minimally) two survey sites in the Thornapple and eastern middle Kalamazoo Valley area. The fact of co-occurrence of northern Bayport and Norwood cherts with the southern exotic cherts in the Portage River area provides tangible evidence of contact between groups within which a wide range of sociocultural information could be transmitted. Our data indicate that this area was the locus of the most intensive interaction during the Middle Woodland.

There is also evidence in our data from the upper Kalamazoo Valley for an eastern route of introduction of the Ohio cherts—Flint Ridge and Upper Mercer chert—into the Grand Valley, where these types are present in significant amounts in the middle Grand Valley at the Early Woodland Arthursburg Hill site (Beld 1993b:7–8) and at Prison Farm (Brashler, Laidler, and Martin 1998:175). Flint Ridge is present as 2.1 percent of debitage in the upper Kalamazoo Valley. It does not occur above 1 percent in the rest of our area, with the exception of the middle St. Joseph Valley, where it was observed at 2.6 percent, reflecting Ohio contacts across the southern tier of counties. Six Middle Woodland points of Flint Ridge chert occur in our sites, whereas none is made

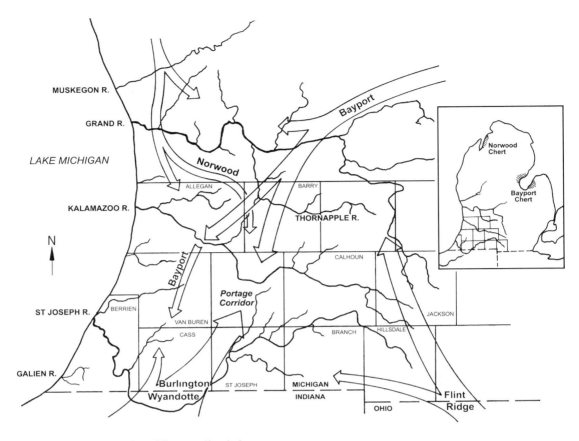

Figure 14.16. Regional Middle Woodland chert sources.

from Upper Mercer chert. High percentages of Upper Mercer debitage were observed at the Barton Lake site on the Portage River and in the Thornapple basin, but we lack good Middle Woodland context for this material.

The area north and west of the Goodall periphery and south of the Kalamazoo Valley has not been extensively surveyed, but available information (including the minor Middle Woodland recovery in the US-31 project sites in the beech-maple forest that characterizes this region) lends support to the view that Middle Woodland sites in this "coastal" zone are few at best. Such north-south contacts as may have occurred here were certainly at a far lower level of intensity than in the Portage-Thornapple Corridor. The corner-notched points in the lower and middle Kalamazoo Valley are almost entirely made from local or northern Michigan cherts. There is little evidence in the lithic data in this westerly region for the interactive dynamic seen in the Portage-Thornapple Corridor.

Discussion and Directions for Future Research

The assessment presented here, particularly new data from the Kalamazoo Valley and Portage-Thornapple Corridor, has demonstrated that the Goodall periphery is a culturally and environmentally distinct region, whereas Middle Woodland Hopewell in the Kalamazoo Valley is affiliated with the Norton tradition. This dichotomy is supported by ceramic comparisons and by projectile point styles and raw materials. These conclusions were anticipated by Mangold (1981b) in his formulation of Goodall and Norton ceramic style zones; our research supports and considerably augments his initial assessment.

Available evidence points to low population density in southwestern Michigan during the Middle Woodland period, with sites in riverine locations and large relatively empty areas to the west of the prairie-oak savanna and in the beech-maple forest in the center of the region. The adaptation of Goodall to oak-hickory forest and prairie locales resulted in spatial separation from the Norton tradition, whatever the real or perceived sociocultural differences between Middle Woodland societies in the St. Joseph and Grand valleys may have been.

Hopewell series ceramics from four of the Kalamazoo sites reflect a primary relationship with the lower Grand River sites and possibly with Sumnerville to the south. It is suggested that this use of the Kalamazoo Valley primarily reflects territorial interchange with the lower Grand, associated with seasonal mobility of these foraging groups. The posited Sumnerville relationship has a limited evidentiary basis and is not well understood. An important and as yet unevaluated question regards the extent to which the Kalamazoo sites may reflect development within a local population that is interacting with neighboring groups to the north. Cultural continuity at the Armintrout-Blackman site in particular seems to suggest change within a resident Kalamazoo Valley population that is differentially influenced over time by exchange relationships and other interaction with Norton tradition groups in the Grand Valley.

At the Mushroom site, however, the ceramic assemblage suggests seasonal movements in and out of the Kalamazoo Valley by small groups from the densely occupied Spoonville area. Given the overall low population density and the high degree of mobility inferred for these Kalamazoo Valley groups, more precise definition of intra- and intersocietal relationships will likely remain elusive. Movement of peoples may have been motivated by desire for social interaction, as well as for subsistence reasons.

Some interaction between the major cultural traditions does seem to have occurred. We have presented evidence for an exchange relationship between Norton and Goodall-related groups within the Portage-Thornapple Corridor. Finished artifacts of Burlington and Wyandotte cherts appear to have reached the Thornapple Valley via the Portage Corridor and the central Kalamazoo Valley, bypassing the western Kalamazoo Valley sites in Allegan County, where these chert types are largely absent. The Cutler site on the Thornapple is important in this context. The Cutler collection contains twenty-five corner-notched points, including six Norton points manufactured from Bayport chert and nine Snyders points from Burlington. Middle Woodland ceramics should be present, but the site has not been test excavated.

The Hart site vessel and the Snyders points made of local chert seem to represent a light Havana footprint in the lower Kalamazoo Valley at an early date within the Middle Woodland period. Interpretation of this component at Hart is complicated by an Early Woodland radiocarbon date, recalling similar ambiguity at the Jancarich village site on the Muskegon (Garland 2000; Prahl 1991). Future work at Hart may permit evaluation of its possible importance for contact with the Havana heartland. Hart may have relevance for the introduction of Havana-Hopewell into the Norton tradition within the kin-based framework of the village fission model put forward by Holman (1990). We continue to believe that the arrival in western Michigan of small groups of people with kin-based ties to Illinois is a necessary, if not sufficient, mechanism for the Hopewell introduction here.

In addition to targeted site excavation in western Michigan, Middle Woodland studies will benefit most directly from progress in several fundamental areas. Chronological control is a pressing concern best addressed by AMS dating of ceramics, as is convincingly demonstrated by Brashler and coauthors in this volume. The AMS option is unfortunately constrained by cost in contexts outside of public archaeology. There is a clear need for the development of ceramic typologies that will strengthen comparisons on both inter- and intra-regional levels; projectile point typology and certain raw material identifications similarly require agreed-upon criteria for classification. Until these basic elements of archaeological practice are strengthened in our area, the important theoretical issues that surround Hopewell studies in western Michigan cannot be adequately or convincingly addressed.

Acknowledgments

Middle Woodland studies in this area have been immeasurably advanced by the Kalamazoo Valley Chapter of the Michigan Archaeological Society, whose members discovered and excavated the Armintrout-Blackman, Fennville, and Hart sites. The senior author is indebted to colleagues for discussions about the Middle Woodland spanning three decades. Bob Kingsley's stimulating analyses of Michigan Hopewell in the 1980s provided major impetus to research by others, and he continues to remind us (Kingsley 1999) about important issues concerning the complex sociocultural landscape in Michigan at the time that Hopewell took root and flourished here. Thanks to Jan Brashler for her wisdom concerning Havana-Hopewell ceramics and to Peggy Holman for discussions about the process of village fission as it might pertain to the Hopewell introduction in western Michigan. Jim Mohow of the Indiana Department of Natural Resources provided useful comments on lithic typology. Thanks also to Meghan Garland for assistance with production of the manuscript.

We especially want to thank Bill Mangold, whose prior research prefigured this study, for generously sharing his broad knowledge of the Middle Woodland and for reading and providing extensive comments on a previous draft of this chapter, by which it was significantly improved. Any errors in terminology and interpretation that remain are the sole responsibility of the authors.

15

Middle Woodland Occupation in the Grand River Basin of Michigan

Janet G. Brashler, Michael J. Hambacher, Terrance J. Martin, Kathryn E. Parker, and James A. Robertson

In this chapter we very briefly review 150 years of research on Middle Woodland occupation in the Grand River valley of west-central Michigan (fig. 15.1). Ultimately we hope to elucidate Middle Woodland cultural processes in an area near the northern- and easternmost boundaries of the Havana and Hopewellian traditions. In reviewing previous research in the area, we place recent excavations at the Prison Farm site (20IA58) and the Converse village site (20KT2) in the context of the earlier work in the area. New information from these sites on temporal relationships, subsistence, lithics, and ceramics allows us to integrate these Middle Woodland occupations with earlier and recent theoretical and analytical frameworks established for the Grand River valley and other regions of the Hopewellian world. Hopewellian occupations in the Grand River area, and other portions of Michigan as well, have long been studied in terms of models and interpretations derived from Illinois and Ohio Hopewell. While in the shadow of these more resplendent expressions of mortuary and subsistence activity, the Grand River region nonetheless offers an opportunity to understand the Hopewellian world near the northern edge of its range.

Previous Research, Models, and Assumptions

Until recently, knowledge of the Middle Woodland period in the Grand River basin was largely based on information gained from the excavation of burial mounds or observations associated with their destruction. The best-known sites in the Grand River valley are the Norton, Converse, and Spoonville mound groups. The Converse mounds, located in Grand Rapids, were largely destroyed by the mid-nineteenth century. Situated just outside of Grand Rapids, the Norton mounds were excavated by various avocational and professional archaeologists from the late nineteenth through the mid-twentieth century, as were the Spoonville mounds and village. The Spoonville mounds were destroyed in the mid twentieth century by residential construction, but the village immediately adjacent to the mounds remains relatively well preserved.

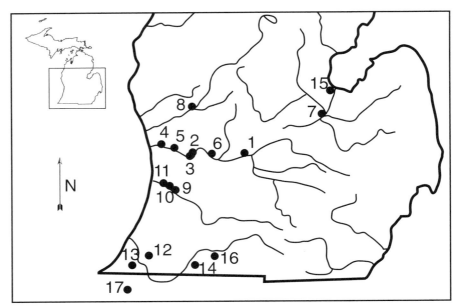

Figure 15.1. Middle Woodland sites in Michigan and adjacent Indiana: 1 = Prison Farm (20IA58); 2 = Converse Mounds (20KT2); 3 = Norton Mounds (20KT1); 4 = Spoonville mounds and village (20OT1); 5 = Zemaitis (20OT68); 6 = Grattan Mounds (20KT3); 7 = Schultz (20SA2); 8 = Muskegon River sites [Brooks (20NE1), Mallon (20NE31), Parsons (20NE100), Palmiteer (20NE101), Schumaker (20NE107), Toft Lake (20NE110), Jancarich (20NE113)]; 9 = Hacklander (20AE78); 10 = Mushroom (20AE88); 11 = Armintrout-Blackman (20AE12); 12 = Sumnerville (20CS6); 13 = Moccasin Bluff (20BE8); 14 = Stroebel (20SJ180); 15 = Kantzler (20BY30); 16 = Marantette (20SJ1); 17 = Goodall (12LE9).

Excavation of Grand River mound groups yielded artifacts and mortuary structures clearly associated with Illinois Havana and Hopewellian worldviews and exchange. Specific evidence pointing to an Illinois Havana-Hopewell relationship included submound log-lined central tombs with ramps and burials associated with ceramic vessels, copper, mica, engraved turtle shell, and other nonlocal materials (Griffin, Flanders, and Titterington 1970; Quimby 1941b). Particularly important indicators of interregional interaction are artifacts of chert from Ohio, Indiana, Illinois, and other areas of Michigan.

The earliest reports of these sites occur in newspapers from the nascent community of Grand Rapids during the 1850s. In the 1870s and 1880s, the systematic, if not scientific, work of avocational archaeologists such as Able Anderson, Frank W. Porter, and Wright L. Coffinberry resulted in explorations of mounds throughout western Michigan and the first descriptions of "mound builder materials" (Coffinberry 1885). The products of these and other excavations in the early twentieth century were the focus of the first professional descriptions of Middle Woodland materials in the Grand River valley. Working with James

Table 15.1. Middle Woodland Grand River Sites

Phase Site	Dating Method
Norton	
Spoonville (20OT1)	[14]C dates, artifact associations
Norton Mounds (20KT1)	[14]C dates, artifact associations?
Zemaitis (20OT68)	[14]C dates, artifact associations
Prison Farm (20IA58)	[14]C dates, artifact associations
Arthursburg Hill (20IA37)[a]	[14]C dates, artifact associations
Converse	
Paggeot (20OT89)	? artifact associations
Grattan Mounds	? artifact associations
Zemaitis (20OT68)	[14]C date, sparse artifacts
Spoonville (20OT1)	[14]C date, artifact associations
Converse (20KT2)	[14]C dates, artifact associations

Source: Following Kingsley 1999.
a. Village component.

B. Griffin, Grand Rapids native son George Quimby defined the Goodall focus based on materials housed at the Kent Scientific Institute, now the Public Museum of Grand Rapids. Quimby (1941a, 1941b, 1943) recognized similarities in ceramics and mortuary practice between Illinois and the Goodall region that encompassed northern Indiana and southwestern Michigan in the Muskegon, Grand, and St. Joseph drainages. Quimby further suggested that Michigan Hopewell had developed out of the Goodall focus. While Brown (1964b:122) reiterated the linkage between Michigan Middle Woodland burial mounds and Havana, he suggested that the "precise cultural relationship . . . was not apparent."

Archaeologists working in the Grand River valley between the 1960s and the 1980s continued to focus primarily on the excavation of mounds (Flanders 1965a; Griffin, Flanders, and Titterington 1970), although excavation at the Spoonville mounds was accompanied by exploration of an adjacent habitation area (Flanders 1965a). Following developing models of Middle Woodland settlement in Illinois, Flanders reasoned that this was the "village" associated with the mortuary facility. In addition, Flanders and students surveyed the lower Grand, seeking habitation sites that could be correlated with the multimound mortuary sites (Flanders, Marek, and Szten 1979). The result of this work was development of a chronological framework and a proposed settlement model anchored by only a few radiocarbon dates from the Grand and other areas of western Michigan and cross-dating by ceramic style (table 15.1).

The Norton phase, dated between 10 B.C. and A.D. 200, was proposed as the phase name for the initial occupation of western Michigan by Hopewellian populations (Griffin, Flanders, and Titterington 1970:189). Sites dating to this time span in the Grand Valley included Norton Mounds, the multicomponent Spoonville village, and the multicomponent, though predominantly Late Woodland, Zemaitis site (Kingsley 1999:150). The Converse phase was proposed for the later Middle Woodland (approximately A.D. 200–400). Sites along the Grand attributed to this phase include the Converse Mounds, Spoonville Mounds and the associated village, Zemaitis, Grattan Mounds, and Paggeot Mound (Kingsley 1999). Of these, only Spoonville, Zemaitis, and Norton have been extensively excavated. The Norton phase corresponds roughly with the Ogden and Bedford phases in the central and lower Illinois Valley, while the Converse phase largely corresponds with the Pike and Steuben phases (Griffin, Flanders, and Titterington 1970; Kingsley 1999). More recently Cantwell (1980) revised the early chronology for central Illinois Havana, suggesting a Caldwell phase between 150 and 50 B.C. followed by the Fulton phase dating between 50 B.C. and A.D. 150. Most researchers in the 1960s through the 1990s maintained that Havana Hopewellian occupation of the Grand Valley was the result of "expansion of Middle Woodland people" out of the central Illinois Valley along the Kankakee and into western Michigan sometime during the Fulton phase (Griffin, Flanders, and Titterington 1970).

By the last decade of the millennium, Middle Woodland research in the Grand River basin had produced a total of forty-seven components: thirty-five camps, seven mounds and mound groups, and five find spots (Brashler and Mead 1996). Middle Woodland occupation appeared to have been concentrated along the lower Grand, where most of the mortuary sites were located. The only site identified as a "village" in the Grand Valley was that associated with the Spoonville mound group (Brashler and Mead 1996; Flanders 1965a). Although occupations were known to be associated with the Norton and Converse mounds, archaeologists believed that they had been largely destroyed. The two mounds known from outside the lower Grand, Grattan and a small mound (20CL3), were located far upstream and appeared to be more closely related to Saginaw Hopewell than to the lower Grand manifestation (Brashler and Mead 1996:220).

Flanders tested approximately half of the forty-seven known Middle Woodland sites identified in the Grand Valley between 1960 and 1989. Most of the Middle Woodland components in the excavated sites unfortunately occur in mixed deposits, some with Early Woodland (and all with Late Woodland) ceramics. Considerable debate occurred throughout the 1970s and 1980s pertaining to the differentiation of Middle from Late Woodland ceramics in these contexts, but it was hampered by few radiocarbon dates and a reliance on models of ceramic production and use borrowed from the Illinois Valley (Brashler 1981, 1991; Flanders 1977; Kingsley 1990).

Until the 1990s, the radiocarbon chronology for Middle Woodland in the Grand Valley was limited to six dates, with two each from Zemaitis, Norton Mounds, and the Spoonville village (table 15.2). Zemaitis and Spoonville are complicated by the presence of a temporally ambiguous ceramic type, Hacklander ware. This type was originally dated to the end of the first millennium at the type site in the Kalamazoo drainage (Garland 1976, 1978; Kingsley 1989), but dates from Zemaitis place Hacklander ware in the Middle and early Late Woodland periods (Brashler and Garland 1993). Hacklander ware has a Middle

Woodland analog in the Princess Point Middle Woodland of southern Ontario (Brashler and Garland 1993). Further complicating the clear association of ceramics with Middle Woodland dates at Zemaitis and Spoonville village is the shallow, compressed nature of the deposits in the areas of both sites from which the dates originate.

Though hampered by a sketchy radiocarbon chronology and few excavated habitation sites, two major problems pertaining to Grand River Middle Woodland occupation have been addressed in the past thirty-five years (Brashler and Mead 1996; Garland and DesJardins 1995; Holman 1990; Kingsley 1981). The first involves the subsistence and settlement strategies of Middle Woodland occupants of the region, and the second addresses the timing and means by which Havana Middle Woodland first appeared in the Grand River valley.

Brown (1964b), Cleland (1966), Kingsley (1981), and others (for example, Brashler and Holman 1999; Prahl 1991) have suggested that the distribution of Havana-related materials in Michigan is associated with the Carolinian biotic province and portions of the Carolinian-Canadian transition zone. Kingsley (1981, 1999), expanding on that observation, applied Illinois Middle Woodland settlement models (Roper 1979; Struever 1968b) to explain the relative lack of Hopewellian occupation in the Kalamazoo drainage to the south of the Grand. Kingsley concluded that Havana Middle Woodland sites in Michigan (including the Grand drainage) were situated in locations with environmental configurations similar to those around Roper's Strategy 2 base settlements in the Sangamon, and therefore that base settlements in Michigan might be year-round occupations, as was the case in Illinois (Kingsley 1981).

Focusing on drainage age and physical character, Kingsley (1981) reasoned that Illinois-derived Middle Woodland populations located in environments with broad floodplains with renewable plant and fish resources associated with adjacent uplands followed a strategy grounded in intensive harvest collecting. Thus, Kingsley suggested, base camps and special camps might be expected along the Grand, despite the fact that only the multicomponent and mixed Spoonville village and Zemaitis sites were known. He also stressed the notion that the settlement pattern and adaptation would have been flexible, responding to local conditions that were similar to those of the Sangamon in a number of ways (broad floodplains, bluffs, resource base, and so forth). Although the intensive harvest collecting model gave way to recognition of Middle Woodland dependence on Eastern Agricultural Complex plants in the Ohio and Illinois regions (Smith 1987), the practice of horticulture in the Grand Valley was seldom raised as a possibility. More critically, it was not until the past ten years that systematic flotation data collected from excavations in the region could be applied to test any Middle Woodland subsistence models.

More recently, Brashler and Holman (1999) explored the farthest extension of Havana ceramics to the north in Michigan, the distribution of which is congruent with the Carolinian-Canadian transition zone. They note that small quantities of Havana-related and more northern Laurel materials appear in the northernmost extension of the transition zone, where the zone consists of a narrow band of Carolinian and Canadian patches. Analysis of site placement within this mosaic of northern and southern habitats suggests that northern Lake Forest and southern Havana Middle Woodland occupants of the transition zone used the area differently and, perhaps, contemporaneously. Intensively occupied Middle Woodland sites, however, are located along the Grand and Muskegon drainages at the southern edge of the transition zone, in proximity to the northernmost extension of the Carolinian and Illinoian biotic provinces from the south.

Finally, recent work by Stretton, Chapman, and Brashler (2000) focused on a series of sites located near Wabasis Creek, a third-order tributary of the Grand River. In this study, based only on surface collections, a significant number of Middle Woodland diagnostic projectiles and ceramics were recovered. The presence of a large number of sites in the hinterlands supports the existence of different seasonal settlement strategies, as suggested by Brashler and Holman (1999) and Egan-Bruhy (2002, 2003).

The fact that subsistence and settlement were oriented around the river and its tributaries suggests that occupations in this area should demonstrate the types of subsistence and settlement found in other areas of the same broad ecological zone. If Illinois models apply throughout the area where we see Havana mortuary and ceramic stylistic markers, subsistence and settlement should include some reliance on cultigens or intensive harvest collecting, base camps, seasonal camps, mortuary sites, and special-function camps (Kingsley 1990, 1999; Roper 1979).

The second series of hypotheses related to Grand River Hopewell that have been debated over the past thirty-five years revolves around the cultural processes that could account for the introduction of Havana Hopewell ceramic styles and mortuary practice into the area. The dominant paradigm suggests that they were introduced through the expansion of Havana groups out of the central Illinois Valley into the Grand River area at approximately 10 B.C. Dating of the introduction of Havana and Hopewell ceramics and burial practices is based on a radiocarbon date from the base (original ground surface) of Mound C at Norton Mounds (Griffin, Flanders, and Titterington 1970:158)—until recently the earliest Havana Hopewell-related date in the Grand Valley. If Havana Middle Woodland in the Grand does not predate 10 B.C., then it seems reasonable that the model of Middle Woodland expansion out of the central Illinois Valley into adjacent regions (Wiant and McGimsey 1986b) may best account for the presence of these diagnostics in the Grand River valley.

Support for a later early Middle Woodland intrusion into the Grand River valley comes from the apparent absence of late Early Woodland and the earliest Havana Middle Woodland ceramics. Until recently no sites had been identified in the Grand River valley with remains dated to between 380 B.C. and 10 B.C., using the averaged dates from Arthursburg Hill (Beld 1994:29; Garland 1986; Garland and Beld 1999:128) and the 10 B.C. Mound C date from Norton Mounds. The reasons for the absence of occupation along the Grand during this period are unclear. How this void is interpreted has significant bearing on our understanding of the timing and processes by which Havana Hopewell Middle

Woodland material remains appear in the region. One possibility is that the Grand was devoid of human population during the last three centuries B.C. Another possibility is that there was a nonceramic Early Woodland presence (Brashler and Mead 1996; Kingsley 1999).

There are, in fact, a few clues suggesting the presence of an indigenous population. First, on virtually every site with Havana Middle Woodland ceramics there are also Early Woodland thick ceramics, suggesting continuity in settlement patterns. Second, there is a 250 B.C. radiocarbon date from the Zemaitis site from a stable surface (Brashler and Garland 1993). Unfortunately, no diagnostic cultural materials (only fire-cracked rock and a few lithics) were recovered from approximately six square meters of deep excavation. Third, there is a single Naples Ovoid sherd from the Ada site, located near Grand Rapids, that stylistically would date to the earliest Middle Woodland in the central Illinois Valley. Finally, recent research at the Prison Farm site narrows the gap between the Early Woodland and the earliest Middle Woodland dates to a period of under 250 years.

A number of scholars (for example, Griffin, Flanders, and Titterington 1970; Kingsley 1999) have suggested that a small subset of ceramics from Norton, Spoonville, and other sites comprises imports into the region, thus supporting the idea that materials from the central Illinois Valley were introduced into the Grand River valley from elsewhere. If these are truly imports, the process of their introduction could have been through exchange related to kinship networks. Alternatively, the imports could have been carried by newcomers into the area. The former suggests at least some in situ population, while the latter suggests migration by Havana Hopewell populations into a largely unoccupied area. Writing about the Bolthouse site, a small occupation site on the Grand, Holman (1990) provides a general model to account for the appearance of Havana Hopewell in the Grand River valley that can accommodate both possibilities. Holman suggests that Hopewellian Middle Woodland expansion into Michigan involved a process of fission whereby groups successful in their environment split when group size exceeded the social and/or economic carrying capacity of the immediate vicinity. The fissioning model provides a mechanism for getting people to the Grand River valley, but it does not address the critical issue of who, if anyone, was in the region when they arrived.

Recent excavations at two sites, Prison Farm (1996–1999) and Converse village (1999–2000), provide data with which to further evaluate the questions of Middle Woodland origins and subsistence/settlement strategies in the Grand Valley. Although analyses of the collections from these two occupation sites are ongoing, we can already refine some of our ideas about Middle Woodland in the Grand River valley.

The Prison Farm Site

The Prison Farm site (20IA58) is situated in the central Grand River valley approximately 100 kilometers from the juncture of the Grand with Lake Michigan. Analysis of an extensive surface collection and continuing analysis of 340 square meters of excavated materials from 1996, 1997, and 1999 field seasons reveals what is probably a seasonal and intermittent Middle Woodland occupation that occurred between 100 B.C. and A.D. 150, based on radiocarbon dates (table 15.2) and diagnostic ceramics and lithics.

Radiocarbon Chronology

Radiocarbon dates from the site are associated with two features, several ceramic sherds, and a midden deposit. Four AMS and two standard radiocarbon determinations date two features (Features 1 and 32) containing four diagnostic rim sherds and associated charcoal. In addition, there are dates on a cross-hatched rim vessel section and associated charcoal and an AMS date on a sherd from the surface collection (Brashler 1998). With three proveniences (two features and a midden deposit) dated so far, the temporal placement of the site can be firmly anchored in the early Middle Woodland period, sometime in the first century B.C. Duration of occupation appears to extend to perhaps the beginning of the later Middle Woodland, sometime around A.D. 200 (table 15.2).

Ceramics

Ceramics from the site are predominantly clunky, round and flat-lipped, noded pots with smoothed cord-marked and smoothed-over cord-marked exteriors. Beveling on rims and dentate stamping occur on relatively few vessels in the assemblage (Brashler 1995; Morrissey, Brashler, and Detz 1998). Several vessels have interior cord marking, but this treatment occurs on relatively thin walled sherds that are unlike Early Woodland Marion or Schultz Thick wares.

Design elements thought to be early in the Havana Middle Woodland sequence (250–150 B.C., late Morton/Caldwell phase)—such as punctates (for example, Sister Creeks Punctated), Neteler crescents, and Morton and Fettie Incised—are missing from or extremely rare in the assemblage. At least one thick vessel was excavated in 1999 that has a series of ragged fingernail impressions or punctates (a Sister Creeks design element) on both the exterior and the interior surfaces of the vessel. With the exception of a single sherd in an avocational collection from the Ada site, there are no diagnostic analogs from the central Illinois Valley such as Naples Ovoid or Neteler Stamped in the Grand River basin.

The best dating of the site based on ceramic style places it in the period between 150 B.C. and A.D. 1. This corresponds to the Fulton phase in the central Illinois Valley (Cantwell 1980; Munson 1986). However, in addition to the near absence of Sister Creeks Punctated, there are other key stylistic motifs and types absent in the Prison Farm assemblage that are found associated with zoned dentate and Havana Cordmarked ceramics in the central Illinois Valley. Specifically, the assemblage lacks incised sherds such as Black Sand, Dane, Fettie, and Morton Incised, which occur in the late Early Woodland and early Middle Woodland in other regions of the Midwest. The absence of these ceramics is curious given the presence of analogs for them in the Saginaw Valley to the east in the form of Shiawassee incised materials from the Schultz site (Fischer

Table 15.2. Grand River Early and Middle Woodland Radiocarbon Dates

Site	Phase	Lab Number	^{14}C Age[a]	Calibrated Age/Ranges[b]
Arthursburg Hill[c]	Early	Beta-69940/CAMS-11183	2450 ±60 B.P.	763 B.C. (519 B.C.) 405 B.C.
Arthursburg Hill[d]	Early	Beta-57440	2420 ±70 B.P.	758 B.C. (413 B.C.) 397 B.C.
Arthursburg Hill[d]	Early	Beta-57441	2310 ±60 B.P.	402 B.C. (389 B.C.) 263 B.C.
Arthursburg Hill[c]	Early	Beta-67202/ETH-11447	2400 ±50 B.P.	519 B.C. (407 B.C.) 397 B.C.
Arthursburg Hill[c]	Early	Beta-69941/CAMS-11184	2280 ±70 B.P.	397 B.C. (377 B.C.) 204 B.C.
Zemaitis[e]	Early (?)[f]	Beta-65115	2200 ±80 B.P.	377 B.C. (337, 324, 202 B.C.) 125 B.C.
Arthursburg Hill[c]	Early	Beta-67203/ETH-11448	2135 ±50 B.P.	197 B.C. (169 B.C.) 62 B.C.
20IA58[g]	Middle: Converse	Beta-113899	2100 ±40 B.P.	195 B.C. (100 B.C.) 5 B.C.
20IA58[g]	Middle: Norton	Beta-113897	2090 ±70 B.P.	355 B.C. (75 B.C.) 290 and 230 B.C. to A.D. 70
20IA58[g]	Middle: Norton	Beta-113898	2020 ±60 B.P.	175 B.C. (5 B.C.) A.D. 110
20IA58[g]	Middle: Norton	Beta-83091	1960 ±40 B.P.	35 B.C. (A.D. 65) A.D. 130
Arthursburg Hill[c]	Middle	Beta-69939	1960 ±70 B.P.	32 B.C. (A.D. 66) A.D. 125
Norton Mound C[h]	Middle: Norton	M-1493	1960 ±60 B.P.	58 B.C. (A.D. 66) A.D. 240
20IA58[g]	Middle: Norton	Beta-113900	1910 ±80 B.P.	50 B.C. (A.D. 100) A.D. 265 and 290 to A.D. 320
20IA58[g]	Middle: Norton	Beta-113894	1910 ±40 B.P.	A.D. 25 (A.D. 100) A.D. 220
20IA58[g]	Middle: Norton	Beta-113896	1890 ±40 B.P.	A.D. 55 (A.D. 120) A.D. 235
Zemaitis[e]	Middle: Hacklander[i]	Beta-65120/CAMS-8329	1890 ±60 B.P.	A.D. 119 (A.D. 215) A.D. 249
Arthursburg Hill[d]	Middle?	Beta-64946	1880 ±60 B.P.	A.D. 76 (A.D. 133, 203, 207) A.D. 236
Zemaitis[j]	Middle: Norton	Beta-6557	1870 ±70 B.P.	A.D. 75 (A.D. 135) A.D. 240
20IA58[g]	Middle: Norton	Beta-113895	1860 ±60 B.P.	A.D. 45 (A.D. 145) A.D. 330
Norton Mound H[h]	Middle: Norton	M-1490	1850 ±100 B.P.	A.D. 71 (A.D. 146, 190) A.D. 324
Spoonville Village[k]	Middle: Norton?	M-1428	1840 ±120 B.P.	A.D. 66 (A.D. 215) A.D. 341
Norton Mound H[h]	Middle: Norton	M-1488	1790 ±160 B.P.	A.D. 71 (A.D. 266, 278, 331) A.D. 426
Spoonville Village[k]	Middle: Converse	M-1427	1735 ±110 B.P.	A.D. 148 (A.D. 266, 278, 331) A.D. 426

Note: Table does not include dates from Converse (see table 15.3).

a. Uncorrected age is measured ^{14}C age.

b. Calibrations run using Stuiver and Reimer (1993) Revised Calib 3.0 ^{14}C age calibration program. The calibrations may vary slightly from reported ranges found in references cited. Ages in parentheses are the calibrated calendar date with maximum and minimum ranges at one sigma bracketing the calendar date.

c. Beld 1994.

d. Beld 1993b.

e. Brashler and Garland 1993.

f. This date is for an aceramic component.

g. Brashler 1998.

h. Griffin, Flanders, and Titterington 1970.

i. This AMS date is the earliest Hacklander ware date.

j. Murphy 1986.

k. Fitting 1975.

1972). In fact, there are no good ceramic analogs or radiocarbon dates for any occupation in the Grand Valley between the late fourth century and the early third century B.C. Arthursburg Hill (20IA37), a late Marion phase earthen enclosure located approximately 10 kilometers east of the Prison Farm site (Beld 1993b, 1994), has a tight series of radiocarbon dates clustering around 390 B.C. The next most recent dates in the Grand River valley are the two early-third-century B.C. dates from Zemaitis.

The gap in both radiocarbon chronology and ceramic style analogs represents "an important unresolved problem" (Garland and Beld 1999) that has significant bearing on the question of Middle Woodland/Hopewellian origins in the Grand River valley.

Lithics

Heavily curated points, scrapers, bifaces, and other tools characterize the lithic assemblage from Prison Farm. The predominant projectile point style is a short-bladed, reworked corner-notched point most closely related to *affinis* Snyders and Norton points, though the latter are represented by only a few specimens (Brashler, Laidler, and Martin 1998; Griffin, Flanders, and Titterington 1970; Justice 1987). The assemblage lacks many of the hallmarks of Illinois Valley Middle Woodland lithic assemblages such as bladelets and bladelet cores, hoes and hoe chips, Snyders points, and cache blades, although some items typical of Illinois assemblages, such as hafted scrapers, are present. Instead, there are heavy choppers and numerous small thumbnail, side, and end scrapers. The lithic assemblage thus has a distinctively local character and does not correspond to early Middle Woodland assemblages from the Illinois Valley in terms of the formal tool categories present.

Other striking characteristics of the lithic assemblage include the mix of nonlocal cherts present and, at Prison Farm, the near absence of any evidence for primary reduction. There are no local chert outcrops near the site, and, with the exception of poor-quality glacial pebble cherts, no raw material is available within 100 kilometers of the site. Bayport, a Michigan chert that outcrops approximately 100 kilometers to the east in the Saginaw Bay area, is the most common raw material, accounting for 50–80 percent of items in all tool and debitage categories (Brashler, Laidler, and Martin 1998). The remaining tools and debitage are made of Wyandotte (Harrison County), Burlington, Flint Ridge, and Upper Mercer from Ohio, Norwood and Lambrix from Michigan, and very small quantities of Kettle Point, a chert that outcrops in Ontario. The diversity of raw materials present at the site suggests that occupants had ties not only to Illinois but also to the east and south into Ohio and Indiana.

Faunal Remains

The large and well-preserved faunal assemblage from the Prison Farm site provides the best opportunity to date to view Middle Woodland animal exploitation patterns in the Grand River valley. Animal remains recovered by Grand Valley State University excavations in 1996, 1997, and 1999, along with those in the Buerl Guernsey collection (Brashler, Laidler, and Martin 1998), total approximately fifty thousand specimens. Collections from 1996 and in the Guernsey collection have been analyzed (Brashler, Laidler, and Martin 1998; Meekhof and Martin 1998), and the 1997 and 1999 materials are currently being analyzed at the Illinois State Museum.

Approximately 40 percent of all identified animal specimens, and nearly 84 percent of the total by weight, are from mammals. The assemblage from terrestrial mammals are dominated by white-tailed deer, which constitute 84 percent of all identified mammal specimens by count and 74 percent by weight. Guernsey's surface collection includes numerous bones and teeth from elk and black bear; succeeding excavations indicate that this is not a reflection of collector bias, as each species is represented by dozens of specimens. Additional terrestrial mammals identified include cottontail rabbit, tree squirrel, canid (wolf or large dog and fox), and raccoon. Aquatic mammals are also numerous in the faunal assemblage, with beaver and muskrat together representing 10 percent of the identified mammal remains.

Birds tend to be underrepresented, with the only identified bones coming from wild turkey and ducks. Although this may reflect taphonomic factors, given the lighter bones of these animals, the scarcity of bird bones is generally consistent with findings at other Woodland period sites in the Grand River valley.

Turtles are well represented at Prison Farm and include snapping and softshell turtles, in addition to the usual suite of semiaquatic pond turtles (Family Emydidae: for example, painted, map, and red-eared turtles). Both the Blanding's turtle and the eastern box turtle also belong to this family, and both are present at Prison Farm. Whereas the box turtle is terrestrial and prefers open woodlands, the Blanding's turtle occurs in shallow ponds, marshes, and river backwaters. Blanding's turtles are noteworthy in that they were selected by prehistoric Michigan Indians for modification into containers, with numerous examples being found at Norton Mounds (Flanders 1965b; Griffin, Flanders, and Titterington 1970). Their carapaces were also apparently made into utensils at Prison Farm, since internal scraping and smoothing are commonly observed.

The greatest insights into local Middle Woodland subsistence practices come from the fish remains. Although all fish specimens at Prison Farm contribute only 9 percent by weight, they constitute more than 52 percent by count. Approximately 99 percent of the identified fish bones are from lake sturgeon. These giant bottom-feeders (as large as 136 kilograms in weight and over 2 meters in length) formerly migrated up the major rivers from the Great Lakes during the late spring and early summer (Hubbs and Lagler 1967:38). The number of individuals is difficult to estimate because the sturgeon's cartilaginous skeleton leaves only pectoral spine fragments and fragile, mostly nondescript dermal bones. Most of the sturgeon bones at Prison Farm are comparable in size to one of the Illinois State Museum's comparative sturgeon skeletons from an individual that weighed 26 kilograms and was approximately 160 centimeters long. The conclusion based on the 1996 faunal assemblage is that lake sturgeon contributed about 85 percent of the usable meat from fish and nearly 10 percent from all animals. The importance of spring fishing is also indicated by the presence of white sucker, redhorse, and walleye. Channel catfish and freshwater drum were also taken when available. At least nine species of freshwater mussel have also been identified, but these contribute only about 1 percent of the identified animal remains.

Unlike the situation at the Middle Woodland Schultz site in the Saginaw Valley (Cleland 1966; Luxenberg 1972), faunal assemblages from mound fill at Norton Mounds and from the Spoonville site suggest that Middle Woodland groups in the Grand Valley concentrated on large mammals and gave much less attention to aquatic resources (Cleland 1966:63–66; Martin 1975). Excavations at the Zemaitis site, upriver from Spoonville, provided the first indications of the great importance of lake sturgeon to Woodland peoples in the Grand Valley and suggested that the anadromous spring-spawning species must have been far more important than any other aquatic resource in western Michigan. Marginal preservation conditions at Zemaitis, however, warrant caution in interpretation. The presence of both Middle and Late Woodland ceramics at Zemaitis also clouds our perspectives on Middle Woodland subsistence (Brashler and Garland 1993). The Prison Farm site, with its clear Middle Woodland temporal position and large assemblage of well-preserved animal remains, offers an unprecedented opportunity to address this question. Although other fish (such as suckers and catfish) were utilized, the heavy concentration on lake sturgeon is distinct from the more balanced riverine procurement strategies followed by Middle Woodland people in the Saginaw Valley. Similarities to the small but growing faunal assemblage from the Arthursburg Hill Earthwork, located 8 kilometers upstream from Prison Farm, suggests that this pattern may have been established at least as early as the Early Woodland period (Martin personal communication 2000; Martin 1993).

In a recent synthesis and review, Kingsley (1999) revisited his previous discussion of Middle Woodland settlement systems in southwestern Michigan where he had applied Struever's (1968b) intensive harvest collecting model to the physiological setting and natural resources in southwestern Michigan (Kingsley 1981:143). Pertinent to our consideration of animal exploitation patterns, we can now suggest that the local adaptation to the strategy of intensive exploitation of selected, high-yielding species on a seasonal basis in the Grand River valley focused on two major species. White-tailed deer were the fundamental terrestrial prey during much of the year, but they were especially important during the autumn. Perhaps nearly as important were anadromous fish that ascended the major rivers of western Michigan to spawn during the spring. Lake sturgeon were especially significant because they constituted large meat units that were readily accessible in the wide and relatively shallow stretches of large rivers, where they congregated to spawn on the gravelly shoals. At these highly visible locations, Middle Woodland people could use spears and possibly weirs to harvest the aquatic giants. Unlike the inland shore fishery that developed farther north during the Late Woodland period (which involved the sophisticated gill-net technology necessary to exploit deepwater fish in open water [Cleland 1982]), the technology for capturing large fish that was employed by Middle Woodland populations in the Grand River valley was relatively simple. This discussion recalls Bruce D. Smith's (1975:137–138) consideration of Middle Mississippian animal exploitation, in which he considers selectivity to reflect high biological potential/reproductive rates, a large amount of edible meat per individual, ease of capture, and seasonal peaks in density levels. In this light, a stable, natural lake sturgeon population was capable of sustaining human exploitation during the Woodland period, and the species came to represent a major resource in the intensive harvest collecting strategy of western Michigan. Floodplain lakes, where present in the Grand River valley, were probably most important during the later months of summer, when the waters receded and made the trapped fish more accessible. In contrast to the Illinois Valley scenario, however, the importance of these backwaters in the Grand Valley remains to be demonstrated.

Botanical Remains

Botanical materials recovered during excavations at the Prison Farm site have provided some important new clues to interactions between Middle Woodland Havana populations and the floristic environment in the western Michigan region. Until now organic remains from Middle Woodland sites in Michigan have tended to be either scarce or not securely linked to Middle Woodland occupations at multicomponent sites.

Lacking data in the Grand River valley, subsistence models for Middle Woodland populations in Michigan were developed by analogy with the better-documented Havana Hopewell systems of the lower Illinois Valley (compare Brown 1964b; Kingsley 1981, 1999), which are based on Struever's (1968b) intensive harvest collecting model. In this framework, the Middle Woodland economy followed a seasonally scheduled round that included exploitation of selected high-yielding resources, including summer-ripening seeds (chenopod [*Chenopodium berlandieri*], sumpweed [*Iva annua*], knotweed [*Polygonum erectum*], and so forth) and fall nut masts. In recent decades, a flood of flotation-derived information has demonstrated that the summer-ripening seeds that formed a central aspect of the intensive harvest collecting model were harvested not from naturally occurring weedy stands but from a suite of native cultivated and domesticated plants.

Flotation-derived data emerging from Middle Woodland sites along major river valleys and their tributaries at the middle latitudes of eastern North America have revealed an economic system flexibly adapted to varying environmental situations, incorporating both cultivated and locally productive wild-plant resources. Although the foundations of this system are found in the Archaic, the contribution of agriculture greatly increased during the Middle Woodland period (compare Arzigian 1987; N. Asch and D. Asch 1985; Fritz 1993; Parker 1989). Corn was also present at this time in some areas, but apparently this crop was not intensively grown.

Situated on a broad levee four meters above the Grand River, the rich loamy soils at the Prison Farm site are ideal for cultivation, as the recent history of this landform clearly shows. Yet the remains of agricultural products are rare, consisting of one sunflower achene of domesticate size in more than 3,400 liters of midden and feature matrix processed by flotation. Obviously, factors other than the availability of soils suitable for crops provided the rationale for repeated Middle Woodland occupations at this locality. At the same time, it does not appear that foods grown elsewhere were regularly processed or consumed here. One sunflower seed and some dried fruit makes a pretty small bag of trail mix.

Varied wild seasonal resources from floodplain and upland forest, wetland, and prairie would have been accessible to people at the Prison Farm site. The largest part of the botanical assemblage consists of a highly diverse array of wood taxa used as fuel, indicating that within a short distance there were forest communities adapted to a range of floodplain soil and moisture conditions. The roster of identified tree types includes hickory, black walnut, butternut, and oak, all potential sources of edible, nutritious, and storable nut masts. In the central Grand Valley, mast-bearing trees were probably scattered, rather than clustered as a concentrated biomass, but in any given fall they would have yielded quantities of fruit sufficient to merit the attention of any resident Havana groups. Diverse nutshell from features and midden reflect the harvesting and processing of nuts from butternut, black walnut, and hickory trees, but nut remains occurred at a low density and ubiquity. It would seem that mast resources, like crops, were neither a motivation for fall occupation nor the focus of any significant subsistence activity. Similarly, edible wild plant resources associated with spring or summer, such as tubers and fleshy fruits, were sparsely represented in the assemblage.

The lack of botanical evidence, and the paucity of cultigens and other plant-based food remains in particular, is consistent with the interpretation that Prison Farm functioned as an important extractive locale where large game animals and select riverine resources, especially anadromous fish, were targeted (Brashler, Laidler, and Martin 1998; Meekhof and Martin 1998). The minimal use of floral resources may correlate inversely with the intensive focus on fauna during a series of warm-season occupations. The Prison Farm site may represent a unique situation in western Michigan, and researchers cannot be certain whether subsistence practices here typify a category of Middle Woodland occupation for the region and where the site might fit in an intensive harvest collecting subsistence round. However, in the St. Joseph River valley of southwestern Michigan, two large Middle Woodland features, one each at the Eidson and Wymer sites, were the only primary refuse pits at either multicomponent site (Garland 1990b). Both pits showed evidence of reuse, had low to moderate densities of taxonomically diverse nutshell, and contained few seeds. Remains of crop plants from the features consisted of a single fragmentary corn cupule. Similarly, at the multicomponent Wymer West site, a series of five pits, some of which may be assigned to the Middle Woodland period, have yielded sparse botanical remains that included a few pieces of nutshell (black walnut) and one fruit seed (Parker 1990). In the Kalamazoo Valley, two heavily sampled pit features at the Armintrout-Blackman site produced abundant wood, scant nut-shell, and no other floral materials. At all of these sites there appears to have been minimal use of plant resources as food, although wood was sometimes intensively exploited for fuel, suggesting that Prison Farm may not be atypical.

Aspects of Middle Woodland horticulture clearly extended north into parts of the lower Great Lakes, including southwestern Wisconsin (Arzigian 1987) and the Saginaw Valley on the east side of Michigan. A domesticated sumpweed achene has been identified from Middle Woodland deposits at the Schultz site, the first record for this crop in Michigan (Katie Egan-Bruhy, personal communication 2000). Also present were chenopod seeds and *Cucurbita pepo* rind fragments. The wild-food spectrum at Schultz included wild rice (*Zizania aquatica*) and an array of nutshell taxa identical to those at Prison Farm but at a much higher frequency. Chenopodium was also identified by Egan-Bruhy from Middle Woodland levels at the Marquette Viaduct locale of the Fletcher site (Lovis et al. 1994; Smith et al. 1994). These components incorporate a wide range of cultivated and wild resources, suggesting mixed or generalized adaptive strategies unlike those of contemporaneous populations in western Michigan.

A pattern of nonintensive use of available plant foods (perhaps related to low population density and mobile settlement strategies), in which cultigens were known but marginally significant, may have persisted from Late Archaic times well into the Late Woodland period in western Michigan. Such a long-term regional adaptation is seemingly reflected in the Havana occupation at the Prison Farm site.

Summary

In sum, Prison Farm offers evidence of an early Havana Hopewell Middle Woodland occupation in the Grand River valley that, along with the Converse site data from the 1999–2000 excavations described below, presents a pattern of animal and plant exploitation substantively different from that seen at contemporaneous Middle Woodland sites in Illinois and Ohio. The settlement and subsistence strategies in the Grand River valley apparent at these two sites suggest a different kind of seasonal mobility and harvesting strategy than was practiced elsewhere in the Hopewellian world.

The Converse Mounds and Village

An unusual opportunity to examine a portion of one of Michigan's largest, yet most poorly understood, Middle Woodland mound and habitation complexes—and to characterize the enigmatic Converse phase—emerged in 1999. Replacement of the US-131 "S-Curve" bridge in downtown Grand Rapids by the Michigan Department of Transportation necessitated excavations at the Converse site (20KT2). Mid- to late-nineteenth-century historic documentation identified an extensive complex of seventeen to twenty-nine mounds and associated habitation areas situated along the west bank of the Grand River

(Demeter and Robinson 1999). Most of the mounds identified in the historic records are burial mounds, although a small number of the mounds were characterized as "kitchen heaps," a nineteenth-century euphemism for large trash or midden deposits.

The village-and-mound complex appears to have stretched for nearly a quarter-mile downstream from the rapids for which the modern city was named. Based on information that survived destruction of the mounds and comparisons with the nearby Norton site and with Illinois Hopewell, the Converse phase was proposed as a later Middle Woodland manifestation in the Grand River valley dating to approximately A.D. 200–400 (Griffin, Flanders, and Titterington 1970; Kingsley 1999:150). Unfortunately, the mounds from which this Norton tradition phase takes its name were destroyed during the early development of Grand Rapids, leaving only a small collection of exotic artifacts, tantalizing descriptions of finds encountered during the leveling of the mounds, and a few maps and drawings sketched many years after the fact. While a number of western Michigan sites have been assigned to the Converse phase (table 15.1; see also Kingsley 1999:150), only one third-century A.D. radiocarbon date from the Spoonville site (20OT1) plus ceramics similar to Baehr/Pike series materials from Illinois support the phase designation (Flanders 1965a).

As a result of nineteenth-century urban land-use patterns in the area, portions of the Converse habitation site have been preserved under historic fill varying from 0.5 meters to 2.0 meters in thickness. During the winter of 1999–2000, Commonwealth Cultural Resources Group, Inc., excavated an area of 115 square meters on the upper terrace (Block A) and about 287 square meters on the lower terrace (Block B), totalling 193 cubic meters of fill, that would be impacted by bridge pier construction. These excavations produced an assemblage of over eighty-three thousand specimens of prehistoric ceramics, lithics, and bone. Carbonized plant remains from sixty-six flotation samples were also analyzed. Diagnostic artifacts recovered from excavations include Late Archaic through Late Woodland materials, although the majority of the artifacts from the site date to the Middle and Late Woodland occupations. A small assemblage from an early- to mid-eighteenth-century Native American occupation, along with a large assemblage of mid-nineteenth- through early-twentieth-century material, was also recovered. The following summary of the Converse site, which focuses on the Middle Woodland component, reflects the results of analyses presented in a technical report and in papers presented at two symposia (Hambacher and Ruggles 2002; Hambacher et al. 2003; Robertson and Hambacher 2002).

The recovered prehistoric artifact assemblages were largely derived from the 30-40-centimeter-thick paleosol preserved on the lower terrace in Block B. Only about 5 percent of the pre-Contact artifact assemblage occurred on the upper terrace in Block A, and it was largely derived from a small natural low spot where the original ground surface had been preserved. The low density of materials in this part of the site may in part be a function of close proximity to the former location of four of the mounds. Approximately 65 percent of the recovered artifacts were associated with the Middle Woodland component, while an additional 30 percent were associated with the early Late Woodland component. A small Early Woodland component, an even smaller Late Archaic component, a single Early Archaic bifurcate-base projectile point, and a small Contact period component complete the Native American artifact assemblage from the site. Only thirty-nine pre-nineteenth-century features, all of which occurred in Block B, were encountered in the excavations. Of these, a refuse pit and a shallow basin were associated with the Early Woodland component. Middle Woodland features included seven hearths, two fire-cracked rock concentrations, one refuse pit, two shallow basins, and a debitage concentration. Two fire-cracked rock concentrations, an earth oven, a refuse pit, and three shallow basins dated to the early Late Woodland period. Eight smudge pits, one hearth, three ash deposits, two dog burials, a large stratified refuse pit, and a shallow basin were associated with the Contact period assemblage.

A series of thirteen radiocarbon dates obtained from the Converse site (table 15.3) complements the artifact assemblage. A radiocarbon date from the base of the paleosol on the lower terrace indicates that the soil in that part of the site began to form around 3060 B.P. Three other radiocarbon dates from this terrace indicate a period of increased flooding around 110 B.C. These dates were derived from below and within a lens of alluvial gravels extending across a portion of a flood chute that apparently once extended along the back edge of the lower terrace. Two other radiocarbon dates of A.D. 870 and A.D. 1710–1720 clearly relate to early Late Woodland and Contact era occupations of the site. The remaining seven radiocarbon dates from the site are AMS dates derived from carbonized residues adhering to Early Woodland and Middle Woodland body sherds. Two of these dates place the small Early Woodland occupation between 800 and 400 B.C. The remaining five radiocarbon dates span the period between 50 B.C. and A.D. 380.

Ceramics

The ceramic assemblage of 4,175 sherds documents the Early Woodland, Middle Woodland, and Zemaitis phase early Late Woodland occupations at the site, spanning the period between the first and twelfth centuries A.D. (Brashler 2002, 2003). A complicating and limiting factor is the highly fragmented condition of the ceramic assemblage. Most of the recovered sherds are less than 4 square centimeters in size, only seventy-two rims are represented, and no significant reconstructable vessel fragments were present. Consequently, attribute analysis, rather than a typological approach, was used in the examination of the ceramics (Brashler 2002). Attributes coded for the ceramics included paste and temper characteristics, sherd thickness, construction technique, surface treatment types, and exterior decoration characteristics. Given the small size of the sherds it is not surprising that most of the ceramic assemblage consists of undecorated fragments. Decoration was present on only 319 sherds (7.6 percent of the total).

The ceramics were subdivided into a series of five primary categories: Early

Table 15.3. Radiocarbon Dates from the Converse Site (20KT2)

Lab Number	^{14}C Age[a]	Calibrated Age/Ranges[b]
Beta-138050[c]	100.2 ±0.7%	100 B.P. (A.D. 1710–1720; A.D. 1880–1910)
Beta-142610[d]	3060 ±40 B.P.	3365–3165 B.P. (1415–1215 B.C.)
Beta-142611[e]	2180 ±50 B.P.	2330–2030 B.P. (380–80 B.C.)
Beta-142612[e]	2240 ±50 B.P.	2345–2130 B.P. (395–180 B.C.)
Beta-142614[e]	2260 ±40 B.P.	2345–2150 B.P. (395–200 B.C.)
Beta-142613[f]	1190 ±50 B.P.	1250–970 B.P. (A.D. 700–980)
Beta-148358[g]	2540 ±40 B.P.	2750–2690 and 2660–2480 B.P. (800–740 B.C. and 710–530 B.C.)
Beta-148359[h]	1890 ±40 B.P.	1900–1720 B.P. (A.D. 40–230)
Beta-148360[i]	2440 ±40 B.P.	2720–2350 B.P. (770–400 B.C.)
Beta-148361[i]	1970 ±40 B.P.	2000–1840 B.P. (50 B.C.–A.D. 110)
Beta-153907[k]	2040 ±40 B.P.	1990–1820 B.P. (40 B.C.–A.D. 130)
Beta-153908[l]	2010 ±40 B.P.	1990–1830 B.P. (40 B.C.–A.D. 120)
Beta-153909[m]	1850 ±40 B.P.	1810–1570 B.P. (A.D. 140–380)

a. Uncorrected age is measured ^{14}C age.

b. Calibrations run using Stuiver et al. 1998. Results are 2 sigma (95% probability) calibrations.

c. Sample was a corn cob (*Zea mays*) recovered from a smudge pit (Feature 23). Result is reported as a percentage of the reference standard rather than an age because the sample contained an average ^{14}C content greater than the modern standard.

d. Dates the initiation of soil development on the T2 terrace, which contains the majority of the intact deposits.

e. These dates bracket a period of increased alluvial activity on the T2 terrace and appear to predate the period of most intense occupation by 250–300 years.

f. Dates an "earth oven" (Feature 64) containing early Late Woodland Zemaitis phase ceramics.

g. AMS date on food residue adhering to a relatively thick, cordmarked exterior/smoothed interior Early Woodland body sherd from Feature 34.

h. AMS date on food residue adhering to a Norton phase smoothed-over cordmarked body sherd recovered from N505 E548, Level 4.

i. AMS date on food residue adhering to a interior-exterior cordmarked Early Woodland body sherd recovered from Feature 38.

j. AMS date on food residue adhering to a Hopewell zoned dentate rocker-stamped sherd recovered from N500 E537, Level 3.

k. AMS date on food residue adhering to a Hopewell zoned incised sherd recovered from N500 E539, Level 3.

l. AMS date on food residue adhering to a Hopewell dentate rocker-stamped sherd recovered from N502 E565, Level 7.

m. AMS date on food residue adhering to a Hopewell crosshatched rim sherd recovered from N501 E508, Level 13.

Woodland (*n* = 41), Middle Woodland (*n* = 627), Late Woodland (*n* = 331), Hacklander ware (*n* = 79), and type indeterminate (*n* = 3,097). The Early Woodland sherds are mostly characterized by interior-exterior cord marking or smoothed cord marking, thick walls (averaging 12.2 millimeters), an even mix of silty and sandy pastes, moderately sized igneous temper, and coil manufacture. These sherds are comparable to other Early Woodland ceramic assemblages in Michigan (Fischer 1972; Garland 1986; Garland and Beld 1999).

Ceramics assigned to the Middle Woodland component represent 56.3 percent of the identifiable sherds from the Converse site. Sherds were assigned to Norton, Hopewellian, Baehr, and Middle Woodland type indeterminate categories based on morphological and decorative characteristics. Slightly less than 10 percent of the Middle Woodland ceramics were classified as Norton phase, characterized as relatively thick with primarily silty pastes, light-colored igneous temper, and smoothed-over cordmarked or cordmarked exteriors (or, rarely, smoothed exteriors). The four decorated Norton sherds included two with nodes, one with straight square dentate stamping, and one with a zoned or incised line. A small number of sherds with shallow dotlike punctates may also belong to this group. In general, the Norton ceramics from the Converse site are comparable to material from the Norton Mounds (Griffin, Flanders, and Titterington 1970) and Prison Farm sites, as well as material from the central Muskegon Valley to the north (Losey 1967; Prahl 1970, 1991) and the Kalamazoo Valley to the south (Garland and DesJardins, this volume).

The majority of the Middle Woodland ceramics from the Converse site were classified as Hopewellian. The 437 body sherds and twenty rims in this group comprise 72.9 percent of the Middle Woodland ceramics from the site. The presence of typical Hopewellian decorative elements, such as plain rocker stamping, incising, combing/brushing, cross-hatching, hemiconical punctates, and zoned lines, were the primary criteria for the identification of these ceramics. Hopewellian sherds also generally exhibited compact sandy pastes with light-colored igneous temper. Two radiocarbon-dated zoned dentate rocker-stamped sherds produced similar dates of A.D. 40 and A.D. 50, while a third zoned incised sherd produced a date of A.D. 60. Not only are these dates about 150 years younger than the traditionally accepted beginning of the Converse phase (A.D. 200–400), they also predate the single Norton phase sherd from the site that was directly dated (table 15.3). On the basis of these dates and comparisons with ceramics from the Prison Farm and Norton Mounds sites, Brashler (2002, 2003) has made a compelling argument for the early introduction of Hopewellian traits into the Grand Valley during the Norton phase (10 B.C.–A.D. 200). These dates also call into question what actually constitutes the so-called Converse phase, its dating, and its utility as a chronological construct. The ceramic data from the site have not only highlighted important technological differences between Havana-related Norton ceramics and Hopewellian ceramics but also, in conjunction with the radiocarbon dates, have provided evidence for the chronological overlap of these two ceramic groups. The data from the Converse site lead us to suggest that the Converse phase, if it is to be retained as an archaeological construct, be shifted to about A.D. 100–300, with its initiation coinciding with a possible shift in ceramic technology and the appearance of Hopewellian ceramic motifs.

A few sherds (n = 7) with very thin walls, limestone temper, and brushed or combed decoration on burnished exteriors appear to represent Baehr wares that were imported into the Converse site. A small number of non-limestone-tempered Baehr-like sherds in the assemblage may represent locally manufactured copies. Although these sherds are not directly dated, their co-occurrence with both Havana-related and Hopewell materials dating to the first century A.D. is analogous to the situation in the lower Illinois Valley discussed by Asch (1997).

Lithics

The lithic assemblage recovered from the Converse site contains 920 chipped stone tools, 89 ground stone tools, 88 cores (mostly exhausted bipolar forms), 42,668 pieces of debitage, and 9,525 pieces of fire-cracked rock (804 kilograms). Although its bulk is composed of debitage and fire-cracked rock, the lithic assemblage is nonetheless impressive in terms of size, and it testifies to the important economically and socially strategic nature of the Converse site. In general, the lithic assemblage from the Converse site can be characterized as a lithic industry that is near the end of its use-life. Many of the tools are broken, the projectile points have been heavily resharpened, there are relatively few unfinished bifaces, most of the cores are exhausted or broken, and the debitage is dominated by late-stage debris from core reduction and toolkit maintenance activities.

While there is a relatively broad range of chipped and ground stone tools from the site, the assemblage is dominated by a relatively narrow range of tools. This fact, coupled with the substantial overlap in the distribution of temporally diagnostic artifacts, suggests that there is a high degree of redundancy in the types and range of activities carried out at the site. The frequency distribution of the projectile points suggests that the contributions of the pre-Middle Woodland and Late Woodland occupations to the overall assemblage were low, accounting for only about 24 percent of the total.

About 40 percent of the 157 recovered projectile points have been associated with the Middle Woodland component of the site. Because of the extensive amount of resharpening on these points they were subdivided into large corner-notched forms with typological affinities to Snyders and Norton varieties and medium-sized corner-notched forms with typological affinities to the Manker and miscellaneous untyped corner-notched varieties. Two Gibson notched points were also identified in the assemblage. Later Middle Woodland points include five Steuben/Lowe series and two Chesser Notched-like points. Data from the Prison Farm site suggest that the six small expanding-stemmed points in the assemblage may be associated with the main Middle Woodland occupation of the site.

Similar to the situation at other Middle Woodland occupations in the lower Grand Valley, raw materials are dominated by locally available chert types (variants of Deer Lick Creek, Lambrix, and miscellaneous gravel cherts). Present at lower densities are other Michigan materials (Bayport and Norwood) and cherts from farther-flung sources, including Upper Mercer, Flint Ridge, Burlington/Avon, and Indiana Hornstone. With the exception of Upper Mercer chert, these chert types are represented in only small amounts.

The chipped stone tool inventory at Converse is heavily slanted towards tools associated with hunting, hide-working, and toolkit fabrication and maintenance activities. The ground stone assemblage provides additional evidence for these activities, but there are also indications of additional processing and manufacturing activities. Once again, a small number of tool types dominates this segment of the lithic assemblage.

Faunal Remains

Faunal material at the site was relatively well preserved and abundant. This summary of the faunal remains focuses on the material recovered from Block B, since most of the fauna from Block A are associated with the Euro-American component of the site (Martin 2002, 2003). Species present in the Block B paleosol reflect the diverse terrestrial and riparian habitats present within close proximity to the site. Mammalian remains, primarily white-tailed deer, dominate the faunal assemblage, accounting for 91.5 percent of the bone from the site. Deer constitute nearly three-quarters of the identifiable pre-Contact period mammal bone. Species occurring in moderate frequencies include beaver, canids, black bear, raccoon, and muskrat. Elk/wapiti, rabbits, woodchuck, squirrels, porcupine, river otter, and voles occur in very low frequencies. The relatively low frequency of bird bone in the assemblage reflects patterns seen in other western Michigan prehistoric sites (Martin 1976; Meekhoff and Martin 1998). Identified avian species from the site are limited to geese, duck, turkey, and probably red-tailed hawk. Reptiles are similarly represented by only a small number of specimens, and turtles, particularly softshell, comprise most of this segment of the faunal assemblage. A small number of bivalve specimens are also present.

Fish remains, 85 percent of which are lake sturgeon, constitute a relatively small proportion of the bone recovered from the site. This may be a function of taphonomic factors. Martin (2002, 2003) argues that the ubiquity of the lake sturgeon remains in the Middle Woodland features, and their relatively even distribution across Block B, indicate that the species was an abundant and important resource at the site. Similar to the situation at the Prison Farm site, exploitation of spring-spawning fish, particularly lake sturgeon, represented an important economic activity at the Converse site. Gar, freshwater drum, redhorse, several species of catfish and bass, bowfin, northern pike, yellow perch, and walleye are represented in comparatively small numbers.

Botanical Remains

Botanical materials from the site were limited in both number and diversity compared to recovered fauna and artifacts. Although the assemblage in general and Middle Woodland floral remains in particular are limited, Egan-Bruhy (2002, 2003) provides some insights into the season of occupation and the nature of Middle Woodland exploitive strategies. Since charcoal occurred in moderate densities across the site, poor preservation does not explain the general lack of floral remains at the site. Identified edible floral resources from Middle Woodland features are limited to eight fragments of nutshell (hickory, acorn, and walnut family), six seeds (chenopod, blackberry/raspberry, and rose family), a rhizome, and a single fragment of maize, the last most likely intrusive from the later Contact period component.

Seasonality

The lack of edible plant remains from the site coupled with the structure of the faunal assemblage suggest that the spring occupation of the site was relatively brief and was focused on the harvesting of lake sturgeon. It further suggests that there was probably no appreciable occupation of the site during the summer or in the fall during the period when nut resources would have been collected. This pattern of exploitation is similar to that seen at the Prison Farm site and suggests a settlement pattern involving considerable seasonal mobility during the Middle Woodland, potentially involving interior sites (Egan-Bruhy 2003). The structure of the tool and debitage assemblages indicates site activities dominated by a relatively narrow range of tasks. The tools are heavily geared towards resource extraction and processing. Whereas the faunal assemblage testifies to the importance of the spring sturgeon fishery, the high frequency of projectile points and end scrapers argues for high levels of hunting and hide processing—activities that are closely associated with the fall, when the meat and hides are in optimal condition and at a time when residentially mobile groups might be making arrangements for dispersal to cold-season encampments. The condition of the tools themselves and the structure of the debitage assemblage indicate high levels of toolkit maintenance, possibly in anticipation of a relatively brief period of heavy use associated with fall hunting. Other segments of the lithic assemblage also argue for some plant resource extraction and processing, although what is being collected and when it is occurring is unclear.

Overall, data from these excavations suggest that the site served as a point of social aggregation during both the spring and the late fall season. Specifically, the intensive sturgeon fishing that occurred during the spring and intensive hunting for deer meat and pelts in the late fall provided the basis for this aggregation. Further, based on a variety of locational and environmental data, it has been suggested that Middle Woodland populations dispersed during the remaining parts of the warm season to interior lakes and headwaters areas (Brashler and Holman 1999; Egan-Bruhy 2002) and possibly to the lower reaches of the major rivers where extensive marshes and swamps were located (Hambacher and Robertson 2002). These periods of social aggregation provided the context for the renewal and reaffirmation of kin and other social ties necessary for maintaining the cohesiveness of residentially mobile hunter-forager societies. Important ritual activities, such as the burial of the dead, would have taken place at these gatherings. Since little in the way of mortuary-related artifacts and activities or interaction sphere goods were recovered from the habitation area of the Converse site, it is in the domestic sphere of Middle Woodland life that these excavations make their greatest contribution.

Other Converse Phase Sites

Several other sites in the Grand Valley might be attributable, primarily on the basis of ceramic styles, to the proposed Converse phase. The most notable is the

Spoonville site (20OT1), which was partially excavated and destroyed in the 1960s (Brashler 1991; Flanders 1965a; Kingsley 1999). Additional excavation at Spoonville in 1990 revealed that deposits at the site are conflated and contain materials dating from the Archaic through Late Woodland periods within approximately 15 centimeters of deposit. However, as in the case of Converse village, a significant portion of the diagnostic ceramic and lithic material does appear to be Middle Woodland. In addition, floral and faunal materials are poorly preserved. Dates from Spoonville range from the first through the early third century A.D., suggesting a later Norton tradition Middle Woodland temporal position.

Several sites contain small quantities of what are probably Hopewellian ceramics with rocker stamping and other diagnostic decorations. This distribution may indicate that populations in the later Middle Woodland period were dispersed. Alternatively, these groups may have followed a highly mobile seasonal round involving interior lakes and marshes (Brashler and Holman 1999; Egan-Bruhy 2003).

Conclusion

The recent work on Middle Woodland occupations in the Grand River valley and other areas to the north in Michigan offer insights regarding the spread and nature of Havana and Hopewell culture in areas outside of Illinois and Ohio. In terms of subsistence, data from the Prison Farm and Converse site support Kingsley's (1990, 1999) hypothesis that Middle Woodland adaptation in this part of Michigan included selection for habitats similar to those occupied in the central and lower Illinois Valley. However, the subsistence choices at these two sites appear to have been focused on animals rather than plants. While evidence of contact between Illinois and Ohio Middle Woodland cultures is present in the Grand Valley (in the form of burial motifs, exotic materials, and ceramic styles), we would like to suggest that the Middle Woodland subsistence strategy evolved in place from a Late Archaic/Early Woodland base. Unfortunately, we have little from the Late Archaic and Early Woodland with which to compare our emerging Middle Woodland subsistence data. A heavy reliance on hunting and gathering appears to have continued along the Grand and the Muskegon through the Late Woodland period, as indicated at sites such as Zemaitis.

If we accept the hypothesis that the subsistence strategy practiced by Grand River Middle Woodland populations evolved in place, then what is the mechanism by which Hopewellian burial practices, exotic goods, and ceramics appeared in the area? Holman (1990) suggested a model to account for Hopewellian traits that involved the fissioning of groups from the central Illinois Valley that moved north but maintained connections to the region through kin ties. Given the paucity of diagnostic Early Woodland ceramics and radiocarbon dates for the period 380–100 B.C., was the Grand River basin empty or was there an indigenous population we have yet to identify? Ceramic data from Prison Farm suggest the presence of Havana Hopewell-like pottery by the first century B.C., but the assemblage also strongly suggests that ceramic manufacturing techniques were not as sophisticated as is typical for Illinois Valley Middle Woodland ceramics, even though Havana tradition diagnostic attributes are present on the majority of the vessels.

Therefore, a persistent unresolved problem involves the dynamics of Hopewellian expansion. We do have a much better understanding of the timing and appearance of groups or ideas and technology in the area than we did even ten years ago. We think we will know perhaps a bit more about the ties between the Grand and the other portions of the Middle Woodland world in the future as collections from both Prison Farm and other Middle Woodland sites in the valley are analyzed and synthesized with the existing data from Norton, Converse, and Spoonville.

An important contribution of recent Prison Farm and Converse site research and recent work by Brashler and Holman (1999) is the idea that a variety of different subsistence strategies were practiced within the Havana and Hopewellian Middle Woodland at its northern edge in Michigan. The fact that various adaptive strategies were employed in different regions of the Hopewellian world may ultimately have some bearing on the very nature of Middle Woodland cultural processes. It might be interesting to consider as a model the flexible adaptive strategies of more recent tribal groups in the Great Lakes area such as the Ojibwe, some of whom were fishers, some horticulturalists, some hunter-gatherers, and some a mix of all three practices.

Finally, to understand Middle Woodland occupation in the Grand River system in Michigan, and indeed other areas, we need to understand what happened locally as well as what happened in the broader context of the Middle Woodland. For too long we in the Grand River valley have been in the shadow of the incomparable cultural material from other regions of the Middle Woodland world. We need to understand what was happening here first and then look at how the relationships between the Grand and other areas during the Middle Woodland can advance our understanding of Middle Woodland cultural processes.

Acknowledgments

The Converse site excavations were funded by the Michigan Department of Transportation (MDOT). Without this funding, the cooperation of MDOT and their regional offices in Grand Rapids, and the logistics capabilities of the Kent County Road Commission these excavations would not have been possible. The Prison Farm excavations were conducted with support from Grand Valley State University. Various colleagues have significantly benefited from conversations, often spirited, with Elizabeth Garland, Robert Kingsley, Barbara Mead, Mark Schurr, and William Mangold. We are particularly indebted to Margaret Holman, who read and commented on several drafts of this document. We are indebted to them and the legacy of the late George I. Quimby and Richard E. Flanders, whose pioneering work in the Grand River valley set the stage for the research in the new millennium.

16

Hopewell Regional Interactions
in Southeastern Wisconsin and Northern Illinois

A Core-Periphery Approach

Robert J. Jeske

The focus of this study is to explore the extent to which a core-periphery model of social interaction can explain the nature of cultural contact and the expression of Hopewellian cultural traits at the northern edge of the Prairie Peninsula, in southern Wisconsin and northern Illinois. Materials recovered from the Alberts site complex (47JE887 and 47JE903) will be used to illustrate long-standing patterns of settlement and interaction between southeastern Wisconsin and northern Illinois populations that played a strong role in the nature of southeastern Wisconsin people's participation in the Hopewell exchange system. Sites in southeastern Wisconsin during the time that Hopewell exchange operated are described as part of the Waukesha phase (Salzer n.d.; Stevenson et al. 1997). The material culture from these sites, particularly the frequency of Steuben Punctated ceramic vessels in association with decorated Havana Hopewell materials, bears a resemblance to the material culture recovered from sites described as part of the Steuben phase in the upper Illinois River valley of northern Illinois. These materials also have some affinity to those recovered from sites of the Havana Hopewell phase from the lower Illinois River valley and seem to have less affinity to material from Trempealeau phase sites in southwestern Wisconsin (Stevenson et al. 1997) and sites of the Frazier phase of the central Illinois River valley (Wolforth 1995). Models using general diffusion or down-the-line trade to explain the distribution of Havana Hopewell sherds cannot explain this discontinuous pattern of ceramic assemblage resemblances. A core-periphery approach, however, may provide a framework for discussing interregional interactions among Hopewellian groups.

A Core-Periphery Approach

Core-periphery models of cultural contact and development derive directly from world systems theory, which was devised by Immanuel Wallerstein (1974) to explain the rise and worldwide spread of European capitalism. Wallerstein suggests that humans interacting (both cooperatively and competitively) with each other across geographical boundaries eventually begin to specialize in the production of certain commodities or services. Advantages conferred on one group by geography may result in that group's eventually gaining a competitive advantage over its neighbors, initiating a hierarchical exchange relationship. As the advantaged group leverages itself above the others through its exploitation of the unequal exchange, it becomes the core, while the others in the exchange system become the periphery. Valuable commodities flow into the core and are reworked, and then the value-added products are shipped back out to the peripheries at great profit to the core. In time, peripheral groups' economies become dependent upon the core, and eventually nearly all cultural relations become structured by this unequal exchange relationship. The core becomes increasingly powerful economically, socially, ideologically, and militarily: in Wallerstein's European case, the Western European core of the fourteenth through nineteenth centuries was able to expand globally through repeated application of this process in continents beyond Europe.

The distinctly materialist and economic approach to culture contact and complexity is naturally intriguing to archaeologists attempting to explain the rise and fall of sociopolitical phenomena through time. Its application to non-state-level societies, however, has been controversial and less than successful for a number of reasons. Wallerstein insisted that trade in bulk goods, rather than luxuries ("preciosities," in his terminology), was the paramount organizing principle on which intergroup contacts were structured. To adapt the world systems approach to chiefdom- or tribal-level societies, where large-scale exchange of bulk goods is poorly demonstrated, researchers have reworked Wallerstein's formulation to allow a better fit with noncapitalist structures. Chase-Dunn and Hall (1991) have termed their approach core-periphery analysis and have gone the farthest to articulate a world systems–derived perspective on the organizational principles of economic exchange among societies. On the nature of exchange, core-periphery researchers have been forced to turn Wallerstein on his head, arguing that it is, in fact, exchange in luxury items valued by elites that structures intergroup competition (for example, Peregrine 1991; Schneider 1991; but see Dincauze and Hasenstab 1989; Frank 1993). Whether using Wallerstein's formulation or a derivative version, archaeologists have met with varying degrees of success in demonstrating the effectiveness of these models for explaining the development of hierarchical social organizations in noncapitalist societies, such as Bronze Age Greece (Frank 1993; Kardulias 1999), the Classic–Post-Classic traditions in the Oaxaca Valley (Feinman 1999), Cahokia (Jeske 1999; Peregrine 1991, 1995), the Inca (Kuznar 1999), the Iroquois (Dincauze and Hasenstab 1989), and seventeenth- and eighteenth-century Native Americans (Kardulias 1990).

Taking exception to the use of world systems theory or core-periphery analysis in noncapitalist systems, Stein (1999) has argued that three basic assumptions of world systems theory (core dominance over periphery, unequal exchange, and culture change caused by long-distance trade) are empirically refuted by ethnohistorical and archaeological evidence. Stein and others have argued that the emphasis on external economic relationships and the relative lack of attention to the internal structuring of cultural systems within the core-periphery relationship are fundamental flaws. The basic notion that the core must dominate the periphery through unequal trade is challenged by Stein and others because it assumes that people in the peripheries are passive victims, lacking agency in the relationship (see Sahlins 1994). Others argue that since trade must be unequal and, essentially, a zero sum game in which the periphery will lose, people in the so-called periphery will not participate (Sella 1977; Stein 1999:157). Stein also suggests that internal dynamics are more likely to cause systemic change than are external trade relations, especially as distance from the core increases, thus undermining the power of the core to influence the periphery.

Stein (1999:159) is also unsympathetic to those who would like to modify Wallerstein's world systems theory into a more generic model of core-periphery interaction: "If we adhere to Wallerstein's original construct, then we have a model which . . . simply does not work for pre- or noncapitalist societies. On the other hand, if we embrace a modified World Systems perspective then we have a construct that gains broad cross-cultural applicability to virtually all interregional networks everywhere, but does so by sacrificing all analytical specificity about how these systems actually work." I agree with Stein (1999:153) that there has been a tendency by some to use world systems theory uncritically to force a "variety of interactional forms and developmental trajectories in to a single theoretical procrustean bed." I suggest, however, that the core-periphery approach championed by Chase-Dunn and Hall (1991) might be a useful approach to describing, and ultimately explaining, non-state-level culture contact at least in some circumstances. The core-periphery perspective may be useful as long as we are careful to avoid simplistically slapping Wallerstein's world systems theory onto the late prehistory of the eastern United States (compare Jeske 1999). Where I must diverge from Stein's critique is where he takes an overly rigid view of core-periphery systems as inherently hierarchically ordered and ignores that complexity such as overlapping and multiple cores are an important aspect even of Wallerstein's formulation (see also Frank 1999). I suggest that we can look at interregional exchange at multiple levels, acknowledge agency on the part of people in peripheries, and assume that each periphery and core will interact with multiple other peripheries and cores to produce a dynamic economic and cultural landscape.

I propose to use a differential core-periphery interaction as a framework within which to describe and analyze the Hopewell phenomenon. In a differential core-periphery relation, unlike in a hierarchical core-periphery model, the core need not actively dominate the periphery either politically or militaristically. Rather, the maintenance of asymmetrical social or economic relationships pulls the peripheral groups into the economic and cultural orbit of the core. This pull may be tempered or even vigorously resisted by people in the periphery, and the rise and decline of multiple cores and peripheries across geographic and temporal spans is expected.

One crucial aspect to understanding culture contact in a core-periphery approach is the ability to bound the system, that is, to define the spatial and temporal limits of the interaction. Hall (1999) proposes four types of boundaries to define the extent of a world system: (1) information and cultural flows, (2) trade of luxury/prestige goods, (3) political/military interaction, and (4) trade of bulk goods. It is important to understand that these boundaries are not isomorphic, that is, information and cultural flow might extend much farther afield than political/military interaction or even trade. The non-coterminal nature of cultural subsystems has long recognized by ethnographers (various authors in Barth 1969) and has recently been emphasized by some archaeologists (for example, Hodder 1982, 1991b; Seeman 1996).

In a core-periphery approach, the system itself is the fundamental unit of analysis: "'societies' are not fundamental units of social organization, but are crystallizations of systemic relations" (Hall 1999:7). It is through an understanding of the nature of culture contact that we can come back to the development of individual regional polities. Of course, to understand the nature of culture contact we need a data set of regional polities—crystallizations—for comparison. This hermeneutic (or at least reflexive) approach to understanding context and content also accords well with much recent literature on appropriate archaeological methods and methodologies (Hodder 1991b; Kosso 1991). At the very least, a core-periphery approach provides a relatively straightforward framework within which we can describe—and perhaps make testable statements about—the nature and direction of prehistoric culture contact within and across specific regions. We can also examine how, if at all, such contact effects change within individual societies. Rather than force all culture contact into a single procrustean bed, I suggest that using a core-periphery analysis of intersocial interaction provides us with a method of discerning what fits and what does not.

Hopewell, or the Hopewell Interaction Sphere, has sparked arguably the most intensive and long-lasting discussion of culture contact in pre-Columbian North America (Brose and Greber 1979; Brown 1961; Caldwell and Hall 1964; Deuel 1952; Pacheco 1996b; Van Gilder and Charles 2003; see also Griffin 1960; Prufer 1964a; Seeman 1979b). Among its many descriptions, Hopewell is often explained, more or less, as localized polities adapting to local social and physical environments, connected within and across regions by some vaguely defined ideological network expressed in panregional stylistic motifs, raw material choices, and artifact forms. However, this network is discontinuous and nonsymmetrical across its geographic scope, at least in the quantities and quality of materials that remain in the archaeological record (for example, Seeman 1979b). The Hopewell Interaction Sphere is also accepted by most to have two geographic centers: Ohio Hopewell of the Scioto River valley of south-central

Ohio, and Illinois Havana Hopewell of the lower Illinois River valley of west-central Illinois (for example, Griffin 1952c, 1978).

To date, no model of Hopewell economic or other relationships has been widely accepted. Our inability to explain (or even describe) Hopewell interactions adequately in part results from the multiple economic, social, ideological, and military histories spanning half a continent and some five hundred years of time that make up Hopewell. A differential core-periphery model of interaction may help to define the mechanisms for the rise and maintenance of this purported asymmetrical movement of goods and ideas within at least a portion of the Illinois Havana Hopewellian space and time framework. If this approach can be shown to be useful at this regional level, higher levels of analysis may also prove fruitful.

In the Illinois Havana Hopewell case, the core area may not be conceived of as an economic magnet dragging the periphery into its orbit as much as it is an economic, social, and biological reproductive pool that attracts the attention of elites in peripheral regions. The use of long-distance trade by elites to restructure social relations within the local community has been suggested as at least one consequence of Hopewell interaction (Charles 1992). Charles argues that Havana Hopewell resulted from the migration of groups from the central Illinois River valley into the lower Illinois River valley, which had been relatively unoccupied during the preceding Early Woodland period (Charles 1992:190). As the valley population increased over time, a mechanism for mediating between new immigrants (most likely lineage groups) and original settlers was needed. Intergroup trade was one such mediator, creating a multitiered social network of junior and senior lineages. Elites could recruit new immigrants using mortuary rituals, including the manipulation of exotic items and materials, as a focal point. The adoption of junior lineages into the original community would increase the status of the original lineages, a process Charles terms levitation.

Mortuary ritual, manipulation of symbolic artifacts, and ritual adoption were common means of structuring intergroup relationships in historic Native American groups (R. Hall 1997). The seventeenth-century French explorers Radisson and Groseilliers were shocked at meeting Ottawa and Dakota Indians in Wisconsin who stripped them, redressed them in furs, wept and shed tears over them as if in mourning for a dead loved one, and covered them in smoke from calumet pipes (R. Hall 1997:1–2). The French explorer Nicolas Perrot also underwent this calumet ceremony upon meeting a group of Iowa, who explained to Perrot that he had been adopted as the chief of the tribe, by virtue of his acceptance of the calumet. The calumet ceremony was a mortuary/adoption ritual used to mediate between unrelated individuals and social groups: "This was the ceremony of the Captain which did not in fact make Perrot the chief of the Iowas except in a symbolic sense. We know now that Perrot was being received as the reincarnation of a dead chief" (R. Hall 1997:3). "The [calumet] ceremony was basically a rite of adoption used to establish a bond of kinship between two respected individuals of different clans and usually of different villages or tribes. Although the adoption was between individuals, the selection . . . was a community decision and the ceremony required support from the community and extended family. . . . This form of adoption between communities contrasted with that within a community that was associated mainly with mourning" (R. Hall 1997:50, see also 1991:30).

According to Charles (1992), Hopewell elites also needed a medium to maintain and develop within-group relationships. The manipulation of symbols indicative of status and affiliation served as justification for the social order, and trade in exotic items was one way of obtaining such symbols. Those who controlled the manipulation of mortuary ritual and exotic symbols could maintain or increase their individual status within the group. The creation and maintenance of this system of elite/non-elite individuals and senior/junior lineages was fueled by the manipulation of symbolic artifacts and materials, including exotic items obtained through trade. Ritual—especially rites of mourning, adoption, obligation, and affiliation—played a central role in mediating social relations within historic midwestern Native American groups (Hall 1997:85). Indeed, the roots of well-recorded historic mortuary rituals can be traced by material culture remains back to the Middle Woodland period (Hall 1997:18–19, 50–51, 57–58).

From the core-periphery viewpoint, once elites are able to manipulate trade (particularly in the context of mortuary ritual) for personal aggrandizement and status elevation, external trade becomes central to the maintenance of internal social relations. This trade forges ties among elites across regions; many of these relationships may be of a competitive nature. Increasing status of elites via trade connections promotes recruitment of new individuals and groups in alliance formation, again increasing the status of elites and their lineages within communities as well as increasing the status of communities within regions. If one or a group of closely related communities gains a competitive edge over other communities, it may then be seen as a core, able to structure and manipulate economic and other interactions to its advantage.

The economic and political structure described above is inherently unstable. With little ability to control or constrain the movements of others, elite power brokers have to rely upon their individual or lineage reputation to maintain their external contacts and internal status. Intercommunity competition with other elites may result in social fragmentation and the forging of new ties with other regions, which may well undermine previous alliances. Core elites may be abandoned by their trade partners in the periphery for another individual or group that promises more attractive alliances. With less certainty of obtaining desired alliances, the core elites may lose their ability to manipulate internal social relations.

At the same time that elites in core communities are increasing competition to attract new recruits and the symbolic and economic resources necessary to continue their own positions, those elites in the peripheral region will be seeking ways to increase their own competitive advantage both within their own community and across communities. They have incentive to engage in trade beyond that with core elites—not only trade in material items, but also trade in highly charged symbolic items and the rituals that surround them. If successful, these peripheral elites may elevate themselves and their lineages to a position equal to or more attractive than those of their erstwhile core partners. The result is a continual cycling of core and peripheral relations among and between related but competing polities, as well as the diffusion, adoption, and adaptation of individual rituals and mythologies that surround particular artifacts.

The nature of such competitive trade and alliance formation helps explain the discontinuous or patchwork geographic distribution of related material culture among Hopewell sites. Trade and exchange with elites in polities that bypasses one's nearest neighbors may be a way to effectively undermine one's closest and most dangerous competitors for regional dominance. By establishing alliances in groups beyond one's neighbors, those neighbors must operate on multiple fronts of competition, possibly lessening their immediate threat in local politics. It also provides a long-distance safe haven if local conditions warrant a move owing to either localized resource failure or physical conflict with competitors. Ethnohistoric and historic examples of Illini, Shawnee, and Miami making long-distance movements to safe havens during times of warfare are common (M. Brown 1975:1; Callender 1978a, 1978b; Hall 1997:16).

In this scenario, we can see that external trade does play an important role in internal social construction and reconstruction, that core control of peripheries need not be a direct function of Stein's (1999) power-distance decay formulation, that individuals within both the cores and the peripheries have active agency in the construction of these exchange networks, and that the rise and fall of competing cores and peripheries is expected. Moreover, the history of any individual group, lineage, or person will have a strong impact upon which groups, lineages, and people engage one another in these competitive/cooperative exchanges.

Hopewell in Southeastern Wisconsin

The Hopewell phenomenon of southeastern Wisconsin and northeastern Illinois provides a case study for a perspective of core-periphery, elite competition, and historical trajectories. I will present the general knowledge of the region, as well as data from the Alberts site in Jefferson County, Wisconsin. I will then discuss how these data fit into a core-periphery model of intersocietal interaction in the Midwest during the Middle Woodland period.

Southeastern Wisconsin Environment

Southeastern Wisconsin comprises most or all of ten counties that lie between Lake Michigan and the Rock River in Wisconsin (fig. 16.1). The region is on the northern edge of the Prairie Peninsula; immediately to the north is the tension zone between deciduous and boreal forest zones, and to the south is the boundary between deciduous forest and prairie (Glocker 1979; Transeau 1935). This climatic and environmental division across southern Wisconsin undoubtedly

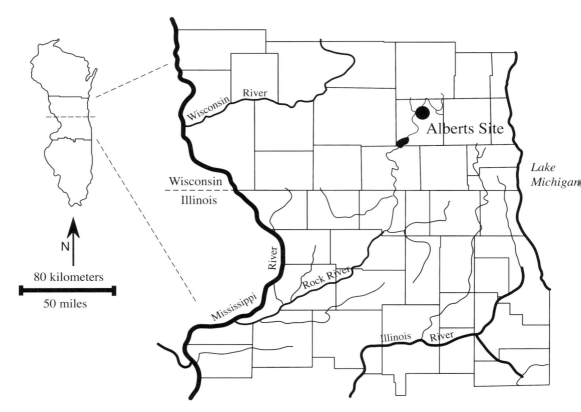

Figure 16.1. Location of the Alberts habitation site (47JE903).

had important implications for prehistoric settlement during the Early and Middle Woodland periods (Boszhardt, Theler, and Kehoe 1986:250–251; Salzer 1986b:239). Surface topography is characterized by a wide variety of glacial features, including deep ground, terminal, and recessional moraines, drumlins, kames, eskers, and boulder trains (Dutton and Bradley 1970; Goldstein and Flick 1992). Limestone deposits do outcrop in places along the Rock and Milwaukee rivers (Mikulic and Kluessendorf 1982).

Unlike the Illinois or Scioto Valley centers of Hopewell efflorescence, the region is not dominated by one large, mature stream. The complex nature of glacial deposition and ice damming at the end of the Pleistocene had left the region with a variety of water drainages. In the eastern portion of the region, major streams run roughly parallel to Lake Michigan between end moraines. The central and western portions of the region are dominated by the Rock River, which flows southwest until it joins with the Mississippi River in northwestern Illinois. The region is thus connected to the known Hopewellian world largely through north–south water routes: the Rock River to the Mississippi, the Fox and DesPlaines Rivers to the upper Illinois River, and the shore of Lake Michigan to the upper Illinois (via a short portage to the DesPlaines). East–west travel across southern Wisconsin is impeded by the numerous north–south-trending rivers and large areas of wetlands. This north–south riverine system may have had a significant impact on settlement and social interactions that extend deep into the past.

The Waukesha Phase

The Middle Woodland period in southern Wisconsin has been separated into three phases: the Trempealeau (circa A.D. 100–200) and Millville (circa A.D. 200–500) phases of southwestern Wisconsin (Stevenson et al. 1997) and the Waukesha phase (circa 100 B.C.–A.D. 250) of southeastern Wisconsin. Defined by McKern as the Waukesha focus in 1942, the Waukesha phase is best described by Salzer (n.d.), who notes certain similarities between Waukesha phase sites to the North Bay phase reported by Mason for Door County (Mason 1966), the Nokomis phase in north-central Wisconsin (Salzer n.d.; Salzer and Stock 1974), and Steuben phase sites from the upper Illinois River valley in northern Illinois (Wolforth 1995).

No radiocarbon dates have been recovered from Waukesha phase sites, but the North Bay phase has been radiocarbon dated from 200 B.C. to A.D. 250 and the Nokomis phase from circa 600 B.C. to A.D. 250 (Stevenson et al. 1997). Through cross-dating to ceramics from the North Bay and Millville phases, the Waukesha phase can be dated to circa A.D. 100–300 (Salzer n.d.:109–110; Stevenson et al. 1997). In addition, two reliably dated sites from northern Illinois suggest that the Steuben phase dates to circa 100 B.C. to A.D. 150 (McGimsey 1988; Walz, Hedman, and Mullen 1998; Wolforth 1995).

Pottery of the Waukesha phase includes three local wares: Kegonsa Stamped, Shorewood Cord Roughened, and Highsmith Plain. Nonlocal wares found include Havana Zoned, Steuben Punctated, Sisters Creek Punctated, Baehr, Neteler Crescent Stamped, and Classic Hopewell. Local variants of these wares are distinctive in terms of lip form, vessel size, and the rounded pebbles occasionally used as temper. Vessels tend to be small to medium-size conoidal jars. Cordmarked surfaces are generally smoothed or partially smoothed. Lips are seldom cordmarked and are typically beveled to the interior. Punctates are placed on the interior, with resulting exterior nodes. Dentate stamping, small punctates, and rocker stamping are all found on the local wares.

Waukesha phase ceramic assemblages are similar to Trempealeau phase assemblages but may be distinguished by different frequencies of certain traits; for example, cord-wrapped-stick impressions are prevalent in Waukesha materials, while dentate and rocker stamping is more common in Trempealeau ceramics. Wolforth (1995) provides further evidence for a Waukesha/Trempealeau distinction in the relatively high frequency of Steuben Punctated sherds in the former and a relatively small number in the latter. Waukesha phase sites have much in common with sites from the upper Illinois River valley, in particular a relatively high proportion of Steuben Punctated sherds in association with decorated Havana sherds (Wolforth 1995). While the Steuben Punctated sherds indicate an affiliation with Havana Hopewell sites in the Illinois River valley, Waukesha phase mortuary sites contain fewer grave goods and less elaborate mounds than those found in Illinois.

Although there are also general style similarities between Waukesha phase materials and Door County North Bay ceramics, Salzer (n.d.:113) separates them on the basis of vessel size (North Point vessels being larger) and the "sharp distinction in the manners in which the decorative element is worked into designs." Salzer (n.d.:114) also differentiates Waukesha phase from north-central Wisconsin Nokomis phase ceramics by noting the high frequency of horizontal finger-trailed over cordmarked vessels at Nokomis phase sites. Neither North Bay nor Nokomis phase sites yield any frequency of Steuben Punctated sherds, but North Bay ceramics have been found at Nokomis phase sites and vice versa.

In sum, it is likely that Trempealeau, Nokomis, North Bay, Waukesha, and Steuben phases are all roughly coterminous. Nokomis and North Bay ceramics share similarities with each other that they do not share with the others, and the same is true for Waukesha and Steuben phase material. Trempealeau seems more closely linked stylistically with Mississippi Valley groups.

Diagnostic projectile points of the Waukesha phase include Waubesa and Adena contracting-stem forms, Norton and Snyders variants, and Steuben and Monona Stemmed forms. Wyandotte chert from southern Illinois and Indiana is found at some sites, as is Knife River flint from North Dakota. Some obsidian artifacts have been reported from surface collections in Racine County (Salzer n.d.:97). Polyhedral blade cores and bladelets are found, as are a variety of utilized flakes, scrapers, and other nondiagnostic tools. Salzer (n.d.) argues that the Waukesha phase is distinguished from North Bay in part because North Bay assemblages are generally manufactured from local lithic material and contain a high proportion of bipolar materials. Bipolar manufacture is absent from Waukesha phase assemblages.

Although habitation sites of the Waukesha phase are not well known, they range from seasonal encampments, such as Pitzner and Trillium (Goldstein 1980b, 1983; Lax 1982), to larger village sites, such as Highsmith and Cooper's Shores (Lippold 1973; Salzer n.d.; Wiersum 1968). Features such as pits, hearths, and post molds have been recovered from Middle Woodland occupations at these sites, but no well-defined houses have been reported and no site has been sufficiently excavated to provide spatial data.

Site placement indicates that wetland and forest-edge resources were preferred. Faunal data suggest that deer were the most common prey, followed by a wide assortment of large- and small-bodied fish. In addition, small mammals such as muskrat, raccoon, and chipmunks were commonly taken. Shellfish and turtles were utilized, but few bird bones have been recovered. Floral remains include goosefoot, hackberry, blackberry, and sunflower seeds, as well as hickory and hazel nuts.

On the basis of the large size and locations of the Highsmith and Cooper's Shores sites, Goldstein (1992) has suggested that seed cultivation may have been a part of the Waukesha phase diet; there is no direct evidence for this premise at this time. Likewise, there is little evidence for a significant amount of corn (*Zea mays*) in the diet at this time, based on the values of ^{13}C ratios in skeletal samples from Wisconsin Trempealeau phase sites (Baerreis and Bender 1984; Bender, Baerreis, and Steventon 1981).

Burials are generally found within mounds, some of which are reported to be up to 4 meters in height. Mounds are found singly or in groups and are often found in association with Late Woodland Effigy Mound groups, such as at Big Bend Mound Group Number 2 (Brown 1923; Lapham 1855). Mortuary ritual at Waukesha phase sites is poorly understood, but several examples of burial in tombs under conical mounds have been noted. Extended, flexed, sitting, and bundle burials are all part of the Waukesha phase repertoire, with more than one form noted in the same mound—a situation similar to that seen in lower Illinois Valley mounds (for example, Charles, Leigh, and Buikstra 1988). Grave goods are relatively uncommon but include corner-notched points, bone pins, freshwater pearl and shell bead necklaces, animal teeth, cut deer mandibles, platform and other pipe forms, ceramic vessels, copper celts, copper beads, cut human mandibles, and white clay face coverings (Salzer n.d.).

At the Big Bend Mound Group Number 2, Lafayette Ellarson found a subfloor stone burial chamber with a single skeleton (Brown 1923:94). The skull of the skeleton was reportedly found between its legs. Two stone pipes were also recovered, including a unique form. A second mound in the same group contained a subfloor pit and associated earthen ramp. At least seventeen individuals were recovered from the tomb. They had been placed in subfloor tombs (possibly log lined and covered by limestone slabs) and showed body treatments that ranged from extended to bundled disarticulations, with some cremation possible. Norton points, freshwater pearls, and bone tools were recovered. At the Racine Mound Group, excavation of a large conical mound exposed seven sitting burials in a subfloor pit, which also yielded Havana ware pottery (Salzer n.d.).

Waukesha Phase Landscape Use

We can draw some conclusions about Waukesha phase lifeways, albeit from limited data. Goldstein (1992), echoing Lippold (1973), makes a strong point about the richness of the wetland resources in the region. She suggests that Middle Woodland sites are associated with wetlands and the presence of stream confluences, noting that most sites have many confluences near them and that larger sites have primary confluences in their immediate vicinity. She notes that along the Rock and Crawfish rivers, sites are found at the intersections of marsh, oak forests, and oak openings. Ceramic-bearing sites are generally found on the inside bends of the streams and between 240 meters and 244 meters in elevation. These locations are not river terraces per se but appear as "a distinctive flat rise immediately above and adjacent to the wetlands or floodplain" (Goldstein 1992:158). She also notes that when one finds Middle Woodland pottery at these locations, one generally finds Early and/or Late Woodland pottery as well, suggesting consistent use of resources throughout the Woodland period.

Goldstein (1992:158–159) suggests that Waukesha phase people followed a pattern of fall/winter exploitation of wetland resources using dispersed camps with a larger or more permanent base camp (or village) near major rivers or possibly even outside the region.

Waukesha Phase Subsistence

Subsistence data are even more limited than settlement data. The general lack of systematically collected, flotation-supplemented subsistence data cripples any discussion of diet and resource selection.

The Alberts Site

The Alberts site (fig. 16.2), in Jefferson County, is actually a complex of several occupations along the east bank of the Rock River, north of its confluence with Johnson Creek (Jeske and Kaufmann 2000). A small, spring-fed stream separates the two major components of the site. Immediately adjacent to the river and associated marshlands is 47JE903, a predominantly Late Woodland occupation. Up on a small terrace is 47JE887, consisting of one linear and one conical mound. The conical mound contains Late Archaic, Middle Woodland, and Late Woodland features. Slightly farther up and away from the river is a surface scatter containing Woodland, Mississippian, and early historic materials. Although this portion of the site complex has been surface-collected over the years, it has never been systematically collected or excavated.

The habitation area along the river, excavated in 1964 through 1968 by Richard Slattery, yielded five features (fig. 16.3). The site is very sandy and has been cultivated only once in the twentieth century. It is not known if it had been cultivated previously or had always been in pasture. Pit 1 was a refuse pit 1.4 meters in diameter and 1.14 meters deep that yielded significant portions of a thick, grit-tempered vessel (fig. 16.4). The interior of the vessel displays stamped impressions, similar to those seen on the exterior of Kegonsa Stamped vessels. The exterior of the vessel shows heavy cord marking and fingernail impressions. A Late Archaic/Early Woodland Durst point and an unidentified stemmed point were also recovered from the pit. Pit 2 was a refuse pit 66 centimeters in diameter and 71 centimeters deep. Aside from some charcoal and fire-cracked rock, the pit yielded a single, Late Woodland Madison ware sherd. Pit 3 was a large pit, 2.4 meters long, 1.14 meters wide, and 81 centimeters deep. This pit yielded charcoal, fire-cracked rock, and portions of several Late Woodland vessels, including a Starved Rock Collared vessel (Hall 1987b). It also yielded one small rim sherd that appears to be from the Langford series (Brown 1961). There is a high probability that this feature is actually several superimposed pits. Pit 64-1 is also probably a multiple-use feature. The pit seems to have been bell shaped, 1.5 meters in diameter and 1.2 meters deep. A series of Late Woodland sherds came from the upper meter of deposits, along with a charcoal sample that has a radiocarbon date of A.D. 960 ±70 B.P., which is calibrated to calendrical year A.D. 1020–1160. At the bottom of the pit, a grouping of heavy cord-roughened

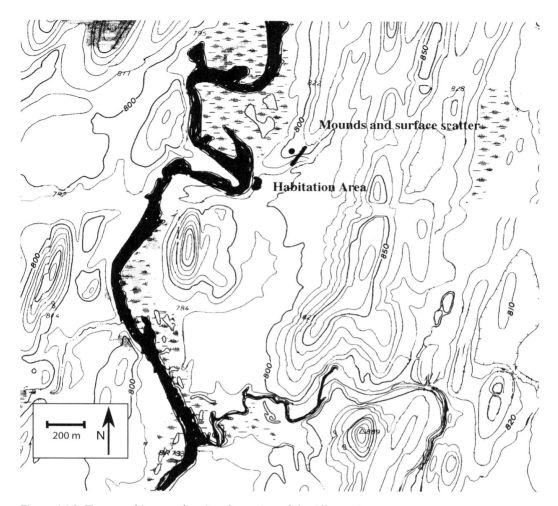

Figure 16.2. Topographic map showing the setting of the Alberts site.

sherds and a Middle Woodland point lay upon a base of white clay (fig. 16.4). The Middle Woodland vessel bears a close resemblance to a Middle Woodland vessel found at the LaSalle County Home site near Starved Rock, in the upper Illinois River valley (Jeske and Hart 1988:75, Figure 6.9a). The Illinois vessel is associated with a radiocarbon date of 1690 ±160 B.P. (A.D. 210–540, calibrated; compare Jeske and Hart 1988:177–184). Pit 64-2 contained no diagnostic material.

The conical mound (fig. 16.5) of 47JE887 was tested by Slattery in 1968. The mound is approximately 6 meters in diameter and at the time was less than 25 centimeters in height. The original mound height is unknown, but given that the area is thought to have been cultivated very infrequently, the mound was probably never very conspicuous. Slattery excavated a series of units measuring 1.5 × 1.5 meters (5 feet × 5 feet) across the mound. Near the center of the mound, at

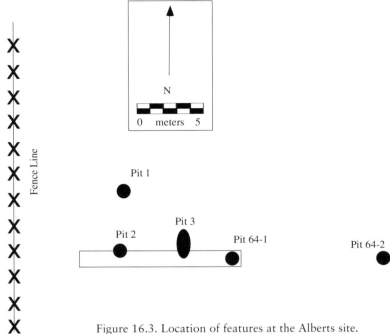

Figure 16.3. Location of features at the Alberts site.

a depth of 40 centimeters, a large boulder was encountered (fig. 16.6). The boulder weighed nearly 19 kilograms and had been set on top of a Havana-style pot, apparently after the pot had been badly burned (figs. 16.6, 16.7). Near the large rock, towards the center of the mound, was a mixture of smooth gravel and clay that extended from 45 centimeters to 112 centimeters below ground surface. No artifacts or bone came from this feature. Another cluster of sherds, apparently the base of the Havana vessel, was encountered in this same excavation unit at a depth of 63 centimeters. At the south edge of the mound, a large pit filled with fire-cracked rock and burned clay measured 1 meter in diameter and 1 meter deep. A thick layer of charcoal at 55 centimeters below ground surface yielded a radiocarbon date of 2730 ±70 B.P. (930–810 B.C., calibrated). Aside from a few chert flakes, no artifacts were recovered from the feature.

Immediately to the east of the mound site, the surface of a cultivated field has yielded diagnostic points from the Late Archaic; points and ceramics from the Early, Middle, and Late Woodland periods; sherds from both shell-tempered Oneota and grit-tempered Langford upper Mississippian ceramics; and brass tinklers and kaolin pipes from historic times. In particular, a Hopewellian platform pipe and several bladelets (the latter probably made from Burlington chert) were recovered. The pipe, found less than 20 meters from the excavated mound, is almost certainly from flint clays obtained near Sterling, in the Rock River valley of northwestern Illinois (Hughes, Berres, and Farnsworth 1998; Slattery n.d.). The quarry for the pipestone is thus located downstream from the Alberts site, approximately 125 kilometers to the south-southwest. Burlington chert is

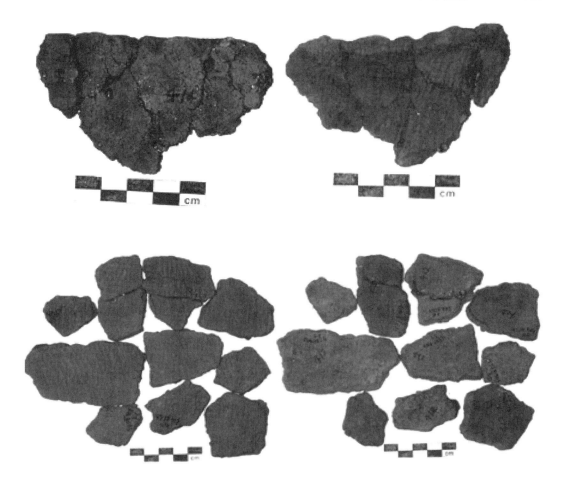

Figure 16.4. Alberts site ceramics. *Top*: cordmarked exterior, Kegonsa Stamped-like stamping on interior; *bottom*: Middle Woodland vessel found on white clay foundation.

found in outcrops along the Illinois and Mississippi River valleys and their tributaries, southwest of the Alberts site (Ferguson and Warren 1992; Rick 1978).

The Middle Woodland component of the Alberts site is consistent with the description of Waukesha phase material culture outlined above. Goldstein (1992:158) has suggested that virtually all Middle Woodland sites in southeastern Wisconsin are multicomponent, and the Alberts site complex fits this description. In fact, both portions of the site complex are multicomponent: the habitation area (47JE903) contains features from the Early, Middle, and Late Woodland periods, as well as a possible Mississippian occupation; while a Middle and/or Late Woodland mound (47JE887) overlies Late Archaic/Early Woodland and Middle Woodland features. Late Woodland sherds are incorporated into upper portions of earlier features. Associated with the excavated Middle Woodland mound is a linear mound, presumably a Late Woodland ef-

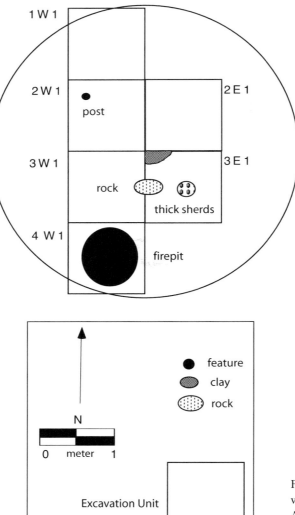

Figure 16.5. Map of excavated mound at the Alberts site (47JE887).

figy. Immediately adjacent to the mounds is a surface scatter containing artifacts from a wide variety of time periods. This multiple occupation of the locale represents some important, long-standing connection within the overall pattern of settlements within the region.

The conical mound at 47JE887 is not a burial mound per se. No bones, grave features, or other obvious signs of mortuary ritual were recovered from the mound. The mound seems more like a small pedestal than a traditional conical mound and appears to have been associated with fire. The Havana-like pot was burned before a 20-kilogram rock was placed upon it. It is not likely that the location of this burning episode so close to the Early Woodland fire pit—and the subsequent covering and incorporation of the vessel and rock into the mound—

Figure 16.6. Finds from mound at the Alberts site. *Top*: large rock in center of mound; *bottom*: crushed Havana-Hopewell vessel.

Figure 16.7. Rim sections of crushed Havana-Hopewell vessel from figure 16.6.

was accidental. Moreover, the lack of evident mortuary remains and the central-
ity of fire and burning within mounds is a pattern that continues into the Late
Woodland Effigy Mound culture. Unfortunately, there is no profile of the
mound structure, so it is not possible to reconstruct its original construction or
any later modifications, additions, or intrusions.

There are similarities in mortuary ritual between Alberts and other southern
Wisconsin sites. White mud was puddled over the faces of two bodies at the
Outlet site, located 46 kilometers to the west on Lake Monona (Hall 1997:19;
Salzer n.d.). Two features of the Alberts site—one within the mound and the
other in 47JE903—are white clay features. Immediately adjacent to the crushed
Havana pot is a deep well of clay and smooth pebbles. In addition, a white clay
deposit at the base of Feature 64-1, outside of the mound, served as a base for
the deposition of a Middle Woodland vessel and projectile point.

The use of white mud strengthens the argument that certain aspects of historic Native American behavior and ritual may be seen in earlier Hopewell
ritual. Hall connects the puddled white mud from the Outlet site to the Native
American Earth Diver myth as well as to Potawatomi beliefs that "when
drowned persons were found with white clay in their mouth, nostrils and eyes
that it was a sure sign that the horned water panther had drowned them. The
story of such a drowning is said to be a reason that the Potawatomis feared Lake
Koshkonong" (Hall 1997:19). The puddled white mud of the Alberts site, located 18 kilometers north of Lake Koshkonong, strengthens Hall's interpretation of the expression of Earth Diver mythology at Waukesha phase sites. The
clay in this case, and especially the association of clay with smooth river- or lake-

bed pebbles (compare Hall 1997:19–23), is not associated with any individual corpse, perhaps suggesting a linkage of Earth Diver ritual and corporate or lineage validation.

Hall (1997) goes further, suggesting that the deep black mud forming the base and enclosing bodies in the central tombs of several mounds in the Steuben phase Utica Mound site in the upper Illinois River valley (Henricksen 1965) is also an expression of the Earth Diver myth. The use of such black mud is also found at later effigy mound sites throughout their range and distribution (Hall 1997).

One thing that is clear is that the Alberts site is definitely not the product of a single archaeologically defined time period. It seems to represent an ideological and/or cultural model of ritual behaviors that extend beyond our definitions of archaeological cultures. The Alberts site seems to represent a long-standing indigenous set of rituals with the addition of some new details; the Hopewell expression at the site seems to continue ritual burning associated at this locale, rather than being a simple diffusion of mortuary ideology that comes in from outside the local group. Despite the long-term continuity of local ritual belief, the connection of the Alberts site to Illinois Havana Hopewell is clearly documented by the Havana pottery, the Illinois pipestone pipe, and, perhaps, the material expression of the Earth Diver myth by the white clay.

The Alberts Site and Core-Periphery Approaches to Culture Contact

How then, may we characterize the Alberts site, and other Waukesha focus sites in southeastern Wisconsin, from a core-periphery perspective? We must first begin with a definition of where the core, if one exists, is located. A plausible case may be made that the lower Illinois River valley was the predominant core area during the Middle Woodland time period for the central Midwest.

Charles (1992) has argued that the origin of Hopewell ritual in the lower Illinois Valley stems from a migration of people from the central Illinois Valley into the nearly unoccupied lower Illinois Valley at the beginning of the Middle Woodland period. As the valley filled, mounds served as territorial beacons, while mortuary ritual, centered on mound construction and maintenance as well as manipulation of exotic artifacts and symbols, served to recruit new immigrants into the social orbit of previously established lineages. These new immigrants became junior lineages, effectively elevating the predecessor lineages to the status of senior lineages, forming social hierarchies where previously none had existed. These elite lineages manipulated mortuary ritual for their own social replication, which encouraged the production of selected items for exchange with other elites outside of the lower Illinois Valley—for example, in the central and upper Illinois Valley, portions of the Mississippi Valley, and even beyond. There is no doubt that the density of mounds and the intensity of mortuary ritual and symbolic manipulation represented by sheer quantities of exotic artifacts and materials was centered in the lower Illinois Valley. If economic activity writ large—that is, symbolic as well as bulk or food economics—follows from this suggested pattern of social and cultural hierarchy and complexity, then the lower Illinois Valley can be seen as a core.

The lower Illinois Valley is not necessarily the only core area. Chase-Dunn and Hall (1991:12) envision systems that include multicore and nested core configurations. Multicore systems are those where multiple geographic locations have populations and economic centers that may vie for dominance (for example, Spain, France, and England in sixteenth- through nineteenth-century Europe). Nested core systems are those where the roles of core and periphery may be blurred or changed at any one time as geographic power relations shift through time. In a nested system, it may be possible that the same group may be peripheral to one core, while acting as a core to another. By changing the scale of analysis we can see how the world system affects internal social change at the local level, as well as change at regional levels.

Among Hopewellian societies interacting in the midwestern United States, the lower Illinois River valley between 50 B.C. and A.D. 300 was undoubtedly a core area, but the central Illinois Valley and perhaps even the Starved Rock area of the upper Illinois Valley may have shifted from peripheral status to the status of secondary cores at different times within this same period. Groups in the American Bottom region may have remained in a peripheral status to the lower Illinois Valley throughout the 350-year period of Hopewell exchange (see Fortier, this volume). On a much larger regional scale, the Scioto in Ohio and lower Illinois River valleys operated as separate cores in a multicore system, certainly interacting at the level of information exchange, if not exchange in material culture or genes. The nature of that interaction is beyond the scope of this chapter.

The Alberts site in southeastern Wisconsin is a good example of a peripheral site within a bounded, multicore system. If we shift our focus away from the largest scale of analysis, the major actors in our core system are the lower, central, and upper Illinois River valleys, southwestern Wisconsin, and southeastern Wisconsin. To follow out the trajectories of the regions in this core-periphery system, one needs to determine how the internal structure of the periphery is manipulated by the economics of the core in the exchange of goods and ideas. To return to Chase-Dunn and Hall (1991), there are four aspects to the trade that connect core and periphery: (1) trade of bulk goods; (2) political/military interaction; (3) trade of luxury/prestige goods; and (4) information and cultural flows.

We can begin our investigation of the relationship between southeastern Wisconsin and the lower Illinois River valley by examining trade in bulk goods. There is no evidence for trade in any kind of bulk goods during the Middle Woodland period, although the lack of evidence for trade in perishable goods does not prove that they were not exchanged. Given what we do know about Middle Woodland settlement and subsistence, there is no theoretical reason to suspect the need for long-distance trade in bulk items, although it cannot be ruled out.

The second aspect is interesting, if somewhat similar to the first issue. There may be little reason to think that lower Illinois Valley elites projected a strong military presence in southeastern Wisconsin. However, there is little reason to think that they could not have done so. Historical evidence indicates that Native Americans traveled long distances to carry out military raids while maintaining long-standing blood feuds. The historic Miami, generally located in northern Illinois and across Indiana, maintained hostile relations with the Dakota Sioux of the plains and the Chickasaw of the Southeast (Callender 1978c). Perhaps more tellingly, the burning of the Grand Village of the Kaskaskia, in the upper Illinois River valley, was only one of several raids carried out by the Iroquois between 1680 and 1700. These extremely effective forays, which fundamentally restructured Miami and Illinois territorial boundaries, economics, and social organization, represent an extension of military power of some seven hundred miles or more by a nonstate society.

Although the historic Iroquois raids were fueled by Native American incorporation into the European world system, oral traditions from many tribes indicate that such feuding has pre-Columbian roots. Ethnographic and archaeological evidence also suggests patterns of violence that extend far into the past, including Hopewellian societies in the lower Illinois River valley (Callender 1978c:682; Charles, Leigh, and Buikstra 1988; Kineitz 1995:196–197; Milner 1995; Seeman 1988). It is not unreasonable to think that long-distance raiding by Hopewellian groups in the lower Illinois Valley could have been a credible threat to groups considerable distances to the north. Stein's (1999:163) "power decays with distance" dilemma may not be critically important to non-state-level societies because of the destabilizing effect that a single raid or several intermittent military raids can have on small-scale societies.

Violence was likely part of Havana Hopewellian life (Charles, Leigh, and Buikstra 1988). Unlike Mississippian groups, whose arrows entered into the body with enough force to penetrate bone, the spear and club repertoire of Middle Woodland societies means that violent death will tend to be underrepresented in Hopewell skeletal collections. A number of investigations into Havana Hopewell cemeteries do, however, indicate trauma such as parry fractures on ulnae and depression fractures on skulls (Conner and Link 1991:31–35; Frankenberg, Albertson, and Kohn 1988; Perino 1961:55). The fairly common occurrence of decapitated individuals, usually male, in Hopewell mortuary contexts may also be an indicator of intergroup violence, although it may represent a mortuary practice unknown in historic times. Moreover, at this point there is no way to differentiate externally induced violence (that is, warfare) from internal feuding or homicide. Nonetheless, there is reason to believe that a core group may well have had the capability of impacting the economic and social structure of groups in peripheral areas through military means during the Middle Woodland period.

The third aspect, trade in luxury goods, is one for which we have much evidence. Waukesha phase sites have yielded nonlocal goods associated with

Hopewell, although the quantity of materials is considered paltry compared to that of regions such as Illinois or even southwestern Wisconsin (Salzer n.d.; Stevenson et al. 1997). The Alberts site has yielded three such artifact classes: several Burlington chert bladelets, a Hopewell platform pipe from Illinois, and a number of Havana-like ceramics. Alberts site occupants were participating in the exchange of durable luxury goods, albeit on a relatively infrequent basis.

The final area of interaction, information and culture flow, is also one in which the Alberts site figures well. Of primary concern are the Havana-like vessel that was burned and then crushed by the boulder, and the white clay features of the mound and village areas. The meaning of such burning and crushing is not yet understood, and we shall return to the white clay later in this chapter. At this point, it is important to note that the ceremonial context of the Havana-like vessel is a context that had been present at that site for perhaps the previous thousand years. It is also important to understand that the nature of the ceremony demonstrated by the burned and crushed Havana pot, outside of a burial context, is unusual. It suggests not that elites at Alberts had taken on the ideological and social manipulative roles hypothesized by Charles (1992) for the lower Illinois Valley elites but that they had introduced an element of long-distance contact into ceremonial behavior already understood and practiced by local people.

The use of a Havana-like vessel for ceremonialism at the Alberts site has implications for our core-periphery perspective. Waukesha focus sites commonly yield Havana Hopewell sherds in association with Steuben Punctated sherds. Wolforth (1995) has shown that Steuben Punctated sherds are dominant in ceramic assemblages during the middle and later portions of Middle Woodland in the upper and lower Illinois Valley regions. He confirms Struever's argument that Steuben Punctated is a microstyle zone in the upper Illinois Valley and defines a Steuben phase for northern Illinois, developing from an earlier Utica phase. The latter phase is represented by Classic Hopewell vessels, while the former is represented by a large proportion of Steuben Punctated in association with Havana Hopewell wares. The distinction between the Steuben and Waukesha phases, if it exists, is not known at this time, but they seem quite similar. When one compares the distribution of Steuben Punctated as a dominant ware, the upper Illinois Valley is clearly the largest cluster of the distribution. The Rock River area near Lake Koshkonong is another concentration, as is the lower Illinois Valley. Steuben Punctated wares do not dominate in the central Illinois Valley and southwestern Wisconsin (Wolforth 1995:38).

I suggest that this distribution has bearing on the issue of the rising and falling of nested cores during the Middle Woodland period. We do know—based on neutron activation analyses—that vessels, as well as ideas, were being exchanged (Fie 2000; chapter 23, this volume). Fie notes that in her sample of Havana Hopewell sherds, a Steuben vessel from the lower Illinois Valley had a 98 percent probability of having been produced in the upper Illinois Valley, in the area of Starved Rock. The exchange of Steuben Punctated vessels was not simple down-the-line trade, however. If neighbors simply exchanged with neighbors, we would expect a drop-off curve from a center to the periphery. This was not the case, however. During the middle stages of the Middle Woodland period, Steuben Punctated vessels were passing around or through the central Illinois Valley but were not stopping there. It seems that a second core in the upper Illinois Valley arose and began to interact directly with the lower Illinois Valley core, perhaps peripheralizing the central Illinois Valley.

Southeastern Wisconsin became part of the periphery of the upper Illinois Valley core (and by extension, the lower Illinois Valley) late, probably after A.D. 100. To understand the nature of the interactions, it becomes necessary to consider the long-standing culture history of the region. Stevenson and colleagues (1997) note that the strong presence of Early Woodland Lake Farms phase sites extends in southeastern Wisconsin until A.D. 100. Unlike Charles's (1992) scenario for the lower Illinois Valley at 100 B.C., there was no migration into a depopulated area during the Middle Woodland of southeastern Wisconsin. The emergence of Middle Woodland symbolism and artifact types occurred as a modification to previously long-held ceremonial behaviors by a relatively large and stable population. Hopewellian symbolic behaviors occurred at the same places that Late Archaic and Early Woodland ceremonies had been conducted.

Southwestern Wisconsin, by contrast followed a different historic path during this period. It has been argued that Trempealeau phase Middle Woodland bears more resemblance to central Mississippi River valley material culture than it does to that of southeastern Wisconsin. Similarly, in the later stages of the Middle Woodland period, sites in southwestern Wisconsin show material culture similarities to Weaver phase materials of western and south-central Illinois. The difference between the participation by populations in southwestern versus southeastern Wisconsin with their southerly neighbors may be accounted for by direct connection of the former with groups along the Mississippi River, drawing them more completely into the lower Illinois system. While obviously related, groups in the two corners of southern Wisconsin clearly seem to have looked to different sources for intersocietal contacts.

The lack of radiocarbon dates hampers our understanding of the duration of the contact between groups in southeastern Wisconsin and those in the upper Illinois Valley. However, it is likely that the Waukesha phase extends to at least A.D. 300. Between A.D. 300 and 600 B.C., when effigy mounds construction began, sites such as Klug in Ozaukee County yield transitional, fabric-impressed ceramics and Steuben points (Van Langen 1986). However, it is again important to note that virtually all Late Woodland sites in southeastern Wisconsin are set on top of Early and Middle Woodland occupations. There is little evidence for large population movements or reorganizations during the Middle to Late Woodland transition. (See also Richards and Jeske 2000.) Yet it may be possible to see that external contact with the Illinois Valley did alter some aspects of peripheral, Wisconsin populations.

At the Alberts site, the Late Woodland population (represented by both early and late ceramic wares) put their linear mound immediately adjacent to a physically very inconspicuous earlier mound, continuing the ceremonial use of this otherwise undistinguished section of river terrace that had lasted for over a thousand years. The people who built effigy mounds did so in an area that effectively defines the northern edge of the Illinois River valley Havana Hopewell periphery. Rather than search for simple ecological explanations for the construction and use of Effigy Mounds and their placement on the landscape, it makes more sense to think of their builders as peripheral populations continuing, albeit modifying, long-term ceremonialism in the face of interactions with core elites from the Illinois Valley (compare Goldstein 1995; Hurley 1975). Areas containing sites of the Trempealeau phase, Waukesha phase, and North Bay phase—all of which have some connection with the Hopewellian world—were later used as effigy mound sites. The Nokomis phase sites of north-central Wisconsin, where the presence of some southern Illinois cherts and ceramic assemblages are somewhat similar to those from Waukesha phase sites (Salzer 1986b), demonstrate some contact with the Hopewellian world, which Chase-Dunn and Hall (1991) might call the "deep periphery." This region appears to be the northern extent of the Effigy Mound culture (Stevenson et al. 1997).

Conclusion

The Alberts site, as viewed through world systems theory, hints at the nature and extent of culture contact between southeastern Wisconsin groups and southern populations between A.D. 100 and 300. It is obvious that radiocarbon dating and systematic excavations at Middle Woodland sites in southeastern Wisconsin are necessary to make more substantial any of the observations or speculations offered here. Future research conducted in a core-periphery framework will, I suspect, be fruitful, but several questions need to be addressed.

The extent and duration of communications and ideological contact between southeastern Wisconsin and other regions must be investigated by systematic analyses of ceremonial and other symbolic behaviors found at Waukesha focus sites. How much external ideological contact may result in internal restructuring of a society is very much open to debate.

The exchange of luxury items needs to be formally investigated. Neutron activation analysis and petrographic examination of presumably nonlocal ceramics and pipestone is one avenue towards pinpointing the direction and nature of nonlocal social contacts. It is argued here (and elsewhere) that such external trade in exotic items may strongly effect internal reorganization within societies.

Reexamination of skeletal material for the presence of violent trauma would bring an otherwise important, but relatively neglected, area of social behavior to light. Assessment of the nature and extent of violence in Middle Woodland societies is critical for understanding the dynamics of long-distance contact, alliance, and avoidance behaviors. Even small-scale, guerilla-style raiding may have a strong impact upon the internal organization of a peripheral polity.

Trade in bulk goods may or may not be a moot issue at this time. It is hard to see that such trade would effectively organize long-distance social relations during the Middle Woodland. However, that does not mean that we should ignore its potential completely.

Ultimately, no amount of theory building of any sort will be useful until modern, systematically excavated data from a substantial number of sites in southeastern Wisconsin and northern Illinois are available for testing and evaluation. To that end, new programs of exploration must be initiated in this region, and elsewhere, if we are to ever comprehend the phenomenon that we refer to today as Hopewell.

Acknowledgments

Many thanks to Richard Slattery, who excavated the Alberts site and provided access to his collections, notes, and photographs. Also, Kira E. Kaufmann spent considerable time and effort to sort, inventory, and conduct preliminary analysis on the ceramics from the site.

17

Reconsidering the Context of Hopewell Interaction in Southwestern Wisconsin

James B. Stoltman

The archaeological recovery of Hopewell-related artifacts in burial mounds in the upper Mississippi Valley dates at least to the 1880s (Thomas 1894:47–93), but it was only as a result of the mound explorations of Will C. McKern (1929, 1931, 1932) in southwestern Wisconsin four decades later that ties to Hopewellian cultures farther south were recognized. As a reflection of the Hopewellian affinities that he saw in both his own recently excavated mounds and those excavated earlier by Thomas, McKern (1942) formally created the Trempealeau focus (later redefined as a phase; Stoltman 1979:137). Following McKern's insight, subsequent mound excavations in neighboring portions of northwestern Illinois and northeastern Iowa revealed two closely related complexes, now referred to, respectively, as the Nickerson (Bennett 1945:121) and the McGregor phase (Logan 1976:155). In each of these three cases the primary basis for phase definition was mortuary evidence derived from burial mounds, with close cultural affinities clearly evident with sites of the Havana tradition of the Illinois Valley. The goal of the present chapter is to reevaluate the status of one of these phases, Trempealeau, in light of recent research in southwestern Wisconsin that has focused upon residential rather than mortuary sites. In pursuing this goal the generally held view that the Trempealeau phase was the sole cultural context in southwestern Wisconsin within which Hopewell interaction had occurred will be critically evaluated.

The Trempealeau Phase as Originally Conceived

The recognition of Trempealeau as a phase (Stoltman 1979), following the principles laid down by Willey and Phillips (1958), was based primarily upon the contents of sixty-two previously excavated burial mounds from seven sites along the Mississippi River from Prairie du Chien to the vicinity of La Crosse, Wisconsin (McKern 1931; Thomas 1894). These seven sites—Flucke, Vilas, Courtois, Sioux Coulee, Battle Island, White's Mounds, Shrake II and Trempealeau Lakes—still constitute the main database by which the Trempealeau phase is known (fig. 17.1). More recent excavations in Mounds 4 and 26 of the Trempealeau Lakes (Schwert) mound group by Freeman (1968) and at the Overhead mound in La Crosse by Gallagher and colleagues (1981) enriched but did not alter this basic mound-based picture of the Trempealeau phase.

Most of the artifacts reported from these mounds are specialized grave goods rarely found outside of burial contexts. McKern (1931:200) reported two "campsites" at Trempealeau Lakes, but the relatively few artifacts in the Milwaukee Public Museum collections suggest that no substantive excavations were conducted at these sites. Only three decorated sherds from these campsites are present in the Milwaukee Public Museum collections, all from "Campsite l," and all three are illustrated in McKern's publication. One rim is of the Havana series type Naples Stamped (McKern 1931:Plate 43, no. 5), while the other two are body sherds, possibly from the same vessel, that have the qualities of Levsen Stamped, a Linn series type (McKern 1931:Plate 44, nos. 11 and 13).

In 1966, excavations at Trempealeau Lakes explored Mounds 4 and 26 and opened twenty-five units in a nearby residential area referred to as Second Lake Village (Freeman 1968). Three (uncalibrated) radiocarbon dates were derived from these excavations (Bender, Bryson, and Baerreis 1968:165): 1590 ±60 B.P. (A.D. 360; WIS-236); 1610 ±65 B.P. (A.D. 340; WIS-237); and 270 ±55 B.P. (A.D. 1680; WIS-240). The ceramics from this site appeared to constitute "a pure Linn series assemblage" (Stoltman 1979:137). On the basis of these observations, and the two radiocarbon dates that show contemporaneity with the Millville site (WIS-240 is clearly unacceptable), it seemed clear that the Second Lake Village was a Millville phase community, thus most likely postdating the Hopewellian mounds at Trempealeau Lakes (Stoltman 1979:130, 137).

Because reliably identified cultural assemblages—"associated set(s) of contemporary artefact-types" (Clarke 1968:230)—from habitation sites played virtually no role in its formulation, the Trempealeau phase as conceived in 1979 was problematic from the outset. The "fleshing out" of the Trempealeau phase was heavily based upon analogies with the Illinois Valley (for example, Baker et al. 1941; Cole and Deuel 1937; Deuel 1952; McGregor 1958) and nearby portions of the Mississippi Valley in Illinois (for example, Bennett 1945; Herold 1971) and Iowa (for example, Logan 1976). On this basis it was presumed that ceramics of the Havana series (Griffin 1952c) would serve as the most reliable indicators of Trempealeau phase habitation sites. The presence of Hopewell series vessels at White's Mound, Shrake Mound 39, and Trempealeau Lakes was, of course, a major contributing factor to McKern's initial recognition of Hopewell interaction in southwestern Wisconsin (McKern 1931), but the overall scarcity of such vessels and their nearly exclusive occurrence in burial mound contexts in Wisconsin renders them of little practical value for identifying Trempealeau phase habitation sites. To a lesser extent certain lithic artifact types—especially prismatic blades and projectile points related to the Snyders, Norton, Gibson, Manker, Clear Lake, and Marshall types (Montet-White 1968)—were also assumed to be associated with the Trempealeau phase, again more so by analogy with Illinois than by occurrence in habitation site assemblages in southwestern Wisconsin. Thus, as of 1979, the Trempealeau phase was, for the most part, a mortuary complex to which had been added a series of

Havana-related artifact types that would presumably be found at habitation sites.

Seeking Confirmation of the Trempealeau Phase

My involvement in the search for Trempealeau phase habitation sites grew gradually in the context of a program of survey and excavation commenced on behalf of the University of Wisconsin–Madison in the Prairie du Chien locality in 1978. Almost no archaeological research had been conducted in this locality since Cyrus Thomas' pioneering excavations (Thomas 1894). During the three seasons of 1883, 1885, and 1887, Thomas' agents had investigated at least thirty-five mounds in and near Prairie du Chien. Because only written descriptions of selected artifacts, mostly specialized grave goods, and almost no illustrations were included in the final report (Thomas 1894:47–77), determining cultural affiliation of these mounds is problematic. Thus, the first goal of our fieldwork was to establish a firm cultural sequence based upon stratigraphic and radiometric evidence from local habitation sites that would complement and provide the necessary framework within which to contextualize Thomas' sites. In pursuing this goal, we conducted pedestrian surveys of all of the major landforms in the locality, including the low, seasonally inundated floodplain and its many islands (for example, Theler 1987), the high Pleistocene terrace on which Prairie du Chien is situated (for example, Stoltman 1990), and the coulees and uplands bordering the Prairie du Chien terrace (for example, Arzigian 1981; Theler 1981).

We were eventually able to define a series of local Woodland phases: Indian Isle, Prairie, Millville, Mill, and Eastman (Arzigian 1987; Stoltman 1990; Theler 1987). Our biggest frustration in this research, however, involved a failure to find firm evidence of the elusive Trempealeau phase; while the expected Havana ceramics and presumably associated projectile point types were turning up in both our surface collections and our test excavations, we were unable to isolate them in assemblages. For example, between 1978 and 1990 the surface surveys and test excavations at sixteen datable Woodland sites in the Prairie du Chien locality produced 244 Havana sherds from among 1,897 rim and decorated body sherds (Stoltman 1990:246). Yet, despite the relative abundance of the Havana series (13 percent of our ceramic sample), such sherds were always found intermixed with other types in surface collections or, upon excavation, scattered widely throughout the culture-bearing deposits: in neither the surface collections nor the test excavations did we encounter a pure Havana (= Trempealeau?) assemblage.

Our excavations at the Bloyer site (47CR339) perhaps best exemplify this problem. This site is especially relevant because it lies on the western edge of the terrace upon which are located two of the Middle Woodland mound groups tested by Thomas: Flucke and Vilas (Thomas 1894:Plate I, Figure 1). In addition it had produced the most Havana sherds ($n = 51$) of any site in our sample. Eight 2-x-2-meter units were excavated at this site in 1980. Artifacts were recovered

Table 17.1. Mean Depth of Major Ceramic Series from Excavations at the Bloyer Site (47CR339)

Ceramic Series	Number of Sherds	Mean Depth
Madison	88	32.8 cm = Level 4
Linn	230	48.0 cm = Level 5
Havana	48	50.4 cm = Level 6
Prairie	31	50.6 cm = Level 6

to depths of approximately one meter in sandy sediments that showed no discernible internal stratigraphic differentiation, other than a gradational color change with depth from dark gray to gray to tan. A number of pit features were exposed, but no middens, living floors, buried A-horizons, or other stratigraphic surfaces were encountered. As a result, excavations were conducted in arbitrary 10-centimeter levels. In total, 4,109 sherds (not counting one nearly complete Late Woodland vessel) were recovered, scattered throughout the upper 80 centimeters. Since the contents of arbitrary levels cannot be treated as assemblages (a topic discussed at length in Stoltman 1974:65–69), the mean depth of these sherds by ceramic series was computed as the best available method by which to seek evidence of temporal trends (table 17.1).

As can be seen from table 17.1, the mean depths of the ceramic series conform to expectations based upon the presumed association of each series with one of the sequential cultural phases, from oldest to youngest, of Prairie, Trempealeau, Millville, and Eastman. This literal interpretation of the mean depths, however, is putting too fine a spin on the data. Clearly, the differences between the Prairie and Havana series are minuscule. More reasonable interpretations of these data are either that the Prairie and Havana ceramics are essentially the same age or that subsequent mixing during later occupations has obscured their chronological relationship.

As of 1990 the Trempealeau phase remained as much an inferred as a demonstrated archaeological taxon in southwestern Wisconsin. Because of this state of affairs, at least three alternative views of the Trempealeau phase are viable: (1) population densities were so low and mobility so high that no nucleated settlements formed, (2) the extant archaeological record is seriously biased, or (3) expectations about the formal content of the phase are flawed. The paucity of single-component Trempealeau habitation sites with pure Havana ceramic assemblages supports the first view. Those favoring the second view believe that Trempealeau hamlets or villages are "out there" but remain to be found. The third alternative holds that many "mixed" sites, such as Bloyer and the recently excavated DEET Thinker and Cipra sites (Johansen et al. 1998), near Wauzeka on the Wisconsin River east of Prairie du Chien (fig. 17.1), are rather less mixed than has been generally believed. The existence of varying degrees of stylistic and contextual intermixing among the presumably sequential Prairie, Havana, and Linn ceramic series coupled with the highly variable radiocarbon dates showing considerable overlap among them (Stoltman 1979:130; 1986:134–

Figure 17.1. Location of main sites discussed in the text.

135) supports this alternative. Accepting this view, however, forces us to consider seriously the possibility that there is no such thing as a Trempealeau phase assemblage with purely Havana series ceramics in southwestern Wisconsin. At issue is the basic question of whether or not the Havana ceramic series is temporally discrete in southwestern Wisconsin vis-à-vis the Prairie and Linn ceramic series or overlaps one or both of the latter in time.

Prairie and Trempealeau: Coeval or Sequential Phases?

The two available (uncalibrated) radiocarbon dates for the Prairie phase—1880 ±80 B.P. (A.D. 70; WIS-1275) and 1890 ±80 B.P. (A.D. 60; WIS-1309)—raise the distinct possibility of contemporaneity with the Havana tradition (Stoltman 1986:134–135). Collins and Forman (1995) have recently put forth further support for this view, based upon excavations of the Buck Creek Mounds in Clayton County, Iowa (fig. 17.1). At the base of Mound 1 at Buck Creek, evidence of Prairie phase mortuary activity was encountered beneath a later Allamakee phase (Millville-related) mantle. Two (uncalibrated) radiocarbon dates (Collins and Forman 1995:69–70) from the base of Buck Creek Mound 1 date the Prairie component to 1890 B.P. ±150 (A.D. 60; ISGS-3150) and 1840 ±160 B.P. (A.D. 110; ISGS-3149).

A second, recently excavated site in northeastern Iowa, Dolomite Ridge (13DB428), has also produced data relevant to this issue (Collins 1996; fig. 17.1). In the West Block of this site, sandy, Prairie-like ceramics were recovered in association with grit-tempered Havana-like body sherds and Sister Creeks-like punctated (both annular and oblique) sherds. That these materials constitute a valid assemblage is supported by the close parallels that can be observed with the ceramics recovered from the buried A-horizon at 47CR100 (see fig. 17.6 below; Collins 1996:69). The two (uncalibrated) radiocarbon dates obtained from features in the Dolomite Ridge West Block are only slightly earlier than other Prairie phase dates (Collins 1996:107–108): 2140 ±50 B.P. (190 B.C.; Beta-92900) and 2110 ±50 B.P. (160 B.C.; Beta-92901).

Yet another site with evidence suggestive of contemporaneity of the Prairie and Trempealeau phases is Mound l at the Overhead site in LaCrosse (Gallagher et al. 1981). Beneath this mound remnant was a subfloor tomb with classic Hopewell-related burials associated with copper beads, bear canines, Knife River flint bifaces, and a platform pipe, among other grave goods (Gallagher et al. 1981:25–28). A single (uncalibrated) radiocarbon date, unfortunately on bone, from the burial pit was 2130 ±80 B.P. (180 B.C.; Beta-1916) (Gallagher et al. 1981:29). The associated ceramics, all recovered from the mound fill, included three vessels: one incised-over-cordmarked (forty-one sherds), a second bossed-over-cordmarked (twenty-nine sherds), and a single "Havana-like" body sherd (Gallagher et al. 1981:31–32). Considering that the mound "seemed totally free of intrusive materials" (Gallagher et al. 1981:25), and if its contents are accepted as a valid assemblage (a reasonable but fallible inference), it is difficult not to see here an intermixture of Prairie and Trempealeau stylistic attributes.

Recent research at 47CR100 (fig. 17.1) has provided two additional lines of evidence—one stratigraphic, the other typological—also supporting the contemporaneity of Prairie and Havana ceramics. The site of 47CR100 is situated on a two-pronged alluvial fan on the north side of Mill Coulee about 400 meters east of the coulee mouth (fig. 17.2). Mill Coulee opens onto the Prairie du Chien terrace 2 kilometers north of the Prairie du Chien city limits, at the north edge of the Courtois mound group excavated by Thomas (1894:63–68).

Following its discovery through pedestrian survey in 1979 (Theler 1981), the site was the scene of recurrent excavations in 1980 (Arzigian 1987; Theler 1987:99–107), 1983 (Stoltman 1990), and 1993. The excavations of 1980 focused on the cultivated portion of the site on the southern end of the largest (that is, western) fan arm, where surface collections had been especially rich. These excavations revealed a series of features just beneath the plow zone, including a hearth, a shell lens, and two shell-filled pits attributable to the Millville phase (Arzigian 1987; Theler 1987:99–107). Two (uncalibrated) radiocarbon dates from these features are 1670 B.P. ±70 (A.D. 280; WIS-1335) and 1620 ±70 (A.D. 330; WIS-1308) (Steventon and Kutzbach 1983:157).

By contrast the excavations of 1983 focused primarily upon the upslope (that is, northern) portions of the site that were in pasture and had apparently never

Figure 17.2. View north across Mill Creek (foreground) and Mill Coulee road onto the alluvial fans on which 47CR100 is located. Students in the plowed field near the foot of the western fan indicate the site of the 1980 excavations; students in the wooded pasture beyond are near the 1983 block excavations atop the western fan arm. The shell middens shown in figure 17.3 are located in the swale directly behind the cars. The vessel illustrated in figure 17.7 was recovered from atop the right fan arm in the pasture just to the right of the field of view.

been cultivated (fig. 17.2). While excavations were in progress on the main arm of the fan, the serendipitous recognition of clam shell fragments in the back-dirt of a groundhog burrow in the unlikely location of the swale between the two fan arms (fig. 17.2) prompted test excavations that confirmed an earlier report by Charles E. Brown (1912:167) that an "Aboriginal shell heap formerly existed in Mill Coulee."

The 1983 excavations in "the Mill Coulee shell heap" consisted of only two 2-x-2-meter units, but they revealed an extraordinarily clear-cut series of strata, including not one but two superimposed shell middens that were in turn underlain by a buried soil (Stoltman 1990; fig. 17.3). There was seemingly clear-cut cultural stratigraphy associated with the physical strata. In the 20–30 centimeters of colluvium above the upper shell midden were Late Woodland ceramics and triangular projectile points. In the upper shell midden was a unique component dominated by Lane Farm Cord-Impressed ceramics that became the primary basis for defining a new early Late Woodland (Mill) phase. Separated from the upper shell midden by a 20-centimeter level of sandy colluvium was the second shell midden, containing classic Millville phase ceramics (fig. 17.4).

Figure 17.3. View of the north walls of the two 1983 2–meter units excavated into the "shell heap" portion of 47CR100.

Another colluvial layer, this time up to 30 centimeters thick, separated the lower shell midden from a dark, buried A-horizon in which were Havana sherds (fig. 17.5). Had we finally isolated a Trempealeau phase component? While the cultural stratigraphy seemed clear and unambiguous, the artifact densities in the two lowest components (the lower shell midden and the buried soil) were low. Clearly, more extensive excavations into these lower levels were warranted.

Various circumstances conspired to prevent further work at the site until a decade later, but in 1993 we were able to return. After reestablishment of the 1983 grid system, the 1993 excavations at the Mill Coulee shell heap consisted of a series of seventeen 1-x-1-meter units, plus two 2-x-2-meter units in a block surrounding the two 2-x-2-meter units previously excavated. A full report of these excavations is in progress, but for the purposes of this chapter I shall focus primarily upon the ceramic stratigraphy, especially the materials recovered from the Middle Woodland levels, that is, the lower shell midden and the buried A-horizon.

Of the thousands of sherds recovered from the Mill Coulee shell heap excavations, 279 diagnostics—that is, rims and decorated body sherds—constitute the main basis of the analysis. These diagnostic sherds were assigned to individual vessels, sixty-seven in number, and the vessels each were then assigned to a specific excavation level following a few simple rules: (1) if a vessel was represented by only one sherd, the context of that sherd was, of course, its assigned level; (2) when a vessel was represented by sherds from two or more levels, the recovery context was considered to be that from which the majority of sherds had come; and (3) when a vessel was represented by equal numbers of sherds

Figure 17.4. Linn ware (Millville phase) sherds from 47CR100. All are from the lower shell midden (Shell 2) or the adjacent colluvial layers above and below Shell 2, except Vessel 36 (*middle row, right*) and Vessel 35 (*lower row, left*), which are both from the buried A-horizon.

Figure 17.5. Havana ware sherds from the buried A-horizon at 47CR100.

Table 17.2. Stratigraphic Distribution by Ceramic Series of the Sixty-seven Vessels Recovered at the Mill Coulee Shell Heap Site (47CR100)

Stratum	Collared	Madison	Other	Lane Farm	Linn	Havana	Prairie	Totals
Above Shell 1	4	16	3		1			24
Shell 1		3		9	1			13
Between Shells				2	3	1		6
Shell 2			1		5			6
Below Shell 2		1			4	2	1	8
Buried A-horizon					2	4[a]	4	10
Totals	4	20	4	11	16	7	5	67

a. Includes Sister Creeks–like vessel shown in fig. 17.6.

from two or more levels (so the majority rule could not be applied), the recovery context was either the midpoint of the distribution or, for two levels, the cultural stratum involved (that is, one of the two shell middens or the A-horizon). Table 17.2 shows the stratigraphic distribution of the sixty-seven vessels as thus determined.

The upper shell midden (Shell 1) is the denser and more extensive of the two, encountered in sixteen of the twenty-one excavation units. It effectively sealed the underlying cultural materials over most of the excavated portion of the site (fig. 17.3). Two (uncalibrated) radiocarbon dates from the upper shell midden (Stoltman 1990:251) seem to reliably place the age of this early Late Woodland (Mill phase) deposit circa A.D. 750: 1200 B.P. ±70 (A.D. 750; WIS-1692) and 1180 B.P. ±70 (A.D. 770; WIS-1585). The lower shell midden, while not yet directly dated, contains a virtually pure Millville ceramic assemblage (fig. 17.4). All vessels with primary recovery contexts within the Shell 2 midden are Levsen Stamped types, except for one unique rocker-stamped and incised rim with an interior channel that is Baehr-like in many ways (table 17.2).

The lowest cultural materials, those associated with the buried A-horizon that are analogous to the Dolomite Ridge West Block ceramics (Collins 1996:69), are our primary concern here (figs. 17.5 and 17.6). The depth to this horizon from the ground surface ranges between 60 centimeters and 1 meter. As can be seen from table 17.2, the ceramics with primary recovery contexts in this horizon include ten vessels: four Prairie series, four Havana series (the annular-punctated, Sister Creeks–like vessel [fig. 17.6, lower right] is included in this category), and two Linn series. There is little doubt that the Prairie and Havana vessels antedate Shell 2, since eleven of the twelve vessels (including seventy-one of the seventy-five sherds involved) have their primary recovery context below that stratum. The sole exception, a bossed, plain body sherd from between the shell middens, was assigned to the Havana series with considerable trepidation (table 17.2). That these two ceramic series are unambiguously pre-Shell 2, and thus pre-Millville, in age is securely documented here, and that they both occur in the same buried stratum is certainly consistent with the view that they were contemporary. Their coexistence in a buried A-horizon, however, cannot be accepted as conclusive proof of contemporaneity because such soils could only

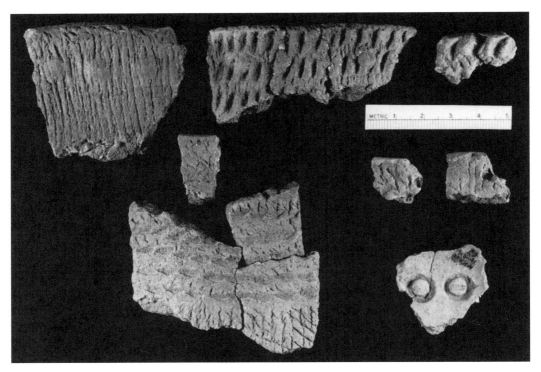

Figure 17.6. Stylistically Early Woodland vessels from the buried A-horizon at 47CR100; all are sand-tempered (that is, Prairie ware) except the Sister Creeks–like vessel in lower right.

have formed under a protracted period of nondeposition during which a mature vegetative cover had become established. Thus, prior to its eventual burial, this soil would have provided a reasonably stable surface upon which sequential occupation by prehistoric peoples could have occurred without enough elapsed time for intervening sediments to have accumulated.

One aspect of the two ceramic series is certain: their technological and stylistic attributes are markedly different. The Prairie series vessels have highly sandy pastes and are sand-tempered (all vessels in fig. 17.6 except the Sister Creeks–like vessel), while the Havana series vessels have far less sandy pastes and are tempered with coarse fragments of crushed igneous rock (fig. 17.5, plus the Sister Creeks–like vessel in fig. 17.6). This suggests that distinctly different ceramic-making traditions were involved.

The two Linn series vessels from the buried A-horizon (fig. 17.4) present a different problem. Because vessels of this series are the most widely scattered of any in the sample—indeed, they are found in all strata—the likelihood of some postdepositional displacement is high. Considering that the peak frequency of Linn vessels is in Shell 2, and that twelve of the sixteen Linn vessels were recovered from Shell 2 and the two adjacent colluvial levels, it is reasonable to view the primary stratigraphic context of the Linn series at this site to be in and around the Shell 2 stratum (table 17.2). Considering this, the two Linn vessels with primary recovery contexts within the buried A-horizon can reasonably be considered as intrusive from above.

The second line of evidence from 47CR100 pertaining to the issue of cultural interaction (that is, contemporaneity) between the Prairie and Havana traditions involves a nearly complete ceramic vessel that was recovered from a shallow pit feature exposed at a depth of 40 centimeters on the second alluvial fan located 20 meters east of the swale in which the superimposed shell middens were found (on the fan arm just right of the field of view in fig. 17.2). It is a jar with a single row of nodes between two horizontal lines that were trailed over a cordmarked surface (fig. 17.7). Between the upper trailed line and the lip are a series of parallel, oblique stamped impressions that appear to be from a cord-wrapped tool. The same tool impressions occur on the vessel interior on the upper rim. Based upon petrographic observations of a thin section of this vessel, its temper can be reliably identified as sand. The flattened lip has a thickness that ranges mostly between 6 and 8 millimeters, with 8.2 millimeters being the maximum value measured. This unique vessel seems clearly to be the product of a potter who knew of both the Prairie and the Havana ceramic tradition: on the one hand its incised-over-cordmarking and bosses on a sand-tempered paste are typically Prairie, while on the other its cord-wrapped-tool stamping, bosses, and fairly thick vessel walls are Havana-like.

Charred encrustations from the interior of this vessel returned a (uncalibrated) radiocarbon date of 1890 ±60 B.P. (A.D. 60; WIS-2377/CAMS-24675).

Figure 17.7. Unique vessel from the eastern fan arm of 47CR100.

This date is well within the range of the radiocarbon ages of both the Havana tradition of Illinois (for example, Asch 1976:9–10; Farnsworth and Studenmund 1999; McGimsey et al. 1985:102) and the Prairie phase (for example, Collins and Forman 1995:69–70; Stoltman 1986:134) and is thus consistent with the view that Prairie ceramics were still being manufactured in southwestern Wisconsin when cultural interaction had begun with the Havana tradition. Interestingly, the only available radiocarbon date from the Albany site in Whiteside County, Illinois, the largest Hopewellian site in the upper Mississippi Valley (Conner and Link 1991:34), also falls in the first century A.D.: 1930 B.P. ±70 (uncalibrated; A.D. 20; ISGS-2112). In light of the combined radiometric, contextual, and stylistic evidence summarized above it is suggested that the contemporaneity of Illinois' Havana tradition and Wisconsin's Prairie phase deserves serious consideration.

Trempealeau and Millville: Coeval or Sequential Phases?

As defined in 1979, the Trempealeau and Millville phases were considered to be sequential Middle Woodland phases, the former characterized predominantly by Havana series ceramics and Hopewell mortuary ceremonialism and the latter predominantly by the Linn ceramic series, at a time postdating the main period of Hopewell interaction (Stevenson et al. 1997:157–164; Stoltman 1979:134–139; see also Benn 1978, 1979; Logan 1976). The stratigraphic evidence at sites like Bloyer and 47CR100 is consistent with this view that the primary period of Linn series manufacture postdates that of the Havana series. While the periods of primary production may be sequential, however, what about the possibility that there was an overlap in the manufacture of the two series? In the following discussion three lines of evidence—radiometric, typological, and contextual—will be examined in order to illuminate the issue of cultural interaction (that is, contemporaneity) between the Havana tradition of Illinois and the Millville phase of Wisconsin.

First, the available radiocarbon dates definitely show temporal overlap with the Havana tradition of Illinois, which falls generally within the interval 150 B.C.–A.D. 300–400 in uncalibrated radiocarbon years (Asch 1976:9–10; Farnsworth and Studenmund 1999; McGimsey et al. 1985:102). For example, thirty "good" Millville dates recorded earlier (Stoltman 1979:130) range from A.D. 70 to A.D. 620 (uncalibrated radiocarbon years). At least thirteen of these dates have central values between A.D. 130 and A.D. 300, and if the 2-sigma range is considered, fully twenty-five of the thirty have ranges that extend before a conservative A.D. 300 upper limit for the Havana tradition. It is difficult to avoid the conclusion that the Havana tradition and the Millville phase were at least partly coeval.

There is also considerable stylistic/typological evidence to suggest that Hopewell-related practices in Illinois were still in vogue during the Millville phase. In particular the highly distinctive practice of interior rim channeling that is characteristic of both Hopewell and Baehr ceramic types in Illinois (Griffin

1952c:114–120) is extremely common within the Linn ceramic series, especially on the Levsen Stamped and Marquette (formerly Lane Farm) Stamped types (Stoltman 1979:Figure 18.7, a–d and i–l; Stoltman and Christiansen 2000:500). In addition there is at least one rim from the Millville site (Stoltman 1979:Figure 18.7m) that is an unmistakable copy of a crosshatched Hopewell rim, complete with punctates beneath the cross-hatching and a channeled interior (compare Griffin 1952c:117). It is possible to view such types as holdovers in southwestern Wisconsin after the main period of Hopewell interaction, but ultimately it is simpler, and thus preferable, to see some of them as originating in the context of direct cultural contacts between Hopewell-related peoples of Illinois and Millville peoples of Wisconsin.

There is also contextual evidence to suggest that the manufacture of Linn series ceramics had begun while the Havana series was still being produced and/ or traded into southwestern Wisconsin. Much of this evidence, such as the two Levsen Stamped vessels in the buried A-horizon at the Mill Coulee shell heap, is open to alternative interpretations that are extremely difficult to resolve given the current archaeological record. Are such vessels contemporaries of the Havana vessels found on the same horizon; were they deposited there shortly after the Trempealeau peoples vacated the site but before new slope-wash deposits buried the soil; or were the Levsen vessels postdepositional intrusions from above caused by rodents or some other disturbance?

Recent excavations in the Wisconsin River valley near Wauzeka, about 8 miles upstream from Prairie du Chien, have inspired Johansen and colleagues (1998:314) to propose, in no uncertain terms, that "Millville and Trempealeau wares do not stand in a sequential relationship." The basis for this claim was the recovery of Havana and Linn ceramic types in close association buried beneath more than 1 meter of alluvial fan deposits at the DEET Thinker and Cipra sites. This interpretation is not entirely compelling, considering that occupations at one of the sites, DEET Thinker, "are not separated by sedimentary units but rather have been sorted by biomechanical processes in the soil" (Johansen et al. 1998:208). Furthermore, buried soils at both sites, from which most of the artifacts were recovered, could have provided stable surfaces on which sequential occupations could have been superimposed prior to the deposition of additional sediments (Johansen et al. 1998:209). Perhaps more than anything the views expressed by the authors are an indication of the frustrations all researchers in the region are feeling concerning the Trempealeau phase, which is looking more and more like a chimera.

In this context I would like to revisit the Second Lake Village. In preparing the symposium paper on which this chapter is based, I was able to examine more carefully the ceramics and other artifacts recovered by Freeman in 1966. On the basis of this reexamination, I have no hesitation in reasserting the general validity of my original impressions of this assemblage as being derived from a single-component Millville community. However, its "purity" is in need of reconsideration! The vast majority of pottery from this site—twenty-eight of thirty-three vessels, three with channeled rims—can be assigned to the Levsen and Spring

Figure 17.8. Five vessels with channeled rims from Second Lake Village.

Hollow types of Linn ware (fig. 17.8). In addition there is one unique incised-over-plain vessel; one Prairie Bossed vessel; one probable Naples Stamped vessel; one Hopewell-like vessel with a channeled rim and a row of punctates at the base of the channel but no other decoration (fig. 17.8, bottom row center); and one noteworthy Baehr-like rim that has a broad interior channel and appears to have brushed decoration and limestone temper (fig. 17.8, top right). Also present in the Second Lake Village collections were three prismatic blades of Burlington chert; a small flake of muscovite; and a flake of Cochrane chert that, according to Freeman (personal communication 2000), matches the material from which some of the mortuary bifaces recovered in Mound 4 were made.

If all of these materials are accepted as parts of a single Millville village assemblage dating to the early 300s A.D., as appears reasonable considering the available radiocarbon dates (see above), then a number of significant insights follow. First, the peoples of Second Lake Village had direct contacts with peoples of the Havana tradition, as evidenced by a number of numerically minor but culturally significant ceramic features, as well as the presence of imported prismatic blades. Second, Freeman was correct in her long-standing belief that the people who occupied Second Lake Village were also the builders of nearby Mound 4 of the Trempealeau Lakes group. These conclusions present, however, a major dilemma for the current systematics—namely, the attribution of a classic Trempealeau phase burial mound to people of the Millville phase. If Free-man's view is accepted, as I propose to do here, the current construct of the Trempealeau phase must be revised or abandoned.

Conclusion

Two problems in particular have bedeviled efforts to comprehend the Trem-pealeau phase: (1) none of the classic burial mounds has been reliably radio-carbon dated, so their precise ages remain unknown; and (2) habitation site assemblages have been notoriously difficult to associate with the Hopewellian mounds of Wisconsin. In the absence of a resolution of these problems, most research over the past two decades has been conducted under the supposition that habitation sites with cultural assemblages closely similar to those of Ha-vana tradition peoples of Illinois are what we should be finding. Instead, the habitation sites encountered, even when stratified, seem invariably to produce "mixed" assemblages, that is, a certain number of presumably Trempealeau artifacts (such as Havana ware or Manker points) accompanied by Prairie and/ or Millville artifacts as well.

It is time to consider more seriously the possibility that southwestern Wiscon-sin is located beyond the primary geographic boundaries of the Havana tradi-tion, whose representation in southwestern Wisconsin was always partial and variable in both time and space. Under this view, there are unlikely to be any "pure" Havana assemblages unless a site-unit intrusion should eventually be discovered (none is currently known). Instead, the habitation sites of southwest-ern Wisconsin dating from shortly before A.D. 1 to circa A.D. 400 can be pos-tulated to manifest a continuum of cultural development from the Prairie phase to the Millville phase into which Havana influences were differentially intro-duced as a result of intermittent, but persistent, cultural interaction. At the early end of this continuum (perhaps by 100 B.C.; see Collins 1996), and perhaps enduring in geographically marginal areas, pure Prairie assemblages will be found. After A.D. 1, and perhaps only in mainline settings, "mixed" assem-blages with evidence of Prairie and Havana interaction may be found, as, for example, at Mill Coulee. Then, after circa A.D. 200 or so, and as a by-product of this cultural interaction, Levsen Stamped and other Linn series types will dominate assemblages, and the "mixing" seen would now involve the latest stages of the Havana tradition and the Millville phase as manifest, for example, at Second Lake Village.

In terms of human behavior the picture being suggested is one involving intermittent, persistent, but always small-scale, face-to-face human interaction between agents of the Havana tradition and, for lack of a better term, members of the local Mississippi Valley tradition. It seems highly likely that the major initiatives for cultural interaction between the two regions stemmed from Ha-vana peoples, but in behalf of whom—various corporate kin groups seem most likely—is not known. It is also likely that visitors from the south came often into southern Wisconsin but stayed for only short periods. The procurement by trade

of various exotic materials (such as copper, obsidian, Knife River flint, Wyoming chert and quartzite, and bear canines for which the Wisconsinites may
have served as middlemen) is a likely motive for the southerners to come north
(for example, Boszhardt 1998a; Clark 1984). Thus, it is reasonable to suggest
that various social mechanisms, such as reciprocal gift exchange, spouse exchange, the establishment of real and fictive kinship ties, and the establishment
of formal trading partnerships, would have been employed to facilitate and
perpetuate peaceful cultural interaction. Perhaps some of the visitors died in
Wisconsin, while others shared their beliefs about death, afterlife, spirituality,
and other such issues during the periods of co-residence, thus inspiring some of
the local peoples to adopt Hopewellian mound-building practices. If, then, it
was primarily the local peoples who built the Hopewellian mounds in Wisconsin, it would be reasonable to expect their everyday cultural assemblages to
conform to Prairie phase parameters early and to Millville phase parameters
later, with perhaps a variable amount of Havana tradition admixture in both
cases. In such a scenario the cultural context of Hopewell interaction in southwestern Wisconsin was *both* the Prairie and the Millville phase.

So, what is to become of the Trempealeau phase? Born as a partial (that is,
mortuary) complex and never properly "fleshed out" with habitation site assemblages, it seems an especially good candidate for relegation to the ranks of
the retired, along with one of its major proponents (who also happens to be the
author of this chapter).

This reconsideration of the status of the Trempealeau phase highlights an
important problem in all efforts to infer past human behavior from the present
archaeological record, namely, the extraordinary difficulty in defining valid archaeological assemblages reliably. All efforts to infer past human behavior from
the archaeological record depend first and foremost upon the supposition that
the artifact inventory, at whatever spatial scale (whether activity area, stratum,
or site) represents the remains of the activities of a single group of people during
a continuous period of occupancy. Insofar as the spatial locus of concern was
occupied at more than one continuous period of time (whether by the same
group or different social groups) and insofar as that spatial locus was subjected
to postdepositional disturbances, the integrity of assemblages will be adversely
affected. The inevitable result will be unreliable inferences concerning the human activities conducted at the specified spatial locus. As exemplified by Second
Lake Village or the various strata at 47CR100, it is often virtually impossible to
demonstrate conclusively that associated sets of artifact types (even when stylistically disparate) recovered from carefully excavated contexts are actually contemporaneous, that is, valid assemblages (for example, Clarke 1968:230). Because of this inherent ambiguity in the archaeological record, the alternatives of
assemblages versus palimpsests must always be competitively considered in our
efforts to understand past human behavior. In the case of the Trempealeau phase
considered here, it is suggested that the prevailing view that most of the extant
artifact collections are best interpreted as mixtures from multiple cultural contexts (that is, are palimpsests) ought to be rejected in favor of the alternative

view that many of these (like Second Lake Village) are better viewed as valid assemblages. The overriding lesson of this study, then, is summed up best in the title of T. C. Chamberlin's (1965) classic paper: inferences about past human behavior derived from the archaeological record should always be evaluated, and persistently reevaluated, within an evolving framework of "multiple working hypotheses."

18

The Land between Two Traditions

Middle Woodland Societies of the American Bottom

Andrew C. Fortier

The historical processes that brought into being the Middle Woodland traditions of the American Bottom are still largely unknown. As a crossroads at the
confluence of three major rivers, the American Bottom surprisingly never
emerged as a Hopewellian focal point, nor did it function as a major gateway or
transaction center for the movement of interaction sphere exotics. Although
there are over a hundred Middle Woodland sites identified in this locality, there
are to date no confirmed mound centers and only a handful of Hopewell Interaction Sphere exotics excavated from villages or campsites. Yet this area has
yielded evidence of Middle Woodland people who inhabited the American Bottom over the course of a half millennium, from cal 150 B.C. to A.D. 350. There
is evidence that groups in this area participated in the Hopewell Interaction
Sphere exchange system (Fortier et al. 1989; Struever 1964), perhaps even serving at times as agents of goods interaction, but the level of participation was
minor compared to that of their more northerly and southerly neighbors.
American Bottom Middle Woodland groups were never populous, but by cal
A.D. 50 a local residential population had emerged. Although these people
originated from northern Havana traditions, after cal A.D. 50 they became a
unique blend of northern Havana/Hopewell traditions and southern Illinois
Crab Orchard traditions, and arguably were in the process of developing their
own identity in the region.

During the early 1960s, Struever (1964:92) proposed the term "shatter zone"
for areas of northern and southern Middle Woodland tradition overlap (fig.
18.1). In Illinois, examples included the Cache River valley, the Carlyle Reservoir locality, and the middle Wabash River valley. Although sharing some of the
characteristics of a shatter zone, the American Bottom was regarded by Struever
(1965) as belonging to the so-called Snyders microzone of the Havana tradition.
With the exception of the Munson (1971) and Harn (1971) surveys in 1961,
however, very little was actually known about Middle Woodland assemblages in
the American Bottom, especially their affiliations with either the northern Havana or the southern Crab Orchard tradition. Over the past twenty years this
situation has been dramatically reversed.

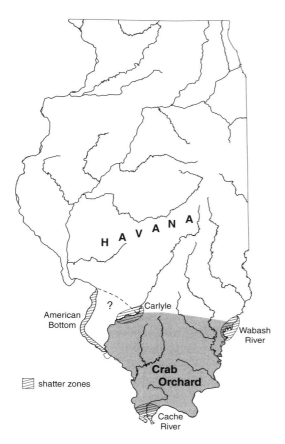

Figure 18.1. Havana/Crab Orchard tradition "shatter zones."

In examining the origins of Middle Woodland settlement in the American Bottom we must first start with the diverse and discontinuous nature of Early Woodland habitation in this area. Marion, Black Sand, Morton, Florence, and Columbia cultures have been identified, dating from 800 B.C. to 150 B.C. (Emerson and Fortier 1986; Fortier 2001; Fortier, Emerson, and Finney 1984). Their settlements are found mostly in the low-lying paludal environments of the Mississippi River floodplain, in the higher elevations of the Wood River terrace, and, in the case of the Marion or Carr Creek cultures, also along the creek valleys of the uplands. These cultures overlap in time, and in a few isolated cases, such as on the Wood River terrace, their remains co-occur (Emerson and McElrath 2001; Evans et al. 2000). The extent of interaction among them is unknown. Their ceramic assemblages are distinct, and mixing of decorative styles or technologies, such as the use of temper and pastes, is not observable. Black Sand, Florence, and Columbia cultures do share some elements of lithic technology and style, including the use of contracting-stemmed points and humpback scrapers, but chert procurement patterns vary widely. There is evidence, for example, that Black Sand groups had access to southern Illinois cherts such as Cobden/Dongola, while Florence and Marion groups almost exclusively utilized high-quality Burlington cherts from nearby Missouri quarries. Settlements also vary widely among these groups. Black Sand and Marion occupations consist of scatters of materials or, in some cases, middens, but pits are rare. These ephemeral settlements appear to represent short-term extractive camps. In contrast, the Florence site yielded a large circular structure, pits, and stone hearths (Emerson, Milner, and Jackson 1983). However, Florence culture occupations in the American Bottom must have been short-lived, as remains are extremely rare. Finally, subsistence practices, although poorly represented at most Early Woodland sites, suggest a pattern of wild seed, nut, and tuber procurement.

Whether the earliest Middle Woodland Havana-like cultures of the American Bottom were derived directly from Black Sand populations to the north or the south cannot be resolved in the American Bottom. The first Middle Woodland settlers arrived from the north sometime around cal 150 B.C. and were not spawned from local Early Woodland traditions (Fortier 1995). The thick-walled, sand/grit-tempered dentate stamped and cordmarked jars of the early Middle Woodland Cement Hollow phase are nearly identical to early Havana types found in the central Illinois River valley (Finney 1983). It is noteworthy that these early Middle Woodland immigrants occupied the same kind of landscapes as their Early Woodland predecessors, preferring low-lying sandy environments in the middle of the floodplain (Emerson and Fortier 1986): Black Sand remains were identified at the Holding site (Fortier et al. 1989), while Marion remains were found in the vicinity of the Truck #7 site (Fortier 1985). The Cement Hollow culture was predominantly floodplain adapted, with virtually no evidence of upland occupation. The wild plant and nut subsistence focus was virtually identical to Early Woodland practices, with no evidence for domestication or complex horticultural practices.

To date, only a few sites from the early Middle Woodland period have been excavated, including a large residential campsite (Petite Michele) and several smaller extractive camp locations (Fortier and Ghosh 2000). Available survey information indicates that populations were sparse and widely dispersed across the floodplain during this period.

The best excavated example of a relatively large settlement from this early period is the Petite Michele site in northern St. Clair County (Fortier 2004), dating to approximately cal 50 B.C. Eighty-six pit features were excavated, including two with burials. The ceramic assemblage includes typical Havana-type pottery, with large, thick-walled zoned, curvilinear, linear, and dentate stamped jars (Havana Zoned var. Dentate Stamped) being most frequent. Naples Ovoid, Naples Stamped, Neteler Stamped, Schafner Pinched, and a dentate version of Fettie Incised also occur, along with the more mundane Havana Cordmarked and Plain vessels. Heavy food residues on all these pots indicate their use as cooking vessels. The lithic assemblage includes large Snyders points and scrapers, Waubesa-like contracting-stemmed bifaces, large disc scrapers, a handful of lamellar blades, and a mix of bifacial and unifacial scrapers. Virtually none of these artifact types occurs in Early Woodland assemblages in this area.

There are several somewhat unusual aspects to the Petite Michele lithic assemblage worth noting. First, there is an unusually high percentage of southern Illinois–derived Cobden/Dongola chert in this assemblage, totaling nearly 20 percent of both tools and debitage. There are even a number of flakes and core fragments with intact cortex, indicating the importation of raw material to the site. In the context of a northern-derived ceramic assemblage, this lithic source suggests broad interaction or movement of materials over relatively long distances (in particular, contact with southern Illinois). Similarly indicative of interaction is the occurrence of several copper tool fragments, including a miniature celt fragment. Extraregional materials have heretofore been restricted to the subsequent Holding or Hopewell phase in this area. A few other items indicating possible Hopewell interaction activities are a chert bird effigy, mica and fluorite fragments, ground galena, and a piece of ground schist. Similar items have not been recovered from any other Cement Hollow phase occupations in this area, nor have possible copper working activities and nonlocal chert raw material manipulation been previously recognized. Petite Michele gives every indication of being an encampment of intrusive trans-Mississippi River travelers, perhaps even representing early agents of the Hopewell Interaction Sphere in the tri-river confluence.

The subsequent Holding phase, cal A.D. 50 to A.D. 150, is marked by dramatic shifts in settlement type, ceramic style and technology, lithic technological formats, and subsistence practices. The derivation of such a wholesale shift involving so many different lifeway practices is seemingly enigmatic, but similar changes in Hopewell cultural dynamics were occurring over the entire Midwest and Southeast at this time. Specific American Bottom aspects of this technological and stylistic transformation in material culture include the appearance of a lamellar blade industry, including both Fulton and Cobden preparation technologies (McNerney 1987; Montet-White 1968; Morrow 1987); an increase in chert type diversity, including the use of extralocal materials and an emphasis on local colorful cherts; the development of a small-tool tradition, including many new formal types of blade and flake tools (Fortier 2000b); the use of chert hoes; a general downsizing of bifaces and scrapers; the introduction of new hafted biface types; use of limestone and grog in addition to grit and sand tempers; the appearance of ceramic bowls and thin-walled jars, often decorated with elaborate Hopewell design motifs; the appearance of clay human and animal figurines and clay ear spools; and, finally, the use of exotic nonlocal materials such as obsidian, mica, copper, and fluorite, at least at the larger settlements (fig. 18.2). In the American Bottom, exotics take the form of finished copper awls and miniature celts, obsidian blades, miniature limestone bowls, sandstone cones, fired clay reel ear spools, clay figurines, and chert bird effigies. Several platform pipes have been reported from the Horseshoe Lake #2 or Bobby Becker site (Harn 1971:26; Pauketat, Rees, and Pauketat 1998:41), and a possible pipe fragment was observed during the destruction of a Middle Woodland mound at the Gehring site (T. Pauketat, personal communication, 2000). Missing from this complex are marine shell, copper ear spools, panpipes, drilled animal canines, and modified bone.

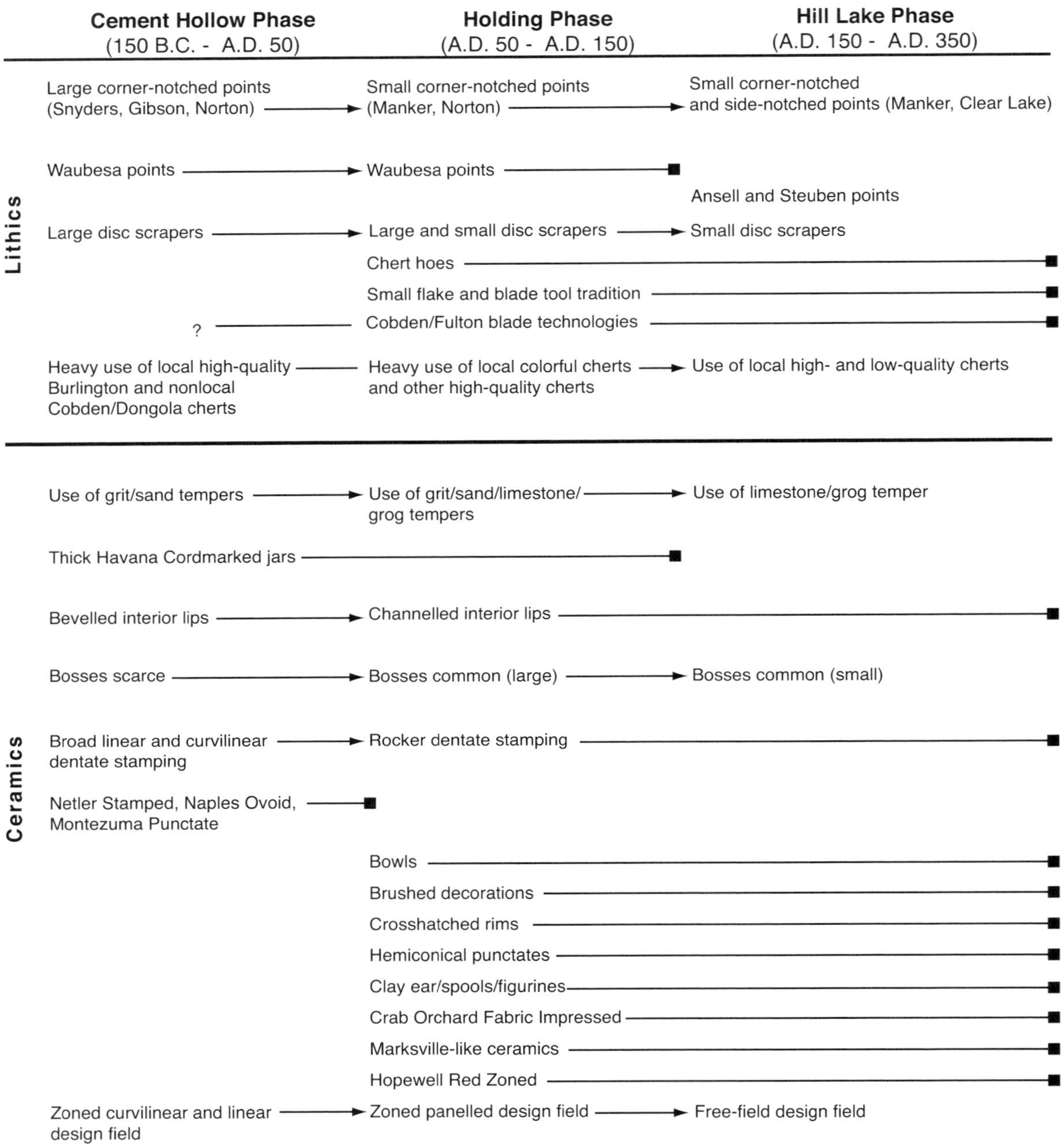

Lithics

Cement Hollow Phase (150 B.C. - A.D. 50)	Holding Phase (A.D. 50 - A.D. 150)	Hill Lake Phase (A.D. 150 - A.D. 350)
Large corner-notched points (Snyders, Gibson, Norton) →	Small corner-notched points (Manker, Norton) →	Small corner-notched and side-notched points (Manker, Clear Lake)
Waubesa points →	Waubesa points → ■	
		Ansell and Steuben points
Large disc scrapers →	Large and small disc scrapers →	Small disc scrapers
	Chert hoes ——————————————— ■	
	Small flake and blade tool tradition ——— ■	
? —————	Cobden/Fulton blade technologies ——— ■	
Heavy use of local high-quality Burlington and nonlocal Cobden/Dongola cherts ———	Heavy use of local colorful cherts and other high-quality cherts →	Use of local high- and low-quality cherts

Ceramics

Cement Hollow Phase	Holding Phase	Hill Lake Phase
Use of grit/sand tempers →	Use of grit/sand/limestone/grog tempers →	Use of limestone/grog temper
Thick Havana Cordmarked jars ——————————— ■		
Bevelled interior lips →	Channelled interior lips ——————————— ■	
Bosses scarce →	Bosses common (large) →	Bosses common (small)
Broad linear and curvilinear dentate stamping →	Rocker dentate stamping ——————————— ■	
Netler Stamped, Naples Ovoid, Montezuma Punctate ——— ■		
	Bowls ——————————————————— ■	
	Brushed decorations ———————————— ■	
	Crosshatched rims ————————————— ■	
	Hemiconical punctates ———————————— ■	
	Clay ear/spools/figurines—————————— ■	
	Crab Orchard Fabric Impressed ————— ■	
	Marksville-like ceramics ————————— ■	
	Hopewell Red Zoned ————————————— ■	
Zoned curvilinear and linear design field →	Zoned panelled design field →	Free-field design field

Figure 18.2. Diachronic trends in American Bottom Middle Woodland lithic and ceramic assemblages.

In the midst of this multifaceted technological revolution, there is evidence that horticultural practices were simultaneously becoming more sophisticated. Maize has been identified at the Holding site (Riley et al. 1994), and there is a marked increase in the number of starchy seed domesticates at all Middle Woodland sites from this phase. Cucurbits, tobacco, and sunflower have also been identified, and there is an increase in the use of hazelnuts over the previously preferred black walnut and hickory nut groups. Finally, there is a significant increase in the plant diversity index, again generally at the larger settlements. Hunting and generalized seasonal foraging also constituted important components of the Hopewellian economic system, as indicated by small campsites located in both the uplands and the floodplain of the American Bottom (Fortier and Ghosh 2000). In contrast to the previous Early Woodland and early Middle Woodland subsistence practices, the appearance of this new, diverse plant-use complex amounts to a virtual horticultural revolution (Fortier 1998).

In terms of ceramic style there is a shift away from the broad dentate patterns of design to more finely executed motifs, including the use of hemiconical punctates, narrow incised lines, rocker stamps, small nodes, and brushing (Maher 1989, 1996). Multiple zoned bands, with a variety of motifs within the bands, produce a rigid paneled effect. Design patterns are often repetitive but also occur in opposition (fig. 18.2). This iconographic representation appears throughout the Midwest at this time and is clearly a form of regionally based symbolic communication system (Seeman 1995). We may hypothesize that we are in fact viewing a kind of cosmological alphabet whose letters we have yet to decipher. In any case, this ideographic system reaches its peak in the middle portion of the Hopewellian renaissance and is a defining hallmark of this period.

I have previously detailed the decline and disappearance of much of this complex over the following 250 years of Middle Woodland settlement in the American Bottom (Fortier 1998). This long-term process follows the general collapse of the Hopewell cultural manifestation throughout the Midwest at this time. The most enigmatic aspect of this historical process in the American Bottom is the almost complete abandonment of multiple, and apparently unconnected, technologies and practices. This breakdown of technologies and various stylistic and subsistence practices is still poorly understood. It may involve a long-term resistance or disaffiliation with cultures to the north and south, or perhaps it happened suddenly near the end of the period. The coeval cessation of hazelnut use, abandonment of blade technology, and dramatic shifts in design presentation and motif use on pots are not explained by existing models of Hopewellian collapse. If these subsistence and technologically-based assemblages are contrasted with those of the immediately subsequent Late Woodland assemblages, it is clear that almost all practices related to what we identify as Middle Woodland disappear completely from the American Bottom landscape, sometime around cal A.D. 350 (McElrath and Fortier 2000).

Before offering some speculations on this problem, I would like to backtrack to the period of Hopewellian ascendancy or apical technological diversity. As I have outlined, the shift from early Middle Woodland to Hopewell was dramatic.

The earlier period is essentially Havana-related in origin and cultural affiliation. It is clearly intrusive from the Illinois River valley. Even in this early period, however, there are a few design elements in the ceramic assemblage that are unique to the American Bottom. For example, large Havana Cordmarked and Plain jars sometimes display unbevelled, rounded lips with either exterior or interior lip decoration (Maher 1996). These jars are also generally unnoded, unlike their counterparts to the north. The vessel walls on the larger jars are generally thinner than on similar Illinois Valley jars. Some contain only grit temper, while none is completely sand-tempered. One Cement Hollow phase vessel from the Mund site is even tempered with Missouri River Clinker fragments (Finney 1983:57). There is also some use of grog, a technological practice that is extremely rare in the north. Overall, however, the typical Cement Hollow assemblage still mostly resembles Havana ceramic assemblages found to the north.

By the Holding and Hill Lake phases, some uniquely American Bottom elements characterize the Middle Woodland tradition of this area (fig. 18.3). Ceramic assemblages include a mix of Hopewell-Havana and Crab Orchard types. There are at least sixteen American Bottom types in this area and roughly the same number that parallel types recognized in the Illinois River valley (Maher 1989). Fabric-impressed Crab Orchard types constitute a third group. The use of multiple tempering agents is a unique characteristic of this locality, and, with the exception of the Crab Orchard pottery, differences in temper account for most of the typological variability. Grog-tempered vessels dramatically increase in frequency and occur alongside limestone-, grit-, and grit/sand-tempered vessels. Even Crab Orchard pottery, which is typically grog-tempered to the south, is grit- and sand-tempered in the American Bottom (Butler and Jefferies 1986).

In terms of lithics there appears to be much greater diversity in chert sources in the American Bottom than in other areas of Illinois (Stafford 1985a), including the selection of numerous types of local colorful cherts such as Ste. Genevieve reds and purples, Old Blue, Fern Glen reds and greens, and Grimes Hill. Heat treatment of local cherts to enhance color is also an important element of chert manipulation in this area, although this practice occurs elsewhere as well.

The lamellar blade tool industry seems more diverse in the American Bottom than it is to the north or south, as is the technology used to produce blades. At least five distinct blade core types have been recognized at the Dash Reeves site (Fortier 2000a), including classic examples of both Fulton and Cobden techniques, as well as local multidirectional techniques on wedges and irregular-shaped cores. At Dash Reeves, blades are made on virtually any chert type available, including coarse, nonlustrous local Salem cherts. There are a small number of obsidian blades, although given the absence of cores or debitage, it is doubtful that these were actually manufactured in the American Bottom. Blade tools are diverse, by no means restricted to simple razorlike cutting functions. Needlelike microdrills, bifacial blade drills, perforators, and gravers are among the formal types manufactured during this period (Fortier 2000b). Blades also tend to be

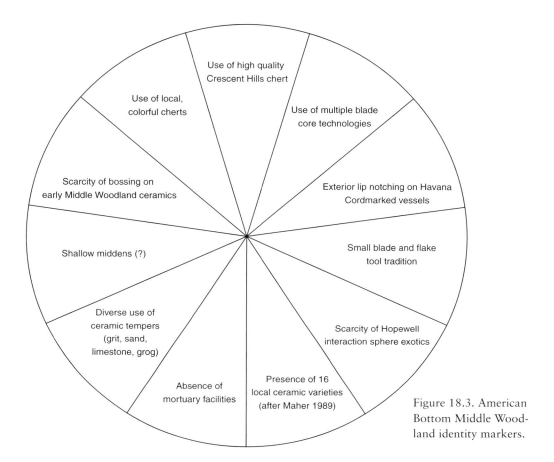

Figure 18.3. American Bottom Middle Woodland identity markers.

Labels within figure (clockwise from top):

Use of high quality Crescent Hills chert

Use of multiple blade core technologies

Exterior lip notching on Havana Cordmarked vessels

Small blade and flake tool tradition

Scarcity of Hopewell interaction sphere exotics

Presence of 16 local ceramic varieties (after Maher 1989)

Absence of mortuary facilities

Diverse use of ceramic tempers (grit, sand, limestone, grog)

Shallow middens (?)

Scarcity of bossing on early Middle Woodland ceramics

Use of local, colorful cherts

shorter than their counterparts to the north and often have unusually broad platforms. Blades occur in both village and camp contexts and constitute a multifunctional utilitarian tool industry. This is in contrast to their proposed primary uses in ceremonial contexts to the north, a proposition that probably warrants reexamination in that area.

The American Bottom is characterized by a scarcity of Middle Woodland mounds and an absence of elaborate mortuary paraphernalia. It should be pointed out, however, that earlier Munson/Harn surveys in this area identified at least fifteen possible Middle Woodland mounds in the northern American Bottom (Harn 1971:24). Unfortunately, none of these has ever been adequately examined or had its Middle Woodland affiliations confirmed. Seven of these mounds are reportedly associated with the Grassy Lake site. Later investigations by Southern Illinois University at Edwardsville at one of these mounds, however, produced evidence of much later (cal A.D. 850–900) Sponemann phase materials (Kelly 2000:152; Witty and Kelly 1993:Figure 6a). Maher (1996) also tested several possible Middle Woodland mounds (Wanda, West, and Gehring) in the area but likewise failed to confirm their Middle Woodland associations. A Hill Lake phase mortuary area was recently uncovered at the Horseshoe Lake site

(Pauketat, Rees, and Pauketat 1998). The burials were not found in mound or tomb contexts, however (T. Pauketat, personal communication, 2000). In short, there is nothing in the American Bottom that rivals the extensive mound centers of the Illinois River valley; Twenhafel or nearby village sites such as Hiser, Cleiman, Gorham, Pottery Creek, and Bunselmeyer that have from one to four associated mounds in the Jackson Bottom; or some of the larger mound groups, such as Kraske, known from the central Kaskaskia River.

According to Munson (1971:8), another distinguishing characteristic of Middle Woodland sites in the American Bottom may be the presence of shallow midden deposits. Harn (1971:27) made the same observation and further speculated that population levels were either too low in the American Bottom to sustain anything but short-term settlement or that resources were not sufficient to maintain large villages for extended periods of time. However, both models may be too simplistic and are predicated on the assumption that village middens are typically accretional in nature. In reality, at many Middle Woodland sites middens actually occur as specific dump zones—often located, for example, in natural swales or abandoned creeks adjacent to living areas. The main midden at Dash Reeves, for example, which measured 30–50 centimeters deep, was found in a creek channel (Fortier 2000a). Adjacent to this creek, materials accreted on the settlement living surface to less than 10 centimeters in depth. At the Holding site, materials were not allowed to develop to any depth in the central living area, as they were apparently swept to the edges of the occupation (Fortier et al. 1989). Some of the midden deposits excavated from Illinois River valley sites have been found in adjacent creek or swale contexts, although there are many examples of deep accretional middens in living areas as well (Stafford and Sant 1985b; Wiant and McGimsey 1986b). In short, we need to carefully distinguish between the various forms of midden debris at sites. Further study of midden forming processes is clearly needed in all areas of the state before we can assuredly say that shallow middens are an American Bottom hallmark.

The pattern of Middle Woodland mound distribution in the American Bottom parallels that of the Jackson Bottom and Crab Orchard tradition. With the notable exception of the Twenhafel complex, single mounds located in proximity to floodplain village settlements are typical. There are no known bluff-base villages with mounds situated on surrounding bluff crests in either the American Bottom or Jackson Bottom. That practice is more typical of the Illinois River valley. Whether this is a specific Crab Orchard or generic Mississippi River trench practice is unknown, but it does highlight another possible American Bottom tie to southern practice (Hofman and Morrow 1984).

In summary, it is obvious that the American Bottom does not merely represent some kind of frontier outpost of either the northern Havana/Hopewell or the southern Crab Orchard tradition. It is not clear, however, whether the sometimes subtle differences in technology, style, or mortuary programs that are recognizable in the archaeological record are significant enough to warrant the creation of a separate American Bottom Middle Woodland tradition. At the very least I would argue that the American Bottom was undergoing a transformation that was leading towards the development of its own identity. It is clear, however, that the historical processes behind this transformation were inexplicably altered, and this American Bottom identity was never fully established. It is important to observe that the differences between this area and traditions to the north and south also go far beyond the simple nuances of Struever's (1965) ceramic-based regional microstyle traditions. Clearly differences in subsistence practices, mortuary behavior, lithic technology, and so on, need to be evaluated when distinguishing between such traditions and local historical processes.

Almost from the very outset of Middle Woodland occupation of the American Bottom, certain genealogical practices or identity hallmarks were formed that made this locality unique in the Midwest. This probably occurred because the American Bottom was a geographic crossroads. It was also an unstable locality because of its susceptibility to flooding. In addition, traditions, by their natures, are not conservative entities and are subject to a constant renegotiation process (Pauketat 2001). Hopewell hegemony was probably unstable and more variable across the central Midwest than is often admitted. The efflorescence of Hopewell technological and stylistic diversity, which came into being and ultimately passed away over a three- to four-hundred-year period, was a process of renegotiated ideology and social practice that we archaeologically identify as encapsulated in material things. The actual tradition-forming historical processes of renegotiation were specifically carried out by means of staged rituals, mortuary behavior, fandango/trade fairs, giveaways, adoption ceremonies, and intermarriages. These historical processes also involved such local variables as the available natural resources, differential access to those resources, changing social relations, inventions and adaptations, and differential understanding of or access to the regional Hopewellian Zeitgeist. Historical chance may also have played a role, as occurs in the sometimes unpredictable acts of personality or human agency, or in unpredictable changes in resource availability. Each Middle Woodland locality in the Midwest essentially developed through time according to how each of these factors was renegotiated or integrated into existing local traditional practice. Each locality may have developed its own identity, involving linkage and perhaps, at times, resistance to a perceived Midwest Hopewellian cultural hegemony.

It is apparent that American Bottom populations did not participate in all Hopewellian practices, especially in the area of mortuary behavior and certain aspects of exchange. Were they merely out of the loop? Are we seeing a form of resistance to neighboring traditions with which they did not maintain close affinity? Or were ties maintained through the kinds of historical processes that leave little archaeological evidence? I have argued elsewhere (Fortier 1995, 1998; McElrath and Fortier 2000) that near the end of the Middle Woodland period the American Bottom was completely abandoned. There is, in fact, no gradual transition to Late Woodland in this locality. Late Middle Woodland and early Late Woodland settlements do not co-occur. Moreover, virtually all of the hallmarks of Middle Woodland technological, stylistic, settlement, and ideological traditions disappear by cal A.D. 350–400 and are not observable in

subsequent Late Woodland assemblages. Contact with the southern Crab Orchard tradition also ends abruptly.

McElrath and I (2000) have speculated that a probable population retreat
occurred at the end of the Middle Woodland period, upriver, to centers that were
still participating in Hopewellian ceremonialism or, perhaps, to centers that
were attempting to maintain regional social bonds in the midst of crumbling
interaction relationships. Population levels were always relatively low in the
American Bottom, so this migration may have been gradual and probably involved only a limited number of groups. Given the number of large village and
ceremonial centers in the Illinois River valley and northern Mississippi River
trench, that area no doubt served as a magnet for people living along the fringes
of those valleys. Moreover, the cultural trajectory north of the American Bottom
indicates a gradual transition from Middle Woodland to Late Woodland, more
than any other area in proximity to the American Bottom. It therefore represents
a likely reservoir for the subsequent Late Woodland repopulation of the American Bottom after cal A.D. 400.

If our migration model is correct, then relationships between the Illinois and
adjacent Mississippi valleys and the American Bottom must have been closer
during the late Middle Woodland period than the archaeological record now
reveals. This suggests that while differences in material culture may vary from
locality to locality, ideological and/or social ties or appropriational processes
(Fortier 1998) may actually have been more important in terms of how cultural
boundaries were perceived by Native Americans in the past. Finding ways of
archaeologically documenting what may amount to nonmaterial patterns of
prehistoric ethnicity, however, remains an elusive challenge.

19

Kansas City Hopewell

Middle Woodland on the Western Frontier

Brad Logan

Since first defined by Waldo Wedel (1943b), the Kansas City Hopewell culture, a Middle Woodland variant of the lower Missouri Valley, has been compared to Havana Hopewell of the lower Illinois River valley. Later investigators dated its appearance to circa A.D. 1 and attributed it to the migration of groups from the latter region (Griffin 1967:186; Johnson 1976a:12, 1979; Shippee 1967; Wedel 1943b:206). Subsequent parallel developments in ceramic and lithic technologies in the two localities through the early Late Woodland period (circa A.D. 400–600) were attributed to continued contact and information exchange (Chapman 1980; Johnson 1976a, 1979, 1992). Recently, O'Brien and Wood (1998) discounted the development of Kansas City Hopewell in terms of this historical, as opposed to adaptive, process. They interpret the complex as the result of increased social interaction among indigenous, increasingly sedentary groups along the Missouri River and the sharing of widely recognized "information laden symbols," particularly with regard to ceramic motifs (O'Brien and Wood 1998:219–221). This supralocal communication is seen as an attempt to mitigate risks, such as periodic food shortages, inherent in hunter-gatherer-gardener adaptations to the physical environment. The roots of this process lay in horticultural experimentation through the Archaic and Early Woodland periods that, in the Midwest, reached a critical threshold with regard to various demographic or environmental factors circa 200 B.C. (Braun 1986, 1987; Braun and Plog 1982; Brown 1985; O'Brien 1987).

It is apparent that Kansas City Hopewell was an adaptation to a local physical and social environment different from that of the Havana Hopewell in some respects but one that, like the latter, exemplified variations in a broadly similar pattern of Middle Woodland adaptive responses to the Prairie Peninsula (Brown 1991:206–210). For example, the importance of large valley backwater/wetland habitats to Hopewell subsistence and settlement is evident in both regions. It is not yet clear, however, that the preceding Late Archaic and Early Woodland adaptations in the Kansas City locality, as yet poorly understood, were essential precursors of an indigenous Middle Woodland development like that in the lower Illinois Valley (Johnson 1992; Johnson and Johnson 1998:201–203).

While not yet fully understood, the distinctions and similarities between Havana, seen as a core Hopewell manifestation (Braun 1986), and Kansas City, perceived as peripheral to it (O'Brien and Wood 1998:221), are critical to explaining Middle Woodland development as a whole. Previous researchers have either viewed Kansas City Hopewell locally, emphasizing its settlement-subsistence system with regard to its physical milieu (Johnson 1976a, 1979; Reid 1980), or extralocally, as an imitative but indigenous expression of a broader development initiated elsewhere (Braun 1986; Braun and Plog 1982; O'Brien and Wood 1998). A key difference between these views regards the origin of Middle Woodland in the Kansas City locality: one accepts the seemingly simplistic cause of migration and subsequent local adaptation, while the other dismisses migration and attributes the appearance of Middle Woodland to the "radiation" (Braun 1987:172) of a systemic set of responses to resource productivity, flexibility, and risk management with its own internal dynamic. In this chapter I will critique aspects of both the local and the extralocal view in the light of current data from the lower Missouri Valley.

Origins

O'Brien and Wood (1998:198–199) discount the immigration of a Havana tradition population from the lower Illinois Valley as the origin of Kansas City Hopewell, as well as that of two comparable Middle Woodland complexes in central Missouri: the Big Bend and Lamine localities (Kay 1979; Kay and Johnson 1977). Instead they offer three alternatives to explain similarities in (exclusively ceramic) traits between these regions: intraregional trade, diffusion of technical knowledge, and independent invention. The last explanation is rightly eliminated as highly improbable given the similarity in ceramic decorative motifs that are occasionally quite elaborate. The first alternative is eliminated on the grounds of some dissimilarity in decorative motifs and a difference in paste that points to local ceramic production. In accepting the second alternative, they suggest that "the evidence, at least in the case of Havana decoration, strongly supports imitation over either of the other(s)" (O'Brien and Wood 1998:199). Such imitation is explained, following the argument of Braun (1986) and Braun and Plog (1982), as the result of "continuously increasing social interaction among large numbers of similarly organized or 'peer' local residential aggregates, across several ecologically similar regions" (Braun 1986:186, cited in O'Brien and Wood 1998:221). This adaptive argument is more broadly expressed in a precedent concept proposed by Brown (1991:191–192), who recognized a "Prairie Peninsula interaction sphere . . . an area in which societies at different levels of adaptation have an organized means of social and cultural accommodation to each other."

Dismissal of migration as a viable hypothesis to explain Kansas City Hopewell is premature. It cannot be refuted simply because it invokes a historic process not currently in vogue among archaeologists (for example, Brown 1991: 20–21; compare Anthony 1990, 1997). At present, we do not have sufficient data ("facts") for adequate testing, particularly with regard to the critical Early Woodland period in the Kansas City locality.

O'Brien and Wood (1998:221) note that there is "no evidence of Hopewellians moving up the Missouri River to form colonies in Saline and Cooper Counties or farther west in the Kansas City area." The absence of intervening settlements might be explained by the lack of preferred terrain, such as lowland terraces in proximity to wetland habitats that were well stocked with fish during times of flood, or to a general lack of survey data pertaining to upland settings that might contain transient camps (James Brown, personal communication, 2000; compare Brown 1991:61, 80–81). It might also reflect a "chain migration" pattern, in which migrants follow earlier migrants to a specific locale, leapfrogging intervening areas that are unfamiliar (Anthony 1997:26). In this case, the paltry evidence of Early Woodland culture in the Kansas City locality, the ceramics of which are comparable to the Black Sand pottery of the Illinois River valley, may be testimony to a pioneer migration followed by a more substantial wave of migrants circa A.D. 1. As is discussed later, however, there remains a substantial temporal gap between Early and Middle Woodland manifestations in the Kansas City area.

The comparison of Middle Woodland manifestations in the Kansas City area and west-central Illinois by O'Brien and Wood (1998) is restricted to ceramics, the similarities and differences of which can as easily be attributed to migration and culture drift (compare Brockington 1977). Mortuary practices among Middle Woodland groups in Missouri are examined in the context of risk management via the control of access to goods and whether this is reflected in the differential treatment of the dead (that is, ascribed versus achieved status). They do not account for the appearance in the Kansas City locality circa A.D. 1 of a Middle Woodland complex that consists of a developed suite of "Hopewellian" traits that have no documented local precedents: mound burial; prolonged residence of base-camp settlements; significant use of native domesticate plants; embossed and dentate stamped decorative treatment of large, conical based vessels; a lithic assemblage that contains corner-notched dart points of the Norton, Manker, and Steuben types, as well as circular and blocky scrapers; and a worked bone assemblage that includes turkey bone awls and antler tine tools. Some of these traits have clear antecedents in the lower Illinois Valley; with the exception of corner-notched points (for example, at the DB site [Hatfield 1998; Logan 1998b]), none has yet been recorded at any Late Archaic or Early Woodland site in the Kansas City locality.

If "supralocal communication" with Middle Woodland groups in the Havana tradition area was of importance to the Kansas City Hopewell, then we might expect some expression of this in the form of Hopewell Interaction Sphere goods. Yet exotic items indicative of this exchange are rare in the Kansas City locality, and most have been recovered from nonmortuary contexts, in contrast to their frequent inclusion as grave goods in the Hopewell core areas (Johnson 1979; Struever 1964; Struever and Houart 1972). Recent investigations, particularly excavations at the Quarry Creek site (see below), have not significantly

Figure 19.1. Interaction sphere–like artifacts from the Quarry Creek site. *Top row, left to right*: top, bottom, and oral views of pipe fragment from the midden above the pit features shown in figure 19.6; *bottom row*: miniature copper celt from the large pit shown in figure 19.6. Scale bar is 3 centimeters long.

augmented the number of interaction sphere artifacts from Kansas City Hopewell sites described a generation ago (Johnson 1979). They include a platform pipe fragment that appears to be made of local paste and a miniature copper celt (fig. 19.1). Only two other examples of the latter are known from the region, both from the Renner site (Shippee 1967:Figure 51; Wedel 1943b:49, Plate 11). Chapman (1980:44) illustrates another from a Wakenda phase (central Missouri) site, perhaps reflecting the occasional movement of these items up the Missouri River from Illinois. From the perspective of archaeologists working in the Hopewell core areas, Middle Woodland populations in the Kansas City locality appear peripheral to the interaction sphere. Alternatively, however, they can be seen as independent of the core area, reflecting their purposeful separation from the Havana tradition.

Recognizing the potential pitfalls of the antiquated "trait-listing" approach (wherein, for example, settlement patterns are weighted equally with turkey bone awls), I consider the contrast between the Kansas City Hopewell variant and those of its local predecessors as too compelling at this time to discount the migration hypothesis. Instead, the comparison is consistent with the identification of the variant as a "site unit intrusion" (Willey et al. 1956), a concept still useful for identifying archaeological manifestations of immigrant groups (compare Logan 1998a; Ritterbush and Logan 2000). It is possible that the contrast is more apparent than real because we have virtually no evidence of any residents in the Kansas City locality for a period of 100–200 years prior to the appearance of the Middle Woodland population. The few reliably radiocarbon dated Early Woodland sites in the area (Logan 1990:105; Schmits 1989:227–228) indicate a hiatus from 250 B.C. to A.D. 50 (based on a one sigma range of ≤100 years), with the generally accepted origin of Kansas City Hopewell circa A.D. 1. Even given a local Woodland population during that time, support for the "regional interaction for risk management" hypothesis of Middle Woodland origin still requires evidence of increasing reliance on horticulture. Such a trend is considered necessary, if not sufficient, for the development of Hopewell adaptations in the core areas of Illinois and Ohio (Braun 1987). At present, remains of native cultigens in the floral assemblages from Early Woodland sites in the Kansas City locality are scant (Adair 2000b).

The contrast between the different views on the origin of Kansas City Hopewell may reflect our tendency to dichotomize interpretive approaches. Other than the perception that historical hypotheses such as migration are considered descriptive rather than analytical (Brown 1991:20), there is no reason to consider historical and adaptive interpretations as exclusive. There are many historic accounts of migration in the Prairie Peninsula (for example, Bauxar 1978), and while many are attributable to the influence of the fur trade or dislocations directly or indirectly caused by Euro-American expansion, it is unlikely that these are the only instances since its peopling during the Paleoindian period. Indeed, at least one example of a significant movement of populations in the Prairie Peninsula during the Late Prehistoric period is represented by the rapid Oneota expansion in the thirteenth century A.D. throughout that region and into the Central Plains (Boszhardt 1998b; Fishel 1999; Henning 1998; Logan 1998a; Ritterbush and Logan 2000). Thus, what appear to be mutually exclusive hypotheses might be complementary if we posit the following to explain Kansas City Hopewell: fissioning of an expanding population in the lower Illinois locality, chain migration of the daughter group via the Missouri Valley to the Kansas City locality, and subsequent maintenance of ties with the parent group for the reasons suggested by Braun (1986, 1987; Braun and Plog 1982; compare Johnson 1992:134).

Settlement-Subsistence Pattern Models

In the 1960s and 1970s, archaeologists from the University of Kansas conducted extensive investigations at Hopewell sites in the Kansas City locality (Johnson 1974, 1976a, 1976b, 1979, 1981). All focused on villages and camps and provided the basis for the settlement-subsistence pattern models discussed here. Although several bluff-top burial mounds have been excavated (Larsen and O'Brien 1973; Shippee 1967; Tjaden 1974; Wedel 1943b, 1959), it is notable that Kansas City Hopewell sites do not include ritual camps like Napoleon Hollow in the Illinois River valley (Wiant and McGimsey 1986b). Most of these sites excavated by the University of Kansas were located in Platte County, Missouri, particularly along Brush Creek (fig. 19.2). The results of these investigations, in conjunction with the earlier works of Wedel and others, provided the basis for Johnson's (1976a, 1981) model of the Kansas City Hopewell settle-

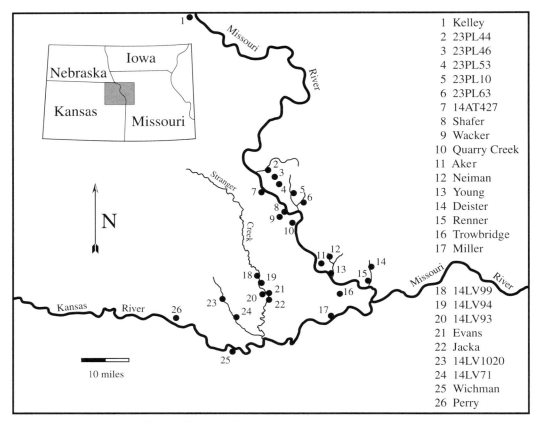

Figure 19.2. Map of Middle Woodland settlement sites in the Kansas City locality.

ment-subsistence system. The model was derived from sixteen Hopewell sites in Missouri but only two in Kansas: Trowbridge (Bell 1976; Johnson 1976a) and Kelley (Katz 1969). As a result, little was known about this Middle Woodland variant on the western side of the Missouri River. Data from more recent excavations at the Quarry Creek and McPherson sites on the Fort Leavenworth reservation; review of other, long neglected sites in nearby Salt Creek valley (Witty and Marshall 1968); and information from surveys in Stranger Creek valley now permit revision of the Kansas City Hopewell settlement-subsistence models and the correction of earlier views about the nature and extent of the Hopewell cultural manifestation in Kansas.

The Johnson Model

Johnson's (1976a) model posits the initial establishment of large villages at the mouths of Missouri River tributaries, such as Renner at Line Creek and Young at Brush Creek, circa A.D. 1. Responses to population expansion by about A.D. 250 included settlement of villages in similar settings northward along the Missouri River and of ancillary camps upstream along its tributaries. The latter were short-term satellites that facilitated the acquisition and processing of foodstuffs to sustain permanent villages at the tributary mouths. By A.D. 500, population pressure on resources exceeded the critical maintenance threshold of the permanent village–ancillary camp system; the response was a shift to occupation of smaller, seasonal settlements.

Johnson recognizes four plant communities as critical to Hopewell settlement: (1) the Missouri Valley floodplain forest, (2) the oak-hickory forest along the bluffs lining the valley, (3) an open woodland zone beyond the bluffs, and (4) tall-grass prairie in the higher uplands. Tributary valleys crosscut these zones, facilitating their exploitation, and led to the location of satellite camps near their headwaters. Floral and faunal remains from sites including Renner, Deister, Young, and Trowbridge indicate that resources of the oak-hickory woodlands figured prominently in Hopewell subsistence and settlement decision making. Noting the few Hopewell sites then known west of the Missouri River as compared to their apparent concentration along tributaries on the eastern side, Johnson (1976a) attributed the contrast to the effect of fires, driven by prevailing southwestern winds, which diminished the extent of oak-hickory woodlands in that area.

The Reid Model

Reid (1980) also emphasized the importance of oak-hickory woodland resources to the Kansas City Hopewell. He noted in particular the low proportion of aquatic resources in faunal assemblages from sites such as Trowbridge and Young and their much higher frequency in assemblages from Havana Hopewell sites in Illinois. The slight contribution of aquatic resources to the Kansas City Hopewell economy reflected the fickle nature of Missouri River meanders, the effect of the river's high turbidity on various animals, and the short life span of backwater niches. Reid's conclusion regarding Hopewell adaptations in the Kansas City locality emphasized socioeconomic, rather than ecological, factors. Despite this, he invoked perceived environmental constraints to explain a contrast in subsistence practices between Kansas City and Havana Hopewell.

Kansas City Hopewell: A View from the Kansas Side

Trowbridge (figs. 19.2, 19.3), a 20,000-square-meter Hopewell settlement in Wyandotte County, Kansas, has long appeared anomalous with regard to its physical setting. It is located within the oak-hickory upland forest a short distance from the Kansas and Missouri rivers, at the junction of two spring-fed tributaries of Brenner Heights Creek, a Missouri River confluent (Bell 1976:17). Johnson (1976a:9) suggested that the Kansas River was a natural barrier for the site against periodic fires that elsewhere in Kansas restricted oak-hickory habitat and Hopewell settlement. Reid (1980:41) believed that Trowbridge reflected unique logistical concerns of resource procurement that overrode those more typical of tributary valley settings at villages such as Renner and Young. The resources of its inter-river woodland setting were as easily exploited from its location on south and west bluff slopes.

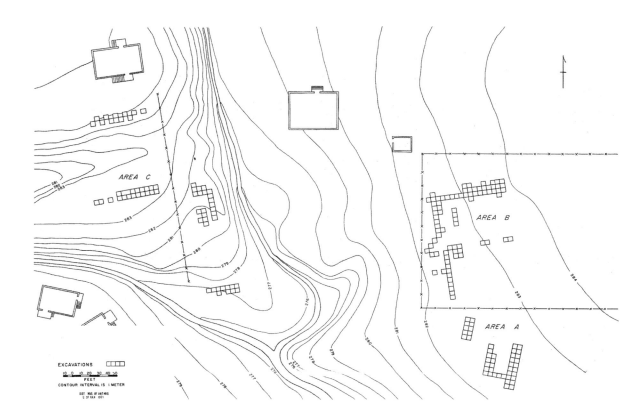

Figure 19.3. Map of the Trowbridge (14WY1) site on Brenner Heights Creek (University of Kansas, Museum of Anthropology Archives). Note the location of Areas A–C with respect to the stream and compare with figure 19.5.

In fact, Trowbridge appeared anomalous only because so little was known about Hopewell sites west of the Missouri River, contrary to Johnson's (1976a:8) suggestion that the contrast between the two sides of the trench could not be attributed to survey bias. Much of what we know about Kansas City Hopewell from Missouri sites comes from the unsystematic surveys of J. Mett Shippee and R. B. Aker, avocational archaeologists who focused on the eastern side of the valley between Kansas City and St. Joseph. Aker (personal communication 1991), in particular, was quite candid about his preference for surveys in Platte County, Missouri.

In reality, Kansas has more Hopewell sites than are generally appreciated. Sites there fall into three general stream settings: (1) the western loess bluffs of the lower Missouri Valley and its tributaries, (2) Stranger Creek basin, and (3) the Kansas River valley westward as far as the mouth of the Delaware River.

Western Loess Bluffs and Tributaries

The western loess bluffs and tributaries is that region of oak-hickory woodland northward from the confluence of the Kansas and Missouri rivers to the Kansas-

Nebraska border. The Trowbridge and Kelley sites approximate the region's southern and northern limits respectively. Though the area between them has not been systematically explored, investigations near the center of this reach reveal its potential for Hopewell research.

Oak-hickory woodland, which figured prominently in Hopewell subsistence and settlement, was not as restricted in this area as Johnson (1976b) suggested. Kuchler (1974), in his map of the natural potential vegetation of Kansas (generally applicable to the region throughout post-Hypsithermal time), delineates a substantial belt of this community along the Missouri River valley (fig. 19.4). The distribution of soil types, whose profiles record their formation under prairie or woodland vegetation, also shows the prevalence of the latter community

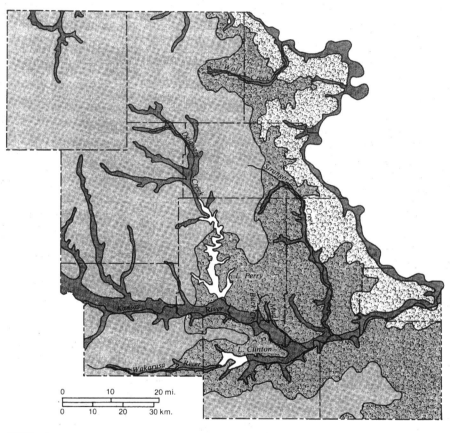

Bluestem prairie (*Andropogon—Panicum—Sorghastrum*).

Oak-hickory forest (*Quercus—Carya*).

Mosaic of bluestem prairie and oak-hickory forest.

Forest-savanna (*Populus—Salix*) and freshwater marsh (*Spartina*).

Figure 19.4. Natural potential vegetation of northeastern Kansas (based on Kuchler 1974).

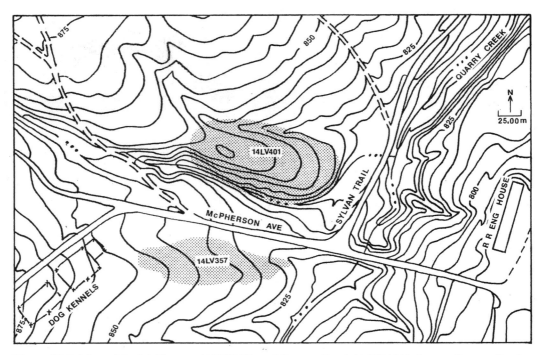

Figure 19.5. Map of the McPherson (14LV357) and Quarry Creek (14LV401) sites on Quarry Creek (from Logan 1993).

west of the Missouri River. For example, the soils of Leavenworth County, Kansas, suggest a prairie-woodland ecotone that would have supported a Hopewellian population (Logan 1985:75–80). Similarly, log data from the 1830 survey of the Delaware-Kickapoo reservation boundary, which provides a transect from the Missouri River to the Delaware River, shows extensive bluff-top hardwood and floodplain forest communities (Logan 1985; compare Asch and Asch 1986:430 for the application of similar survey data to the Middle Woodland as first-order approximations of past vegetation).

Several Hopewell sites have been recorded in Leavenworth County, particularly in the Salt Creek drainage and on the adjacent Fort Leavenworth reservation. The most extensively investigated sites here are Quarry Creek and McPherson, situated on terraces opposite each other along a spring-fed stream (figs. 19.2, 19.5). Both sites, recorded separately yet containing comparable Hopewell components, should be considered as one, referred to hereafter as Quarry Creek. Together they cover more than 20,000 square meters. As the most recently and systematically excavated Middle Woodland site in the Kansas City locality, Quarry Creek warrants summary discussion.

Quarry Creek

In 1988, archaeologists from American Resources Group excavated units totaling 7 square meters in what was the McPherson component, revealing one pit feature and several artifacts indicative of Kansas City Hopewell occupation (Wagner et al. 1989). In 1991, the Kansas Archaeological Field School excavated test units and a trench that totaled 33 square meters in the original Quarry Creek component (Logan 1993). The excavations revealed six trash-filled pit features, four within a 4-square-meter area (fig. 19.6), suggesting a relatively high density of storage facilities and a correspondingly prolonged occupation. A series of relatively undisturbed middens (fig. 19.7) also yielded a varied and abundant cultural assemblage, including a large, well-preserved faunal sample that reflects exploitation of woodland-riverine resources.

Four radiocarbon assays date Quarry Creek circa A.D. 210–540, again suggesting prolonged occupation (Logan 1993:184–188). Other temporal data support this range, including the relative frequencies of ceramics ($n = 99$; Cook 1993) of the three phases of Kansas City Hopewell: Trowbridge (circa A.D. 1–250), Kansas City (circa A.D. 250–400), and Edwardsville (circa A.D. 400–600) (Johnson 2001; compare Logan 1993:184–188). The low number ($n = 3$) of rims of Trowbridge phase ware (decorated with bosses and cord-wrapped stick, dentate, or plain stick impressions) is consistent with the beginning of the radiometric range. The even proportion of rims of Kansas City phase ($n = 48$; crosshatching or rocker marks and punctates; that is, Chapman's [1980] Renner Crosshatched) and Edwardsville phase rims ($n = 46$; rims crenelated or lacking

Figure 19.6. Concentration of pit features in 4-square-meter area below midden at the Quarry Creek site (from Logan 1993).

Figure 19.7. View of the Quarry Creek site during the 1991 Kansas Archaeological Field School excavation (from Logan 1993). The low mound in the background, which counters the natural gradient of the terrain, is one of a series of middens. The features shown in figure 19.6 are by the seated people to the right.

decorative treatment) suggests that the Quarry Creek occupation spanned at least parts of both phases. Absence from the projectile point/knife assemblage (*n* = 45) of both Snyders dart points/knives and Scallorn arrow points, the former diagnostic of the Trowbridge phase and the latter postdating A.D. 500 in the region (Johnson 1974, 1976b), is also consistent with the radiocarbon range (Raymond, Rothman, and Logan 1993:141).

In its topographic setting, its spatial extent, and the nature of its deposits, Quarry Creek is like Trowbridge. Both are near spring-fed streams that feed minor tributaries of the Missouri River, and both offer easy access to Missouri Valley floodplain resources. Despite the terrace setting of Quarry Creek, both are accurately described as being in an "upland" context in that they are not in the immediate vicinity of a navigable tributary. Trowbridge is 6 kilometers from the Kansas and Missouri rivers, Quarry Creek just 1 kilometer from the latter. Quarry Creek, 21.5 meters above the Missouri River floodplain, was secure during times of flood and, as we will see, within a short distance of upland and lowland habitats with varied resources.

Salt Creek Valley Sites

Hopewell sites were recorded in the lower Salt Creek valley during a brief survey by archaeologists from the Kansas State Historical Society in 1966 (Witty and Marshall 1968). The goal of that survey was to discover Fort Cavignial, an eighteenth-century French fur-trading post recorded by such Missouri River explorers as Stephen Long, Meriwether Lewis, and William Clark. Prehistoric sites were recorded incidentally, and only a few were tested—including the Wacker sites (14LV301 and 14LV302) and Shafer (14LV316), all near the confluence of Salt Creek and Plum Creek (fig. 19.2).

The Wacker sites are on a bluff slope overlooking Plum Creek and on the summit of the ridge above it. Limited excavations at both locations yielded small samples of Middle Woodland ceramic and lithic material (Witty and Marshall 1968:18–25). More intriguing is Shafer, evidence of which is limited to that portion of it exposed along a cut bank of Plum Creek (Witty and Marshall 1968:41–44). Material recovered includes a large vessel fragment of Renner Crosshatched ware and other Hopewell sherds, a few chipped stone tools and pieces of debitage, and a small sample of deer bone. These artifacts, primarily from a pit feature, were found at a depth of 3 meters in what appears to be a buried soil. The excavators did not fully appreciate the significance of its deep burial below the shared floodplain of the Salt Creek and Missouri River valleys. It is in just such a setting that Johnson (1976b) predicts the location of a Hopewell base camp. Since Hopewell people are not known to have used isolated storage pits, it is likely that the portion of the Shafer site exposed in 1966 is but a fraction of a much richer deposit. Shafer points to the potential for other buried Hopewell settlements in similar contexts along both sides of the trench.

The Salt Creek–Fort Leavenworth area offered easy access to resources in a variety of communities, including floodplain woodlands, grasslands, and wetlands and upland hardwoods and prairie (fig. 19.8). Historical documents from this area provide analogs for the Middle Woodland period that dispute Reid's (1980) assertion of the relative unimportance of aquatic habitats in the Missouri Valley. As noted earlier, Reid suggested that the river too frequently erased backwater or other wetland niches, limiting any contribution of their animal resources to Hopewell subsistence. Today, the Missouri River here forms a conspicuous meander called the Weston Bend, named for the river town on the Missouri side opposite Kickapoo Island. It is now fixed to some extent by levees and the effects of post–World War II dam construction upstream. However, maps predating that construction show no significant change in the meander except for the presence of Kickapoo Island near Salt Creek. The 1948 USGS topographic quadrangle shows that the northern branch of the river that had defined this "island" was abandoned by that date but that its general configuration had otherwise not changed from its depiction on an 1854 map of the military reservation (fig. 19.9).

The general configuration of the Weston Bend noted above also appears on several late eighteenth- and early to mid nineteenth-century maps. All show a large island on the northern portion of the meander, a broad eastward bend, and a rather sharp southward turn at the confluence of Quarry Creek. A generalized depiction of the meander appears on the Indian Office map of 1797, attributed to the surveyor John Evans and used by Lewis and Clark during their ascent of the Missouri River with the Corps of Discovery in 1804–1806 (Moulton

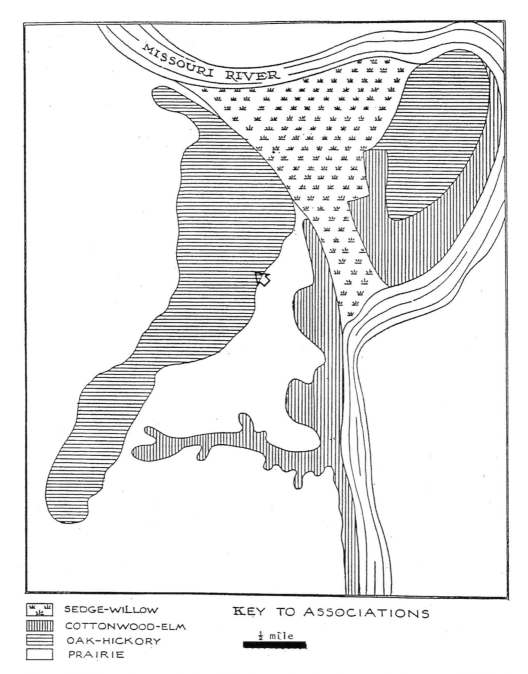

KEY TO ASSOCIATIONS

SEDGE-WILLOW	
COTTONWOOD-ELM	
OAK-HICKORY	
PRAIRIE	

½ mile

Figure 19.8. Vegetation associations of the Quarry Creek catchment (site is at arrow tip). Modified from Brumwell 1941.

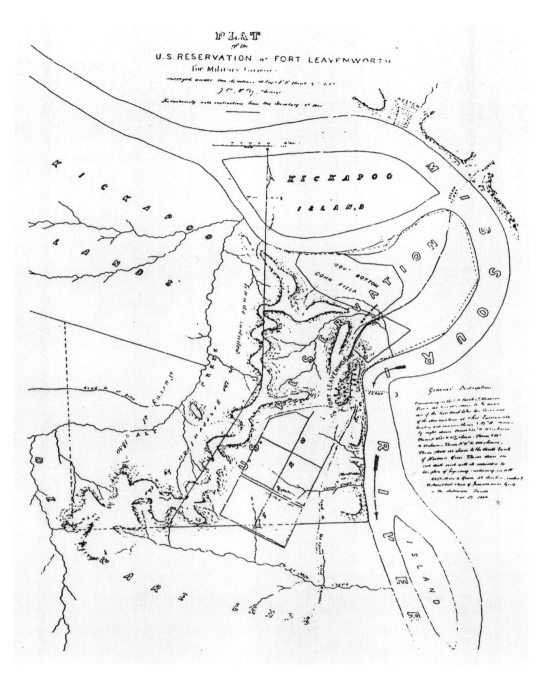

Figure 19.9. The Weston Bend of the Missouri River on the 1854 plat of Fort Leavenworth (Fortifications Map File, Drawer 131, Sheet 8; Records of the Office of the Chief of Engineers, Record Group 77; National Archives, Washington, D.C.).

1983:Map 5). A more detailed map of the Fort Leavenworth area later made by Clark was among the twelve sheets, now lost, that covered that part of their journey from Camp Dubois, on the Illinois side of the Mississippi River, to Camp White Catfish, above the mouth of the Platte River (Moulton 1983:7). Still, Clark's compass bearings in his field notes for July 2, 1804, the day the corps navigated this meander (see Moulton 1986:341–343), even given the difference in declinations used then and now, describe the meander much as it is shown on later nineteenth-century maps (that is, from N 10° W to N 34° E, passing what Clark called Turkey Creek, now believed to be Corral Creek, about 2 kilometers south of the Quarry Creek confluence; thence N 10° W to N 46° W, passing the lower end of Kickapoo Island, then called "Wau-car-ba war-canda-da or Bear Medesin [sic] Island"). The meander appears on the map of the Delaware and Ottawa lands surveyed in 1830 and 1832 by Isaac and R. McCoy (Kansas State Historical Society archives, see Logan 1985:108), on Nicollet's map of 1842 based on surveys (particularly those of John C. Fremont) in 1836–1840 (Nicollet 1976), on the Fremont-Gibbs-Smith map that is based on a "Fremont" printed map of 1845 (Barry 1972:131, 197, 604; Morgan and Wheat 1954), on Hutawa's map of 1842 (Barry 1972:408), on the map of Captain L. C. Easton based on his 1849 exploration (Easton 1953), and on the Gunneson-Preuss map based on the Stansbury expedition that same year (reproduced in Barry 1972:819).

The most striking evidence of the stability of the Weston Bend is its sharp southward turn at the confluence of Quarry Creek, shown on the Indian Office map and described in the first pair of Clark's compass bearings. This distinctive bend is shown in detail on an 1875 map of Fort Leavenworth (fig. 19.10) that shows Quarry Creek draining a marshy portion of the Missouri River floodplain through a series of distributaries. That occupants of the Quarry Creek site targeted such a wetland habitat is evident in the remains of various aquatic and marshland animals in its faunal assemblage (Logan and Banks 1993). Comparable habitats may have been available at oxbows like Mud Lake, just southeast of the Quarry Creek confluence and on the opposite side of the Missouri River.

The Missouri River in the Kansas City locality has often coursed its floodplain, creating and destroying islands like Kickapoo and making sloughs like Mud Lake (Moulton 1986:336–354, particularly editor's notes). While geomorphological research is needed to determine whether Weston Bend, or something like it, existed in Middle Woodland times, the historical evidence of its persistence and its associated wetland habitats suggests that the Missouri Valley could have offered important resources for a resident Hopewell population.

The contrast in the relative frequencies of wetland resources versus woodland and edge game (for example, deer, raccoon, and turkey) between Kansas City Hopewell faunal assemblages and those of the lower Illinois Valley may reflect relative population densities in those regions. Greater population pressure on other game along the lower Illinois River may have encouraged greater reliance on aquatic and other lowland animals. This inference requires careful analysis in the light of at least one relatively low estimate of population density

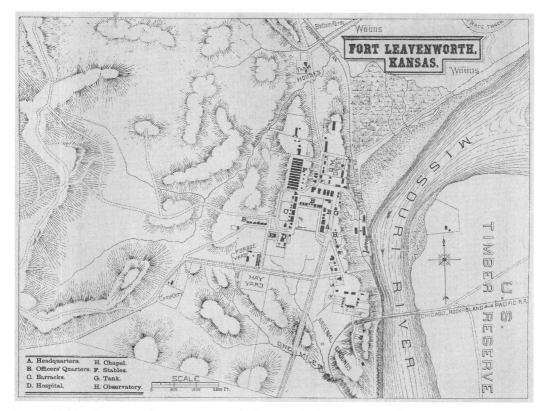

Figure 19.10. 1875 map of Fort Leavenworth showing the lower portion of Weston Bend and Quarry Creek (Kansas State Historical Society).

in the lower Illinois Valley. Asch (1976) suggests a density of only 1.6 persons per square mile on the basis of mortuary data. This estimate, however, may be misleading given the concentrated nature of populations suggested by extensive base camps such as Apple Creek in that region. Parmalee, Paloumpis, and Wilson (1972:59) note that even occupation of a settlement such as Apple Creek by no more than 100 persons could have significantly impacted the local deer population, requiring reliance on other game and occasional moves to other localities. Perceptions of "crowding" and resource depletion may have contributed to decisions regarding group fissioning. Such factors are also more consistent with Reid's assertion that socioeconomic factors, rather than ecological ones, account for general Late Holocene adaptations in either locality.

Kansas River and Stranger Creek Sites

Kansas City Hopewell sites are known west of the Missouri River trench (fig. 19.2), though few have been excavated. The westernmost sites are on the Newman Terrace in the Kansas River valley: one near the mouth of the Delaware River (Perry, 14JF314) and another near the mouth of the Wakarusa River

(Wichman, 14DO1). Their large valley locations suggest a strategy for the exploitation of riverine resources. Certainly, the Kansas River valley setting would have facilitated transportation and communication among local populations. Interestingly, extensive surveys and excavations of Woodland sites in the Delaware and Wakarusa river valleys have not recorded any significant evidence of Hopewell activity. For example, no Middle Woodland sites have been recorded at Clinton Lake on the Wakarusa River (Logan 1987). Of 115 Woodland sites at Perry Lake on the Delaware River, only one has yielded Hopewell pottery (Schmits 1987:207; Witty 1983:206–209). Unless valley aggradation has buried sites below the reach of agricultural disturbance and archaeological surface survey and testing, we can assume that the base settlement–satellite camp model described by Johnson (1976a) does not apply to the Kansas valley sites. It is not clear whether this dearth of Hopewell material reflects temporal differences or differences in resource/habitat distribution.

There are eight known Kansas City Hopewell sites in Stranger Creek basin, east of the Delaware Valley. The last major tributary of the Kansas River before its confluence with the Missouri River, Stranger Creek shares its eastern divide with Salt Creek and other west-bank tributaries of the Missouri. It would have offered to Middle Woodland residents of the Missouri tributaries access to what may have been the westernmost extent of the oak-hickory community (fig. 19.4). Of the sites in this watershed, five are along the trunk stream, and the balance are along its tributaries (Logan 1981, 1985, 2004). Evans (14LV1079) and Jacka (14LV1080), the most recently recorded of these sites, exemplify site burial below the Holliday Terrace in that valley. Here, recent scouring of the floodplain has exposed abundant lithic and ceramic artifacts of Middle Woodland age (Logan 2004). Evans and Jacka, like the Shafer site, attest to the need for geoarchaeological investigation for better delimitation of the distribution of Middle Woodland sites in the Kansas City locality.

With the exception of the Schultz "phase," a geographically disjunct and poorly understood complex in the vicinity of Manhattan and Junction City that has Hopewellian overtones, particularly with regard to mortuary features and their associated artifacts (Eyman 1966; O'Brien 1972; O'Brien et al. 1979; O'Brien, Larsen et al. 1973; Parks 1978; Schultz and Spaulding 1948), the geographic distribution of Middle Woodland sites in northeastern Kansas closely correlates with that of the oak/hickory–tall grass ecotone. This probably reflects the importance of woodland-riverine resources to the subsistence system of Kansas City Hopewell populations.

An appreciation for the contrast between the woodlands along the Missouri River and the tall-grass prairie west of the Stranger Creek divide can be gained by reading the accounts of presettlement Euro-American visitors to the region (Logan 1985). For example, in 1723, Etienne Véniard de Bourgmont, accompanying the Kansa westward from their Missouri River village on a bison hunt, described the "beautiful prairie," spotted with "some clumps of trees . . . from time to time" along the upper portion of Stranger Creek (Margry 1886:411–

412). In 1846, Francis Parkman (1946:24) struck out westward from Fort Leavenworth on the Oregon Trail and described "prairies as green as an emerald, expanding before us mile after mile, wider and more wild than the wastes Mazeppa rode over." Thirteen years later, Horace Greeley (1963:37–38) described the bluffs along Stranger Creek as "generally timbered with oak, etc." and that as "we pass[ed] out of the valley . . . rising to the slightly rolling prairie, and henceforth for forty miles to Topeka our way lies generally through a gently heaving sea of grass, with timber generally visible along the watercourses on either side." Just as these travelers from a woodland environment were struck by the expanse of tall-grass prairie beyond Stranger Creek, so must have been their woodland-adapted Hopewell predecessors. It appears that Hopewell groups in the latter region chose not to venture far beyond the oak-hickory community.

Conclusion

In sum, there is no support for the hypothesis that Kansas City Hopewell was an indigenous development in response to risk management in "imitation" of comparable adaptations in the lower Illinois River valley. While this premise is viable on logical grounds, there is no evidence of any immediate Early Woodland precursor from which the variant could have been derived. That Kansas City Hopewell developed from Middle Woodland migrants from the lower Illinois Valley Havana tradition remains a viable interpretation, given the current status of Kansas City Hopewell as a "unit intrusive" (Lathrap 1956) phenomenon. While these hypotheses are exclusive with regard to Kansas City Hopewell origins, they may apply in a complementary fashion to explain the adaptive process of that variant. Maintenance of regional interaction between a migrant, daughter group in the Kansas City locality and a parent population in the lower Illinois Valley may have followed the "risk management" scenario.

The Missouri and Kansas valleys were the focus of major Hopewell settlements. Large settlements were at the mouths of tributaries and in certain upland settings. While well-known sites like Renner and Young are on terraces, the location of the Shafer site suggests that some extensive settlements may be buried below floodplains and alluvial fans beyond the reach of surface surveys. The existence of Quarry Creek indicates that Trowbridge was not a singular exception to Johnson's model of tributary villages and village-satellites. Its presence in a setting less targeted by traditional archaeological surveys in this region, which generally focus on larger tributary valleys, suggests that additional sites may be found in other low-order drainages. Our understanding of Hopewell settlement along the lower Missouri Valley is constrained by the limited nature of past surveys, the fortuitous discoveries of some sites, and the lack of geoarchaeological investigations in the valley itself. Large valleys contained relatively stable backwater niches that supplemented Hopewell subsistence economies with varied aquatic and marshland resources. The western boundary of Kansas City Hopewell was near the mouths of the Delaware and Wakarusa rivers. The close correlation between the distribution of sites and the oak/hickory–tall grass eco-tone reflects the importance of woodland-riverine resources to Middle Wood-land populations.

Despite a solid foundation of understanding about Middle Woodland adap-tations in the Kansas City region, much remains unknown. Rapid Euro-Ameri-can settlement of the lower Missouri Valley in the nineteenth century led to the discovery of its prehistoric sites. Purposeful but unsystematic surveys by a few avocational archaeologists in the first half of the twentieth century increased the site inventory and led to recognition of Kansas City Hopewell. Since 1937, limited surveys and the few extensive excavations of a handful of professionals have increased our understanding of the variant. However, recent work on the western side of the Missouri River has shown that the Kansas City locality is still a frontier ripe for the archaeological exploration of Middle Woodland.

Section 3

New Approaches
to Hopewell Material Culture

The third section comprises a set of chapters (20–26) that reflect new or refined approaches to the material culture of Hopewell. While many of these chapters (Burks and Pederson; Van Nest; Fie; Holt; Hall) tend to focus on a single region or even a site, the questions they ask or the techniques employed have relevance in the larger domain. Other chapters (Hughes; Brown) address the Hopewell world as a whole. The materials studied and the approaches employed vary greatly, but as such they represent the array of opportunities still open to productive research.

What is most striking about this section is the range of approaches employed. Several chapters explore traditional material categories—lithics (Hughes), ceramics (Fie), and fauna (Holt)—but with a sophistication of methods or models that greatly expands our understanding of Hopewellian dynamics. This is particularly the case with Burks and Pederson's analysis of debris at the Hopewell Mound Group and Van Nest's exploration of burial mound composition and location in the lower Illinois Valley. As has long been the case, Robert L. Hall and James A. Brown are most adept at thinking outside the Middle Woodland (or any other) box, and their chapters push the Hopewell envelope in the most intriguing directions.

20

The Sources of Hopewell Obsidian

Forty Years after Griffin

Richard E. Hughes

> The lesson here is that identifying objects with the "naked" eye is not good enough; wherever . . . checked by chemical-physical studies, the results have been somewhat surprising.
> **Griffin 1997:414**

Since Squier and Davis (1848) brought obsidian to the attention of prehistorians, speculation has abounded on the place, or places, from which it may have been obtained and imported into Hopewell archaeological sites. Rau (1873) thought the obsidian must have derived from Mexico, while Holmes (1903:194) opined that it may have come from "the Rocky Mountains, Oregon, or Mexico," though he subsequently inclined toward a Mexican origin (Holmes 1919:227). Mills (1907:144), Moorehead (1922:133), Willoughby and Hooton (1922:97), and Shetrone (1926:43, 1930:206) favored the Yellowstone National Park region of Wyoming. In the succeeding years there emerged such conviction that the Rocky Mountain region was the source for Hopewell obsidian that historians (Lilly 1937:29) and even writers of children's books (Scheele 1960:38) repeated it as fact before any chemical analysis was done. Right up to the time the first neutron activation analyses were conducted, disagreement still existed. Bell (1959:137) doubted that "obsidian found in Ohio came from the Yellowstone Wyoming quarries," and Prufer (1964b:93; see also Prufer 1964a:75, 1965:132) wrote that Hopewell obsidian "was obtained either from what is now the U.S. Southwest or from the Yellowstone region of the Rocky Mountains." As is now well known, neutron activation analyses conducted nearly four decades ago by Griffin and his associates (Gordus et al. 1967; Gordus, Griffin, and Wright 1971; Griffin and Gordus 1967; Griffin, Gordus, and Wright 1969) provided instrumental support for the latter view, and today it is commonly held that Yellowstone was the source for Hopewell obsidian (e.g., Brose 1994:224; Fagan 1991:372; Griffin 1981:9, 1983b:263; Jennings 1989:238; Morse and Morse 1983:164; Seeman 1979b:300; Wright 1972:5).

In light of this compelling geochemical evidence, it might not be clear why one would spend time analyzing more obsidian from Hopewell contexts. My initial interest in Hopewell was that it provided a dramatic geographic contrast to the obsidian sourcing research I have conducted in the Far West. The terms "source" and "sourcing" studies, as used herein, refer to research concerned with establishing chemical correlations between geologic parent materials and archaeological artifacts. I use the term "source" as shorthand for "chemical type" and "geochemical type" with the understanding that the actual geographic extent of the geologic parent ("source") material may be variable depending on formation process (dome-and-flow versus ash-flow tuff origin) and posteruptive secondary distribution (see Hughes 1998 for discussion). By midwestern standards the Far West is obsidian-rich; there are literally hundreds of places where artifact-quality obsidians can be obtained from geologic outcrops or secondary deposits. Although there are cases where glasses were conveyed 200–300 kilometers from the source, such long-distance movements are comparatively rare given the availability of alternative high-quality glasses near at hand. By contrast, in the obsidian-poor Great Plains and Midwest, the closest sources of obsidian to sites near Columbus, Ohio, are about 2,200 kilometers (Jemez Mountains, New Mexico) to 2,400 kilometers (Obsidian Cliff, Wyoming) away (but see Brose 1990 for watercraft-based adjustments to these distances). Consequently, it seemed that Hopewell sites could provide a sharp geographic contrast to the relationship between resources and consumers investigated in the Far West.

In addition, obsidian studies in the Far West support the view that social ranking can be inferred from the differential distribution of obsidians from nearby versus distant sources as measured by their representation in different classes of obsidian artifacts (Hughes 1978, 1989). For example, in sites in northwestern California and southwestern Oregon, large obsidian bifaces were exclusively fashioned from parent obsidian source materials located as far as 300 kilometers from the sites, while all utilitarian implements (points, drills, flakes) were manufactured from obsidian from the closest available source. Burial associations supported this general relationship between distance and value, and only high-status individuals (inferred on the basis of grave associations) were accompanied by artifacts made from distant obsidians. From this vantage point, the Hopewell case again carries intriguing implications. Numerous scholars have commented on the strong evidence for social ranking during Middle Woodland times, appealing in part to the presence of long-distance "exotic" artifacts in Hopewell graves. Control over access to valued extralocal resources was probably crucial to reinforcing the social distinctions between segments of Hopewell communities; thus, display of highly valued, scarce items could be envisioned as emblematic of the prestige, influence, and "connections" of the owners and their families or lineages.

The Hopewell material also provided an opportunity to look more generally at the relationship between artifact class and obsidian source. Because of the lessons learned in California and the Great Basin, researchers in these areas have come to recognize the importance of stratifying obsidian samples by artifact class prior to assessing the significance of sourcing data. By contrast, it appears that those interested in such research in the Midwest have largely considered

Figure 20.1. Obsidian bifaces from Hopewell Mound 17, Ross County, Ohio. Photograph reproduced by permission of the Ohio Historical Society.

obsidian to be a unitary "exotic" long-distance resource and have so far not seriously entertained the possibility that different classes of artifacts recovered from Hopewellian and other Middle Woodland period sites may have been fashioned from different sources of obsidian, which may have been introduced into, and circulated among, archaeological sites in different ways.

Hopewell, of course, carries more general theoretical significance because it is one of the best examples of an obsidian conveyance system that apparently appeared without antecedents, flourished, and then ceased. Although obsidian has recently been documented in Early Woodland contexts in Wisconsin (Stoltman and Hughes 2004), I am unaware of any obsidian recovered elsewhere from preceding Adena or subsequent Late Woodland sites (compare Greber and Ruhl 1989:191; Griffin 1965:146). Therefore the Hopewell case provides an opportunity to study a short-lived system and understand its organization.

All of these factors conditioned my analyses of Hopewell obsidian. From collections housed at the Field Museum of Natural History, the Smithsonian Institution, the Ohio Historical Society, the National Park Service (Hopewell Culture National Historical Park), the Peabody Museum of Archaeology and Ethnology, and the Cincinnati Museum, I was able to obtain for study more than 400 specimens and subject them to geochemical analysis using nondestructive energy dispersive x-ray fluorescence (EDXRF) spectrometry (see tables 20.1 and 20.2). This sample included some truly spectacular and unique obsidian artifacts (see figs. 20.1–20.3).

The number of samples tabulated in tables 20.1 and 20.2 is more than six times larger than was previously reported for all Hopewell/Middle Woodland

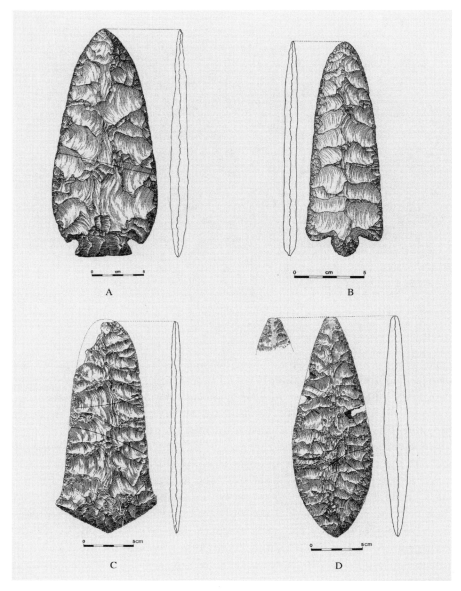

Figure 20.2. Obsidian artifacts from Mound City and the Hopewell Mound Group and their sources: (A) Mound City specimen 260/52, Bear Gulch; (B) Mound City specimen 260/53, Obsidian Cliff; (C) Hopewell Mound Group specimen 56823, Obsidian Cliff; (D) Hopewell Mound Group specimen 56833, Obsidian Cliff.

period obsidians (Gordus, Griffin, and Wright 1971; Griffin, Gordus, and Wright 1969). Unfortunately, the current sample lacks exact provenience for many of the Field Museum specimens excavated by Warren K. Moorehead (1922) from the Hopewell Mound Group in Ohio. Many samples, in fact, are today attributed in museum collections only to the "Hopewell Mound Group."

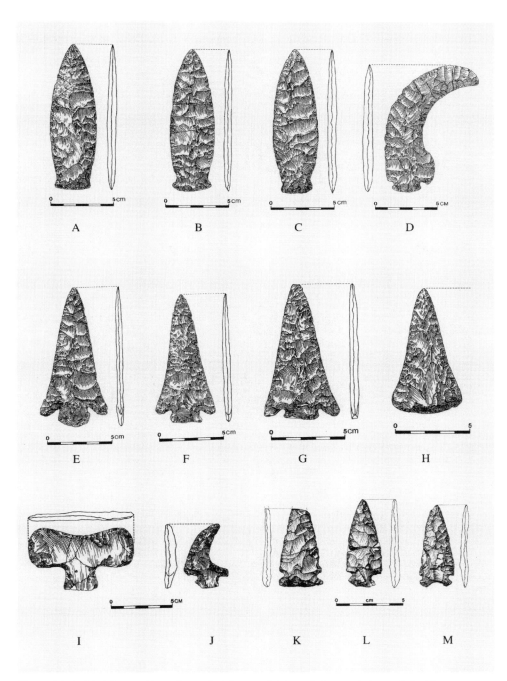

Figure 20.3. Obsidian artifacts from the Hopewell Mound Group, Seip, and the Turner Mound and their sources: (A) Hopewell Mound Group specimen 56774–B, Bear Gulch; (B) and (C) Hopewell Mound Group specimens 56774–C and 56774–D, Obsidian Cliff; (D) Hopewell Mound 25 specimen 283/386, Obsidian Cliff; (E)–(H) Hopewell Mound Group specimens 56772–A, 56772–B, 56772–C, and 56780–A, Obsidian Cliff; (I) and (J) Seip Mound specimens 957/174 and 957/63, Obsidian Cliff; (K)–(M) Turner Mound specimens 29830, 29835, and 29832, Obsidian Cliff.

Table 20.1. Summary Results of EDXRF Analysis of Obsidian from Archaeological Sites in Ohio

| Site | Artifact Class | Obsidian Source (Chemical Type) | | | |
		Obsidian Cliff	Bear Gulch	Other	Total
Hopewell, Mound 11 (*n* = 29)	Formal Tools[a]	9	0	0	9
	Debitage[b]	20	0	0	20
Hopewell, Mound 17 (*n* = 56)	Formal Tools	44	3	0	47
	Debitage	9	0	0	9
Hopewell, Mound 25 (*n* = 42)	Formal Tools	17	5	0	22
	Debitage	20	0	0	20
Shetrone, Mound 17 (*n* = 1)	Formal Tools	1	0	0	1
	Debitage	0	0	0	0
Hopewell, No. Loc. (*n* = 42)	Formal Tools	34	8	0	42
	Debitage	0	0	0	0
Mound City, Mound 13[c] (*n* = 32)	Formal Tools	15	2	0	17
	Debitage	15	0	0	15
Mound City, Mound 2 (*n* = 1)	Formal Tools	0	1	0	1
	Debitage	0	0	0	0
Mound City, Mound 7[d] (*n* = 3)	Formal Tools	3	0	0	3
	Debitage	0	0	0	0
Mound City, 1963 exc. (*n* = 2)	Formal Tools	1	0	0	1
	Debitage	1	0	0	1
Seip Earthworks (*n* = 10)	Formal Tools	3	7	0	10
	Debitage	0	0	0	0
Stubbs Earthworks[e] (*n* = 30)	Formal Tools	7	0	0	7
	Debitage	22	1	0	23
Turner Mound (*n* = 12)	Formal Tools	12	0	0	12
	Debitage	0	0	0	0

Note: Each sample was analyzed for seven trace elements (Zn, Ga, Rb, Sr, Y, Zr, and Nb, with supplementary analyses for Ba, Mn, and $Fe_2O_3^T$ when necessary) with composition estimates generated in quantitative units (i.e., parts-per-million and weight percentage). Details of the nondestructive EDXRF technique appear elsewhere (Hughes 1986, 1988, 1994). Because of the summary nature of this paper it was not possible to present quantitative data supporting the artifact-to-obsidian source (chemical type) attribution for each specimen. Representative chemical data for Obsidian Cliff and Bear Gulch obsidians appear in Anderson, Tiffany, and Nelson 1986, Hughes and Fortier 1997:84–87, and Hughes and Nelson 1987.

a. "Formal tool" category included biface fragments, bladelets and bladelet fragments, cores, and exhausted cores.

b. "Debitage" included flakes (some with utilized but not intentionally flaked edges) and shatter.

c. Totals combined from Burial 3 (*n* = 2), Depository 5 (*n* = 1), and Mica Grave (*n*= 29) occurrences. Total excludes one specimen (MOCI 4157) from an unknown obsidian source.

d. Total includes one biface from Burial 3 and two bifaces from Burial 12.

e. Total includes thirteen specimens from the surface of sites 33WA256 (*n* = 6), 33WA257 (*n*=2), 33WA258, 33WA260, 33WA360, 33WA362, and one no. loc./site location unknown (*n* = 1 each), and seventeen specimens from the Marvin Julien surface collection from 33WA302.

Table 20.2. Summary Results of EDXRF Analysis of Obsidian from Archaeological Sites in Illinois, Indiana, and Wisconsin

State	Site	Artifact Class	Obsidian Cliff	Bear Gulch	Malad[a]	Total
			Obsidian Source (Chemical Type)			
Illinois	American Bottom ($n = 4$)	Formal Tools[b]	3	1	0	4
		Debitage[c]	0	0	0	0
	Baehr-Gust ($n = 30$)	Formal Tools	0	0	0	0
		Debitage	21	8	1	30
Indiana	Mann ($n = 102$)[d]	Formal Tools	2	55	0	57
		Debitage	2	43	0	45
Wisconsin	Flucke Mound 1 ($n = 2$)	Formal Tools	1	1	0	2
		Debitage	0	0	0	0
	Sue Coulee	Formal Tools	0	1	0	1
	Mound 7 ($n = 1$)	Debitage	0	0	0	0
	White Group	Formal Tools	1	0	0	1
	Mound 10 ($n = 1$)	Debitage	0	0	0	0
	Schwert Mound 19 ($n = 1$)	Formal Tools	0	1	0	1
		Debitage	0	0	0	0
	Nicholls Mound ($n = 1$)	Formal Tools	1	0	0	1
		Debitage	0	0	0	0

a. A single flake from Baehr-Gust was manufactured from Malad obsidian from southeastern Idaho (see fig. 20.4).
b. "Formal tool" category included biface fragments, bladelets and bladelet fragments, cores, and exhausted cores.
c. "Debitage" included flakes (some with utilized but not intentionally flaked edges) and shatter.
d. Includes ninety-nine specimens from the Charles Lacer Jr. collection and three specimens from the Glenn A. Black Laboratory of Archaeology, Indiana University.

Results of Analysis of Obsidian from Ohio ($n = 260$)

One hundred seventy specimens were analyzed from the Hopewell Mound Group; EDXRF analysis indicates that the vast majority of specimens (91 percent; 154 of 170) were fashioned from volcanic glass of the Obsidian Cliff chemical type. Thus, the general conclusion put forth over thirty years ago by Griffin, Gordus, and Wright (1969) on the basis of only sixty-three samples was corroborated by recent research using a sample many times larger (table 20.1).

The real significance of these recent results is not revealed at this coarse scale but may reside instead in finer-grained analysis. When the sample was stratified by artifact class, separating formal artifacts (large bifaces, "spear points," projectile points, cores, bladelets, and recognizable fragments) from debitage (flakes and shatter), 13 percent (16 of 121 specimens) of the formal artifact sample from the Hopewell Mound Group was determined to have been fashioned not from Obsidian Cliff material but from volcanic glass of the Bear Gulch chemical type (Hughes and Nelson 1987) in the southern Centennial Mountains of eastern Idaho, about 110 kilometers southwest of Obsidian Cliff (see fig. 20.4).

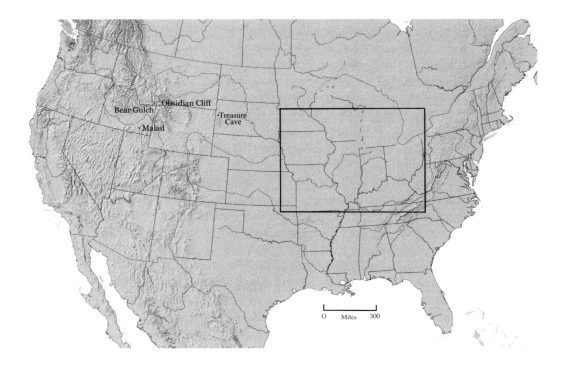

Figure 20.4. Location of major obsidian sources for artifacts recovered from Hopewellian sites (Bear Gulch, Malad, Obsidian Cliff). Also shown is the Treasure Cave site, which contained obsidian flakes sourced to Obsidian Cliff. The outlined area is detailed in figure 20.5.

To appreciate the importance of this distinction, recall that when neutron activation analyses were first conducted, two groups of obsidian—discriminated on the basis of sodium/manganese ratios—were identified in Hopewellian assemblages: a Group 150, representing the Obsidian Cliff source in Yellowstone National Park; and a Group 90, assumed also to be located within Yellowstone (Griffin, Gordus, and Wright 1969:13; Wright 1972:5; Wright, Griffin, and Gordus 1969:28). Subsequent research showed, however, that Group 90 did not represent geologic obsidian located within Yellowstone National Park, but instead an obsidian source to the east in the southern Centennial Mountains area of eastern Idaho (Wright, Chaya, and McDonald 1990), which Hughes and Nelson (1987) termed Bear Gulch. Thus, this source-use contrast identified in Ohio sites is noteworthy because obsidian of the Bear Gulch chemical type was not represented by a single piece of debitage examined ($n = 49$ pieces). While a chi square test showed that this source-use dichotomy was not significant at the 0.05 level, the results are very provocative since the patterning was undetected in previous research.

This same artifact class/obsidian source relationship obtained when other nearby sites were analyzed (fig. 20.5). At Mound City, all debitage examined

Figure 20.5. Hopewell sites that produced obsidian artifacts sourced for this study.

was made from Obsidian Cliff glass (n = 16), while 14 percent of the formal artifact sample (three of twenty-two specimens) was fashioned from Bear Gulch obsidian. The formal artifact percentage frequency for Bear Gulch obsidian at Mound City would have been much higher if the number of Obsidian Cliff samples in the Mica Grave (Mound 13) were reduced. All of these badly broken and burned fragments could have derived from as few as one or two bifaces. The lower Bear Gulch percentage frequency resulted because each specimen analyzed by EDXRF (including fragments and complete artifacts) was treated as a discrete occurrence. Of all Ohio Hopewell sites examined to date, Seip shows the most extreme departure from source-specific frequencies observed at other sites. The sample size from Seip is regrettably small (n = 10), and unfortunately, no obsidian debitage apparently occurred at the site. However, seven of the ten formal artifacts (70 percent) analyzed were manufactured from Bear Gulch obsidian; two Ross Barbed points (spears) and a bear-claw effigy were made from Obsidian Cliff glass.

Only two other Ohio sites with reasonably large samples of obsidian have been examined, and both are located along the Little Miami River in southwestern Ohio. All twelve projectile points recovered from the Central Altar of Mound 3 (Willoughby and Hooton 1922:46–48, 58, Plate 16a) at the Turner Mound were made from Obsidian Cliff volcanic glass, as were twenty-nine of thirty debitage and tool fragments analyzed from the Stubbs Earthworks cluster (see Genheimer 1997).

Results of Analysis of Obsidian from Illinois (n = 34)

Outside the Ohio Hopewell "core" area, a different relationship appears to obtain between obsidian source and artifact class. As Wray (1952:154) and Griffin (1952b:360) had observed, "Illinois area obsidian specimens are found at more sites [than in Ohio] but very few specimens come from any one site. They are shaped from obsidian cores in the local projectile point and blade styles, [and] they do not seem to be traded from Ohio to the Illinois area" (Griffin 1983b:268). Although the specimens have not yet been geochemically analyzed, the large number of obsidian samples reported from Napoleon Hollow (Wiant and McGimsey 1986a:332) now somewhat alter this summation.

The sample analyzed recently from Baehr-Gust adds some important new data (table 20.2). Eight of the thirty flakes (27 percent) analyzed were manufactured from Bear Gulch obsidian, a sample fraction nearly identical to that identified in a much smaller collection (*n* = 4) of obsidian tools recently examined from the American Bottom (25 percent Bear Gulch, 75 percent Obsidian Cliff; Hughes and Fortier 1997). Analyses of much larger collections (like that from Napoleon Hollow) should be undertaken to explore the relationship further, but the Illinois obsidian patterning does appear, as Griffin suggested, to be different from that identified in Ohio. Aside from the dearth of large obsidian bifaces in Illinois, the most obvious difference between the two areas is the absence of Bear Gulch obsidian in any sample of debitage analyzed from Ohio and, by contrast, the strikingly high relative frequency of Bear Gulch obsidian in formal and debitage samples in Illinois. A single flake from Baehr-Gust was manufactured from Malad obsidian, from southeastern Idaho (see fig. 20.4). To my knowledge, this is the first geochemically documented occurrence of this source material east of the Mississippi River, although the obsidian recently has been identified in much later deposits in Arkansas (Hughes, Kay, and Green 2002).

Results of Analysis of Obsidian from Indiana (*n* = 102)

Obsidian samples from the Mann site in southwestern Indiana near the Ohio River (fig. 20.5) recently became available for analysis, providing crucial comparative data for the virtually unknown area between Illinois and Ohio (compare Muller 1986:98–108). In their pioneering pilot study, Griffin, Gordus, and Wright (1969:13) reported the results of analysis of a single flake from Kellar's (1979) excavations at the Mann site, attributing it to the "90 Group from the unknown source in Yellowstone Park." The 90 group has now been identified as Bear Gulch (Hughes and Nelson 1987). For this study, I was able to analyze a considerably larger sample of obsidian from Mann, most of it collected from the site's surface by Charles Lacer Jr.

The results of EDXRF analysis of the Mann site sample were truly remarkable and unanticipated (table 20.2), particularly in light of Griffin's (1979:268) speculation that all the obsidian came from Yellowstone. Of 102 samples analyzed, 96 percent were manufactured from obsidian of the Bear Gulch chemical type; a mere 4 percent were made from Obsidian Cliff volcanic glass. This pattern is precisely the opposite of that observed in Ohio, where Obsidian Cliff was the dominant obsidian in the formal tool category at most sites (except Seip and, perhaps, Mound City; see above). Likewise, the Mann site results differ from Illinois, where the percentage frequency of Obsidian Cliff glass also is much higher (70–75 percent at sites studied so far). In light of such strong contrasts with Hopewell sites in Illinois and Ohio, the dominance of Bear Gulch obsidian at the Mann site may indicate that this obsidian was procured through a different route (or network) than those utilized at neighboring Hopewell sites, that it came to Mann either earlier or later than the obsidian analyzed from Illinois and Ohio sites, or that obsidian at Mann was used in social/ceremonial contexts not widely shared or participated in by other Hopewell communities. These alternatives are not mutually exclusive.

Results of Analysis of Obsidian from Wisconsin (*n* = 6)

Thomas (1894) recovered four obsidian artifacts from excavations at three mounds in the Prairie du Chien area of Crawford and Vernon Counties, Wisconsin. EDXRF analysis shows that two of these were manufactured from Obsidian Cliff obsidian; the other two were made from Bear Gulch volcanic glass (McKern 1931:Plate LX. Left to right:cat. no. 115501, 115502 [Flucke Group Mound 1], no. 115446 [Sue Coulee Mound 7], and no. 88340 [White Group Mound 10]. 115501 and 115446 are Bear Gulch obsidian; 115502 and 88340 are made from Obsidian Cliff glass. Sample 88340 also appears in Thomas 1894 [Figure 39]). McKern's (1931) excavations in the Trempealeau Lakes region yielded two obsidian artifacts, one (cat. 36185 from Schwert Mound 19; McKern 1931:Plate LIX, no. 2) made from Bear Gulch obsidian, the other (cat. 33056 from Nicholls Mound; McKern 1931:Plate LIX, no. 1) fashioned of volcanic glass from Obsidian Cliff. No obsidian flakes or other obsidian artifact fragments were reported from any of these sites.

Discussion

The results of this study may prompt a rethinking of the long-standing account of how obsidian was procured and conveyed to Hopewell sites. As all Hopewell scholars know, over four decades ago Griffin (1965) set forth an intriguing explanation for the presence of obsidian in Hopewell sites, what he termed the "one shot" hypothesis. He suggested that obsidian could have made its way to Hopewellian sites in Ohio and Illinois by either of two means: by "inter-tribal trade, or (as a result of a single trip to Yellowstone) by a group of adventurer-traders" (Griffin 1965:146). With respect to the first alternative, he reasoned that if "inter-tribal trade from Yellowstone was in effect we might expect to find significant amounts of obsidian from a fairly large number of Middle Woodland sites between the Upper Mississippi and the Rocky Mountains. This is not now the case" (Griffin 1965:147). Neither is it the case as of this writing. Although many more obsidian artifacts—mostly flakes—have been recovered and sourced from Middle Woodland temporal contexts between the upper Mississippi and the Rocky Mountains over the past forty years (for example, Anderson, Tiffany, and Nelson 1986; Baugh and Nelson 1988), I doubt that these would qualify as "significant amounts of obsidian from a fairly large number of sites" in Griffin's view. There are usually very few specimens from any one site, and precise dating is also a problem. However, a potentially important "new" site, Treasure Cave (39LA504) in the northern Black Hills of South Dakota, reportedly contains thousands of obsidian flakes, some of which were sourced to Obsidian Cliff (Hughes 2000b; see fig. 20.4).

On the basis of information available at the time he wrote, Griffin seemed inclined to the other alternative—a single-trip scenario:

> It could be argued that the total amount of obsidian from Hopewellian sites might have been obtained on one trip to Yellowstone (and) if it was but one shipment then the probable redistribution point was the Hopewell site itself which produced more obsidian than all the rest of the finds combined. . . . The number of sites in Illinois, Iowa and Wisconsin which have produced obsidian points, cores and flakes would suggest that the flint knappers of these sites must have obtained the raw material either from Ohio, or from the "traders" on their way back to Ross County, Ohio. The implications of this 'one shot' hypothesis would be that Hopewellian obsidian was obtained, distributed, and consumed within a relatively short span of time, say 25 to 50 years. (Griffin 1965:146–147)

There is no question that a serious problem with evaluating these alternatives is the remarkably short time, perhaps only one hundred to two hundred years in duration (Griffin 1965:146), attributed to the appearance of obsidian in Hopewell sites. If obsidian in Ohio Hopewell sites was restricted to the period between A.D. 0 and A.D. 200, it is not now possible to falsify Griffin's hypothesis using obsidian hydration analysis (Hughes 1992), although the implications of the "intertribal" trade alternative can be addressed at least indirectly with distributional data. Doubtless because of the monumental quantity of obsidian debris recovered from a burial-associated cache in Mound 11, both Shetrone (1926:40–43, 1930:207–208) and Griffin (1965:146, 148, 1983b:263) regarded Hopewell Mound 11 as the principal manufacturing center and redistribution point for obsidian found at other Ohio Hopewell sites. Shetrone (1926:43) believed that "the fine obsidian implements found in Mound 25 were fashioned on the site of the Hopewell Group," and Griffin (1983b:263) wrote that this "burial (from Mound 11) I regard as being that of the individual who produced the magnificent Hopewell obsidian spears of which there were between 250 and 500 in altar 2 in Mound 25 at Hopewell." Braun, Griffin, and Titterington (1982:88) concluded "that the few other obsidian artifacts in Ohio were the result of exchange with the individual buried alone with the remains of his 'wealth.'"

If the "one shot" hypothesis is correct and virtually all the obsidian introduced into Ohio Hopewell sites arrived first at Mound 11, then one would expect to find formal obsidian artifacts made from Bear Gulch obsidian at Mound 11 in roughly the same proportions as at other Ohio Hopewell sites. To date, no Bear Gulch obsidian has been geochemically identified from Hopewell Mound 11 or, as debitage, at any other Hopewell mound site; but because so few samples from the Mound 11 cache have been chemically characterized ($n = 29$), the case is far from closed. If all, or a disproportionately large amount, of the debitage and artifact fragments from the Mound 11 cache turn out to be Obsidian Cliff volcanic glass (as it all has, to date), then this feature obviously could not have been the source for the Bear Gulch obsidian spears recovered from Mounds 17 and 25 at Hopewell (table 20.1). In light of the apparent conflict with obsidian sourcing data, the alternative is that if obsidian did come to Mound 11 in one shot, all of it was from Obsidian Cliff. If so, this would render consistent the view of Griffin and others that the master craftsman buried in Mound 11 was responsible for the manufacture of the large spears found at other mounds in the Hopewell group (since most of these were made from Obsidian Cliff glass), but this scenario would be inadequate to account for the presence of Bear Gulch obsidian spears in Mounds 17 and 25 at Hopewell and at Mound City.

Current distributional data lend themselves to both synchronic and diachronic alternatives, neither of which is mutually exclusive of the other. On the synchronic level, even if the material originally was obtained via a one-time expedition, once it arrived east of the Mississippi the observed distributions suggest that obsidian did not have a single "function" among communities participating in the Hopewell phenomenon, as Griffin (Braun, Griffin, and Titterington 1982:88; 1965:147–148) observed, but may have marked social and/or ceremonial relations differently in discrete interacting communities. The absence of Bear Gulch debitage in Ohio Hopewell sites suggests that even if Bear Gulch and Obsidian Cliff glass were obtained in one shot, Bear Gulch obsidian was accorded treatment different from that of Obsidian Cliff, perhaps signaling the operation of these glasses in different ceremonial contexts or as differential status markers.

These distributional differences also lend themselves to diachronic interpretation. If obsidian came to Hopewell sites on more than one occasion, it is likely that some of the differences observed are time-dependent. In this case, source-use disjunctions may reflect not only the variable social and/or ceremonial contexts of obsidian use, but also changes in these contexts through time reflexive of the incorporation of "new," or more distant and valuable, sources of obsidian into the network. For example, the absence of Bear Gulch obsidian debitage in Ohio Hopewell sites may be such an indication if the greater distance involved in its procurement translated into greater intrinsic value in different social/ceremonial contexts. Although Bear Gulch obsidian is more distant from sites in the Scioto Valley than is Obsidian Cliff, it could be argued that the additional distance is not particularly significant if viewed from a "long-distance" versus a "short-distance" perspective. However, it is worth noting that access from the east to Bear Gulch, regardless of how people actually got there, is more difficult than access to Obsidian Cliff.

Fine-grained temporal control will be required to evaluate these alternatives since it may be, for example, that Bear Gulch obsidian was imported only later in Middle Woodland times, further amplifying preexisting distance/value relationships. Conversely, Bear Gulch may have been employed earlier in the period, only later to be replaced by "cheaper" Obsidian Cliff glass. If so, the value of existing Bear Gulch artifacts may have increased, and the absence of this glass as debitage may reflect this high value. In either case, the virtual absence of Bear Gulch debitage in Ohio sites could be taken to support the view that artifacts made from this glass were imported as finished pieces, not manufactured locally as Obsidian Cliff debitage at Hopewell Mound 11 suggests. To the extent that any of these relationships are found to obtain, they would tend to support the view that exchange (or resource procurement forays) took place over a longer period of time than would follow from the one-shot hypothesis, as Hatch and colleagues (1990) and Stevenson, Abdelrehim, and Novak (2004) have suggested. *How much* longer is difficult to say at present.

Regardless, it is now abundantly clear that Yellowstone National Park (that is, Obsidian Cliff, Wyoming) was not the sole source for obsidian found at Ohio Hopewell and other Middle Woodland sites. Obsidian of the Bear Gulch chemical type in eastern Idaho accounts for a small but significant fraction of formal artifacts in Ohio sites and an even higher percentage of tools and debitage in Illinois, and it dominates in both formal tool and debitage samples analyzed thus far from Indiana. Formal tools in the Wisconsin mounds are evenly split between Bear Gulch and Obsidian Cliff, but the apparent absence of obsidian debitage in these sites hinders comparisons with adjacent Hopewellian assemblages. The source-specific mix of tools and debitage in Illinois appears more similar to that of Iowa sites (Anderson, Tiffany, and Nelson 1986) than to that of sites in Ohio (compare Griffin 1965:147–148), but the dominance of Bear Gulch obsidian in the Mann site collection from Indiana has no counterpart anywhere east of the Mississippi during Middle Woodland times. These distributional differences are persuasive and difficult to reconcile with the view that obsidian was introduced to Hopewell populations on only a single occasion.

I have touched generally on some implications of the meaning of these differences, but consider them provisional in light of dramatic differences in sample size and site function or functions, uncertain temporal contexts of the obsidian finds within some of the larger sites, and broader issues of assemblage contemporaneity across several states. These problems notwithstanding, an explicit focus on obsidian source-use variability by artifact class may be one way to identify previously undisclosed patterning within the long-distance conveyance network or networks that brought obsidian to Hopewell and allied Middle Woodland populations; it may also help us understand the variable contexts in which obsidian circulated once it arrived. The source-specific differences in formal tool and debitage distributions documented here among sites in the Illinois, Indiana, Ohio, and Wisconsin Hopewell areas provide general corroboration for the "marked variation both within and between regions . . . through which quantities of scarce raw materials and finished goods moved" and for the existence of "networks of different types . . . on different scales" noted by Struever and Houart (1972:79). More generally, these results suggest that there is still much to be learned from continued problem-oriented analyses of obsidian from well-dated Middle Woodland contexts.

Acknowledgments

Numerous colleagues have provided information and assistance through the years this study has been in progress. Foremost among them, N'omi Greber has freely provided assistance and encouragement at every turn, for which I am most grateful. James VanStone (Field Museum), Martha Otto (Ohio Historical Society), Stephen Williams (Peabody Museum, Harvard), Thomas Kehoe (Milwaukee Public Museum), Donald Ortner and Bruce Smith (National Museum of Natural History, Smithsonian Institution), Noel Justice (Glenn Black Laboratory, Indiana University), and Frank Cowan and Robert Genheimer (Cincinnati Museum Center) approved specimen loans from their respective institutions for this study. I particularly appreciate the generosity of Charles Lacer Jr. for allowing me to analyze specimens from his collection from the Mann site, and I am likewise indebted to Anne-Marie Cantwell and Julie Zimmerman Holt for providing specimens from Baehr-Gust. Without the help and cooperation of all these individuals and institutions, this study literally could not have been completed. I also appreciated discussions and correspondence with James Brown, Mark Seeman, Michael Wiant, and the late James B. Griffin and Howard Winters regarding Middle Woodland obsidian, and other assistance from Frank Cowan, Andrew Fortier, Michael Fosha, Michael Hambacher, Jennifer Pederson, Bret Ruby, and James Stoltman. Ben Hughes prepared figures 20.4 and 20.5 herein, and Robert Pengelly drafted figures 20.2 and 20.3. Special thanks to Jodie O'Gorman and Jane Buikstra for inviting me to participate in the stimulating "Perspectives on Middle Woodland at the Millennium" conference and to Doug Charles for his patience while I revised and expanded my conference paper.

21

The Place of Nonmound Debris at Hopewell Mound Group (33RO27), Ross County, Ohio

Jarrod Burks and Jennifer Pederson

Most research in Ohio Hopewell archaeology falls into one of two broad categories: (1) the nature of ceremonial activity at Hopewell earthworks, or (2) Hopewell community organization and day-to-day life. The first topic has been extensively studied through numerous excavation projects at Hopewell mounds and earthworks, most of which were conducted prior to the 1930s. While many modern discussions of Hopewell ceremonialism derive from more recent projects (for example, Baby and Brown 1964; Brown 1982; Greber 1983), much of the modern literature concerning Hopewell ceremonialism is based on the results of the earlier excavations (for example, Cowan 1996; Greber 1976; Greber and Ruhl 1989; Lepper 1989). Because of the more rigorous demands of the data required by modern archaeological research, studies of Hopewell ceremonialism in Ohio have been somewhat restricted in scope (Brown 1982).

Though overshadowed by the study of earthworks and ceremonialism, research concerning the daily lives of the Hopewell people also began during the formative years of archaeological excavation techniques and standards of record keeping. Early accounts of Hopewell habitation and economy were based on deposits inadvertently found outside of and between the mounds during major earthwork excavation projects. This nonmound debris inside of or adjacent to the earthworks—such as at Hopewell Mound Group, for example—has long been a primary reference for evidence of Hopewell habitation (for example, Fischer 1974; Griffin 1979, 1997; Moorehead 1922; Squier and Davis 1848). Detailed research on an Ohio Hopewell habitation site from outside an earthwork complex was not published until 1965 (Prufer 1965). Few similar efforts at understanding Ohio Hopewell daily life followed (compare select chapters in Brose and Greber 1979; Dancey 1991; Kozarek 1987; Wymer 1987a), until a recent set of volumes explored the topic (Dancey and Pacheco 1997b; Pacheco 1996b).

Recent salvage work at the remains of certain Ohio Hopewell earthwork sites has brought discussions of Hopewell habitation back to the earthworks. At sites such as Fort Ancient and Stubbs in Warren County and Liberty and Seip Earthworks in Ross County, Hopewell debris and subsurface features have been documented inside and outside of embankments, as well as under them (Baby and Langlois 1979; Connolly 1997; Coughlin and Seeman 1997; Cowan, this volume; Genheimer 1997; Greber 1997). In the past this nonmound evidence of Hopewell occupation was loosely interpreted as the remains of village sites (for example, Moorehead 1922). While this debris clearly represents some form of occupation, the nature and duration of these occupations have yet to be intensively studied.

In this chapter we turn our attention to the nonmound debris at Hopewell Mound Group in Ross County, Ohio. Over the past twenty years, numerous clusters of nonmound debris have been located within and adjacent to the earthworks. Basing his conclusions on an extensive survey of the area within and surrounding the earthworks, Seeman (1981a) hypothesized that the nonmound debris at Hopewell Mound Group is indicative of scattered, short-term occupations. Through an intensive study of newly recovered nonmound debris from select clusters, this chapter serves to further test Seeman's hypotheses and to more thoroughly explore the nature of nonmound debris at this important Hopewell earthwork. In documenting the nature of Hopewell occupation at earthwork sites, the study of nonmound debris explores the ceremonial activities that took place between the mounds and buildings and provides evidence of a little-studied aspect of Hopewell community organization in Ohio.

Background to the Problem

Scholars have used Hopewell earthwork complexes to debate the nature of Hopewell habitation practices since the early nineteenth century. In the early stages of Hopewell research, the great geometric earthworks and burial mounds of central and southern Ohio attracted the most attention. Caleb Atwater (1820) was one of the first to contemplate the habitation practices of the Hopewell. He surmised that the earthworks, with their many gateways and interior ditches, made poor defensive works and therefore must have served a ceremonial rather than a domestic purpose. Thirty years later, Ephraim Squier and Edwin Davis (1848) revisited the idea of the Hopewell earthworks as defensive constructions. For example, they envisioned Hopewell Mound Group as a fortified town, with religious and domestic areas enclosed in its protective embankments and ditches. In this scenario, Hopewell earthworks acted as both habitation and ceremonial center. Lewis Henry Morgan carried this line of thought to an extreme in his 1881 treatise, *Houses and House-Life of the American Aborigines*. Morgan portrayed the embankments of Hopewell earthworks as building platforms for immense long houses, as depicted in his reconstruction of life at the High Bank Works (Morgan 1881).

At the turn of the twentieth century, Gerard Fowke (1902) explored the widely ranging, functional explanations that existed for the earthen enclosures of Ohio. From defensive works or game preserves to dwelling foundations, Fowke carefully reviewed every explanation, and each was discounted in turn based on the existing evidence. The only way to finally explain the sometimes vast and complex earthworks of the Ohio region, he advised, was to conduct more investigations "of the embankments, ditches, and included areas, to a depth at or below any level which was disturbed by the Mound Builders" (Fowke 1902:155–158). Whether in response to this suggestion or not, many of the major earthwork complexes of Ohio were excavated, and reexcavated, over the next forty years.

In addition to intensifying their examination of earthwork sites, early-twentieth-century archaeologists also began to broaden their research to include the areas surrounding the mounds and earthworks. For example, in their reports on excavations at Hopewell Mound Group, both Warren K. Moorehead (1922) and Henry C. Shetrone (1926) recorded the location of nonmound debris within the earthworks. For these two researchers, the presence of such debris inside the earthworks suggested the existence of villages or towns. However, neither Moorehead nor Shetrone discussed or described these artifact deposits beyond simply noting their location. While Moorehead thought that the earthworks had served as village and burial sites for the Hopewell, Shetrone was unimpressed with the amount of nonmound debris inside the earthworks and considered it inconsistent with their size (Shetrone 1926:112).

By the 1950s, Ohio archaeologists had begun to entertain the possibility that Hopewell people may have lived in other places across the landscape, as well as at their ceremonial centers (for example, Morgan 1952). A lack of evidence for Hopewell habitation sites outside the earthworks, however, meant that researchers had to rely upon nonmound debris from earthwork sites for their interpretations of Ohio Hopewell domestic life (for example, Griffin 1952b). The extensive deposits of debris at Fort Ancient inside the North Fort and outside to the northeast, south of the parallel walls, was in the 1940s and 1950s taken as solid evidence supporting the presence of villages within and next to earthworks (Morgan 1946).

In the early 1960s, a new era of Hopewell settlement studies was initiated when Olaf Prufer addressed the possibility of Hopewell habitation away from earthwork complexes in Ross County. During his Scioto Valley survey, Prufer's crew identified approximately twenty concentrations of Hopewell debris outside and away from the earthworks and burial mounds in their survey area (Blank 1965; Prufer 1965, 1967). In fact, the first well-documented Hopewell habitation, the McGraw site, was excavated as a result of this survey (Prufer 1965). Prufer concluded that the Hopewell must have occupied small settlements in the hinterlands of their "vacant" earthworks, an idea that is now referred to as the hamlet hypothesis (Dancey and Pacheco 1997a; Pacheco 1988, 1993). Thus, in the early to mid 1960s, archaeologists began to shift their focus away from earthwork complexes in the study of Hopewell habitation.

Despite Prufer's success and his call to conduct surveys of other regions, it was not until the mid to late 1980s that archaeologists began to more intensively search for the remains of Hopewell settlements away from the earthworks (for example, Dancey 1991; Genheimer 1984; Kozarek 1987; Pacheco 1988, 1993). In a recent volume on Hopewell community structure, Dancey and Pacheco (1997a) used information from over ninety Hopewell settlements in the formulation of their dispersed sedentary community model of Hopewell community organization. This model proposed that the Hopewell people had lived in small, sedentary settlements on the terraces of main stream valleys and at the convergence of intermittent streams in the uplands surrounding the earthwork sites. Each earthwork was the focal point of a community's mortuary and socio-ceremonial life.

In conjunction with continued exploration of Hopewell habitation sites, many archaeologists are turning back to the earthworks in an effort to salvage what remains before urban development and modern agricultural practices totally erase this aspect of the Hopewell. Recent studies of earthwork sites such as Fort Ancient (Connolly 1997), the Liberty Earthworks (Coughlin and Seeman 1997), and the Stubbs Earthworks (Cowan, this volume; Genheimer 1997) are finding that Hopewell earthwork complexes are literally covered in nonmound artifactual debris and the subtle remnants of occupation. What differs among these earthworks, however, is how this material is recorded, studied, and interpreted.

Hopewell Mound Group

Hopewell Mound Group, located on the North Fork of Paint Creek about 8 kilometers west of the town of Chillicothe, Ohio, has been a focus of nonmound debris studies intermittently over the past twenty-five years. The known features of the earthwork complex consist of embankments, ditches, mounds, the remains of submound structures, borrow pits, and nonmound artifact concentrations and subsurface features. Figure 21.1 shows the location of many of these features and is a compilation of maps made by Squier and Davis (1848), Cowen (1882 [in Greber and Ruhl 1989]), and Shetrone (1926). Greber (1999b) has recently georeferenced the various maps of Hopewell Mound Group and has found them to contain numerous discrepancies. Thus, the map in figure 21.1 is an approximation of features documented over the past two hundred years. While we have fit this map to a recent global positioning system (GPS) survey of extant earthworks at the site (our map north is UTM [Universal Transverse Mercator] north), a modern field resurvey has yet to be completed.

The earthwork complex is made up of four sets of embankments. The main embankment is a large, irregular wall that hugs the edges of the second terrace and the top of the ridge at the north edge of the site. This embankment is broken by as many as six gateways. At the time the site was first extensively mapped in the 1840s, the embankment enclosed 45 hectares with more than 3 kilometers of mounded earth varying in height from 1.5 to 2 meters (Squier and Davis 1848). A ditch surrounded the embankment on the east, west, and north sides, representing the source for the bulk of the embankment fill.

A small square (6.5 hectares) composed of six wall segments is attached to the east side of the main embankment. Four of the gateways allowing access to the square, including the opening to the interior of the main embankment, were blocked by mounds. Two smaller, geometric earthworks occur on the inside of

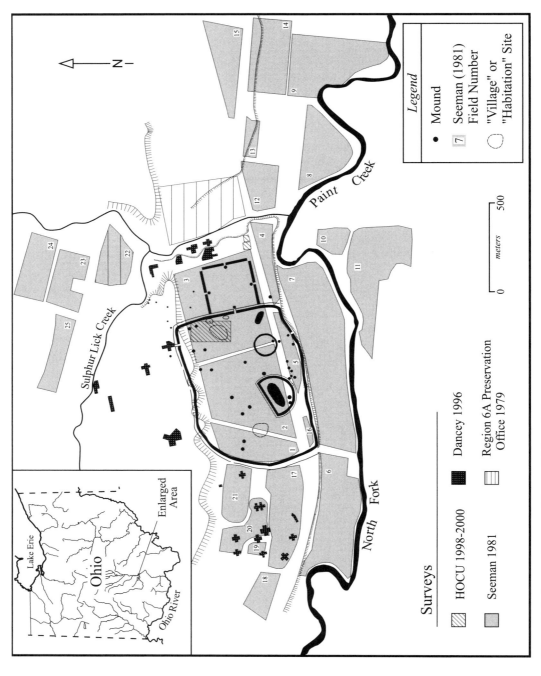

Figure 21.1. Surveyed areas at Hopewell Mound Group.

the main embankment. A circular embankment, approximately 150 meters in diameter, lies adjacent to the second largest mound (Mound 23) in the complex. A half circle, approximately 175 meters across and originally nearly 1 meter in height, surrounds the largest mound on the site (Mound 25) and is located about 150 meters west of the circle.

As many as forty-three mounds of various sizes were once scattered within and around the site's embankments, including the largest known Hopewell mound, Mound 25. While many of these mounds have been documented through excavation and survey, some have yet to be relocated by modern surveys. Six new mounds proposed by Seeman (1981a) are not depicted in figure 21.1. It is highly likely that the early surveys of Squier and Davis, Moorehead, and Shetrone overlooked some of the smaller mounds. Squier and Davis omitted numerous mounds from their maps, and by the time Moorehead began excavations in the early 1890s, many of the smaller mounds had already vanished beneath the plow. Today fewer yet are visible at the surface. Along with the mounds, a number of borrow pits were recorded inside the main embankments and on top of the terrace along the northern edge of the site. There are clearly too few recorded borrow pits, however, to account for the vast amounts of sediment in the mounds. Recent geophysical surveys in various areas of the site have relocated at least one "lost" mound (Mound 1) and perhaps some new borrow pits (Pederson and Burks 2001).

Finally, nearly every archaeologist who has worked at Hopewell Mound Group has commented on the prehistoric debris scattered about the earthworks. Squier and Davis (1848) were the first to map nonmound debris within the northeastern portion of the main embankment. This apparent concentration of debris then appeared on the maps of Moorehead (1922) and Shetrone (1926), where it was labeled as the location of a "Village Site" and a "Habitation Site," respectively. An additional concentration of debris also appears in the western half of the main embankment on the maps of Moorehead and Shetrone.

The Natural Setting

The majority of the embankments and mounds at the site are situated on a Wisconsinan terrace consisting predominantly of limestone and shale gravel (Hyde 1921). To the west, the North Fork of Paint Creek cuts through 100-meter-high hills of Bedford shale surrounded by terminal end moraine deposits of sand and gravel 15 to 30 meters thick. Along and underneath the northern edge of the earthworks this end moraine deposit rises approximately 20 to 30 meters. South and east of Hopewell Mound Group, toward the Scioto River, 90–120-meter-high hills of Portsmouth, Cuyahoga, and Sunbury shales dominate a landscape sculpted by Illinoian-age glaciers. Illinoian drift can be found 12 to 15 kilometers to the east, in the hills flanking the far side of the Scioto River floodplain.

Previous Archaeological Research

Hopewell Mound Group was first mapped and described by Caleb Atwater (1820). While Atwater's map is far from complete, it does convey the enormity of the earthworks. Atwater also suggests that the mounds represent cemeteries. This conclusion is perhaps based on the excavation of mounds from similar sites elsewhere that did contain burials.

Squier and Davis (1848) performed the first intensive survey of the earthworks and mounds at Hopewell Mound Group in 1845. At the time of their survey, the earthworks were owned by W. C. Clark and were named the "Clark's Works." They did not become the Hopewell Mound Group until the publication of Moorehead's 1891–1892 excavations in 1922. The Squier and Davis map has been the basis for nearly every subsequent map, although much confusion has resulted from later researchers' (for example, Moorehead and Shetrone) departing from the mound numbers as originally designated. In addition to surveying the earthworks, Squier and Davis also conducted the first documented excavations at the site in four of the mounds. These excavations produced some of the first evidence of the exotic and finely crafted artifacts located in Hopewell mounds. Despite the site's numerous ceremonial contexts, Squier and Davis (1848) placed the Clark's Works in their "works of defence" category.

In 1891 Warren Moorehead (1892, 1922), under charge from Frederick W. Putnam of Harvard University to find materials for the upcoming World's Columbian Exposition, moved his excavations from the site of Fort Ancient on the Little Miami River to the Clark's Works. While at Hopewell Mound Group (which was renamed after the site's then-owner, Mordecai Cloud Hopewell), Moorehead excavated at least fifteen mounds. Moorehead's map has additional mounds not depicted on the Squier and Davis map and is supposedly based on a new plan of the earthworks produced by Clinton Cowen in 1892 (Moorehead 1922:83; a copy of the original Cowen map appears in Greber and Ruhl 1989: 15). Cowen's map closely matches our recent GPS measurements of extant sections of the main embankment walls. The results of Moorehead's excavations electrified researchers' interest in what became known as the Hopewell culture. The materials excavated by Moorehead in 1891–1892 and displayed in Chicago at the Columbian Exposition are now curated at the Field Museum in Chicago. On the basis of his numerous mound excavations and the two significant surface scatters of Hopewell debris noted on his map by the term "Village Site," Moorehead (1922:85) concluded that Hopewell Mound Group represented a "fortified town or city" with ceremonial and habitation areas enclosed within an earthen wall.

In 1922 Henry Shetrone, of the Ohio Historical Society, returned to Hopewell Mound Group to finish what Moorehead had started three decades earlier. By the time Shetrone was finished in 1925, nearly every mound at Hopewell Mound Group had been excavated, some two or three times. Shetrone's (1926) findings built on those of Moorehead: Hopewell Mound Group represented a massive ceremonial center with evidence of habitation inside the earthworks. Beyond the reference to these habitation areas inside the earthworks, however, neither Shetrone nor Moorehead spent much effort in describing the materials found in these supposed "village" deposits.

Not until the late 1970s did archaeologists once again begin to focus their attention on the area surrounding the earthworks and mounds. In 1980 Seeman (1981a, 1981c) directed a survey of 178 hectares within and in the vicinity of the embankments. Using a combination of surface collection and the study of aerial photographs, Seeman was able to relocate most of the known mounds and earthworks. The surface collections also produced information concerning the general scatter of Hopewell debris around and within the earthworks, which will be described in greater detail below. Shortly after Seeman's survey, the Archaeological Conservancy purchased a large portion of the site.

In the early 1990s, Seeman returned to Hopewell Mound Group with Greber for two field seasons of work on Mound 23 (Greber and Seeman 1993, 1995). The goal of the Mound 23 project was to identify intact deposits potentially useful in further developing a culture history of earthwork construction and use. In 1992 a conductivity meter was used for remote sensing the mound area in an effort to locate the mound edges and identify internal features. The following year, a sequence of sediment cores was removed from potential cultural anomalies identified by the remote sensing. Portions of an intact submound building floor were encountered. The results of this work clearly show the utility of remote sensing for documenting degraded mounds, as well as the degree of preservation present at Hopewell Mound Group despite two centuries of accelerated erosion.

A more recent survey by Ohio State University archaeologists, developed and directed by Dancey (1996a), has refined and expanded knowledge of the debris scatter around Hopewell Mound Group. In a series of 449 shovel tests conducted at twenty-one locales in the vicinity of the earthworks, Dancey documented seven clusters of Hopewell debris, including some fairly heavy concentrations. For example, the Datum H locale, located 300 meters northeast of the square enclosure (fig. 21.2), yielded ninety-three artifacts from 28 shovel tests. Importantly, 30 percent of these artifacts are prehistoric ceramics, which suggests a more significant accumulation of possible habitation debris than was previously known in the vicinity. On the basis of these preliminary data, Dancey concluded that the available evidence did not refute his dispersed sedentary community model of Hopewell settlement (Dancey and Pacheco 1997a). He further tentatively suggested that Datums A, C, D-E-F, H, and O represent hamlets (Dancey 1996a:24). The debris recovered from Dancey's Datums A, C, D, E, F, H, and K are further discussed in subsequent sections.

In 1997 the National Park Service began acquiring portions of Hopewell Mound Group, starting with the Archaeological Conservancy parcel. Since 1998 archaeologists from Hopewell Culture National Historical Park have been conducting surveys initiated by Ruby in the vicinity of Moorehead's east "Village Site" (Burks and Pederson 1999; Pederson and Burks 2000). To date, only low-density debris has been found in the area of the supposed village site. Small test pits in the edges of the main embankment near the northern edge of the square have also uncovered intact Hopewell pit and posthole features below the

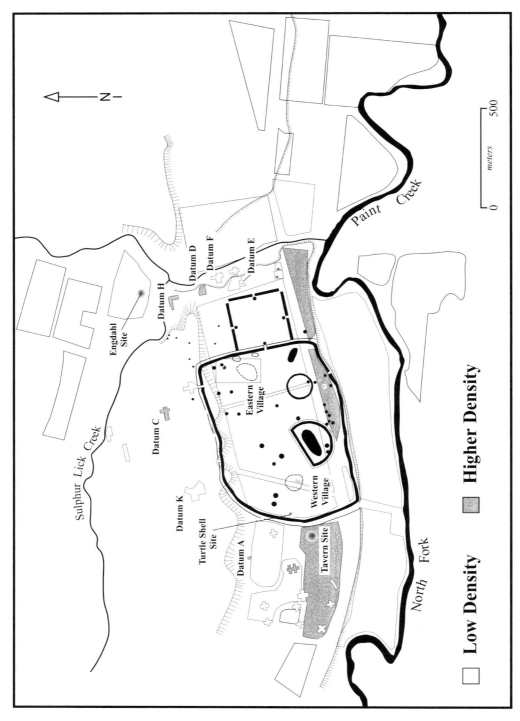

Figure 21.2. Distribution of nonmound debris in surveyed areas at Hopewell Mound Group.

embankment. Despite nearly two hundred years of plowing and excavation, there are still many preserved nonmound features at Hopewell Mound Group.

Analysis

Most studies of nonmound debris at Hopewell earthworks have used the artifact as the material unit of analysis and, especially in Ross County, the agricultural field as the primary unit of spatial analysis. While artifacts and agricultural fields have initially served to identify the general location and composition of nonmound debris, more specific units of analysis are necessary to further our understanding of nonmound debris. The following two sections present a summary of nonmound debris studies at Hopewell Mound Group over the past twenty-five years. First we summarize a pedestrian survey conducted by Seeman and use his conclusions as the basis for a set of hypotheses that provide expectations of nonmound debris located by additional survey at Hopewell Mound Group. Second, these hypotheses are tested using debris collected during intensive shovel testing by Dancey (1996a) from 1994 through 1995 and by the Hopewell Culture National Historical Park (HOCU) from 1998 through 2000 (summarized below). We then use various artifact attributes, as well as more inclusive artifact classes, to clarify the nature of the nonmound debris and to develop interpretations of its meaning, thus testing our hypotheses.

Pedestrian Survey (1980): Generating the Hypotheses

Over the past twenty-five years, approximately 200 hectares have been surveyed around and within Hopewell Mound Group using a variety of techniques, including pedestrian survey, shovel testing, coring, and remote sensing. The Kent State University pedestrian survey provides the greatest coverage. One of the primary goals of this survey was to obtain "data bearing on the configuration of Hopewell settlement in the southern Ohio area" (Seeman 1981c:1). To this end, the 1980 crew conducted a surface pickup of 178 hectares using a 6-meter transect interval. Agricultural field boundaries defined the units of collection, except in cases where discrete artifact clusters were identified.

Figure 21.1 shows the agricultural fields (in gray) in which the 1980 survey was conducted. Each field was given a unique number, and artifact clusters were named. The results shown in figure 21.2 provide a simple graphic summary of the survey. A wide range of field sizes in various physiographic settings was surveyed. In general, ten of the twenty-five fields surveyed produced debris indicative of Hopewell occupation—including, for example, bladelets, bladelet cores, and Hopewell projectile points. Of these ten fields, three (dark gray in fig. 21.2) contained more than ten artifacts per hectare. Six discrete concentrations of Hopewell debris were identified and collected separately from the general field collection lot. The locations of these clusters (for example, the Turtle Shell site) are shown in figure 21.2 as darker areas.

Figure 21.3 is a detailed summary of the artifacts collected by field and cluster. The frequencies provided in this matrix represent the results of one surface collection event per context. Except for the Engdahl site data, this matrix is populated with data generated by the Kent State University survey. The Engdahl site was recorded in 1979 and contains a small cluster of Hopewell artifacts (Ohio Archaeological Inventory form 33RO184).

Using the data in figure 21.3, Seeman (1981c) made a number of conclusions pertinent to discussions of nonmound debris at Hopewell Mound Group. First, while the area of the earthworks is covered in a low-density scatter of Hopewell debris, much of the debris is confined to the nonalluviating terrace on which the bulk of the earthwork is located. The debris density also seems to decrease with distance from the main embankments. Second, concentrations of debris occur both inside and outside the embankments, but these two cluster contexts are characterized by a different set of Hopewell artifacts. Most notably, bladelet use seems to have occurred at a higher frequency inside the embankments, while bladelet cores are more common outside the earthwork. Seeman suggested that this distribution might have resulted from the differential location of bladelet production and use. Obsidian and large cache blades (similar to the more than eight thousand found in Mound 2) occur almost exclusively inside the earthworks. Finally, the 1980 survey was unable to locate any concentrations of debris commensurate with the remains of a village-sized occupation, despite the debris cluster located in the area of Moorehead's west "Village Site." Thus, while Seeman concluded that the Hopewell clearly spent time at the earthworks for mourning, feasting, and other ceremonial activities, he found no evidence contradicting the vacant-center model of Hopewell community organization as originally proposed by Prufer (1964b, 1967).

On the basis of the results of Seeman's survey, we present two hypotheses concerning the Hopewell debris found in nonmound areas at Hopewell Mound Group. These hypotheses serve to focus attention on the nature of nonmound debris and direct research towards understanding the variability in non-mortuary-related occupations at the site. We use the word *occupation* to initially avoid value-laden words such as habitation, which inherently invest the debris with connotations of function prior to testing. Each hypothesis entails certain expectations of the archaeological record in the nonmound areas. These expectations are evaluated with independent data acquired since the Kent State survey. While none of the archaeological surveys at Hopewell Mound Group was set up specifically to generate and test hypotheses without bias, we believe that the surveys maintain enough independence that we may use the later surveys to evaluate hypotheses generated from the Kent State data. The junior author is currently conducting a more systematic and statistically valid test of the use of nonmound space inside the embankments at the site.

Hypothesis 1: Discrete occupation episodes are detectable in the archaeological record at Hopewell Mound Group

The Kent State surface collections demonstrate the presence of debris in many areas inside of and outside of the earthwork. While Seeman (1981c) was unable to identify clusters of debris in many of the survey units, six concentrations were

	Surface Condition	Mound 2 Type Cache Blades	Bladelet	Bladelet Core	Hopewell Point	Middle Woodland Point	Other Points	Debitage	Pottery Sherd	Celt	Biface Fragment	Other Stone Tools	Bone	Non-Hopewell Diagnostic	Collection Area Size (ha)	Hopewell Artifact Density per Hectare
West Village (1)	E	0	13	1	1	1	0	149	0	0	12	4	0	1	5	36.2
Turtle Shell (1)	E	0	5	0	0	0	0	19	0	0	4	0	1	0	0.05	560
Field 2	E	3	12	0	1	0	1	53	0	0	6	2	0	3	16	4.9
Field 2 SE Portion	E	0	0	0	0	0	0	7	1	0	2	0	0	0	na	na
Field 3 East	E	0	6	4	1	0	1	39	0	0	0	3	0	0	12	4.5
Field 3 West	E	0	1	2	0	0	0	15	1	0	1	2	0	0	6	3.7
East Village (3)	E	0	4	0	0	0	0	23	0	0	1	1	0	0	na	na
Spring Locale (3)	E	0	8	0	0	1	0	18	0	0	1	1	0	0	na	na
Field 4	E	1	4	0	1	0	0	40	0	1	6	2	0	2	2	28
Field 5	E	1	6	0	0	0	0	55	0	0	6	3	0	5	3.2	22.2
Fields 6&7	E	0	0	0	0	0	0	4	0	0	0	0	0	0	42.9	0.09
Field 8	FG	0	0	0	0	0	0	6	0	0	2	0	0	0	5.3	1.5
Field 9	E	0	0	0	0	0	0	12	0	0	1	1	0	1	13.8	1
Field 10	P	0	0	0	0	0	0	0	0	0	0	0	0	0	1.6	0
Field 11	VP	0	0	0	0	0	0	0	0	0	0	0	0	0	14.6	0
Field 12	P	0	1	1	0	1	0	5	0	0	3	0	0	1	4.1	2.7
Anderson Barn Site (13)	E	0	0	0	0	0	0	41	0	0	3	0	0	2	0.2	220
Field 14	F	0	0	0	0	0	0	6	0	0	2	0	0	2	6.1	1.3
Field 15	F	0	0	0	0	0	0	3	0	0	0	0	0	0	5.3	0.6
Field 16	E	0	1	0	0	0	0	2	0	0	0	0	0	0	0.4	7.5
Field 17	E	0	5	2	0	0	0	59	0	0	9	1	0	0	6.1	12.5
Tavern Site (17)	E	0	1	2	0	0	0	20	0	0	0	0	0	1	0.05	480
Field 18	G	0	0	0	0	0	0	0	0	0	0	0	0	3	1.6	0
Field 19	G	0	0	0	0	0	0	0	0	0	0	0	0	0	1.2	0
Field 20	E	0	1	2	0	0	0	7	1	0	2	0	0	2	5.3	2.5
Field 21	E	0	4	2	0	0	0	24	0	0	6	3	0	4	5	7.8
Field 22	G	0	2	0	1	1	0	14	1	0	0	5	0	1	6	3.9
Field 23	VG	0	0	0	0	0	0	1	0	0	1	0	0	1	5.3	0.4
Field 24	VG	0	0	0	0	0	0	0	0	0	0	0	0	0	3.6	0
Field 25	VG	0	0	0	0	0	0	0	0	0	0	0	0	0	8.1	0
Engdahl Site (22)	P	0	1	0	0	1	0	7	0	0	1	0	0	1	na	na

Figure 21.3. Results from the 1980 survey reported by Seeman (1981a): E = excellent, VG = very good, G = good, FG = fair to good, F = fair, P = poor, VP = very poor. Parentheses in first column indicate field location of cluster.

noted at various points around the earthwork. The presence of dispersed, low-density and higher-density, clustered debris suggests that discrete occupations may yet be detectable despite nearly two hundred years of plowing. To better identify variability in the location and composition of these clusters, a more complete collection of artifact classes must be made; for example, the 1980 surface collections did not record fire-cracked rock frequencies.

Discrete occupations represent either single-episode visits to the earthworks confined to a specific locale or repeated use of a specific locale over time. These clusters can be as small as 400 square meters with relatively few artifacts on the ground surface. Thus, any survey intending to locate these discrete occupations must utilize a small sampling interval. Differentiating between the remains of a single occupation episode and the overlapping debris from multiple occupations is a more difficult task that we leave for a future study. Controlling for time is a major obstacle to any kind of research at Hopewell earthwork sites, as many were occupied and built over hundreds of years.

Hypothesis 2: Space use varied across the earthworks and is dependent on the occupation's location inside of or outside of the earthworks

Hypothesis 2 suggests that the space delimited by the earthworks provided a context for different sets of activities. For example, the inside of the earthwork may have been restricted to ceremonial use only, while the outside was used during ceremonies, in gearing up for ceremonies, and for habitation. This hypothesis requires an intensive comparison of debris from interior and exterior earthwork contexts. Variability in the presence of certain classes of debris, such as pottery or fire-cracked rock, represents differences in site formation processes and the range of activities that took place at each occupation locus. Differences in space use should also be evident in the debris from making, using, and maintaining tools. Such evidence is best documented in chipped stone debris, as it is the least affected by the postdepositional impacts of plowing and tends to be the most abundant.

Shovel-test Surveys (1994–2000): Testing the Hypotheses

Two field projects were completed in the past decade to document nonmound debris at Hopewell Mound Group. In 1994 and 1995, Ohio State University (OSU) conducted shovel-test surveys at a number of locales around the periphery of the earthworks (Dancey 1996a); from 1998 through 2000, HOCU archaeologists surveyed both inside and outside the earthworks. Both projects used variable-interval shovel testing and 0.64-centimeter (quarter-inch) mesh screens to successfully locate and sample debris clusters. Samples of microartifacts were also collected from many of the clusters, but microartifact sample processing has yet to be completed. Initial work with these samples shows that microartifacts are present in varying quantities.

The following description of the recent surveys presents an artifact analysis of the items collected and curated in the HOCU curation facility. Nonmound cluster (NMC) assemblages were created in two ways. Each of the OSU collection locales, or datums, is treated as a separate assemblage that consists of the materials from all shovel tests excavated at that locale. The HOCU NMC assemblages include materials from a selection of shovel tests excavated in two survey areas. The HOCU cluster boundaries were established using the SURFER® software package to plot the total frequency of artifacts per shovel test across the surveyed areas. Clusters were visually identified based on artifact density and the presence of diagnostic Hopewell artifacts (for example, bladelets). The HOCU NMC assemblages were then pulled together from those shovel tests within the higher-density areas. We acknowledge the fact that creating artifact assemblages using a site-based technique has inherent limitations and biases. Hopewell use of the landscape surrounding Hopewell Mound Group is best addressed using a nonsite approach (*sensu* Dunnell and Dancey 1983). Such nonsite approaches minimize bias and assign equal importance to all artifacts, regardless of density. Instead of creating assemblages by attempting to define site boundaries, nonsite approaches use arbitrary units of space as the primary analytical unit. Our preliminary study, while essentially site based, serves to test two simple hypotheses and inform future nonsite surveys and analyses of Hopewell Mound Group and other earthwork sites.

We divided each assemblage into basic artifact classes, including fire-cracked rock, pottery, debitage (all debris related to chipped stone reduction), bladelets, bifaces, and bone. Interestingly, no bifaces or other stone tools, aside from one biface fragment found inside a feature within the earthworks, were found at any of the clusters. We then subjected the debitage to a more intensive attribute analysis to characterize the basic stages of reduction present in each assemblage.

Largely on the basis of lithic reduction experiments, a number of chipped stone debris attributes are deemed useful for tracking the stages and trajectory of lithic reduction (for example, Ingbar, Larson, and Bradley 1989; Magne and Pokotylo 1981; Mauldin and Amick 1989; Shott 1994; Tomka 1989). In our analysis, we coded for a selection of these debris attributes, including the presence or absence of cortex on platforms and the dorsal surfaces of complete flakes, the number of platform facets on complete and proximal flakes, the number of flake scars on the dorsal surfaces of complete flakes, and the overall size of debris based on the length of the longest axis of each piece. Together these attributes allow us to characterize the degree of lithic reduction and the points in the reduction sequence represented by cluster debitage: larger pieces of debris with cortex and few flake scars dorsally or on platforms are typical of the early stages of reduction; small debris with few or no cortex-covered surfaces and more numerous flake scars represent the later stages. While sample size limits the statistical significance of our debris comparisons, we believe that these debitage attributes provide an accurate overall estimate of the nature of lithic reduction in the tested assemblages.

The results of our analysis appear in figure 21.4. Each nonmound context is presented in terms of its general assemblage composition and the five debitage attributes. Other information is also provided, including the average number of artifacts per shovel test and a projected density of debris per hectare. Density

Nonmound Context	Size of Area Tested (ha)	Number of Shovel Tests	Total Artifacts	Fire-cracked Rock	Pottery	Debitage	Bladelets	Biface	Bone	Platform Cortex (cortex/n)	Flakes w/ Dorsal Cortex (cortex/n)	Platform Facets (range/average)	Dorsal Flake Scars (range/average)	Debris Size Classes 1–2	Debris Size Class 3 and up	Artifacts per Shovel Test	Estimated Artifacts per Hectare	Cluster Relative Density (CRD)
NMC 1	0.05	20	313	76%	4%	18%	2%	0%	0%	2 / 16	3 / 38	0-2 / 1.3	1-6 / 2.4	88%	12%	15.7	6260	4.99
NMC 2	0.02	9	61	49%	12%	26%	2%	0%	11%	1 / 7	2 / 12	0-3 / 1.2	0-10 / 4.6	94%	6%	6.8	3050	4.32
NMC 3	0.2	11	103	56%	10%	17%	2%	0%	15%	1 / 3	5 / 14	0-3 / 1	1-3 / 2	83%	17%	9.4	515	3.68
Datum A	0.009	8	76	85%	0%	12%	3%	0%	0%	3 / 3	3 / 4	0-1 / 0.7	0-1 / 0.5	33%	67%	9.5	8444	4.9
Datum C	0.013	12	42	64%	12%	24%	0%	0%	0%	0 / 0	1 / 1	1-2 / 1.5	0 / 0	90%	10%	3.5	3231	4.05
Datum D	0.012	12	17	53%	0%	35%	12%	0%	0%	0 / 4	0 / 6	1-3 / 2.3	- / 4	100%	0%	1.4	1417	3.29
Datum E	0.039	65	42	38%	0%	57%	5%	0%	0%	4 / 9	6 / 17	0-2 / 1.3	0-4 / 1.2	79%	21%	0.7	1077	2.88
Datum F	0.017	38	12	42%	0%	50%	8%	0%	0%	0 / 3	0 / 3	0-2 / 0.7	2-4 / 3	100%	0%	0.3	705	2.33
Datum H	0.021	28	93	35%	30%	29%	2%	0%	0%	1 / 8	0 / 15	0-3 / 1.3	2-5 / 3	96%	4%	3.3	4429	4.16
Datum K	0.017	11	21	9%	0%	86%	5%	0%	0%	0 / 12	0 / 16	0-3 / 1.1	2-8 / 3.7	89%	11%	1.9	1235	3.37
Feature 3	na	na	177	na	66	40	14	0	48	0 / 16	2 / 33	0-4 / 1.8	0-7 / 2.9	86%	14%	na	na	na

Figure 21.4. Comparison of nonmound context attributes at Hopewell Mound Group. Platform cortex = complete flakes plus proximals; flakes with dorsal cortex = all flakes; platform facets = complete flakes plus proximals. Dorsal flake scar counts were conducted on complete flakes only; debris size classes include all debitage only.

estimates are standardized for varying field methodology using a technique developed for this research (cluster relative density; see below).

The OSU Survey

Out of the twenty-one locales OSU tested in the immediate vicinity of the earthworks, seven produced diagnostic Hopewell artifacts (Datums A, C, D, E, F, H, and K). The locations of these locales in relation to the Kent State and HOCU survey units are shown in figure 21.2. Datums C and K are located on the upland plateau to the north of the earthwork; Datums D, H, and part of E are situated on the same terrace as the majority of the earthworks and overlook the floodplain of an intermittent stream (Sulphur Lick Creek); and Datums F and the remainder of E sit on the floodplain of this same stream.

Figure 21.4 presents a summary of the artifact analysis for these contexts. Four of the tested areas are covered by a low-density debris scatter (Datums D, E, F, and K), while three (Datums A, C, and H) contain concentrations proportional in density to the clusters Seeman identified (for example, Turtle Shell and Tavern sites). Most of the variability in general debris among these contexts occurs in terms of the relative frequency of pottery, debitage, and fire-cracked rock. Except for Datum H, there seems to be a negative correlation between fire-cracked rock and debitage. At some locales, such as Datums A and C, fire-cracked rock dominates the assemblage. In other assemblages, such as Datums E and K, debitage is the most prevalent debris class. Datum H stands out from the rest in two ways: (1) it was the most productive locale, with ninety-three total artifacts (although Datum A had the highest number of artifacts per shovel test); and (2) it produced a high percentage of pottery in addition to fire-cracked rock and debitage. While the high relative frequency of pottery at Datum H may have resulted from sampling error—the edges of the cluster were not defined and thus the entire cluster was not representatively sampled—the presence of twenty-eight pottery sherds sets it apart from the other clusters.

The debitage study of the OSU debris indicates predominantly late-stage reduction. Only Datums A and E produced debitage with a high incidence of platform and dorsal cortex as well as low numbers of platform facets and dorsal flake scars. This debris also tended to be larger in overall size. The debitage from the remainder of the contexts was largely free of cortex, exhibited higher numbers of platform facets and dorsal flake scars, and was small in size.

In sum, the OSU survey found diagnostic Hopewell artifacts in seven of the twenty-one locales tested. These seven locales were situated in a variety of physiographic settings. Three contained relatively high densities of nonmound debris. Two of these three are located on opposite sides of the earthworks on the main terrace, and the third is situated north of the earthworks on the upland plateau. Most of the debitage assemblages suggest only late-stage lithic reduction, while two are more typical of early-stage reduction.

The HOCU Survey

From 1998 through 2000, HOCU archaeologists tested for nonmound debris in an additional 3.5 hectares in two areas of the site using 50-×-50-centimeter shovel tests (fig. 21.1). A light scatter of debris was found in both survey areas, and three Hopewell artifact clusters were defined. The first area lies less than 100 meters east of the earthwork's square enclosure (fig. 21.5). This area was tested in preparation for the construction of new interpretive facilities. Shovel tests were initially excavated at 10-meter intervals. In areas where the debris seemed to increase in density, the testing interval was reduced to 5 meters. Importantly, a 10-meter interval ably located small debris clusters but was insufficient for providing large artifact samples. The 5-meter interval allowed us to better define cluster edges and acquire a larger artifact sample.

Nonmound Cluster 1 is the larger of the two clusters in the interpretive area. It covers approximately 0.05 hectares and produced 313 artifacts from twenty

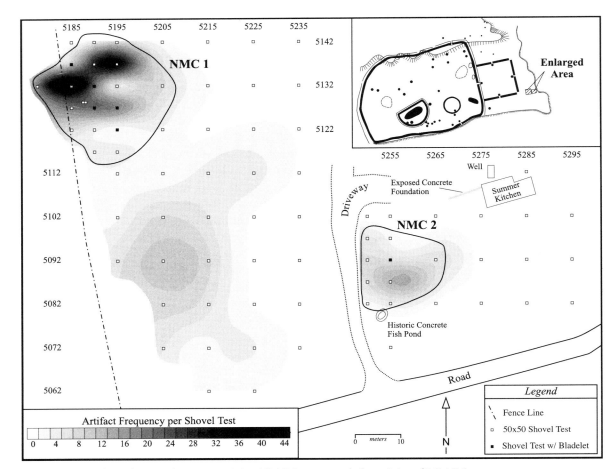

Figure 21.5. Enlarged view of area containing NMC (nonmound cluster) 1 and NMC 2.

shovel tests—the highest number of artifacts per shovel test of any cluster (fig. 21.4). While this cluster contained seven bladelet fragments and eleven small pottery sherds, the bulk of the debris was fire-cracked rock. A few of the shovel tests encountered small pieces of wood charcoal, but no tools or animal bone were found. The debitage from NMC 1 (fig. 21.4) is consistent with a middle- to late-stage reduction assemblage. Eighty-eight percent of the debitage falls into the small size class, and an overwhelming majority lack platform or dorsal cortex. Despite their overall small size, the whole flakes also have a relatively high number of dorsal flake scars on average.

Nonmound Cluster 2 is located 40–50 meters southeast of NMC 1 and consists of sixty-one artifacts recovered from just nine shovel tests. While NMC 1 is situated in a plowed field, NMC 2 was found in the house yard of a nineteenth-century farmstead. The assemblage composition of NMC 2 is also slightly different than NMC 1 in that there is a more even representation of artifact classes.

Pottery is more prevalent in the NMC 2 assemblage, and seven bone fragments were found. The bone may be historic given this cluster's proximity to the historic farmstead. Even without the bone, this cluster's lower relative frequency of fire-cracked rock and higher amounts of pottery and debitage distinguish it from NMC 1. Once again, other than one bladelet, no tools were found. The debitage of NMC 2 looks much like that of NMC 1, except that a higher percentage of objects were small in size and the complete flakes had twice as many dorsal flake scars on average.

The second area tested by HOCU archaeologists is located in the inner northeast corner of the main enclosure (fig. 21.1). This area has long been of interest to archaeologists, as it includes one of the two supposed village sites on the inside of the earthworks as noted by Squier and Davis (1848), Moorehead (1922), and Shetrone (1926). In 1998 HOCU archaeologists, under the direction of Ruby, initiated a shovel-test survey in the vicinity of the east "Village Site." In 1999 the authors began a geophysical remote sensing survey in this area to locate the northern junction of the main embankment and the square. In the summer of 2000 we greatly expanded the initial shovel-test survey and conducted additional remote sensing in the vicinity of Mound 1, which has been "lost" since before Moorehead's excavations in the early 1890s.

Figure 21.6 shows the location of debris across 106 shovel tests in the Mound 1/east "Village Site" area. A 20-meter shovel test interval was used initially, but this was reduced to 10 meters when higher-density debris was encountered. Several shovel tests were excavated in the deflated remains of the embankment to confirm its presence and test for remaining integrity. While this section of embankment is much reduced in height from plowing and erosion, the shovel tests revealed that the embankment's very bottom is still intact and covers subembankment features. For this study, we consider only the debris from those shovel tests located in nonmound contexts on the inside of the embankment.

Ten of the 106 shovel tests, scattered across the survey area, contained bladelets, and the majority had at least one piece of fire-cracked rock. No significant clusters of debris were found in the area containing the supposed village site. However, an arc of debris was found surrounding the southern half of Mound 1. The artifacts from the higher-density shovel tests (eleven shovel tests) in this cluster were singled out and combined as the NMC 3 assemblage. A pit feature (Feature 3) was also encountered along the southern edge of NMC 3. The artifacts from this feature are presented separately in figure 21.4.

The NMC 3 assemblage is very similar to those of NMC 1 and 2 in terms of object size and presence of cortex, but the number of platform facets and dorsal flake scars is slightly lower on average. While the estimated number of artifacts per hectare is much lower than for the clusters outside the earthwork, the number of artifacts per shovel test falls in between NMC 1 and 2. This highlights one of the basic problems in comparing survey data collected with different techniques (for example, shovel testing versus pedestrian survey) at different sampling intervals. To compensate for variability in shovel test frequency and den-

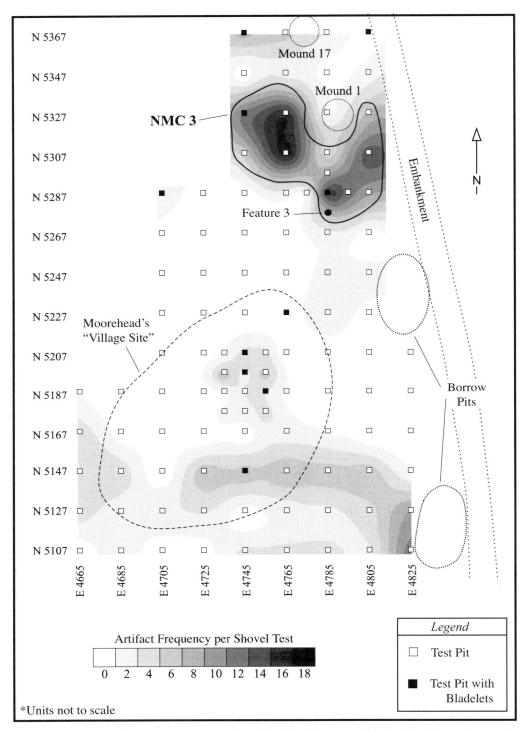

Figure 21.6. East "Village Site"–area test pits and artifact frequency distribution. Feature 3 contained bladelets.

sity, we have created a density index that accounts for the size of the area tested, artifacts per shovel test, and estimated artifacts per hectare, where

Cluster Relative Density (CRD) = log (artifacts per shovel test × estimated artifacts per hectare)

When sample unit frequency and density are accounted for, NMC 3 (CRD = 3.68) is clearly less dense than the two clusters outside the embankments (fig. 21.4).

Feature 3 is an oval (50 × 75 centimeters), undulating-bottomed basin that extended approximately 45 centimeters below the surface. It was encountered when additional shovel tests were excavated at 10-meter intervals along the southeastern edge of NMC 3. The Feature 3 artifacts analyzed for this research must be considered a sample of those actually present, since the feature has been highly impacted by plowing and flotation samples have yet to be fully analyzed. The raw counts presented in figure 21.4 at least represent the major trends in feature content and provide an interesting comparison with plow-zone debris.

The most prominent difference between the Feature 3 assemblage and the other assemblages is the high incidence of bone, pottery, and bladelets. While many of the sherds were cordmarked body fragments, tetrapodal vessel feet and simple-stamped and diamond-check-stamped sherds were also found. No decorated pottery was found in the plow-zone contexts of the other clusters. Numerous pieces of fire-cracked rock, as well as debitage and pottery, were found in the plow zone above this feature. The debitage attributes are consistent with those from the other clusters. The overwhelming majority of the debitage is small and lacks any evidence of cortex.

Discussion

In 1980 a survey of Hopewell Mound Group by Kent State University found that the earthworks and their adjacent areas contained widespread evidence of prehistoric occupation. Much of this debris was reported as an undifferentiated, low-density scatter punctuated by infrequent, higher-density clusters. These debris scatters were interpreted as representing the remains of intermittent habitations by Hopewell groups who traveled to the earthworks for the purpose of participating in ritual and ceremonial activities (Seeman 1981a, 1981b). Following Seeman's conclusions, we have presented two hypotheses related to the Hopewell occupation of Hopewell Mound Group. First we hypothesized that evidence of discrete occupation episodes is present and detectable in the archaeological record. Second, these nodes of occupation were hypothesized to differ in content, especially when those from inside the earthworks are compared to those from the outside. In testing these hypotheses, we intensively studied assemblages from ten new locales, both within and adjacent to the earthworks, paying special attention to specific attributes present on the chipped stone debris.

During both Dancey's 1994–1995 survey and the 1998–2000 HOCU survey, discrete clusters of Hopewell artifacts were identified. Thus, we cannot reject our first hypothesis. Hopewell Mound Group contains numerous, detectable clusters of Hopewell occupation. Regarding Hypothesis 2, our analyses show that these clusters do vary in their size, intracluster density, and relative frequency of major artifact classes (that is, fire-cracked rock, pottery, debitage, bone, stone tools, and bladelets). The remainder of this chapter will be devoted to exploring the nature of the variability in the nonmound debris clusters.

Size

Except for the west "Village Site," which is not yet well defined, all of the known occupation areas at Hopewell Mound Group are smaller than 0.5 hectares. In fact, many are substantially smaller. Of the three nonmound clusters identified by the HOCU survey, NMC 3 was the largest at 0.2 hectares, while the clusters on the exterior of the earthwork cover 0.05 hectares (NMC 1) and 0.02 hectares (NMC 2). The locales tested during the OSU survey are also small, ranging from 0.009 to 0.039 hectares. Additional testing at some of these locales (for example, Datum A) is necessary if definitive cluster boundaries are to be drawn. Compared to documented Hopewell habitation sites, these debris clusters are tiny. Of the forty-eight open-air habitation sites reported by Dancey and Pacheco (1997a:Table 1.1), the average site size is 0.62 hectares (ranging from 0.03 hectares to 4.5 hectares), which is nearly four times larger than the average of NMC 1-3 and the clusters presented in figure 21.3. Thus, the occupation clusters at Hopewell Mound Group differ markedly in size from documented habitation sites.

The Hopewell Mound Group clusters also differ in size compared to clusters adjacent to other earthwork complexes, such as those surrounding the Stubbs Earthwork in Warren County. Based on controlled and uncontrolled surface collections, twenty-eight Hopewell clusters have been identified within a mile of the Stubbs Earthwork (Genheimer 1997). These clusters range in size from 0.05 hectares to 4.3 hectares, with an average of 1.19 hectares, making them comparable in size to habitation sites and much larger than the clusters at Hopewell Mound Group. Debris from other surveyed earthworks, such as the Liberty Works in Ross County, also seems to be found in larger clusters (Coughlin and Seeman 1997).

It is not clear whether the small size of the debris clusters at Hopewell Mound Group relative to habitation clusters and those at other earthwork sites reflects actual cultural variability, site formation factors, or differences in sampling methodology. We would argue that most surveys conducted in the vicinity of Ohio Hopewell earthwork complexes lack the resolution to define the smaller-scale occupations identified at Hopewell Mound Group. For this reason, other characteristics of debris clusters must also be considered.

Density

Artifact density is a more difficult archaeological quality to compare from one study to another. Different survey and excavation techniques produce highly varied density data. Cluster relative density (CRD) is an attempt to standardize the density data from the various shovel-test surveys at Hopewell Mound Group (see above and fig. 21.4). The number of artifacts per shovel test or the number of artifacts per area tested do not alone adequately characterize artifact density when comparing data from areas tested using different shovel test intervals. For example, NMC 3 (9.4) seems to be denser than NMC 2 (6.8) when considering only the number of artifacts found per shovel test. However, an estimate of the artifacts per hectare suggests that NMC 2 (3,050) is many times denser than NMC 3 (515). What sets the two clusters apart is the size of the area tested and the density of shovel tests. At NMC 2 we used a 5-meter interval across an area of only 0.02 hectares, and at NMC 3 a 20-meter interval was used to test a much larger area. Our measure of CRD standardizes density data across variable interval testing grids by factoring in the number of shovel tests conducted, the area tested, and the total number of artifacts found. The CRDs of NMC 2 (CRD = 4.32) and NMC 3 (CRD = 3.68) correctly show that NMC 2 is a denser concentration of artifacts than NMC 3.

When considering the above factors of sampling method and site formation at Hopewell Mound Group, a simple pattern emerges. A rather abrupt decrease in density at about 300–400 meters out from the earthworks is apparent in figure 21.2. The outermost shovel-test blocks to the east and north of the earthworks do not contain Hopewell artifacts, whereas those blocks closer to the earthworks generally do.

A similar pattern is evident in the Kent State University surface data when the density of Hopewell artifacts per hectare is considered for each of the surveyed fields. Fields closer to the embankments have a higher number of artifacts per hectare than do those more distant. Three fields in particular—4, 5, and 17—stand out. Field 4 has an artifact density three standard deviations higher than the average of all surveyed fields. This is likely evidence signifying the differential use of space for this area of the earthworks. Fields 5 (> 2 s.d.) and 17 (> 1 s.d.) support the presence of a significantly higher density of debris near the outside of the embankments. These two fields also happen to be those on the second terrace closest to the floodplain and the outside edge of the embankment. A noticeable decrease in surface artifact density is apparent at about 300–400 meters from the edges of the embankments.

Two other density patterns are evident in the surface-collected data that did not show up in the shovel-test data. First, the general scatter of debris from the fields inside the embankments is much lower than that from the fields immediately adjacent to the outside edges of the embankments. While this difference may in part be accounted for by the large size of the fields found inside the earthworks, even the smaller interior fields (for example, Fields 5 and 16) have a lower density of artifacts per hectare than nearby fields just beyond the embankments (for example, Fields 4 and 17).

In addition to differences in interior versus exterior artifact densities, landform also seems to play a role in the density of Hopewell artifacts. If we assume that artifacts in the floodplains of the North Fork have not been obscured by alluvium or disturbed by floodwaters, the floodplains did not accumulate any detectable Hopewell debris (Seeman 1981a, 1981c). None of the fields surveyed in the floodplains—even those adjacent to the embankments—exceeds a density of three artifacts per hectare. Likewise, the fields in the uplands to the north of the earthworks (Fields 22–25) also have low artifact densities. While this suggests that the uplands were not a favored landform for use by the Hopewell, the low artifact densities in this area could just as likely be a factor of their distance from the embankments.

Similar artifact density patterns have been found at other Hopewell earthwork complexes. When the agricultural field has been used as the survey unit, such as at the Mound City Group (Burks and Pederson 1999; Lynott and Monk 1985; Seeman 1981b) and the Liberty Earthworks (Coughlin and Seeman 1997), Hopewell artifact density tends to decrease with distance from the earthworks. At the Stubbs Earthwork, where individual clusters are the unit of analysis, cluster density is significantly lower 1.5 kilometers away from the embankments as compared to just south of the embankments along Bigfoot Run (Genheimer 1997).

Based on data from Hopewell Mound Group, and similar patterns at a number of other Hopewell earthwork complexes, nonmound artifact density exterior to the embankments seems to be inversely related to distance from the earthworks. Since the amount of surface area available for occupation generally increases with distance from the earthworks, it follows that artifact density (a measure of artifacts per unit area) decreases. In situations where the surface area for occupation near an earthwork is limited, as at Fort Ancient (Connolly 1997), Hopewell artifacts and features are especially dense. Thus, Hopewell occupation events at Fort Ancient could have been just as short-term and intermittent as we suggest for Hopewell Mound Group, but confined to a smaller area.

Artifacts

Fire-cracked rock and lithic debitage, with pottery and bone as a very minor component, dominate most of the nonmound debris clusters at Hopewell Mound Group. In general, the clusters fall into four groups: those with high and low relative frequencies of fire-cracked rock and those with and without pottery. Fire-cracked rock has not been regularly recorded or collected by the various surveys at Hopewell Mound Group, but it clearly represents more than just passing occupation of a given area. While the OSU and HOCU surveys counted and collected fire-cracked rock, it was noted but not quantified by the Kent State surveys. Thus, the general distribution of this artifact class across the surveyed areas is not well understood. In those areas where fire-cracked rock was regularly collected, it is nearly ubiquitous. Fire-cracked rock represents less than half of the assemblage in only five of the eleven clusters presented in figure 21.4. In two of these four clusters (NMC 2 and Datum H), the lower fire-cracked rock frequencies can be accounted for by a more even spread of artifact class frequencies, suggesting a more intensive occupation of the Datum H area, especially. The remaining fire-cracked rock–poor assemblages (Datums E, F, and K) lack pottery and consequently have a higher relative frequency of debitage.

While some of these differences in the relative frequency of fire-cracked rock may result from sample bias in assemblage size per cluster, they are also a factor of preservation and prehistoric rates of deposition. Fire-cracked rock was likely deposited as both a sheet midden and in pit features. Pit features like Feature 3 near NMC 3 contain vast amounts of fire-cracked rock that, when disturbed by the plow, can produce fairly dense clusters of plow-zone debris. Such deposits can represent a single depositional event or can be the result of repeated reuse of an area. More work is needed at the Hopewell Mound Group clusters before questions of occupation duration and reoccupation can be addressed.

Woodland period pottery is also heavily affected by plow disturbance. Most plow-zone-context pottery sherds from Hopewell Mound Group are 2 centimeters or less in diameter and heavily eroded. The location of NMC 2 in close proximity to a historic house probably minimized pottery breakage caused by plowing, and yet the pottery from this cluster is also small and very weathered. The similarity between pottery found at NMC 1 and NMC 2 suggests that perhaps plow-zone breakage is not as pervasive as has been feared.

Known Hopewell habitation sites, such as Murphy (Dancey 1991), McGraw (Prufer 1965), and 33FR895 (Aument and Gibbs 1991) have highly variable debris profiles. The Murphy site (Murphy I in Dancey and Pacheco 1997a:Table 1.1) is located on a terrace along Raccoon Creek in Licking County, Ohio, approximately 100 kilometers northeast of Hopewell Mound Group. The deposit was plowed for at least 150 years prior to excavation, and the debris profile looks somewhat similar to those from the clusters at Hopewell. The Murphy assemblage is dominated by chipped stone tools and tool-making debris (>20,000), with just 858 ceramic sherds. As with the nonmound clusters, bladelets comprised a very small percentage of the assemblage at Murphy (approximately 1 percent). However, the similarities end there. Over 400 bifaces were found at Murphy, and debris from all stages of reduction was abundant. While attribute analyses of the debitage have yet to be conducted, the high frequency of early-stage biface reduction debris distinguishes the Murphy debitage from that of the nonmound clusters. Dancey (1991:55) attributes the presence of all stages of biface reduction to the site's proximity to the Flint Ridge quarries, 19 kilometers to the west of the Murphy site.

Site 33FR895, which consists of a structure, external pit features, and a debris scatter, is a Hopewell habitation located in the uplands of Franklin County, Ohio, 60 kilometers north of Hopewell Mound Group. This site was also extensively plowed prior to excavation, and the bulk of the assemblage was found in a plow-zone context. Of the 1,373 recovered artifacts (not including fire-cracked rock), the chipped stone assemblage comprises the majority of the material remains with 1,215 items. Only 149 sherds were recovered. Bladelets represent a somewhat larger fraction of the total debris at 11 percent. As at Murphy, virtually no faunal material was recovered. The proportion of debitage to pottery and bladelets is very similar to that found at the Hopewell debris clusters. While Aument and Gibbs (1991:42) suggest that the debris at 33FR895 represents at least two time periods, the use of Vanport chert (which would likely have been brought in from the Flint Ridge quarries approximately 85 kilometers to the east) is most likely attributable to Hopewell lithic reduction activities. The majority of the Vanport debris is made up of "secondary and tertiary thinning flakes," which typically have little to no cortex and are relatively small in size. The eight complete bifaces recovered represent early to middle stages of biface reduction. An additional thirty-nine biface fragments were also found in the plow zone. More than half of the complete and fragmented bifaces were made from chert types commonly found in the streambeds and glacial till in close proximity to the site. In sum, the occupants of 33FR895 were clearly less focused on biface production as compared to those who lived at Murphy. The debris profile at 33FR895 looks very similar to those of the nonmound clusters at Hopewell Mound Group, except for the bifaces, but the age of these bifaces is unknown. A more informed comparison of the nonmound cluster assemblages at 33FR895 cannot be conducted until an intensive attribute analysis of the debris from this site has been completed.

The cultural deposits at the McGraw site were recovered from a minimally disturbed, sealed midden located on the slope of a low rise in the Scioto River floodplain 15 kilometers southeast of Hopewell Mound Group (Prufer 1965). Pottery sherds ($n = 9,946$) dominate the assemblage, followed by animal bone (n = approximately 6,400) and chipped stone tools and debris (n = approximately 2,000). Bifaces and 233 complete and fragmented bladelets (approximately 1 percent of the assemblage) were also recovered. The debitage assemblage from McGraw also has not been studied at the attribute level, but it was sorted according to material type. Fifteen percent of the debitage is nonlocal in origin (Vanport or Harrison County, Indiana, chert), with the remainder representing more-local raw materials. Other objects were also found, including numerous scraps of mica, celt fragments ($n = 2$), gorget fragments ($n = 2$), worked copper ($n = 1$), fragments of terra-cotta figurines ($n = 5$), a sandstone hemispherical cone, and numerous worked bone implements. Some of these objects, such as the copper and figurine fragments, are more typically found in ceremonial contexts. Fire-cracked rock was not reported in Prufer's volume beyond the statement that it was "common throughout the midden" (Prufer 1965:101).

While the McGraw assemblage may represent only one area (probably the garbage dump) of a larger Hopewell habitation site, the vast amounts of pottery sherds and the wide array of miscellaneous objects set it apart from any of the other plow-zone assemblages considered in this chapter. McGraw is most unlike other Hopewell habitation sites in the number of pottery sherds preserved in its unplowed midden. Other unplowed Middle Woodland–era sites in Ohio, such as the Strait site in northern Fairfield County, have also produced substantial amounts of pottery (Burks and Dancey 2000), attesting to the potential for assemblage bias caused by over a hundred years of plowing.

Summary and Conclusions

The past twenty-five years of research clearly show that, like most other Ohio Hopewell earthworks, Hopewell Mound Group has significant quantities of

Hopewell debris inside and outside of its embankments. Most models of Ohio Hopewell community organization (for example, Dancey and Pacheco 1997a) assume that Hopewell earthwork centers were vacant for much of the year. Visits by small and large groups for mortuary, social, and seasonal ceremonial events were likely short-term and periodic, yet some researchers still refer to the debris clusters at Hopewell Mound Group as Hopewell habitation sites—in other words, permanent domestic habitations.

Hopewell habitation sites appear to differ from the debris clusters at Hopewell Mound Group in two important ways. First, Hopewell habitation sites are much larger, with higher concentrations of debris. Of all of the clusters known at Hopewell to date, Dancey's Datum H is perhaps the only candidate for a habitation site, and it is located well outside the site's embankments. Second, the Hopewell Mound Group clusters differ from habitation sites in their significant lack of stone tools and tool diversity, particularly regarding bifaces. The cluster assemblages exhibit a very restricted range of artifact classes, consisting almost entirely of fire-cracked rock, lithic debitage, and very small amounts of weathered pottery. Similar-sized clusters with such meager assemblages are commonly overlooked in most surveys in Ohio.

We conclude that much of the known Hopewell debris surrounding and contemporaneous with Hopewell Mound Group represents the remains of small, short-term camps inhabited by groups visiting the earthworks to participate in the varied social and ceremonial events that took place there throughout the year. Such repeated short-term occupations would have likely produced widely scattered clusters of low-density sheet midden, each perhaps associated with a select number of subsurface features. Thus far no subsurface features have been tested from one of these clusters outside the earthwork. Nevertheless, low artifact diversity suggests that a very limited amount and/or range of activities occurred at these occupation sites. The consistent presence of fire-cracked rock (a sign of heating and cooking), small debitage (a sign of tool maintenance), and small amounts of pottery (indicative of minimal breakage during storage or cooking) all point to everyday kinds of activities at these clusters. However, the low artifact densities suggest only short-term occupation and a limited range of activities. Future projects at Hopewell Mound Group and other earthwork centers owned by the National Park Service are slated to more intensively test these nonmound clusters and clarify the Hopewell use of space.

Acknowledgments

We gratefully acknowledge the advice and assistance of the individuals who read and provided comments on various drafts of this chapter, including Carrie Andreson, Albert Pecora, Charles Stout, and Dawn Walter. Their keen eyes and insight helped us iron out some of the major kinks. Bill Dancey and Mark Seeman were kind enough to provide us access to their research and unpublished manuscripts. However, any mistakes, misinterpretations, or inconsistencies remain our own.

22

Rediscovering This Earth

Some Ethnogeological Aspects of the Illinois Valley Hopewell Mounds

Julieann Van Nest

> . . . so the ceremony requires the presence of a woman to direct a certain few rites where a man may not properly perform. This was done by a woman named Chaúi (Lump-Forehead). In previous ceremonies, in which she fulfilled this office, she cut the so-called "ditch," an important element of the altar. In the ceremony under consideration, she directed Sósoni, Hisénibe (Singing-Woman), and Waánibe in this rite. The reason why this so-called "ditch" is cut by women, is because the woman who ascended to the Heavens and became the wife of Sun-Boy, dug a similar hole at the time that she rediscovered this earth.
> **Dorsey 1903:27**

The Illinois River valley Hopewell mounds (fig. 22.1), dating to circa 2,050–1,750 uncalibrated radiocarbon years ago (Asch 1997; Farnsworth and Asch 1986), are noteworthy for an extraordinary variety of ethnogeological attributes ranging in scale from minute inclusions to earthen constructions visible from space. In this chapter I explore how some of these cultural constructions may have articulated with the natural landscapes at these sites in the overall context of world-renewal ritual (Hall 1979, 1997). That the Hopewellian cosmos was vertically partitioned into three worlds—this world, above, and below—is symbolically represented by where the mound groups were situated, as well as by the earthen compositions of the mounds themselves. Inasmuch as some of the earthen elements crucial to the plan of Illinois Hopewell mounds have earlier Archaic antecedents in the Illinois Valley, it can be argued that it was in this particular physical landscape, under geohistorical conditions of circa 2,050 years ago, that a kind of mound building arose that was closely integrated with world-renewal ritual (Buikstra and Charles 1999; Buikstra, Charles, and Rakita 1998). Whether or not or to what degree Illinois Hopewell mounds are similar or dissimilar to those in Ohio and elsewhere remains to be critically examined.

Why did Illinois Hopewell rise and fall when and where it did? It is the premise of this chapter that some clues are to be found in the geological as well as the anthropological record. Many questions remain concerning the meaning of these mounds, and any direct comparisons made between Illinois Hopewell

Figure 22.1. Map of Illinois showing the mound groups mentioned in the text.

and later groups regarding the use of soils and earthen materials could serve as well to demonstrate how radically things have changed as to show linkages to a former past. It is readily apparent that the Illinois Hopewell way of building mounds ceased at the end of the Middle Woodland period (circa 1750 B.P.), yet some of the ritual elements may have carried on, as Hall (1979, 1997) has suggested.

Although some have looked to the ethnographic record of southeastern Indians for insight into the symbolism behind the earthen elements in these mounds, an equally rich source may be found in the more northerly and Plains groups now in areas usually thought of as peripheral to Hopewell. Perhaps it is a case of cultural conservatism that some of the elements of Hopewellian world-renewal ritual survived for so long in those groups that by design or by historical accident were ultimately able to remain marginal to subsequent developments in the Mississippian world.

The ethnographic record certainly has not been a significant source of hypotheses for the field of geology, to say the least. But whether or not Hall's assertions are true, they are certainly plausible. They therefore constitute legitimate grounds for hypothesis building, following a long-standing tradition in the earth sciences in which all plausible alternative hypotheses must be examined (Chamberlin 1890, 1897; Gilbert 1886). Because much of what follows serves to amplify Hall's original observations, it is incumbent upon us to formulate new hypotheses amenable to scientific testing: (1) the Illinois Hopewell mounds were built during a time of very large regional floods, and (2) the overarching earthen theme involved in mound construction was the use of newly made or newly transformed ground. The first impacted decisions about how and where the mounds would be built; the second constituted but a portion of an elaborate set of symbolic acts by the living to create the world anew.

Ethnographic Vestiges of a Distant Past?

Hall (1979, 1997) has argued that certain aspects of world-renewal ritual documented in historical ethnographic writings may be the splintered remnants of earlier Woodland period burial mound ceremonialism. Of particular interest for this chapter are two themes discussed by Hall and briefly reviewed again here—namely, the creation of this world by Earth Diver, and certain elements of the Arapahoe and Cheyenne Sun Dance, especially the acquisition and use of sod blocks (Dorsey 1903, 1905, 1910; see also Charles, Van Nest, and Buikstra 2004).

Described by Leeming and Page (1998:77) as "easily the most prevalent type of Native American creation story," the Earth Diver myth generally involves a primordial world covered by water. Animals dive until one is successful in bringing up a small amount of mud, from which the earth grows and is subsequently populated. "They have a droll theory of the Creation, for they think that a pregnant woman fell down from heaven, and that a tortoise . . . took this pregnant woman on its back, because every place was covered with water; and that the woman sat upon the tortoise, groped with her hands in the water, and scraped together some of the earth, whence it finally happened that the earth was raised above the water. They think that there are more worlds than one, and that we came from another world" (Megapolensis [1644]1996:45). This early, but short, account in a letter sent back home captures the main Earth Diver theme, namely, the creation of this world from a dab of subaqueous mud. In more elaborate accounts, mud is brought up from below only with great difficulty:

> It was agreed that the duck-creatures should receive her on their interknit wings and lower her gently to the surface below. The great turtle from the under-world was to arise and make his broad back a resting-place. It was as had been agreed and the woman came down upon the floating island.
>
> Then did the creatures seek to make a world for the woman and one by one they dove to the bottom of the water seeking to find earth to plant upon the turtle's back. A duck dived but went so far that it breathed the water and came up dead. A pickerel went down and came back dead. Many creatures sought to find the bottom of the water but could not. At last the creature called Muskrat made the attempt and only succeeded in touching the bottom with his nose but this was sufficient for he was enabled to smear it upon the shell and the earth immediately grew, and as the earth-substance increased so did the size of the turtle. (Parker 1923:62)

Citing several archaeological examples, Hall (1979:260) has suggested that the use of "special soil" such as "clay, marl, muck or mud" in Hopewell mounds may have been representative of the primordial mud brought up by Earth Diver, in large part because these deposits are thought to have been obtained from springy or wet-ground areas. These deposits tend to occur in limited burial contexts involving very small volumes relative to overall mound volume. The most striking example is still the widely cited "black burial mould" (Kelly and Cole 1931:326) found in nine of the twenty mounds at Utica (fig. 22.1), in the upper Illinois River valley (Henricksen 1957, 1965). Generally this custom is attributed to the more northerly Illinois groups (Griffin 1945; Herold 1971; Walker 1952; Winters 1961), but its use to the south in Illinois might be expanded if more could be known about vague references to "black soils" (see for example, the summary of historical references to mound sediments and structures compiled by Buikstra [1998]).

The relatively small volumes of these "special soils" are compatible with the typically small amounts of primordial mud brought up by Earth Diver. But what about the soil materials used to build the rest of these mounds? Generally there has been little historical description or sampling of mound fill, and usually it is thought to have been obtained with little difficulty from the surrounding terrain. This assumption may be largely inaccurate, as discussed below.

If the "special soils" are representative dabs of primordial earth brought up by Earth Diver, then perhaps there are other elements of this myth that are also relevant to the interpretation of the Illinois Hopewell mounds. We should not overlook the fact that the antecedent condition for Earth Diver is a place covered by water and lacking land. When, if ever, might such conditions have existed, in reality or metaphorically? As argued below, if one takes a geological rather than a historical perspective, it is not difficult at all to imagine very large floods that would have completely inundated the riverine environment, effectively rendering it inaccessible, perhaps for relatively long periods of time. For societies whose economies were otherwise very much centered on riverine resources, such flood events might well have profoundly impacted worldviews. In essence, riverine environments are destroyed and recreated, more or less simultaneously. When receding, large floods leave the indelible marks of a physically reorganized floodplain, a situation that in turn probably has more than minor ecological impacts (positive and negative) on important floodplain resource zones.

The recent documentation of extensive use of sod blocks in Illinois Hopewell mounds (Van Nest et al. 2001; see below) raises a number of additional questions for which ethnographic insights might prove useful in helping to explain their occurrences. As Hall (1979, 1997) has noted, sod blocks were crucial elements of the altars constructed during the Cheyenne and Arapahoe "Sun Dance" ceremonies. Dorsey (1910:651) regarded the ceremony as one of "rebirth or re-animation," or world-renewal, and in this the Cheyenne and Arapahoe ceremonies differed from some of the other ceremonies subsumed under the rubric of "Sun Dance" (Hall 1997:19–20; Schlesier 1990). Although its current form (as recorded in written forms) may have developed only in protohistoric times, Schlesier (1987) argues that many of the elements of the ceremony have deep Asiatic-American roots. Schlesier (1987:145) has presented a hypothetical reconstruction of a premound "spirit lodge" that might have been erected as part of mound-building activities at the Swift Creek mounds (Middle Woodland, Sonota Complex) in South Dakota. This structure is not unlike some of the reconstructions suggested for premound structures found at or near the base of many Illinois Hopewell mounds (see review in Buikstra, Charles, and Rakita 1998:68–74). Although the diameter of the mound may be compatible with such a structure, the archaeological report by Neuman (1975) does not substantiate the presence of any post molds, either around the circumference of the mound or indicating the four central posts suggested by Schlesier's reconstruction.

In the Arapahoe Sun Dance, or Offerings Lodge ceremony, two turf-side up sod blocks were placed near a small, rectangular "ditch," the outer boundary of which was lined by two painted wooden billets. Ultimately the sod blocks became the receptacles into which were placed symbolic branches (Dorsey 1903:104–111, Plate LII). In the Cheyenne ceremony, five inverted (turf-side down) sod blocks were arranged first in a rectangular array, then rearranged into a semicircular array at the head of a small rectangular "ditch." These sods also became the receptacles into which symbolic branches were placed. In addition, the ditch was filled with dry sand to a depth of about one-half inch (Dorsey 1905:132–147, Figure 68).

Hall (1997:23) has likened the rectangular ditch in these ceremonies to a symbolic grave, although that is not the symbolism specifically given by either the Arapahoe or the Cheyenne. The ditch, billets, and bent-pole coverings were said to be symbolic of a ceremonial tepee or sweat lodge, and it was also said that "from earth similar to that removed from this ditch were made man and woman" (Dorsey 1903:120). Notwithstanding Hall's (1997:22) synthetic interpretation that the "sods in the Cheyenne and Arapahoe Sun Dances explicitly represent lumps of mud brought from beneath the primordial sea by mythical Earth Divers and have explicit associations with toes" (namely the five toes of most earth divers), Dorsey (1903:119) gave several meanings for the sods in the Arapahoe ceremony: present earth–future earth, father-mother, sky-earth, and hands of father-mother. Grinnell (1923:258) recorded that the "placing of the sods represented an act of the Creator when He made the earth" and that "the sods represented the ground which supports us."

It is not supposed that the described meanings attached to the use of sods in these ceremonies would be the same as or even remotely similar to the meanings attributed to sods in the Illinois Hopewell mounds. Great structural differences are readily apparent: two sods in the Arapahoe ceremony, five in the Cheyenne ceremony, and probably thousands in some Illinois Hopewell mounds. Rather, the point is that the sods in these ceremonies played an important symbolic role in the larger world-renewal ceremony, and their use and acquisition was infused with much ritual. With this in mind, a final ethnographic note relates the potential symbolic importance of the source of the sods. In the Arapahoe ceremony documented by Dorsey (1903), the sod blocks were obtained from a specifically selected place at some distance from where they were used, despite the fact that sod blocks per se could have been easily obtained nearby:

[The party] left in single file toward the southeast, their object being to secure the two pieces of sod, which were to be used in the construction of the altar. Their line of march was single file, "like geese." When they had reached the field where good sod was to be found they halted. Cheáthea offered a prayer, whereupon Sósoni and Waánibe took a knife and cut out two circular pieces of sod, one about fourteen and the other about sixteen inches in diameter.

The two sods were placed on a blanket, which was carried by four young men, and they all started back for the lodge again, going in single file, and making a circular motion, in imitation of geese. This motion was especially intended to represent the different motions made by geese as they fly high in the summer and winter flight, for as they travel a long distance, so do the Arapaho, for the earth is wide. (Dorsey 1903:104)

Allogenetic Nature of Mound Fills

One of the most striking geological aspects of the Illinois Valley Hopewell mounds is the allogenetic nature of the mound fills, coupled with a general lack of borrow pits from which fill may have been quarried. As used herein, the term *allogenetic* refers to the situation in which the fills used to construct the mound were not obtained in the areas immediately adjoining the mounds but were quarried elsewhere. Occasional and casual references to this phenomenon can be found in many historical documents, but the degree to which entire mounds may have comprised allogenetic fills is only now becoming apparent (Van Nest et al. 2001).

Recent geoarchaeological investigations, including detailed topographic surveys and review of all available historical aerial imagery, demonstrate that there is no surficial evidence for borrow areas at the Illinois Valley Hopewell sites. But the absence of borrow pits alone does not establish that the mounds are composed of allogenetic fills. Mound fill may have been obtained by scraping the surface soils in the area around the mound, or it may have been obtained by digging small holes whose depressions are no longer visible at the surface. It is now known that near-surface sources did not provide the fills at the three sites for which new, detailed geoarchaeological databases are available (Mound House, Kamp, and Baehr; see fig. 22.1).

At the Mound House site, for example, quantitative data on soil texture for the <2-millimeter fraction from a representative suite of 160 samples show almost no overlap between mound fills and the underlying and surrounding Illinois River sand ridge upon which the mound was built (Van Nest et al. 2001:Figure 5). The fills investigated at Mound House contain substantially more silt and clay than the sand ridge deposits and classify as loams and silt loams, while sand ridge soils and sediment are sandy loams, loamy sands, and sand.

Analysis of the gravel-sized fraction (>2 millimeters) of nonartifactual natural rock at Mound House also clearly separates mound fills from the surficial

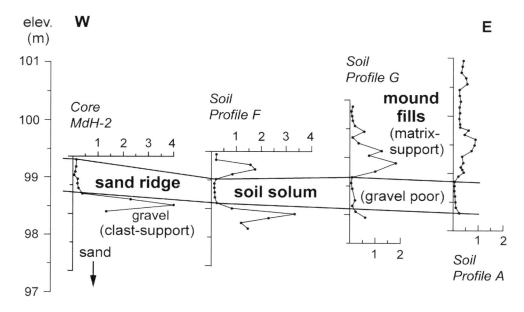

Figure 22.2. Gravel content of selected mound and off-mound soil columns, Mound 1, Mound House site, Greene County, Illinois (data from Van Nest 1998:147). Horizontal axes measure the number of granules (2–4 millimeters) per kilogram of soil (X1000).

sand ridge deposits, the latter being almost devoid of gravel for the upper 50–75 centimeters (fig. 22.2). The presence of gravel in the fill at Mound House is significant because it occurs as clasts in a matrix-supported deposit (that is, the clasts are supported by the <2-millimeter matrix, not by each other as they would be in a clast-supported deposit). Beds of clast-supported gravel are present at depths varying between 0.5 meters and 1.5 meters below the surface of the sand ridge at Mound 1 (the "spike" of gravel in the lower portions of the graphs in figure 22.2), and this deposit does rise to the surface north of the mound group. Even so, the excavation or scraping out of a (now-invisible) borrow pit into these deposits, in which all the soil then subsequently became admixed (changing from clast-supported to matrix-supported, with an accompanying decrease in gravel density) would result in relatively clay-depleted textures still not compatible with the mound fill, requiring additions from yet a third source of mud (comprising silt and clay). Although the possibility that the mound fills have hybrid textures because they have been deliberately or accidentally mixed by anthropogenic processes cannot be ruled out, I favor the more parsimonious explanation that the poorly sorted, matrix-supported nature of the fill reflects its geological source area. Such deposits on floodplains are not very common from a sedimentological point of view. Gravel implies that the deposit was not far from its channel source, and its poorly sorted character is suggestive of conditions of high-energy flow containing much sediment.

Today the Illinois River channel is about 0.5 kilometers west of Mound 1 at the Mound House site. The source of fill for this mound has not been located, probably because it no longer exists. Three new radiocarbon dates from deep deposits of alluvium west of the mound group (and inside the artificial levee) show that historic alluvium exceeds a thickness of 5.05 meters (ISGS-4413 and ISGS-4414, both historic) for at least 200 meters east of the current Illinois channel. Closer to the Mound House sandbar (260 meters east of the present-day Illinois River channel) a radiocarbon date of 1557 ±50 B.P. (ISGS-A0094) was obtained on uncarbonized plant macrofossil material from 4.90 meters below the surface. Taken together, these dates demonstrate that the current set of thick floodplain deposits immediately west of the mound group postdates mound construction and that at approximately 2,050 years ago when the mounds were built, the main channel of the Illinois River adjoined the site immediately to the west.

Given these paleogeographic conditions, the postulated sources of flood deposits did not necessarily require an extraordinary effort to quarry or transport, the distances involved being possibly as little as a few hundred meters. Nonetheless, it remains clear that the easiest and most convenient sources of fill for Mound 1 at Mound House were not used, and the question of why matrix-supported, pebble-rich deposits were selected still begs explanation. On the basis of available data, it can be hypothesized that selection was for what were then newly made flood deposits.

Sod Blocks as Mound Fill

Another striking aspect of the Illinois Valley Hopewell mounds is the extensive use of sod blocks as construction material to build internal mound structures (Van Nest et al. 2001). At Kamp Mound 9 this earthen structure was called the "primary mound" (Struever 1960), and because the surface of the structure led up to an opening into a centrally located burial chamber or crypt, Perino (1968a) called them "ramps" at the Pete Klunk Mound Group (see also Buikstra and Charles 1999:Figure 9.6; Charles 1992:Figure 1; Charles, Van Nest, and Buikstra 2004:Figure 3.3). Charles (1992) has suggested that the shape and size of these internal structures so influenced final mound form that it is possible even in pedestrian surveys to distinguish Hopewellian mounds from later Woodland mounds in the lower Illinois Valley.

Based on published accounts there appears to be at least four basic variations on the structure of the Hopewellian mortuary crypts in Illinois (fig. 22.3). The major architectural elements potentially involved in various combinations include a rectangular crypt with or without log sides or outlines, a log roof, and a roofing cover of slab-shaped stones. As reviewed by Brown (1979), the crypts were reused and the stone covering probably served to deter scavengers. The simplest form involves a covered subfloor pit (fig. 22.3a). In this case, the soil excavated from the pit is evidently not involved in a crypt/ramp structure. A slight modification to this theme is excavation of a subfloor pit, followed by use of the soil materials from the pit to raise the height of the wall (fig. 22.3b). The last two examples involve the use of loaded fills (sod blocks or compositional

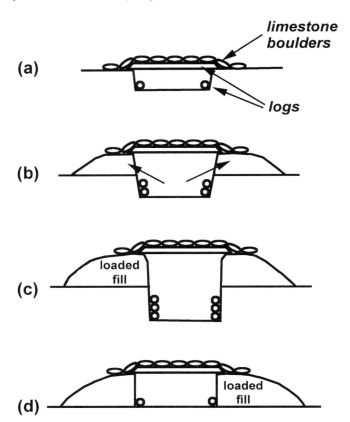

Figure 22.3. Schematic cross sections illustrating structural themes of Hopewellian mortuary crypts in Illinois. The portions labelled "loaded fill" in (c) and (d) commonly comprise sod blocks.

loads, see below) as a construction material. In figure 22.3c, a structure built of loaded fills adds height to a subfloor pit, and in figure 22.3d, the entire structure is aboveground. It is abundantly clear that some (or all) of these forms co-occur within the same mound groups, but whether or not they hold any temporal implications needs further resolution. Charles, Leigh, and Buikstra (1988) have suggested that within the series of five Middle Woodland mounds at Elizabeth there may be a temporal trend toward increasing complexity, not only of the central ramp/crypt structures, but of other attributes as well, from what was probably the earliest mound on the distal end of the ridge, to what is probably the latest mound on the more proximal end of the ridge.

The fills comprising the ramps are often described as being "loaded" (or "basket-loaded"), but this term refers to at least two fundamentally different kinds of fill that need to be distinguished if we are to gain a fuller appreciation of mound structures. Following the simple classification of fills recently proposed by Van Nest and colleagues (2001:635) these include compositional loads and sod blocks; both are well represented in the Illinois Hopewell mounds.

Compositional loads are those that can be distinguished on the basis of soil, sedimentary, or archaeological attributes, including color, texture, structure, and other sedimentary or soil features inherent from the source, as well as by

incidental or deliberate inclusions of distinctive artifactual or ecofactual remains. Compositional loading implies variation in the potential source areas,
including both natural and anthropogenic sources, and whether or not the
source areas were differentiated vertically by digging or laterally by obtaining
fills from different areas. One of the earliest published photographs of loaded
mound fill in Illinois (Leighton 1930:Figure 3) is the fill exposed in one of the
walls made by the commercial tunneling activity at the Ogden-Fettie site in the
central Illinois River valley (fig. 22.1). These are clearly compositional fills,
described by Leighton (1930:69) as "lumpy and of different colors of yellow,
rusty-brown, drab, and light-gray, as if it had been intimately mixed before it
was placed." Leighton's illustration is the same photographic image used by
Cole and Deuel (1937:Plate XXb), though inverted and cropped somewhat,
illustrating that these heterogeneous compositional fills give the observer no
ready sense of which way was up in the illustrated profile segment.

A closer look at loaded fills that are sod blocks reveals that the color contrast
between light- and dark-colored soil material actually exists within each load,
and each load (each sod block) represents the upper portions of the surface soil
profile present on the ground from which the blocks were cut and quarried (Van
Nest et al. 2001). The sod blocks used to build the internal earthen ramp structures were almost invariably stacked upside down. The individual sod loads
appear multicolored because the A-horizons of these soils were thin (2–10 centimeters thick) and dark, while the soil horizons beneath them were substantially lighter colored. The key characteristic for distinguishing sod-block loads
from compositional loads is the gradational boundary between dark and light
soil horizons that occurs within the individual sod blocks, in contrast to the
sharp or clear outer boundaries that define each sod block. If the light- and dark-
colored soil materials were from separate sources, as in compositional loads, the
boundaries that circumscribe each load would likely have sharp rather than
gradational boundaries. Sod blocks can be seen in a number of published photographs from several sites: Elizabeth (Charles, Leigh, and Buikstra 1988:Figure
5.26); Klunk (Perino 1968a:Figures 17 and 18); Knight (Griffin, Flanders, and
Titterington 1970:Plate 59); Liverpool (Cole and Deuel 1937:Plate 18); and
Mound House (Van Nest et al. 2001:Figure 3). Archival photographs of Kamp
Mound 9 show that the primary mound structure there was also made mostly of
sod blocks, with at least one intriguing area of compositional fills that involve
dark-colored sediment intermixed with shell fragments.

Variations in sod properties (color, texture, shape) show that some of these
were compound structures composed of sets of blocks, in arrangements whose
detailed geometries were not captured in earlier excavations. For example, in a
single 2-×-2-meter test excavation at Mound House (Square 80), at least two
rows, and possibly three, of stacked blocks of sod were revealed by more careful
excavation. Reexamination of archival photographs of the primary mound at
Kamp Mound 9 also show that this structure is composed of at least three major
sets of sods. Evidently the structures termed ramps are substantially more complex internally than a simple embankment of soil stacked against or forming the

walls of the central crypt or crypts, even if the final ramp surfaces may have served as a route of entry into the crypt.

The sources of the sod blocks used in the Illinois Hopewell mounds remain enigmatic. Like many of the other fills, they too are allogenetic to the landforms upon which the mounds were built (Van Nest et al. 2001). Most of the sod blocks are characterized by thin, dark A horizons only a few centimeters thick regardless of the parent materials from which they were cut, whether those soil materials were pebbly flood deposits, as at Mound House, or upland loessial soils, such as the sod blocks that have now been documented by coring in Kamp Mounds 1, 2, 6, 7, and 10 and in the remnant of Kamp Mound 9. Sod blocks very similar to those at Kamp have also been documented by coring at Baehr Mound 1, far to the north of Kamp in Brown County, in the central Illinois Valley (Van Nest 2000). Published photographs of sod blocks at Klunk Mound 2 (Perino 1968a) also suggest close similarities to those at Kamp and Baehr.

Elsewhere it has been hypothesized that the sod blocks used in the Illinois Hopewell mounds do not have good modern matches or analogs because they may have been cut from youthful soils that formed under a grassy turf cover on what was anthropogenically transformed ground (Van Nest et al. 2001). Hypothetical possibilities include the surfaces of mounds or other earthen structures, or spaces cleared in the forest canopy that allowed formation of a grassy vegetative cover. The first possibility implies the presence of preexisting mounds, yet we do not know at this time what, if any, temporal significance should be given to sod-block structures.

Crib-Form Log Tombs?

Recognition that sod blocks could be used to form relatively stable walls of the crypt raises a subsidiary question concerning the use of logs in the Illinois Hopewell mortuary crypts. Early historical notations suggested that many of these mortuary crypts were log structures (Kelly and Cole 1931:340; Snyder 1895), and when the McKern/midwestern taxonomic system emerged, "crib-form log tombs" became one of the few mound structural features listed among the "diagnostic traits of the Hopewellian Phase" by Cole and Deuel (1937:222). Later Wray (1952:154) would write that "the Early Hopewell burial complex has been commonly referred to as the 'log crypt' type of mound." Wray's citations include no actual descriptions of log structures other than those given by Cole and Deuel, who listed three examples. Two of these were at Liverpool and the third was the large mound at Ogden-Fettie, and none of them was actually excavated by their field parties. The log structures at Liverpool were said to comprise logs stacked three (or four) high in one instance, but in the other instance, it was only one log high (Cole and Deuel 1937:133–134). The listing for Ogden-Fettie appears to be even more conjectural. J. L. B. Taylor's 1929 plan map of the Ogden-Fettie tunneling operation shows a rectangular "imprint of logs" outlining a grave in the northwestern part of the tunnel (Shields n.d.:37). Moorehead (1929:168–169) was skeptical of the Liverpool accounts and wrote that "although we carefully interviewed the owners and other interested persons, and particularly a Mr. Solomon, who did the actual digging, we were unable to secure a satisfactory account of the so-called log tombs and the stone tomb."

Use of the word *crib* suggests a structure more substantial than it may have actually been, implying either that the roof was supported by the crib walls or that the crib walls were meant to retain soil to keep it from entering the chamber. Collapse of the roof and erosion of the walls of the crypt would indeed be two potentially legitimate problems, but each is alleviated substantially if the walls are built of sod blocks. That the logs did not support the roof was a point clearly made by Perino (1968a:16), and if a cribbing was not necessary to hold back soil, what then was the purpose of the logs? If we liken this architectural phenomenon to the lining of the rectangular "ditch" by two ceremonial log billets in the Arapahoe Offerings Lodge ceremony, perhaps some of the log features in the Illinois Hopewell mounds, especially the ones that cannot be demonstrated to have been more than one log high, served in part to symbolically mark a space whose meaning is not readily apparent.

Basal Mound Prepared Surfaces

The use of the phrase "prepared surface" and related phrases in the historical literature on mounds appears to encompass a wide variety of phenomena—everything from clearing away topsoil to actual earthen constructions, and ranging in spatial scales from areas covering much or all of the mound base to limited small deposits within graves. Inasmuch as they are mostly earthen constructions, all mounds could be viewed as a series of "prepared surfaces," broadly defined. To aid analyses, Greber (1996) has provided a useful categorization of the wide variety of deposits associated with Ohio Hopewell mounds. Among the kinds of deposits discussed are "prepared floors" that include a range of situations from the (relatively) simple removal of the top soil layer to expose a harder subsoil surface, to actual construction of earthen floors that become the sites of subsequent activities.

In Illinois Hopewell mounds, removal of the top soil layer prior to mound construction is difficult to confirm from historical records of excavations that lack reliable soil observations and study. It is clear, however, that it did take place at some mound groups—for example, at Elizabeth (Charles, Leigh, and Buikstra 1988)—but not at others, including the three sites that I have examined (Mound House, Kamp, and Baehr), where premound soil A horizons are very well preserved beneath the mounds. One of the mound structural traits listed by Cole and Deuel (1937:222) is "surface leveled, sand lines laid down." Four central valley mound groups were cited, including Liverpool and Ogden-Fettie (fig. 22.1).

Excavation at Liverpool Mound F°77 provided a particularly striking example of a "sand line" that became one the stratigraphic keystones for Illinois archaeology. The profile exposed by University of Chicago excavations showed that the "sand line" separated the "black sand" deposit (or soil) beneath the mound from loaded fills (probably sod blocks) in the mound above it (Cole and Deuel 1937:Plate XVIII). Evidently, the A horizon of the premound soil at this mound (the "black sand") beneath the thin layer of sand was well preserved. Deuel trenched a nearby mound (F°78) the following year, 1932, to gain supplemental data, and he sought the advice of soil scientist E. A. Norton and geologist M. M. Leighton. Leighton (1932) recorded that the "original profile shows about two feet black, sandy loam, grading down through dirty brown to brown gravel at depth of 4' below 'sand line.' Calc. sand occurs at depth of about 6' below 'sand line.'" Leighton's notes are important because they show that the premound soil was pedogenically leached of carbonates to a depth of about 1.8 meters, yet, significantly, mound fill above the sand line was calcareous and "made up of lumpy material with secondary lime gathered from the adjacent lowland swampy soil, as shown by root canals lined with red iron oxide." Calcareous fills and sod blocks suggest that these two mounds at Liverpool mostly if not entirely comprise allogenetic fills.

A more recent review of prepared surfaces in Illinois Hopewell mounds (Bullington 1988) focuses largely on positive constructional features, made from at least two kinds of soil materials (sand and loessial silt loams). An example of the latter was found at Elizabeth Mound 6, where a thin layer (3–5 cm) of "C horizon loess" was laid out in a circular area 18 meters in diameter, over which the central tomb and its associated ramps were built (Leigh, Charles, and Albertson 1988:59). While the "sand line" at Liverpool is a striking example when seen in profile, perhaps the best published illustration of the phenomenon appears in the overview photograph of Mound 478 at the Dickison Group near Peoria, where prior to mound construction a "thin layer of yellow sand [was] spread over an oblong area about 40 by 45 feet" (Walker 1952:18, Plate I). It is to these sand layers in particular that we now turn our attention.

"Those Mysterious Seams of Sand"

> [Squier and Davis] describe it as having in its composition two strata of sand, separated from each other by a foot or more of intervening earth, and continuous throughout the structure to the ground; and that those mysterious seams of sand had never to that time, been broken. Mr. Moorehead, who subsequently removed the entire mound, found the sand strata intact, excepting in the centre where the previous exploring work had been done. He adds the fact that this mound, as well as all the others in that group, had "been constructed on a hard burnt floor"; and that on this floor prepared by fire the flints were found "lying in little pockets or bunches of twelve to fifteen each with layers of sand between each mass." (Snyder 1894:319)

John Francis Snyder, a medical doctor based in Virginia, Illinois, spent a great deal of time exploring the archaeology of the region. His many contributions to

Illinois archaeology have been previously discussed, and some of his scientific articles have been reprinted (Elkin 1953; Farnsworth 2004; Walton 1962). Of particular interest to this study are Snyder's 1890s excavations at the Baehr Mound Group on the Illinois River south of Beardstown in Brown County, Illinois (fig. 22.1; see also Holt 2000 for a review of archaeological investigations at Baehr). As an educated person in the latter half of the nineteenth century, Snyder probably possessed knowledge of a number of natural history topics. It is evident from his writings that he was at least familiar with the geology of the Beardstown area, so that his observations about the soils and ecofactual materials encountered in his archaeological excavations are still worth consideration today when viewed in the historical context of 1890s geology. It is, however, equally clear from his writings that Snyder also envied and was strongly influenced by previous archaeological findings in Ohio, and we must weigh the possibility that researchers were then, not unlike they are today, very adept at finding what they set out to look for. A careful reading of Snyder's articles, for example, reveals a number of discrepancies in mound structural details at Baehr that suggest he was either writing solely from an imperfect memory or embellishing details to make some specific point. With these caveats in mind, and to the extent that Snyder found what he said he found, a number of interesting aspects of the Baehr mounds are relevant to this study.

Layers of sand in the mounds particularly intrigued Snyder, but he used them primarily for their stratigraphic utility. In the quoted passage beginning this section, Snyder refers to work by Warren K. Moorehead at the Hopewell Mound Group in Ohio, where several thousand ovoid disks of dark-colored flint ("hornstone") were found near the base of a mound. Snyder also found thousands of "hornstone" disks in Baehr Mounds 1 and 2 (reviewed in Morrow 1991 and Morrow, Elam, and Glascock 1992). For Baehr Mound 1, he wrote,

> The initial step in rearing this stupendous monument—comprising not less than 30,000 cubic yards of earth—was laying down on the alluvial soil an oval-shaped layer of clay, ten feet in width by eighteen feet in length, and less than a foot in thickness. *Over this, and extending beyond the limits of our excavation, the surface had been covered with sand,* and the whole area burnt by a long continued fire, in which many human bones were incinerated. On the center of the clay oval were then laid three large hornstone nodules close together, and around and over these, as far as the clay oval extended, was a mass of black hornstone implements, that apparently had been thrown down in lots of from 6 to 20, *with sand over and between each lot,* as though to isolate them from each other. (Snyder 1895:79, emphasis added)

In agreement with the terminology of his day, Snyder's "clay" deposits are silt or silt loam loess deposits from the bluff located immediately west of the mounds. For Snyder, the fact that the sand strata in the mounds were uninterrupted became one of his main lines of evidence that the large caches of artifacts found in the Hopewell mounds, including Baehr, were votive offerings never meant for use in this world. Although to reach this conclusion may have been Snyder's primary reason for mentioning the sand at all, the presence of this sand layer does have other interesting ramifications, especially in light of new geoarchaeological data for Baehr Mound 1 (Van Nest 2000).

Two solid sediment cores measuring 2.5 inches (6.3 centimeters) in diameter were extracted from the eastern, riverside flank of Baehr Mound 1 in 1999, recovering 2.07 meters and 1.34 meters of undisturbed mound fill. In both cores, mound fill is a series of stacked inverted sod blocks that buries a thin (1–3 centimeters) layer of brown sand, which in turn rests abruptly on top of the premound soil developed into silt loam and silty clay loam alluvial fan deposits. Coring shows that fan deposits extend to a depth of at least 6.5 meters before bottoming out on sand and gravel.

The premound soil beneath Baehr Mound 1 exhibits A-E-Bt-BC soil horizonation, suggesting that if it were a surface soil today, it would probably classify as an Alfisol in the U.S. Soil Taxonomic System. Given its relative degree of development and the climatic and geomorphologic conditions under which it formed, the pedogenic features of this soil likely took at least 2,000–3,000 years to develop (Bettis 1992), and it did so mainly if not exclusively under a forested vegetation (Fehrenbacher et al. 1984). This millennial time frame for fan stability, and hence soil formation, is compatible with geomorphologic studies suggesting that most alluvial fan activity dates to the early and mid Holocene, with landform equilibrium established by the late Holocene (Hajic 1990a, 1990b; Styles 1985; Van Nest 1997). Thus we may conclude on the basis of these two lines of evidence (soil and geomorphic) that the surface of the Baehr alluvial fan had long been a stable geomorphic surface prior to mound construction and that it harbored a relatively closed-canopy forest prior to its use as a Middle Woodland ritual space. Also readily apparent is the observation that, despite superficial textural similarities (they are all silt loams), soils like this premound soil were not the source of the sod blocks used in the mound structure built on top of the sand layer. In addition to its inherent pedogenetic association with the underlying E- and Bt-horizons, the A-horizon of the premound soil is relatively thick, compared to the thin A-horizons exhibited by the succession of inverted sod blocks placed above the sand layer. No E- or Bt-horizon-derived soil materials were noted in the more than 3.5 meters of recovered sod-block mound fill. Additionally, none of the sod-block fills is calcareous, ruling out sources that might truncate the C-horizons of the Peoria Silt, such as the one originally suggested by Snyder (quarrying into the side of the bluff). Where and how these sod blocks came into existence remains enigmatic (Van Nest et al. 2001). They are remarkably similar in outward form and internal composition to those recently documented at the Kamp Mound Group in Calhoun County.

Although the "oval-shaped layer of clay" was probably completely excavated and does not occur in the cores, Snyder (1895:79, quoted above) did note that the margins of the sand layer extended beyond the limits of his excavation, so it seems quite reasonable to infer that the sand recovered in the recent cores is in fact the same sand that Snyder saw. The Baehr core sections provide modern, tangible evidence that with little or no disruption, the premound soil surface beneath this mound was sealed, concluding its use, by the careful addition of a sand layer. Following this act in short succession, the first of several sod blocks were stacked upside down to build an internal mound structure.

The sand recovered at the base of Baehr Mound 1 is a clean, very well sorted, medium sand lacking pebbles. One can only speculate on what its purpose was or what it may have meant to the builders of the mound. We can, however, note that it was clearly selected for some reason and that its source was very definitely someplace other than the immediate surrounds of the mound area. For Baehr, the most likely options include sources in high-level Pleistocene sand terraces located on the other side of the river valley, or alternatively, the sand may have been quarried from what would have then been newly deposited Illinois River channel sand, such as one might see in overbank flooding, especially when crevasse splays form (for a landform analog, see the crevasse splay feature in figure 22.8 below).

Here it is worthwhile to briefly reflect on what otherwise might seem like a trivial point of distinction regarding implications of the use of the words *floor* and *surface*. Despite the fact that the sand layer at Baehr Mound 1 forms the base of the mound, it was perhaps neither a floor nor a surface. Judging by this and other examples, we may deduce that the sand layer probably served to seal what was a ritual space (see also Charles, Van Nest, and Buikstra 2004:55). Loose sand such as that used at Baehr could not have been left exposed to the weather for long, nor would it have lasted long were it trod upon. Some may derive meaning from the fact that the sand is "clean" sand—that is, sand with little mud (silt and clay) or gravel—or that it has a "light" color, but to these prospects should be added the possible significance of source area. Perhaps sands such as these were quarried from what were at the time newly made flood deposits, symbolically representative of the regenerative nature of large floods. In either case, construction of such a sand layer can be seen as an effective end to a prior world and the beginning of a new world, one that is represented in part by sod blocks. The sod blocks are placed upside down, inverted to the senses of the living in this world but in proper perspective to those placed face-upward in a grave, especially if their passage to another world was through the air, as is suggested by the ornigraphic nature of Hopewell burial art.

This brief summary of some of the fills comprising the Illinois Hopewell mounds shows that they are nothing short of extraordinary. The presence of allogenetic fills and the many complicated questions raised by the presence of sod blocks clearly establish that the mounds are not simply earthen monuments constructed on the basis of least-effort principles, in which any soil materials might have been satisfactory. It is increasingly apparent that almost all of the soils in these mounds must have carried symbolic meaning to those who built the mound. Initial results suggest selection for flood deposits and more broadly, other forms of newly made or newly transformed ground (Van Nest et al. 2001).

With this working hypothesis in mind, the search for the sources and the meanings of the fills comprising the Hopewellian mounds in Illinois inevitably leads one to reconsider these mounds at even broader landscape scales.

Mound Groups Located near Paleoflood Features

Hopewell mounds in the lower Illinois Valley occur primarily as groups located in three main physiographic settings (fig. 22.4): (1) upland bluff crests, (2) valley margin fans or high terraces, and (3) highwater islands surrounded by floodplains (sensu stricto). In the past, the latter two settings have been combined into a single group called "floodplain" mounds, meaning in essence those mounds within the bedrock valley and not in the uplands, irregardless of the many non-floodplain landforms within the valley.

One of the most striking differences between Ohio and Illinois Valley Hopewell sites is the paucity of earthworks at the latter. Only two Illinois Hopewell groups (Golden Eagle and Ogden-Fettie; see fig. 22.1) are known to contain earthworks in addition to mounds. Because these two groups also happen to be located near key river junctions (the Mississippi and Illinois, and the Illinois and Spoon rivers, respectively), they are considered in greater detail below with regard to paleoflood features. Many other groups also have intriguing settings, but space does not permit their consideration here; rather, it is hoped that similar observations at all of the sites might stimulate further geoarchaeological field research.

The Illinois Valley sites occur along many fundamentally different river reaches. When considering flood histories we must not only take stock of what it is we already know about these individual areas, but also consider what it is

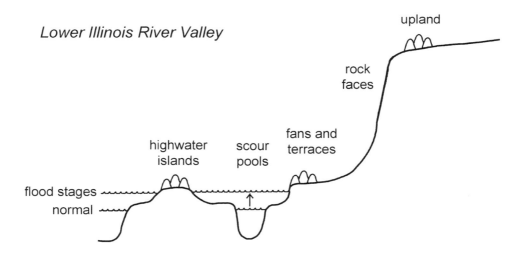

Figure 22.4. Diagrammetric representation of the major landscape settings of the Illinois Valley Hopewell mound groups.

we can expect to know about past geological events at scales relevant to the three-hundred-year span of the Middle Woodland period. Because of a long history of multidisciplinary archaeological research, the Illinois River valley and adjoining segments of the Mississippi have some of the best Holocene geological databases anywhere in North America (Butzer 1977, 1978; Hajic 1985, 1990a, 1990b; Leigh 1992; Styles 1985; Van Nest 1990, 1997). Even so, a number of questions whose answers will require more fieldwork readily arise when these geological histories are pressed to serve in such a precise chronological framework.

Data from the Sny Bottom portion of the Mississippi River valley (fig. 22.1) suggest that the Middle Woodland period was a time of very large floods that were probably significantly larger than those known for the Historic period (Van Nest 1997). Recent excavation of the stratified Middle Woodland C. House archaeological site near Hannibal, Missouri (O'Gorman 2003), provides a new series of radiocarbon dates that firmly anchor the timing of these events in the Sny Bottom. How these floods impacted the Illinois River is less well known, but it seems quite likely that these very large floods were regional in scope. Recent data from the Gulf of Mexico indicate a large influx of freshwater (that is, a "megaflood") at this time (Brown, Kennett, and Ingram 1999), and more generally, this was a time of relatively large floods in the upper Mississippi basin (Knox 1985, 1988, 1995, 2000).

Given the geohistorical condition of large floods, and as the examples below illustrate, it can be seen that some mound groups were positioned to provide proximity to water that would have been there only during high river stages (fig. 22.4). Additionally, some groups appear to have been positioned next to large floodplain scour pools.

Golden Eagle Site

The Golden Eagle site is located near the Mississippi River about 8 kilometers upstream from its current junction with the Illinois River at Grafton (fig. 22.1). William McAdams (1881:718) mentioned the site as noteworthy for the presence of earthworks in addition to mounds. Since then, a number of investigators have examined the site, although relatively little of this research has been published. According to records archived at the Center for American Archeology (CAA), James Marshall noticed the earthwork on a 1937 aerial photograph and relocated it on the ground in 1969. Following this discovery, researchers associated with the Foundation for Illinois Archaeology (the CAA's predecessor) conducted field surveys and limited excavation in 1970. That and other work since has shown that Terminal Archaic, Middle Woodland, and Late Woodland period artifacts are present at various locales across the surface of this large multicomponent site.

The earthworks at Golden Eagle are readily visible on most available imagery of the site area (fig. 22.5). Major geomorphologic features in the Golden Eagle area include the island-braided channel of the Mississippi River, the Illinois/ Mississippi River floodplain ("Calhoun Point" on the Illinois side), the late

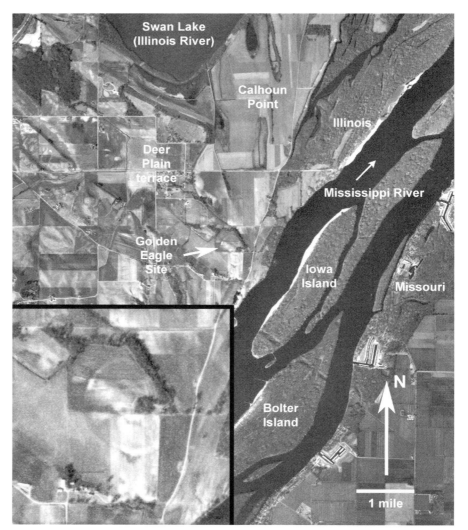

Figure 22.5. Portion of a 1990 black-and-white aerial photograph (USGS NAPP 2198–345) of the Golden Eagle site, Calhoun County, Illinois. The inset at the lower left is the same image with the site area enlarged.

Pleistocene Deer Plain terrace (Rubey 1952), and dissected uplands south and west of the site. The site is situated on the edge of the Deer Plain terrace overlooking the southern tip of the Calhoun Point floodplain, which is underlain by Late Holocene alluvium (Hajic 1990b). Of special note are the relict scour pools represented by elongate, teardrop-shaped depressional features that trend north–south across Calhoun Point (fig. 22.5).

Detailed topographic survey of the Golden Eagle site also documents a scour pool there as well (fig. 22.6). Survey conditions were generally very good when data for the map were obtained using Total Station surveying technology (April 1998). Map interpretation is complicated somewhat by the presence of readily

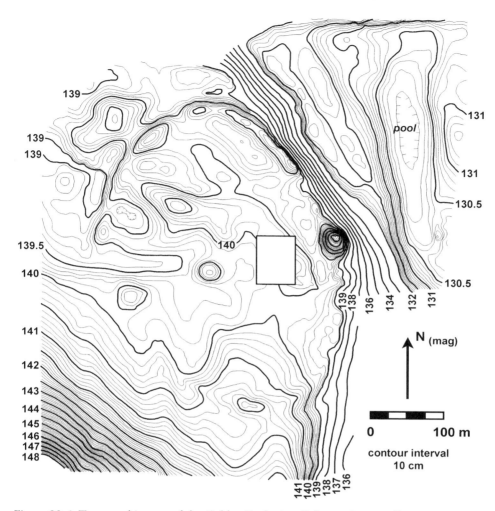

Figure 22.6. Topographic map of the Golden Eagle site, Calhoun County, Illinois.

erodible, low, broad sand dunes and sand sheets that mantle the surface of the Deer Plain terrace in this area. Nonetheless, the survey clearly shows that the earthworks at Golden Eagle comprised two ditch segments, each with an internal embankment. Along with four and possibly eight conical mounds, the embankment encloses an oval area whose long axis measures about 440 meters and whose short axis measures about 280 meters, giving an axial ratio of about 1.6. The circumference of the earthwork is about 1,160 meters. The eastern riverside "entrance" to the earthwork is marked by a large (2.7 meters high) central mound that remains in good condition because it is located in a forested area that probably was never cultivated. This forested area, visible in figure 22.5, is the relatively steep and high (8–10 meters) scarp of the Deer Plain terrace (fig. 22.6). All of the other mounds in the group have been historically modified by plowing and/or other farm activities. The western landward entrance to the enclosure is marked by a slight topographic depression between two low conical mounds. Inside the earthwork is a single distinct mound that is situated about two-thirds of the distance back from the terrace edge entrance.

Today the enclosure opens out onto a fairly large tract of floodplain, begging the question, where was the main river channel circa 2,050 years ago? Perhaps the Mississippi was somewhat closer to the site, but the Illinois River is unlikely to have adjoined it. Although there are no radiocarbon dates dating the alluvium that underlies this floodplain, recent excavations at the Persimmon site on the southern bank of Swan Lake (fig. 22.5) document the presence of near-surface stratified Early to Late Woodland remains, strongly suggesting that the bulk of the alluvium beneath Calhoun Point in the area of Golden Eagle was in place by Hopewellian times.

The now-infilled scour pool at Golden Eagle is a less-than-spectacular flood-plain puddle that retains the last of the receding floodwaters. But when it first formed (by scour during a flood), it would have been much deeper. How deep remains to be seen by subsurface exploration, but judging by analogous situations in the modern Mississippi (Goodwin and Masters 1983), depths up to 15–25 meters would not be surprising. The presence of a scour pool in front of the site demonstrates the presence of high-velocity, turbulent water. Thus it can be inferred that during high river flood stages, the Golden Eagle site was not only located precisely at the junction of the Illinois and Mississippi rivers, but was also situated to overlook a flood scour pool.

Another noteworthy feature revealed by the Golden Eagle map is the situation of the relatively undisturbed mound located right at the terrace edge (fig. 22.6). The riverward side of this large mound exhibits topographic lines that show a distinctive outward-facing anomaly, or a "bulge" away from the terrace edge. Similar topographic "bulges" have recently been recognized for the terrace-edge mounds at the Kamp Mound Group in Calhoun County, where archival records and photographs associated with the 1959 excavation of Mound 9 by Struever (1960) show that an earthen, wedge-shaped platform like that schematically illustrated here in figure 22.7 was constructed to support the secondary portion of that mound (Van Nest and Asch 2001). Seemingly extra effort to build such earthen platforms shows a purposeful placement of the mounds as near to the terrace edge as possible, with a decided orientation to the floodplain. Like Golden Eagle, the Kamp Mound Group also overlooks a relict flood scour pool.

Ogden-Fettie Site

The Ogden-Fettie site (Cole and Deuel 1937) is located in the central Illinois River valley in Fulton County (fig. 22.1). This group of more than thirty mounds is situated near the junction of Sepo Creek and the Spoon River (fig. 22.8), about 6 kilometers from the present-day mouth of the Spoon River near Havana. Munson (1967) suggested that a pentagonal ditch without an embankment enclosed some but not all of the mounds at Ogden-Fettie. The shape of a pentagon was based on field reconnaissance and examination of aerial images.

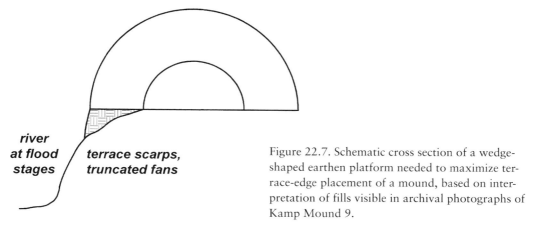

*river
at flood
stages*

*terrace scarps,
truncated fans*

Figure 22.7. Schematic cross section of a wedge-shaped earthen platform needed to maximize terrace-edge placement of a mound, based on interpretation of fills visible in archival photographs of Kamp Mound 9.

Topographic mapping in 1976 reported by Shields (n.d.:91) suggested that the enclosure was complete and that "the enclosure does at least roughly approximate a pentagonal pattern," although as drawn it more closely approximates a circle. Both investigators noted that the western portion of this mound group had been impacted to varying degrees by historical disturbances, including railroad and drainage ditch constructions. Then, as today, the ditch was most readily apparent east of the big mound (F°175), less so to the south. In April 1999, the ditch could not be traced as a complete enclosure on the ground.

The two images dating to 1957 and 1963 reproduced in the Munson (1967) article appear to be the same images available for this study (the collection of historical agricultural and soil images curated by the Map and Geography Library at the University of Illinois–Urbana-Champaign). A better-quality image of the site dating to August 6, 1950 (fig. 22.8), shows the ditch at Ogden-Fettie less ambiguously. Taken shortly after a Spoon River flood, this image also illustrates an extensive series of crevasse splays deposited where the Spoon enters the Illinois floodplain. These splay features appear light colored (high reflectance) because they primarily are composed of sand and hence are well-drained soils. The inset shows the ditch as it appears on the same image only enlarged for better viewing. In this image the ditch appears as an oval or egg-shaped partial enclosure, with the large mound (F°175, with trees) situated approximately where the ditch would go if it formed a complete enclosure. This configuration gives an axial ratio of about 1.6, not unlike the situation at Golden Eagle.

Immediately to the southeast of the oval at Ogden-Fettie is an area of low ground (fig. 22.8). Shields (n.d.) has stated that this is the area that Clyde Ogden believed was a large borrow pit. The location of this possible borrow pit at Ogden-Fettie is in relatively the same riverward position as the natural relict scour pool at Golden Eagle, raising the intriguing possibility that perhaps the Ogden borrow area not only is humanly made, but also was constructed as much to produce a pool as to produce a source of mound fill. In any case this feature deserves much closer attention as being part of the built landscape at the site.

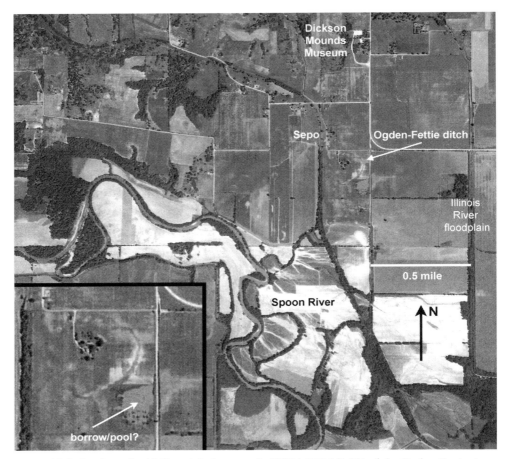

Figure 22.8. Portion of a 1950 aerial photograph (USDA RZ-2G-50) of the Ogden-Fettie site, Fulton County, Illinois. The inset at lower left is the same image with the site area enlarged.

Like Golden Eagle, the Ogden-Fettie group is not presently located on any major river course but instead looks out over an expanse of floodplain sediment. This perspective changes dramatically when one considers very high-level flood stages and a paleolandscape setting in which the Ogden-Fettie site would have been situated precisely at the junction of the Spoon and Illinois rivers. How did the river systems in the Ogden-Fettie area respond to large floods? Apparently not by excavating large scour pools and building longitudinal bars and islands as in some other river segments, such as the lower Illinois near Golden Eagle. Instead, the meandering Spoon River, which has built a large fluvial fan at its junction with the Illinois Valley, accommodates increased flood discharges by bursting its levees through crevasses, resulting in large sand splays, such as the 1950 splay shown in figure 22.8.

Many people saw the now-infilled tunnel and chamber walls exposed in the commercial and research tunnels dug into the large mound (F°175) at Ogden-Fettie, yet few bothered to record in any detail the composition of this mound.

Awed by the complexity of this earthen structure, Morris M. Leighton, then the chief of the Illinois Geological Survey and deeply interested in the soils comprising the Illinois mounds, would ultimately note only that the soils were "too complicated to be adequately described in this paper" (Leighton 1930:69). Leighton's field notes (1928) indicate that sand deposits were found in several stratigraphic contexts; most notably, "near the base of the mound, about 2 feet above the old soil, the Indians spread a thin layer of sand before building the remainder of the structure" (Leighton 1930:69). Did the builders of this mound choose sand from a river splay? And if so, was the sand layer at Ogden-Fettie similar to that found at Baehr Mound 1, and might it have carried a similar meaning?

Discussion

It is now possible to begin to consider the three general physiographic settings of the mound groups (fig. 22.4) as also reflecting, at larger landscape scales, the tripartite division of the Hopewellian cosmos seen by Buikstra and Charles (1999) in other aspects of these mounds. As has been shown, some mound groups were built on the edge of truncated alluvial fans or terraces, seemingly to offer direct access to water that would have been there only during large floods. Sites like Golden Eagle and Kamp in the lower valley are associated with relict flood scour pools, geomorphic features that would have attained their maximal depths during or shortly after large flood events, and prior to being infilled relatively rapidly with sediment. Scour pools add an appreciable vertical depth to what is otherwise a rather flat floodplain surface, and perhaps for this portion of Illinois, water (especially deep water) represented the underworld. Or perhaps the pools provided challenging depths for reenactment of the key events of the Earth Diver myth. Alternatively, meaning might be gleaned from the fact that scour pools are intimately linked with the formation of bars and islands in the river channel, the excavated pools being a major source of the sediment deposited onto the islands; in this way, one may think of scour pools as the inverse of islands. Both are highly dynamic landforms that are remolded and reshaped during floods, and in essence, they are both partially destroyed and then newly recreated during the same geological flood event. Thus, some fills may have been selected from flood deposits as representative of the newly rejuvenated floodplain.

Some groups like Mound House (and probably Liverpool as well) were situated in the floodplain such that they became completely surrounded by water, that is, they became islands at high river stages. Counterposed to these floodplain settings—especially in the bedrock-controlled lower valley with its well-defined rock bluffs—are bluff-top mound settings that command spectacular river valley vistas and overviews of the valley landforms below. Thus the river-edge fan and terrace sites can be seen to occupy an intermediary position, one that possibly allowed simultaneous access to both the upper and the underworld, and like this world, might be regarded as a "mirror" to both.

The tripartite landscape pattern may be reinforced when we reconsider the various mound fill compositions in these landscape settings. Thus it is noteworthy that Mound House, an island of mounds during floods, is composed of allogenetic riverine flood deposits. Likewise, the upland Klunk mound comprises allogenetic loessial soil materials. Considered alone, both compositions could be interpreted as reflecting relatively nearby source areas for mound fill. But consider also the composition of Kamp Mound 9, a large and complex mound located in an intermediate landscape position that seemingly has a mixture of both riverine and loessial soils. The report by Struever (1960) and archival materials show that this mound had an aboveground tomb made largely of sod blocks, with some photographic evidence that part of this structure was made of dark, clay-rich materials intermixed with shells. Clean brown sand is included in some of the tomb fill. The "primary" mound was then covered with secondary cappings, first of loessial soils, followed by a "blue gumbo" (dark-colored clay-rich material).

Few to none of the earthen materials used at Kamp Mound 9 were obtained from the alluvial fan upon which the mound was built. Indeed, this allogenetic aspect to the Illinois Hopewell mounds seems to be the most pervasive earthen theme, and perhaps this is the strongest argument that the source of the fills held symbolic importance to the builders. What these sources were and what meanings might have been attached to them pose challenging research questions not necessarily beyond the reach of archaeological science. Detailed geoarchaeological studies can begin to tell us *what* was chosen, not just as an end in itself or as a means of confirming what has been reportedly found elsewhere, but as a primary means of enriching phenomena in need of more than a passing explanation. Toward this end, this chapter has brought together a number of observations suggesting that the Illinois Hopewell mounds were built during a period of very large floods and that many of their compositions reflect selection of mound fill representative of newly made earth.

Acknowledgments

This essay draws on the multidisciplinary knowledge base built over several decades through the efforts of many affiliated with the Center for American Archeology in Kampsville, Illinois. Geoarchaeological research at the Mound House site was supported by National Science Foundation Grant SBR-9729956 to the volume editors, Douglas K. Charles and Jane E. Buikstra. Geoarchaeological research at the Baehr site was facilitated by Julie Zimmerman Holt, and at the Kamp Mound group by D. Asch, S. Struever, Bonnie Styles, and M. Wiant. Mapping of the Golden Eagle site was funded by the Center for American Archeology and was conducted by the volume editors and R. Hickson.

23

Visiting in the Interaction Sphere

Ceramic Exchange and Interaction in the Lower Illinois Valley

Shannon M. Fie

Studies of Middle Woodland exchange traditionally focus on goods associated with the Hopewell Interaction Sphere. However, the attention given to these exotic items strongly influences our models of Middle Woodland interaction. The concern of this chapter is the implied hierarchical organization of Middle Woodland exchange networks that often results from the emphasis on ritual caches and "prestige chain" distributions. The current study, in contrast, examines the exchange of more modest goods within less formal spheres of interaction.

Ceramics can provide more direct evidence of the parties involved in exchange than other artifact classes. Like many exotic goods, ceramics are potentially sourceable to regions within the interaction sphere. In contrast to Hopewell goods, ceramic vessels were presumably not socially restricted items, and their short use-lives implicate few transaction events. Evidence of ceramic exchange may therefore offer important clues into the parties, distances, and organization involved in long-distance exchange.

Based on stylistic and compositional data, the current study documents the presence of exotic ceramics in six lower Illinois River valley sites. The presence of exotic sherds throughout the settlement system is then taken as evidence for ceramic exchange. The stylistic and compositional data also indicate that exotic-looking vessels were occasionally manufactured within the lower valley region. Together, these patterns suggest that Middle Woodland interaction included networks of interaction that linked small families through visitations and the exchange of subsistence-maintenance goods.

The Organization of Middle Woodland Exchange

Exchange remains a valuable concept for studies of prehistoric interaction. Foreign goods provide important evidence of political, economic, social, and ideological relationships between prehistoric populations. These items offer a means to explain the spread of cultural traits within and between populations and to understand more fundamental changes in cultural systems. Given the explanatory power of exchange models, it is not surprising that much Middle Woodland research has focused on the goods, materials, and concepts associated with the Hopewell Interaction Sphere (for example, Seeman 1979b; Struever and Houart 1972). The attention given to these apparent prestige items continues to influence models of Middle Woodland exchange and interaction.

Models of exchange are based on the commodities they include. The attention given to Hopewell artifact distributions strongly conditions our perceptions of the participants, contexts, and organization of Middle Woodland exchange. However, models based on only limited suites of goods account for only limited spheres of interaction. The significance placed on Hopewell goods fosters perceptions that Middle Woodland exchange centered on structured interactions between elite members of distant social groups.

Items associated with Hopewell are presumed to have been "valuable" in Middle Woodland social systems. Their strong association with mortuary programs suggests that they were used to mark and reinforce status in Middle Woodland social systems (Struever and Houart 1972:49). The scarcity of these items in burial deposits, and their resulting value, is thought to correspond with use by high-status segments of Middle Woodland social groups (for example, Braun 1986:118; Brose 1979:8; Buikstra 1984:222–223; Prufer 1965:132). The conveyance of Hopewell exotics among high-ranking individuals conforms well to a "prestige chain" mode of distribution (*sensu* Renfrew 1975:50, 1977:77).

Valuables are transported greater distances from their source than are more mundane goods. The value of these items restricts the number of likely recipients while concurrently extending the range of their distribution. Whereas down-the-line exchanges of less valuable materials are envisioned as balanced and reciprocal, prestige transactions often take the form of gift giving among important personages. Not intended for mundane use, such valuables are rarely retained by the receiver; their social and material value makes them more serviceable as gifts in subsequent interactions. Ultimately such items are consumed in mortuary contexts, although some may be deposited in other contexts through accidental loss or breakage. The cumulative effect is a more gradual fall-off distribution than results from down-the-line exchange (Renfrew 1975:50, 1977:77). Although these items are rarely envisioned as components of serial transactions, the transitory possession of valuable Hopewell "gifts" is fully consistent with their perceived roles in Middle Woodland exchange and interaction.

Middle Woodland exchange is typically modeled as interaction organized around political, economic, religious, or social principles (see Vickery 1996). When based on Hopewell artifact distributions, these organizing principles implicate structured relationships and/or complex sociopolitical organizations.

Political models of exchange recognize a centralized authority capable of concentrating goods and labor as part of centralized redistribution. In Middle Woodland studies, large deposits of exotic materials at mound centers have been interpreted as evidence of centralized authority, as well as stockpiles for ensuing redistributions (for example, Griffin 1965:146; Morrow 1988:82; Struever and Houart 1972:69, 71, 74). Centralized redistribution implies a high level of cultural complexity and provides much of the basis for inferences of chiefdom-level development within the Scioto region (for example, Seeman 1979a; Struever 1965:212–214). More recently, such political models have fallen from favor (for example, Greber 1996:152, 162), and interest in Hopewellian interaction has shifted to reciprocal transactions between groups.

The exchange of Hopewell goods is currently modeled as part of alliance-building strategies (for example, Braun and Plog 1982; Brose 1979:8; Brown 1985:222–224; Ford 1979:237; Seeman 1992b:35). Between socially distant groups, the display of Hopewell symbols likely facilitated communication and the procurement of desirable materials (Braun 1986:122–123; Braun and Plog 1982:510–511; Braun, Griffin, and Titterington 1982:62–64; Seeman 1995). Once acquired, these items were employed within more parochial spheres to entice alliances with other regional groups (for example, Braun 1977:94; Brose 1979:7; Ford 1979:237–238), as well as to reinforce status (for example, Struever and Houart 1972:49) and validate positions of leadership (for example, Bender 1985a:55; Seeman 1995:136). As an alliance-building pursuit, the context of interaction was likely formal and accompanied by presentation and pageantry. Accordingly, the conveyance of Hopewell exotics continues to be modeled as part of ceremonial activities often associated with the interment of the dead.

Despite the obvious symbolic importance of many Hopewell artifacts, explanations for their distributions have also been framed in economic terms. Much of this discussion, however, derives from similarities drawn between Struever and Houart's "transaction center" model and "central place" frameworks (for example, Seeman 1979b:386). Though Struever and Houart clearly associate Middle Woodland exchange with social, political, economic, and ceremonial activities (Struever and Houart 1972:61–63), their model is now strongly linked with economic motives (for example, Seeman 1979b:245, 247, 386; Vickery 1996:120).

According to Struever and Houart's transaction center model, Hopewell goods and concepts passed through a nested hierarchy of interactions. Within this scheme, exotics were introduced into a region via a gateway or "regional transaction center" and then passed to "local transaction centers," where they were distributed to local communities and eventually consumed in status display and mortuary ceremony. While the notion of a singular hierarchical system of interaction is now dismissed (Seeman 1979b:408–411), Middle Woodland exchange continues to be viewed as a series of organized acquisitions and apportionments.

Envisioned within a hierarchy of interactions, Hopewell artifact distributions again imply highly organized systems of exchange. While one may question whether mortuary deposits reflect economic activities, Middle Woodland mound groups nevertheless become identified with the production and distribution of particular artifact types. Mound groups with relatively high numbers of an artifact type, for example, become equated with a central node in the manufacture and distribution of that type (for example, Braun, Griffin, and Titterington 1982:88; Griffin 1965:146; Morrow 1988:82; Seeman 1979b:310–379; Struever and Houart 1972:68, 71, 77; Vickery 1996:122). Sites with fewer examples are in turn understood as recipient locales. Though based on relatively few artifacts, the association of smaller sites with mound "centers"—and their subsequent linkage to other, more distant centers—results in the semblance of organized, hierarchical networks of exchange.

Ceremonial models assume that exotic materials were transported to ritual centers where they were laid down as offerings, rendered into valued objects for use in ceremonial activities (Vickery 1996:210), or used in the manufacture of other ritually charged items (for example, Odell 1994:144). While ceremonial models do not necessarily involve complex sociopolitical organizations, they do emphasize mortuary contexts and the few high-ranking individuals with whom such items were interred (Vickery 1996:122).

In the ceremonial models, individuals associated with Hopewell artifacts presumably held important roles in their ritual use. Among potentially competing social groups, rituals would have imposed a structure on interaction that helped diffuse social tension and reinforced cooperation (Brose 1979:7; see also Braun 1986:122–123; Braun and Plog 1982:510; Conkey 1985:303–305; Wobst 1977:337). Participation within these activities was facilitated by the display and use of widely understood symbols that affiliated distinct groups with a common set of cultural references. At death, individuals associated with these important rituals and symbols were buried in a manner consistent with their position.

Social models have largely been neglected as explanations for Middle Woodland exchange. Of the four explanatory frameworks, models of socially motivated exchange assume the least amount of organization or social complexity. In contrast to political, economic, and ceremonial models, social models emphasize voluntary participation at mound centers and less formal interactions among participants, such as feasting and exchange. When traveling to mound centers, individuals and small groups likely carried supplies of local materials that they exchanged with other groups or contributed to ritual offerings (Vickery 1996:120–121). Though often overlooked, the relevance of social models is demonstrated by Vickery (1996), who found that the occurrence of several exotic flints in Ohio sites was best explained by the movement of small social groups.

The lack of attention given to social models reflects a broader neglect of subsistence-maintenance commodities in models of Middle Woodland exchange. Several models of Middle Woodland exchange are predicated on the need to secure important resources (for example, Brose 1979:8; Cleland 1976:71; Ford 1979:237–238; Seeman 1979a:45–47). Yet with the exception of feasting, the exchange of subsistence-maintenance materials continues to be viewed as ancillary to prominent formal exchanges. Often the procurement of mundane commodities between groups is modeled as direct acquisitions through agreements of access (for example, Braun 1977:94; Brose 1979:8).

Goods made of raw materials such as cherts occur in Middle Woodland sites in larger quantities and with greater regularity than other exotic materials. However, their importance in Middle Woodland exchange is often eclipsed by interest in more distant geologic materials such as obsidian or Knife River flint (for example, Griffin 1975:142; Seeman 1979b:291). When used in distributional studies, occurrences of foreign chert in habitation sites become linked to mound centers (such as Baehr-Gust, Collins, and Havana in Illinois and the Hopewell site in Ohio) through caches of exotics found within the mounds. The spatial distributions of these materials are consequently interpreted as the by-products of down-the-line exchanges emanating from central distribution nodes, where Middle Woodland populations maintained preferential access to these raw materials (for example, Morrow 1988:78–79; Struever and Houart 1972:74; Vickery 1996:122–123; Winters 1984:12).

Despite the importance of materials such as cherts in local and regional interaction, Middle Woodland research remains focused on the long-distance exchange of materials and symbols identified with the Hopewell Interaction Sphere. The emphasis on these highly visible items, however, addresses only a limited sphere of interaction that underscores status goods, organized transport, and elite involvements.

Assessment of this characterization is currently hampered by an inability to identify the actual participants in exchange networks. Several studies have documented patterns in the distribution of Hopewell artifacts (for example, Seeman 1979b, 1995; Struever and Houart 1972). However, their numbers are too low to do more than suggest general patterns of interaction. Consequently, inferences of intergroup contact rely on appeals to the likely avenues of transport (for example, Griffin 1965:146–147; Struever and Houart 1972:Figure 1; Walthall, Stow, and Karson 1980:23). Yet as commodities within a "prestige chain" of exchange (*sensu* Renfrew 1975:50), Hopewell goods had a distribution that probably resulted from a series of transactions involving multiple parties and extending across substantial distances. Models of Middle Woodland exchange would undoubtedly benefit from a better understanding of the parties involved in these and other interactions. Archaeological signatures of these participants would improve our insights into the organization of interregional exchange networks.

Pottery constitutes an ideal data set for such an investigation. First, ceramic sherds are common artifacts and are found on Middle Woodland sites in large numbers. Middle Woodland pottery is also constructed with materials and methods that often produce contrasting compositional signatures (for example, Carr and Komorowski 1995; Cogswell, Neff, and Glascock 1998; Cogswell et al. 1995; Elam et al. 1992; Mainfort et al. 1997; Yeatts 1990). While stylistic decorations on the vessels (or sherds) provide a means to identify potential exotics, they may also suggest source areas not yet identifiable compositionally. Finally, ceramic vessels are short-lived implements (Shott 1996) that presumably passed through only a limited number of transactions. Accordingly, ceramics should provide more direct evidence of the parties involved in exchange than do other artifact classes.

Ceramics in Middle Woodland Exchange Networks

Ceramics typically receive only nominal consideration in models of Middle Woodland exchange. Arguments for only the limited circulation of ceramics result largely from models derived from principles of market economics—for example, bulk, production costs, demand, availability, and transport costs (Fry 1980:3; see also Brumfiel and Earle 1987:4; Clark 1979; Drennan 1984a, 1984b:31; Hodder 1974; Renfrew 1977). Ceramic vessels, which are relatively large, heavy, fragile, and locally available, are unlikely commodities of exchange (for example, Drennan 1984b:29). Instances of their transport and exchange should be limited to "luxury" vessels (Drennan 1985:892). It is not surprising that discussions of Middle Woodland vessel exchange focus on the movement of finely made Hopewell jars (for example, Braun, Griffin, and Titterington 1982:62–64; Struever and Houart 1972:76–77). Arguments for the exchange (and frequent copying) of Hopewell vessels draw support from widespread standardization in vessel form, technology, and stylistic motifs (for example, Braun 1977:174; Farnsworth 1973:31–32).

In practice, the identification of foreign vessels relies heavily on contrasts with local production norms. In Ohio, for example, contrasts with paste and decoration provide the basis for the identification of exotic vessels at Seip (Prufer 1968:14, 78), Tremper (Prufer 1968:46), Turner (Prufer 1968:14), Mound City (Prufer 1968:52, 54, 57; Seeman 1979b:378–379), and possibly Newcastle and Esch (Seeman 1979b:378–379). While foreign vessels may be expected in the heartland of Hopewell interaction, exotic ceramics are also reported in other areas of the interaction sphere.

In the Havana tradition, Hopewell (and Baehr) vessel distributions concentrate in the central and lower regions of the Illinois Valley. These areas are therefore understood as primary source areas for several types of small special-purpose vessels. Consequently, only ceramics that markedly contrast with local Hopewell styles, such as the simple-stamped tetrapodal vessel at Meppen (Fecht 1955; Griffin 1958:13), are recognized as foreign. Away from the central and lower valleys, exotic vessels are more readily identified.

In southern Michigan, for example, Flanders (1979:113–114) described two limestone-tempered vessels from the Spoonville sites as "quite obviously manufactured elsewhere." While he did not specify where these vessels originated, Flanders (1979:114) noted the resemblance of one to the quadrilobate vessel from Knight Mounds (Griffin, Flanders, and Titterington 1970:Plate 68). Similar observations are made for southern Wisconsin. On the basis of vessels reported by Thomas (1894:83) and McKern (1931:Plates 45–47), Stoltman (1979:135) states that "so specific are the similarities of these vessels to Illinois types, including the presence of limestone temper, which is otherwise extremely rare in Wisconsin, that one is inclined to consider many to be direct imports from Illinois."

In the upper Illinois Valley, foreign Hopewell vessels are also identified at Utica Mounds based on the lack of "continuity in design or method of application" (Henriksen 1965:58). With regard to the two Hopewell Zoned Dentate vessels (Mounds 1 and 8, Group 1) and the Montezuma Punctate vessel (Mound 1, Group 1) Griffin, Flanders, and Titterington (1970:8) suggest that they "probably were made in the lower Illinois Valley."

Utilitarian vessels are less frequently identified in Middle Woodland exchange interactions. At the Havana site in the central Illinois Valley, McGregor (1952:83) recognized nine sherds as foreign; these were identified as Neteler Stamped, Mason Plain, Hummel Stamped, and unnamed fabric-impressed. Of these, the limestone-tempered Hummel Stamped sherd was singled out as "probably derived from farther south in the Illinois River Valley" (McGregor 1952:84).

In the lower Illinois Valley, small numbers of fabric-impressed sherds are reported at a number of sites, including Pool (Epstein 1958:37–40), Smiling Dan (Morgan 1985:Table 12.1), Napoleon Hollow (Morgan 1986:385), Loy and Crane (Farnsworth and Koski 1985:Table 5.1), Macoupin (Rackerby 1983:Table 2), and Peisker (Staab 1984:167). Their occurrence in the Illinois Valley—coupled with the identification of Havana and Hopewell sherds in Crab Orchard assemblages such as Twenhofel (Flanders 1965a:194–195, as cited in Seeman 1979b:378), Sugar Camp Hill (Maxwell 1951:170), and Wilson Mounds (Neumann and Fowler 1952:214)—suggests occasional transport of utilitarian vessels between these regions.

Until recently, the identification of "trade vessels" relied on visual assessments of decoration and paste. Not all researchers accept that ceramic vessels circulated during the Middle Woodland period, and this disagreement results in inconsistent and sometimes conflicting identifications. The current study therefore utilizes compositional and stylistic data to document the presence of foreign ceramics—and presumably foreign persons—within the lower Illinois Valley.

Compositional and Stylistic Analysis of Middle Woodland Ceramics

In this study (derived from analyses originally detailed in Fie 2000), ceramic sherds and samples of raw clay were analyzed to identify the transport and exchange of Middle Woodland pottery within the lower Illinois Valley (fig. 23.1). For this analysis, the selection of site assemblages targeted functionally different site types (*sensu* Struever 1968a, 1968b). In all, 313 ceramic sherds were chosen from four habitation sites and two transaction centers (table 23.1). The habitation sites consisted of Smiling Dan (Odell 1985b:325; Stafford 1985c:447–455; Stafford and Sant 1985a:31; Styles, Purdue, and Colburn 1985:435), Sandy Creek Church (Struever 1968a:Figure 15), Apple Creek (Struever 1968a:201–206, 245–246, 1968b:297–304, 307), and Macoupin (Rackerby 1983), while the transaction centers were represented by Mound House (Buikstra, Charles, and Rakita 1998; Struever and Houart 1972:63; see also Struever 1968a:216–217, 1968b:308) and Peisker (Struever and Houart 1972:63–64, Figure 3; see also McGimsey and Wiant 1986:540; Struever 1968a:211–212, 1968b:300–305). These contrasting occupational contexts

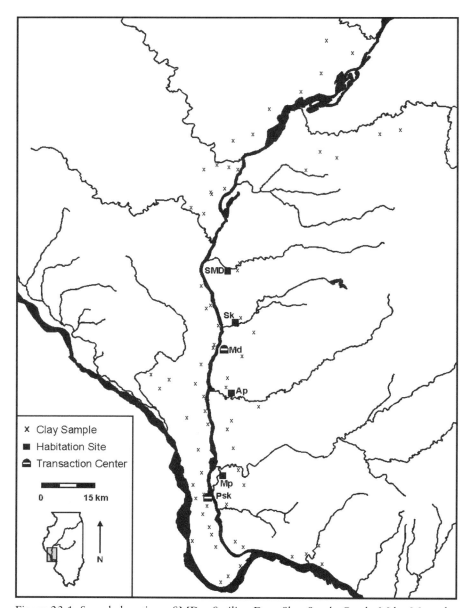

Figure 23.1. Sample locations: SMD = Smiling Dan; Sk = Sandy Creek; Md = Mound House; Ap = Apple Creek; Mp = Macoupin; Psk = Peisker.

provide a backdrop against which the occurrence of foreign sherds may be assessed. From these assemblages, individual sherds were chosen so as to maximize the explanatory capability; this choice emphasized large decorated Middle Woodland sherds (see Bishop, Rands, and Holley 1982:279; Carr and Komorowski 1995:740).

Prior to destructive sampling, each sherd was classified and coded for decorative and technological attributes. Efforts to classify samples within Griffin's (1952c) ceramic typology met with some difficulty, and individual sherds could

Table 23.1. Breakdown of Analyzed Sherd Samples by Site and Ware

Ware Category	Mp	Ap	Psk	Sk	Md	SMD	Total
Havana	44	28	37	22	22	18	171
Havana-Hopewell	0	1	1	1	0	1	4
Havana-Pike	0	2	0	0	0	5	7
Havana-Other	0	1	2	0	1	2	6
Hopewell	0	1	3	9	1	7	21
Bluffdale/Grigsby Rockered	0	3	1	2	1	3	10
Baehr	4	2	2	4	4	4	20
Pike	5	16	3	5	4	14	47
Pike-Havana	0	0	1	1	0	3	5
Pike-Other	0	0	0	1	0	0	1
MW Fabric Impressed	5	0	2	0	2	0	9
MW Simple Stamped	0	0	0	0	0	1	1
MW Type Indeterminate	0	1	0	1	0	0	2
Early Woodland	1	0	0	3	2	0	6
Late Woodland	0	2	1	0	0	0	3
Total	59	57	53	49	37	58	313

Note: Mp = Macoupin, Ap = Apple Creek, Psk = Peisker, Sk = Sandy Creek, Md = Mound House, SMD = Smiling Dan; MW = Middle Woodland.

not always be readily assigned to a ware category. Following Morgan's (1985: 189–213) precedent, several combination ware designations (for example, Havana-Pike) were created to account for sherds that exhibited traits associated with more than one ware. For the compositional analysis, these hybrid designations were structured according to, first, their paste and temper characteristics and, second, their form and/or decoration. The type assignments also relied heavily on the conventions employed by Morgan (1985:189–215, 1986:372– 387). His scheme corresponded closely with Griffin's (1952c) typology but also accounted for more recently defined wares and their types (for example, Bluffdale Rockered, Grigsby Dentate Rockered).

The ceramic sample consists primarily of sherds representing the four major Middle Woodland wares found in lower Illinois Valley sites: Havana, Hopewell, Pike, and Baehr. The sherd sample also includes several examples of less common ceramics that suggest relationships with other regions. For example, Sister Creeks Punctated, Neteler Stamped, and Naples Ovoid Stamped sherds represent early Havana types, and their presence in lower valley sites may reflect historical relationships with the central Illinois Valley. The center of Steuben Punctated occurs in the upper Illinois Valley (Wolforth 1995:39), and the two examples from Apple Creek may confirm contacts with groups in this region. To the south, the fabric-impressed sherds indicate interaction with Crab Orchard groups, while the Brangenburg rim and simple-stamped sherd suggest contacts farther south.

Analytical Methods

The composition of ceramic materials can be determined through a variety of techniques (see Bishop, Rands, and Holley 1982:290–292; Rice 1987:392–

404). In the current study, elemental concentrations were determined using instrumental neutron activation analysis (INAA) at the Missouri University Research Reactor (MURR). Neutron activation is a highly sensitive technique capable of simultaneously measuring numerous trace and major elements. Moreover, the suitability of this technique for discriminating ceramic source areas has already been established in several areas of the Midwest (for example, Clark, Neff, and Glascock 1992; Elam et al. 1992). To maintain comparability with these studies, sample preparation and analysis followed the procedures utilized at the MURR facilities, including the production of briquettes from the eighty-two samples of raw clays (see Glascock 1992).

Of the thirty-three elements determined for these samples, eleven elements were omitted from the original study (Fie 2000) owing to erratic detection, elemental enrichment, or the likelihood of postdepositional alteration. Two additional elements, hafnium and zirconium, correlated with the silt fraction in the paste (Fie 2000:409; Neff et al. 1992:67) and were eliminated in order to include the clay samples. The concentrations of the remaining twenty elements were transformed to $\log_{10}$ values to compensate for differences in magnitude between the major and trace elements (Glascock 1992:16). To identify groupings within this matrix, the data were subjected to a series of statistical analyses including cluster analysis, principal components analysis, and Mahalanobis distance analysis.

Preliminary partitioning of the data was accomplished using cluster analysis with the groupings based on squared-mean Euclidean distances and average link clustering (see Glascock 1992:17). Dendrograms generated from the cluster analysis revealed a number of sherd and clay samples with only weak affiliation to individual sites or the total sherd and clay sample. Though compelling, these results were considered preliminary as cluster analysis may produce incorrect groupings.

Cluster analysis assumes that the analyzed variables are independent of each other (Shennan 1988:200). Strong correlations among the variables result in either an overestimate or an underestimate of the Euclidean distance coefficient and consequently produce hyperspherical groupings (Bishop, Rands, and Holley 1982:320; Glascock 1992:17; Shennan 1988:200). Such interelement correlations are common in compositional data and are present in the current data set (see Fie 2000:Table 40). Additional analysis therefore relies on principal components analysis, a statistical technique that is sensitive to interelement relationships (Shennan 1988:246).

Principal components analysis is a highly valued statistical technique in the investigation of compositional data and one commonly used to identify and clarify source-related groupings. Following the conventions adopted at MURR, the calculated principal components were based on the variance-covariance matrix across the entire data set with principal components scores also calculated for individual samples (see Glascock 1992:18).

Scatter-plots generated for the first few principal components corroborated the cluster analyses. Many of the sherd and clay samples that displayed a weak affiliation in the dendrograms also exhibited only marginal association in the principal components scores generated for individual site samples, the total sherd sample (n = 313), and the combined sherd and clay sample (n = 395). More quantitative assessment of the data patterning was accomplished using Mahalanobis distance analysis. Because Mahalanobis distance incorporates both the distance of data points and the rate for dispersion from a group's centroid, it was used to calculate the probability of a sample's membership within different lower valley sample groups.

The inclusion of significantly different samples may, however, adversely affect the results of multivariate analyses by extending the distribution of samples and causing them to appear more similar to each other (Mainfort et al. 1997:47). On the basis of cluster analysis results, twenty-one clay samples were removed from the data set: SFC-403, SFC-405, SFC-407, SFC-409, SFC-419, SFC-421, SFC-431, SFC-436, SFC-437, SFC-442, SFC-444, SFC-450, SFC-452, SFC-453, SFC-454, SFC-462, SFC-464, SFC-467, SFC-468, SFC-469, SFC-474. Principal components were then recalculated for the remaining samples. Through the use of Mahalanobis distance, a probability of membership (p-value) was calculated for each sherd within its parent site sample of sherds, the total sherds (n = 313), and the combined sherd and clay sample (n = 374).

The statistical analysis of the compositional data finds that most of the sherds are affiliated with the lower Illinois Valley, albeit some only minimally. At the same time, several sherds invariably occur as outliers within their parent site sample, within other site samples, and within the data set as a whole; their relationship to the other lower valley samples is best illustrated on a biplot of the elements chromium and thorium (fig. 23.2). Distinct from the general compositional patterning, these nineteen Middle Woodland sherds are considered the remnants of vessels manufactured outside the study area (table 23.2). While several of the stylistically less common sherds are included among the outliers, several others appear to be local. Understanding these patterns requires some consideration of the occurrence of foreign sherds among lower Illinois Valley settlement types as well as the styles represented among the local and exotic ceramics.

Discussion

The outliers include several sherds that are stylistically similar to vessels more common outside the lower Illinois Valley: Naples Ovoid Stamped and Sister Creeks Punctated (central Illinois Valley), Steuben Punctated (upper Illinois Valley), and several of the fabric-impressed sherds (southern Illinois). The remaining compositional outliers consist of Havana types and one example of Pike, which are styles at home in the lower Illinois Valley.

Historically, the identification of exotic Middle Woodland ceramics has focused on Hopewell and Baehr vessels (for example, Braun, Griffin, and Titterington 1982:62–63; Farnsworth 1973:31–32; Struever and Houart 1972:74–77). It is therefore notable that no Hopewell or Baehr vessels are identified among the outliers; all are compositionally local to the lower Illinois Val-

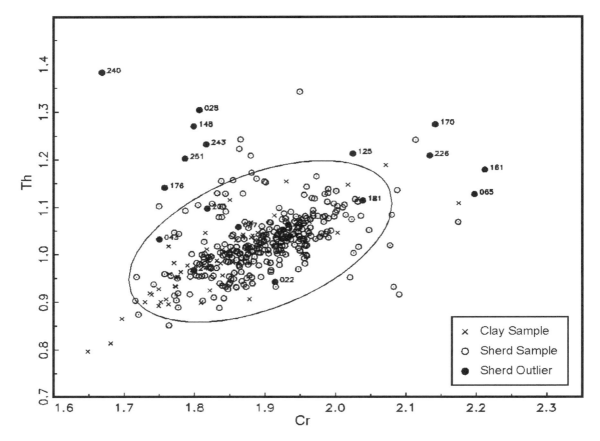

Figure 23.2. Biplot of chromium and thorium concentrations for the sherd and clay samples.

ley. Studies of ware distributions within the Havana tradition (Griffin 1952a:15; Struever and Houart 1972:76–77; Taylor 1958:205) and arguments for their exchange (Struever and Houart 1972:76–77) link the manufacture of Baehr and several Hopewell types to the Illinois Valley, specifically to its lower reaches. Thus, there is little reason to expect imported specimens within this region to be of Hopewell or Baehr types.

The compositional analysis indicates that vessels were transported into the lower Illinois Valley during the Middle Woodland period. But, as Mark Seeman (1979b:276–278) rightly asks, "Is the presence of nonlocal ceramics a function of trade or a by-product of it?" In other words, while foreign vessels may result from exchange, they may also result from activities that follow from exchange or socioceremonial interaction. The current data support both inferences. The occurrence of exotic vessels at both transaction centers, Peisker and Mound House, is to be expected if foreign groups participated in political, economic, ceremonial, or social activities at these locales. However, the presence of foreign sherds in all four of the habitation sites samples suggests that, once introduced into the region, some vessels were acquired and incorporated into local domestic assemblages.

Table 23.2. Membership Probabilities for the Middle Woodland Compositional Outliers

ID	Site	Site Sherds	All Sherds	All Samples	Orifice Diameter (cm)	Vessel Rim Present	Sample Description
SFS-022	Mp	0.0	0.0	0.0	—	—	MW fabric impressed
SFS-028	Mp	0.0	0.0	0.0	24	5%	Havana Plain
SFS-037	Mp	0.2	0.0	0.0	—	—	Naples Cordwrapped-Stick Stamped
SFS-043	Mp	0.2	0.0	0.0	22	6%	Havana Plain
SFS-065	Ap	0.0	0.0	0.0	34	11%	Steuben Punctated
SFS-125	Psk	0.0	0.0	0.0	—	—	MW fabric impressed
SFS-148	Psk	0.0	0.1	0.0	28	6%	Havana Plain
SFS-161	Sk	0.0	0.0	0.0	—	—	Naples Ovoid Stamped
SFS-170	Sk	0.0	0.0	0.0	30	3%	Hummel Dentate Stamped
SFS-176	Sk	0.0	0.0	0.0	28	3%	Neteler Plain Stamped
SFS-181	Sk	0.0	0.0	0.0	—	—	Sister Creeks Punctated
SFS-200	Md	0.0	0.0	0.0	—	—	Naples Cordwrapped-Stick Stamped
SFS-226	Md	0.0	0.0	0.0	—	—	Pike Brushed/Scratched/Combed
SFS-227	Md	0.0	0.0	0.0	40	5%	Havana Plain
SFS-240	Md	0.6	0.0	0.0	26	3%	Havana Plain
SFS-242	Md	0.0	0.0	0.0	22	4%	Havana Plain
SFS-243	Md	0.4	0.0	0.0	38	3%	Havana Plain
SFS-251	Md	0.0	0.0	0.0	—	—	Havana Cordmarked
SFS-284	SMD	0.0	0.0	0.0	—	—	Havana-Pike Cordmarked

Note: Membership probabilities based on Mahalanobis distance calculations using 20 principal components; samples were jackknifed prior to probability calculations. Mp = Macoupin, Ap = Apple Creek, Psk = Peisker, Sk = Sandy Creek, Md = Mound House, SMD = Smiling Dan; MW = Middle Woodland; ID = sample identification number.

Marriage alliances, while plausible, do not adequately explain this distribution. To assess the biological relationship of Middle Woodland populations within the lower Illinois Valley, Buikstra (1976:46–57, 1980:289–290) compared the skeletal remains from Gibson, Klunk, Bedford, and Peisker. Analyses of both metric and nonmetric trait frequencies found no significant differences between the adjacent Klunk and Gibson mound populations but significant differences between Gibson-Klunk and Bedford, and between Gibson-Klunk and Peisker. Additional analysis of the Gibson-Klunk interments revealed considerable stability in the frequency of these skeletal traits over time. Together, these analyses suggest localized and somewhat biologically isolated communities within the lower Illinois Valley throughout the Middle Woodland period (Buikstra 1980:295, 1984:227). The persistence of significant epigenetic differences between populations separated by as little as 15 kilometers raises serious doubt as to whether marriage alliances were regularly conducted over more substantial distances. While marriage alliances may have occasionally transpired between distant groups, they apparently did not occur with sufficient regularity to confound the biological data. Accordingly, marriage alliances are an unlikely explanation for the ubiquity of foreign vessels in the analyzed lower Illinois Valley sites.

The compositional outliers provide a compelling argument for the exchange of Middle Woodland ceramics. However, an assertion that foreign vessels result from organized shipments or down-the-line distributions is difficult to support. Pottery vessels, and utilitarian vessels in particular, are fragile tools and subject to breakage during use and transport (see Shott 1996 for a summary of vessel use-life data). As short-term implements, utilitarian vessels presumably passed through few exchange transactions. Their long-distance transport likely occurred *with* groups as part of a basic domestic assemblage. If this reasoning is applied to the outliers, the identified exotic ceramics apparently resulted from direct contact between parties from southern, central, and northern Illinois. While the locations of these interactions remain unknown, the presence of foreign groups in the lower Illinois Valley is suggested by several of the stylistically "exotic" sherds.

"Copying" is a frequently evoked explanation for vessels that exhibit uncommon styles on local pastes (for example, Braun 1986:123; Maxwell 1951:170; Morgan 1985:213; Neumann and Fowler 1952:226). In the Wabash Valley, for example, Neumann and Fowler (1952:225–226) identified the zoned stamped Hopewell sherds at the Hubele village as local products on the basis of similarities in paste and tempering materials with the local Crab Orchard ceramics. In southern Michigan, Flanders (1979:114), while recognizing two limestone vessels as foreign, also noted, "A quadrilobate burial vessel with a good classic Hopewell rim form was also recovered, but with grit temper and probably locally produced." Two Hopewell vessels from the Paggeot site were similarly characterized as "grit tempered and probably locally manufactured" (Flanders 1979:113).

Occasionally, exotic vessels are seen as the prototype for copies of vessel forms or decoration: "In the upper Illinois valley and eastward along the Kankakee, pottery of the Baehr-Pike types was brought in, and local pottery products were made with the same decorative features" (Griffin, Flanders, and Titterington 1970:9). In many instances, however, the actual producers of locally made but exotic-looking vessels remain unnamed: "A very small number of sherds were identified as Crab Orchard Fabric Impressed [at Smiling Dan]. . . . Although some of the vessels represented by these sherds may have originated outside the lower Illinois valley, it is suspected that most are a reflection of local manufacture" (Morgan 1985:213). Given the presence of exotic ceramics in the lower valley, it is conceivable that the stylistically "exotic" ceramics also result from the presence of foreign groups in the region.

Simple-stamped ceramics are rare in Illinois Valley sites, although one sherd is reported at Peisker (Staab 1984:167) and a complete vessel is known from the Meppen mounds in southern Calhoun County (Fecht 1955; Griffin 1958:13). Fabric-impressed Crab Orchard–like sherds are more regularly reported but still constitute less than 1 percent of the ceramics recovered from sites in the Illinois Valley (for example, Epstein 1958:37–40; Farnsworth and Koski 1985:Table 5.1; McGregor 1952:83–84; Morgan 1985:213, 1986:385, 395, 402; Rackerby 1983:Table 2; Staab 1984:167; Struever 1960:61). Owing to the low frequencies of these types in the lower Illinois Valley it was assumed that the analyzed examples would be compositionally "foreign."

In addition to their unusual surface treatment, other attributes contribute to

Table 23.3. Select Attributes for the Steuben Punctated, Simple-stamped, and Fabric-impressed Sherds

ID	Site	Aplastics	Interior Surface	Exterior Surface	Lip Form	Orifice (cm)	Vessel Rim Present	Node (mm)
SFS-065[a]	Ap	grit	plain	plain, punctated	interior beveled	34	11%	—
SFS-111	Ap	sand	plain	plain, punctated	interior beveled	13	5%	—
SFS-292	SMD	sand	plain	simple stamped	exterior beveled	26	5%	9
SFS-009	Mp	fine sand	plain	fabric impressed	—	—	—	—
SFS-022[a]	Mp	grit (mafic)	plain	fabric impressed	flattened	—	—	—
SFS-034	Mp	grit, fine sand	plain	fabric impressed	rounded	22	8%	—
SFS-036	Mp	fine sand, clay	plain	fabric impressed	—	—	—	—
SFS-040	Mp	grit, fine sand	fabric	fabric impressed	flattened	—	—	—
SFS-124	Psk	clay/grog	fabric	fabric impressed	rounded	22	16%	13
SFS-125[a]	Psk	grit	plain	fabric impressed	—	—	—	—
SFS-235	Md	sand	plain	fabric impressed	—	—	—	—
SFS-255	Md	grit (mafic)	plain	fabric impressed	—	—	—	—

Note: Mp = Macoupin, Ap = Apple Creek, Psk = Peisker, Md = Mound House, SMD = Smiling Dan
a. Compositional outlier.

the assumption that the simple-stamped and fabric-impressed sherds are foreign in origin (table 23.3). The simple-stamped sherd, for example, exhibits a flattened lip beveled slightly to the exterior and nodes placed 9 millimeters below the lip. Several rare traits also occur on the fabric-impressed sherds and include fabric-impressed interior surfaces, flat and rounded rims, and a high node placement of 13 millimeters below the lip. These attributes contrast with the analyzed Havana sherds, which are characterized by flattened rims typically beveled to the interior (*n* = 90 of 126), a plain interior surface (*n* = 182 of 187), and node placement averaging 24.3 ±8.3 millimeters below the lip (*n* = 60). Despite these contrasts with regional norms, the simple-stamped sherd and at least two of the nine fabric-impressed sherds (SFS-022 and SFS-125) are compositionally "local" (table 23.4).

While initially perplexing, these results may be understood with reference to the Massey and Archie ceramic assemblages. Situated in the uplands east of the lower Illinois Valley (fig. 23.3), the Massey and Archie sites are notable for high frequencies of fabric-impressed sherds and for the absence of both Havana and Pike sherds (Farnsworth and Koski 1985). Detailed examination of these assemblages found that as many as one-third of the fabric-impressed sherds lack Crab Orchard–like paste characteristics, such as grog and/or mafic temper (Farnsworth and Koski 1985:128). Following their analysis of the pottery, Farnsworth and Koski (1985:225) concluded that these two sites represent rural homesteads occupied by family groups that migrated into the area. During their residency near the lower valley, these groups apparently continued to produce ceramics in their traditional Crab Orchard style. Thus while all are stylistically exotic, some of these fabric-impressed sherds were manufactured from local raw materials.

These findings offer an intriguing explanation of the "local" simple-stamped and fabric-impressed sherds. Previous interpretations of such sherds ascribe the amalgam of exotic styles and local pastes to "copying" behavior. The composi-

Table 23.4. Membership Probabilities for the Steuben Punctated, Simple-stamped, and Fabric-impressed Sherds

ID	Site	Site Sherds (%)	All Sherds (%)	All Samples (%)	Sample Description
SFS-065	Ap	0.0	0.0	0.0	Steuben Punctated
SFS-111	Ap	33.4	97.8	99.4	Steuben Punctated
SFS-292	SMD	20.9	35.2	66.5	MW simple stamped
SFS-009	Mp	99.7	99.1	98.6	MW fabric impressed
SFS-022	Mp	0.0	0.0	0.0	MW fabric impressed
SFS-034	Mp	75.1	64.2	79.0	MW fabric impressed
SFS-036	Mp	76.3	77.1	90.4	MW fabric impressed
SFS-040	Mp	0.8	0.4	2.1	MW fabric impressed
SFS-124	Psk	0.0[a]	0.0	0.0	MW fabric impressed
SFS-125	Psk	0.0	0.0	0.0	MW fabric impressed
SFS-235	Md	22.7	61.4	83.0	MW fabric impressed
SFS-255	Md	7.5	43.3	48.3	MW fabric impressed

Note: Membership in Middle Woodland ware type probabilities based on Mahalanobis distance calculations using 20 principal components. Mp = Macoupin, Ap = Apple Creek, Psk = Peisker, Md = Mound House, SMD = Smiling Dan, MW = Middle Woodland.
a. Membership probability >5% in another site sample.

tional analysis confirms that several of the stylistically less common ceramics were made from lower Illinois Valley materials, and the obvious contrasts with local surface treatments may be attributed to copying behavior. However, other stylistic attributes suggest that these sherds are not simply imitations of exotic ceramic types. Rather, the subtle deviations in rim form and node placement from regional Havana norms connote differences in more basic production modes (Plog 1990:61; Sackett 1985:157–159; Wiessner 1985). These sherds are therefore interpreted as products of local manufacture by itinerant foreign producers.

This is not to insinuate that foreign groups commonly took up residence in the lower Illinois Valley. Rather, these data suggest that interregional visitation by small family groups was a regular component of Middle Woodland interaction. During these travels some implements were inevitably broken during regular use and discarded. At the same time, other containers, along with more prestigious goods, were exchanged between local and visiting groups. Depending on the duration and demands of travel, ceramic production was occasionally required to replace broken vessels. Vessels that were made to supplement a depleted inventory accompanied itinerant groups on their return trip (although some were undoubtedly consumed en route). Though manufactured from foreign materials, these vessels would be stylistically consistent with their "local" assemblage. At the same time, vessels produced out of social and ceremonial obligation were left behind with host groups. While appearing stylistically exotic, these vessels would exhibit the same compositional signature as the local ceramics manufactured from these same raw materials.

The available ceramic data strongly support this interpretation. First, all of the foreign sherds identified in the compositional analysis represent cooking or storage vessels. Most of the foreign sherds identified in the study represent Ha-

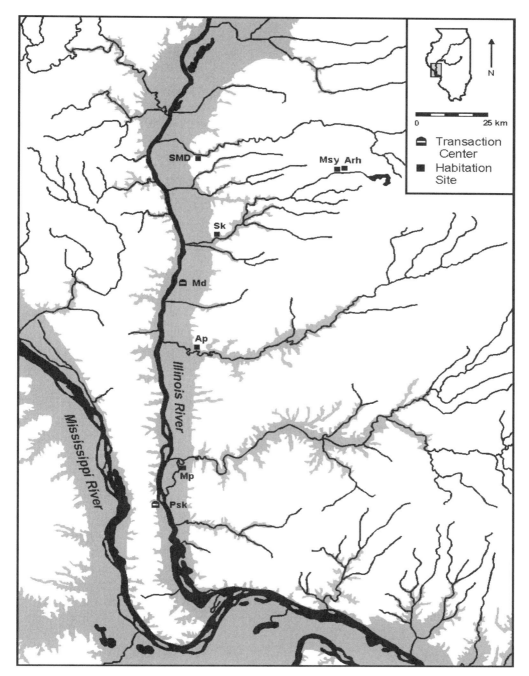

Figure 23.3. Site locations: SMD = Smiling Dan; Msy = Massey; Arh = Archie; Sk = Sandy Creek; Md = Mound House; Ap = Apple Creek; Mp = Macoupin; Psk = Peisker.

vana types: Neteler Plain Stamped (SFS-176), Sister Creeks Punctated (SFS-181), Havana Plain (SFS-028, 043, 148, 227, 240, 242, 243), Havana Cord-marked (SFS-251, SFS-284), Naples Stamped (SFS-037, SFS-161, SFS-200), Steuben Punctated (SFS-065), and Hummel Dentate Stamped (SFS-170). The remaining three outliers consist of one Pike (SFS-226) and two fabric-impressed sherds (SFS-022, SFS-125). In the lower Illinois Valley, large Havana and Pike vessels are widely regarded as cooking and/or storage containers. In southern Illinois, Crab Orchard or Jackson ware is considered the functional equivalent of Havana (Neumann and Fowler 1952:225).

The size data also support a utilitarian function for these vessels. The orifice diameter for the foreign rim sherds ranges between 22 centimeters and 40 centimeters, as compared to 8–42 centimeters for the sample as a whole ($n = 180$) (Fie 2000:Table 19). Additionally, three of the exotic sherds (SFS-125, 148, and 243) exhibit charred residue on their interior surface. Thus, while some of these vessels were evidently exchanged, these larger vessels also suggest ongoing sub-sistence-maintenance activities.

Finally, Middle Woodland ceramic production is generally assumed to have been a female enterprise. Some support for this assumption can be drawn from the strong association of ceramic vessels with female burials (Leigh 1988:199). In at least one instance, a serrated shell was also interred with an adult female (and two juveniles) and may represent an association of females with tools of ceramic manufacture (see Odell 1994:116–117). Moreover, a review of the eth-nographic literature finds that ceramic production at the household level is strongly associated with women (Skibo and Schiffer 1995). While arguments have been made for standardization in Hopewell vessels (for example, Braun, Griffin, and Titterington 1982:63), there is little evidence for ceramic produc-tion above the household level.

If one assumes that women made Middle Woodland vessels, the itinerant manufacture of vessels suggests that women were regular members of traveling companies. Taken together, itinerant manufacture and use of vessels suggest that journeys were not limited to expeditions by adventurous explorers (for ex-ample, Brose 1990:110; Griffin 1965:146; Seeman 1979b:300) but that they also included visits to adjacent regions by small family groups. These visitations would have afforded opportunities to engage in less formal exchange activities and establish more direct partnerships with other groups. Such relationships may have provided access to more desirable goods or simply secured hospitality during future travels. The exchange of more mundane goods such as ceramic vessels and lithic raw materials suggests efforts to establish and maintain more familiar ties between distant family groups. While providing more direct access to distant goods, the resulting lattice of interaction would have bolstered more formal relationships between regional groups.

Conclusion

This sketch of Middle Woodland interaction differs from many ceremonial, political, and economic models based on Hopewell mortuary goods. Models of exchange are strongly influenced by the commodities they entail. For the Middle Woodland period, the attention given to Hopewell goods fosters perceptions that exchange centered on prestige goods, elite engagements, and formal interactions.

Using compositional and stylistic data, this study succeeds in documenting "foreign" pottery within six Middle Woodland sites in the lower Illinois Valley. Because of their occurrence in both floodplain mound groups (that is, transaction centers) and habitation sites, these exotic sherds are interpreted as the products of exchange. Whether ceramic vessels or their contents were valued, their acquisition was presumably not socially restricted and suggests a network of non-elite exchange. Additional insight into this interaction was drawn from locally made "exotic" ceramics. Though few in number, these sherds suggest that vessels were also manufactured in the lower Illinois Valley by visiting domestic groups.

Of the four models discussed, these results conform best to expectations of socially motivated exchange. Political models currently focus on the use of exchange goods as tokens in intergroup alliances. A symbolic importance of exotic goods is similarly emphasized in ideological models of exchange. If the exchange of Middle Woodland ceramics was politically or ideologically motivated, we would expect the circulation of stylistically standardized Hopewell vessels. Contrary to expectations, none of the twenty-one Hopewell (or twenty Baehr) sherds in the lower Illinois Valley sample was identified as exotic. Rather, all nineteen compositional outliers derived from utilitarian vessels.

The presence of foreign domestic ceramics such as Havana, Pike, and Crab Orchard suggests that these vessels were part of economic activities. Economics-based models of material distributions predict that these large containers were unlikely commodities of exchange. In addition to being bulky and fragile, these items were also locally available. It is possible that these vessels contained highly desirable commodities that warranted long-distance transport in large ceramic containers. Until such goods are identified, it is assumed that the exchange of foodstuffs via ceramic containers was related to their use in social activities.

The regular exchange of utilitarian ceramics, as well as lithic raw materials, suggests that subsistence-maintenance materials were more important in Middle Woodland exchange networks than is generally appreciated. Their inclusion in exchange also connotes the participation of a broad segment of Middle Woodland social groups and the movement of small family groups between regions. While challenging the emphasis placed on high-status exotics, these findings also complement previous models of Middle Woodland exchange. The movement of groups across the landscape, their engagement in food-related activities, and the exchange of ceramic vessels suggest a sphere of interaction that was important for sustaining social relationships among Middle Woodland populations. Taken together, these findings advance a more inclusive model of Middle Woodland interaction that recognizes multiple scales of interaction, a breadth of commodities, and the participation of all social group members.

24

Animal Exploitation and the Havana Tradition

A Comparison of Animal Use at Mound Centers and Hamlets in the Illinois Valley

Julie Zimmermann Holt

A review of the archaeological literature reveals disagreement regarding the nature of the socioeconomy in the Havana tradition of the Illinois Valley (Holt 2000:Chapter 3). This disagreement might be collapsed into two simple models that differ primarily in the level of complexity they portray in the Havana socioeconomy and in how they explain the role of mounded sites in the Havana settlement system. The first model presents the Havana socioeconomy as essentially egalitarian. Each settlement was responsible for its own subsistence, and mounded sites were vacant ceremonial centers used for ritual (primarily mortuary) and feasting. The second model emphasizes evidence of stratification in the Havana socioeconomy (compare Winters 1993). Non-elites supported an elite class of ritual specialists and craft specialists, particularly in terms of subsistence. The elites resided at mounded sites, which were protourban centers of ritual, trade, and craft manufacture.

This chapter summarizes results of a zooarchaeological analysis that tests these two models (Holt 2000). This analysis compares faunal data from Middle Woodland mound centers and hamlets; it also compares faunal data from Middle Woodland Havana sites with faunal data from early Late Woodland White Hall and Weaver sites. By making a diachronic comparison, this analysis will examine the Havana socioeconomy and its collapse as indicated by the changing role of animal products at the Middle to Late Woodland transition.

Methods

The Middle Woodland sample includes the Ogden-Fettie, Baehr-Gust, and Peisker mound centers (Corwin 1968; Holt 2000). The Napoleon Hollow site is considered an early version of a mound center in this analysis because of its association with the Elizabeth mounds (Styles and Purdue 1986). Smiling Dan is a small Middle Woodland hamlet with no mounds (Styles, Purdue, and Colburn 1985). The early Late Woodland sample comprises the Baehr-Gust, Newbridge, and Rench sites (Holt 2000; Martin and Masulis 1993; Styles 1981).

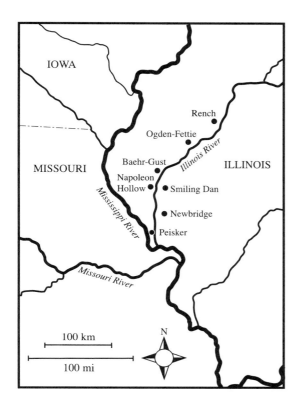

Figure 24.1. Locations of selected Middle and early Late Woodland sites in the lower and central Illinois Valley. After Yingst 1990; Owens 1994.

Of these sites, Peisker, Newbridge, Napoleon Hollow, and Smiling Dan are located in the lower Illinois Valley; Baehr-Gust (or the Baehr site) lies at the juncture of the central and lower Illinois valleys; and Ogden-Fettie and Rench are located in the central Illinois Valley (fig. 24.1). All of these sites are situated on floodplains with easy access to the Illinois River, streams, and/or backwater lakes; they also had ready access to upland resources.

Methods of identification are comparable for most of these sites, with the possible exception of Peisker (Corwin 1968). Because of possible differences in methods of taxonomic identification for Peisker, consideration of that sample is limited to the analysis of white-tailed deer element representation. Methods of collection are roughly comparable for most of these sites, although half-inch (127 millimeters) mesh, rather than quarter-inch (64 millimeters) mesh, was used at Peisker and Newbridge (Corwin 1968; Styles 1981). This source of variation is not believed to have a significant effect on the analysis reported here (Holt 2000).

In this analysis five lines of zooarchaeological evidence are examined: species representation, element representation, seasonality data, the number of bones recovered per volume of soil excavated, and the percentage of bone and shell artifacts. Styles and Purdue (1991) performed a similar analysis, examining samples from Smiling Dan, Napoleon Hollow, and Elizabeth. Their purpose was to compare faunal use at Havana ritual and secular sites, but they did not consider the effects of social stratification in their analysis.

There are ambiguities inherent in this type of analysis. Both models to be tested can create very similar zooarchaeological signatures; in particular, zooarchaeological evidence of feasting and tribute can be difficult to distinguish (Holt 2000; compare Jackson and Scott 1995). However, the consideration of multiple lines of evidence will help mitigate such ambiguities. We might also distinguish between these signatures based upon their broader archaeological context.

Results

Species Representation

The first line of evidence to be considered is species representation. The first model suggests that occupants of outlying settlements procured their own food, so species representation should reflect locally available fauna. Species representation at Havana centers should stand out if these were centers of ritual and feasting. This pattern might change at the end of the Middle Woodland period as ritual feasting became less important or perhaps decentralized.

The second model suggests that occupants of outlying settlements procured their own food but also provided animal products to the centers. Therefore, we should expect a greater variety of species at Havana centers, since in effect the catchment area of a mound center is equal to the sum of all its supporting sites' catchment areas. In particular, we should expect ritual and possibly exotic species, as well as species that might represent choice meat. This pattern should change at the end of the Middle Woodland period as outlying settlements withdrew their support from the mound centers.

Analysis of species representation supports certain aspects of both models but overall fits better with the first model. This analysis considered both vertebrate taxonomic richness, which is defined here as the number of distinct vertebrate taxa at the level of genus, and taxonomic richness for mussels, which is defined here as the number of distinct mussel taxa at the level of species (Holt 2000:166–167; compare Styles and Purdue 1991). Greater numbers of species were not found at Havana centers, as was predicted by the second model (table 24.1). Instead, taxonomic richness among these samples was found to correlate positively with sample size (figs. 24.2, 24.3): the positive correlation between richness and sample size is highly significant for vertebrate taxa (r_p = .8654; p = .0055) and for mussels (r_p = .9165; p = .0014).

This pattern does not explain why some sites—namely, the Havana centers—have smaller sample sizes than others (compare Plog and Hegmon 1993; Styles and Purdue 1991). This question will be addressed below in the analysis of bone frequency.

Menhinick's index (D_{Mn}) is a measure of taxonomic richness that considers sample size (Magurran 1988:11, 129). Calculation of Menhinick's index for these samples shows that relative richness varies, but it does not vary by either site function or time period (table 24.1). For example, among the Havana vertebrate samples, the Baehr-Gust center is the richest, but the Smiling Dan hamlet

Table 24.1. Taxonomic Richness at Selected Havana, White Hall, and Weaver Sites

Site and Component	Vertebrates			Mussels		
	Taxonomic Richness[a]	Sample Size[b]	D_{Mn} [c]	Taxonomic Richness[d]	Sample Size[e]	D_{Mn} [c]
Napoleon Hollow (H/C)	33	6,697	0.40	1	4	0.50
Ogden-Fettie (H/C)	29	3,457	0.49	2	2	1.41
Baehr-Gust (H/C)	28	1,228	0.80	15	79	1.69
Smiling Dan (H/V)	53	7,728	0.60	10	58	1.31
Baehr-Gust (WH)	58	10,405	0.57	14	99	1.41
Newbridge (WH)	58	6,371	0.73	23	188	1.68
Rench (W)	71	17,355	0.54	15	180	1.12

Sources: Holt 2000:Tables 5.8 and 5.9; Martin and Masulis 1993:Table 10.2; Styles 1981:Table 16; Styles and Purdue 1986:Table 19.2; Styles, Purdue, and Colburn 1985:Appendix 16.1.
Note: H = Havana, WH = White Hall, W = Weaver, C = center; V = village or hamlet.
a. Number of distinct taxa at the level of genus (but not including *Homo* and *Sus*).
b. Screened number of identified species (NISP) identified minimally to class.
c. Menhinick's index (D_{Mn}) = richness divided by the square root of sample size (Magurran 1988:11, 129).
d. Screened NISP identified minimally to genus.
e. Number of distinct taxa at the level of species.

is richer than the Napoleon Hollow and Ogden-Fettie centers. The relatively low richness of Napoleon Hollow and Ogden-Fettie is probably the result of poorer preservation and, consequently, lower rates of taxonomic identification at those sites (see below and Styles and Purdue 1986).

Most if not all of the taxa represented in these samples could have been procured within several kilometers of each site. Exotic species, such as marine

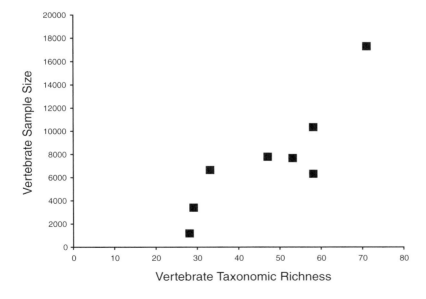

Figure 24.2. Vertebrate taxonomic richness versus sample size.

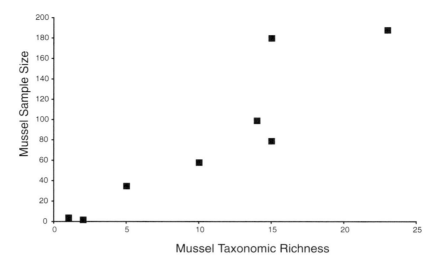

Figure 24.3. Mussel taxonomic richness versus sample size.

shellfish and roseate spoonbills, are sometimes found in Havana Hopewell mortuary contexts (for example, Styles and Purdue 1991). None was found in any of the nonmortuary contexts considered in this analysis.

This analysis also examined the number of ritual taxa found at these sites. "Ritual taxa" are defined here as taxa commonly found in mortuary contexts but rarely found in habitation contexts, such as carnivores and birds of prey (Styles and Purdue 1991). To correct for variation in sample size, numbers of ritual taxa are compared using a "ritual index." A ritual index is simply the number of ritual taxa in a sample divided by the total number of vertebrate taxa (that is, vertebrate taxonomic richness, or the number of distinct vertebrate taxa at the level of genus) for that sample (Holt 2000:167–168). Comparison of ritual indices shows that Havana centers and hamlets have relatively consistent numbers of ritual taxa present (table 24.2). This finding is not consistent with either model, both of which suggest that relatively greater numbers of ritual taxa should be found at mound centers than at outlying sites. Comparison of ritual indices also shows that relatively more ritual species are found at Havana sites than White Hall/Weaver sites. This finding is consistent with both models, which suggest that traditional ritual practices broke down at the end of the Middle Woodland period.

Ritual taxa are found in very small numbers in all of these samples, which is expected since these are nonmortuary contexts. There is no correlation, however, between the number of ritual taxa and sample size ($r_p = -.1533$; $p = .7170$), nor is there a correlation between the number of ritual taxa and vertebrate taxonomic richness ($r_p = -.1820$; $p = .6662$). Thus we might conclude that the relative number of ritual taxa at these sites is culturally meaningful and probably not simply a result of sampling bias. A probable hawk bone and three eagle bones from Baehr-Gust were all terminal phalanges, a striking pattern of ele-

Table 24.2. Ritual Species at Selected Havana, White Hall, and Weaver Sites

Site and Component	Species	Number[a]	Ritual Index[b]
Napoleon Hollow (H/C)	bobcat	1	.03
Ogden-Fettie (H/C)	bear	1	.03
Baehr-Gust (H/C)	eagle, cf. hawk	2	.07
Smiling Dan (H/V)	screech owl, barred owl, bobcat	3	.06
Baehr-Gust (WH)	eagle	1	.02
Newbridge (WH)	none	0	.00
Rench (W)	barred owl	1	.01

Sources: Holt 2000:Tables 5.8 and 5.9; Martin and Masulis 1993:Table 10.2; Styles 1981:Table 16; Styles and Purdue 1986:Table 19.2; Styles, Purdue, and Colburn 1985:Appendix 16.1.
Note: H = Havana, WH = White Hall, W = Weaver, C = center, V = village or hamlet.
a. Number of ritual species identified.
b. Number divided by vertebrate taxonomic richness (see table 24.1).

ment representation that seems unlikely to have occurred by chance. The terminal phalanx is found in the claw on a bird's foot; an owl bone from an undated context at Baehr-Gust was also an element from the foot, a tarsometatarsus (see Holt 2000: Table 5.22). The bear specimen from Ogden-Fettie was a tooth, but it was a premolar (bear canines are commonly found in mortuary contexts).

Finally, this analysis considered the abundance of species preferred for feasting, such as dogs, elk, or deer. Ethnohistoric records indicate that dog meat was eaten at feasts in some Native American societies (for example, Snyder 1991); we might hypothesize that venison was preferred at feasts since the meat of large game conveys prestige in many Western and non-Western societies (for example, Bogan 1983). This analysis shows that dogs and elk are relatively more abundant at Havana mound centers than at the Havana hamlet and also more abundant at Havana sites than White Hall/Weaver sites (tables 24.3, 24.4; figs. 24.4, 24.5). These results suggest that feasting was more common at Havana mound centers than at Havana hamlets and that traditional feasting practices became less important or otherwise changed at the end of the Middle Woodland period. These results are largely consistent with both models.

Table 24.3. Percentages of Elk at Selected Havana, White Hall, and Weaver Sites

Site and Component	%NISP	%MNI
Napoleon Hollow (H/C)	0.15	5.00
Ogden-Fettie (H/C)	0.14	4.00
Baehr-Gust (H/C)	0.24	1.16
Smiling Dan (H/V)	0.04	0.57
Baehr-Gust (WH)	0.05	0.28
Newbridge (WH)	0.00	0.00
Rench (W)	0.10	0.23

Sources: Holt 2000:Tables 5.8 and 5.9; Martin and Masulis 1993:Table 10.2; Styles 1981:Table 16; Styles and Purdue 1986:Table 19.2; Styles, Purdue, and Colburn 1985:Appendix 16.1.
Note: Elk elements as a percentage of the vertebrate screened sample identified minimally to class. H = Havana, WH = White Hall, W = Weaver, C = center, V = village or hamlet, NISP = number of identified species, MNI = minimum number of individuals.

Table 24.4. Percentages of Canids at Selected Havana, White Hall, and Weaver Sites

Site and Component	%NISP	%MNI
Napoleon Hollow (H/C)	0.01	2.50
Ogden-Fettie (H/C)	0.03	1.00
Baehr-Gust (H/C)	0.65	2.33
Smiling Dan (H/V)	0.30	0.95
Baehr-Gust (WH)	0.38	0.41
Newbridge (WH)	0.03	0.13
Rench (W)	0.10	0.70

Sources: Holt 2000:Tables 5.8 and 5.9; Martin and Masulis 1993:Table 10.2; Styles 1981:Table 16; Styles and Purdue 1986:Table 19.2; Styles, Purdue, and Colburn 1985:Appendix 16.1. *Note*: Canid elements as a percentages of the vertebrate screened sample identified minimally to class. Specimens identified are *Canis* sp., cf. *C. familiaris*, and *C. familiaris* (a single specimen identified as cf. *C. latrans* from Newbridge is not included; no other specimens in any of these samples were identified as *C. latrans*, cf. *C. lupus*, or *C. lupus*). H = Havana, WH = White Hall, W = Weaver, C = center, V = village or hamlet, NISP = number of identified species, MNI = minimum number of individuals.

Table 24.5. Percentages of White-tailed Deer at Selected Havana, White Hall, and Weaver Sites

Site and Component	%NISP	%MNI
Napoleon Hollow (H/C)	4.1	20.0
Ogden-Fettie (H/C)	5.8	12.0
Baehr-Gust (H/C)	6.0	7.0
Smiling Dan (H/V)	6.8	7.8
Baehr-Gust (WH)	1.9	1.5
Newbridge (WH)	4.8	1.0
Rench (W)	15.5	2.4

Sources: Holt 2000:Tables 5.8 and 5.9; Martin and Masulis 1993:Table 10.2; Styles 1981:Table 16; Styles and Purdue 1986:Table 19.2; Styles, Purdue, and Colburn 1985:Appendix 16.1. *Note*: White-tailed deer elements as a percentage of the vertebrate screened sample identified minimally to class. Samples from Baehr-Gust and Ogden-Fettie include fragments of vertebrae, ribs, and costal cartilage identified as large mammal, to make data from these sites comparable with data from other sites. H = Havana, WH = White Hall, W = Weaver, C = center, V = village or hamlet, NISP = number of identified species, MNI = minimum number of individuals.

Trends related to the consumption of white-tailed deer are slightly different (table 24.5; fig. 24.6). Deer are no more common at Havana mound centers than at the Havana hamlet, which is not consistent with either model. However, it is important to remember that deer meat was a staple during this period, and its consumption would not have been limited to feasts. As with elk and dog, the relative number of deer decreased through time. Decreases in numbers of deer, elk, and dogs are in part related to an increase in numbers of fish through time (table 24.6; fig. 24.7). Fish were much more important in the White Hall/Weaver diet than in the Havana diet (for example, Styles 2000). Intensification of this resource was probably an expedient way to feed a growing population.

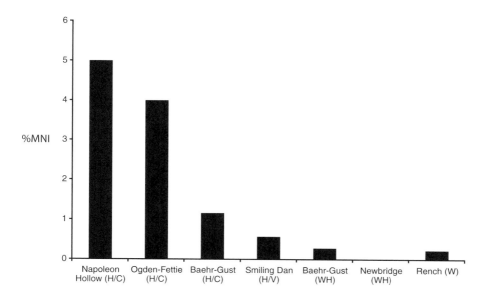

Figure 24.4. Percentages of elk: H = Havana, WH = White Hall, W = Weaver; C = center, V = village or hamlet; MNI = minimum number of individuals.

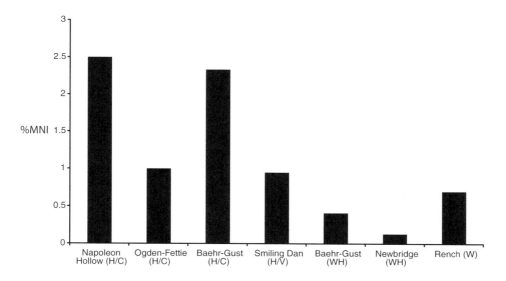

Figure 24.5. Percentages of canids: H = Havana, WH = White Hall, W = Weaver; C = center, V = village or hamlet; MNI = minimum number of individuals.

Table 24.6. Percentages of Fish at Selected Havana, White Hall, and Weaver Sites

Site and Component	%NISP	%MNI
Napoleon Hollow (H/C)	0.7	27.5
Ogden-Fettie (H/C)	10.2	53.0
Baehr-Gust (H/C)	20.7	53.5
Smiling Dan (H/V)	19.3	51.6
Baehr-Gust (WH)	79.4	80.7
Newbridge (WH)	63.4	81.5
Rench (W)	35.4	70.1

Sources: Holt 2000:Tables 5.8 and 5.9; Martin and Masulis 1993:Table 10.2; Styles 1981:Table 16; Styles and Purdue 1986:Table 19.2; Styles, Purdue, and Colburn 1985:Appendix 16.1.
Note: Fish elements as a percentage of the vertebrate screened sample identified minimally to class. H = Havana, WH = White Hall, W = Weaver, C = center, V = village or hamlet, NISP = number of identified species, MNI = minimum number of individuals.

Element Representation of White-tailed Deer

The second line of zooarchaeological evidence to be considered is element representation of white-tailed deer. Given that deer were so important to the prehistoric diet, analysis of deer element representation is probably a more useful way to look for evidence of feasting on deer meat than is analysis of deer bone abundance. In other words, while consumption of deer meat was ubiquitous, consumption of the best parts of the deer might more directly signal feasting or tribute. But what were the best parts of the deer? There is little if any mention in ethnohistoric records of which venison cuts were considered the best. The com-

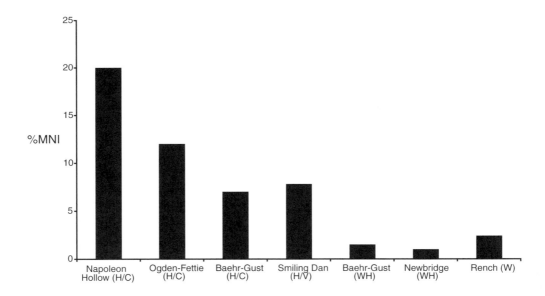

Figure 24.6. Percentages of white-tailed deer: H = Havana, WH = White Hall, W = Weaver; C = center, V = village or hamlet; MNI = minimum number of individuals.

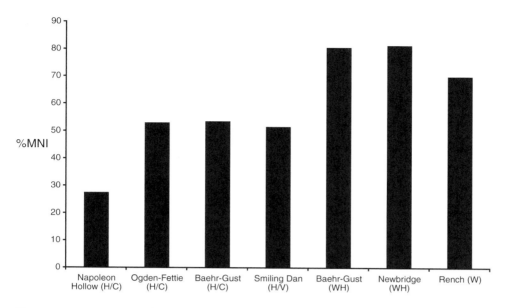

Figure 24.7. Percentages of fish: H = Havana, WH = White Hall, W = Weaver; C = center, V = village or hamlet; MNI = minimum number of individuals.

mon practice in Illinois Valley and American Bottom studies is to rank elements using the Food Utility Index, or FUI (for example, Kelly 1997; Styles and Purdue 1991). The FUI ranks elements according to meat, marrow, and grease content, based upon data gathered by Binford from a single caribou (Metcalfe and Jones 1988). Deer elements will be ranked here using meat and marrow data collected more recently from several white-tailed deer (Holt 2000, 2004; Madrigal and Holt 2002).

The first model suggests that settlements were self-sufficient; hence, all elements of the deer should be present at most sites, with no correlation between element abundance and meat yields. However, if feasting occurred at Havana mound centers, we might expect to find a positive correlation between element abundance and meat yields at centers, assuming that meat was brought to the mound centers bone-in.

The second model suggests that non-elite inhabitants of Havana hamlets supplied venison to elite inhabitants of Havana mound centers. If meat is again assumed to have been transported bone-in, this model suggests that Havana outlying sites should exhibit a negative correlation between element abundance and meat yields. Havana mound centers should exhibit the opposite pattern: positive correlations between element abundance and meat yields. If this system of tribute collapsed at the end of the Middle Woodland period, as the second model suggests, then White Hall and Weaver sites would have been self-sufficient and should exhibit no correlation between element abundance and meat yields.

Table 24.7. Correlation Coefficients (r_p) and Levels of Significance (p) between MAU and Meat Yields, Marrow Yields, and Bone Density

Site and Component Subsample	MAU:Meat				MAU:Marrow				MAU:Bone Density	
	Gross Yield		Return Rate		Gross Yield		Return Rate			
	r_p	p	r_p	p	r_p	p	r_p	p	r_p	p
Napoleon Hollow (H/C)										
Whole sample	-.12	.72	-.16	.63	.93	.00	.90	.00	na	
Hillside	-.06	.87	-.17	.62	.95	.00	.93	.00	na	
Floodplain	-.21	.54	.05	.89	.61	.08	.60	.09	na	
Feature 9	-.48	.14	-.46	.15	.79	.01	.64	.06	na	
Ogden-Fettie (H/C)	-.51	.10	-.18	.59	.08	.84	.13	.75	.45	.01
Peisker (H/C)										
Havana	.20	.55	-.10	.77	.64	.06	.89	.00	.12	.53
Havana-Pike	-.12	.73	-.06	.87	.10	.80	.31	.42	.18	.32
Baehr-Gust (H/C)										
All features	-.37	.26	.08	.81	.79	.01	.71	.03	-.09	.64
Feature 1 (1987)	-.51	.11	.04	.91	.59	.09	.57	.11	-.02	.93
Smiling Dan (H/V)										
Whole sample	-.10	.78	-.09	.78	.37	.32	.35	.36	na	
Stream channel	-.41	.21	-.23	.50	.45	.22	.47	.20	na	
Features	.16	.64	.03	.94	.30	.43	.26	.51	na	
Baehr-Gust (WH)	-.32	.34	-.06	.86	.72	.03	.64	.06	.21	.25
Newbridge (WH)										
Whole sample	-.09	.80	-.03	.93	.10	.80	.25	.52	na	
Midden	.21	.53	.08	.82	.21	.59	.51	.16	na	
Features	-.27	.43	-.09	.78	.05	.89	.14	.72	na	
Rench (W)	.03	.92	-.08	.81	.96	.00	.98	.00	.03	.89

Sources: Corwin 1968:Table 4; Holt 2000:Table 5.25; Martin and Masulis 1993:Table 10.4; Bonnie Styles, personal communication 1999.
Note: Sample sizes (number of elements or bone part kinds) = 9 for meat, 11 for marrow, and 31 for bone density. Elements and bone part kinds with zero counts are factored into the correlations. Boldface type indicates statistically significant. H = Havana, WH = White Hall, W = Weaver, C = center, V = village or hamlet, MAU = minimal animal unit, na = not available

This analysis suggests that neither model is well supported by the zooarchaeological record. However, before patterns of element abundance can be evaluated, it must first be determined whether preservation conditions have affected them. The presence or absence of density-mediated attrition was determined for these samples by testing for correlation between element abundance (measured by Minimal Animal Unit, or MAU) and bone density (Lyman 1994). Most of the samples show a weak positive correlation between MAU and bone density, but only the correlation for Ogden-Fettie is statistically significant (table 24.7). This suggests that density-mediated attrition has adversely affected the samples from Ogden-Fettie.

Correlations between element abundance (measured by MAU) and meat yield for most Havana samples approach zero, providing no evidence of the transport of meat to or from sites (table 24.7). One exception is a significant negative correlation at the Havana Ogden-Fettie mound center, not the positive correlation predicted by both models. However, this negative correlation is possibly the result of poor preservation conditions at Ogden-Fettie (see above).

Correlations between element abundance and meat yields for White Hall/ Weaver sites also approach zero. This suggests self-sufficiency at these sites, as predicted by both models. In sum, there is no strong evidence for the transport of meatier bone to or from any of the sites analyzed here.

In contrast, every site, regardless of function and regardless of age, exhibits a positive correlation between element abundance (MAU) and marrow yields; in most cases, the correlation is statistically significant (table 24.7). The preference for marrow-rich bone at these sites probably had nothing to do with feasting or tribute. Marrow was a valuable resource in a diet otherwise low in fat. While marrow-poor bones would typically have been discarded at the time of butchery, marrow-rich bones would have been retained because further processing was required to exploit them to their fullest (Holt 2004; Madrigal and Holt 2002).

This analysis reaches a different conclusion regarding deer element representation at Napoleon Hollow than Styles and Purdue (1986, 1991) reached in their analysis. When elements are ranked according to the FUI, Napoleon Hollow exhibits a high percentage of high-utility bones, from which Styles and Purdue inferred that meaty bone was brought to Napoleon Hollow for feasting. This analysis shows that the bones from Napoleon Hollow were not especially meaty but were instead marrow-rich, as bones were at most sites analyzed. The difference in results between their analysis and this one is probably attributable to two factors: first, the FUI is based on data from caribou, whereas data used in this study are derived from the target species, white-tailed deer; and second, the FUI is based on combined meat, marrow, and grease data, whereas this analysis considers meat and marrow separately.

Seasonality Data

The third line of evidence to be considered is seasonality data. The first model portrays Havana mound centers as vacant ceremonial centers, so we might expect limited seasonal use of these sites compared to hamlets. The second model suggests that mound centers were inhabited, so whatever pattern of seasonal use is seen at outlying sites should also be seen at mound centers.

This analysis finds little to no evidence from any of these sites that they were occupied during the winter (Holt 2000). Remains from a six-month-old deer (age determined by tooth eruption) recovered from Smiling Dan indicate a winter kill and possibly winter occupation at that site (Styles, Purdue, and Colburn 1985:433). It is possible that Middle and early Late Woodland people left these floodplain sites and moved to upland hunting camps during the winter. However, the paucity of evidence for winter occupation at these sites is attributable at least in part to the nature of the faunal data: there are few types of faunal data available in this region that are positive indicators of winter occupation. Most of the species on which we base seasonality assessments are either migrating birds or cold-blooded species, which are either absent or less accessible during winter. Positive evidence for winter occupation in this region is primarily limited to the presence of individual deer, such as that from Smiling Dan, which are shown by

Table 24.8. Frequency of Animal Remains at Selected Havana and White Hall Sites

Site and Component Subsample	Mean Vertebrate Frequency	Range of Vertebrate Frequency
Napoleon Hollow (H/C)		
Hillside ($n = 1$)	5.3	
Floodplain ($n = 1$)	9.3	
Vertical-sided pit ($n = 1$)	14.5	
Ogden-Fettie (H/C)		
Plow zone ($n = 1$)	1.2	
Midden ($n = 1$)	6.2	
In-slanting-sided pits ($n = 3$)	6.1	1.6–12.0
Basined pit ($n = 1$)	5.7	
Baehr-Gust (H/C)		
In-slanting-sided pits ($n = 4$)	24.3	8.6–58.8
Smiling Dan (H/V)[a]		
Stream channel ($n = 1$)	~ 4	na
Decreasing-sided pits ($n = 16$)	~ 5	na
Parallel-sided pits ($n = 7$)	~ 11	na
Conical pits ($n = 10$)	~ 14	na
Baehr-Gust (WH)		
In-slanting-sided pits ($n = 7$)	44.0	5.7–105.1
Vertical-sided pit ($n = 1$)	18.0	
Basined pit ($n = 1$)	93.7	

Sources: Holt 2000:Table 5.31; Styles and Purdue 1986:Tables 19.1 and 19.2; Styles, Purdue, and Colburn 1985:Figure 16.1.

Note: Animal remains as vertebrate NISP (number of identified species present) per 10 liters of matrix. H = Havana, WH = White Hall, W = Weaver, C = center, V = village or hamlet, na = not available.

a. Means and ranges for Smiling Dan were reported graphically rather than as numbers, so the means presented here are approximated.

dental aging or epiphyseal fusion to have died in the winter. Unfortunately, few complete mandibles were recovered from these sites, and few bones have ages of fusion narrow enough to be of use as precise seasonal indicators. Given the nature of the evidence, then, it is not surprising that there is slim evidence for winter occupation at all of these sites.

There is, however, good evidence from all of these sites that they were occupied during the spring, summer, and fall, based on abundant remains of migrating birds and cold-blooded species (Holt 2000). Thus we can say that all of these sites were occupied for most, if not all, of the year. There is no evidence that centers were vacant throughout most of the year, as predicted by the first model. Instead, analysis of seasonality data offers better support for the second model, since similar patterns of use are indicated for Havana centers and outlying sites.

Number of Bones per Volume of Sediment

The fourth line of evidence to be considered is number of bones per volume of sediment excavated, or bone frequency. The first model suggests that bone frequencies at Havana mound centers should be lower than at outlying sites since centers were vacant throughout most of the year (Styles and Purdue 1991). The second model suggests that bone frequencies should be higher at Havana mound centers than at other sites, since the elite inhabitants of the Havana centers would have had greater access to animal products (Bogan 1983).

In the analysis of species representation above, it was noted that sample sizes were smaller at the Havana centers than at other sites (table 24.1). This observation might seem to support the expectations of the first model, if we infer from those smaller sample sizes that fewer bones actually made their way into the Havana centers (that is, centers were vacant throughout most of the year). However, this inference is not supported by this analysis of bone frequencies (table 24.8).

A comparison of Smiling Dan, Napoleon Hollow, Ogden-Fettie, and Baehr-Gust shows great variation in bone frequencies at these sites (bone frequencies were not available for the other samples). Baehr-Gust has by far the highest frequencies, Smiling Dan and Napoleon Hollow have comparable frequencies, and Ogden-Fettie has very low frequencies. There is no patterning evident here regarding Havana centers versus hamlets or regarding Havana versus White Hall sites, so these patterns do not clearly relate to predictions of either model. Instead, these patterns probably relate more to taphonomic conditions at these sites than to rates of bone deposition. Taphonomic conditions would include preservation conditions and rates of sedimentation.

Preservation conditions certainly affect these frequencies, although to what extent it is impossible to say with precision. The positive correlation between bone density and element abundance at Ogden-Fettie indicates that density-mediated attrition adversely affected that sample (see above and table 24.7). We might therefore conclude that poor preservation is to some extent responsible for the low bone frequencies at Ogden-Fettie. Bone preservation at Baehr-Gust was good, and there is no evidence of significant density-mediated attrition in the Baehr-Gust samples (table 24.7). Good preservation conditions at Baehr-Gust were therefore probably responsible at least in part for the high bone frequencies at Baehr-Gust. Without bone density data for Napoleon Hollow and Smiling Dan, it is difficult to say how bone frequencies at those sites might have been affected by preservation conditions (but see Styles and Purdue 1986). Data on sediment acidity from all of these sites could be used to examine preservation conditions more precisely.

Another important variable in bone frequency per volume of sediment is the rate of sedimentation (for example, Holliday 1992; Kidwell 1986). Obviously, the rate of sedimentation can be highly variable among sites (for example, a floodplain versus an upland site) and even within sites (for example, an alluvial fan versus a natural levee, or feature versus nonfeature sediments). A geomorphologist might be able to estimate with some accuracy the rate of sedimentation for natural deposits, but estimating the rate of sedimentation for cultural deposits is more difficult. In any case, it would be simplistic to compare bone frequencies per volume of sediment without also considering rates of sedimentation, which is beyond the scope of the present analysis.

Bone frequency is high at Baehr-Gust regardless of time period and regardless of location. This may indicate that inhabitants of Baehr-Gust had greater access to animal products, as suggested by the second model. However, the second model would lead us to expect that Havana bone frequency at Baehr-Gust should be greater than White Hall bone frequency at Baehr-Gust. Instead, White Hall bone frequencies are generally much greater than Havana bone frequencies. The Havana features and White Hall features are found in proximity to one another, so preservation conditions are comparable. The Havana occupation might have been less intense than the White Hall occupation at Baehr-Gust (consistent with the expectations of the first model). The differences in bone frequency between Havana and White Hall samples might also be a result of changing patterns of settlement organization and garbage disposal. The shallow pits and sheet middens typical of Havana sites created more opportunities for the decay of food refuse than did the deep pits typical of White Hall sites (William Green, personal communication, 1999).

In sum, bone frequencies at these sites do not support either of the proposed models. Smiling Dan and Napoleon Hollow have comparable bone frequencies (Styles and Purdue 1991), despite different hypothesized functions. Compared to those sites, Baehr-Gust has very high bone frequencies and Ogden-Fettie has low bone frequencies. We might hypothesize that this is due to some extent to better preservation conditions at Baehr-Gust and poorer preservation conditions at Ogden-Fettie. Bone density data from Smiling Dan and Napoleon Hollow and sediment acidity data from all sites could be used to test this hypothesis further. In addition, data on rates of sedimentation for the specific proveniences excavated are also needed if meaningful comparisons of bone frequency per volume of sediment are to be made. In short, a more sophisticated understanding of taphonomic conditions is needed to permit meaningful comparisons of bone frequencies from one site to the next, and even from one feature or midden deposit to the next.

Percentage of Bone and Shell Artifacts

The fifth and final line of zooarchaeological evidence to be considered is percentages of bone and shell artifacts, including both finished tools and manufacture refuse. Artifact categories used here include modified turtle shell, pointed bone, modified antler, other modified bone, and modified mussel shell. The first model suggests that Havana centers were vacant ceremonial centers and not inhabited for any length of time. This implies that Havana mound centers should have relatively fewer tools and less evidence for artifact manufacture. The second model portrays Havana mound centers as protourban centers of craft manufacture and trade. If bone and shell artifacts were among the products manufactured and traded at centers, we should expect to find higher percentages of such artifacts or more abundant evidence of their manufacture at Havana mound centers than at hamlets.

Results of this analysis show generally low percentages of bone and shell artifacts at all sites and do not support either model (table 24.9). Havana centers do not stand out with either low percentages of bone and shell artifacts (as

Table 24.9. Percentages of Bone, Antler, and Shell Artifacts at Selected Havana, White Hall, and Weaver Sites

Site and Component	Turtle Shell	Pointed Bone[a]	Cervid Antler	Other Bone	Mussel Shell
Napoleon Hollow (H/C)	0.3	>0.1	none	none	none
Ogden-Fettie (H/C)	1.1	0.3	0.4	none	none
Baehr-Gust (H/C)	0.5	0.3	none	1.1	1.3
Smiling Dan (H/V)	0.9	0.1	>0.1	?[b]	none
Baehr-Gust (WH)	0.3	0.1	>0.1	>0.1	none
Newbridge (WH)	1.0	0.2	>0.1	1.5[c]	3.2
Rench (W)	0.2	1.0	0.2	0.3	9.4[d]

Sources: Holt 2000:Table 5.32; Martin and Masulis 1993:Table 11.1; Styles 1981:Table 26; Styles and Purdue 1986:Table 19.9; Styles, Purdue, and Colburn 1985:415–422; Table 16.3.
Note: Percentages for bone and antler are calculated by dividing the number of modified specimens by vertebrate sample size. Percentages for mussel shell are calculated by dividing the number of modified specimens by mussel sample size. (See table 24.1 for vertebrate and mussel sample sizes.) H = Havana, WH = White Hall, W = Weaver, C = center, V = village or hamlet.
a. Includes so-called awls, shuttles, pins, and needles.
b. Counts of modified bone for Smiling Dan include bones cut during butchery (Styles, Purdue, and Colburn 1985:Table 16.3) and so are not presented here.
c. This percentage is based on 93 "complete bone artifacts" and 1 bone "gaming piece." The true percentage of modified bone at Newbridge is potentially much higher, since the figure here does not include "numerous fragments of modified bone," which accounted for 4.8% of Newbridge midden bone and 2.2% of Newbridge feature bone (Styles 1981:201–202). (Because actual counts were not given, the percentage of vertebrate NISP cannot be calculated for this table.)
d. Most shell artifacts (16 out of 17) from Rench were shell "hoes."

predicted by the first model) or high percentages of bone and shell artifacts (as predicted by the second model). Two White Hall/Weaver sites, Newbridge and Rench, stand out with high percentages of shell artifacts, and Rench also has high percentages of pointed bone artifacts. Although these patterns give insight into activities that took place at these sites during the early Late Woodland period, they are not relevant to our understanding of the Havana socioeconomy. In sum, neither model of the Havana socioeconomy is supported by analysis of bone and shell artifacts at these sites.

Summary and Conclusions

This analysis shows that differences between faunal samples from Havana mound centers and hamlets, and between Havana samples and White Hall/ Weaver samples, are for the most part subtle. This analysis does not adequately support either of the two proposed models of the Havana socioeconomy.

Analysis of species representation finds little difference between Havana mound centers and hamlets. More feasting may have taken place at Havana centers than at Havana hamlets, based on slightly larger percentages of elk and dogs at mound centers, but there is no evidence at Havana centers of an elite social group that would have been provided with animal products from a large area. These findings are more consistent with the expectations of the first model than with those of the second model. Analysis of species representation also suggests that rituals involving animals and feasting were more important at Havana sites than at White Hall/Weaver sites. A decline in ritual and feasting at this time is consistent with expectations of both models.

Analysis of white-tailed deer element representation provides no evidence of feasting or elite tribute at Havana mound centers. Element representation is essentially similar at Havana mound centers and hamlets, and at White Hall/ Weaver sites, suggesting that all of these sites were self-sufficient in terms of venison production. This conclusion is also more consistent with the expectations of the first model than with those of the second model.

Analysis of seasonality suggests that all of these sites were occupied for most if not all of the year. The same patterns of seasonal use seem to characterize all of the sites considered, regardless of hypothesized function. In short, seasonality data suggest that centers were not "vacant ceremonial centers." This conclusion is more consistent with the predictions of the second model than with those of the first model.

Analysis of bone frequency suggests that the number of bones recovered per volume of sediment does not vary with site function as expected. Instead, bone frequency varies in part with taphonomic conditions. This conclusion has no bearing on either of the models tested here.

Finally, analysis of bone and shell artifacts suggests that such items are equally abundant at Havana mound centers and hamlets. This finding is contrary to the predictions of both models, since the first model predicts that fewer artifacts will be found at Havana centers and the second predicts that more artifacts will be found at Havana centers.

In sum, the results of this analysis suggest a new model for the role of animal products in the Havana socioeconomy. Both Havana mound centers and hamlets were occupied throughout most of the year. The occupants of these sites were self-sufficient in acquiring animals for food and other purposes, and they were self-sufficient in bone and shell artifact production. From a faunal perspective, the only apparent difference between Havana mound centers and hamlets is that more feasting may have taken place at mound centers, as indicated by the presence of slightly greater percentages of elk and dog remains. Faunal data alone provide no evidence for Havana social stratification.

Most patterns of animal exploitation remained unchanged at the end of the Middle Woodland period: early Late Woodland sites were occupied throughout most of the year, and their inhabitants were self-sufficient in acquiring animals and in producing bone and shell artifacts. The most obvious change in animal exploitation at this time was an increase in fish consumption, which was probably a means of increasing food production. More subtle changes in animal exploitation at this time, which were probably more directly related to the demise of the Hopewell Interaction Sphere in the Illinois Valley, were changes in feasts and rituals involving animal products. These feasts and rituals were less frequent at White Hall and Weaver sites, or perhaps they were simply different.

That is, feasts and rituals surely took place on early Late Woodland sites, but they were no longer recognizable as Hopewell.

Acknowledgments

This chapter summarizes research originally reported in my dissertation (Holt 2000), which was supported in part by grants from the Wenner-Gren Foundation (Gr. 5881) and the National Science Foundation (SBR-9704018). More details, including a full account of the faunal remains recovered from Baehr-Gust and Ogden-Fettie, can be found in Holt 2000. I would like to take this opportunity to once again thank my committee members: Pam Crabtree, Anne-Marie Cantwell, Bill Green, Bonnie Styles, and Rita Wright. Thanks especially to Bonnie for assembling and making available unpublished data on deer-element representation at Napoleon Hollow, Smiling Dan, and Newbridge. And finally thanks also to the late Howard Winters, for inspiring this project in the first place.

25

The Enigmatic Copper Cutout from Bedford Mound 8

Robert L. Hall

Reading the *Central States Archaeological Journal* many years ago I found an article by Gregory Perino on pre-Columbian artifacts of native copper. One of the illustrations was of a Hopewellian copper cutout that he had found in Mound 8 of the Bedford Group in Pike County, Illinois (Perino 1968b:Figure 74d). Five years later in the same journal I read an article by William Mangold (1973) that reinterpreted the symbolism of the creature that appears on so-called birdstones. Birdstones belong in that transition era between the Late Ar-chaic and Early Woodland periods of eastern United States prehistory. I found each of these articles to have importance in themselves and cited them separately in my own writings (Hall 1985, 1997). Only recently have I recognized the relevance of Perino's article to Mangold's, and that is the subject of the present chapter.

Perino's copper object (fig. 25.1a) is 18 centimeters long and was found near the right shoulder of an elderly adult (sex not determined) interred in Mound 8. It was cut in an intricate outline and was given more details by indentations punched into the surface of the copper. In his manuscript report on the Bedford excavation Perino (n.d.) compares part of the design to "two hawk-like heads with eyes and with beaks slightly open."

The bird interpretation, however, leaves much of the detail of the copper cutout unexplained. This interpretation is also inconsistent with the location of three large holes that were apparently meant to attach the object to something. If the object was meant to be suspended, then the cutout, as illustrated, was upside down. If one inverts the illustrated cutout (fig. 25.1b) a different impres-sion is obtained; rather than a pair of birds, it looks something like a buffalo head. The horns are there, and the eyes, mouth, and nostrils seem to be there, but there is something more that does not belong. If the cutout was meant to represent a buffalo, then it was a buffalo with four prominent caninelike teeth in its upper jaw—not two, like carnivores, but four! In any case, buffaloes are not carnivores. If this was a buffalo it would have to have been some mythical, supernatural buffalo, certainly not an ordinary one.

Was the cutout meant to represent a pair of birds? Was it meant to represent a supernatural buffalo? Was it meant to represent an animal that *does* have the

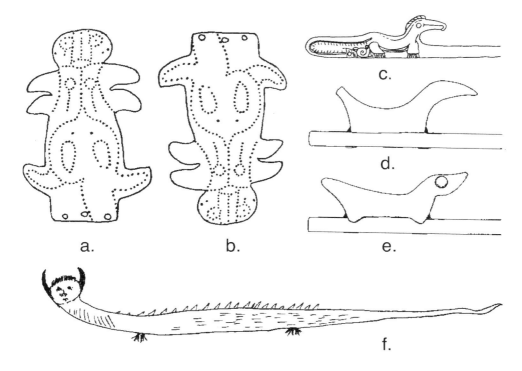

Figure 25.1. Prehistoric representations of bird- and crocodilian-related creatures: (a) Bedford Mound 8 copper cutout as originally oriented by Perino, resembling two birds back to back (after Perino 1968a:Fig. 74d); (b) Bedford cutout reoriented to resemble horned caiman (after Perino 1968a:Fig. 74d, inverted); (c) carved bone atlatl grip from Coclé, Panama, in the form of a bird-headed crocodilian (from Hall 1997:Fig. 14.5a, after Lothrop 1937:Fig. 66a); (d) birdstone shown as an atlatl grip (from Hall 1997:Fig. 14.5d, after Hinsdale 1925:Plate XX-5); (e) quadrupedal birdstone shown as an atlatl grip (from Hall 1997:Fig. 14.5e, after Hinsdale 1925, Plate XXI-3a); (f) alligator perceived by the eighteenth-century Santee Dakota of Minnesota as the horned buffalo-snake, as it appears in version 1 of Captain Jonathan Carver's manuscript journals (after Parker 1976:97).

equivalent of four upper caninelike teeth, like the caiman? Caimans are not found in North America, however. Could it represent, instead, all of these possibilities at the same time? If so, what would be the logic of such a combination?

Composite Birds

The most famous two-headed bird representation in Illinois is the now well-known shell falcon pendant from the Liverpool Lake site in Mason County, Illinois. Found by Karen Sank in a submerged circular feature also containing sherds of the Late Woodland Maples Mills type, this pendant represents a falcon with two heads facing away from each other. Sank and Sampson (1994) compare this shell to a range of two-headed bird images in shell, copper, and stone with associations ranging from Archaic to Mississippian in age. There is no question that these objects represent a class of ritual objects with a long history in the greater Mississippi Valley from Illinois to Louisiana. What is not clear is the significance of the icon.

Figure 25.2. Pawnee eagle war charm in the collections of the Field Museum, Chicago (cat. no. A47894, acc. no. 3848), drawn as displayed.

To the above group may be added an article formerly on display in a gallery of the Field Museum in Chicago. This is a Pawnee bundle perhaps a century and a half old at most (fig. 25.2). The item is a pair of eagle skins bound together with their heads facing outward and their bodies joined, wrapped in the spotted hide of an unborn fawn. Little is known of the origin of this bundle other than that it was called a war charm; that it was collected in Oklahoma; and that it was once exhibited, retired from display, and subsequently found in storage at the museum in 1950. At that time it was unnumbered but accompanied by its original display card.

The contents of the eagle skins are revealing. One eagle contained a hide bag filled with tobacco; the other eagle contained an ear of corn. Among the Pawnee, maize had a female association. The Pawnee honor so-called Mother Corn ears representing the earth, for instance. Tobacco, by contrast, has a widespread male association (Hall 1977). It would have been logical for the Pawnee to construct a charm using the skins of a pair of eagles with one eagle representing earth or female associations and the other, sky or male associations, because in the Pawnee Hako or Calumet ceremony the calumets were also used in pairs, one with female associations and the other with male associations, and each festooned with a fan of eagle feathers (Hall 1997:Figure 7.1). This combination amounted to a cosmogram representing earth and sky. The covering of fawn skin contributes to this impression because a fawn's spots symbolize the stars of the night sky, as do those of spotted felines like the bobcat.

One of the oldest recognizable cosmograms in eastern North America could be the birdstone (fig. 25.1d). The name "birdstone" describes this object's obvious appearance fairly well, except that when feet are represented on birdstones they are four in number, as was long ago pointed out by William Mangold (1973). Elsewhere I have given reasons for believing that the birdstone was an atlatl grip of a type whose form was that of a composite bird and crocodilian, a combination also found archaeologically on a functional atlatl in Panama and on a flute representing an atlatl in Vera Cruz, Mexico (Hall 1983:49, Figures 4b, 4i, 5c; Hall 1997:115–116, Figure 14.5). Such an object had the head of a crocodilian and the body of a bird or vice versa, the latter in the case of the birdstone, so called (fig. 25.1d–e). Crocodilians figure importantly in Mesoamerica in stories of the creation of the earth and sky and in South America with the creation of food plants (for example, Boas and Boas 1973:195–200; Lathrap 1973:91–105).

Caimans

What the Bedford Mound 8 cutout appears like to me, when seen suspended from its holes as a pendant, is a representation in copper of the skull of a caiman done by someone who knew the caiman only from its skeletal form (fig. 25.3). The nasal opening of the caiman skull is clearly shown on the copper cutout as a lenticular outline bracketed by four small circles, two of which very clearly have what look like little tails, and these tails correspond to the sutures that terminate at the foramina found around the nasal opening of the caiman. In some caimans, like the Central American *Caiman sclerops,* the four lower caninelike teeth project upward into these foramina and pass completely through the upper jaw. Crocodiles proper and alligators do not have this particular pattern of four holes through the upper jaw. Below the nasal opening on the cutout are three lines that correspond to a separation of the bones of the upper jaw forward of the nasal opening. This is a condition that can be found on old dried caiman and crocodile skulls warped with age in storage because of the weakness of the bones at this point. Crocodilians have four prominent, projecting teeth in the lower jaw and four in the upper jaw. The four most prominent upper teeth are represented on the copper cutout as protruding sideways. This could be just an artistic convention, but it corresponds in fact to an actual condition observed on the skulls of old crocodilians; the upper and lower teeth become directed outward or sideways (Neill 1971:Figure 129).

Examples of the genus *Caiman* are found neither in the Caribbean islands nor in Mexico north of the Isthmus of Tehuantepec, so any awareness of that taxon on the part of any Indian group in the United States would necessarily indicate some form of contact, direct or indirect, across the Gulf of Mexico from Central

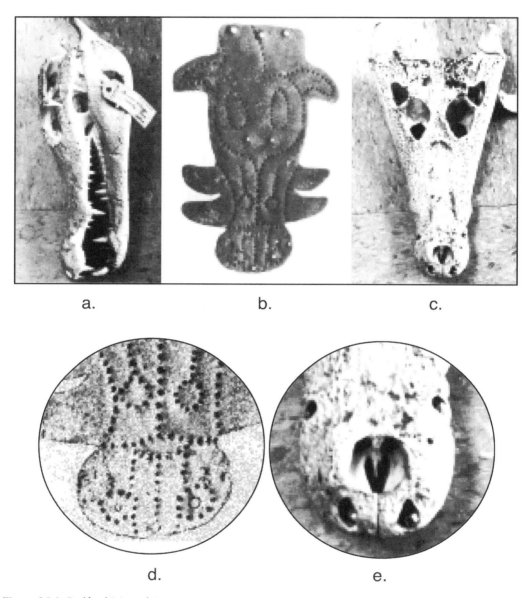

Figure 25.3. Bedford Mound 8 copper cutout compared with skeletal heads of *Caiman sclerops* from Colombia: (a) lateral view of *C. sclerops*, collections of the Field Museum, Chicago; (b) Bedford cutout from Perino 1968a:Fig. 74d; (c) dorsal view of *C. sclerops*, collections of the Field Museum, Chicago; (d) detail from view b, digitally enhanced; (e) detail from view c.

America. As for alligators, there is no doubt that at least some northern Mississippi Valley Indians were aware of this reptile. Captain Jonathan Carver spent parts of the years 1766 and 1767 among the Santee or Eastern Dakota in Minnesota. While there, Carver copied a Santee representation of a "serpent of a monsterous shape and size which they call *Tautongo Omlishco* which signifies

in English the buffeloe snake, it having horns (and four feet and claws like a
bear) they say 'tis three fathoms [5.5 meters] long near as big round as a buffaloe
with a black head and tail; the middle from neck to tail is red having somthing
like fins on the back" (Parker 1976:98–99; spelling as in the original). The body
was unmistakably crocodilian, but the head was more human in aspect, or perhaps bovine but presenting a foreshortened frontal view, and with horns (fig.
25.1f). The clue to the buffalo snake's identity as an alligator and not as just
another northern water monster is found in Carver's caption: "The Buffeloe
Snake Seen *toward the South Sea*, by the Naudowessee [Sioux] Esteemed by
them a God" (Parker 1976:97, emphasis added).

Spirit Buffaloes and Water Monsters

Bedford Mound 8 was a Hopewell mound built near the beginning of the first
millennium of our era. Not until shortly before the arrival of French explorers
did the modern buffalo (*Bison bison*) begin to appear commonly in the Holocene archaeological record in Illinois. There is, however, a Late Prehistoric site
in the Chicago area from which an artifact with two engraved buffaloes was
recovered. This is the Anker site, a component of the Huber phase of the Oneota
culture. Anker is believed to date to the late precontact period (Bluhm and Liss
1961:Figure 65). The artifact from Anker is a stone smoking pipe. The buffalo
is no ordinary buffalo, however. This is clear from the relative locations of the
ears and the horns. On a natural buffalo the horns are located between the ears.
On the Anker site buffalo engravings the horns are located outside of the ears.
I do not consider this to be a mistake. I believe that the Anker site buffaloes are
some form of spirit buffalo. It was an iconographic convention for Indians to
add horns to a creature to indicate that it was supernatural, so when a creature
normally had horns it may have been the rule to switch the position of the horns
and ears to mark its supernatural character. Images of buffaloes with ears and
horns reversed occur also on two engraved catlinite tablets from the Bastian site
near Cherokee, Iowa (Bray 1963:Figures 12, 21).

    Water monsters in the northern Mississippi Valley commonly take the form
either of horned serpents or of horned pantherlike creatures. The element common to both is the very long tail, which may be used to whip rivers and lakes into
foaming waves. A third variety of water spirit is a little harder to characterize.
Among the Eastern Dakota there were several kinds of *unktehi* or water spirits.
Some were horned snakes. The one that figured in the origin myth of the
Wahpeton Dakota Medicine Society was singled out as different: "Jingling
Cloud . . . specified that this was a four-footed, long-tailed monster with shiny
horns, somewhat resembling a buffalo. Neither this monster nor its mate were
buffalo color, but their heads were white like snow. I suspect this of being related
to the 'underneath panther spirit' of the Menominee and Ojibwa, and the 'water
spirit' of the Winnebago" (Skinner 1920:339n).

    The Cheyenne believed in the existence of a bull-like water monster called an
ahke, and the Blackfeet, in a similar "water bull" (Grinnell 1972:2:98–99). In

view of the buffalolike form of certain water spirits I thought again about the Bedford mound copper cutout. It looked superficially like a buffalo, but in detail it resembled the skull of a caiman, except for the horns, which no natural crocodilian has but a supernatural crocodilian can have. The Santee Dakota did, of course, place horns on their representation of the alligator as the buffalo-snake (fig. 25.1f).

The Bedford site copper cutout has several interpretations that do not really conflict one with another. Viewed one way it can be seen as a pair of birds positioned back-to-back. Positioned another way it is the skeletal head of a caiman, later possibly perceived as, even if not originally meant to represent, a water monster of buffalo form. This optical illusion recalls the imagery of the Milky Way, believed to have been seen by the Classic period Mayas vertically in winter as the World Tree and horizontally during the summer as a cosmic monster of crocodilian form (Freidel, Schele, and Parker 1993:87–89). It is not difficult to imagine that Perino's cutout was a rendering in copper of a holy relic standing for some mystery of Hopewellian cosmology. The primary element, however, is the caiman, a creature no Hopewellian had possibly ever actually seen in nature.

Gulf-Caribbean Interactions

Thomas Myers (1978) has seen as an interaction sphere, by that name, the kind of intergroup relationships that connected Central America and adjacent South America in Formative period times (compare Myers 1981). For a period beginning at least as early as the Late Archaic–Early Woodland transition in North America I recognize a circulation of ideas within the Gulf and Caribbean borderlands of southeastern North America, Mesoamerica, and Central America. I see the cosmic monster ("birdstone") form and single-hole-type atlatl grips as two products of this circulation, as I do those flutes of the *vorsat* type that were prototypes of latter-day courting flutes in the eastern United States (Hall 1997:114–118, Figures 14.4, 14.5, 14.7). Another product would be the stone blocked-end tube pipe, which I see as a skeuomorphic transformation of the Mesoamerican cane smoking tube (Hall 1997:119–120, Figure 14.6). The cosmic monster form of atlatl grip is important as a witness to the early presence through the area of the idea of a dragon of combined crocodilian and bird form that was a personification of the sky, earth, and waters, however differently that creature came to be later perceived through the Early and Middle Woodland periods.

The defining feature of the Bedford Mound 8 caiman is the set of four holes surrounding the nasal opening. A similar pattern is found on the face of a composite creature engraved on a human femur found in Mound 25 of the Hopewell type site in Ohio. These are four dots bracketing the toothy human grin of an animal that Willoughby (1935) saw as the Algonquian culture hero Michabo, the Great Hare, outfitted with deer antlers and the nose of a roseate spoonbill

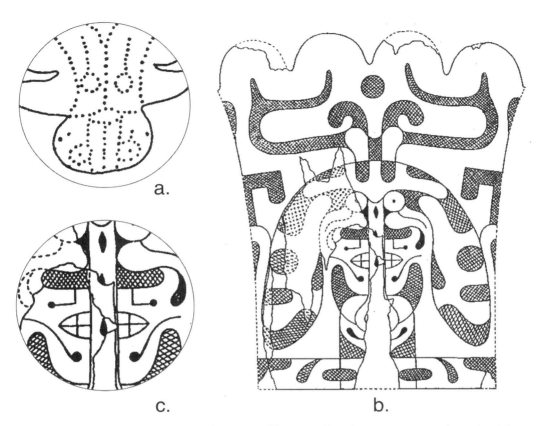

a.

c.   b.

Figure 25.4. Hopewellian imagery with pattern of four maxillary foramina portrayed: (a) detail from Bedford Mound 8 copper cutout (after Perino 1968a:Fig. 74d, inverted); (b) design on an engraved human femur from Mound 25 of Hopewell Mound Group, Ohio (from Moorehead 1922:Fig. 22); (c) detail from the preceding.

(fig. 25.4b). Greber and Ruhl (1989:199–200, 221) have since provided reasons for believing that the ears once perceived to be those of a rabbit are actually those of a deer. The Mound 25 face would seem to be that of an antlered human or anthropomorphized spirit-being whose mouth was bracketed with the four tooth holes of a caiman and whose nose was a flute in the form of the bill of a roseate spoonbill (fig. 25.4c). The roseate spoonbill did seasonally migrate north to the latitude of the Ohio Valley in Hopewellian and more recent times. The roseate spoonbill was known firsthand by Hopewellians (Parmalee and Perino 1971). By contrast, knowledge of the genus *Caiman* had to come from contacts outside of the area of the Hopewellian Interaction Sphere. The deer attributes of the Mound 25 figure need not diminish the caiman aspect of the human face. The Celestial Monster of Classic Maya cosmology, for example, had a crocodilian head, the ears of a deer, and hooved deerlike feet (Schele and Freidel 1990:408).

The Hopewellian Great Tradition

The concept of the Hopewellian Interaction Sphere has for years provided the dominant framework within which interregional Middle Woodland relationships have been discussed. The mechanism of this interaction sphere, as Caldwell (1964:138) conceived it, had its basis in connections of a "mortuary-ceremonial or religious kind." Peaceful interregional connections were facilitated by a widely shared ideology related to death, burial, mourning, and perceptions of the afterlife that constituted a major part of the Hopewellian Great Tradition (Hall 1997:156). In early contact times such a mechanism existed in Spirit Adoption in mourning and as employed in the ritual known as the Calumet of the Captain (Hall 1997:41, 81–82, 157, 163).

Caldwell was concerned with the organizing principle that permitted small, local and regional traditions to connect and interact peacefully under the umbrella of a great tradition. Calumet ceremonies of the Hako type that succeeded the Calumet of the Captain were adoption ceremonies derived in part from, but not explicitly related to, adoption in mourning. Adoption in the Pawnee Hako ceremony involved a symbolic reconception of the candidate mediated by the introduction of a breath from the supreme Pawnee spirit-being Tirawahat. Because the adoptee appears to have also represented the earth, the ceremony was simultaneously a ritual of earth renewal (Hall 1987a:35; Hall 1997:54, 57, 85, 163–165, Figure 19.3).

Tirawahat was said to have represented the arch of the sky and the expanse of the heavens, but in a Skidi Pawnee story of the origin of the calumet pipe stem, Tirawahat had the form of a giant water serpent with an eagle plume on its head (Hall 1997:84). This puts Tirawahat in the category of cosmic beings identified with both sky and earth, such as the beast with crocodilian body and bird head represented on atlatl grips of the "birdstone" type (see above). Tirawahat's breath was introduced into the candidate by means of a calumet in the form of an arrow stem representing a wind pipe. The stem was outfitted with a duck head instead of either an arrow point or a pipe bowl. In the Calumet of the Captain the spirit breath would have been introduced using a long, perforated pipe stem with a working pipe bowl.

Spirit Adoption in mourning is just one special example of adoption. Another would be adoption by a spirit patron as practiced in group puberty rites. I see the uniformity of pattern of "birdstone" atlatl grips as indicative of a shared spirit patron prevalent in societies at the time of the Late Archaic–Early Woodland transition. One model would be a boys' initiation rite as practiced in the Vaupés River area of Colombia. There boys were initiated as a class and symbolically adopted by a resurrected ancestral water serpent—an anaconda—in a rite utilizing a cigar to represent the penis of the group's anaconda ancestor. The smoking of the cigar by the group reaffirmed alliances between kinship groups (Hall 1997:120–121; Hugh-Jones 1979:139, 154, 249, 293; Reichel-Dolmatoff 1971:118). Initiation within a class can lead to an age-grade organization of males.

Among the Hidatsa of the northern Plains, one of the two age-graded societies that a pubescent youth might join was the Stone Hammer Society. This society had as its symbol a staff with a stone "hammer" attached (Bowers 1965:179–180). The staff of the Stone Hammer Society of the closely related Crow tribe had a perforated oval wooden "hammer" set partway down its length, not at the end like a club or hammer but well down the shaft like the bannerstone on an atlatl (Hall 1977:507–508, Figure 3b, after Lowie 1956:Figure 12). Were this "hammer" made of stone, any archaeologist seeing one would recognize its likeness to a bannerstone, as did Harlan I. Smith almost a century ago (Lowie 1913:186–187). When about thirty boys aged twelve or above were available to establish a new society, they would buy the rights to the society from its current members. "Purchase was by an organized group from an organized group, the relationship between the two groups being that of 'father-son'" (Bowers 1965:181).

The great variety of forms of the Hopewellian effigy platform pipe strikes me as the product of a transition from class puberty rites to the more individualized kind of rite based upon solitary vision quests and the seeking of personal spirit guardians of diverse character, as found in postcontact times. This transition would have been expedited if the original shared spirit patron was usurped as the patron of, say, a shamanic society or elite lineage. I have suggested just such an origin for God K as a patron of Mayan royal lineages (Hall 1997:122). The relationship of a guardian spirit and vision quest candidate was that of adopting father and adoptee, while the patron of an elite lineage can be perceived as an apical ancestor exclusive to that lineage and legitimizing its leadership. The abundance of crocodilian icons at the beginning of the Early Woodland period and their presence but relative scarcity in Hopewellian imagery may signal a retreat from egalitarian access to an ancestral supreme being and the emergence of elite lineages or privileged religious associations.

Conclusion

The cutout from Bedford Mound 8 is a rendering in copper of the dorsal view of the skull of a crocodilian of the genus *Caiman* with the additional possibility that when inverted it was seen also as a double-eagle or double-falcon. Crocodilians of the genus *Caiman* are not found in nature north of the Isthmus of Tehuantepec, so it is likely that the subject skull arrived as such through some chain of intermediary transfers. Crocodilians figured in the cosmology of many aboriginal peoples within this interaction area and when combined in imagery with a bird were part of a composite cosmic monster or dragon featured on atlatls from Panama to the southeastern United States, where such grips appear in the early literature as "birdstones." A defining characteristic of the caiman skull is a pattern of four holes bracketing the nasal opening that receive the four longer teeth of the lower jaw. This pattern is also found around the mouth of a composite being with human, bird, and deer attributes engraved on a human femur found in Mound 25 of the Hopewell Mound Group in Ohio. This suggests that the Bedford Mound 8 caiman-bird imagery was not a unique phenomenon but rather a previously unsuspected aspect of Hopewellian cosmology.

The Hopewellian Interaction Sphere was made possible by religious understandings that constituted the Hopewellian Great Tradition shared by smaller regional and local traditions in the eastern United States. The mechanism of the Hopewellian Interaction Sphere may have included Spirit Adoption as a part of mourning and world-renewal ritual. The role of a plumed reptilian supreme being in a derived adoption ritual may be a late survival of a reptilian-related cosmology that influenced the belief systems of terminal Late Archaic and Early Woodland times from the direction of tropical America. This cosmology had a material survival in birdstones that represented a composite earth and sky deity who possibly also figured as a spirit patron in group initiation rituals.

Acknowledgments

I wish to acknowledge the kindness of Gregory Perino and James Brown for affording me access to a copy of the manuscript report on Perino's Bedford mound excavations. I wish also to thank the Field Museum Department of Zoology, Division of Amphibians and Reptiles, for granting me access to their collections of crocodilians for examination and photographing.

Alice Kehoe provided me with valuable critical comment on an earlier version of this chapter, and N'omi Greber has through the years steered me away from numerous shoals of misinterpretation in matters Hopewellian. Above all I want to thank Gregory Perino for his example and guidance in many matters when, forty-plus years ago, I was settling into my role as a neophyte Illinois field archaeologist.

26

The Shamanic Element in Hopewellian Period Ritual

James A. Brown

The grandeur of Hopewellian earthworks and the skill level evinced in some of their specialty crafts have been a continual source of wonder to archaeologists. At the outset this wonderment was translated into scenarios of civilization attributable to a bygone "mound builder race." With the incorporation of the Hopewell cultural phenomenon into a continuous Native American history, attention turned to other historical factors. At first, Hopewell became merely a product of a diffusionary pulse from the center of high culture in Mesoamerica. But the midwestern location of the Hopewellian florescence demanded additional factors to make the location plausible. Maize agriculture—of Mexican origin, of course—became that ingredient (Martin, Quimby, and Collier 1947). The problem presented by the location soon led to the ecological approach, which attempted to spell out the special conditions that made Hopewell (and the Ohio form in particular) possible, with or without maize agriculture (Prufer 1964a, 1964b). As our knowledge has grown, the issue has not gone away. Instead, the disparity between the minuscule scale of Ohio Hopewell settlement and the monumental scale of the neighboring earthworks has become all the more obvious (Pacheco 1996b). What we have is a rather uncomfortable fit between the monumental constructions from Ohio and the surrounding thinly distributed population of small-scale farmers and foragers. The scale of economic and political activity is well below any expectation held of a civilization.

The result has been a scramble to fit the two aspects of the settlement pattern together, all the while remembering that the gardening economy lacked the productive capacity of Mississippian period maize agriculture (Smith 1992b). The discordance is particularly acute in the debate over whether or not Hopewellian societies, in Ohio in particular, were governed by hierarchical principles, that is, whether or not they were ruled by chiefs (for example, Braun 1979, 1981; Tainter 1977, 1983). In this chapter I invite the reader to entertain a perspective that departs from the usual by examining the impact that ritual specialists may have had. Although Hopewellian studies have greatly benefited from an ecological approach and the sociology of burials, it is time to insert some cultural content into the subject. Creating content is not without its perils, particularly when standards of evidence are not agreed upon. Furthermore, at the time depths we are considering, the direct historical approach becomes problematical. Ethnographic analogy offers more reliable means of accessing cultural content, but here the very nature of this form of analogy stresses the absence of content (Stahl 1993; Wylie 1985). Fortunately, we are rescued from this impasse by the very plausibility that religious practitioners included, if they were not indeed dominated by, shamans. These specialists stand in a privileged position that allows them to dominate social activity in particular contexts. The object of this chapter is to draw out the shamanistic element in Hopewellian archaeology by centering remarks on the pipe-smoking complex and concluding with some observations on implications of shamanistic practices for interpreting certain high-status Hopewell burials.

Shamans in the Past

An account of shamanistic leadership in the Hopewellian period is not very commonplace, as one might expect. To write such an account requires awarding a prominence to the ideological component of small-scale political economies that is not customarily done in Eastern Woodlands archaeology. Some of the cultural consequences of having a major component of ritual activity dominated by shamans and shamanistic practices will be spelled out below.

Recent scholars have come to appreciate the creative role played by shamans in human culture. In their trance state, shamans actively remold received cultural concepts and extend, in effect, the current repertoire of beliefs and practices. For instance, their authority derived from journeys into the supernatural could inspire the images of both humans and animals with horns and antlers. Thus, the appearance of deer antlers in Hopewell and early Mississippian headgear should not be surprising. There is no need to raise the specter of kingship, as Warren K. Moorehead (1922) once did.

As a group healer a shaman has a clear role. But how does this role enlarge itself to assume larger social import? For one thing, shamans take on the role of specialized practitioners in the importation of a complex liturgy. The elements of such a liturgy are expressed materially in the complex rules by which earthworks were assembled. Byers (1996) has attempted to interpret the diversity of earthworks as various iterations upon a basic set of rules. The metrical consistency among various dimensions of earthworks is an additional feature that makes sense as rule driven (Marshall 1996; Romain 1996, 2000). And lastly there is the evidence that both prominent landmarks and solstitial observations serve as orientation for key alignments (Romain 1996; Seeman 2000; Seeman and Branch, this volume).

Shamans and Shamanism

The term *shamanism* has come to refer to very diverse sets of beliefs and practices (Bowie 2000). Two stances toward the subject dominate the literature (Bowie 2000; Lewis-Williams 2004). One restricts the term to a set of historically conditioned cultural practices—specifically, those of Arctic shamanism (for example, Kehoe 2000). This is its classic locus, wherein the most consistent cultural patterning is exhibited. Elsewhere variability is so extreme as to resist useful characterization.

Eliade (1964), more than any other individual in the English-speaking world, promoted shamanism as an ecstatic religion. Hultkrantz (1979:85–86) has observed that this religious meaning does not conform well to North American practice. "'The religious pattern,' in North and South America, is 'somewhat inappropriately called shamanism,' owing to the crucial roles played by the medicine man, or shaman, in the spiritual and ceremonial life of the indigenous community. Yet not all medicine men in the New World are shamans in a strict adherence to this concept [regarded by Hultkrantz as a 'religious configuration'], which presupposes ecstasy to be the main technique in achieving communication with the spirit world. Therefore, he feels that this term should be used to signify the shaman's worldviews and ritual performance instead of denoting 'an entire religious pattern'" (Ripinsky-Naxon 1993:70).

The other approach, which is less concerned with internal consistency, concentrates on the history of a small set of very specific shamanistic features (for example, Lewis-Williams 2002, 2004). This approach makes its focus those features that take a characteristic material form. Archaeologists, in particular, gravitate toward ways in which the material can be paired with the nonmaterial. An altered state of consciousness is one of these features that have a very specific material signature. Nonetheless, this feature is not consistently distributed among ritual specialists who, at one time or another, may have been characterized as shamans.

Lewis-Williams (2002) has been in the forefront of students of shamanism in advocating a focus on altered states of consciousness as evincing the most promising connection to the archaeological record. For one thing, he posits a "perception of alternative reality that is frequently tiered." This gives rise to the belief by hunter-gatherers "in spiritual realms above and below the world of daily life." For another, he states, "The behavior of the human nervous system in certain altered states creates the illusion of dissociation from one's body (less commonly understood in hunting and gathering shamanistic societies as possession by spirits)" (133). He summarizes:

> Shamans use dissociation and other experiences of altered states of consciousness to achieve at least four ends. Shamans are believed to contact spirits and supernatural entities, heal the sick, control the movements and lives of animals, and change the weather. These four functions of shamans, as well as their entrance into an altered state of consciousness, are believed to be facilitated by supernatural entities that include: variously conceived supernatural potency, or power, and animal-helpers and other categories of spirits that assist shamans and are associated with potency. (Lewis-Williams 2002:133)

The four shamanistic functions identified above are logically emergent from altered states of consciousness. Of these, the curing function has come in for some misunderstanding since nonshamanistic medicine men and women are found to treat patients in North America. It seems clear, however, that where an illness can "be connected directly to some accident or misfortune—a broken bone or a wound, for example"—a medicine man is typically called upon (Hultkrantz 1985:334–335).

Shamans treat an illness lacking any such ostensible cause as having a supernatural origin. Two kinds of origin are widely acknowledged. One is the intrusion of a "foreign spirit or object." The second is the loss of one's soul, after it has either been drawn away or has wandered into the world of the supernatural. "Regardless of its precise cause, illness was the result of an intervention by the supernatural into the natural world. To cure illness, and heal the victim, was to restore the patient to this world. Healing required a deep understanding of the ways of the supernatural" (Goodman 1993:23).

Shamans in Small-scale Societies

The focus upon small-scale societies, including hunter-gatherers, is strategically necessary to direct analysis productively by confining cultural variability to a minimum (Lewis-Williams 2002, 2004). In moving from his primary focus on Upper Paleolithic hunter-gatherers, Lewis-Williams has paved the way for productive exploration among settled Near Eastern farmer-foragers. An examination of Middle Woodland practices is only a short step away, but a certain cautionary note has to be struck here. We have to separate the material culture of shamans reliably from that of ordinary medical arts on the one hand and priestly functions on the other. This is particularly acute in those cases where societies have become sufficiently complex to have a significant priestly component in their rituals.

The cross-cultural study by Bourguignon (1973, 1977) has affirmed that shamans are the major ritual specialists among hunter-gatherers. In what she called "possession societies," these groups are relatively small, sometimes semi-sedentary, with a mean size of less than a thousand. Decision making resides at the local level. These possession societies are likely to be mobile hunter-gatherers, which she defined as those who derive at least 46 percent of their diet from foraging (Bourguignon 1973:43). Shamanistic practice does not involve alteration of outward behavior. Where spirit possession does manifest itself in character and personality change, she designates a very different pattern called "possession trance."

Bourguignon elaborated on this distinction:

[T]he shaman who acquires power, and the witch as well, do not impersonate spirits, do not abdicate their own identity; even the patient who is diminished in some sense by spirit-intrusion illness remains himself. Those who through some form of possession acquire powers for good or for evil have these powers supplement their own; their selves are strengthened rather than displaced. A shaman's chances for achievement are enhanced by the acquisition of spirit power. His relation with the spirit is not dependent on the group; rather, he has most likely obtained it on his own, in his own dealings with the spirit. (Bourguignon 1973:30)

In contrast, "[p]ossession trance, by offering a decision-making authority in the person of a medium, revealing the presumed will of the spirits, allows persons oppressed by rigid societies some degree of leeway and some elbow room. As such, possession trance may be said to represent a safety valve, of sorts, for societies whose rigid social structures cause certain stresses" (Bourguignon 1973:31).

This distinction helps us understand why in small-scale acephalous societies shamans attain the importance they do. In societies without leaders, the fame and notoriety that shamans acquire place them in the forefront of local and even regional networks. By virtue of their elevated status and their specialized spiritual powers, shamans are in a position to take charge over a range of problematic personal issues that potentially plague all human societies. As we will see below, it is conceivable for shamans to have interests in constructing outsized earthworks. However, once chiefly institutions (to say nothing of those belonging to the state) appear, very different forms of materialization can be expected. The scale, large though it might be, is one that is capable of comprehension solely from ground-level observation.

Shamanistic Evidence

Who Are the Honored Few?

Shamans have the potential to serve as social mediators in large assemblies of people. The outsized scale of the larger Hopewellian earthworks suggests that social aggregations were significantly larger than the everyday population level. This has relevance to the well-known exclusiveness of precious objects in Hopewellian graves. The strongly concentrated distribution of obsidian bifaces readily comes to mind, although Seeman (1979b) has documented the same pattern among other artifact classes and earthworks themselves. In the burial sociology of Hopewellian grave goods, a long-standing debate involves the issue of social status and presence of chieftaincies. What we might consider as an unacknowledged alternative to the egalitarian/hierarchical dichotomy is the achieved prestige of shamans and persons inducted into societies involving shamanistic performances. Perhaps varying skills and adeptness in handling various hallucinogens may be a criterion for differentiation. Even simple healers could comprise a rank in such a set. In no sense is this ranking inherited, however; in such a set children should be rare.

Just how the preferential treatment of male and female dead might be patterned is something that needs to be modeled. Research should be directed towards teasing out subsidiary patterns favoring one or the other model. But the achieved status model in which shamanistic skills provide the mode for differentiation does affect one's perspective towards a general pattern of unique assortments of grave goods. Although certain categories of objects (for example, copper sagittal headdresses) are found repetitively, the number and kind of objects found in graves is generally unique.

Transformational Imagery

An outstanding example of transformational imagery is the Wray pipe from the Newark area. A seated man wearing ear spools and with hair coifed in a Hopewellian manner is clothed in a bearskin with the bear head as a headdress (Dragoo and Wray 1964). The human head lying in his lap with long, flowing hair calls to mind the head grasped by the birdman of the Mississippian period. At the Turner site the assemblage of engraved human bone provides another instance. Here animal and human parts are combined in such a manner to admit of several different combinations, many of them referencing transformation individually. The ensemble itself revolves around the theme of transformation, an archetypical shamanistic feature.

Shamanistic Artifacts

What is noteworthy in the Hopewellian case is the mobilization of craft expertise to materialize in technically difficult media imagery that undoubtedly had sources in shamanistic visions. One can start the list with "natural" objects that are found in Hopewellian sites: quartz crystals, fossils, and suggestively shaped rocks and minerals (for example, Willoughby and Hooton 1922). Even the diagnostic cross-hatching on a cambered rim has a shamanistic connection. If one were to draw upon Mississippian period imagery, this decorative device would be none other than a snake coil, and a supernatural one at that (Phillips and Brown 1978). I venture this suggestion to indicate some of the lines that could be pursued in the future if one were to draw from the repertoire of cross-culturally noted imagery of shamanistic trance states.

Smoking Pipes

One of the more consistently found artifacts is the Hopewellian smoking pipe. "The enormous symbolic value of the pipe derived partly from the close association between its stem and the shaman's device for sucking illnesses from patients" (Goodman 1993:35). Wilbert (1987:122) credits Birket-Smith (1929: 37–39) with the observation that the smoking pipe in the Americas and throughout most of the world had "developed from the secular and ritual drinking tube via the shamanic sucking tube" (see also von Gernet and Timmons 1987). The elbow pipe and the tubular pipe predominate north and west of the southern plains and in the Southwest. In those latter areas, cigarettes and alternative forms of tobacco use predominate (Driver and Massey 1957:263)

Platform pipe bowls are either worked into the body of an animal effigy or are unembellished (the "monitor" form). The presence of either form is sufficient in itself to denote a Hopewellian context, or at least one of that period. It is possible that this popular artifact could be a product of widespread recreational smoking. The pipe's prevalence would then be little more than an indication of popularity. But this is unlikely considering the degree to which the cultivation and use of tobacco was surrounded by ritual constraint (von Gernet 1992b). Indeed, in postcontact time almost any gift required an obligatory offering of tobacco, usually but not invariably smoked. As von Gernet (1992b) observed, there was a pervasive and obligatory cementing of gifts and obligations with tobacco-involved puffs of smoke. Such puffing, particularly through a long pipe stem, need not entail bringing smoke into the lungs.

But Hopewellian pipes are no mere smoking tubes. The bowl is positioned on a base that serves as a convenient hand support. The bowls are upright rather than horizontally continuous with the stem, as in a cigar or cigarette; rather, the bowl is positioned to direct the smoke upward. In postcontact ritual this smoke is likened to a message delivered skyward to the divine (Paper 1988). The column of smoke is positioned symbolically by gesturing to the four directions, or blowing smoke to these directions, thereby seating the column of smoke at the world axis, temporarily though that might be. Parenthetically, the slow-burning sacred fires of the Southeast produced a similar message by offering a gift to the ascendant powers within a quadrate axis defined by logs (Paper 1988). Interestingly, the platform pipe held in the hand replicates in miniature a fire constructed on a horizontal surface.

The manner in which platform pipes were used has more to tell us. By analogy with the compound bowl and pipe-stem set that is typical of postcontact ritual pipes, Hall (1977, 1997) has argued that pipe stems were inserted into the borehole of the mouthpiece. This places the stone pipe well away from the smoker's lips with some degree of dilution from the full effects of the nicotine smoke. Indeed, a long pipe stem is shown in the pictograph panel at the Gottschall Shelter (Salzer 1987). Unlike Mississippian and postcontact pipe-stem bores, however, there is to my knowledge no signs of wear in the boreholes of Hopewellian pipes. The stem holes in platform pipes also have much smaller diameters than is the case with Mississippian period pipes. While the latter are easily large enough to accommodate a pipe stem, only the slenderest of reeds could fit into the end of Hopewellian platform pipes. This leads me to conclude that the mouth was placed directly against the distal end of the stone pipe platform. Not only does this place the smoker's lungs and lips into closer contact with the burning tobacco, it also has the effect of placing the smoker directly in front of—and often eye-to-eye with—the animal effigy. The resulting intimacy could not help but enhance the effect of the hallucinogenic experience. It makes sense that Mississippian and Historic period L-shaped pipe bowls were fitted with long stems, since a hallucinogenic experience may not have been intended, merely a gift of smoke to the empyrean divine as Paper (1988) has argued (von Gernet 1992a, 1992b).

The imagery of Hopewellian pipes figures into this picture in a telling way. The animal species composition has been a subject that many have commented upon. Penney (Brose, Brown, and Penney 1985:194) thought that each effigy represented images of personal spirit guardians. Searching more ambitiously, DeBoer (1997) recently undertook a pattern analysis of the species groups into which animal effigy pipes from Tremper and Mound City Mound 8 could be placed (Mills 1916, 1922). He was impressed by the predominance of birds and animals that include water as part of their habitat. He concluded that animal effigies could be partitioned into three relatively equal groups if liminal animals such as the bear were opposed to categories of birds and water animals. From this trichotomy he drew attention to the implicit structural oppositions present in his model.

Regardless of the satisfaction that algebraic formulations might bring to this patterning, there is another way in which the animal distributions could be viewed. This alternative rests on shamanistic values associated with specific animals and even broad taxonomic groupings such as the birds. This recalls von Gernet's (von Gernet 2000; von Gernet and Timmins 1987) thesis. The hallucinogenic states to which shamans subject themselves, including smoking particularly potent tobacco, routinely involve sensations of flight and diving (or swimming) during the journey of the soul. The effigies of birds thus become tutelaries. Birds also are guardians against evil intrusions. Indeed, in postcontact times the hawk and the raven, particularly commonplace effigy subjects, held very specific roles having to do with the living and the dead in many cosmologies. The Bedford Mound pipe has the beak of a raven resting on the outline of a human head in profile incised on the surface of the proximal end of the pipe stem (Perino n.d.). Among the swimming animals, frogs, otters, beavers, and other species represent analogues to the access that the soul has to the underwater domain. In some cases turtles have importance as bearers of hexagonal plates in their carapace (Ripinsky-Naxon 1993:125). The number six is associated with the sides of quartz crystals and a perfect and complete world order derived from the four cardinal directions and the upper and under worlds.

The bear represents something different again. Hultkrantz (1989) has observed that both the brown bear and the grizzly bear take on the role of the archetypical healer in the animal kingdom. Medicine men impersonate this animal in their role as shamanistic healers. The premier importance of the bear probably derives from the circumboreal bear cult. What makes the bear particularly feared is his resemblance to a human when hung and stripped of his skin. Thus, the animals given effigy form are not animals having economic importance. Rather, they emphasize animals that could plausibly have been encountered in the supernatural realm and the tutelaries that a shaman might have brought to this realm as protection. As a consequence, these animals come to have enormous powers attributed to them through their capacity to help or hinder shamanic quests.

Lastly, one should bear in mind the fragmented mode in which the pipes of the famous caches from Tremper and Mound City Mound 8 were disposed (Mills 1916, 1922). Here Gundersen's (Gundersen and Brown 2002; Montgomery, Gundersen, and Mathien 2001) research has shown that they were not simply smashed; rather, they were deliberately allowed to explode. The mode of destruction alone suggests a show, one that would work well in a shamanistic performance. Of course, we have to consider carefully the implications behind wide-scale destruction of both elaborately crafted goods and found objects. The whole range of consumed grave goods can be considered as gifts to the super-natural. In certain cases these gifts could be an attempt to foster the reproduction of these and other objects for human use in the future.

Shamanistic Aerial View

In a paper titled "Plant Hallucinogens, Out-of-body Experiences and New World Monumental Earthworks," Dobkin de Rios (1977) advanced the thesis that in three distinct areas of the Americas a connection existed between the remains of monumental earthworks and the presence of plant hallucinogens and out-of-body experiences. These were the Adena/Hopewell culture of the midwestern United States, the Olmec of the Gulf Coast of Mexico, and the Nazca culture of southern Peru. She drew upon the association between monu-mental, "difficult-to-interpret" earthworks with periods and places where hal-lucinogenic plants and the instruments of their use were clearly present and available. More specifically, she argued that the often colossal scale of these earthworks was prompted by the "aerial gaze" that commonly accompanies out-of-body experiences, which are routinely undertaken by shamans (Dobkin de Rios 1977:237). She reasoned, "The purpose of such expenditures of time and labor was to make known certain cosmological messages not only to super-natural forces, but to members of the community, as well as other shamans in conflict with the social group" (Dobkin de Rios 1977:237). Shamans undertook such trances routinely to acquire their healing arts (Goodman 1993:23). Her argument was articulated by drawing on the commonplace experiences of hal-lucinogen users, that they fall into a disassociated state and have an exosomatic experience. The aerial voyage is the common form this state takes.

Following from this, Dobkin de Rios rested her argument on two points. One, the shaman performs as a psychopomp, that is, as "the spiritual guardian of a community who is obliged to confront and combat his group's adversaries. A major part of his activity includes healing disease and neutralizing those mis-fortunes which have occurred to members of the community through the machi-nations of enemies" (Dobkin de Rios 1977:246). Two, the common experience of flying has its material correlate in earthworks:

> One need not fly in the air to really fly. Thus, the New World massive earthworks, difficult for the Westerner to conceptualize visually outside of an airplane voyage, are perhaps more simply explicable as the projection by the shaman of the animal or totem familiar from the heights of ecstasy through which he soars. . . . Given the arguments for the militant nature of the shaman, protecting his community against the evildoings of others, as well as his role as intermediary with the supernatural, such monumental earthworks in this analysis are viewed as constructed to warn rival sha-mans of the powers that were controlled by the psychopomp of a given area, to reaffirm supernatural contact and maintain social solidarity. Enormous expenditures of labor and cooperation, needed to construct such earthworks (extended perhaps from generation to generation), reaf-

firmed the bonds that link men together. Ties of cooperation maintain intragroup harmony and are important in small-scale societies. Finally, in the case discussed in this article, the symbolic form of the image mounds consisted of elements of ritualized belief already present in the plastic arts of the particular cultures in question. (Dobkin de Rios 1987:246–247)

It is possible to add to Dobkin de Rios' argument by indicating that colossal-sized earthworks appear only in certain culture-evolutionary stages. What is important about these earthworks is that they are difficult to comprehend from an earthbound viewpoint and are most likely to appear at a time before the emergence of institutionalized religions and the political apparatus of centralized control. Here her use of the Olmec case confuses the argument because this society is now regarded as more complex politically than the other two. However, a Middle American relationship probably holds true if one were to make use of Early Formative instances. The Olmec case has the benefit of alerting us to the impact that shamanistic practices have in both chiefdoms and early states (Chang 1983).

Using the same basic perspective, Krupp (1997:17) defined a connection "between the architecture of the universe, the pattern of nature, the fabric of society, and the personal environment," a kind of worldview that he called "cosmovision." The way Krupp (1997:17) uses this concept, cosmovision "integrates these notions and forges a system of relationships between the cosmic and the divine with human society and individual destiny. Ideas about the structure of the world, about the rhythms of time, and about the origin of the cosmos are all combined into a ceremonial landscape."

Tobacco as a Hallucinogen

Winter has summarized the pharmacological properties of tobacco succinctly:

Nicotine and the other alkaloids [principally nornicotine] are biphasic drugs: in small doses they increase locomotor activity and vigilance and allow more rapid, enhanced learning. They are also stimulants, while at the same time they provide selective calming and relaxing effects, serve as hunger and thirst suppressants, and are analgesics. In large doses they produce visions, hallucinations, trances, seizures, color blindness, catatonia, and even death (Siegal 1989:96; Wilbert 1987:19).

Regular use of tobacco, even in small doses as a stimulant, increases tolerance and rapidly leads to habituation and eventually to addiction. As the effects of the regular use of nicotine wear off—be they the pleasant, calming effects of small doses or the intoxicating effects of massive doses—withdrawal symptoms set in, with opposite effects: tension, restlessness, irritability, increased hunger, insomnia, inability to concentrate, and intense craving for more tobacco. The ingestion of more tobacco relieves these symptoms (nicotine reaches the brain within seven seconds of the ingestion of smoke), thereby producing a cycling between satiation and withdrawal, which defines the state of physical addiction (Siegal 1989:96). (Winter 2000c:327)

This portrayal of the effects of tobacco use may appear strange to those whose sole experience is with the low nicotine content of commercially available tobacco. But *Nicotiana rustica* is in a different category. "Weed tobacco," as it is commonly called, has many more times the nicotine content of commercially marketed *N. tabacum* cigarettes, and *N. quadrivalis* has even less than *N. tabacum* (Winter 2000b).

"The narcotic effect of *N. rustica* was well known to the Natchez Indians, who gave it to their intended victims of sacrifice to stupefy them before the rite of strangulation. In the United States today *N. rustica* is used only in the manufacture of insecticides because of its high nicotine content, and farmers keep close lookout for it because it can be poisonous to cattle and sheep" (Robicsek 1978:46). Over a period of five months, von Gernet (1995) smoked this kind of tobacco in a pipe resembling Huron ones. His experience was that smoking definitely induced hallucinations. After a period of acclimation, the hallucinogenic effect persisted consistently throughout the trial period. Importantly, at first he experienced extreme nausea and other unpleasant symptoms, but by the end of the experimental period his body had acclimated itself to the experience. He attempted to grow, cure, and prepare his tobacco in a manner that replicated Huron practices.

From this single case, it is possible to draw two conclusions. First, *N. rustica* is fully capable of producing hallucinatory experiences. Second, it is definitely "stronger" than commercially available varieties of *N. tabacum*. This conclusion seems to be at variance with the report that tobacco smoking among Native Americans is nonhallucinatory, merely "offering smoke" (Paper 1988; but see von Gernet 1990). Von Gernet (1995, 2000) reports that addictive smoking was on record ethnographically.

Questions of Tobacco Usage

Since the publication of Wilbert's (1987) influential study, shamanistic use of tobacco in North America has tended to become elided with his characterization of the South American "tobacco shaman." Wilbert (1987:182) cites the Fox and Winnebago ethnographic data to draw a portrait of the Great Spirit complex of the Woodland Indians as "based on the intoxicating effects of the tobacco plant."

Winter (2000b:267) categorically dismissed the transfer of tobacco shamanism into North America, at least in postcontact times, stating that contemporary tobacco shamanism is not known "north of the southernmost tribes of Mesoamerica." Furthermore, "Most medicine men and women and other leaders in North America do not . . . ingest such large amounts of nicotine that it produces hallucinations, visions, trances, and other states of altered consciousness" (Winter 2000b:266). He goes on to state that "in general the average Native American medico-religious practitioner does not use tobacco to enter a trance state, although he or she does use it for many other purposes" (Winter 2000b:267).

There are indications in the archaeological record, which Winter (2000b: 266) does not dispute, that visions were intimately connected with the pipe-smoking complex in precontact times (see Springer 1981). Von Gernet (1992a, 2000) has argued that a high point in this vision-seeking tobacco-smoking complex took place during the Adena and Middle Woodland periods. He notes that the formal similarity of Late Archaic tubular pipes with the sucking tubes of shamans implies that they "were once symbolically and functionally equivalent" (von Gernet 2000:73). He found psychoactive substances to be associated with birds and cited a variety of other iconographic links and miscellaneous practices as well (von Gernet 2000:73).

The derivation and close connection that Crow Indians make to the stars implies that even their nicotine-poor quadrivalian tobacco is a vision-producing substance, even though that usage has not been explicitly reported (Lowie 1920). Lastly, there is the biphasic reaction to heavy dosage that conforms to an extent to the message conveyed in the Pawnee rite of Hako and the social function of the Calumet ceremony that cannot be accidental. Both were employed to rename individuals as if they had been reborn or had been resuscitated from the dead (Hall, this volume). Conformity to Wilbert's characterization of the typical trance experience is striking. He states,

> Whereas hallucinogens are particularly effective in providing the vivid imagery that illustrates the shaman's celestial journey, nicotine, the biphasic drug in tobacco, is exceptionally well suited to manifest the continuum of dying, which begins with initial nausea, heavy breathing, vomiting, and prostration (illness); continues with tremors, convulsion, or seizure (agony); and ends with peripheral paralysis of the respiratory muscle (death). Progressive blockade of impulse transmission of autonomic ganglia and central stimulation are the primary pharmacological conditions of this journey toward death whence, if appropriately dosed, the shaman is granted safe return thanks to the prompt biotransformation of nicotine in the body. (Wilbert 1987:157)

The effects of tobacco in combination with other substances have not been actively considered. Janiger and Dobkin de Rios (1976) have pointed out that some herbal cigarettes have tested out with much higher nicotine content than tobacco itself. Rather than testifying to an adulteration of tobacco, herbal concoctions could actually be even more hallucinogenic than pure tobacco.

The very democratization of tobacco smoking can be hypothesized as encouraging the use of progressively milder hallucinogens, including less-nicotine-rich tobacco. This scenario would fit the shift from stronger to weaker hallucinogens in the Pecos River valley. For another reason von Gernet's experience with *N. rustica* suggests a practical condition set on its use. Strong tobacco requires bodily conditioning, and such conditioning has the potential necessity for requiring guidance from others in its use. This applies particularly to other more powerful hallucinogenic substances. One of these, datura, is notoriously unpredictable in its effects from dose to dose. Thus a mild and relatively predictable nicotine source may have selective advantages in opening its use to a much larger number of clients by freeing them from the necessity of undergoing a somatic conditioning under the tutelage of a sponsor.

In support of this model I cite the appearance of certain hallucinogen sources early in the history of the Eastern Woodlands and their absence from the record by contact time. I need only point to the copper wand of the deadly amanita (fly agaric, probably *Amanita muscaria*) found at Mound City (Mills 1922; see also Devereaux 1997:117; Romain 2000). Second, datura in the form of jimsonweed grows commonly in the humid forests of the Eastern Woodlands, but its use was restricted to a single instance among eastern-shore Algonquian at the dawn of contact. Thus the dangerous sources of hallucinogens were used under strict guidelines early in history and phased out with replacement from a less dangerous source whose use remained more easily controlled by the user.

Tobacco in the Eastern Woodlands

Only recently has the history of tobacco use in the Eastern Woodlands become an active subject of research. Fine-scale recovery now practiced through flotation recovery has resulted in the accumulation of a useful archaeological seed record. Even so, in all likelihood the quantitative importance of tobacco is greatly underestimated (Wagner 2000). It is clear that tobacco was present around A.D. 150 in Middle Woodland contexts and may well occur even earlier. Although the number of seeds is minuscule, this does not necessarily imply that tobacco was unimportant. The nearly microscopic seeds require particularly fine recovery methods, ones that are not commonly employed (Asch and Asch 1985b, 1985c; Riley, Edging, and Rossen 1990; Wagner 2000). Another promising avenue is chemical analysis of pipe bowl residues, but such analysis has been underutilized so far (Wagner 2000). Except for the earliest pipe records, the reported incidence of tobacco remains mirrors the history of stone pipes in the East.

More than one species is a contender for the tobacco present in Middle Woodland times. *Nicotiana rustica* is the time-honored candidate because it was grown and used throughout the Eastern Woodlands at the time of European contact (Ford 1985a; Riley, Edging, and Rossen 1990:529–530; von Gernet 1995; Winter 2000b). Von Gernet (2000) has provided a thorough review of the ethnohistoric record. On the western flank of the rustica distribution lie two cultivated varieties of another tobacco species, *N. quadrivalis* (alternatively called *N. bigelovii*). The two varieties of tobacco were *N. quadrivalis* var. *quadrivalis* (Pursh.) East and *N. quadrivalis* var. *multivalis* (Lindley) East (Winter 2000b). Rustica and quadrivalian tobaccos had very different botanical histories (Winter 2000a, 2000c). The latter is indigenous to California and arid western North America, with outliers in the Missouri River valley (Winter 2000a). Rustica tobacco, by contrast, is a domesticate belonging to a separate subgenus introduced into the Eastern Woodlands from Mesoamerica sometime before European contact (von Gernet 2000). So far, firm archaeological evidence has not been forthcoming on the timing of the entry of this species into eastern North America.

The use of more than a single species of tobacco has been reported repeatedly and continues to this day. Typically, as in the case of the Crow Indian practice, one was open for broad consumption while the other was reserved solely for specialists in ritual contexts (Adair 2000a; Winter 2000b, 2000c). In the case of the Crow Indians, "tall tobacco" (var. *quadrivalis*) was relatively unrestricted in use, whereas "short tobacco" (var. *multivalis*) is so sacred that it was not even smoked (Lowie 1920; Winter 2000b:286–292).

Haberman (1984) was the first to identify quadrivalian tobacco from Late Woodland contexts in the Missouri Valley. Although this identification has been questioned, Fritz has identified the same species from the Lohmann phase borrow pit deposits beneath Cahokia Mound 51 dating from A.D. 1050–1100 (Pauketat et al. 2002; Wagner and Fritz 2002). These identifications place the arid western indigenous species in the Midwest prior to 1100. *Nicotiana rustica* has also been identified tentatively as early as the Middle Woodland period (Asch and Asch 1985b, 1985c; Wagner 2000:186–188; but see Adair 2000b: 182–183). In the model of tobacco history offered by Winter (2000c:322–325), *N. quadrivalis* was present north of the Rio Grande before *N. rustica* arrived. New data are needed to address the question of whether one or both species were available in Middle Woodland times.

Although the two taxa differ greatly in nicotine content, both were exploited for their ample capacity to induce trance states (Winter 2000c). Despite the much lower nicotine content of quadrivalian tobacco compared with that of tabacum or rustica, the narcotic effect is dependent upon the dosage consumed.

Conclusion

Interest in Hopewellian high-status burials is propelled by the observed number of high-value burial goods on or near the dead and an underlying concern with how to explain the scale of planning and the dedication of labor implied by the heavy earthmoving. The hereditary authority explanation has come under increasing criticism only to leave a gap between observed grandeur and economic and demographic reality. Filling this gap is the prospect that high-status burials are at minimum a product of shamanic ritual and may specifically reflect the mortuary marking of highly honored practitioners. This should alert us to the prospect that the leadership question may be a product of a poverty of models. This chapter presents a brief for the material expression of persons actively engaged in altered states of consciousness. These expressions include the tobacco pipe-smoking complex; the large-scale earthworks; the various bird, bear, and human transformational imagery; and artifacts widely connected with otherworldly power quests. These individuals are the very ones whose acknowledged otherworldly sources of power would have given them the requisite authority to direct the labor of assembled audiences to shamanistic performances in the direction leading to earthmoving operations of impressive scale.

Section 4

Recreating Hopewell: Commentaries

The final two chapters are commentaries on the preceding contents of this volume, providing both an inside and an outside critique. Bruce Smith writes from the perspective of one who has a long history of looking at aspects of Hopewell across the Eastern Woodlands of North America. Robert Chapman provides a view from outside North America, bringing to bear his experience with similar issues in European Neolithic archaeology. The two chapters together provide a fitting conclusion to a volume entitled *Recreating Hopewell*, and both perspectives should prove thought-provoking for Hopewell researchers.

27

Household, Community, and Subsistence in Hopewell Research

Bruce D. Smith

In the more than two decades since the publication of the Chillicothe Conference volume (Brose and Greber 1979), research on Middle Woodland period Hopewell societies has witnessed a substantial resurgence, particularly in the south-central Ohio Hopewell heartland. As is amply documented by many of the chapters in this volume, recent and ongoing surveys and excavations, as well as reconsideration of long-curated collections and documents, have yielded substantial new information on Hopewell earthen enclosures, mounds, and settlements. Along with this steady stream of new information, researchers are also employing a variety of new perspectives, at different scales of analysis, in an effort to gain a better understanding of Hopewell societies. Building on a long and rich tradition of research, these recent efforts are bringing a range of difficult and complex problem domains into sharper focus. Several new explanatory frameworks and general models have been proposed and challenged. A number of new research topics have surfaced, others have been recast or set aside, and some questions have proven to be as difficult and intractable in eastern North America as they are in other regions of the world.

Within the broad array of Hopewell research questions currently being addressed, I think that there are three broad and overlapping problem domains that, while having attracted considerable interest over the last twenty years, still hold great potential for future research:

1. Hopewell habitation sites. There is still a great deal to be done in terms of expanding and refining the baseline standards and criteria of comparison to be used in profiling and differentiating the small settlements of Hopewell households (whether they be termed base camps, farmsteads, homesteads, or hamlets), as well as exploring the full range of variation and diversity that existed.

2. Hopewell subsistence. A number of interesting challenges remain regarding the general placement of Hopewellian subsistence economies on the broad conceptual and developmental landscape extending from hunting and gathering well over into low-level food production (Smith 2001) and also in documenting and understanding the full range of diversity that existed across space and time.

3. Hopewell corporate integration. Unraveling the social and temporal contexts of construction and use history of earthwork enclosures, mounds, great houses, and other community structures is perhaps the most challenging problem facing Hopewell archaeologists today, as it involves exposing and understanding the occupational and ceremonial episodes recorded adjacent to corporate or community-based constructions of earth and wood, within the zone of intersection between the household/domestic and corporate/sacred spheres of Hopewell society.

Providing a shared backdrop of consideration for all three of these high-potential problem domains are the standard archaeological issues of establishing appropriate referent classes of comparison and defining temporal and spatial scales of analysis. Imbedded within this space-time scale issue, of course, is the central, long-intractable multiscalar challenge of establishing contemporaneity: which of the Hopewell habitation sites and associated corporate centers (that is, mounds, enclosures, "big houses," and other ceremonial or ritual constructions [Greber 1979a, Greber et al. 1983]), were active at any particular point in time?

N'omi Greber (this volume) outlines the overall temporal and spatial parameters of Ohio Hopewell and directly addresses the obstacle of establishing contemporaneity of earthwork enclosures on a regional scale. Spanning approximately four hundred years, or about twenty generations, the Hopewell phenomenon endured in Ohio for twice the period the United States has been in existence, and during that four-century span, hundreds of enclosures and other corporate group structures were constructed and served as focal points of polity integration. Greber's discussion highlights the difficulties involved in any efforts at temporal placement of these earthworks with any degree of accuracy, and the associated problems in addressing questions of developmental overlap, contemporaneity, and temporal sequencing of big house and enclosure construction and use when viewed at regional and subregional scales of analysis. Authors of many of the other chapters in this volume address similar problems of temporal placement and contemporaneity, and this challenge is clearly of central importance to any attempts to impose abstract conceptual models of Hopewell community structure and interpolity interaction on the reality of the final archaeological record. It is simply not yet possible to tease apart, in a comprehensive and systematic way, what existed during any particular Hopewell generation from the confusing mass of end-point accumulation. While dating techniques such as long-count radiocarbon dating and dendrochronology are up to the task of providing generation-scale temporal resolution and establishing when individual Hopewell corporate structures were active (for example, Wills 2000), several factors hinder their successful application, including the absence of appropriate materials for dating (for example, well-preserved posts capable of yielding cut dates) and the long and complex construction and use history of many Hopewell enclosures (Greber, this volume; Riordan, this volume). It is clear that establishing a regional-scale chronology at a generational level of resolution for any Hopewell societies will remain a long-term challenge.

Greber also addresses the issue of establishing subregional referent classes as she sorts Ohio Hopewell enclosures into three general formal categories and identifies three separate drainage-based geographical subregions. In so doing, she follows a well-traveled interpretive process in archaeology. Contexts of understanding and explanation in the discipline are often constructed and shaped through straightforward comparative analysis within and between variously partitioned referent classes (for example, Brown 1979). This general compare-and-contrast process—in which individual examples (for example, particular enclosures or other sites) are considered against a backdrop of comparison provided by sets of other previously described examples—is both a contextual and a relative undertaking, as particular examples gain their set or category "identity," their "label," in terms of their perceived degree of similarity to or divergence from various established classes or categories. Such efforts at pattern recognition also obviously involve an interest in generalization, of being able to discuss and interpret a set of similar examples in terms of their salient shared features, rather than having to consider each as a totally unique entity. Drawing more encompassing descriptions, general overall profiles of entire example sets, is also the core of any effort toward being able to predict, that is, to project such characterizations beyond what is already known into the broad realm of what has not yet been uncovered. While efforts to develop general descriptions or predictive models have in recent years been critiqued as being "reductionist" or "essentialist," and as masking underlying patterns of variation, such general profiles or models in fact play an essential foundation and starting point role in the recognition of such patterns of variation. The value and the purpose of such categorical characterizations are not simply to allow larger polity-, region-, or "culture"-scale profiles. They are also proposed to encourage and provoke scholars toward further follow-up revision, refinement, and expansion of such broader categorical descriptions and to chart patterns of variation through time and across the natural and cultural landscapes of the past. In each of the three problem domains identified earlier, for example, the ongoing pursuit of a better understanding of Hopewell in Ohio and elsewhere can be seen to involve a continual unfolding dialectic between recognizing shared commonalities and distinguishing differences, between lumping and splitting, and between both the recasting of existing categories and the recognition of new ones. Driven by new information, new perspectives, and shifting scales of analysis, this ongoing dialectic is particularly evident in the recent research and writing on Hopewell habitation sites, as exemplified in a majority of the chapters in this volume.

Hopewell Habitation Sites

In their chapter in this volume (as well as in their 1997 edited volume, *Ohio Hopewell Community Organization*), William Dancey and Paul Pacheco take a major step in shaping and focusing ongoing and future research on Ohio Hopewell at a polity scale of analysis by proposing a comprehensive general model of how these societies or communities were organized on the landscape. Drawing, I think, on their research at the Murphy locality as well as on Prufer's (1964a,

1965) prescient formulations four decades ago, which in turn were influenced by proposed "vacant center" models of Mayan settlement patterns of the 1960s, Dancey and Pacheco (1997a:8) have proposed a "dispersed sedentary community model of Ohio Hopewell." Their model involves largely vacant centrally placed ritual precincts, "sacred centers of community life" (earthworks, mortuary structures) that are in turn surrounded by individual household units dispersed in isolated but sedentary hamlet settlements. While Dancey and Pacheco do identify other settlement pattern constituents, that is, "activity loci, specialized camps, public works, and symbolic places" (Dancey and Pacheco 1997a:8), it is the isolated, fully sedentary and stable, individual household settlements—the hamlets—that are the central, if dispersed, element of their general model.

One of the more surprising aspects of Dancey and Pacheco's formal model of Ohio Hopewell community organization and hamlets is that it is presented as an intentionally indigenous formulation, independent and freestanding. It is characterized as being neither derived from nor influenced by any of the other numerous Middle Woodland period settlement-pattern models proposed over the past thirty-five years (for example, Faulkner 1973; Fortier et al. 1989; Morse and Morse 1983; Struever 1968a; Toth 1979; Walthall 1980; summarized in Smith 1992a, 2002). As Dancey and Pacheco present this initial, independent, stand-alone Ohio Hopewell model, with acknowledgments to Prufer and both indirect and direct reliance on rather distant Mayan referents (Dancey and Pacheco 1997a:12), they also recognize that it is a first approximation, a work in progress, rather than any sort of final word on the subject. One of their primary aims is to establish an initial general baseline for comparison, which, if successful, would encourage more focused subregional-scale research and the future documentation of patterns of spatial and temporal variation: "[We] hope . . . that publication of this volume will stimulate systematic research on a local scale throughout the area of Ohio Hopewell" (Dancey and Pacheco 1997a:19); "[O]ur model simplifies what, through advances in testing, undoubtedly will prove to be more complex" (Dancey and Pacheco 1997:8).

Judging from a number of the conference papers, many of which appear as chapters in this volume, Pacheco and Dancey have been very successful in provoking reaction and stimulating further research on the nature of Ohio Hopewell habitation sites (for example, how dispersed, how permanent, and how variable are they?). Lazazzera's (2000) description and analysis of a cluster of house structures offers evidence for a relatively long-term multihousehold Hopewell settlement inside the earthen embankment at the Fort Ancient site, contrary to the expectations of the "dispersed-sedentary" model. At the same time, both Frank Cowan (this volume) and Richard Yerkes (this volume) take issue with the idea that any Ohio Hopewell settlements, either adjacent to earthworks or farther out, approached sedentary status. Alternatively, they propose that the small dispersed habitation sites of Ohio Hopewell societies were much more fleeting in duration, representative of frequent household-level seasonal relocations on the landscape.

Pacheco and Dancey (this volume), in turn, reiterate and defend their model relative to other proposed interpretive profiles for Ohio Hopewell, while also acknowledging emerging evidence for substantial variation in, or deviation from, the expectations of their general model. Given the still quite limited amount of actual excavated information available regarding Ohio Hopewell habitation sites, it is quite likely that ongoing debates regarding the relative strengths and interpretative merits of different polity structure models will continue at a healthy pace for some time to come. I think that the shaking-out process for these alternative Ohio Hopewell models could be productively shortened and the parameters of debate sharpened if future domestic-sphere research focused at the household scale of analysis was carried out within the context of comparison with close-at-hand referent classes of well-established research. Pacheco and Dancey account for their lack of reference to research on Hopewellian habitation sites outside of Ohio up until now as appropriate in that Ohio Hopewell is qualitatively distinct from other Middle Woodland societies, making what is known about non-Ohio Middle Woodland settlements irrelevant to understanding the Ohio Hopewell "core." While the massive scale of the corporate labor projects undertaken by a substantial percentage of Ohio Hopewell groups certainly set them apart from other Middle Woodland societies of the eastern United States, this does not negate the strong likelihood that the basic building blocks of "Hopewellian" societies, small dispersed single-family-household settlements, would have shared a number of general organizational similarities over a broad area, particularly given that they reflect generally comparable adaptations to deciduous midlatitude riverine ecosystems. It is interesting to note, in this regard, that the general profile of Ohio Hopewell single-household or hamlet settlements presented by Dancey and Pacheco (1997a) compares quite comfortably to a more general profile of settlement components proposed as comprising the broadly applicable archaeological signature of the "Hopewellian household unit" (Smith 1992a, 2002).

In any case, even if Ohio Hopewell habitation sites were in some way substantively, qualitatively distinct from those of other Middle Woodland societies (which I doubt), it would still be worthwhile to consider the general research design and problem orientation employed with some success over the past thirty years by archaeologists excavating both Middle Woodland and Mississippian period single-household settlements across eastern North America, from Illinois to Alabama. In terms of research design, for example, three aspects of Ohio Hopewell habitation sites as summarized by Pacheco and Dancey (this volume) would seem to be significant in terms of future work on Hopewell hamlets in general: the high percentage of hamlets identified only on the basis of surface debris scatters; the paucity to date of fully exposed, substantially intact settlements; and the continuing absence of very many well-defined house structures at outlying household settlements. Given this, I would argue that considerable opportunities still exist in Ohio and elsewhere for the identification of largely intact, minimally disturbed small habitation sites, ideally to be followed by their complete block exposure and excavation. It is the identification, excavation, and detailed profiling of such household settlements that is essential for Pacheco and Dancey to be able to expand their initial general model to encompass and accommodate patterns of variation that existed across time and space. Such full-exposure efforts at outlying Ohio Hopewell farmsteads like Murphy I and Marsh Run (Pacheco and Dancey, this volume) underscore the value of recovering as complete as possible archaeological records of small habitation sites, a now fairly standardized approach that extends back at least to the early 1970s for both Middle Woodland (Faulkner 1982) and Mississippian (Smith 1978) period sites. Two Illinois sites, Holding (Fortier et al. 1989) and Smiling Dan (Stafford and Sant 1985b), provide more recent non-Ohio examples of comprehensive excavations of Hopewellian household settlements having complex internal occupational histories. Smiling Dan, in particular, would appear to provide an interesting case-study comparison to the Murphy locale household settlement cluster or hamlet. Of comparable relevance to Ohio Hopewell, extensive plow-zone stripping, trenching, and multiple block excavation efforts on a number of terraces along the Duck River underscore the challenges inherent in identifying all of the sometimes widely dispersed elements of Middle Woodland occupancy and resolving issues of contemporaneity (for example, the Parks, Eoff I, and McFarland sites). Parks (Faulkner and McCullough 1982) and Eoff I (Faulkner 1982) in particular provide a number of interesting comparisons to the Jennison Guard site along the Ohio River (Kozarek 1997).

Dancey and Pacheco outline a very interesting and plausible developmental scenario for small dispersed households that involves multigenerational residential stability and sedentism, with tributary mouth household clusters and upstream strings of individual household settlements representing the sequential, overlapping generational occupations of a single family, as "children leave the parental household to form independent [but nearby] residences" (Dancey and Pacheco 1997a:8–9, Figure 1.3). It will of course be difficult to ever convincingly establish, in the absence of skeletal DNA evidence, the genetic intergenerational connection between the households that created such river terrace/ tributary mouth settlement clusters (hamlets) and upstream strings. I think it is a quite plausible general assumption to make, however, that Hopewell single-family-household settlements throughout the Eastern Woodlands of the United States comprised a spatial-temporal fabric of stable, long-term kin-based occupation of particular parcels of river or stream valley real estate and adjacent upland resource catchment zones.

Although Dancey and Pacheco do touch on the topic of duration of occupation of household settlements, primarily as a way of accounting for variability in the profile or archaeological signature of such sites (Dancey and Pacheco 1997a), there has been little discussion of the actual house structures of Hopewell single-family settlements in regard to assessing length of site occupation. This is not surprising, given that few house structures have been identified at outlying Hopewell hamlets in Ohio. Recent excavations within and adjacent to Ohio Hopewell enclosures, however, have exposed abundant evidence of a range of structure forms, including possible habitation structures with rectangular outline and exhibiting wall post and wall trench construction (Cowan, this volume; Lazazzera 2000). The careful excavation of houselike structures at the Stubbs earthwork (Cowan, this volume) is particularly significant in regard to detecting house structures of Ohio Hopewell households and to the question of duration of site and structure occupation. At least fifteen "houselike" single-post rectangular structures were documented at distances of 20–300 meters from the Stubbs earthwork, with superimposed post patterns at some locations showing evidence of sequential construction episodes. Many of these structures had been built within shallow house basins using wall trench construction. Often, only faint traces of wall trenches could be detected, and apparently because of topsoil removal prior to house construction it may be difficult in many situations to recognize very subtle soil color differences between wall trenches, post molds, and surrounding subsoil. These faint traces of wall trench house construction at the Stubbs earthwork raise a number of interesting questions. Are such difficult-to-discern, shadowy archaeological signatures often all that can be expected to remain as evidence of habitation structures of Ohio Hopewell households? Were posts removed, or structures ever burned, on being abandoned? How often might they have been rebuilt, with wall trenches redug and wall posts replaced? Are wall trench houses very common in Ohio Hopewell contexts? Are they functionally distinct from single-wall post structures? For Mississippian and early Historic periods across the Southeast, wall trench construction is often viewed as reflecting a more substantial, more permanent house structure involving greater labor investment. Wall trench houses are sometimes proposed as cold-season structures, particularly when they are found with internal hearths and storage pits and paired in a single-household settlement with a wall post "warm-season" structure (for example, Smith 1978:29, 1995:231–233). I would be hesitant at this point, however, to employ variation in house form or construction methods observed in Hopewell contexts as a measure of relative "permanence" or sedentism, particularly given the often rather sketchy house structure signatures documented at even the most substantial Hopewellian farmsteads in other regions of the eastern United States (Smith 1992a:220–239). Interestingly, Cowan (this volume) argues that the numerous "houselike" structures at Stubbs and other Hopewell centers are "not the places of everyday domestic abode." He concludes, based on the limited abundance and variety of associated debris, that such house structures reflect brief "guest house" occupations. In a discussion of refuse disposal patterns and off-site ravine refuse dumps at Middle Woodland sites in both the American Bottom and the lower Illinois Valley, however, Fortier (this volume) cautions against equating limited midden accumulation with short-term habitation episodes, providing another example of the value of looking beyond Ohio for comparative case-study situations.

A fairly extensive literature exists on the likely life span of pole, thatch, and wattle house structures (summarized in Smith 1995:236–241). Structures unprotected by daub are likely to succumb to insect infestation and decay in less than five years, while those having a clay covering could have a full-generation life span of several decades, although a decade or less (and with considerable variability expected), is a good general life-span envelope. There are, of course, a number of other approaches to estimating duration of household settlements (other than house structure life span), including ceramic use-life and breakage-rate measures (Pauketat 1989); size, abundance, and reexcavation of pits (Hanenberger 1990:385); and artifact assemblage profiles.

This question of duration of occupation is one of a set of a half-dozen or so interrelated questions that together comprise an overall problem orientation that has helped to structure research on Mississippian single-household settlements for the past thirty years (see Smith 1995:225). A similar set of basic overlapping research topics would help to focus the future excavation, analysis, and interpretation of Hopewell single-household settlements in Ohio and elsewhere, and to shape the next generation of corrections, critiques, expansions, and variations on the alternative general models proposed for Middle Woodland settlement systems in Ohio and elsewhere:

1. seasonality of occupation;
2. range of activities carried out;
3. size and composition of the occupying group;
4. duration of occupation;
5. subsistence base of the occupying group;
6. integration of household settlements within larger socioeconomic contexts;
7. indications of higher-order extraction of time, labor, and energy resources from dispersed household settlements.

This list is not meant to imply that Hopewell researchers have not been addressing these interrelated issues, but rather, to suggest that it would be worthwhile to explicitly structure future research within more formal logical frameworks of archaeological inference and to take full advantage of the wide range of different approaches and relevant data sets for each of these problem areas that have been employed over broad expanses of space and time, with varying degrees of success, by archaeologists interested in single-family-household settlements.

There are a variety of ways, for example, of framing and addressing the question of sedentism or permanence of occupation of small household settlements throughout the annual cycle, and a variety of different criteria or test implications of seasonality of occupation have been proposed. Cowan (this volume) presents a very interesting potential measure of occupational duration or sedentism, involving the relative abundance of formal bifaces, bladelets, and expediency flake tools in chipped stone tool assemblages. It will be interesting to see how Cowan's ratio lines up with other measures of relative sedentism, on a case-by-case, site-by-site basis. Do bladelets simply substitute for expediency flake tools in overall site artifact and feature assemblages that are otherwise quite comparable? When available, do potentially "ritually loaded" craft-specialty bladelets make the profane transition over into utilitarian duty as substitutes for flakes? Or do sites that differ in terms of flake versus bladelet abundance also consistently present quite different overall feature and artifact assemblage profiles?

Weighing the relative strength of supporting arguments for alternative hypotheses regarding the sedentary nature of Hopewell sites clearly should not be reduced to a simple "either-or" consideration of a single criterion or a simple choice between sedentary versus nonsedentary. Rather, a full profile assessment of all of the relevant indicators of seasonality of occupation should be carried out within a context of carefully defined alternative categories. At the present time, however, a polarity would appear in large part to be driving discussions of Ohio Hopewell settlements: either Hopewell households were very mobile and occupied numerous locales (and houselike structures) throughout the year (for example, Cowan, this volume; Yerkes, this volume), or they lived in permanent year-round hamlets of fully sedentary households (Dancey and Pacheco, this volume). Excavations of small Hopewellian habitation sites both in Ohio and in other midlatitude regions of the eastern United States, however, provide a range of possibilities that encompasses both of these extremes.

Excavated evidence from small Hopewellian habitation sites in Ohio and in many other regions of the Eastern Woodlands, from Kansas City to the Duck River, appear to cluster closely with the Pacheco and Dancey model (for example, Fortier, this volume; Logan, this volume; Ruby, this volume; Smith 2002). In contrast, recent research in more northerly areas is yielding a growing body of evidence for a range of less sedentary, more seasonal Middle Woodland habitation sites, likely linked to exploitation of seasonally abundant wild plant and animal resources, with a lesser reliance on crop plants. In their summary of Goodall tradition settlements in northern Indiana, for example, Mangold and Schurr (this volume) describe a seasonal pattern of movement between riverine marsh and marsh-edge settings and shorter-term upland sites targeting wetland resources, concluding that "occupations in the Kankakee Valley were shorter-term than was the case for sites in the central and lower Illinois Valley." Further, Mangold and Schurr (this volume) argue, "While populations may have briefly aggregated on the marsh margins and islands for up to several months at a time, the idea that mound group sites represent some sort of permanent agricultural settlement severely overestimates the degree of sedentism in the Goodall settlement system." Similarly, Garland and DesJardins (this volume) describe mostly small, seasonal Middle Woodland encampments along the southwestern Michigan drainages of the St. Joseph and Kalamazoo Rivers, with only the Simpson site on the Portage River perhaps representing a more substantial longer-term occupation. Farther north, in the Grand and Muskegon valleys of western Michigan, Brashler and colleagues (this volume) present a general Middle Woodland model of more permanent base camps near major rivers and dispersed fall and winter exploitation of upland resources. Excavation of the Prison Farm site on the Grand River provided evidence of intermittent warm-season occupation targeting both sturgeon and white-tailed deer.

The ongoing polarized debate regarding the relative permanence of Hopewell settlements in Ohio also serves to focus attention on the nature of the still largely underdocumented shorter-term camps and limited-activity sites of Hopewell groups in Ohio and elsewhere. If Yerkes (this volume) is correct, such sites should be abundant and should reflect a seasonal round of brief occupational episodes keyed to seasonal availability of resources across a range of river valley and upland habitats. I think it is far more likely, however, that most short-term Ohio Hopewell sites will fall into the category of cold-season upland hunting camps that were tethered to growing-season household hamlets. This general category of cold-season habitation sites, which has been a fairly standard component of settlement-pattern models for many different time periods and regions of eastern North America, could be expected to exhibit considerable diversity, with the length of occupation and the size and composition of occupying groups varying from year to year and from region to region in response to a range of cultural and environmental factors (for example, Carskadden and Morton 1997). If Hopewell households, or segments of them, in Ohio or elsewhere shifted residence to varying degrees from year to year between growing-season hamlets and upland cold-season camps, it would be difficult to identify or quantify such shifts through analysis of hamlets alone, since there are so few clear seasonal markers of occupation for the winter months. Griffin (1979:278) posed this problem quite eloquently more than twenty years ago: "Someone ought to investigate where many of these populations *hibernated* because they seem to have operated only in the spring, summer, and fall." This difficulty in distinguishing between permanent year-round Ohio Hopewell household settlements and less sedentary and more variable alternatives serves to open up the middle ground of interpretive categories that should be considered between the options of "full sedentism" and "full mobility" and also serves to underscore the need for more excavation and focused, full-profile problem-oriented analysis of intact hamlets and short-term seasonal settlements.

Hopewell Subsistence

In his contribution to this volume, Richard Yerkes poses another set of either-or categorical options for Ohio Hopewell under the general heading of subsistence: were they hunter-gatherers or agriculturalists? For more than a decade, however, most researchers writing on the topic have recognized that there are more than these two choices, and Hopewell economies have been placed somewhere out in the vast conceptual middle ground between hunting-gathering and agriculture. A number of scholars have explored and charted this in-between landscape in general terms (for example, Ford 1985b; Harris 1989, 1990, 1996; Smith 2001; Zvelebil 1993, 1995, 1996), but questions still remain regarding the most appropriate terms and labels to be used in describing it. One might easily be "bedeviled by confusion over the meanings attributed to such terms as agriculture, cultivation, domestication, and food production" (Harris 1989:11). The hunting-gathering and agriculture borders on either side of this middle ground have also been variously and often rather vaguely drawn, but several straightforward boundary definitions can help in the general characterization, labeling, and placement of Hopewell subsistence: hunting-gathering-foraging groups are defined as relying exclusively on wild species of plants and animals, whereas agricultural societies derive at least 30 to 50 percent of their annual caloric intake from domesticates (Smith 2001). A number of terms have been used to describe Hopewell as well as other societies that appear to fall between these boundary lines for hunting-gathering and agricultural econo-mies—for example, complex or affluent hunting-gathering, incipient agricul-ture, horticulture, cultivation, gardening, plant husbandry, farming, food pro-duction, and so forth (Bender 1985b; Dancey and Pacheco 1997a; Ford 1979, 1985b; MacNeish 1991; Smith 1992a; Stoltman and Baerreis 1983; Wymer 1997). Of all of these different labels and characterizations, "food production" is in my opinion the most useful in that most scholars have employed it in a generally consistent manner over the past sixty years. Food procurement (hunt-ing-and-gathering economies) and food production thus constitute a first-order division. Food production can then be further subdivided into agriculture (do-mesticates more than 30–50 percent of annual caloric budget) and low-level food production. Within this classification system, Hopewell societies are nei-ther hunter-gatherers nor agriculturalists but fall comfortably onto the land-scape of low-level food production.

Once this polarizing, hunting-gathering/agriculture debate is bypassed in this manner, and the middle ground is opened up, several interesting if obvious ques-tions regarding the subsistence economies of Hopewell societies come into clearer focus as promising areas of future research. Given the initial, general low-level food production profiles that have now been developed for Hopewell societies in Ohio and other midlatitude areas of the Eastern Woodlands (for example, Dancey and Pacheco 1997a; Ford 1985b; Fortier, this volume; Pacheco and Dancey, this volume; Ruby, this volume; Smith 2002; Wymer 1997), for example, what patterns of variation will be discerned in the future through detailed comparison of individual household settlements? Was the adaptive stance of Ohio Hopewell households as uniform and as stable, and their environmental settings as homogenous across Ohio, as Pacheco and Dancey (this volume) suggest, or were there substantial differences from house-hold to household? Styles' (1981) site catchment studies of Illinois early post-Hopewell faunal assemblages have shown considerable variation in the econo-mies of individual household settlements, which appear to have been strongly shaped by relative species abundance of close-in habitat zones. It will be interest-ing to see to what extent patterns of variation in household economies of Ohio Hopewell societies correlate with different environmental settings across Ohio and with specific site catchment profiles. While certainly difficult, it would also be interesting to see if Ohio Hopewell household economies vary in affluence due to any number of factors, including relative richness of the resource catch-ment zone and the size, composition, and competence of individual households and their position in society (for example, in regard to craft specialization, at-tained positions of authority, and so forth). On a larger scale, it will also be interesting to see to what extent the documented pattern of regional variation in the relative importance of different crop plants in the economies of Middle Woodland societies across the East continues to hold up, as the admittedly small sample of analyzed sites in Ohio and other regions is increased. This question of the extent to which Middle Woodland societies in different regions of the East emphasized different crop plants (that is, chenopod, erect knotweed, little barley, maize, marsh elder, maygrass, squash, and sunflower; Smith 1992a:207) and how much intraregional, between-household variation existed also serves to raise the more general issue of the nature and range of variation in Hopewell reliance on crop plants across space and time. Did any Hopewell societies or individual households approach the agricultural border zone of 30–50 percent reliance on crop plants? Unfortunately, it is still difficult to establish with any degree of confidence the relative range of dietary contribution of crop plants to Hopewell groups and their exact role within the larger context of continuing reliance on wild plant and animal species.

Just as interesting, of course, is the growing body of negative evidence regarding the very limited to nonexistent reliance on crop plants by Middle Woodland societies situated north of about latitude 40° north (for example, Brashler et al., this volume; Garland and DesJardins, this volume; Mangold and Schurr, this volume). Similarly, societies south of latitude 34–35° north exhibit a lower dependence on food production and crop plants (Fritz 1990). These societies north of 40° and south of 35° provide an interesting adjacent and contemporary referent class to the more crop-reliant Hopewell societies of the intervening 35–40° north latitude band. Somewhat farther afield, the various responses by Late Archaic through Basketmaker societies of the American Southwest, as they differentially layered elements of both indigenous and introduced low-level food production strategies onto preestablished hunting-and-gathering economies, provide an interesting full-profile context of comparison for Eastern Woodlands Hopewell groups (Smith 2005).

It is, of course, the low-level, food-production-fueled societies that flourished across the midlatitude temperate forest zones of Europe during the Mesolithic to Neolithic transition, however, that provide the most compelling opportunities for full-profile comparison with midlatitude Hopewell "farmers." Within the economic sphere, for example, how do these respective European and eastern North American societies, occupying roughly similar deciduous forest ecosystems, match up in terms of relative reliance and seasonal focus on both various classes of wild taxa (for example, mast, nut, and seed harvests; migratory waterfowl; fish; small and medium-sized mammals; and deer) and small-seeded crop plants (Harris 1996; Price 2000; Zvelebil 1993, 1995, 1996)? Beyond the economic sphere, a range of other broad brush-stroke societal similarities could be pursued, including ideology and worldview, material culture, spatial organization of households and communities, corporate labor projects, trade, craft specialization, and so forth.

The Zone of Intersection

One of the most intriguing and as yet largely unexplained aspects of Hopewell society involves the organizational context within which individual household units participated in integrative corporate labor projects, including, most notably, the construction of community-scale wooden and earthen structures (Smith 1992a:243). It is also within this zone of intersection between the household/domestic and corporate/sacred spheres of Hopewell, particularly in Ohio, that some of the most interesting recent research has been undertaken, particularly at Stubbs (Cowan, this volume), at the Hopewell Mound Group (Burks and Pederson, this volume), and at the Fort Ancient site (Connolly 1997; Lazazzera 2000).

This work raises a number of general aspects or logical categories of inquiry regarding the conceptual, behavioral, and spatial zone of intersection between dispersed single-family household units and community nodes of integration and corporate labor. From the perspective of outlying household settlements, for example, how was their contribution of labor to community building projects structured and scheduled? While some households would have been within easy day-trip distance of their corporate labor commitments, many others would have had to relocate, for a period of time, adjacent to the community construction site. Did individual households fulfill their labor commitments as part of a larger kin-based unit? Perhaps the multihousehold tributary valley–scale kin groups proposed by Dancey and Pacheco (1997a) and loosely grouped under the "hamlet" label formed the suprahousehold kin-unit basis of corporate labor contributions in Ohio and beyond. What was the duration of such "multihousehold/hamlet" residential relocations to construction sites? Was it a few weeks, a few months, or longer? At what seasons of the year were they scheduled? Were their labor contributions measured in terms of time spent, or dirt moved? Did entire households relocate, or were corporate labor levies targeted at particular age-grade and gender categories? Was corporate labor carried out in intensive, short, seasonal bursts, involving sizable segments of the total community, or did construction take a more measured pace, with various multihousehold "tributary hamlet"–scale groups cycling through the corporate labor pool? It is at least theoretically possible that test implications and archaeological correlates of such alternative patterns of community labor-pool scheduling might actually be evident in the archaeological record. One might fantasize, for example, about uncovering an ordered linear sequence of settlements along the outside edge of Ohio Hopewell geometrical earthworks, which paralleled and marked the progress of its construction and reflected the size, composition, organization, and duration of such corporate labor construction crews. Given its scale, extent, and relative isolation, the "Great Hopewell Road" (Lepper, this volume) would appear to offer ample opportunities to investigate the sociopolitical settlement signatures of Ohio Hopewell community construction projects.

Judging from the nature of the evidence for occupation within 300 meters of the Hopewell Mound Group, however, documenting the nature of visits to ceremonial centers by outlying household units may prove challenging. In their synthesis analysis of surface collections and shovel-testing studies carried out over the past twenty-five years, Burks and Pederson (this volume) find little evidence of habitation sites of any substantial duration. Despite reflecting a relatively wide range of domestic activities, the low-density debris clusters adjacent to the Hopewell site are quite variable in composition, providing support for Seeman's (1981c) model of short-term occupational episodes by small groups participating in ritual and ceremonial activities.

The cluster of house structures described by Lazazzera (2000) at the Fort Ancient site, in contrast, comes close, in many respects, to an abstract prediction profile of what one might expect for a "labor-levy" settlement at the scale of a tributary-stream, multihousehold kinship-grouping "hamlet" scale of organization. The arrangement of the rectangular rounded-corner habitation structures in circular fashion around an apparent open plaza suggests both contemporaneity and a suprahousehold kin grouping, while the presence of a variety of attributes characteristic of outlying "sedentary" hamlets supports Lazazzera's domestic habitation designation (that is, evidence of structure repair and/or rebuilding, midden dumps, hearths and central earth ovens, storage and other pit features). This arrangement of houses and households at Fort Ancient, along with another nearby householdlike feature described by Lazazzera, as well as those discussed by Connolly (1997), raises a number of other interesting aspects of the functional role and classification of structures in the zone of intersection between the sacred and the mundane in Ohio Hopewell society (Connolly 1997:269). Does the house cluster at Fort Ancient represent the long-term relocation of outlying households related to their work on the Fort Ancient earthwork, or could it instead be a "permanent" settlement of a kin group that resided at Fort Ancient? There is certainly no reason to necessarily expect Ohio Hopewell earthworks to be pristine and sacred precincts that witnessed only temporary encampments of outlying households as they cycled through the community labor pool. If some segments of an extended Hopewell community did reside full time in the close vicinity of earthworks and mortuary precincts, is there any way to distinguish between them and outlying households that were cycling through? Would such resident households and multihousehold societal segments have enjoyed differential status within Hopewell societies and perhaps have played some role in the organization and coordination of community ritual and labor? If so, what material culture and structural/contextual correlates of such differential status and responsibility might be expected to distinguish these households from the general populace? A complex and probably overlapping array of different public or community roles can be considered in the abstract as having been filled, in part or in various combinations, by one or more individuals and largely played out within the zone of intersection. Who served as the repository of architectural and geometrical knowledge, and who designed and staked out the varied construction templates? Who followed through with the scheduling and oversight of construction? Where did the responsibility lie for the provisioning of the labor force? Who scheduled and managed feasts and other ceremonies, at various scales of community inclusion, that marked the completion of sequential construction stages? How were the acquisition of exotic raw materials and the manufacture of ritual objects and mortuary goods accomplished? Who oversaw the proper conduct and associated rituals of mortuary programs (Brown, this volume)?

Taken together, these and other complex and potentially overlapping roles, and the range of corporate initiatives and activities that they framed, should no doubt in turn be reflected in equally complex and overlapping structural and material-culture correlate patterns within the zone of intersection. As a result, I think it will continue to be a challenge for some time to come to further develop full-profile "functional" characterizations and categories, at various levels of generalization, for "houselike" structures and other delimited activity areas of this zone of intersection (for example, circular wooden enclosures, stone pavements, and so forth). Given the very limited number of such structurally defined activity areas that have as yet been uncovered in the vicinity of Hopewell earthworks and mound centers, and the considerable diversity of forms that have been observed, it is still too early to either attempt very detailed pattern recognition or to be too specific or too confident in structural or activity set characterizations. Lazazzera (2000), for example, is appropriately careful in her assessment of the structure cluster at Fort Ancient. Weighing a number of similarities to the admittedly still small referent class of outlying household settlements in terms of structures, features, material culture assemblages, and refuse disposal patterns, she concluded that the Fort Ancient cluster most likely reflects long-term domestic habitation. In the absence of opportunities for comparison to other, finer-scale referent classes within the general category of "domestic habitation," however, it is difficult to say whether the location of the house cluster inside the earthwork at Fort Ancient serves to distinguish it as representing a "resident" group as opposed to being the signature of an outlying suprahousehold unit temporarily coalesced to fulfill corporate labor obligations. Similarly, it is difficult to recognize any distinguishing artifactual or structural correlates of various suprahousehold corporate roles (for example, the shaman; see Brown, this volume) or responsibilities that might distinguish this structure cluster as being different from the "ordinary" household clusters that might be predicted, if not yet documented.

In the same way that Lazazzera's (2000) internal structure cluster at Fort Ancient provides a basis on which to frame an initial general outline of expectation of what corporate labor-levy multihousehold settlements might look like, so too does another structure she describes provide a template for what public structures that were the focus of ceremonies associated with corporate labor might look like. This structure's larger size, more substantial construction, evidence of at least five episodes of rebuilding and renewal, spatial isolation, and placement close to the embankment wall all suggest a ceremonial function. Its apparent ceremonial function in turn opens up consideration of other general conceptual classes or categories of structures and associated activities in the zone of intersection, both domestic and ceremonial. If such ceremonial structures and other ritual spaces (for example, pavements or wooden enclosures) were the location of ceremonies of social integration and interaction, and if they drew in outlying households to mark completion of different segments of corporate labor projects, what would the temporary housing of the visiting households look like? How would the archaeological signatures of such temporary ritual-centered visitations differ from those of longer-term domestic habitation clusters, either resident or corporate labor-levy related (for example, Burks and Pederson, this volume; Cowan, this volume)? Depending on how often and for how long outlying households were drawn in for labor contributions, as opposed to various ceremonies, there might have been considerable overlap in the use (and archaeological signatures) of houses in regard to these general classes of activities.

On a related question, where did responsibility rest for the procurement and preparation of feasting foods to sustain visiting households during ceremonies, and to what degree was this distinct and separate from the necessary long-term provisioning of corporate labor-levy groups? Certainly the recent quite provocative pollen profiles from Fort Ancient ponds that indicate that stands of small-seeded crop plants may have been grown within the earthwork (McLaughlan 2000b) raises the possibility that resident households may have been involved in provisioning corporate labor crews. If so, it will necessitate a substantial expansion of our interpretation of what went on within the walls of Ohio Hopewell enclosures.

In a similar manner, it might also remain difficult to accurately discern or differentiate between the various ceremonial roles of individual public structures and spaces in the zone of intersection. It would seem reasonable to invoke spatial proximity and to assume that structures and other ceremonial spaces (and the activities they witnessed) adjacent to or within earthwork enclosures were associated with construction ceremonies in the same way that structures adjacent to or within burial mounds were linked to mortuary programs. But few if any Ohio Hopewell scholars would express much confidence that there is as yet even a basic understanding of the full range of community ceremonies carried out in the zone of intersection, much less the extent to which they can be structurally, spatially, temporally, and conceptually distinguished.

To add further complexity to the zone of intersection, one need only add in a number of other structural forms, including variously scaled wooden post enclosures, sweat houses, crematory structures, charnel houses, and specialized workshops (Jefferies, this volume). It is important to keep in mind the considerable opportunities for creative variation in the organizational structure and coordination of Hopewell corporate labor and other efforts of social integration, both through time and between communities: "The view of Hopewell communities as evolving but relatively stable landscapes suggests many possible alternatives for inter- and intra-community interaction" (Lazazzera 2000).

Future progress toward understanding the organizational structure of Hopewell corporate labor and community integration should also benefit from new explanatory frameworks formulated for generally comparable situations in other regions. Perhaps most interesting and potentially applicable in this regard is Wills' (2000) recent provocative reassessment of the organizational context of corporate labor in Chaco Canyon during the eleventh and twelfth centuries A.D. Wills' insights regarding Chaco Canyon are relevant to Ohio Hopewell, I would argue, not only in terms of providing an interesting and plausible explanatory context for Hopewell community integration and corporate labor contexts, but also in underscoring the value of broadly and actively seeking out potentially applicable research and referents beyond eastern North America.

In stark contrast to the currently prevailing consensus consisting of competitive leadership models proposed by competition theorists over the past two decades, Wills (2000:24, 41–42) argues that social labor for communal production in Chaco society between A.D. 1020 and 1140 in fact reflected "communitas," the central importance of domestic life and a suppression of internal competition and competitive ritual that was achieved by emphasizing "cyclical, repetitive obligations to the community as a whole and by removing wealth from the control of individuals" (Wills 2000:24). Such corporate labor efforts were standardized, intensive, seasonal, repetitive, and part of a calendrical cycle of community activity, with scheduling based in part on structurally embedded astronomical alignments. Such massive, communal construction projects "exceeded the lifetime of any community member, and indeed, probably continued through multiple generations, indicating that the organization and conduct of this activity were not linked to any particular person or leader but rather were ingrained in Chacoan social structure" (Wills 2000:35). Wills further observes that such calendrical collective-labor commitments involved large numbers of participants coordinated in a predictable, stable ritual pattern of corporate activity, with the allocation of social labor building efforts broken down into many discrete projects carried out by different social subunits (Wills 2000:35–36). Rather than necessitating a strong central authority, Wills argues, decision making was likely structured within small networks of nonoverlapping "patches," with each patch free to pursue its own solutions to assigned construction tasks. When combined, collective ritual and patched decision-making networks could provide an effective solution for nonliterate societies involved in massive long-term construction projects involving the coordination of small, dispersed, relatively autonomous production units:

If the construction process was conceptualized by the participants as a ritual activity, predictable in time and space, its purpose sanctified and symbolic of corporate obligation, then those production roles could have been identified with roles in the ritual system. A calendrical cycle of group participation in predictable, standardized activities would have at least reduced the coordination complexity, and may have enhanced its efficiency. . . . The results of such a collective process could be quite impressive but need not have involved very much institutionalized structure or an elaborate political organization. (Wills 2000:38)

While the conceptual framework of community interaction, ritual systems, and the contexts of group labor outlined by Wills was developed for specific application to Chaco Canyon, I think it can also be seen to have considerable potential application to Hopewell societies, particularly in Ohio. There are a number of other interesting parallels between the two that are worthy of mention. In both places, for example, harvesting and transporting a substantial number of large timbers as construction materials played a central role in corporate labor. Wills has the luxury of being able to accurately chart the pace of such harvesting, transport, and construction through hundreds of great-house dendrochronological dates, in contrast to the situation in Ohio, where any fine-grain chronology of Hopewell corporate construction is still a distant dream. Another interesting point raised by Wills, which would appear relevant to both Chaco and Hopewell, is that the organizational properties of the ritual system itself, rather than any individuals or segments of society, may have driven new construction projects and that cycles of construction would have become self-perpetuating: "[O]nce the organization for producing great houses [or Hopewell earthworks] was in place, it continued to generate these buildings or enlargements of them for as long as labor (or energy) was available" (Wills 2000:39).

Discussion

As the contributions to this volume clearly indicate, new research initiatives from different perspectives and at different scales of analysis hold great promise for yielding new insights regarding the Middle Woodland period societies of eastern North America, particularly within the three broad and overlapping problem domains discussed above: (1) the organizational structure and archaeological signatures of Hopewell households and larger kin-group units; (2) the nature of subsistence economies of the midlatitude band between latitude 35° and 40° north, which combined low-level food production with a strong reliance on wild species of plants and animals; and (3) the social and temporal contexts of construction and use history of earthworks, mounds, and mound-capped wooden structures, including the organization of household units within corporate frameworks of cooperation and integration, as reflected in the structures and activity areas of the zone of intersection.

There is, admittedly, only very limited archaeological information as yet available from different regions of the East for any of these three problem domains. As a result, new information such as the inside-the-embankment pond pollen profiles (Mclaughlan 2000b) and structure clusters (Lazazzera 2000) at Fort Ancient can rapidly and substantially sharpen our perspectives and interpretations. Within the first two of these problem domains, a range of different general models of Hopewell subsistence economies and household, hamlet, and community organization has been outlined and provides a significant foundation for future research. It will be important over the next decade or so to keep in mind that these initial general models are a first approximation. Their substantial value will be in encouraging and expanding documentation of spatial and temporal diversity in Hopewell subsistence and the distribution of households across the landscape. One would hope that they will not be used to submerge and obscure variation under general monolithic labels but rather will be employed as templates of expectation for seeking the patterns of variation that exist. Rather than posing simple either-or questions to be answered with new excavations and new evidence (for example, were Hopewell societies sedentary or mobile, hunter-gatherer or agricultural?), these models should instead frame and focus future research on a range of more specific questions and encourage the search for relevant archaeological test implications. As the amount of available information increases, analysis and interpretation, as well as debate and discussion, should continue to naturally migrate away from initial models toward more specific and more detailed second-generation sets of alternatives that encompass and coalesce around emerging patterns of variation in subsistence and community structure that developed across the Eastern Woodlands through the Middle Woodland period.

In the remaining and perhaps most exciting problem domain, which involves the life history and sociopolitical context of construction of Hopewell corporate structures, first-generation general models are just beginning to take shape. In this volume, Brown, Byers, Greber, Lepper, Pacheco and Dancey, Seeman and Branch, and Van Nest have outlined thoughtful and provocative interpretive viewpoints on these general topics, and recent and ongoing excavations within the zone of intersection of Hopewell societies is providing a wealth of relevant new information. It is clear that Hopewell societies will continue to offer difficult and often frustrating intellectual challenges for many future generations of scholars, providing complex historical developmental and sociopolitical organizational puzzles, and as yet unrecognized temporal-spatial patterns of variation. A constant stream of newly uncovered data and relevant new ideas and perspectives from research conducted across the East, as well as work focused on societies far removed from Hopewell in time and space, will provide ample fuel for this ongoing search for understanding.

28

Middle Woodland/Hopewell

A View from beyond the Periphery

Robert Chapman

What do the chapters in this volume tell us about the current state of Middle Woodland archaeology and Hopewell studies? Such a question might seem rather presumptuous, perhaps even pointless, coming as it does from a nonspecialist with a limited knowledge of the archaeological record of the eastern United States. I was invited to the conference by Jane Buikstra to give a plenary address and, in her words, "reflect on funerary behavior and trade, from your own perspective and experience from your side of the big pond." Having survived that ordeal, I now want to recast my comments and criticisms in a way that I hope will be useful to Middle Woodland/Hopewell specialists. I try to identify what I think are the main themes of study and how they have changed over recent decades, as well as situating them within the wider context of theoretical and methodological issues in contemporary archaeology. How do the archaeological records of the living and the dead and of exchange in Middle Woodland North America and Neolithic Europe compare with each other? How useful is such a comparison? There is evidence that European approaches have become more influential in Middle Woodland archaeology in the past decade (for example, Buikstra, Charles, and Rakita 1998), and I would like to highlight some critical problems with their application. I offer this view from beyond both the Hopewell core and periphery in the hope that (1) the comparative approach to these themes is of interest to Middle Woodland/Hopewell archaeologists, and (2) it might provoke discussion about the current state of Middle Woodland/Hopewell archaeology. The focus of this chapter is deliberately selective and by no means covers all the approaches presented in this volume.

Taking the Pulse of Middle Woodland/Hopewell

There have been several major conference publications on Middle Woodland/ Hopewell archaeology in modern times (for example, Brose and Greber 1979; Dancey and Pacheco 1997b; Pacheco 1996b), as well as seminal papers (for example, Struever and Houart 1972) and analyses of mortuary rituals and ceremonialism (for example, most recently Buikstra, Charles, and Rakita 1998).

Reading these publications makes it clear that two models have set the agenda for Middle Woodland/Hopewell archaeology in the past four decades. The first of these is Olaf Prufer's vacant center model (renamed by Dancey and Pacheco as the dispersed sedentary community model) for Ohio Hopewell settlement patterns. This still provokes debate nearly forty years after it was proposed in a doctoral dissertation (for an overview see Dancey and Pacheco 1997a). Both excavation and surface survey have been used to evaluate the utility of the model for the distribution of Hopewell populations at the beginning of the first millennium A.D.

Second, the economic and social relationships among these Ohio populations, and between what have become known as the Hopewell core and periphery, have been pursued using the model of the interaction sphere, first proposed by Caldwell (1964) and then elaborated for Hopewell by Struever and Houart (1972). Whether we view the interaction sphere in terms of basic economics or of more ideological and symbolic factors, it is still widely used and has undoubtedly led to much research on Hopewell artifacts.

I would also argue that the theoretical basis of Hopewell and Middle Woodland studies during the past four decades has tended to be ecological and focused on whole social systems, usually of a neo-evolutionary kind, whether tribal or chiefdom societies. It has also been proposed that exchanges of goods functioned to build and maintain the social alliances required as "insurance" in case of subsistence difficulties (Brose 1979), although other scholars have argued that the "exotic" goods used in these exchanges occurred in numbers that were too limited to fulfill this function (Spence, Finlayson, and Pihl 1979). Characterization analyses have been widely employed to document the nature and extent of these exchange networks. Overall I have the impression that through much of the 1960s, 1970s, and 1980s, Hopewell and Middle Woodland studies were focused on ecological systems; on the infrastructure rather than the superstructure; on materialism rather than idealism; and, with Robert Hall (for example, 1976, 1979) as the principal exception, with comparatively little attention devoted to ideology. As Van Gilder and Charles have expressed it, "Hopewell, as a 'cultural' phenomenon, has been increasingly viewed as an epiphenomenon" (2003:121).

In publications of the 1990s, leading right up to and including the present volume, I see evidence for greater concern with symbolism and ideology; with sacred space and cosmology; and with the "knowledgeable actors," factions, classes, age and gender groups of practice and structuration theory, rather than the social types of neo-evolutionary theory (for example, Buikstra, Charles, and Rakita 1998:77–95). As Brown (this volume) puts it, "it is time to insert some cultural content" into Hopewellian studies. These changes are beginning to be seen more widely in the eastern United States, as, for example, in recent books on the Mississippian by Emerson (1997a), Pauketat and Emerson (1997), and from a slightly different perspective, Muller (1997).

In all these cases there is much wider citation of, and influence from, English literature of what is called postprocessual archaeology. However, I would not want to argue that this implies that postprocessualism is the most "evolved" of the three "types" of archaeology (traditional, processual, postprocessual) and that it is now going to "triumph" in the eastern United States.

First, as I argue elsewhere (Chapman 2003), I am unhappy with this static and mutually exclusive typology of archaeology and of archaeologists. It struggles to account for variation in archaeological theory and practice within Anglo-American archaeology, let alone in the non-English-speaking archaeologies that are overridden by intellectual colonialism or marginalized by language and publication (see also Politis 2003). Individual archaeologists are allowed no freedom of thought and action, no agency, in the pursuit of their research. It is as if we imagine them trapped within hermetically sealed paradigms. As I have tried to document in relation to models of society and social change, ongoing traditions of thought such as neo-evolutionism, Marxism, and practice theory have become more permeable as archaeologists have adopted concepts from other traditions and tried to build intellectual bridges between them (Chapman 2003:33–70). Others have also argued that processual and postprocessual archaeologies are more compatible than has been claimed in the past (for example, Hodder 1991a:37, 1999:12; Preucel 1991, 1995; Tschauner 1996; Van Pool and Van Pool 1999).

Second, and in line with these arguments, Hegmon (2003:217) argues that "theoretical allegiance is not a major issue" in North American archaeology, as concepts associated with the British postprocessualism of the 1980s (for example, symbolism, meaning, agency, gender, internal causes of social change, focus on more specific causes and historical sequences, as well as the search for generalization) have been integrated into mainstream practice, what she calls "processual-plus" archaeology. In surveying contemporary archaeology in North America (including examples from Middle Woodland/Hopewell), Hegmon (2003:219) notes "an openness and dynamism that result from dialogue across theoretical lines," rather than the maintenance of incommensurable paradigms.

Given this wider context, as well as my observations above, I would suggest that changes in the past decade mark potentially the most radical shift in Middle Woodland/Hopewell archaeology since the 1960s and early 1970s. It may not yet be as radical as the changes seen in major recent monographs on the Mississippian, but that is very much in the hands of local practitioners.

A Theoretical Aside

This recognition of archaeological pluralism, in both thought and deed, is not meant to imply that we can adopt a "mix and match" approach whereby everything is compatible and intellectual bridges create a unified theoretical and methodological landscape. I will pause for a moment to give an example of what, for me personally, would be a bridge too far, as this also affects what I am going to discuss later in this chapter.

There is a critical aspect of what is known as postprocessual archaeology that is rooted in idealism: ideas are argued to exist independently of matter. The actions of people are determined by their interpretation of other people's actions. People respond to symbols, give meaning to them (whatever the meaning given to them by other people), and act according to their perception of these meanings. It is then argued that reality has no existence independent of the meanings that people give to symbols and signs. Reality does not exist; it is constructed. This rules out the evaluation of ideas against an exterior world of experience, as required by any science (whether hard or soft, natural or social).

I would argue that this perspective is both subjective and relativist and that the material world is independent of our perceptions, as proposed by realism; this is humorously defined by the philosopher of science Mario Bunge (1996: 335) as "the epistemology that all of us adopt tacitly when not under the influence of narcotics or anti-scientific philosophies"! I also try to follow the principles of materialism, by which I mean that "everything in the world is material or concrete, ideas being bodily (brain) processes" (Bunge 1996:282). We make use of symbols, and we give meaning to them, but this process occurs in the context of material constraints. Trigger (1998:8) has cited Childe in his point that "humans adapt to a symbolic world rather than to a real one . . . [but] this symbolic world has to correspond to the real one to a very considerable degree if a society was to survive." This does not mean that we neglect ideas and symbolism but that we follow the tradition of materialism and ground ideas and ideologies in the material factors of production and reproduction.

Categorization: The Link

What has all this talk of theory got to do with the topic of this volume? The link is categorization. In the Hopewell literature that I read, as in that of other areas and periods, human behavior and the activities of archaeological research are categorized, or polarized: life versus death, domestic versus ritual, settlement archaeology versus the archaeology of death, sacred versus secular landscapes, social versus subsistence, basic production versus exchange. We divide behavior up into these analytical categories, we specialize in their study, and yet we often neglect to mention that these are our categorizations, given our enculturation in present-day capitalist societies. Yet we know from anthropology that noncapitalist societies in modern times structure their existence in entirely different ways. Somehow we have to reconstruct very different pasts and be wary of overrigid categorizations that prevent us from reaching these other pasts. In studying death, we cannot neglect life, the contexts in which decisions were made about mortuary rituals, and the less exclusive divisions that were made between the living and the dead in past societies. In studying exchange and trade, we cannot neglect their relationships to production and deposition in the archaeological record.

A good example of the critique of such categorization is contained in Brück's (1999a, 1999b) study of the Bronze Age archaeological record in southern England. She argues against the assumption that ritual is "a distinct sphere of practice, separated spatially, temporally and conceptually from more day-to-day activities" (Brück 1999a:319). Instead ritual permeates daily practice in noncapitalist societies. This recognition affects our ability to make clear, exclusive distinctions between "settlement" and "ritual" sites in the archaeological record. To illustrate this, Brück (1999b:54–60) shows the difficulty in identifying a distinct category of "domestic" artifacts in Early Bronze Age contexts: for example, what is often regarded as "domestic" material (quern fragments, cooking pots) is found widely on henge monuments, which are usually attributed some kind of "ritual" function, and Beaker coarse pottery is found in contexts ranging from artifact scatters to burials and henges.

A similar approach is followed by Bradley, who argues against the conception of ritual as "something set apart from daily life, protected from scrutiny by its specialized procedures and connected with religious belief and the supernatural" (Bradley 2003:11) and which "involved special people, special places and a distinctive range of material culture" (Bradley 2003:13). Instead ritual, at least as far as it is studied in later prehistoric Europe, is viewed as action or practice in everyday life. Bradley cites several examples, such as the Neolithic enclosure at Sarup in Denmark, where the division of cultural materials into "utilitarian" and "nonutilitarian" types is done on an arbitrary basis to define successive "ritual" and "settlement" phases of occupation of the site. Interestingly, Bradley (2003:6–8) also documents how interpretation of the Neolithic henge monument at Durrington Walls in southern England has oscillated between that of a specialized ritual site and that of a major domestic settlement during the past three decades. Even the original excavator of the site has changed his mind about this on more than one occasion!

These issues of categorization will recur throughout this chapter. Having set the scene, I will now compare approaches to the study of the living and the dead in Neolithic Europe with those exemplified in this volume and elsewhere for Middle Woodland/Hopewell societies. What similarities and differences are there? How relevant and useful is such comparison? How far do such studies meet my materialist and realist expectations? And where does this leave the first of the two major models that have set the agenda for Middle Woodland/Hopewell archaeology? I begin with Neolithic Western Europe, so that readers can see how I am looking at Middle Woodland/Hopewell through the eyes of my own experience.

The Living and the Dead: Neolithic Western Europe

The archaeological record of Europe from circa 7000 B.C. seems to show two broad patterns of agricultural adoption (Whittle 1996). From Greece and the Balkans in the southeast through Central Europe to the Paris basin in the northwest, we see evidence of agricultural colonization, of radical changes in subsistence, settlement patterns, and material culture. In central and northern Italy, Spain and Portugal, much of France, the Low Countries, southern Scandinavia, and the British Isles, the adoption of cereal agriculture and stock breeding took place among indigenous populations of hunters and gatherers (for example, Arias 1999).

According to the "availability model" of Zvelebil and Rowley-Conwy (1986), the adoption of a full-scale agricultural economy in the absence of colonization took place over generations, centuries, and even millennia, depending not just on the local resource potential, but also on the social and economic structures of local populations of hunters and gatherers. For example, in many areas of Iberia, cave sites continued to be occupied and wild animals heavily exploited, and full-scale sedentism focused on open-air settlements, storage pits, and so forth did not appear for over a millennium. In southern Scandinavia there was no need for the immediate adoption of agriculture, given the broad spectrum of wild resources exploited by increasingly territorial, reduced-mobility hunters and gatherers. Even when cereal agriculture and stock breeding were fully adopted, there was no automatic movement to sedentism.

For much of Western Europe we cannot project back into the Early Neolithic the modern image of a rural, cleared landscape of sedentary villages surrounded by extensive field systems. For example, on the chalk downlands of Wessex there is evidence from pollen diagrams, faunal and floral remains, and artifact scatters of small-scale, scattered clearings in the pine and hazel woodland in the Early Neolithic and mobile populations depending heavily on animal husbandry. In the Stonehenge region this pattern is observed in the thousand years preceding the construction of the first monument at the end of the fourth millennium B.C., but farming does not appear to have become the most significant part of subsistence until the late third millennium B.C. (Cleal and Allen 1995). A similar trend is visible in the evidence from the Avebury region (Whittle 1997:140).

There are, however, exceptions to this model, most notably in areas of Ireland. Cooney (2000:20–51) has shown recently the widespread evidence for cereal production in the fourth millennium B.C., associated with field systems that seem to have been used for both arable cultivation and cattle grazing. There is also variation in the extent of woodland clearance and dependence on agriculture, as is shown not only for Ireland, but also for other areas of the British Isles. These observations lead Cooney to propose that the Wessex model of small cleared areas, perhaps connected by paths and trails through a mainly forested landscape, with wild and domesticated plant and animal resources being exploited somewhere along the spectrum between full mobility and sedentism, is only one regional model for Neolithic societies in Britain. Whatever the local situation, the dominant architecture in these Neolithic landscapes, whether in Britain or in adjacent areas of northwestern Europe, consisted of what are called ritual or funerary monuments.

Before we look at these ritual and funerary sites, let us pause and consider what exactly we mean by the use of the term *monuments*. The clearest definition I can find is the following: "a structure or edifice intended to commemorate a notable person, action or event." The key word is "*commemorate*," and the implications are that the structure will survive in time and that it acts as a symbol. It does not have to be a funerary monument, and by definition it does not have to be built on the grand scale.

What archaeologists define as monuments, however, tend to be large and the product of communal surplus labor: the pyramids of Giza, the Pyramid of the Sun at Teotihuacán, or the ziggurat at Ur. Archaeological monuments are conspicuous by their visibility in, and dominance over, the human landscape. They provide focal points for ritual activities. They may be manipulated by successive generations as they are rebuilt, enlarged, or even destroyed. New monuments of different style may be superimposed on old ones. In such ways the past is appropriated, changed, or even eradicated (Bradley 1993, 1998). Look at the destruction of monuments in the former Yugoslavia as part of the strategy of ethnic cleansing, or the statues of Saddam Hussein that were toppled in front of television cameras during the recent Iraq war. Monuments may also embody the appropriation of the distant and the exotic (for example, nineteenth-century colonial funerary monuments in Calcutta built in neo-Classical styles [Curl 1980]). Whether constructed exclusively as part of mortuary rituals or not, monuments are potent symbols to be used as part of social strategies.

Monuments in Neolithic Western Europe took a variety of forms (for examples of all the forms mentioned here, and many of the sites, see Bradley 1993). Earthen long mounds, some exceeding 40–50 meters in length, were erected over comparatively small timber and stone chambers for the deposition of single individuals or the members of local lineages in areas such as Poland, Denmark, northern France, and southern Britain. Other funerary monuments were covered by round mounds and either had sealed, central stone chambers or access via entrance passages. Many of these megalithic monuments stand today in proud isolation, dominating the landscape, any covering mounds long removed. In some cases, such as at Barnenez in northern France, multiple tombs were eventually incorporated in one impressive monument, with a stepped stone cairn that would have been visible for miles.

In addition to these funerary monuments, timber and stone circles and alignments were constructed mainly in the British Isles, northwestern France, and western Iberia. In Brittany there were individual, now collapsed, standing stones, such as at Locmariaquer, and parallel alignments of standing stones that extended for nearly 4 kilometers across the landscape at Carnac (Burl 1985). Stone circles vary in size and impressiveness, from coastal examples covered by rising sea levels, as seen at Er Lannic in Brittany (Burl 1985), to everybody's favorite, Stonehenge in southern Britain. What now becomes noticeable at places like Carnac and Stonehenge is the development over generations and centuries of what have been called "sacred landscapes," where monuments of different type and date are concentrated, appropriated, incorporated, or superseded. For example, the Carnac alignments incorporate at least two preexisting long barrows, rising up and over their mounds.

Finally, there is a series of "ritual" monuments that are increasingly specific to the British Isles. Causewayed enclosures—so called because of the interrupted ditches and internal banks that surround them—are known from circa 4000 B.C. (as are the earthen long barrows), and they are also known from adjacent areas of northwestern Europe. There is consistent evidence for feasting, exchange, and mortuary rituals from the ditches of these enclosures, leading to debates about the extent to which such sites could have been used for "domestic" purposes. In addition, from about 3500 B.C. in Britain there are the so-called cursus monuments, consisting of parallel ditches and banks: in the case of the Dorset cursus, some 80 meters apart and running 10 kilometers across the landscape. As with the Carnac alignments, the Dorset cursus was built in an earlier landscape of settlement and barrows and incorporated two barrows into it. Still later, the third millennium B.C. saw the construction of "henge" monuments, enclosed by deep ditches and external banks and with timber or stone circles inside them. The most famous of these henges are at Stonehenge and Avebury.

Stability and change are exhibited in the "life histories" of monuments. As has been pointed out many times before (for example, Barrett 1994), the monuments that we see today were not necessarily conceived as such. Indeed, to neglect their sequences of construction is to neglect their individual histories. For example, the final monument that we see today at Stonehenge did not dominate the landscape in its initial phase of construction; this dominance was not achieved until some five hundred years later (Cleal and Allen 1995). As the stone monument we see today, it then lasted for a thousand years, giving a sense of permanence while major changes in society and culture took place in the surrounding region.

Barrett (1994) and Edmonds (1993) also make the point that we focus our attention on the physicality of monuments, on their finished form at various stages, but that the very acts of construction of these stages were also important, in terms of the expenditure of social labor and the maintenance or creation of social relations. These phases of construction—each in turn a potential phase of destruction—often embody evidence for feasting, the deposition of specific artifacts, and the manipulation of remains of the dead.

The extent to which the monumental places of Neolithic Western Europe can be referred to as "ritual" rather than "secular" landscapes is a matter of debate, especially given the critical points made above about categorization. For Stonehenge, for example, the distribution of both monuments and surface materials suggests that what we would call "ritual" and "secular" (or "domestic") activities took place across the same landscape with no clearly demarcated spatial divisions (Cleal and Allen 1995).

In addition to the kinds of studies of the living and the dead that have been mentioned so far, there are approaches to the analysis of Neolithic monuments that need to be mentioned here. First, there is the search for origins. Shared monumental forms imply shared cultures or belief systems, and the spread of these populations or ideologies is measured by typological analysis. One problem with such typological analysis is that the normal assumption of increasing complexity of form with time has been shown by radiocarbon dating not to work for the earliest types of megalithic tombs in southern Scandinavia (Persson and Sjögren 1995).

Second, there is the use of indices of energy expenditure in the construction of these monuments and in the production of the grave goods and offerings that are deposited in them. Renfrew (1973b) argued that the sequence of monuments in southern Britain during the Neolithic documented an increase in energy expenditure and, by inference, in social complexity. Some of the barrow mounds, for example, were clearly much greater in size than was necessary for covering and supporting the burial chamber.

Third, European megalithic tombs have been treated as territorial markers, as material expressions of group identity and of the presence of the ancestors, and thus as claims of access to resources such as land (Renfrew 1973a, 1976; Chapman 1981, 1995). Using megalithic tombs as surrogate settlements, Renfrew (1973b) divided up the landscape of the islands of Arran and Rousay into hypothetical territories. What is open to question in such an analysis is the extent to which the tombs actually map the location of settlements and whether, as has been discussed above, the basis of the economy was full-scale sedentary agriculture at this time. Such tombs may have been associated with particular groups of people (and their ancestors), but they were not necessarily the centers of defended areas.

For the moment I will leave aside a fourth approach, namely that of phenomenology, but I will turn to this after looking at what Middle Woodland/Hopewell studies might glean from the landscape of the living and the dead in Neolithic Europe.

The Living and the Dead: Middle Woodland/Hopewell

I hope that the reader will already have noticed some of the resonances between the archaeological records of Neolithic Western Europe and Middle Woodland/Hopewell of the Eastern Woodlands of North America. These are especially visible in the subsistence-settlement systems that are dominated by monuments, the historical emphasis on these monuments as centers for "ritual" activity, and the reference to "sacred" landscapes. In both areas the study of the monuments has moved from an initial focus on their origins (the megalith/mound builders) to ones based on their social, territorial, and ritual contexts. In looking from my European home to Middle Woodland/Hopewell, I would like to discuss the subsistence-settlement system and then make some brief comments on chronology and on categorization.

Pacheco and Dancey (this volume) reaffirm the details of their updated version of Prufer's (1964a) model for Ohio Hopewell. According to this model, low-density, dispersed, but sedentary communities of households—with subsistence based on a diet of wild animals and plants, as well as a small range of domesticates—came together at "socially prescribed central places" at particular times to maintain and reaffirm social interaction and integration founded on lineage-based descent groups. In contrast, both Cowan (this volume) and Yerkes (this volume; see also Yerkes 2002a) argue against sedentism, with the construction of earthworks and the rituals associated with them being the means by which social integration was maintained. Notice that the broad function of the earthworks is the same, but the societies building them are more at the mobile, tribal, and hunter-gatherer end of the spectrum, rather than the sedentary, farming, chiefdom-level societies often portrayed for Neolithic Europe. Clearly this is a focus of ongoing debate (see below), but I would point out that (1) the evidence from Britain and Ireland cited above allows for more than one subsistence-settlement system associated with early monument construction, and (2) the size and composition of the area covered by Middle Woodland/Hopewell would surely have supported more variation than is seen in a simple mobile hunter-gatherer/sedentary farmer dichotomy.

How can research move forward to clarify the nature of the subsistence-settlement system or systems at this time? Both Cowan (this volume) and Burks and Pederson (this volume) show one way, which is via closer examination of artifact scatters and nonmound structural evidence found inside and adjacent to the earthwork sites. Surface survey, coring, and testing are going to have to be accompanied by larger-scale excavation to allow clearer definition and interpretation of occupation types and densities, as well as of the nature of deposition (for example, structured, placed, dumped, "killed") of material culture. How far do the earthworks demarcate activity differences? How far are any such distinctions imposed or changed by the construction of all or parts of these earthworks? Other lines of evidence include seasonality of occupation, feasting, and differences in access to production, as analyzed by Holt (this volume) on the basis of faunal remains from the Illinois Valley (interestingly, arguing against the existence of a "vacant" ceremonial center for this region). The burials (to which I return below) can also provide critical data on biological distance, diet, and mobility (at least between birth and death), as has been demonstrated for Neolithic Europe.

This brings us to chronology. Using the European experience, I have argued above that monuments are palimpsests of construction and structural remodelling over time ("life histories") and that they embody the materialization of social practices through social labor. The individual acts of construction are not additions based on some predetermined plan but draw on, sustain, or change the commemorative symbolism. European archaeologists have developed detailed sequences of monument use, based upon both small- and large-scale excavations and upon radiocarbon dating. One of the benefits of the latter has been to show how monument forms do not necessarily "evolve" in neat sequences but overlap and may be contemporary with each other (for example, Persson and Sjögren 1995). Dating on human bone has enabled us to refine the chronologies of use and deposition in funerary monuments, as well as to measure differences in diet, biological distance, and mobility.

Reading through the chapters I could not help but notice the number of authors who stress the sketchy relative and absolute chronologies of Middle

Woodland/Hopewell throughout the eastern United States. Both types of chronologies are necessary to track construction phases and labor investment in monuments and the deposition of material culture within them, let alone the extent to which monuments at different phases were as visible or dominant in the landscape as they appear in their final stages. For the major Ohio Hopewell sites, Greber (2003:89) sums it up succinctly in stating elsewhere that "radiocarbon dates cannot yet verify the construction sequence at any site, nor fix the generation that acquired each exotic material, nor establish the relationships among the sites through time." As she points out here (Greber, this volume), we do not know the number of enclosures that were in use at the same time. It is clear from her chapter in this volume, as well as from those of Riordan and Van Nest (compare Buikstra, Charles, and Rakita 1998), that the detail of relative chronology also has much to tell us about the symbolic aspects of monument construction (for example, the color of deposits), which can be expressed at a very fine scale of individual layers that are concealed within the final monument.

Clearly the refinement of the relative and absolute chronologies of Middle Woodland/Hopewell sites is a major challenge, but one that will illuminate the study of monuments at a variety of scales (for example, local/regional) and in relation to a variety of problems. As I mentioned above, the analysis of later prehistoric human burials in Europe has provided an efficient source of short-lived samples for AMS radiocarbon dating, coupled with data on diet (through carbon and nitrogen isotopes) and mobility (through the analysis of strontium and oxygen isotopes). If such material is preserved from the "classic" Hopewell burials associated with the "exotic" goods, then there is a means to date their deposition.

This is the point at which North American readers may take a deep breath, knowing the political complexities of excavation and analysis of burials, and ignore the last paragraph. I have no idea of the practicalities of securing both the materials and the permission to analyze them. All I can do here is note the advantages to research to carry out such dating and analysis, alongside other dating on short-lived samples (see Greber 2003 for examples).

Finally, I return to categorization. Several authors in this volume address the issue, directly or indirectly. At both Tunacunnhee (Jefferies, this volume) and Mann (Ruby, this volume), the excavators note the absence of any clear spatial distinction between "ritual" and "domestic/mundane" activities, although the definition of these different categories is left open. The distinction between "domestic" sites and the "vacant ceremonial centers," which has underpinned one of the two main models for Middle Woodland/Hopewell archaeology, is also problematic, given the arguments presented above about ritual as practice in daily life. Clearly activities did take place in and around these "centers." The use of the term "sacred landscape" has appeared in publications on both sides of the Atlantic, and while it moves us away from such thought, it still separates the "sacred" as ritual in some form from the "domestic." It would be far better to follow Seeman and Branch (this volume) and use the term "cultural landscape." Taking all these examples together, theoretical and empirical reasons can be produced to argue that the kinds of categories that we use to "do" Middle Woodland/ Hopewell archaeology, as elsewhere in the study of precapitalist societies, require both scrutiny and revision. Let us take landscape as an example and see what we might learn from its current study in Western Europe.

Experiencing Monuments and Landscapes

Within the past decade, the focus of the study of Neolithic monuments in Britain in particular has changed. Instead of their study in terms of origins, social complexity, and territory, the emphasis has switched to their implications for a sense of place, that is, of culturally constructed landscapes that embody the ancestors, are manipulated through time, and are invested with symbolic meaning (for example, Ashmore and Knapp 1999; Brück and Goodman 1999; Cooney 2000; Thomas 1991); of their links to cosmology (for example, Whittle 1997); and most important, of their use to "orchestrate human experience" (Bradley 1993:48). Landscape is viewed as a context for the enculturation of each generation (Cooney 2000:6).

According to this perspective, the division between culture and nature is blurred, and landscape is experienced differently by individuals and groups depending upon their age, gender, class, and so forth (for example, Thomas 1991): there are many landscapes, and these may be contested by such groups (for example, Bender 1992). What are also blurred are the kinds of formal distinctions I mentioned earlier, such as those between ritual and domestic spheres. The meaning of monuments and, indeed, of the cultural landscape as a whole varies according to the position, context, and knowledge of people. Monuments may also change their meaning through time, even though they have the same form. The archaeological study of meaning in monuments and landscapes has been approached through phenomenology, defined by Tilley as "the understanding and description of things as they are experienced by a subject" (1994:12). This "experiential" view is contrasted to the "bird's eye view" of monuments (Cooney 2000:91), by studying them from the inside as opposed to the outside, experiencing them rather than observing them.

This argument develops to point out that the form and layout of monuments in the landscape have the potential to determine different experiences, as well as patterns of social inclusion and exclusion. This gives rise to questions such as who had access to particular monuments, what could be seen of the ritual activities that were carried out inside monuments by those outside (for example, Barrett 1994), and how did the layout of monuments determine the experience of them by people of different social groups? How did movement to, between, in, and around monuments determine different experiences (for example, Bender 1992)? In Bradley's (1993:48) words, patterns of movement in and around monuments are "formalized." In the case of Neolithic monumental tombs, the size and layout of internal passages and chambers meant that few individuals could participate in some of the rituals, and many would not be able to observe the rituals from outside. Access to the art within them, and the symbolism it embodied, was also restricted by available space and light (Bradley 1989). In henges, the substantial banks around them prevented people outside from witnessing the rituals taking place inside (Barrett 1994). Knowledge and experience are argued to have been part of strategies of social power.

Examples of this phenomenological approach include Tilley's (1994) studies of tomb and cursus monument locations in Wales and southern Britain and Barrett's (1994) study of movement along one of the main access routes, the stone-lined Kennett Avenue, to the henge monument at Avebury. One detailed observation is that visibility of the interior of the monument is restricted not only by the topography and the surrounding bank, but also by the design of access: the avenue approaches the monument obliquely, and only at the last moment does it change direction to face one of the entrances (Barrett 1994:15–17).

There is no doubt in my mind that this new approach has highlighted different and interesting new data about British Neolithic monuments. The observation that tomb interiors are restricted in size and access is not, of course, a new or stunning observation, but detailed studies of other monuments—showing how far the interiors, or even the monuments as a whole, were visible from which directions and over what distances—have yielded illuminating insights. Indeed, the visibility of such monuments is sometimes accentuated by the use of building stone of striking or contrasting colors (Jones 1999). The focus is now on these monuments and their surrounding landscapes in three rather than two dimensions. Even subtle changes in microtopography can make a marked difference to our understanding of monument location.

The problem, for me, is the subjectivity that examples of this approach can embody, the relativism that they can imply, and the idealism that focuses purely on changes of meaning. I have read student dissertations recently in which claims are made for the visibility, or otherwise, of prominent parts of the landscape, summer and winter solstices, and so forth, without a robust methodology. Fleming (1999) has taken Tilley (1994) to task for failure to give detailed attention to sample quality and observational rigor in his study of the location of Welsh megalithic tombs in relation to natural places in the landscape. He also criticizes Tilley for not proposing alternative hypotheses for the observed tomb locations. It is one thing to define a pattern of site location in relation to the landscape, but it is quite another to evaluate which is the more reliable explanation for that pattern. A more sound methodology compares the actual location of monuments against points in the landscape where they do not occur (for example, Watson [2001] on the location of henge monuments in Britain).

The subjectivity of experience, and the notion that we may share such subjectivity with individuals and groups in quite different cultural and historical contexts, has also been criticized. For example, Criado and Villoch (2000:212) argue against what they call "transcultural subjectivity" and the attempt to reconstruct (experience) the prehistoric meanings of monuments. Instead they prefer to analyze the constraints and opportunities of landscapes (for example, in terms of visibility, patterns of movement, ease of access) against the cultural imposition of Neolithic monuments.

What is more, we are into research overload on ritual monuments without a secure grounding in the material world of production. For example, as I mentioned earlier in this chapter, causewayed enclosures in Denmark have been argued to show more evidence of what we call domestic activity through time. To explain this, Hodder (1988:71) proposes that "the idea of settlement agglomeration and communal centers first came about in a ritual context" and that "later practical activity could build on the initial statement" of ritual activity. Assuming that we can make such clear distinctions between ritual and domestic (see above), how did this settlement agglomeration come about? How did production support this? Where is the material basis for this change in "ideas"? Unless we can answer these questions, I fear that we will not approach a fuller understanding of prehistoric monuments.

If we avoid notions of "transcultural subjectivity" and a pursuit of "meaning" based on idealism, then how might these approaches be useful to Middle Woodland/Hopewell archaeology? Given that the landscape is cultural (and as such plays a role in enculturation) and that earthworks and enclosures occupy prominent positions in that landscape, we can propose that their location and layout were important in this process. Where exactly were they located, and why there in preference to other possible locations? How did their layout "map on" to topography and microtopography (in the latter case, quite subtle distinctions can make all the difference on a local scale)? How were movement and access formalized and constrained? How visible were these monuments across the landscape and from which directions? Could they be seen from the "domestic" sites? How visible were activities being carried out inside the earthworks to anyone outside of them? Given the assumption that all communities used these earthworks for purposes of social integration, we might expect them to be large enough to contain such populations and to be visible to as many people as possible. How far did vegetation impede visibility? Were all earthworks located in clearings? How did their visibility in the landscape change with (to use Riordan's [this volume] concepts) successive additions, augmentations, and alterations? While I understand that such questions, if they are to be tackled in the field, face up to the problems of earthwork preservation, these are not insuperable. There are the records of early explorers and excavators of earthwork sites, and these give us more than a simple two-dimensional picture. Observations that such an earthwork location is visible from varying distances and directions are of value, even without precise data on its original height.

Exchange as a Category: The Hopewell Interaction Sphere Revisited

I cannot remember exactly when I first heard of the Hopewell Interaction Sphere (HIS). Both Winters (1968:219) and Struever (1968b:308) cited the concept, but I think that it was the late David Clarke who suggested I read the paper by

Struever and Houart (1972). Among a group of contemporary graduate students, I was interested in explanations for the styles of Beaker pottery and the distributions of Beaker assemblages in third-millennium B.C. Central and Western Europe. The paper by Struever and Houart seemed to provide us with a new concept and an analogy for some of the patterns that we were trying to understand in our own data. Clarke (1976) led the way, replacing talk of Beaker "cultures" with that of a Beaker "network," of "prestige" and "social status," although he cited neither Caldwell (1964) nor Struever and Houart (1972). Although the formal process of citation was lacking (but see Case 1977:79), the concept of the interaction sphere had now been "translated" from the Midwest to the European continent (as was suggested by Caldwell [1964]). Struever and Houart's (1972:47) seminal paper began by rejecting the concept of "a unitary 'Hopewell Culture' that stretched from New York to Kansas, from Michigan to Florida." Although distinctive artifact types, raw materials, and mortuary practices occurred across this area of eastern North America, there was regional variation in cultural forms and ecological adaptations. The HIS concept accounted for interregional interaction between localized cultures. By their (distant) sources, shared styles, forms, energy expenditure, and depositional contexts, the distinctive HIS materials were interpreted as "status-specific objects which functioned in various ritual and social contexts (including burial) within community life" (Struever and Houart 1972:49). As opposed to local "subsistence technologies," the HIS artifacts "functioned in the social subsystem where they served integrational or social maintenance tasks" (Struever and Houart 1972:50). The material exchanges by which such social integration was maintained occurred through a hierarchy of regional and local transaction centers.

Much of the detail of Struever and Houart's paper was devoted to the identification of such centers, given problems with Hopewell chronology, and with recognition of regional differences in the frequencies and distributions of Hopewell artifacts (Struever and Houart 1972:57, Table 1). The extent to which these differences were "real" or the result of differences in research activity was not, I think, made clear. Local specialization in artifact production was also identified, as, for example, in the case of the ceremonial spears, obsidian, quartz, and mica artifacts at the Hopewell site (Struever and Houart 1972:69). The complexity in the data patterning suggested that the Hopewell Interaction Sphere "was not a single homogenous unit . . . throughout the area from New York to Kansas, Michigan to Florida" but instead "a number of interaction networks, of different types and on different scales" (1972:60).

As I stated earlier, the Hopewell Interaction Sphere has become one of the two major "agenda-setters" of Middle Woodland archaeology during the last three decades. It has been subjected to critique and revised in the form of a symbolic and ideological system (Seeman 1979b), as well as stimulating stylistic (for example, Braun 1991b), distributional, and compositional analyses. Like all the concepts that we use in the social sciences, the challenge is to see how far the Hopewell Interaction Sphere remains useful in accommodating new data, in bringing order and structure to it, and in enabling us to tackle interesting questions at different scales of analysis.

A good example of new data comes in the form of source characterization studies of obsidian, one of the best-known Hopewell exotics. The total number of pieces from Middle Woodland/Hopewell sites has now risen to several thousand, and those analyzed to source, as Hughes (this volume) reports, have risen to four hundred, a marked increase over the results published by Griffin, Gordus, and Wright (1969) and Hatch and colleagues (1990). In some cases there are marked concentrations of obsidian, as for example in the 136 kilograms of artifacts and debitage found in Hopewell Mound 11, but elsewhere the majority of the material comes from superficial contexts, as in the Illinois Valley.

This issue of sample size and context is important, as has been shown in the central Mediterranean during the Neolithic. There, competing sources existed on four islands, from which raw materials and finished products were supplied by sea and land to communities within hundreds of kilometers, but only exceptionally up to nearly a thousand kilometers away. Tykot (1996) has recently demonstrated how increased sample size of provenanced obsidian has expanded the range of sources found in contemporary use at the same sites. Intensive surface collection and excavation has also increased the sample size of artifacts and debitage from individual sites (for example, the potential for "thousands" of obsidian pieces, based upon surface collection, at Gaione in northern Italy [Tykot 1996:67]). As a result, the patterning that has to be explained in terms of the processes of trade and interaction has become more complex. Changes in that patterning through time have to be incorporated into any models. The early "down-the-line" model of Hallam, Warren, and Renfrew (1976) has to be revised to accommodate the larger sample size of obsidian and sourced obsidian.

The characterization analyses reported by Hughes (this volume) strengthen the hypothesis that multiple source locations were exploited for Hopewell obsidian, although over 90 percent still come from Yellowstone, some 2,400 kilometers away. Source use may be related to artifact class, thereby suggesting a rationale for the selection of pieces for source characterization. Differences also exist in the extent to which obsidian is worked and reworked on Hopewell sites, either by source type (the Bear Gulch material comes in as finished products) or by region (the Ohio Hopewell "core" as opposed to the "periphery"). When these factors are taken into account alongside obsidian hydration dating (Hatch et al. 1990), as well as the problems of chronological resolution, it looks increasingly difficult to sustain Griffin's "one-shot" hypothesis.

A focus only on exotics gives us a limited picture of exchange networks, although Fie's (this volume) analyses of pottery from the Illinois Valley will help to widen our knowledge of the scale, intensity, direction, and distance of movement of material goods. But beyond characterization, and all the problems raised in its interpretation (for example, Earle and Ericson 1977; Ericson and Earle 1982), there are arguments that spatial patterns of artifacts were ones of deposition first and exchange second, and that the distributions of artifacts cannot be understood outside of their contexts of production, exchange, and deposition. Once again the categorization of archaeological materials and specialisms has gotten in the way of a more holistic analysis.

The best example of this approach that I know from European archaeology is the work of Perlès (1992) on exchange and the organization of production in Neolithic Greece. Although published over ten years ago, it is still a model of analysis to which few have aspired. Perlès analyzed the production, circulation, and deposition of a variety of artifacts and raw materials, from the flaked stone industries through fine pottery wares to ornaments and rare exotica. For example, production was broken down into parameters such as the localization of production centers, technical knowledge and investment, the level of specialization, the stylistic investment, and the quantities actually produced. Comparisons were then made between different periods of the Neolithic. These data on production were then compared with the use and deposition, as well as the circulation and distribution, of each raw material and artifact.

As a result of these analyses, Perlès (1992:149) observes that the differences between the stone assemblages, pottery, and ornaments and exotica are such that "they invalidate the hypothesis of a single exchange system, operating in terms of an invariable mode of exchange and fulfilling a single socioeconomic function." Thus the stone tools were the products of specialist knappers, exchanged with an economic purpose between all segments of the populations, and were not being used in symbolic or ritual contexts; the pottery developed in a mainly nonutilitarian context, with regionally distinctive styles, and seems to have been used in the context of social interaction and alliance; while the ornaments and scarce exotica were the result of at least some specialized production, were used in a symbolic or ritual context, and were exchanged over long distances in small numbers, as predicted by the prestige goods model of exchange. Changes are also observed between the successive periods of the Neolithic over three and a half thousand years.

Apart from the need to link production, exchange, and deposition, what does all this mean for the Hopewell Interaction Sphere? New analyses bear out Struever and Houart's (1972) idea of multiple interaction networks of different types and scales. The kinds of compositional analyses that were lacking when they wrote their paper have multiplied in the past thirty years. Alternative proposals of the mechanisms by which goods circulated and were deposited in the Middle Woodland period have been put forward. But is the concept of the Hopewell Interaction Sphere still of any use to us?

I am reminded of the fact that when the modern discipline of archaeology first developed in Western Europe, it was based on a system of technological stages, from Stone Age to Bronze Age to Iron Age. These were subdivided during the later nineteenth and earlier twentieth centuries. Then attention shifted to variation between populations within these stages, leading to a focus on the definition of regional "cultures." By the 1960s and 1970s, the extent to which these cultures defined "peoples" was severely questioned, and we turned our attention to society and processes of change. The terminology of technological stages and cultures still permeates the literature, however. They are taken as "given," even though the theoretical assumptions on which they were based have been questioned. We still see books published on the Neolithic (for example, Thomas 1991; Whittle 1996) or Bronze Age (for example, Harding 2000). The proponents of the latest theoretical approaches propose novel interpretations using the same units of analysis, the cultures, as the authors they criticize. The best examples of this are Hodder's (1990) book on early European agriculture and Thomas' (1996) book on Neolithic societies.

Ideally our units of analysis should relate in some explicit way to the questions we are asking, the theories we employ, and the scale of our analyses. We should also be looking to see how far existing units stand up to the test of subsequent data accumulation. Logically there should be both replacement of such units and the addition of new ones to existing units. My impression of the archaeological world is that we are often better at the latter than the former.

The Hopewell Interaction Sphere has been a potent concept, in that it has stimulated three decades of archaeological research. It remains widely used as a taxonomic unit, a "building block" of research in the eastern United States, and it is embedded in the archaeological literature. Scholars appear to be content to follow Caldwell and Struever and Houart in recognizing a large-scale unit of interaction between regional "cultures." The model that lay behind the concept of the Hopewell Interaction Sphere has stimulated research on characterization, on production and style, on elite and non-elite interaction, and on competitive trading alliances, as we have seen in these chapters. The result is that the structure and content of the Hopewell Interaction Sphere (that is, the archaeological record that requires interpretation) have become more complex. The focus now moves to the nature and scale of interaction; the organization of production, exchange, and deposition; and the expression of identity (whether of culture, gender, class, and so forth) from the interregional to the regional and from the top to the bottom. Instead of being concerned with models that move down through regional centers, attention is switching, I suggest, to models that build on local social practices, on production, and on social reproduction and move upwards (just as in the study of European Beakers). How such local practices combined to create panregional patterning could be one of the major challenges facing research on the Hopewell Interaction Sphere during coming decades.

Challenges for the Future

As I have finished the last section by mentioning one challenge for future research on Middle Woodland/Hopewell, I end this chapter by suggesting five other such challenges:

1. the closer study of categories of thought, moving away from Western dichotomies such as ritual/domestic and sacred/secular;

2. the use of multiple lines of evidence to evaluate contrasting hypotheses on the subsistence-settlement system(s) of Middle Woodland/Hopewell;

3. the refinement of relative and absolute chronologies, allowing among other things more detailed accounts of the life histories of monuments;

4. the (re-?)insertion of cultural content, but with methodological rigor; and

5. the wider study of material goods beyond the famous interaction sphere exotics and the detailed relationship of their production, exchange, and deposition in the archaeological record.

Acknowledgments

I am indebted to Jane Buikstra for the invitation to attend the conference on "Perspectives on Middle Woodland at the Millennium," to the Center for American Archeology for covering my travel expenses and accommodation at Pere Marquette, and to Doug Charles for support and patience while I revised my paper for publication. I am grateful to Richard Bradley for reading through the chapter and suggesting some helpful revisions. I would also like to thank all the delegates for making a stranger feel so welcome. I enjoyed the conference immensely and learned a lot about Middle Woodland archaeology. Thank you all!

Bibliography

Abbe, C. 1869. The Earthworks of Fort Ancient. Unpublished manuscript and map on file at the Cincinnati Museum Center Research Library, Cincinnati, Ohio.

Adair, M. J. 2000a. Tobacco on the Plains: Historical Use, Ethnographic Accounts, and Archaeological Evidence. In *Tobacco Use by Native North Americans*. Edited by J. C. Williams, 171–184. Norman: University of Oklahoma Press.

———. 2000b. Woodland Period Farming in the Plains: Ethnobotanical Data and AMS Dates. Paper presented at the Plains Anthropological Conference, St. Paul.

Adams, W. R. 1949. *Archaeological Notes on Posey County, Indiana*. Indianapolis: Indiana Historical Bureau.

Ahler, S. R. 1992. The Hansen Site (15Gp14): A Middle/Late Woodland Site near the Confluence of the Ohio and Scioto Rivers. In *Cultural Variability in Context: Woodland Settlements of the Mid-Ohio Valley*. Midcontinental Journal of Archaeology Special Paper No. 7. Edited by M. F. Seeman, 30–40. Kent, Ohio: Kent State University Press.

Allman, J. C. 1957. A New Late Woodland Culture for Ohio—The Lichliter Village Site near Dayton, Ohio. *Ohio Archaeologist* 7:59–68.

Anderson, D. C., J. A. Tiffany, and F. W. Nelson. 1986. Recent Research on Obsidian from Iowa Archaeological Sites. *American Antiquity* 51:837–852.

Anderson, D. G. 1998. Swift Creek in Regional Perspective. In *A World Engraved: Archaeology of the Swift Creek Culture*. Edited by J. M. Williams and D. T. Elliott, 274–300. Tuscaloosa: University of Alabama Press.

Anderson, D. G., and R. C. Mainfort Jr. 2002a. An Introduction to Woodland Archaeology in the Southeast. In *The Woodland Southeast*. Edited by D. G. Anderson and R. C. Mainfort Jr., 1–10. Tuscaloosa: University of Alabama Press.

———, eds. 2002b. *The Woodland Southeast*. Tuscaloosa: University of Alabama Press.

Anonymous. 1925. An Archaeological Find. *Indiana History Bulletin* 2:16.

Anthony, D. W. 1990. Migration in Archaeology: The Baby and the Bathwater. *American Anthropologist* 92:895–914.

———. 1997. Prehistoric Migration as Social Process. In *Migrations and Invasions in Archaeological Explanation*. BAR International Series 664. Edited by J. Chapman and H. Hamerow, 21–32. Oxford: Oxford University Press.

Apfelstadt, G. A. 1971. Kuester Site Report. Manuscript on file, Glenn A. Black Laboratory of Archaeology, Indiana University, Bloomington.

———. 1973. Preliminary Investigations at the Kuester Site. *Proceedings of the Indiana Academy of Science* 82:86–90.

Arias, P. 1999. The Origins of the Neolithic along the Atlantic Coast of Continental Europe: A Survey. *Journal of World Prehistory* 13:403–464.

Arzigian, C. M. 1981. The Archaeology of Gran Grae: A Survey of the Valley and Headlands of a Small Stream in the Driftless Area, Crawford County, Wisconsin. *Wisconsin Archaeologist* 62:207–246.

———. 1987. The Emergence of Horticultural Economies in Southwest Wisconsin. In *Emergence of Horticultural Economies of the Eastern Woodlands*. Center for Archaeological Investigations, Occasional Paper No. 7. Edited by W. F. Keegan, 217–242. Carbondale: Southern Illinois University at Carbondale.

Asch, D. L. 1976. *The Middle Woodland Population of the Lower Illinois River Valley: A Study in Paleodemographic Methods.* Scientific Papers, No. 1. Evanston, Ill.: Northwestern University Archeological Program.

———. 1997. The End of Hopewell in Illinois: A Mortuary Site Chronology. Unpublished manuscript in author's possession.

Asch, D. L., and N. B. Asch. 1978. The Economic Potential of *Iva Annua* and Its Prehistoric Importance in the Lower Illinois River Valley. In *The Nature and Status of Ethnobotany.* Museum of Anthropology, Anthropological Papers 67. Edited by R. I. Ford, 301–340. Ann Arbor: University of Michigan.

———. 1985a. Archeobotany. In *Massey and Archie: A Study of Two Hopewellian Homesteads in the Western Illinois Uplands.* Research Series, Vol. 3. Edited by K. B. Farnsworth and A. L. Koski, 162–220. Kampsville, Ill.: Center for American Archeology.

———. 1985b. Archeobotany. In *Smiling Dan: Structure and Function at a Middle Woodland Settlement in the Illinois Valley.* Research Series, Vol. 2. Edited by B. D. Stafford and M. B. Sant, 327–401. Kampsville, Ill.: Center for American Archeology.

———. 1985c. Prehistoric Plant Cultivation in West-Central Illinois. In *Prehistoric Food Production in North America.* Museum of Anthropology, Anthropological Papers 75. Edited by R. I. Ford, 149–203. Ann Arbor: University of Michigan.

Asch, N. B., and D. L. Asch. 1985. Archeobotany. In *Deer Track: A Late Woodland Village in the Mississippi Valley.* Technical Reports 1. Edited by C. R. McGimsey and M. D. Conner, 44–117. Kampsville, Ill.: Center for American Archeology.

———. 1986. Woodland Period Archeobotany of the Napoleon Hollow Site. In *Woodland Period Occupations of the Napoleon Hollow Site in the Lower Illinois River Valley.* Research Series, Vol. 6. Edited by M. D. Wiant and C. R. McGimsey, 427–512. Kampsville, Ill.: Center for American Archeology.

Ashmore, W., and A. B. Knapp, eds. 1999. *Archaeologies of Landscape: Contemporary Perspectives.* London: Routledge.

Aston, M. 1985. *Interpreting the Landscape: Landscape Archaeology in Local Studies.* London: B. T. Batsford.

Aston, M., and T. Rowley. 1974. *Landscape Archaeology.* Vancouver: Douglas, David, and Charles.

Atwater, C. 1820. Description of the Antiquities Discovered in the State of Ohio and Other Western States. In *Archaeologia Americana: Transactions and Collections of the American Antiquarian Society,* Vol. 1, 105–267. Philadelphia.

Aument, B. W. 1992. Variability in Two Middle Woodland Habitation Sites from the Central Ohio Uplands. Paper presented at the 57th annual meeting of the Society for American Archaeology, Pittsburgh.

Aument, B. W., and K. Gibbs. 1991. *Phase III and Phase IV Data Recovery Survey of 33Fr895 and 33Fr901 on the Wal-Mart Property in Grove City, Franklin County, Ohio.* Report on file, Ohio Historic Preservation Office, and submitted to Wal-Mart Stores by Archaeological Services Consultants.

Baby, R. S., and J. A. Brown. 1964. Re-examination of the Mound City Group. Paper presented at the 29th annual meeting of the Society for American Archaeology, Chapel Hill, N.C.

Baby, R. S., and S. M. Langlois. 1979. Seip Mound State Memorial: Nonmortuary Aspects of Hopewell. In *Hopewell Archaeology: The Chillicothe Conference.* Edited by D. S. Brose and N. B. Greber, 16–18. Kent, Ohio: Kent State University Press.

Baerreis, D. A., and M. M. Bender. 1984. The Outlet Site (47DA3): Some Dating Problems and a Reevaluation of the Presence of Corn in the Diet of Middle and Late Woodland Peoples in Wisconsin. *Midcontinental Journal of Archaeology* 9:143–154.

Baker, F. C., J. B. Griffin, R. G. Morgan, G. Neumann, and J. L. B. Taylor. 1941. Contributions to the Archaeology of the Illinois River Valley. *Transactions of the American Philosophical Society* (n.s. 32, part 1).

Baker, S. W. 1978. The Gilead Site (33MW19): A Middle Woodland Component in North Central Ohio. *Ohio Archaeologist* 28:12–15.

———. 1993. 33PK153: Site Comparisons and Interpretation. In *Phase III Re-examination of Selected Prehistoric Resources and Phase II Testing of Flood Prone Areas Impacted by the Proposed PIK-32–13.55 Project in Seal Township, Pike County, Ohio (PID. 7563)*. Columbus: Cultural Resources Unit, Bureau of Environmental Services, Ohio Department of Transportation.

Barnes, G. L., and G. Dashun. 1996. The Ritual Landscape of "Boar Mountain" Basin: The Niuheliang Site Complex of North-Eastern China. *World Archaeology* 28:209–219.

Barrett, J. C. 1994. *Fragments from Antiquity: An Archaeology of Social Life in Britain, 2900–1200 BC*. Oxford: Blackwell.

Barry, L. 1972. *The Beginning of the West: Annals of the Kansas Gateway to the American West, 1540–1854*. Topeka: Kansas State Historical Society.

Barth, F., ed. 1969. *Ethnic Groups and Ethnic Boundaries: The Social Organization of Culture Differences*. Boston: Little, Brown.

Basso, K. H. 1996. *Wisdom Sits in Places: Landscape and Language among the Western Apache*. Albuquerque: University of New Mexico Press.

Baugh, T. G., and F. W. Nelson. 1988. Archaeological Obsidian Recovered from Selected North Dakota Sites and Its Relationship to Changing Exchange Systems in the Plains. *Journal of the North Dakota Archaeological Association* 3:74–94.

Bauxar, J. J. 1978. History of the Illinois Area. In *Handbook of North American Indians*, Vol. 15, *Northeast*. Edited by B. G. Trigger, 594–601. Washington, D.C.: Smithsonian Institution Press.

Becker, M. S. 1999. Reconstructing Prehistoric Hunter-Gatherer Mobility Patterns and the Implications for the Shift to Sedentism: A Perspective from the Near East. Ph.D. dissertation, Department of Anthropology, University of Colorado, Boulder.

Becker, M. S., and F. Wendorf. 1993. A Microwear Study of a Late Pleistocene Qadan Assemblage from Southern Egypt. *Journal of Field Archaeology* 20:389–398.

Beld, S. G. 1991. 20GR14: A Middle Woodland Site in Gratiot County, Michigan. *Michigan Archaeologist* 37:255–264.

———. 1993a. *Lyons Township Archaeological Survey, S-92–313*. Report on file in the Office of the State Archaeologist, Bureau of Michigan History, Michigan Department of State.

———. 1993b. Site 20IA37 (Arthursburg Hill Earthworks), Lyons Township, Ionia County, Michigan. In *Lyons Township Archaeological Survey, S-92–313*. Edited by S. G. Beld, 3–82. Report on file in the Office of the State Archaeologist, Bureau of Michigan History, Michigan Department of State.

———. 1994. Site 20IA37, Lyons Township, Ionia County, Michigan. In *Ionia County Archaeology, Phase II, S-93–319*. Edited by S. G. Beld, 2–39. Report on file in the Office of the State Archaeologist, Bureau of Michigan History, Michigan Department of State.

Bell, P. 1976. Spatial and Temporal Variability within the Trowbridge Site, a Kansas City Hopewell Village. In *Hopewellian Archaeology in the Lower Missouri Valley*. Publications in Anthropology, No. 8. Edited by A. E. Johnson, 16–58. Lawrence: University of Kansas.

Bell, R. E. 1959. More on Obsidian in Ohio. *Ohio Archaeologist* 9:137.

Bender, B. 1985a. Emergent Tribal Formation in the American Midcontinent. *American Antiquity* 50:52–62.

———. 1985b. Prehistoric Developments in the American Midcontinent and in Brittany, Northwest France. In *Prehistoric Hunter-Gatherers: The Emergence of Cultural Complexity.* Edited by T. D. Price and J. A. Brown, 21–57. San Diego: Academic Press.

———. 1992. Theorising Landscapes, and the Prehistoric Landscapes of Stonehenge. *Man* 27:735–755.

Bender, M. M., D. A. Baerreis, and R. L. Steventon. 1981. Further Light on Carbon Isotopes and Hopewell Agriculture. *American Antiquity* 46:346–353.

Bender, M. M., R. A. Bryson, and D. A. Baerreis. 1968. University of Wisconsin Radiocarbon Dates IV. *Radiocarbon* 10:161–168.

Benn, D. W. 1978. The Woodland Ceramic Sequence in the Culture History of Northeastern Iowa. *Midcontinental Journal of Archaeology* 3:215–283.

———. 1979. Some Trends and Traditions in Woodland Cultures of the Quad-State Region in the Upper Mississippi River Basin. *Wisconsin Archaeologist* 60:47–82.

Bennett, J. W. 1945. *Archaeological Explorations in Jo Daviess County, Illinois.* Chicago: University of Chicago Press.

Bense, J. 1998. Santa-Rosa Swift Creek in Northwest Florida. In *A World Engraved: Archaeology of the Swift Creek Culture.* Edited by J. M. Williams and D. T. Elliott, 247–273. Tuscaloosa: University of Alabama Press.

Berry, J. W. 1976. *Human Ecology and Cognitive Style: Comparative Studies in Cultural and Psychological Adaptation.* New York: Sage Books.

Bettarel, R. L., and H. G. Smith. 1973. *The Moccasin Bluff Site and the Woodland Cultures of Southwestern Michigan.* Museum of Anthropology, Anthropological Papers 49. Ann Arbor: University of Michigan.

Bettis, E. A., III. 1992. Soil Morphologic Properties and Weathering Zone Characteristics as Age Indicators in Holocene Alluvium in the Upper Midwest. In *Soils in Archaeology: Landscape Evolution and Human Occupation.* Edited by V. T. Holliday, 119–144. Washington, D.C.: Smithsonian Institution Press.

Bildstein, K. L. 1987. *Behavioral Ecology of Red-Tailed Hawks (Buteo Jamaicensis), Northern Harriers (Circus Cyaneus), and American Kestrels (Falco Sparverius) in South Central Ohio.* Biological Notes, No. 18. Columbus: Ohio Biological Survey.

Binford, L. R. 1962. Archaeology as Anthropology. *American Antiquity* 28:217–225.

———. 1964. A Consideration of Archaeological Research Design. *American Antiquity* 29:425–441.

———. 1971. Mortuary Practices: Their Study and Their Potential. In *Approaches to the Social Dimensions of Mortuary Practices.* Memoirs of the Society for American Archaeology, Vol. 25. Edited by J. A. Brown, 6–29. Salt Lake City: Society for American Archaeology. (Also issued as *American Antiquity* 36 [3, part 2].)

———. 1980. Willow Smoke and Dog's Tails: Hunter-Gatherer Settlement Systems and Archaeological Site Formation. *American Antiquity* 45:4–20.

———. 1982. The Archaeology of Place. *Journal of Anthropological Archaeology* 1:5–31.

———. 1983. *In Pursuit of the Past: Decoding the Archaeological Record.* New York: Thames and Hudson.

Birket-Smith, K. 1929. Drinking Tube and Tobacco Pipe in North America. *Ethnologische Studien* 1:29–39.

Bishop, R. L., R. L. Rands, and G. R. Holley. 1982. Ceramic Compositional Analysis in Archaeological Perspectives. In *Advances in Archaeological Method and Theory*, Vol. 5. Edited by M. B. Schiffer, 275–330. New York: Academic Press.

Blackman, M. J. 1992. The Effect of Natural and Human Size Sorting on the Mineralogy and Chemistry of Ceramic Clays. In *Chemical Characterization of Ceramic Pastes in Archaeology*. Monographs in World Archaeology, No. 7. Edited by H. Neff, 113–124. Madison, Wisc.: Prehistory Press.

Blair, E. H. 1916. *The Indian Tribes of the Upper Mississippi Valley and Region of the Great Lakes*. Cleveland: Arthur H. Clark.

Blank, J. E. 1965. The Brown's Bottom Site, Ross County, Ohio. *Ohio Archaeologist* 15:16–21.

Blosser, J. K. 1996. The 1984 Excavation at 12D29S: A Middle Woodland Village in Southeastern Indiana. In *A View from the Core: A Synthesis of Ohio Hopewell Archaeology*. Edited by P. J. Pacheco, 54–68. Columbus: Ohio Archaeological Council.

Bluhm, E. A., and A. Liss. 1961. The Anker Site. In *Chicago Area Archaeology,* Bulletin 3, 89–137. Urbana: Illinois Archaeological Survey.

Boas, O. V., and C. V. Boas. 1973. *Xingu: The Indians, Their Myths*. New York: Farrar, Straus, and Giraux.

Bogan, A. E. 1983. Evidence for Faunal Resource Partitioning in an Eastern North American Chiefdom. In *Animals and Archaeology,* Vol. 1, *Hunters and Their Prey*. BAR International Series 163. Edited by J. Clutton-Brock and C. Grigson, 305–324. Oxford: Oxford University Press.

Boszhardt, R. F. 1977. Wisconsin Radiocarbon Chronology—1976, Second Compilation. *Wisconsin Archaeologist* 58:87–143.

———. 1982. Wisconsin Radiocarbon Compilation Update, 1981, Mississippi Valley Archaeology Center, Inc. *Wisconsin Archaeologist* 63:128–152.

———. 1998a. Additional Western Lithics for Hopewell Bifaces in the Upper Mississippi River Valley. *Plains Anthropologist* 43:275–286.

———. 1998b. Oneota Horizons: A La Crosse Perspective. *Wisconsin Archaeologist* 79:196–226.

Boszhardt, R. F., J. L. Theler, and T. F. Kehoe. 1986. The Early Woodland Stage. *Wisconsin Archaeologist* 67:243–262.

Bourguignon, E. 1973. Introduction: A Framework for the Comparative Study of Altered States of Consciousness. In *Religion, Altered States of Consciousness, and Social Change*. Edited by E. Bourguignon, 3–35. Columbus: Ohio State University Press.

———. 1977. Altered States of Consciousness, Myths, and Ritual. In *Drugs, Rituals, and Altered States of Consciousness*. Edited by B. M. Du Toit, 7–23. Rotterdam: A. A. Balkena.

Bowers, A. W. 1965. *Hidatsa Social and Ceremonial Organization*. Bulletin 194. Washington, D.C.: Bureau of American Ethnology. (Reprint, Lincoln: University of Nebraska, 1992.)

Bowie, F. 2000. *The Anthropology of Religion*. Oxford: Blackwell.

Bradley, R. 1989. Darkness and Light in the Design of Megalithic Tombs. *Oxford Journal of Archaeology* 8:251–259.

———. 1991a. Monuments as Places. In *Sacred and Profane*. Monograph 32. Edited by P. Garwood, D. Jennings, R. Skeates, and J. Toms, 135–140. Oxford: Oxford University Committee for Archaeology.

———. 1991b. The Pattern of Change in British Prehistory. In *Chiefdoms: Power, Economy, and Ideology*. Edited by T. K. Earle, 44–70. Cambridge: Cambridge University Press.

———. 1993. *Altering the Earth: The Origins of Monuments in Britain and Continental Europe*. Edinburgh: Society of Antiquaries of Scotland.

———. 1996. Long Houses, Long Mounds, and Neolithic Enclosures. *Journal of Material Culture* 1:239–256.

———. 1998. *The Significance of Monuments*. London: Routledge.

———. 2003. A Life Less Ordinary: The Ritualization of the Domestic Sphere in Later Prehistoric Europe. *Cambridge Archaeological Journal* 13:5–23.

Braidwood, R. J. 1963. The Agricultural Revolution. *Scientific American* 203:130–141.

Branch, J. R. 2000. Patterns of Mound Distribution: The Cultural Landscape of Ross County, Ohio. M.A. thesis, Department of Anthropology, Kent State University, Kent, Ohio.

Brandy, L. W. 1976. Terrestrial Vertebrates. In *Environmental Analysis of Central Ohio—An Initial Approximation*. Edited by D. Anderson and C. King, 1–255. Columbus: Ohio Biological Survey.

Brashler, J. G. 1981. *Early Late Woodland Boundaries and Interaction: Indian Ceramics of Southern Lower Michigan*. Publications of the Museum, Anthropological Series, Vol. 3, No. 3. East Lansing: Michigan State University.

———. 1991. The Spoonville Site (20OT1): A New Look at Old Data. Paper presented at the Midwest Archaeological Conference, La Crosse, Wisconsin.

———. 1995. The Prison Farm Site, 20IA58: A Middle Woodland Occupation in West Central Michigan. Paper presented at the Midwest Archaeological Conference, Beloit, Wisconsin.

———. 1998. Excavations at the Prison Farm Site. Paper presented at the Midwest Archaeological Conference, Muncie, Indiana.

———. 2002. What Is the Converse Phase? Ceramics and Chronology at 20KT2. Paper presented at the 67th annual meeting of the Society for American Archaeology, Denver.

———. 2003. Ceramics. In *Phase III Archaeological Data Recovery for the U.S. 131 S-Curve Realignment Project, Grand Rapids, Michigan*. Report No. R-0446. Edited by M. J. Hambacher, J. G. Brashler, K. C. Egan-Bruhy, D. R. Hayes, B. Hardy, D. G. Landis, T. J. Martin, G. W. Monaghan, K. Murphy, J. A. Robertson, and D. L. Seltz, Section 5.0, 1–57. Report submitted to the Michigan Department of Transportation, Lansing, by Commonwealth Cultural Resources Group, Jackson, Michigan.

Brashler, J. G., and E. B. Garland. 1993. The Zemaitis Site (20OT68): A Stratified Woodland Occupation on the Grand River in Michigan. Paper presented at the Midwest Archaeological Conference, Milwaukee.

Brashler, J. G., E. B. Garland, and W. A. Lovis. 1994. Recent Research on Hopewell in Michigan. *Wisconsin Archaeologist* 75:2–18.

Brashler, J. G., and M. B. Holman. 1999. Middle Woodland Adaptation in the Carolinian/Canadian Transition Zone of Western Lower Michigan. Paper presented at the Midwest Archaeological Conference, East Lansing, Michigan.

Brashler, J. G., M. R. Laidler, and T. J. Martin. 1998. The Prison Farm Site (20IA58): A Woodland Occupation in the Grand River Basin of Michigan. *Midcontinental Journal of Archaeology* 23:143–197.

Brashler, J. G., and B. E. Mead. 1996. Woodland Archaeology in the Grand River Basin. In *Investigating the Archaeological Record of the Great Lake State: Essays in Honor of Elizabeth Baldwin Garland.* Edited by M. B. Holman, J. G. Brashler, and K. Parker, 181–249. Kalamazoo, Mich.: New Issues Press.

Braun, D. P. 1977. Middle Woodland–(Early) Late Woodland Social Change in the Pre-historic Central Midwestern United States. Ph.D. dissertation, Department of Anthropology, University of Michigan, Ann Arbor.

———. 1979. Illinois Hopewell Burial Practices and Social Organization: A Re-examination of the Klunk-Gibson Mound Group. In *Hopewell Archaeology: The Chillicothe Conference.* Edited by D. S. Brose and N. B. Greber, 66–79. Kent, Ohio: Kent State University Press.

———. 1981. A Critique of Some Recent North American Mortuary Studies. *American Antiquity* 46:398–416.

———. 1983. Pots as Tools. In *Archaeological Hammers and Theories.* Edited by J. A. Moore and A. S. Keene, 107–134. New York: Academic Press.

———. 1986. Midwestern Hopewellian Exchange and Supralocal Interaction. In *Peer Polity Interaction and Socio-Political Change.* Edited by C. Renfrew and J. F. Cherry, 117–126. Cambridge: Cambridge University Press.

———. 1987. Coevolution of Sedentism, Pottery Technology, and Horticulture in the Central Midwest, 200 B.C.–A.D. 600. In *Emergent Horticultural Economies of the Eastern Woodlands.* Center for Archaeological Investigations, Occasional Paper No. 7. Edited by W. F. Keegan, 153–181. Carbondale: Southern Illinois University at Carbondale.

———. 1988. The Social and Technological Roots of "Late Woodland." In *Interpretations of Cultural Change in the Eastern Woodlands during the Late Woodland Period.* Occasional Papers in Anthropology, No. 3. Edited by R. W. Yerkes, 17–38. Columbus: Ohio State University.

———. 1991a. Are There Cross-Cultural Regularities in Tribal Social Practices? In *Between Bands and States.* Center for Archaeological Investigations, Occasional Paper No. 9. Edited by S. A. Gregg, 423–444. Carbondale: Southern Illinois University at Carbondale.

———. 1991b. Why Decorate a Pot? Midwestern Household Pottery 200 B.C.–A.D. 600. *Journal of Anthropological Archaeology* 10:360–397.

Braun, D. P., J. B. Griffin, and P. F. Titterington. 1982. *The Snyders Mounds and Five Other Mound Groups in Calhoun County, Illinois.* Museum of Anthropology Technical Reports 13. Ann Arbor: University of Michigan.

Braun, D. P., and S. E. Plog. 1982. Evolution of "Tribal" Social Networks: Theory and Prehistoric American Evidence. *American Antiquity* 47:504–525.

Braun, E. L. 1916. Physiographic Ecology of the Cincinnati Region. In *Ohio Biological Survey,* Vol. 2, No. 3, Bulletin No. 7, 121–128. Columbus: Ohio State University.

Bray, R. T. 1963. Southern Cult Motifs from the Utz Oneota Site, Saline County, Missouri. *Missouri Archaeologist* 25.

Brewer, R. 1980. *Vegetation of Southwestern Michigan at the Time of Settlement.* Kalamazoo: Department of Biological Sciences, Western Michigan University.

Brine, L. 1894. *Travels Amongst American Indians, Their Ancient Earthworks and Temples; Including a Journey in Guatemala, Mexico and Yucatan, and a Visit to the Ruins of Patinamit, Utatlan, Palenque and Uxmal.* London: Sampson Low, Marston and Company.

Brinton, D. G. 1890. Folk-Lore of the Modern Lenape. In *Essays of an Americanist. I. Ethnologic and Archaeologic. II. Mythology and Folk Lore. III. Graphic Systems and*

Literature. IV. Linguistic. Edited by D. G. Brinton, 181–192. Philadelphia: David McKay.

Brockington, P. E. 1977. Culture Drift and Kansas City Hopewell Stone Tool Variability: A Multisite Analysis. Ph.D. dissertation, Department of Anthropology, University of Kansas, Lawrence.

Bronson, B. 1977. The Earliest Farming: Demography as Cause and Consequence. In *Origins of Agriculture.* Edited by C. R. Reed, 23–48. The Hague: Mouton.

Brose, D. S. 1977. *An Historical and Archaeological Evaluation of the Hopeton Works, Ross County, Ohio.* Report to the National Park Service (GX-6115–6–0410). Lincoln: Midwest Archaeological Center.

———. 1979. A Speculative Model of the Role of Exchange in the Prehistory of the Eastern Woodlands. In *Hopewell Archaeology: The Chillicothe Conference.* Edited by D. S. Brose and N. B. Greber, 3–8. Kent, Ohio: Kent State University Press.

———. 1990. Toward a Model of Exchange Values for the Eastern Woodlands. *Midcontinental Journal of Archaeology* 15:100–136.

———. 1994. Trade and Exchange in the Midwestern United States. In *Prehistoric Exchange Systems in North America.* Edited by T. G. Baugh and J. E. Ericson, 215–240. New York: Plenum Press.

Brose, D. S., J. A. Brown, and D. W. Penney. 1985. *Ancient Art of the American Woodland Indians.* New York: Henry N. Abrams.

Brose, D. S., and N. B. Greber, eds. 1979. *Hopewell Archaeology: The Chillicothe Conference.* Kent, Ohio: Kent State University Press.

Brose, D. S., and N. M. White. 1979. *Archaeological Investigations of Prehistoric Occupation in Caesar Creek Lake: Clinton, Greene, and Warren Counties, Ohio.* Cleveland: Cleveland Museum of Natural History.

Brown, C. E. 1912. Fourth Addition to the Record of Wisconsin Antiquities. *Wisconsin Archaeologist* (o.s.) 10:165–185.

———. 1923. Waukesha County: The Southern Townships. *Wisconsin Archaeologist* 2:69–119.

Brown, J. A. 1961. *The Zimmerman Site: A Report on Excavations at the Grand Village of the Kaskaskia.* Report of Investigations, Vol. 9. Springfield: Illinois State Museum.

———. 1964a. The Identification of a Prehistoric Bone Tool from the Midwest: The Deer-Jaw Sickle. *American Antiquity* 29:381–386.

———. 1964b. The Northeastern Extension of the Havana Tradition. In *Hopewellian Studies.* Scientific Papers 12. Edited by J. R. Caldwell and R. L. Hall, 107–122. Springfield: Illinois State Museum.

———, ed. 1968. *Hopewell and Woodland Site Archaeology in Illinois.* Bulletin 6. Springfield: Illinois Archaeological Survey.

———. 1971. The Dimensions of Status in the Burials at Spiro. In *Approaches to the Social Dimensions of Mortuary Practices.* Memoirs of the Society for American Archaeology, Vol. 25. Edited by J. A. Brown, 92–111. Salt Lake City: Society for American Archaeology. (Also issued as *American Antiquity* 36 [3, part 2].)

———. 1979. Charnel Houses and Mortuary Crypts: Disposal of the Dead in the Middle Woodland Period. In *Hopewell Archaeology: The Chillicothe Conference.* Edited by D. S. Brose and N. B. Greber, 211–219. Kent, Ohio: Kent State University Press.

———. 1981. The Search for Rank in Prehistoric Burials. In *The Archaeology of Death.* Edited by R. Chapman, I. Kinnes, and K. Randsborg, 25–37. Cambridge: Cambridge University Press.

———. 1982. Mound City and the Vacant Ceremonial Center. Paper presented at the 47th annual meeting of the Society for American Archaeology, Minneapolis.

———. 1985. Long-Term Trends to Sedentism and the Emergence of Complexity in the American Midwest. In *Prehistoric Hunter-Gatherers: The Emergence of Cultural Complexity.* Edited by T. D. Price and J. A. Brown, 201–231. New York: Academic Press.

———. 1986a. Early Ceramics and Culture. In *Early Woodland Archeology.* Seminars in Archeology, No. 2. Edited by K. B. Farnsworth and T. E. Emerson, 598–608. Kampsville, Ill.: Center for American Archeology.

———. 1986b. Food for Thought: Where Has Subsistence Analysis Gotten Us? In *Foraging, Collecting, and Harvesting: Archaic Period Subsistence and Settlement in the Eastern Woodlands.* Center for Archaeological Investigations, Occasional Paper No. 6. Edited by S. W. Neusius, 315–330. Carbondale: Southern Illinois University at Carbondale.

———. 1991. *Aboriginal Cultural Adaptations in the Midwestern Prairies.* New York: Garland Press.

———. 1995. On Mortuary Analysis—With Special Reference to the Saxe-Binford Research Program. In *Regional Approaches to Mortuary Analysis.* Edited by L. A. Beck, 3–26. New York: Plenum Press.

———. 1997a. Comment on "Ceremonial Centres from the Cayapas (Esmeraldas, Ecuador) to Chillicothe (Ohio, USA)." *Cambridge Archaeological Journal* 7:242–244.

———. 1997b. The Archaeology of Ancient Religion in the Eastern Woodlands. *Annual Reviews of Anthropology* 26:465–485.

Brown, J. A., and R. S. Baby. 1966. Mound City Revisited. Unpublished report on file at the Ohio Historical Society, Columbus.

Brown, J. A., and R. K. Vierra. 1983. What Happened in the Middle Archaic? Introduction to an Ecological Approach to Koster Site Archaeology. In *Archaic Hunters and Gatherers in the American Midwest.* Edited by J. L. Phillips and J. A. Brown, 165–195. New York: Academic Press.

Brown, M. K. 1975. *The Zimmerman Site: Further Excavations at the Grand Village of the Kaskaskia.* Report of Investigations 32. Springfield: Illinois State Museum.

Brown, P., J. P. Kennett, and B. L. Ingram. 1999. Marine Evidence for Episodic Holocene Megafloods in North America and Northern Gulf of Mexico. *Paleoceanography* 14:498–510.

Brück, J. 1999a. Ritual and Rationality: Some Problems of Interpretation in European Archaeology. *European Journal of Archaeology* 2:313–344.

———. 1999b. What's in a Settlement? Domestic Practice and Residential Mobility in Early Bronze Age Southern England. In *Making Places in the Prehistoric World: Themes in Settlement Archaeology.* Edited by J. Brück and M. Goodman, 52–75. London: UCL Press.

Brück, J., and M. Goodman, eds. 1999. *Making Places in the Prehistoric World: Themes in Settlement Archaeology.* London: UCL Press.

Brumfiel, E. M. 1976. Regional Growth in the Eastern Valley of Mexico: A Test of the "Population Pressure" Hypothesis. In *The Early Mesoamerican Village.* Edited by K. Flannery, 234–249. New York: Academic Press.

Brumfiel, E. M., and T. K. Earle. 1987. Specialization, Exchange, and Complex Society. In *Specialization, Exchange, and Complex Society.* Edited by E. M. Brumfiel and T. K. Earle, 1–9. Cambridge: Cambridge University Press.

Brumwell, M. J. 1941. An Ecological Survey of the Leavenworth Military Reservation. M.A. thesis, Department of Zoology, University of Kansas, Lawrence.

Buikstra, J. E. 1976. *Hopewell in the Lower Illinois River Valley: A Regional Study of Human Biological Variability and Prehistoric Mortuary Behavior.* Scientific Papers No. 2. Evanston, Ill.: Northwestern University Archeological Program.

———. 1977. Biocultural Dimensions of Archaeological Study: A Regional Perspective. In *Biocultural Adaptation in Prehistoric America.* Edited by R. L. Blakely, 67–84. Athens: University of Georgia Press.

———. 1979. Contributions of Physical Anthropologists to the Concept of Hopewell: A Historical Perspective. In *Hopewell Archaeology: The Chillicothe Conference.* Edited by D. S. Brose and N. B. Greber, 220–233. Kent, Ohio: Kent State University Press.

———. 1980. Epigenetic Distance: A Study of Biological Variability in the Lower Illinois River Region. In *Early Native Americans: Prehistoric Demography, Economy, and Technology.* Edited by D. L. Browman, 271–299. The Hague: Mouton.

———. 1984. The Lower Illinois River Region: A Prehistoric Context for the Study of Ancient Diet and Health. In *Paleopathology at the Origins of Agriculture.* Edited by M. N. Cohen and G. J. Armelagos, 215–234. New York: Academic Press.

———. 1988. *The Mound-Builders of Eastern North America: A Regional Perspective.* Elfe Kroon-Voordracht. Amsterdam: Stichting Nederlands Museum Voor Anthropologie en Prehistorie.

———. 1998. Architectural Details: Sediments and Structures (Appendix 2). In *Staging Ritual: Hopewell Ceremonialism at the Mound House Site, Greene County, Illinois.* Studies in Archeology and History, No. 1. Edited by J. E. Buikstra, D. K. Charles, and G. F. M. Rakita, 101–117. Kampsville, Ill.: Center for American Archeology.

Buikstra, J. E., and D. K. Charles. 1999. Centering the Ancestors: Cemeteries, Mounds, and Sacred Landscapes of the Ancient North American Midcontinent. In *Archaeologies of Landscape: Contemporary Perspectives.* Edited by W. Ashmore and A. B. Knapp, 201–228. Oxford: Blackwell.

Buikstra, J. E., D. K. Charles, and G. F. M. Rakita. 1998. *Staging Ritual: Hopewell Ceremonialism at the Mound House Site, Greene County, Illinois.* Studies in Archeology and History, No. 1. Kampsville, Ill.: Center for American Archeology.

Bullington, J. 1988. Middle Woodland Mound Structure: Social Implications and Regional Context. In *The Archaic and Woodland Cemeteries at the Elizabeth Site in the Lower Illinois Valley.* Research Series, Vol. 7. Edited by D. K. Charles, S. R. Leigh, and J. E. Buikstra, 218–241. Kampsville, Ill.: Center for American Archeology.

Bunge, M. 1996. *Finding Philosophy in Social Science.* New Haven, Conn.: Yale University Press.

Burks, J. J., and W. S. Dancey. 1999. Documenting Terminal Middle Woodland Community Pattern Change in Central Ohio: Aggregated Households at the Strait Site. Paper presented at the Midwest Archaeological Conference, East Lansing, Michigan.

———. 2000. Terminal Middle Woodland Period Settlement Aggregation in the Middle Ohio River Valley: Recent Findings from the Strait Site in Central Ohio. Paper presented at the 65th annual meeting of the Society for American Archaeology, Philadelphia.

Burks, J. J., and J. Pederson. 1999. From Secular to Sacred: A Comparison of Occupation Debris from Middle Woodland Habitation and Earthwork Sites in Central Ohio. Paper presented at the Midwest Archaeological Conference, East Lansing, Michigan.

———. 2000. An Update on Non-Mound Debris Studies at Hopewell Mound Group

(33Ro27), Ross County, Ohio. Paper presented at the Joint Midwest Archaeological and Plains Conference, St. Paul.

Burks, J. J., J. Pederson, and D. Walter. 2002. Hopewell Land Use Patterns at the Hopeton Earthworks. Paper presented at the 67th annual meeting of the Society for American Archaeology, Denver.

Burl, A. 1985. *Megalithic Brittany.* London: Thames and Hudson.

Burland, C. 1968. *North American Indian Mythology.* London: Hamlyn.

Butler, B. M. 1977. The Yearwood Site: A Specialized Middle Woodland Occupation on the Elk River. *Tennessee Anthropologist* 2:1–15.

———. 1979. Hopewellian Contacts in Southern Middle Tennessee. In *Hopewell Archaeology: The Chillicothe Conference.* Edited by D. S. Brose and N. B. Greber, 150–156. Kent, Ohio: Kent State University Press.

Butler, B. M., and R. W. Jefferies. 1986. Crab Orchard and Early Woodland Cultures in the Middle South. In *Early Woodland Archeology.* Seminars in Archeology, No. 2. Edited by K. B. Farnsworth and T. E. Emerson, 523–534. Kampsville, Ill.: Center for American Archeology.

Butzer, K. W. 1977. *Geomorphology of the Lower Illinois Valley as a Spatial-Temporal Context for the Koster Archaic Site.* Report of Investigations, No. 34. Springfield: Illinois State Museum.

———. 1978. Changing Holocene Environments at the Koster Site: A Geo-archaeological Perspective. *American Antiquity* 43:408–413.

Byers, A. M. 1987. The Earthwork Enclosures of the Central Ohio Valley: A Temporal and Structural Analysis of Woodland Society and Culture. Ph.D. dissertation, Department of Anthropology, State University of New York at Albany.

———. 1996. Social Structure and the Pragmatic Meaning of Material Culture: Ohio Hopewell as Ecclesiastic-Communal Cult. In *A View from the Core: A Synthesis of Ohio Hopewell Archaeology.* Edited by P. J. Pacheco, 174–192. Columbus: Ohio Archaeological Council.

———. 1998. Is the Newark Circle-Octagon the Ohio Hopewell "Rosetta Stone?" In *Ancient Earthen Enclosures of the Eastern Woodlands.* Edited by R. C. Mainfort Jr. and L. P. Sullivan, 135–153. Gainesville: University Press of Florida.

———. 1999. Intentionality, Symbolic Pragmatics, and Material Culture: Revisiting Binford's View of the Old Copper Culture. *American Antiquity* 64:265–287.

———. 2004. *The Ohio Hopewell Episode: Paradigm Lost, Paradigm Gained.* Akron, Ohio: University of Akron Press.

Cahen, D., L. H. Keeley, and F. L. van Noten. 1979. Stone Tools, Toolkits, and Human Behavior in Prehistory. *Current Anthropology* 20:661–683.

Caldwell, J. R. 1958. *Trend and Tradition in the Prehistory of the Eastern United States.* Memoir of the American Anthropological Association, No. 88. Menasha, Wisc.

———. 1964. Interaction Spheres in Prehistory. In *Hopewellian Studies.* Scientific Papers 12. Edited by J. R. Caldwell and R. L. Hall, 133–143. Springfield: Illinois State Museum.

Caldwell, J. R., and R. L. Hall, eds. 1964. *Hopewellian Studies.* Scientific Papers 12. Springfield: Illinois State Museum.

Callender, C. 1978a. Illinois. In *Handbook of North American Indians,* Vol. 15, *Northeast.* Edited by B. G. Trigger, 673–680. Washington, D.C.: Smithsonian Institution Press.

———. 1978b. Shawnee. In *Handbook of North American Indians,* Vol. 15, *Northeast.* Edited by B. G. Trigger, 622–635. Washington, D.C.: Smithsonian Institution Press.

————. 1978c. Miami. In *Handbook of North American Indians,* Vol. 15, *Northeast.* Edited by B. G. Trigger, 681–689. Washington, D.C.: Smithsonian Institution Press.

Campbell, J. 1962. *The Mask of God: Oriental Mythology.* New York: Viking Penguin.

Cantwell, A.-M. 1980. *Dickson Camp and Pond: Two Early Havana Tradition Sites in Central Illinois Valley.* Report of Investigations No. 36. Springfield: Illinois State Museum.

Carr, C., and H. Haas. 1996. Beta-Count and AMS Radiocarbon Dates of Woodland and Fort Ancient Period Occupations in Ohio, 1350 B.C.–A.D. 1650. *West Virginia Archaeologist* 48:19–53.

Carr, C., and J.-C. Komorowski. 1995. Identifying the Mineralogy of Rock Temper in Ceramics Using X-Radiography. *American Antiquity* 60:723–749.

Carskadden, J., and J. Morton. 1996. The Middle Woodland–Late Woodland Transition in the Central Muskingum Valley of Eastern Ohio. In *A View from the Core: A Synthesis of Ohio Hopewell Archaeology.* Edited by P. J. Pacheco, 316–339. Columbus: Ohio Archaeological Council.

————. 1997. Living on the Edge: A Comparison of Adena and Hopewell Communities in the Central Muskingum Valley of Eastern Ohio. In *Ohio Hopewell Community Organization.* Edited by W. S. Dancey and P. J. Pacheco, 365–401. Kent, Ohio: Kent State University Press.

Case, H. 1977. The Beaker Culture in Britain and Ireland. In *Beakers in Britain and Europe.* BAR Supplementary Series 26. Edited by R. Mercer and L. Barfield, 71–101. Oxford: Oxford University Press.

Chamberlin, T. C. 1890. The Method of Multiple Working Hypotheses. *Science* (o.s.) 15:92–96.

————. 1897. The Method of Multiple Working Hypotheses. *Journal of Geology* 5:837–848.

————. 1965. The Method of Multiple Working Hypotheses. *Science* 148:754–759.

Chang, K. C. 1983. *Art, Myth, and Ritual: The Path to Political Authority in Ancient China.* Cambridge, Mass.: Harvard University Press.

Chapman, C. H. 1980. *The Archaeology of Missouri, II.* Columbia: University of Missouri Press.

Chapman, J. C. 1973. *The Icehouse Bottom Site, 40MR23.* Department of Anthropology, Report of Investigation, No. 13. Knoxville: University of Tennessee.

Chapman, J. C., and B. C. Keel. 1979. Candy Creek–Connestee Components in Eastern Tennessee and Western North Carolina and Their Relationship with Adena-Hopewell. In *Hopewell Archaeology: The Chillicothe Conference.* Edited by D. S. Brose and N. B. Greber, 157–161. Kent, Ohio: Kent State University Press.

Chapman, R. 1981. The Emergence of Formal Disposal Areas and the "Problem" of Megalithic Tombs in Prehistoric Europe. In *The Archaeology of Death.* Edited by R. Chapman, I. Kinnes, and K. Randsborg, 71–81. Cambridge: Cambridge University Press.

————. 1995. Ten Years After—Megaliths, Mortuary Practices, and the Territorial Model. In *Regional Approaches to Mortuary Analysis.* Edited by L. A. Beck, 29–51. New York: Plenum Press.

————. 2003. *Archaeologies of Complexity.* London: Routledge.

Charles, D. K. 1985. Corporate Symbols: An Interpretive Prehistory of Indian Burial Mounds in West-Central Illinois. Ph.D. dissertation, Department of Anthropology, Northwestern University, Evanston, Illinois.

———. 1992. Woodland Demographic and Social Dynamics in the American Midwest: Analysis of a Burial Mound Survey. *World Archaeology* 24:175–197.

———. 1995. Diachronic Regional Social Dynamics: Mortuary Sites in the Illinois Valley/American Bottom Region. In *Regional Approaches to Mortuary Analysis*. Edited by L. A. Beck, 77–99. New York: Plenum Press.

Charles, D. K., and J. E. Buikstra. 1983. Archaic Mortuary Sites in the Central Mississippi Drainage: Distribution, Structure, and Behavioral Implications. In *Archaic Hunters and Gatherers in the American Midwest*. Edited by J. L. Phillips and J. A. Brown, 117–145. New York: Academic Press.

———. 2002. Siting, Sighting, and Citing the Dead. In *The Space and Place of Death*. Archaeological Papers of the American Anthropological Association, No. 11. Edited by H. Silverman and D. B. Small, 13–25. Arlington, Va.: American Anthropological Association.

Charles, D. K., J. E. Buikstra, and L. W. Konigsberg. 1986. Behavioral Implications of Terminal Archaic and Early Woodland Mortuary Practices in the Lower Illinois Valley. In *Early Woodland Archeology*. Seminars in Archeology, No. 2. Edited by K. B. Farnsworth and T. E. Emerson, 458–474. Kampsville, Ill.: Center for American Archeology.

Charles, D. K., S. R. Leigh, and J. E. Buikstra, eds. 1988. *The Archaic and Woodland Cemeteries at the Elizabeth Site in the Lower Illinois Valley*. Research Series, Vol. 7. Kampsville, Ill.: Center for American Archeology.

Charles, D. K., J. Van Nest, and J. E. Buikstra. 2004. From the Earth: Minerals and Meaning in the Hopewellian World. In *Soil, Stones, and Symbols: Cultural Perceptions of the Mineral World*. Edited by M. Owoc and N. Boivin, 43–70. London: UCL Press.

Chase-Dunn, C., and T. D. Hall. 1991. Conceptualizing Core/Periphery Hierarchies for Comparative Studies. In *Core/Periphery Relations in Precapitalist Worlds*. Edited by C. Chase-Dunn and T. D. Hall, 5–43. Boulder, Colo.: Westview Press.

Childe, V. G. 1952. *New Light on the Most Ancient East*. New York: Praeger.

Church, F., and A. G. Ericksen. 1997. Beyond the Scioto Valley: Middle Woodland Occupations in the Salt Creek Drainage. In *Ohio Hopewell Community Organization*. Edited by W. S. Dancey and P. J. Pacheco, 331–360. Kent, Ohio: Kent State University Press.

Clark, C., H. Neff, and M. D. Glascock. 1992. Neutron Activation Analysis of Late Woodland Ceramics from the Lake Superior Basin. In *Chemical Characterization of Ceramic Pastes in Archaeology*. Monographs in World Archaeology, No. 7. Edited by H. Neff, 255–267. Madison, Wisc.: Prehistory Press.

Clark, F. 1984. Knife River Flint and Interregional Exchange. *Midcontinental Journal of Archaeology* 9:173–198.

Clark, J. E., and M. Blake. 1996. Power of Prestige: Competitive Generosity and the Emergence of Rank Societies in Lowland Mesoamerica. In *Contemporary Archaeology in Theory: A Reader*. Edited by R. W. Preucel and I. Hodder, 258–281. Oxford: Blackwell.

Clark, J. R. 1979. Modeling Trade in Non-literate Archaeological Contexts. *Journal of Anthropological Research* 35:170–190.

Clark, J. V. H. 1849. *Onondaga, or Reminiscences of Earlier and Later Times*. 2 vols. Syracuse, N.Y.: Stoddard and Babcock.

Clarke, D. L. 1968. *Analytical Archaeology*. London: Methuen.

———. 1976. The Beaker Network: Social and Economic Models. In *Glockenbecher-symposion. Oberried 1974.* Edited by J. N. Lanting and J. D. Van Der Waals, 459–476. Bussum/Haarlem: Fibula–Van Dishoek.

Clay, R. B. 1986. Adena Ritual Spaces. In *Early Woodland Archeology.* Seminars in Archeology, No. 2. Edited by K. B. Farnsworth and T. E. Emerson, 581–595. Kampsville, Ill.: Center for American Archeology.

———. 1988. Peter Village: An Adena Enclosure. In *Middle Woodland Settlement and Ceremonialism in the Mid-South and Lower Mississippi Valley: Proceedings of the 1984 Mid-South Conference.* Archaeological Report 22. Edited by R. C. Mainfort Jr., 19–30. Jackson: Mississippi Department of Archives and History.

———. 1991. Adena Ritual Development: An Organizational Type in Temporal Perspective. In *The Human Landscape in Kentucky's Past: Site Structure and Settlement Patterns.* Edited by C. Stout and C. K. Hensley, 30–39. Lexington: Kentucky Heritage Council.

———. 1992. Chiefs, Big Men or What? Economy, Settlement Patterns, and Their Bearings on Adena Political Models. In *Cultural Variability in Context: Woodland Settlements in the Mid-Ohio Valley.* Midcontinental Journal of Archaeology Special Paper No. 7. Edited by M. F. Seeman, 77–80. Kent, Ohio: Kent State University Press.

———. 1998. The Essential Features of Adena Ritual and Their Implications. *Southeastern Archaeology* 17:1–21.

Clay, R. B., and S. D. Creasman. 1999. Middle Ohio Valley Late Woodland Nucleated Settlements: "Where's the Beef?" Paper presented to the meeting on Kentucky Archaeology, Kentucky Heritage Council, Lexington.

Clay, R. B., and C. M. Niquette. 1989. Cultural Overview. In *Phase III Excavations at the Niebert Site (46MS103) in the Gallipolis Locks and Dam Replacement Project, Mason County, West Virginia.* Edited by R.B. Clay and C.M. Niquette. Contract Publications Series 89–06. 10–26. Lexington, Ky.: Contract Resource Analysts.

Cleal, R. M. J., and M. J. Allen. 1995. Stonehenge in Its Landscape. In *Stonehenge in Its Landscape: Twentieth-Century Excavations.* Edited by R. M. J. Cleal, K. E. Walker, and R. Montegue, 464–491. London: English Heritage.

Cleland, C. E. 1966. *The Prehistoric Animal Ecology and Ethnozoology of the Upper Great Lakes Region.* Museum of Anthropology, Anthropological Papers 29. Ann Arbor: University of Michigan.

———. 1976. The Focal-Diffusion Model: An Evolutionary Perspective on the Prehistoric Cultural Adaptations of the Eastern United States. *Midcontinental Journal of Archaeology* 1:59–76.

———. 1982. The Inland Shore Fishery of the Northern Great Lakes: Its Development and Importance in Prehistory. *American Antiquity* 47:761–784.

Cobb, C. R. 1989. An Appraisal of the Role of Mill Creek Chert Hoes in Mississippian Exchange Systems. *Southeastern Archaeology* 8:79–92.

Cochran, D. R. 1996. The Adena/Hopewell Convergence in East Central Indiana. In *A View from the Core: A Synthesis of Ohio Hopewell Archaeology.* Edited by P. J. Pacheco, 340–353. Columbus: Ohio Archaeological Council.

Coffinberry, W. L. 1885. Letter Or Report to F. W. Putnam (?), Peabody Museum [October (?), 1885]. Typed manuscript copy maintained in the Converse Mound (20KT2) file at the State of Michigan State Historic Preservation Office, Lansing. Original manuscript held in Accession File 85–51, Peabody Museum of Archaeology and Ethnology, Harvard University, Cambridge, Massachusetts.

Cogswell, J. W. 1995. *Neutron Activation Analysis of Pottery and Clays from Selected*

Sites in the Upper Illinois River Valley. University of Missouri Research Reactor, final report, samples submitted by R. J. Jeske and M. Lynott.

Cogswell, J. W., H. Neff, and M. D. Glascock. 1998. *Compositional Variation of Pottery and Clays in the Upper Illinois River Valley.* University of Missouri Research Reactor, final report, samples submitted by R. J. Jeske and M. Lynott.

Cogswell, J. W., L. J. Ross, M. J. O'Brien, H. Neff, and M. D. Glascock. 1995. Analysis of Postdepositional Effects on Prehistoric Ceramics from Southeastern Missouri: Implications for Provenance Studies. Poster presented at the 60th annual meeting of the Society for American Archaeology, Minneapolis.

Cole, F.-C., and T. Deuel. 1937. *Rediscovering Illinois: Archaeological Explorations in and around Fulton County.* Chicago: University of Chicago Press.

Coleman, S., and J. Elsner. 1995. *Pilgrimage: Past and Present in the World Religions.* Cambridge, Mass.: Harvard University Press.

Collins, J. M. 1996. *The Archaeology of the Dolomite Ridge Site.* Project Completion Report 19 (10). Office of the State Archaeologist, University of Iowa, Iowa City.

Collins, J. M., and L. Forman. 1995. *Phase III Archaeological Salvage of the Buck Creek Mounds (13CT34 and 13CT36), Local Systems Project GRS-1792(2), Clayton County, Iowa.* Project Completion Report 18 (14). Office of the State Archaeologist, University of Iowa, Iowa City.

Conkey, M. W. 1985. Ritual Communication, Social Elaboration, and the Variable Trajectories of Paleolithic Material Culture. In *Prehistoric Hunter-Gatherers: The Emergence of Cultural Complexity.* Edited by T. D. Price and J. A. Brown, 299–323. Orlando: Academic Press.

Conner, M. D., and D. W. Link. 1991. Archaeological and Osteological Analysis of Mound 38 at the Albany Mound Group (11–Wt-1). *Illinois Archaeology* 3:23–55.

Connolly, R. P. 1996a. Prehistoric Land Modification at the Fort Ancient Hilltop Enclosure: A Model of Formal and Accretive Development. In *A View from the Core: A Synthesis of Ohio Hopewell Archaeology.* Edited by P. J. Pacheco, 258–273. Columbus: Ohio Archaeological Council.

———. 1996b. Middle Woodland Hilltop Enclosures: The Built Environment, Construction, and Function. Ph.D. dissertation, Department of Anthropology, University of Illinois at Urbana-Champaign.

———. 1997. The Evidence of Habitation at the Fort Ancient Earthworks, Warren County, Ohio. In *Ohio Hopewell Community Organization.* Edited by W. S. Dancey and P. J. Pacheco, 251–282. Kent, Ohio: Kent State University Press.

———. 1998. Architectural Grammar Rules at the Fort Ancient Hilltop Enclosure. In *Ancient Earthen Enclosures of the Eastern Woodlands.* Edited by R. C. Mainfort Jr. and L. P. Sullivan, 85–113. Gainesville: University Press of Florida.

Connolly, R. P., and B. T. Lepper, eds. 2004. *The Fort Ancient Earthworks: Prehistoric Lifeways of the Hopewell Culture in Southwestern Ohio.* Columbus: Ohio Historical Society.

Connolly, R. P., and L. E. Sieg. 1996. *1995 Report of Investigations at Fort Ancient State Memorial, Ohio (33WA2),* Vol. 1, *Museum Expansion and Garden Zones.* Columbus: Ohio Historical Society.

Connolly, R. P., and A. P. Sullivan III. 1998. Inferring Activities at Middle Woodland Earthworks with Surface Collection Data. In *Surface Archaeology.* Edited by A. P. Sullivan III, 61–74. Albuquerque: University of New Mexico Press.

Converse, R. N. 1993. The Troyer Site: A Hopewell Habitation Site, and a Secular View of Hopewell Villages. *Ohio Archaeologist* 43:4–12.

————. 1994. The Harness Hopewell Village Sites. *Ohio Archaeologist* 44:4–9.

Cook, E. L. 1993. Ceramic Artifacts. In *Quarry Creek: Excavation, Analysis and Prospect of a Kansas City Hopewell Site, Fort Leavenworth, Kansas.* Museum of Anthropology, Project Report Series No. 80. Edited by B. Logan, 98–129. Lawrence: University of Kansas.

Cooney, G. 2000. *Landscapes of Neolithic Ireland.* London: Routledge.

Corwin, R. N. 1968. Faunas from Four Archaeological Sites in the Lower Illinois Valley. M.S. thesis, Department of Biological Science, Illinois State University.

Coughlin, S., and M. F. Seeman. 1997. Hopewell Settlements at the Liberty Earthworks, Ross County, Ohio. In *Ohio Hopewell Community Organization.* Edited by W. S. Dancey and P. J. Pacheco, 231–250. Kent, Ohio: Kent State University Press.

Count, E. W. 1952. The Earth-Diver and the Rival Twins: A Clue to Time Correlation in North-Eurasiatic and North American Mythology. In *Indian Tribes of Aboriginal America.* Edited by S. Tax, 55–62. Chicago: University of Chicago Press.

Cowan, C. W. 1978. The Prehistoric Use and Distribution of Maygrass in Eastern North America: Cultural and Phytogeographical Implications. In *The Nature and Status of Ethnobotany.* Museum of Anthropology, Anthropological Papers 67. Edited by R. I. Ford, 263–288. Ann Arbor: University of Michigan.

————. 1996. Social Implications of Ohio Hopewell Art. In *A View from the Core: A Synthesis of Ohio Hopewell Archaeology.* Edited by P. J. Pacheco, 128–148. Columbus: Ohio Archaeological Council.

Cowan, C. W., and P. J. Watson. 1992. *The Origins of Agriculture: An International Perspective.* Washington, D.C.: Smithsonian Institution Press.

Cowan, F. L. 1987. Tillage Damage to Lithic Artifacts: Experimental Results. Paper presented at the annual meeting of Northeastern Anthropological Association, Amherst, Massachusetts.

————. 1994. Prehistoric Mobility Strategies in Western New York: A Small Sites Perspective. Ph.D. dissertation, Department of Anthropology, State University of New York at Buffalo.

————. 1999. Making Sense of Flake Scatters: Lithic Technological Strategies and Mobility. *American Antiquity* 64:593–607.

Cowan, F. L., and R. B. Clay. 1998. Ground-Truthing Magnetometry Data at an Ohio Hopewell Site. Paper presented at the Midwest Archaeological Conference, Muncie, Indiana.

Cowan, F. L., R. A. Genheimer, and T. K. Sunderhaus. 1997. Recent Investigations at Fort Ancient's Parallel Walls. *Ohio Archaeological Council Newsletter* 9:15–19.

Cowan, F. L., and T. K. Sunderhaus. 2002. Dating the Stubbs "Woodworks." *Ohio Archaeological Council Newsletter* 14:11–16.

Cowan, F. L., T. K. Sunderhaus, and R. A. Genheimer. 1998. Notes from the Field: An Update from the Stubbs Earthworks Site. *Ohio Archaeological Council Newsletter* 10:6–13.

————. 1999a. In the Shadow of the Earthworks: Architecture and Activities outside Ohio Hopewell Earthworks. Paper presented to the annual meeting of the Eastern States Archaeological Federation, Lebanon, Ohio.

————. 1999b. Notes from the Field: More Hopewell "Houses" at the Stubbs Earthwork Site. *Ohio Archaeological Council Newsletter* 11:11–16.

————. 2000. Wooden Architecture in Ohio Hopewell Sites: Structural and Spatial Patterns at the Stubbs Earthworks Site. Paper presented at the 65th annual meeting of the Society for American Archaeology, Philadelphia.

———. 2003. Up-"dating" the Stubbs Cluster, Sort of . . . . *The Ohio Archaeological Council Newsletter* 15(2): http://ohioarchaeology.org/cowan_10_2003.html.

———. 2004. Earthwork Peripheries: Probing the Margins of the Fort Ancient Site. In *The Fort Ancient Earthwork: Prehistoric Lifeways of the Hopewell Culture in Southwestern Ohio*. Edited by R. P. Connolly and B. T. Lepper, 107–124. Columbus: Ohio Historical Society.

Cremin, W. M. 1980. Kalamazoo Basin Survey, Allegan County, Michigan: Systematic Site Survey in a Varied Environment Utilizing the Transect and Stratified Random Sampling. *Wisconsin Archaeologist* 61:111–119.

———, ed. 1981. *Kalamazoo Basin Survey, 1976–1980*. Archaeological Report No. 11. Kalamazoo: Western Michigan University.

Cremin, W. M., and A. L. DesJardins. 2001. Dieffenderfer: A Late Woodland Ditched Hamlet in Southwest Michigan. Paper presented at the 66th annual meeting of the Society for American Archaeology, New Orleans.

Criado, F., and V. Villoch. 2000. Monumentalizing Landscape: From Present Perception to the Past Meaning of Galician Megalithism (North-West Iberian Peninsula). *European Journal of Archaeology* 3:188–216.

Crites, G. D. 1987. Human-Plant Mutualism and Niche Expression in the Paleoethnobotanical Record: A Middle Woodland Example. *American Antiquity* 52:725–740.

Cross, J. R. 1988. Expanding the Scope of Seasonality Research in Archaeology. In *Coping with Seasonal Constraints*. MASCA Research Papers in Science and Archaeology 5, 55–63. Philadelphia: University of Pennsylvania.

Crumley, C. L., and W. H. Marquardt, eds. 1987. *Regional Dynamics: Burgundian Landscapes in Historical Perspective*. San Diego: Academic Press.

Curl, J. S. 1980. *A Celebration of Death*. London: Batsford.

Cutler, H. G. 1906. *History of St. Joseph County, Michigan*. Chicago: Lewis Publishing.

Dancey, W. S. 1984. The 1914 Archaeological Atlas of Ohio: Its History and Significance. Paper presented at the 49th annual meeting of the Society for American Archaeology, Portland, Oregon.

———. 1988a. The Community Plan of an Early Late Woodland Village in the Middle Scioto River Valley. *Midcontinental Journal of Archaeology* 13:223–258.

———. 1988b. The Murphy Site (33–Li-212): A Middle Woodland Settlement in Raccoon Creek Valley, Licking County, Ohio. In *Moundbuilders' Notes No. 7*. Edited by B. T. Lepper, 1–8. Newark: Moundbuilders State Memorial, Ohio Historical Society.

———. 1991. A Middle Woodland Settlement in Central Ohio: A Preliminary Report on the Murphy Site. *Pennsylvania Archaeologist* 61:37–72.

———. 1992a. Small Site Formation Process and the Hopewell Problem. Paper presented at the Southeastern Archaeological Conference, Little Rock, Arkansas.

———. 1992b. Village Origins in Central Ohio: The Results and Implications of Recent Middle and Late Woodland Research. In *Cultural Variability in Context: Woodland Settlements of the Mid-Ohio Valley*. Midcontinental Journal of Archaeology Special Paper No. 7. Edited by M. F. Seeman, 24–29. Kent, Ohio: Kent State University Press.

———. 1996a. *Hopewell Earthwork Catchment Survey: Interim Report*. Report submitted to the National Park Service, Hopewell Culture National Historical Park, Chillicothe, Ohio.

———. 1996b. Putting an End to Ohio Hopewell. In *A View from the Core: A Synthesis of Ohio Hopewell Archaeology*. Edited by P. J. Pacheco, 394–405. Columbus: Ohio Archaeological Council.

———. 1998. The Value of Surface Archaeological Data in Exploring the Dynamics of

Community Evolution in the Middle Ohio Valley. In *Surface Archaeology*. Edited by A. Sullivan, 3–19. Albuquerque: University of New Mexico Press.

Dancey, W. S., and P. J. Pacheco. 1997a. A Community Model of Ohio Hopewell Settlement. In *Ohio Hopewell Community Organization*. Edited by W. S. Dancey and P. J. Pacheco, 3–40. Kent, Ohio: Kent State University Press.

———, eds. 1997b. *Ohio Hopewell Community Organization*. Kent, Ohio: Kent State University Press.

Dancey, W. S., and J. Pederson. 1999. Late Woodland and Late Prehistoric Village Adaptations in the Middle Ohio Valley. Paper presented at the 64th annual meeting of the Society for American Archaeology, Chicago.

Davis, E. H. 1847. Letter to Ephraim Squier. Ephraim Squier Papers, Reel 1, United States Library of Congress.

DeBoer, W. E. 1997. Ceremonial Centres from the Cayapas (Esmeraldas, Ecuador) to Chillicothe (Ohio). *Cambridge Archaeological Journal* 7:225–253.

DeBoer, W. E., and J. H. Blitz. 1991. Ceremonial Centers of the Chachi. *Expedition* 33:53–62.

Delcourt, P. A., H. R. Delcourt, C. R. Ison, W. E. Sharp, and K. J. Gremillion. 1998. Prehistoric Human Use of Fire, the Eastern Agricultural Complex, and Appalachian Oak-Chestnut Forests: Paleoecology of Cliff Palace Pond, Kentucky. *American Antiquity* 63:263–278.

Demeter, C. S., and E. H. Robinson. 1999. *Phase I Archaeological Literature Review and Above-Ground Assessment of the US-131 S-Curve Crossing of the Grand River in the City of Grand Rapids, Kent County, Michigan, Part 1: Archaeological Evaluation*. Report submitted to the Michigan Department of Transportation by Commonwealth Cultural Resources Group, Jackson, Michigan.

DesJardins, A. L. 2001. An Analysis of the Lithic Assemblage from the Armintrout-Blackman Site (20AE812), Allegan County, Michigan. M.A. thesis, Department of Anthropology, Western Michigan University, Kalamazoo.

De Sonneville-Bordes, D., and J. Perrot. 1954. Lexique Typologique du Paléolithique Supérieur. *Bulletin de la Société Préhistorique Française* 51:327–335.

———. 1955. Lexique Typologique du Paléolithique Supérieur. *Bulletin de la Société Préhistorique Française* 52:76–79.

———. 1956a. Lexique Typologique du Paléolithique Supérieur. *Bulletin de la Société Préhistorique Française* 53:408–412.

———. 1956b. Lexique Typologique Du Paléolithique Supérieur. *Bulletin de la Société Préhistorique Française* 56:547–559.

Deuel, T., ed. 1952. *Hopewellian Communities in Illinois*. Scientific Papers 5. Springfield: Illinois State Museum.

Devereaux, P. 1997. *The Long Trip: A Prehistory of Psychedelia*. New York: Penguin.

Diamond, J. 1999. *Guns, Germs, and Steel*. New York: W. W. Norton.

Dillehay, T. D. 1990. Mapuche Ceremonial Landscape, Social Recruitment, and Resource Rights. *World Archaeology* 22:223–241.

———. 1992. Keeping Outsiders Out: Public Ceremony, Resource Rights, and Hierarchy in Historic and Contemporary Mapuche Society. In *Wealth and Hierarchy in the Intermediate Area*. Edited by F. Lange, 379–422. Washington, D.C.: Dumbarton Oaks Research Library.

Dincauze, D. F., and R. J. Hasenstab. 1989. Explaining the Iroquois: Tribalization on a Prehistoric Periphery. In *Centre and Periphery: Comparative Studies in Archaeology*. Edited by T. C. Champion, 67–87. London: Unwin Hyman.

Dobkin de Rios, M. 1977. Plant Hallucinogens, Out-of-Body Experiences, and New World Monumental Earthworks. In *Drugs, Rituals, and Altered States of Consciousness.* Edited by B. M. Du Toit, 237–249. Rotterdam: A. A. Balkena.

Dorothy, L. G., and E. B. Garland. 1981. *The Portage River Archaeological Survey, St. Joseph County, Michigan.* Department of Anthropology, Archaeological Report No. 8. Kalamazoo: Western Michigan University.

Dorsey, G. A. 1903. *The Arapahoe Sun Dance: The Ceremony of the Offerings Lodge.* Anthropological Series, Vol. 4. Field Columbian Museum Publication 75. Chicago.

———. 1905. *The Cheyenne: II. The Sun Dance.* Anthropological Series, Vol. 9, No. 2. Field Columbian Museum Publication 99. Chicago.

———. 1910. Sun Dance. In *Handbook of American Indians North of Mexico,* Part 2. Smithsonian Institution, Bureau of American Ethnology, Bulletin 30. Edited by F. W. Hodge, 649–652. Washington, D.C.: Government Printing Office.

Douglas, M. 1966. *Purity and Danger.* New York: Praeger.

———. 1970. *Natural Symbols.* London: Barrie and Jenkins.

———. 1975. *Implicit Meanings: Essays in Anthropology.* London: Routledge and Kegan Paul.

———. 1982. *In the Active Voice.* London: Routledge and Kegan Paul.

Dowagiac Daily News. 1888. Mounds Excavated in Sumnerville. Dowagiac, Mich.

Dragoo, D. W. 1963. *Mounds for the Dead.* Annals of the Carnegie Museum, Vol. 37. Pittsburgh.

Dragoo, D. W., and D. E. Wray. 1964. Hopewell Figurine Rediscovered. *American Antiquity* 30:195–199.

Drake, D. 1815. *Natural and Statistical View; Or Picture of Cincinnati and the Miami Country, Illustrated by Maps.* Cincinnati: Looker and Wallace.

Drennan, R. D. 1984a. Long-Distance Movement of Goods in the Mesoamerican Formative and Classic. *American Antiquity* 49:27–43.

———. 1984b. Long Distance Transport Costs in Pre-Hispanic Mesoamerica. *American Anthropologist* 86:105–112.

———. 1985. Porters, Pots, and Profits: The Economics of Long-Distance Exchange in Mesoamerica. *American Anthropologist* 87:891–893.

Driver, H. E. 1972. *Indians of North America.* 2nd revised edition. Chicago: University of Chicago Press.

Driver, H. E., and W. C. Massey. 1957. *Comparative Studies of North American Indians,* Vol. 47, Part 2. Philadelphia: Transactions of the American Philosophical Society.

DUCS (Denison University Capstone Seminar). 1998. *Phase I Environmental Impact Assessment for the Airport Parkway Extension Project, Licking County, Ohio.* Granville, Ohio: Environmental Studies Program, Denison University.

Dunne, M. T., and W. Green. 1998. Terminal Archaic and Early Woodland Plant Use at the Gast Spring Site (13LA152), Southeast Iowa. *Midcontinental Journal of Archaeology* 23:45–88.

Dunnell, R. C. 1980. Evolutionary Theory and Archaeology. In *Advances in Archaeological Method and Theory,* Vol. 3. Edited by M. B. Schiffer, 35–99. New York: Academic Press.

———. 1989. Aspects of the Application of Evolutionary Theory in Archaeology. In *Archaeological Thought in America.* Edited by C. C. Lamberg-Karlovsky, 35–49. Cambridge: Cambridge University Press.

———. 1992. Archaeology and Evolutionary Science. In *Quandaries and Quests: Visions of Archaeology's Future.* Center for Archaeological Investigations, Occasional

Paper No. 11. Edited by L. Wandsnider, 209–224. Carbondale: Southern Illinois University.

Dunnell, R. C., and W. S. Dancey. 1983. The Siteless Survey: A Regional Scale Data Collection Strategy. In *Advances in Archaeological Method and Theory*, Vol. 9. Edited by M. B. Schiffer, 267–288. New York: Academic Press.

Dutton, C. E., and R. E. Bradley. 1970. *Lithologic, Geophysical, and Mineral Commodity Maps of Precolumbian Rocks in Wisconsin*. Madison: University of Wisconsin Geological and Natural History Survey.

Earle, T. K. 1991. Property Rights and the Evolution of Chiefdoms. In *Chiefdoms: Power, Economy, and Ideology*. Edited by T. K. Earle, 71–99. Cambridge: Cambridge University Press.

Earle, T. K., and J. E. Ericson, eds. 1977. *Exchange Systems in Prehistory*. New York: Academic Press.

Easton, L. C. 1953. Capt. L. C. Easton's Report: Fort Laramie to Fort Leavenworth Via Republican River in 1849. Edited by Merrill J. Mattes. *Kansas Historical Quarterly* 20(6):392–416.

Ebbers, B. C. 1990. Reconstruction of the Floristic Environment in Central Berrien County, Michigan, 2000 B.C. to Nineteenth Century A.D. In *Late Archaic and Early Woodland Adaptation in the Lower St. Joseph River Valley, Berrien County, Michigan*. Michigan Cultural Resources Investigation Series 2. Edited by E. B. Garland, 83–107. Lansing: Michigan Department of Transportation and Michigan Department of State.

Echo-Hawk, R. C. 2000. Ancient History in the New World: Integrating Oral Traditions and the Archaeological Record in Deep Time. *American Antiquity* 65:267–290.

Edmonds, M. 1993. Interpreting Causewayed Enclosures in the Past and the Present. In *Interpretative Archaeology*. Edited by C. Tilley, 99–142. Oxford: Berg.

Egan-Bruhy, K. C. 2002. Variability in the Converse Site Woodland and Contact Period Archaeobotanical Assemblage. Paper presented at the 67th annual meeting of the Society for American Archaeology, Denver.

———. 2003. Floral Analysis. In *Phase III Archaeological Data Recovery for the U.S. 131 S-Curve Realignment Project, Grand Rapids, Michigan*. Report No. R-0446. Edited by M. J. Hambacher, J. G. Brashler, K. C. Egan-Bruhy, D. R. Hayes, B. Hardy, D. G. Landis, T. J. Martin, G. W. Monaghan, K. Murphy, J. A. Robertson, and D. L. Seltz, section 7.0. Report submitted to the Michigan Department of Transportation, Lansing, by Commonwealth Cultural Resources Group, Jackson, Michigan.

Elam, J. M., C. Carr, M. D. Glascock, and H. Neff. 1992. Ultrasonic Dissaggregation and INAA of Textural Fractions of Tucson Basin and Ohio Valley Ceramics. In *Chemical Characterization of Ceramic Pastes in Archaeology*. Monographs in World Archaeology, No. 7. Edited by H. Neff, 93–111. Madison, Wisc.: Prehistory Press.

Eliade, M. 1964. *Shamanism: Archaic Techniques of Ecstasy*. New York: Pantheon Books.

———, ed. 1987. *The Encyclopedia of Religion*, Vol. 10. New York: Macmillan.

Elkin, R. E. 1953. John Francis Snyder and Illinois Archaeology. M.A. thesis, Department of History, University of Illinois, Urbana.

Emerson, T. E. 1997a. *Cahokia and the Archaeology of Power*. Tuscaloosa: University of Alabama Press.

———. 1997b. Reflections from the Countryside on Cahokia Hegemony. In *Cahokia Domination and the Ideology in the Mississippian World*. Edited by T. K. Pauketat and T. E. Emerson, 167–189. Lincoln: University of Nebraska Press.

Emerson, T. E., and A. C. Fortier. 1986. Early Woodland Cultural Variation, Subsistence, and Settlement in the American Bottom. In *Early Woodland Archeology*. Seminars in Archeology, No. 2. Edited by K. B. Farnsworth and T. E. Emerson, 475–522. Kampsville, Ill.: Center for American Archeology.

Emerson, T. E., and D. L. McElrath. 2001. Interpreting Discontinuity and Historical Process in Midcontinental Late Archaic and Early Woodland Societies. In *The Archaeology of Traditions: Agency and History before and after Columbus*. Edited by T. K. Pauketat, 195–217. Gainesville: University Press of Florida.

Emerson, T. E., G. R. Milner, and D. Jackson. 1983. *The Florence Street Site*. American Bottom Archaeology FAI-270 Site Reports, Vol. 2. Urbana: University of Illinois Press.

Epstein, J. F. 1958. Ceramics and Ceramic Artifacts of the Pool Site. In *The Pool and Irving Villages: A Study of Hopewell Occupation in the Illinois River Valley*. Edited by J. C. McGregor, 31–63. Urbana: University of Illinois Press.

Ericson, J. E., and T. K. Earle, eds. 1982. *Contexts for Prehistoric Exchange*. New York: Academic Press.

Essenpreis, P. S. 1978. Fort Ancient Settlement: Differential Responses at a Mississippian–Late Woodland Interface. In *Mississippian Settlement Patterns*. Edited by B. D. Smith, 141–167. New York: Academic Press.

Essenpreis, P. S., and M. E. Moseley. 1984. Fort Ancient: Citadel or Coliseum? Past and Present Field Museum Explorations of a Major American Monument. *Field Museum of Natural History Bulletin* June:5–26.

Evans, J. B., M. G. Evans, M. Simon, and T. E. Berres. 2000. *Ringering: A Multi-component Site in the American Bottom*. Research Reports, Vol. 8. Champaign: Illinois Transportation Archaeological Research Program.

Everts, L. H. 1887. *History of St. Joseph County, Michigan*. Philadelphia: L. H. Everts and Company.

Eyman, C. E. 1966. The Schultz Focus: A Plains Middle Woodland Burial Complex in Eastern Kansas. M.A. thesis, Department of Archaeology, University of Alberta, Edmonton.

Fagan, B. M. 1991. *Ancient North America*. New York: Thames and Hudson.

Fairbanks, C. H. 1940a. *Analysis of Sherd Collections from Kolomoki State Park*. Report on file, Southeastern Archaeological Center, Tallahassee, Florida.

———. 1940b. *Report on Archaeological Investigations of 1Ea2 and 1Ea3 at Kolomoki Mounds State Park, Georgia*. Report on file, Southeastern Archaeological Center.

———. 1941a. *Archaeological Site Survey of the Kolomoki Mound Group*. Report on file, Southeastern Archaeological Center.

———. 1941b. *The Excavation of 1ER2 and 1ER3, Kolomoki Group*. Report on file, Southeastern Archaeological Center.

———. 1946. The Kolomoki Mound Group, Early County, Georgia. *American Antiquity* 11:258–260.

Farnsworth, K. B. 1973. *An Archaeological Survey of the Macoupin Valley*. Illinois Valley Archaeology Program, Reports of Investigation No. 26, Research Papers Vol. 7. Springfield: Illinois State Museum.

———, ed. 2004. *Early Hopewell Mound Explorations: The First Fifty Years in the Illinois River Valley*. Illinois Transportation Archaeology Research Program, Studies in Archaeology, No. 3. Urbana: University of Illinois Press.

Farnsworth, K. B., and D. L. Asch. 1986. Early Woodland Chronology, Artifact Styles, and Settlement Distribution in the Lower Illinois Valley Region. In *Early Woodland*

Archeology. Seminars in Archeology, No. 2. Edited by K. B. Farnsworth and T. E. Emerson, 326–457. Kampsville, Ill.: Center for American Archeology.

Farnsworth, K. B., and T. E. Emerson, eds. 1986. *Early Woodland Archeology*. Seminars in Archeology, No. 2. Kampsville, Ill.: Center for American Archeology.

Farnsworth, K. B., and A. L. Koski. 1985. *Massey and Archie: A Study of Two Hopewellian Farmsteads in the Western Illinois Uplands*. Research Series, Vol. 3. Kampsville, Ill.: Center for American Archeology.

Farnsworth, K. B., and S. J. Studenmund. 1999. After the Archaic: A Re-examination of the Woodland and Late Prehistoric Radiocarbon Database from West-Central Illinois. Paper presented at the Midwest Archaeological Conference, East Lansing, Michigan.

Faulkner, C. H. 1972. *The Late Prehistoric Occupation of Northwestern Indiana: A Study of the Upper Mississippi Cultures of the Kankakee Valley*. Prehistory Research Series Vol. 5 (1). Indianapolis: Indiana Historical Society.

———. 1973. Middle Woodland Subsistence-Settlement Systems in the Highland Rim: A Commentary. In *Salvage Archaeology at 40FR47*. Miscellaneous Paper 11. Edited by W. Bacon and N. Merryman, 35–45. Knoxville: Tennessee Archaeological Society.

———. 1982. The McFarland Occupation at 40CF32: Interpretations of the 1975 Field Season. In *Eighth Report of the Normandy Archaeological Project*. Department of Anthropology, Report of Investigations, No. 33. Edited by C. H. Faulkner and M. M. C. R. McCollough, 303–388. Knoxville: University of Tennessee.

Faulkner, C. H., and M. M. C. R. McCollough, eds. 1973. *Introductory Report of the Normandy Reservoir Salvage Project: Environmental Setting, Typology, and Survey*. Normandy Archaeological Project, Vol. 1. Department of Anthropology, Report of Investigations, No. 11. Knoxville: University of Tennessee.

———. 1982. The Investigations of the Parks Site (40CF5). In *Seventh Report of the Normandy Archaeological Project*. Department of Anthropology, Report of Investigations, No. 32. Edited by C. H. Faulkner and M. M. C. R. McCollough, 313–352. Knoxville: University of Tennessee.

Fecht, W. G. 1955. Mound Exploration at Meppen, Illinois. *Central States Archaeological Journal* 2:29–34.

Fehrenbacher, J. B., J. D. Alexander, I. J. Jansen, R. G. Darmody, R. A. Pope, M. A. Flock, E. E. Voss, J. W. Scott, W. F. Andrews, and L. J. Bushue. 1984. *Soils of Illinois*. Agriculture Experiment Station Bulletin No. 778. Urbana: University of Illinois College of Agriculture.

Feinman, G. M. 1999. The Changing Structure of Macroregional Mesoamerica: The Classic-Postclassic Transition in the Valley of Oaxaca. In *World-Systems Theory in Practice: Leadership, Production, and Exchange*. Edited by P. N. Kardulias, 53–62. Lanham, Md.: Rowman and Littlefield.

Fenton, J. P., and R. W. Jefferies. 1991. The Camargo Mound and Earthworks: Preliminary Findings. In *The Human Landscape in Kentucky's Past: Site Structure and Settlement Patterns*. Edited by C. K. Hensley and C. Stout, 40–55. Frankfort: Kentucky Heritage Council.

Ferguson, J. A., and R. E. Warren. 1992. Chert Resources of Northern Illinois: Discriminant Analysis and an Identification Key. *Illinois Archaeology* 4:1–37.

Fidlar, M. M. 1948. *Physiography of the Lower Wabash Valley*. Bulletin 2. Bloomington: Indiana Geological Survey.

Fie, S. M. 2000. An Integrative Study of Ceramic Exchange during the Illinois Valley Middle Woodland Period. Ph.D. dissertation, Department of Anthropology, State University of New York at Buffalo.

Finney, F. A. 1983. Middle Woodland Cement Hollow Phase. In *The Mund Site (11–S-435)*. American Bottom Archaeology FAI-270 Site Reports, Vol. 5. Edited by A. C. Fortier, F. A. Finney, and R. B. Lacampagne, 40–107. Urbana: University of Illinois Press.

Fischer, F. W. 1971. Preliminary Report on the University of Cincinnati Archaeological Investigations, 1970. Ms. on file, Department of Anthropology, University of Cincinnati. Report on File, Ohio Historic Preservation Office, Columbus.

———. 1972. Schultz Site Ceramics. In *The Schultz Site at Green Point: A Stratified Occupation Area in the Saginaw Valley of Michigan.* Museum of Anthropology, Memoirs 4. Edited by J. E. Fitting, 137–190. Ann Arbor: University of Michigan.

———. 1974. Early and Middle Woodland Settlement, Subsistence and Population in the Central Ohio Valley. Ph.D. dissertation, Department of Anthropology, Washington University, St. Louis.

Fishel, R. L., ed. 1999. *Bison Hunters of the Western Prairies: Archaeological Investigations at the Dixon Site (13WD8), Woodbury County, Iowa.* Report 21. Office of the State Archaeologist, University of Iowa, Iowa City.

Fitting, J. E. 1972. Lithic Industries of the Schultz Site. In *The Schultz Site at Green Point: A Stratified Occupation Area in the Saginaw Valley of Michigan.* Museum of Anthropology, Memoirs 4. Edited by J. E. Fitting, 191–224. Ann Arbor: University of Michigan.

———. 1975. *The Archaeology of Michigan*, 2nd edition. Bloomfield Hills, Mich.: Cranbrook Institute of Science.

Fitting, J. E., and C. E. Cleland. 1969. Late Prehistoric Settlement Patterns in the Upper Great Lakes. *Ethnohistory* 16:289–302.

Flanders, R. E. 1965a. A Comparison of Some Middle Woodland Materials from Illinois and Michigan. Ph.D. dissertation, Department of Anthropology, University of Michigan, Ann Arbor.

———. 1965b. Engraved Turtle Shells from the Norton Mounds. *Papers of the Michigan Academy of Science, Arts, and Letters* 50:361–364.

———. 1977. Some Observations on the Goodall Focus. In *For the Director: Essays in Honor of James B. Griffin.* Museum of Anthropology, Anthropological Papers 611. Edited by C. E. Cleland, 144–151. Ann Arbor: University of Michigan.

———. 1979. New Evidence for Hopewell in Southwestern Michigan. In *Hopewell Archaeology: The Chillicothe Conference.* Edited by D. S. Brose and N. B. Greber, 113–114. Kent, Ohio: Kent State University Press.

Flanders, R. E., J. E. Marek, and W. F. Szten. 1979. *An Archaeological Survey of the Lower Grand River Valley, Ottawa County, Michigan, 1978.* Report submitted to the History Division, Michigan Department of State, Lansing, by Grand Valley State Colleges.

Fleming, A. 1999. Phenomenology and the Megaliths of Wales: A Dreaming Too Far? *Oxford Journal of Archaeology* 18:119–125.

Folan, W. J. 1991. Sacbes of the Northern Maya. In *Ancient Road Networks and Settlement Hierarchies in the New World.* Edited by C. D. Trombold, 222–229. Cambridge: Cambridge University Press.

Ford, J. A., and G. R. Willey. 1941. An Interpretation of the Prehistory of the Eastern United States. *American Anthropologist* 43:325–363.

Ford, R. I. 1979. Gathering and Gardening: Trends and Consequences of Hopewell Subsistence Strategies. In *Hopewell Archaeology: The Chillicothe Conference.* Edited by D. S. Brose and N. B. Greber, 234–238. Kent, Ohio: Kent State University Press.

———. 1985a. Patterns of Prehistoric Food Production in North America. In *Prehistoric*

Food Production in North America. Museum of Anthropology, Anthropological Papers 75. Edited by R. I. Ford, 341–364. Ann Arbor: University of Michigan.

———. 1985b. The Processes of Plant Food Production in Prehistoric North America. In *Prehistoric Food Production in North America.* Museum of Anthropology, Anthropological Papers 75. Edited by R. I. Ford, 1–18. Ann Arbor: University of Michigan.

Fortier, A. C. 1985. Middle Woodland Occupations at the Truck #7 and Go-Kart South Sites. In *Selected Sites in the Hill Lake Locality.* American Bottom Archaeology FAI-270 Site Reports, Vol. 13. Edited by A. C. Fortier, 163–280. Urbana: University of Illinois Press.

———. 1992. American Bottom House Types of the Archaic and Woodland Periods: An Overview. *Illinois Archaeology* 5:260–275.

———. 1995. Renaissance and Disequilibrium: Middle Woodland Discontinuities in the American Bottom. Paper presented at the 60th annual meeting of the Society for American Archaeology, Minneapolis.

———. 1998. Pre-Mississippian Economies in the American Bottom of Southwestern Illinois, 3000 B.C.–A.D. 1050. *Research in Economic Anthropology* 19:341–392.

———. 2000a. *The Dash Reeves Site: A Middle Woodland Village and Lithic Production Center in the American Bottom.* American Bottom Archaeology FAI-270 Site Reports, Vol. 28. Urbana: University of Illinois Press.

———. 2000b. The Emergence and Demise of the Middle Woodland Small-Tool Tradition in the American Bottom. *Midcontinental Journal of Archaeology* 25:191–213.

———. 2001. A Tradition of Discontinuity: American Bottom Early and Middle Woodland Culture History Reexamined. In *The Archaeology of Traditions: Agency and Tradition before and after Columbus.* Edited by T. K. Pauketat, 174–194. Gainesville: University Press of Florida.

———. 2004. The Petite Michele Site. An Early Middle Woodland Occupation in the American Bottom. Transportation Archaeological Research Reports, No. 19. Illinois Transportation Archaeological Research Program, University of Illinois, Urbana.

Fortier, A. C., T. E. Emerson, and F. A. Finney. 1984. Early and Middle Woodland Periods. In *A Summary of the FAI-270 Project Contribution to the Culture History of the Mississippi River Valley.* Edited by C. J. Bareis and J. W. Porter, 59–103. Urbana: University of Illinois Press.

Fortier, A. C., and S. Ghosh. 2000. The Bosque Medio Site: A Hopewellian Campsite in the American Bottom Uplands. *Illinois Archaeology* 12:1–56.

Fortier, A. C., T. O. Maher, J. A. Williams, M. C. Meinkoth, K. E. Parker, and L. S. Kelly. 1989. *The Holding Site: A Hopewell Community in the American Bottom.* American Bottom Archaeology FAI-270 Site Reports, Vol. 19. Urbana: University of Illinois.

Fowke, G. 1902. *Archaeological History of Ohio.* Columbus: Ohio State Archaeological and Historical Society.

Fowler, M. L. 1969. Middle Mississippian Agricultural Fields. *American Antiquity* 34:365–375.

———. 1992. The Eastern Horticultural Complex and Mississippian Agricultural Fields: Studies and Hypotheses. In *Late Prehistoric Agriculture: Observations from the Midwest.* Edited by W. I. Woods, 1–18. Springfield: Illinois Historic Preservation Agency.

Fowles, S. M. 2002. From Social Type to Social Process: Placing "Tribe" in a Historical Framework. In *The Archaeology of Tribal Societies.* Archaeological Series 15. Edited by W. A. Parkinson, 13–33. Ann Arbor: International Monographs in Prehistory.

Frank, A. G. 1993. Bronze Age World System Cycles. *Current Anthropology* 34:383–432.

———. 1999. Uses of World-Systems Theory in Archaeology. In *World-Systems Theory in Practice: Leadership, Production, and Exchange.* Edited by P. N. Kardulias, 275–296. Lanham, Md.: Rowman and Littlefield.

Frankenberg, S. R., D. G. Albertson, and L. Kohn. 1988. The Elizabeth Skeletal Remains: Demography and Disease. In *The Archaic and Woodland Cemeteries at the Elizabeth Mound Site in the Lower Illinois River Valley.* Research Series, Vol. 7. Edited by D. K. Charles, S. R. Leigh, and J. E. Buikstra, 103–119. Kampsville, Ill.: Center for American Archeology.

Freeman, J. E. 1968. Hopewell Indians. *Wisconsin Academy Review* 15:5–7.

———. 1969. The Millville Site, a Middle Woodland Village in Grant County, Wisconsin. *Wisconsin Archaeologist* 50:37–88.

Freidel, D. A., and J. A. Sabloff. 1984. *Cozumel: Late Maya Settlement Patterns.* Orlando: Academic Press.

Freidel, D. A., L. Schele, and J. Parker. 1993. *Maya Cosmos: Three Thousand Years on the Shaman's Path.* New York: William Morrow.

Fritz, G. J. 1990. Multiple Pathways to Farming in Precontact Eastern North America. *Journal of World Prehistory* 4:387–476.

———. 1993. Crops before Corn in the East: Regional Patterns of Early and Middle Woodland Period Paleoethnobotany. In *Foraging and Farming in the Eastern Woodlands.* Edited by C. M. Scarry, 39–56. Gainesville: University of Florida Press.

Fry, R. E. 1980. Models of Exchange for Major Shape Classes of Lowland Maya Pottery. In *Models and Methods in Regional Exchange.* Papers No. 1. Edited by R. E. Fry, 3–18. Washington, D.C.: Society for American Archaeology.

Fuller, J. W. 1981. The Development of Sedentary Village Communities in Northern West Virginia. In *Plowzone Archaeology: Contributions to Theory and Technique.* Publications in Anthropology, No. 27. Edited by M. J. O'Brien and D. Lewarch, 187–214. Nashville, Tenn.: Vanderbilt University.

Furst, P. T., ed. 1972. *Flesh of the Gods: The Ritual Use of Hallucinogens.* New York: Praeger.

Gaines, R. V., H. C. W. Skinner, E. E. Foord, B. Mason, and A. Rosenzweig. 1997. *Dana's New Mineralogy.* New York: John Wiley and Son.

Gallagher, J. P. 1992. Prehistoric Field Systems in the Upper Midwest. In *Prehistoric Agriculture: Observations from the Midwest.* Edited by W. I. Woods, 95–135. Springfield: Illinois Preservation Agency.

Gallagher, J. P., K. Stevenson, H. Fassler, C. Hill, M. Mills, T. Morrow, K. Motivans, S. Neff, T. Weeth, and R. Withrow. 1981. *The Overhead Site, 47LC20.* Mississippi Valley Archaeology Center, University of Wisconsin–La Crosse, report prepared for the State Historical Society of Wisconsin.

Garland, E. B. 1976. *Completion Report, Hacklander Archaeological Project 1975 Excavations, Allegan County, Michigan.* Report submitted to the Office of the State Archaeologist, Bureau of Michigan History, Department of State.

———. 1978. Late Woodland Occupation of the Lower Kalamazoo Valley, with Particular Reference to the Hacklander Site. Paper presented at the annual meeting of the Central States Anthropological Society, South Bend, Indiana.

———. 1986. Early Woodland Occupations in Michigan: A Lower St. Joseph Valley Perspective. In *Early Woodland Archaeology.* Seminars in Archeology, No. 2. Edited by K. B. Farnsworth and T. E. Emerson, 47–77. Kampsville, Ill.: Center for American Archeology.

———. 1990a. Early Post-Hopewell Ceremonialism at the Sumnerville Mounds Site

(20CS6): The Brainerd Phase in Southwestern Michigan. In *Pilot of the Grand: Papers in Tribute to Richard E. Flanders,* Part 1. Edited by T. J. Martin and C. E. Cleland. *Michigan Archaeologist* 36(3–4):191–210.

———, ed. 1990b. *Late Archaic and Early Woodland Adaptation in the Lower St. Joseph River Valley, Berrien County, Michigan: The US-31 Berrien County Freeway Project.* Michigan Cultural Resources Investigation Series 2. Lansing: Michigan Department of Transportation and Michigan Department of State.

———. 2000. Report on the Hart Site (20AE860) 2000 Field Season. Report submitted to the Office of the State Archaeologist, Michigan Historical Center, Michigan Department of State, Lansing.

Garland, E. B., and S. G. Beld. 1999. The Early Woodland: Ceramics, Domesticated Plants, and Burial Mounds Foretell the Shape of the Future. In *Retrieving Michigan's Buried Past: The Archaeology of the Great Lakes State.* Bulletin 64. Edited by J. R. Halsey, 125–146. Bloomfield Hills, Mich.: Cranbrook Institute of Science.

Garland, E. B., and A. L. DesJardins. 1995. The Strobel Site (20SJ180), a Havana Middle Woodland Encampment on the Prairie River in Southwestern Michigan. *Michigan Archaeologist* 41:1–40.

———. 1999. *Report on the Hart Site (20AE860) 1999 Field Season.* Report submitted to the Office of State Archaeologist, Michigan Historical Center, Michigan Department of State.

Garland, E. B., and R. G. Kingsley. 1979. *Settlement Pattern Survey in Allegan County, Michigan: 1978 Field Season.* Department of Anthropology, Archaeological Report, No. 4. Kalamazoo: Western Michigan University.

Garland, E. B., and K. E. Parachini. 1981. *Settlement Pattern Survey in Allegan County, Michigan: 1980 Field Season.* Department of Anthropology, Archaeological Report, No. 9. Kalamazoo: Western Michigan University.

Garland, E. B., and D. K. Rhead. 1980. *Settlement Pattern Survey in Allegan County, Michigan: 1979 Field Season.* Department of Anthropology, Archaeological Report, No. 6. Kalamazoo: Western Michigan University.

Garner, D. E., N. E. Reeder, and J. E. Ernst. 1973. *Soil Survey of Warren County.* Columbus: United States Department of Agriculture, Ohio; Ohio Department of Natural Resources, Division of Land and Soils; and the Ohio Agricultural Research and Development Center.

Garwood, P. 1991. Ritual Tradition and the Reconstruction of Society. In *Sacred and Profane.* Monograph 32. Edited by P. Garwood, D. Jennings, R. Skeates, and J. Toms, 10–32. Oxford: Oxford University Committee for Archaeology.

Genheimer, R. A. 1984. *A Systematic Examination of Middle Woodland Settlements in Warren County, Ohio.* Report submitted to Ohio Historic Preservation Office.

———. 1996. Bladelets Are Tools, Too: The Predominance of Bladelets among Formal Tools at Ohio Hopewell Sites. In *A View from the Core: A Synthesis of Ohio Hopewell Archaeology.* Edited by P. J. Pacheco, 92–107. Columbus: Ohio Archaeological Council.

———. 1997. Stubbs Cluster: Hopewellian Site Dynamics at a Forgotten Little Miami River Valley Settlement. In *Ohio Hopewell Community Organization.* Edited by W. S. Dancey and P. J. Pacheco, 283–309. Kent, Ohio: Kent State University Press.

Gibson, J. L. 1986. Earth Sitting: Architectural Masses at Poverty Point, Northeastern Louisiana. *Louisiana Archaeology* 13:201–248.

Giddens, A. 1979. *Central Problems in Social Theory.* London: Macmillan.

———. 1981. *A Contemporary Critique of Historical Materialism.* London: Macmillan.

Gilbert, G. K. 1886. The Inculcation of Scientific Method by Example, with an Illustration Drawn from the Quaternary Geology of Utah. *American Journal of Science* (3rd ser.) 31:284–299.

Glascock, M. D. 1992. Characterization of Archaeological Ceramics at MURR by Neutron Activation Analysis and Multivariate Statistics. In *Chemical Characterization of Ceramic Pastes in Archaeology.* Monographs in World Archaeology, No. 7. Edited by H. Neff, 11–26. Madison, Wisc.: Prehistory Press.

Glocker, C. L. 1979. *Soil Survey of Jefferson County, Wisconsin.* Madison: United States Department of Agriculture Soil Conservation Service and Wisconsin Agricultural Experiment Station.

Goad, S. I. 1979. Middle Woodland Exchange in the Prehistoric Southeastern United States. In *Hopewell Archaeology: The Chillicothe Conference.* Edited by D. S. Brose and N. B. Greber, 239–246. Kent, Ohio: Kent State University Press.

Goldstein, L. G. 1980a. *Mississippian Mortuary Practices: A Case Study of Two Cemeteries in the Lower Illinois Valley.* Scientific Papers, No. 4. Evanston, Ill.: Northwestern University Archeological Program.

———. 1980b. The Pitzner Site. In *A Continuing Archaeological Survey of Portions of the Crawfish and Rock River Valleys near Their Confluence in Jefferson County, Wisconsin.* Archaeological Research Laboratory, Report of Investigations 45. Edited by L. G. Goldstein, 64–82. Milwaukee: University of Wisconsin–Milwaukee.

———. 1981. One-Dimensional Archaeology and Multi-Dimensional People: Spatial Organization and Mortuary Analysis. In *The Archaeology of Death.* Edited by R. Chapman, I. Kinnes, and K. Randsborg, 53–69. Cambridge: Cambridge University Press.

———. 1983. The Trillium Site. In *The Southeastern Wisconsin Archaeological Program: 1982–1983.* Archaeological Research Laboratory, Report of Investigations 68. Edited by L. G. Goldstein, 138–178. Milwaukee: University of Wisconsin–Milwaukee.

———. 1992. Produce a Middle Woodland Study Unit. In *The Southeast Wisconsin Archaeological Project: 1991–1992.* Archaeological Research Laboratory, Reports of Investigations 67. Edited by L. G. Goldstein, 148–189. Milwaukee: University of Wisconsin–Milwaukee.

———. 1995. Landscapes and Mortuary Practices: A Case for Regional Perspectives. In *Regional Approaches to Mortuary Analysis.* Edited by L. A. Beck, 101–124. New York: Plenum.

Goodman, J. 1993. *Tobacco in History: The Culture of Dependence.* London: Routledge.

Goodwin, J. H., and J. M. Masters. 1983. *Sedimentology and Bathymetry of Pool 26, Mississippi River.* Environmental Geology Notes 103. Urbana: Illinois State Geological Survey.

Gordon, R. B. 1969. *The Natural Vegetation of Ohio in Pioneer Days.* Bulletin 3 (2), n.s. Columbus: Ohio Biological Survey.

Gordus, A. A., W. C. Fink, M. E. Hill, J. C. Purdy, and T. R. Wilcox. 1967. Identification of the Geologic Origins of Archaeological Artifacts: An Automated Method of Na and Mn Neutron Activation Analysis. *Archaeometry* 10:87–96.

Gordus, A. A., J. B. Griffin, and G. A. Wright. 1971. Activation Analysis Identification of the Geologic Origins of Prehistoric Obsidian Artifacts. In *Science and Archaeology.* Edited by R. H. Brill, 222–234. Cambridge, Mass.: MIT Press.

Gramly, R. M. 2003. Obsidian Sourcing: An Example from an Hopewell Artifact Assemblage in Ohio. *Amateur Archaeologist* 9:35–41.

Greber, N. B. 1976. Within Ohio Hopewell: Analysis of Burial Patterns from Several Classic Sites. Ph.D. dissertation, Department of Anthropology, Case Western Reserve University, Cleveland, Ohio.

———. 1979a. A Comparative Study of Site Morphology and Burial Patterns at Edwin Harness Mound and Seip Mounds 1 and 2. In *Hopewell Archaeology: The Chillicothe Conference*. Edited by D. S. Brose and N. B. Greber, 27–38. Kent, Ohio: Kent State University Press.

———. 1979b. Variations in Social Structure of Ohio Hopewell Peoples. *Midcontinental Journal of Archaeology* 4:35–78.

———. 1983. Recent Excavations at the Edwin Harness Mound, Liberty Works, Ross County, Ohio. In Midcontinental Journal of Archaeology, Special Paper No. 5. Kent, Ohio: Kent State University Press.

———. 1989. *Ohio Hopewell*. Weston, Conn.: Pictures of Record.

———. 1991. A Study of Continuity and Contrast between Central Scioto Adena and Hopewell Sites. *West Virginia Archaeologist* 43:1–26.

———. 1993a. Considering Some Possible Ecological, Social, and Political Boundaries among Ohio Hopewell Peoples. Paper presented at the 58th annual meeting of Society for American Archaeology, St. Louis, Missouri.

———. 1993b. The Turner Site as Seen from the Scioto Valley. Paper presented at the second annual Conference on Ohio Archaeology, the Ohio Archaeological Council, Chillicothe.

———. 1995. *Some Archaeological Localities Recorded in the Seip Earthwork and Dill Mounds Historic District*. Report submitted to the Midwest Archaeological Center, National Park Service, Lincoln, Nebraska.

———. 1996. A Commentary on the Contexts and Contents of Large to Small Ohio Hopewell Deposits. In *A View from the Core: A Synthesis of Ohio Hopewell Archaeology*. Edited by P. J. Pacheco, 150–173. Columbus: Ohio Archaeological Council.

———. 1997. Two Geometric Enclosures in the Paint Creek Valley: An Estimate of Possible Changes in Community Patterns through Time. In *Ohio Hopewell Community Organization*. Edited by W. S. Dancey and P. J. Pacheco, 207–229. Kent, Ohio: Kent State University Press.

———. 1998a. Geophysics and Archaeology: A Case Study from the High Banks Earthworks, Ross County, Ohio. Paper presented at the 63rd annual meeting of the Society for American Archaeology, Seattle.

———. 1998b. Ohio Hopewell. In *Encyclopedia of North American Prehistory*. Edited by G. E. Gibbon, 601–604. New York: Garland Publishing.

———. 1998c. Seip Earthworks. In *Encyclopedia of North American Prehistory*. Edited by G. E. Gibbon, 753–754. New York: Garland Publishing.

———. 1999a. Combining Geophysics and Ground Truthing at High Banks Earthworks, Ross County, Ohio. *Ohio Archaeological Council Newsletter* 11:8–11.

———. 1999b. Correlating Maps of the Hopewell Site, 1820–1993. Manuscript on file, Hopewell Culture National Historical Park, Chillicothe, Ohio.

———. 2002. A Preliminary Comparison of 1997 and 2002 Limited Excavations in the Great Circle Wall, High Banks Works, Ross County, Ohio. *Hopewell Archaeology: The Newsletter of Hopewell Archaeology in the Ohio River Valley* 5:1-6.

———. 2003. Chronological Relationships among Ohio Hopewell Sites: Few Dates and Much Complexity. In *Theory, Method, and Practice in Modern Archaeology*. Edited by R. J. Jeske and D. K. Charles, 88–113. Westport, Conn.: Praeger.

———. 2005 Adena and Hopewell in the Middle Ohio Valley: To Be or Not to Be. In *Woodland Period Systematics in the Middle Ohio Valley*. Edited by D. Applegate and R. C. Mainfort Jr. Tuscaloosa: University of Alabama Press.

Greber, N. B., R. S. Davis, and A. S. DuFresne. 1981. The Micro-component of the Ohio Hopewell Lithic Technology: Bladelets. *Annals of the New York Academy of Sciences* 376:489–528.

Greber, N. B., J. B. Griffin, T. L. Smart, R. I. Ford, O. C. Shane III, R. S. Baby, S. M. Langlois, S. J. Belovich, D. R. Morse, and K. D. Vickery. 1983. *Recent Excavations at the Edwin Harness Mound, Liberty Works, Ross County, Ohio*. Midcontinental Journal of Archaeology, Special Paper 5. Kent, Ohio: Kent State University Press.

Greber, N. B., and K. C. Ruhl. 1989. *The Hopewell Site: A Contemporary Analysis Based on the Work of Charles C. Willoughby*. Investigations in American Archaeology. Boulder, Colo.: Westview Press.

Greber, N. B., and M. F. Seeman. 1993. *The 1992 Field Season at the Hopewell Site, Ross County, Ohio*. Report on file, Hopewell Culture National Historical Park, Chillicothe, Ohio.

———. 1995. *The 1993 Field Season at the Hopewell Site, Ross County, Ohio*. Report to the Archaeological Conservancy, on file at the Hopewell Culture National Historical Park, Chillicothe, Ohio.

Greber, N. B., and O. C. Shane III. 2003. Studies of the Octagon and Great Circle, High Bank Works. Paper presented at the 68th annual meeting of the Society for American Archaeology, Milwaukee.

Greeley, H. 1963. *An Overland Journey from New York to San Francisco in the Summer of 1859*. Edited by C. T. Duncan. New York: Alfred A. Knopf.

Green, T. J. 1977. Economic Relationships Underlying Mississippian Settlement Patterns in Southwestern Indiana and North-Central Kentucky. Ph.D. dissertation, Department of Anthropology, Indiana University, Bloomington.

Green, T. J., and C. A. Munson. 1978. Mississippian Settlement Patterns in Southwestern Indiana. In *Mississippian Settlement Patterns*. Edited by B. D. Smith, 293–325. New York: Academic Press.

Green, W. E. 1994. *Agricultural Origins and Development in the Midcontinent*. Report 19. Office of the State Archaeologist, University of Iowa, Iowa City.

Gremillion, K. J. 1993. Crop and Weed in Prehistoric Eastern North America: The *Chenopodium* Example. *American Antiquity* 58:496–509.

Griffin, J. B. 1945. The Box Elder Mound in La Salle County, Illinois. *American Antiquity* 11:47–48.

———. 1952a. A Preview of the Ceramic Relationship of the Snyders Site, Calhoun County, Illinois. In *The Greater St. Louis Archaeological Society, Mimeograph 50*, 14–20.

———. 1952b. Culture Periods in Eastern United States. In *Archaeology of Eastern United States*. Edited by J. B. Griffin, 352–364. Chicago: University of Chicago Press.

———. 1952c. Some Early and Middle Woodland Pottery Types in Illinois. In *Hopewellian Communities in Illinois*. Scientific Papers 5. Edited by T. Deuel, 95–129. Springfield: Illinois State Museum.

———. 1958. *The Chronologic Position of the Hopewellian Culture in the Eastern United States*. Museum of Anthropology, Anthropological Papers 12. Ann Arbor: University of Michigan.

———. 1960. Climatic Change: A Contributory Cause of the Growth and Decline of Northern Hopewellian Culture. *Wisconsin Archaeologist* 41:21–33.

————. 1964. The Northeast Woodlands Area. In *Prehistoric Man in the New World.* Edited by J. D. Jennings and E. Norbeck, 223–258. Chicago: University of Chicago Press.

————. 1965. Hopewell and the Dark Black Glass. *Michigan Archaeologist* 11:115–155.

————. 1967. Eastern North American Archaeology: A Summary. *Science* 156(3772): 175–191.

————. 1975. Review of Variation in Anthropology: Essays in Honor of John C. McGregor. *American Anthropologist* 77:142–143.

————. 1978. The Midlands and Northeastern United States. In *Ancient Native Americans.* Edited by J. D. Jennings, 243–301. San Francisco: W. H. Freeman.

————. 1979. An Overview of the Chillicothe Conference. In *Hopewell Archaeology: The Chillicothe Conference.* Edited by D. S. Brose and N. B. Greber, 266–279. Kent, Ohio: Kent State University Press.

————. 1981. The Man Who Comes After; Or, Careful How You Curate the Research Potential of Anthropological Museum Collections. *Annals of the New York Academy of Sciences* 376:7–15.

————. 1983a. The Ceramic Complex. In *Recent Excavations at the Edwin Harness Mound, Liberty Works, Ross County, Ohio.* Kirtlandia, Vol. 39. Edited by N. B. Greber, 39–53. Cleveland: Cleveland Museum of Natural History.

————. 1983b. The Midlands. In *Ancient North Americans.* Edited by J. D. Jennings, 243–301. San Francisco: W. H. Freeman.

————. 1996. The Hopewell Housing Shortage in Ohio, A.D. 1–350. In *A View from the Core: A Synthesis of Ohio Hopewell Archaeology.* Edited by P. J. Pacheco, 4–15. Columbus: Ohio Archaeological Council.

————. 1997. Interpretations of Ohio Hopewell 1845–1984 and the Recent Emphasis on the Study of Dispersed Hamlets. In *Ohio Hopewell Community Organization.* Edited by W. S. Dancey and P. J. Pacheco, 405–426. Kent, Ohio: Kent State University Press.

Griffin, J. B., R. E. Flanders, and P. F. Titterington. 1970. *The Burial Complexes of the Knight and Norton Mounds in Illinois and Michigan.* Memoirs of the Museum of Anthropology, No. 2. Ann Arbor: University of Michigan.

Griffin, J. B., and A. A. Gordus. 1967. Neutron Activation Studies of the Sources of Prehistoric Hopewellian Obsidian Implements from the Middle West. *Science* 158:528.

Griffin, J. B., A. A. Gordus, and G. A. Wright. 1969. Identification of the Sources of Hopewellian Obsidian in the Middle West. *American Antiquity* 34:1–14.

Grinnell, G. B. 1923. *The Cheyenne Indians: Their History and Ways of Life,* Vol. 2. New Haven, Conn.: Yale University Press.

Gundersen, J. N., and J. A. Brown. 2002. The Ceramics of Hopewellian Shamanic Display. Paper presented at the 67th annual meeting, Society for American Archaeology, Denver.

Haberman, T. W. 1984. Evidence for Aboriginal Tobaccos in Eastern North America. *American Antiquity* 42:269–287.

Hajic, E. R. 1985. Landscape Evolution and Archeological Contexts in the Lower Illinois River Valley. *American Archeology* 5:127–136.

————. 1990a. *Koster Site Archeology: Stratigraphy and Landscape Evolution.* Research Series, Vol. 8. Kampsville, Ill.: Center for American Archeology.

————. 1990b. Late Pleistocene and Holocene Landscape Evolution, Depositional Subsystems, and Stratigraphy in the Lower Illinois River Valley. Ph.D. dissertation, Department of Geology, University of Illinois at Urbana-Champaign.

Hale, E. E., Jr. 1980. Archaeological Survey Report, Phase III, LIC-79–12–5. Department of Archaeology, Ohio Historical Society, Columbus.

Hall, R. L. 1976. Ghosts, Water Barriers, Corn, and Sacred Enclosures in the Eastern Woodlands. *American Antiquity* 41:360–354.

———. 1977. An Anthropocentric Perspective for Eastern United States Prehistory. *American Antiquity* 42:499–518.

———. 1979. In Search of the Ideology of the Adena-Hopewell Climax. In *Hopewell Archaeology: The Chillicothe Conference.* Edited by D. S. Brose and N. B. Greber, 258–265. Kent, Ohio: Kent State University Press.

———. 1980. An Interpretation of the Two-Climax Model of Illinois Prehistory. In *Early Native Americans: Prehistoric Demography, Economy, and Technology.* Edited by D. L. Browman, 401–462. The Hague: Mouton.

———. 1983. The Evolution of the Calumet-Pipe. In *Prairie Archaeology: Papers in Honor of David A. Baerreis.* Publications in Anthropology 3. Edited by G. E. Gibbon, 37–52. Minneapolis: University of Minnesota.

———. 1985. The Buffalo as a Water Monster in Midwestern Indian Belief. Paper presented at the annual meeting of the American Society for Ethnohistory, Chicago.

———. 1987a. Calumet Ceremonialism, Mourning Ritual, and Mechanisms of Intertribal Trade. In *Mirror and Metaphor: Material and Social Constructions of Reality.* Edited by D. J. Ingersoll and G. Bronitsky, 29–43. Lanham, Md.: University Press of America.

———. 1987b. Type Description of Starved Rock Collard. *Wisconsin Archaeologist* 68:65–70.

———. 1991. Cahokia Identity and Interaction Models of Cahokia Mississippian. In *Cahokia and the Hinterlands.* Edited by T. E. Emerson and R. B. Lewis, 3–34. Urbana: University of Illinois.

———. 1997. *An Archaeology of the Soul: North American Indian Belief and Ritual.* Urbana: University of Illinois Press.

Hall, T. D. 1999. World-Systems and Evolution: An Appraisal. In *World-Systems Theory in Practice: Leadership, Production, and Exchange.* Edited by P. N. Kardulias, 1–24. Lanham, Md.: Rowman and Littlefield.

Hallam, B. R., S. E. Warren, and C. Renfrew. 1976. Obsidian in the Western Mediterranean: Characterisation by Neutron Activation Analysis and Optical Emission Spectroscopy. *Proceedings of the Prehistoric Society* 42:85–110.

Hambacher, M. J., J. G. Brashler, K. C. Egan-Bruhy, D. R. Hayes, B. Hardy, D. G. Landis, T. J. Martin, G. W. Monaghan, K. Murphy, J. A. Robertson, and D. L. Seltz. 2003. *Phase III Archaeological Data Recovery for the U.S. 131 S-Curve Realignment Project, Grand Rapids, Michigan.* Report No. R-0446. Report submitted to the Michigan Department of Transportation, Lansing, by Commonwealth Cultural Resources Group, Jackson, Michigan.

Hambacher, M. J., and J. A. Robertson. 2002. The Converse Site and Western Michigan Hopewell. Paper presented at the 67th annual meeting of the Society for American Archaeology, Denver.

Hambacher, M. J., and D. L. Ruggles. 2002. I Once Was Lost But Now Am Found: New Insights on Michigan Hopewell from the Converse Site (20KT2), Grand Rapids, Michigan. Symposium organized for the 67th annual meeting of the Society for American Archaeology, Denver.

Hamell, G. R. 1992. The Iroquois and the World's Rim: Speculations on Color, Culture, and Contact. *American Indian Quarterly* 16:451–469.

Hanenberger, N. 1990. The Olszewski Site. In *Selected Early Mississippian Household Sites in the American Bottom*. American Bottom Archaeology FAI-270 Site Reports, Vol. 22. Edited by D. Jackson and N. Hanenberger, 253–424. Urbana: University of Illinois Press.

Hanna, C. A. 1911. *The Wilderness Trail: The Ventures and Adventures of the Pennsylvania Traders on the Allegheny Path*. (2 vols.) New York: G. P. Putnam's Sons, Knickerbocker Press.

Harding, A. F. 2000. *European Societies in the Bronze Age*. Cambridge: Cambridge University Press.

Hargrave, M. L. 1982. Woodland Ceramic Decoration, Form, and Chronometry in the Carrier Mills Archaeological District. In *The Carrier Mills Archaeological Project: Human Adaptation in the Saline Valley*. Illinois Research Paper, Center for Archaeological Investigations. Edited by R. W. Jefferies and B. M. Butler, 1233–1288. Carbondale: Southern Illinois University at Carbondale.

Hargrave, M. L., and B. M. Butler. 1993. Crab Orchard Settlement Patterns and Residential Mobility. In *Highways to the Past: Essays on Illinois Archaeology in Honor of Charles J. Bareis*. Edited by T. E. Emerson, A. C. Fortier, and D. L. McElrath. *Illinois Archaeology* 5(1–2):181–192.

Harlan, J. R. 1994. *The Living Fields: Our Agricultural Heritage*. Cambridge: Cambridge University Press.

Harn, A. D. 1971. *An Archaeological Survey of the American Bottoms in Madison and St. Clair Counties, Illinois*. Reports of Investigations, No. 21, Part 2. Springfield: Illinois State Museum.

Harpending, H., and H. Davis. 1977. Some Implications for Hunter-Gatherer Ecology Derived from the Spatial Structure of Resources. *World Archaeology* 8:275–286.

Harris, D. R. 1989. An Evolutionary Continuum of People-Plant Interaction. In *Foraging and Farming: The Evolution of Plant Exploitation*. Edited by D. R. Harris and G. C. Hillman, 11–26. London: Unwin Hyman.

———. 1990. *Settling Down and Breaking Ground: Rethinking the Neolithic Revolution*. Twaalfde Kroon-Voordracht. Amsterdam: Stichting Nederlands Museum Voor Anthropologie en Praehistorie.

———. 1996. Introduction: Themes and Concepts in the Study of Early Agriculture. In *The Origins and Spread of Agriculture and Pastoralism in Eurasia*. Edited by D. R. Harris, 1–11. Washington, D.C.: Smithsonian Institution Press.

———. 1997. The Origins of Agriculture in Southwest Asia. *Review of Archaeology* 19:5–11.

Harrison, W. H. 1839. A Discourse on the Aborigines of the Valley of the Ohio. *Transactions of the Historical and Philosophical Society of Ohio* 1:217–267.

Hatch, J. W., J. W. Michels, C. M. Stevenson, B. E. Scheetz, and R. A. Geidel. 1990. Hopewell Obsidian Studies: Behavioral Implications of Recent Sourcing and Dating Research. *American Antiquity* 55:461–479.

Hatfield, V. L. 1998. Chipped Stone Tools. In *Prehistoric Settlement of the Lower Missouri Uplands: The View from DB Ridge, Fort Leavenworth, Kansas*. Museum of Anthropology, Project Report Series, No. 98. Edited by B. Logan, 141–166. Lawrence: University of Kansas.

Hawkins, R. A. 1996. Revising the Ohio Middle Woodland Ceramic Typology: New Information from the Twin Mounds West Site. In *A View from the Core: A Synthesis of Ohio Hopewell Archaeology*. Edited by P. J. Pacheco, 70–91. Columbus: Ohio Archaeological Council.

Hays, C. T. 1995. Adena Mortuary Patterns and Ritual Cycles in the Upper Scioto Valley, Ohio. Ph.D. dissertation, Department of Anthropology, State University of New York at Binghamton.

Heart, J. 1789. Accounts of Some Remains of Ancient Works on the Muskingum, with a Plan of These Works. *Columbian Magazine* 1:425–427.

Heckewelder, J. 1881. *History, Manners, and Customs of the Indian Nations Who Once Inhabited Pennsylvania and the Neighboring States.* Philadelphia: Historical Society of Pennsylvania.

Hegmon, M. 2003. Setting Theoretical Egos Aside: Issues and Theory in North American Archaeology. *American Antiquity* 68:213–243.

Henning, D. R. 1998. The Oneota Tradition. In *Archaeology on the Great Plains.* Edited by W. R. Wood, 345–414. Lawrence: University Press of Kansas.

Henriksen, H. C. 1957. Utica Hopewell: A Study of Early Hopewellian Occupation in the Illinois River Valley. M.A. thesis, Department of Anthropology, University of Illinois at Urbana-Champaign.

———. 1965. Utica Hopewell: A Study of Early Hopewellian Occupation in the Illinois River Valley. In *Middle Woodland Sites in Illinois.* Bulletin No. 5. Edited by E. B. Herold, 1–67. Urbana: Illinois Archaeological Survey.

Herold, E. B. 1971. *The Indian Mounds at Albany, Illinois.* Anthropological Papers No. 1. Davenport, Iowa: Davenport Museum.

Hertz, R. 1907. A Contribution to the Study of the Collective Representation of Death. In *Death and the Right Hand,* pp. 27–86. Glencoe, Ill.: Free Press. (1960 translation by Rodney Needham.)

Hiatt, J. W. n.d. Account of Exploration of Mounds in Posey County. Manuscript on file, Glenn A. Black Laboratory of Archaeology, Indiana University, Bloomington.

Higgenbotham, C. D. 1983. An Archaeological Survey of the Lower Wabash Valley in Gibson and Posey Counties in Indiana. Ph.D. dissertation, Department of Anthropology, Purdue University, West Lafayette, Indiana.

Hinsdale, W. B. 1925. *Primitive Man in Michigan.* University Museum Handbook Series, No. 1. Ann Arbor: University of Michigan.

———. 1931. *An Archaeological Atlas of Michigan.* Ann Arbor: University of Michigan Press.

Hively, R., and R. Horn. 1982. Geometry and Astronomy in Prehistoric Ohio. *Archaeoastronomy* 4:S1–S20.

———. 1984. Hopewellian Geometry and Astronomy at High Bank. *Archaeoastronomy* 7:S85–S100.

Hobbs, S. D. 2000. The Stories behind the Great Seal of Ohio. *Echoes* 39:3.

Hodder, I. 1974. Regression Analysis of Some Trade and Marketing Patterns. *World Archaeology* 6:172–189.

———. 1982. *Symbols in Action.* Cambridge: Cambridge University Press.

———. 1988. Material Culture Texts and Social Change: A Theoretical Discussion and Some Archaeological Examples. *Proceedings of the Prehistoric Society* 54:67–75.

———. 1990. *The Domestication of Europe.* Oxford: Blackwell.

———. 1991a. Postprocessual Archaeology and the Current Debate. In *Processual and Postprocessual Archaeologies: Multiple Ways of Knowing the Past.* Center for Archaeological Investigations, Occasional Paper No. 10. Edited by R. W. Preucel, 30–41. Carbondale: Southern Illinois University.

———. 1991b. *Reading the Past.* Cambridge: Cambridge University Press.

———. 1999. *The Archaeological Process.* Oxford: Blackwell.

Hoekstra, T. W. 1972. Ecology and Population Dynamics of the White-Tailed Deer on Crane Naval Ammunition Depot, Indiana. Ph.D. dissertation, Department of Forestry and Conservation, Purdue University, West Lafayette, Indiana.

Hofman, J. L. 1987. Hopewell Blades from Twenhafel: Distinguishing Local and Foreign Core Technology. In *The Organization of Core Technology*. Edited by J. K. Johnson and C. A. Morrow, 87–117. Boulder, Colo.: Westview Press.

Hofman, J. L., and C. A. Morrow. 1984. Chipped Stone Technologies at Twenhafel: A Multicomponent Site in Southern Illinois. In *Lithic Resource Procurement: Proceedings from the Second Conference on Prehistoric Chert Exploitation*. Center for Archaeological Investigations, Occasional Paper No. 4. Edited by S. Vehik, 165–182. Carbondale: Southern Illinois University at Carbondale.

Holley, G. R. 1993. Observations Regarding Sedentism in Central Silver Creek and the Enduring Significance of the FAI-64 Archaeological Mitigation Program. *Illinois Archaeology* 5:276–284.

Holliday, V. T. 1992. Soil Formation, Time, and Archaeology. In *Soils in Archaeology*. Edited by V. T. Holliday, 101–117. Washington, D.C.: Smithsonian Institution Press.

Holman, M. B. 1990. The Bolthouse Site (20OT11/52) and Woodland Settlement in the Grand River Valley. In *Pilot of the Grand: Papers in Tribute to Richard E. Flanders*, Part 1. Edited by T. J. Martin and C. E. Cleland, pp. 171–190. *Michigan Archaeologist* 36(3–4):171–190.

Holmes, W. H. 1903. Aboriginal Pottery of the Eastern United States. Twentieth Annual Report Bureau of American Ethnology, 1898–99. Edited by J. W. Powell, 1–201. Washington, D.C.: Government Printing Office.

———. 1919. *Handbook of Aboriginal American Antiquities, Part I, The Lithic Industries*. Bulletin 60. Washington, D.C.: Bureau of American Ethnology.

Holt, J. Z. 2000. Animal Exploitation and the Middle to Late Woodland Transition: A Comparison of Animal Use at Mound Centers and Hamlets in the Lower and Central Illinois Valleys. Ph.D. dissertation, Department of Anthropology, New York University.

———. 2004. The Havana Socioeconomy and Its Fall: Testing Winters' Model with White-Tailed Deer Remains from the Baehr-Gust Site. In *Aboriginal Ritual and Economy in the Eastern Woodlands: Essays in Memory of Howard Dalton Winters*. Scientific Papers 30 (Illinois State Museum); Studies in Archeology and History, Vol. 5 (Center for American Archeology). Edited by A.-M. Cantwell, L. A. Conrad, and J. E. Reyman, 241–257. Springfield: Illinois State Museum, and Kampsville, Ill.: Center for American Archeology.

Hood, J. E. 1996. Social Relations and the Cultural Landscape. In *Landscape Archaeology: Reading and Interpreting the American Historical Landscape*. Edited by R. Yamin and K. B. Metheny, 121–146. Knoxville: University of Tennessee Press.

Hooge, P. E. 1992. Preserving the Past for the Future. In *Vanishing Heritage*. Edited by P. E. Hooge and B. T. Lepper, 74–92. Newark, Ohio: Licking County Archaeology and Landmarks Society.

Horn, H. 1968. The Adaptive Significance of Colonial Nesting in the Brewer's Blackbird. *Ecology* 49:682–694.

Hosea, L. M. 1874. Some Facts and Considerations about Fort Ancient, Warren County, Ohio. *Cincinnati Quarterly Journal of Science* 1:289–302.

Howard, J. H. 1981. *Shawnee! The Ceremonialism of a Native Indian Tribe and Its Cultural Background*. Athens: Ohio University Press.

Hubbs, C. L., and K. F. Lagler. 1967. *Fishes of the Great Lakes Region.* Ann Arbor: University of Michigan Press.

Hudson, C. 1976. *The Southeastern Indians.* Knoxville: University of Tennessee Press.

Hughes, R. E. 1978. Aspects of Prehistoric Wiyot Exchange and Social Ranking. *Journal of California Anthropology* 5:53–66.

———. 1986. *Diachronic Variability in Obsidian Procurement Patterns in Northeastern California and Southcentral Oregon.* Publications in Anthropology 17. Berkeley and Los Angeles: University of California.

———. 1988. The Coso Volcanic Field Reexamined: Implications for Obsidian Sourcing and Hydration Dating Research. *Geoarchaeology* 3:253–265.

———. 1989. The Gold Hill Site: Evidence for a Prehistoric Socioceremonial System in Southwestern Oregon. In *Living with the Land: The Indians of Southwest Oregon.* Edited by N. Hannon and R. K. Olmo, 48–55. Medford: Southern Oregon Historical Society.

———. 1992. Another Look at Hopewell Obsidian Studies. *American Antiquity* 57:515–523.

———. 1994. Intrasource Chemical Variability of Artifact-Quality Obsidians from the Casa Diablo Area, California. *Journal of Archaeological Science* 21:263–271.

———. 1995. Source Identification of Obsidian from the Trowbridge Site (14WY1), a Hopewellian Site in Kansas. *Midcontinental Journal of Archaeology* 20:105–113.

———. 1998. On Reliability, Validity, and Scale in Obsidian Sourcing Research. In *Unit Issues in Archaeology: Measuring Time, Space, and Material.* Edited by A. F. Ramenofsky and A. Steffen, 103–114. Salt Lake City: University of Utah Press.

———. 2000a. *Geochemical Research Laboratory Letter Report 2000–66.* Portola Valley, Calif.

———. 2000b. X-Ray Fluorescence Analysis of Obsidian Artifacts from Treasure Cave (39LA504) in the North Black Hills of South Dakota. *Geochemical Research Laboratory Letter Report 2000–7.* Portola Valley, Calif.

Hughes, R. E., T. E. Berres, and K. B. Farnsworth. 1998. Revision of Hopewellian Trading Patterns in Midwestern North America Based on Mineralogical Sourcing. *Geoarchaeology* 13:701–730.

Hughes, R. E., and A. C. Fortier. 1997. Identification of the Geologic Sources for Obsidian Artifacts from Three Middle Woodland Sites in the American Bottom, Illinois. *Illinois Archaeology* 9:79–92.

Hughes, R. E., M. Kay, and T. J. Green. 2002. Geochemical and Microwear Analysis of an Obsidian Artifact from the Brown Bluff Site (3WA10), Arkansas. *Plains Anthropologist* 47:73–76.

Hughes, R. E., and F. W. Nelson. 1987. New Findings on Obsidian Source Utilization in Iowa. *Plains Anthropologist* 32:313–316.

Hugh-Jones, S. 1979. *The Palm and the Pleiades.* Cambridge: Cambridge University Press.

Hultkrantz, Å. 1979. *The Religions of the American Indians.* Berkeley: University of California Press.

———. 1985. The Shaman and the Medicine-Man. *Social Science and Medicine* 20:511–515.

———. 1989. Health, Religion, and Medicine in Native North American Traditions. In *Health and Medicine in the World's Religious Traditions.* Edited by L. E. Sullivan, 327–358. New York: Macmillan.

Hunter-Anderson, R. L. 1977. A Theoretical Approach to the Study of House Form. In

For Theory Building in Archaeology: Essays on Faunal Remains, Aquatic Resources, Spatial Analysis, and Systemic Modeling. Edited by L. R. Binford, 287–315. New York: Academic Press.

Huntington, R., and P. Metcalf. 1979. *Celebrations of Death: The Anthropology of Mortuary Rituals.* New York: Cambridge University Press.

Hurley, W. M. 1974. *Silver Creek Woodland Sites, Southwest Wisconsin.* Report 6. Office of the State Archaeologist, University of Iowa, Iowa City.

———. 1975. *An Analysis of Effigy Mound Complexes in Wisconsin.* Museum of Anthropology, Anthropological Papers 59. Ann Arbor: University of Michigan.

Hyde, J. E. 1921. *Geology of the Camp Sherman Quadrangle.* Bulletin 23, 4th ser. Columbus: Geological Survey of Ohio.

Ingbar, E. E., M. L. Larson, and B. A. Bradley. 1989. A Nontypological Approach to Debitage Analysis. In *Experiments in Lithic Technology.* BAR International Series 528. Edited by D. S. Amick and R. P. Mauldin, 117–136. Oxford: Oxford University Press.

Ingold, T. 1987. *The Appropriation of Nature: Essays on Human Ecology and Social Relations.* Iowa City: University of Iowa Press.

Irwin, L. 1994. *The Dream Seekers: Native American Visionary Traditions of the Great Plains.* Norman: University of Oklahoma Press.

Jackson, H. E., and S. L. Scott. 1995. The Faunal Record of the Southeastern Elite: The Implications of Economy, Social Relations, and Ideology. *Southeastern Archaeology* 14:103–119.

Janiger, O., and M. Dobkin de Rios. 1976. *Nicotiana* an Hallucinogen. *Economic Botany* 30:149–151.

Jefferies, R. W. 1975. The Tunacunnhee Site: Evidence of Hopewellian Interaction in Northwestern Georgia. M.A. thesis, Department of Anthropology, University of Georgia, Athens.

———. 1976. *The Tunacunnhee Site: Evidence of Hopewell Interaction in Northwest Georgia.* Anthropological Papers of the University of Georgia, No. 1. Athens: Department of Anthropology, University of Georgia.

———. 1978. Intersite Activity Variability in the Lookout Valley Area of Northwest Georgia. Ph.D. dissertation, Department of Anthropology, University of Georgia, Athens.

———. 1979. The Tunacunnhee Site: Hopewell in Northwest Georgia. In *Hopewell Archaeology: The Chillicothe Conference.* Edited by D. S. Brose and N. B. Greber, 162–170. Kent, Ohio: Kent State University Press.

———. 1982. Debitage as an Indicator of Intraregional Activity Diversity in Northwest Georgia. *Midcontinental Journal of Archaeology* 7:99–132.

Jennings, J. D. 1989. *Prehistory of North America.* 3rd edition. Mountain View, Calif.: Mayfield.

Jeske, R. J. 1999. World Systems Theory, Core Periphery Interactions, and Elite Economic Exchange in Mississippian Societies. In *World-Systems Theory in Practice: Leadership, Production, and Exchange.* Edited by P. N. Kardulias, 203–222. Lanham, Md.: Rowman and Littlefield.

Jeske, R. J., and J. P. Hart. 1988. *Report on Test Excavations at Four Sites in the Illinois and Michigan Canal National Heritage Corridor, La Salle and Grundy Counties, Illinois.* Contributions 6. Evanston, Ill.: Northwestern Archaeological Center.

Jeske, R. J., and K. E. Kaufmann. 2000. The Alberts Site (47je887 & 47je903): Excavations at a Late Archaic through Mississippian Site in Jefferson County. In *The South-*

eastern Wisconsin Archaeology Program: 1999–2000. Archaeological Research Laboratory Report of Investigations 144. Edited by R. J. Jeske, 79–98. Milwaukee: University of Wisconsin–Milwaukee.

Johannessen, S. 1983. Plant Remains from the Cement Hollow Phase. In *The Mund Site (11–S-435).* American Bottom Archaeology, FAI-270 Site Reports, Vol. 5. Edited by A. C. Fortier, F. A. Finney and R. B. Lacampagne, 94–104. Urbana: University of Illinois Press.

———. 1984. Paleoethnobotany. In *American Bottom Archaeology.* Edited by C. Bareis and J. Porter, 197–214. Urbana: University of Illinois Press.

———. 1988. Plant Remains and Culture Change: Are Paleoethnobotanical Data Better Than We Think? In *Current Paleoethnobotany: Analytical Methods and Cultural Interpretations of Archaeological Plant Remains.* Edited by C. A. Hastorf and V. S. Popper, 145–166. Chicago: University of Chicago Press.

Johansen, C., M. Kastell, D. F. Overstreet, and L. A. Brazeau. 1998. *Archeological Recovery at the DEET Thinker (47 Cr 467), Cipra (47 Cr 414), and McCarthy (47 Cr 108) Sites.* Reports of Investigations 294. Milwaukee: Great Lakes Archaeological Research Center.

Johnson, A. E. 1974. Settlement Pattern Variability in Brush Creek Valley, Platte County, Missouri. *Plains Anthropologist* 19:107–122.

———. 1976a. A Model of the Kansas City Hopewell Subsistence-Settlement System. In *Hopewellian Archaeology in the Lower Missouri Valley.* Publications in Anthropology, No. 8. Edited by A. E. Johnson, 7–15. Lawrence: University of Kansas.

———. 1976b. Introduction. In *Hopewellian Archaeology in the Lower Missouri Valley.* Publications in Anthropology, No. 8. Edited by A. E. Johnson, 1–6. Lawrence: University of Kansas.

———. 1979. Kansas City Hopewell. In *Hopewell Archaeology: The Chillicothe Conference.* Edited by D. S. Brose and N. B. Greber, 86–93. Kent, Ohio: Kent State University Press.

———. 1981. The Kansas City Hopewell Subsistence and Settlement System. *Missouri Archaeologist* 42:69–76.

———. 1992. Early Woodland in the Trans-Missouri West. *Plains Anthropologist* 37(139): 129–136.

———. 2001. Plains Woodland Tradition. In *Handbook of North American Indians,* Vol. 13. Edited by W. C. Sturtevant, 159–172. Washington, D.C.: Smithsonian Institution Press.

Johnson, A. M., and A. E. Johnson. 1998. The Plains Woodland. In *Archaeology on the Great Plains.* Edited by W. R. Wood, 201–234. Lawrence: University of Kansas Press.

Johnson, G. A. 1977. Aspects of Regional Analysis in Archaeology. *Annual Review of Anthropology* 6:479–508.

———. 1980. Monitoring System Integration and Boundary Phenomena with Settlement Size Data. In *Archaeological Approaches to the Study of Complexity.* Edited by S. E. Van Der Leeuw, 143–188. Amsterdam: University of Amsterdam Press.

———. 1982. Organizational Structure and Scalar Stress. In *Theory and Explanation in Archaeology.* Edited by C. Renfrew, M. J. Rowlands, and B. A. Seagraves, 389–422. New York: Academic Press.

———. 1987. The Changing Organization of Uruk Administration on the Susiana Plain. In *Archaeology of Western Iran.* Edited by F. Hole, 107–139. Washington, D.C.: Smithsonian Institution Press.

Johnson, K. 1997. *Archaeological Excavations at Kolomoki Mounds State Park, 1995.* Report prepared for the Georgia Department of Natural Resources.

Johnson, M. 1999. *Archaeological Theory: An Introduction*. London: Blackwell.

Jones, A. 1999. Local Colour: Megalithic Architecture and Colour Symbolism in Neolithic Arran. *Oxford Journal of Archaeology* 18:339–350.

Jones, C. C. 1873. *Antiquities of the Southern Indians*. New York: Appleton and Company.

Justice, N. D. 1987. *Stone Age Spear and Arrow Points of the Midcontinental and Eastern United States*. Bloomington: Indiana University Press.

Kaltenthaler, L. 1992. Analysis of the Chert Debitage and Tools from Twin Mounds—A Hamilton County Hopewellian Site. M.A. thesis, Department of Anthropology, University of Cincinnati, Ohio.

Kapp, R. O. 1999. Michigan Late Pleistocene, Holocene, and Presettlement Vegetation and Climate. In *Retrieving Michigan's Buried Past: The Archaeology of the Great Lakes State*. Bulletin 64. Edited by J. R. Halsey, 31–58. Bloomfield Hills, Mich.: Cranbrook Institute of Science.

Kardulias, P. N. 1990. Fur Production as a Specialized Activity in a World System: Indians in the North American Fur Trade. *American Indian Culture and Research Journal* 14:25–60.

———, ed. 1999. *World-Systems Theory in Practice: Leadership, Production, and Exchange*. Lanham, Md.: Rowman and Littlefield.

Karst, F. 1969. Indian Mounds of Indiana. In *Michiana: The Sunday Magazine of the South Bend Tribune,* June 1, 1969, 3–4.

Katz, P. R. 1969. An Analysis of Archaeological Data from the Kelley Site, North-Eastern Kansas. M.A. thesis, Department of Anthropology, University of Kansas, Lawrence.

Kay, M. 1979. On the Periphery: Hopewell Settlement of Central Missouri. In *Hopewell Archaeology: The Chillicothe Conference*. Edited by D. S. Brose and N. B. Greber, 94–99. Kent, Ohio: Kent State University Press.

Kay, M., and A. E. Johnson. 1977. Havana Tradition Chronology of Central Missouri. *Midcontinental Journal of Archaeology* 2:195–217.

Keel, B. C. 1972. Woodland Phases of the Appalachian Summit Area. Ph.D. dissertation, Department of Anthropology, Washington State University, Pullman.

———. 1976. *Cherokee Archaeology: A Study of the Appalachian Summit*. Knoxville: University of Tennessee Press.

———. n.d. Hopewell Influence in the Southern Appalachians. Manuscript on file, Glenn A. Black Laboratory of Archaeology, Indiana University. Bloomington.

Keeley, L. H. 1982. Hafting and Retooling: Effects on the Archaeological Record. *American Antiquity* 47:798–809.

Keener, C. S., and S. M. Biehl. 1999. Examination and Distribution of Woodland Period Sites along the Twin Creek Drainage in Southwestern Ohio. *North American Archaeologist* 20:319–346.

Kehoe, A. B. 2000. *Shamans and Religion: An Anthropological Exploration in Critical Thinking*. Prospect Height, Ill.: Waveland Press.

Kellar, J. H. 1979. The Mann Site and "Hopewell" In the Lower Wabash-Ohio Valley. In *Hopewell Archaeology: The Chillicothe Conference*. Edited by D. S. Brose and N. B. Greber, 100–107. Kent, Ohio: Kent State University Press.

Kellar, J. H., A. R. Kelly, and E. McMichael. 1962. The Mandeville Site in Southwest Georgia. *American Antiquity* 27:336–355.

Kelly, A. R. 1938. *A Preliminary Report on Archaeological Exploration at Macon, Georgia*. Bureau of American Ethnology Bulletin 119. Washington, D.C.: Smithsonian Institution Press.

Kelly, A. R., and F.-C. Cole. 1931. Rediscovering Illinois. In *Blue Book of the State of Illinois, 1931–1932,* 318–341. Journal Printing Company, Springfield, Illinois.

Kelly, A. R., and B. A. Smith. 1975. *The Swift Creek Site, 9 BI 3, Macon, Georgia.* Report on file, Laboratory of Archaeology, Department of Anthropology, University of Georgia, Athens.

Kelly, J. E. 2000. The Grassy Lake Site: An Historical and Archaeological Observation. In *Mounds, Modoc, and Mesoamerica: Papers in Honor of Melvin L. Fowler.* Scientific Papers 28. Edited by S. R. Ahler, 141–178. Springfield: Illinois State Museum.

Kelly, L. S. 1997. Patterns of Faunal Exploitation at Cahokia. In *Cahokia: Domination and Ideology in the Mississippian World.* Edited by T. K. Pauketat and T. E. Emerson, 69–88. Lincoln: University of Nebraska.

Kempton, J. P., and R. P. Goldthwait. 1959. Glacial Outwash Terraces of the Hocking and Scioto River Valleys, Ohio. *Ohio Journal of Science* 59:135–151.

Kennedy, R. G. 1994. *Hidden Cities: The Discovery and Loss of North American Civilizations.* New York: Free Press.

Kent, S. 1991. The Relationship between Mobility Strategies and Site Structure. In *The Interpretation of Archaeological Spatial Patterning.* Edited by E. M. Kroll and T. D. Price, 33–59. New York: Plenum Press.

———. 1992. Studying Variability in the Archaeological Record: An Ethnoarchaeological Model for Distinguishing Mobility Patterns. *American Antiquity* 57:635–660.

Kidwell, S. M. 1986. Models for Fossil Concentrations: Paleobiologic Implications. *Paleobiology* 12:6–24.

Kincaid, C., ed. 1983. *Chaco Roads Project Phase I, a Reappraisal of Prehistoric Roads in the San Juan Basin.* Albuquerque: U.S. Department of the Interior, Bureau of Land Management.

Kineitz, W. V. 1995. *The Indians of the Western Great Lakes, 1615–1760.* Ann Arbor: University of Michigan.

Kingsley, R. G. 1977. A Statistical Analysis of the Prehistoric Ceramics from the Hacklander Site, Allegan County, Michigan. M.A. thesis, Department of Anthropology, Western Michigan University, Kalamazoo.

———. 1978. On the Lack of Hopewellian Occupation of the Kalamazoo River Valley. Paper presented to the annual meeting of the Central States Anthropological Society, South Bend, Indiana.

———. 1981. Hopewell Middle Woodland Settlement Systems and Cultural Dynamics in Southern Michigan. *Midcontinental Journal of Archaeology* 6:131–178.

———. 1989. On the Occurrence of Hacklander Ware in Michigan. *Michigan Archaeologist* 35:61–87.

———. 1990. Rethinking Hopewell Ceramic Typology in Michigan. In *Pilot of the Grand: Papers in Tribute to Richard E. Flanders,* Part 1. Edited by T. J. Martin and C. E. Cleland, 211–232. *Michigan Archaeologist* 36(3–4):211–232.

———. 1999. The Middle Woodland Period in Southern Michigan. In *Retrieving Michigan's Buried Past: The Archaeology of the Great Lakes State.* Bulletin 64. Edited by J. R. Halsey, 148–172. Bloomfield Hills, Mich.: Cranbrook Institute of Science.

Kline, G. W., G. D. Crites, and C. H. Faulkner. 1982. *The McFarland Project.* Tennessee Anthropological Association Miscellaneous Paper 8. Knoxville: University of Tennessee.

Knabenshue, S. S. 1902. The Great Seal of Ohio. *Ohio Archaeological and Historical Quarterly* 10:489–491.

Knight, V. J., Jr. 1990. *Excavation of the Truncated Mound at the Walling Site.* Alabama

State Museum of Natural History, Division of Archaeology, Report of Investigations 56. Birmingham: University of Alabama.

———. 2001. Feasting and the Emergence of Platform Mound Ceremonialism in Eastern North America. In *Feasts: Archaeological and Ethnographic Perspectives on Food, Politics, and Power*. Edited by M. Dietler and B. Hayden, 311–333. Washington, D.C.: Smithsonian Institution Press.

Knox, J. C. 1985. Responses of Floods to Holocene Climatic Change in the Upper Mississippi Valley. *Quaternary Research* 23.

———. 1988. Climatic Influence on Upper Mississippi Valley Floods. In *Flood Geomorphology*. Edited by V. R. Baker, R. C. Kochel, and P. C. Patton, 279–300. New York: John Wiley and Sons.

———. 1995. Late Quaternary Upper Mississippi Alluvial Episodes and Their Significance to the Lower Mississippi River System. *Engineering Geology* 45:263–285.

———. 2000. Sensitivity of Modern and Holocene Floods to Climate Change. In *Past Global Changes and Their Significance for the Future*. Edited by K. D. Alverson, F. Oldfield, and R. S. Bradley. *Quaternary Science Reviews* 19(1–5):439–457.

Kohler, T. A. 1991. The Demise of Weeden Island and Post-Weeden Island Cultural Stability in Non-Mississippian North Florida. In *Stability, Transformation, and Variation: The Late Woodland Southeast*. Edited by M. S. Nassaney and C. R. Cobb, 91–110. New York: Plenum Press.

Kosso, P. 1991. Method in Archaeology: Middle-Range Theory as Hermeneutic. *American Antiquity* 56:621–627.

Kostof, S. 1995. *A History of Architecture: Settings and Rituals*. New York: Oxford University Press.

Kozarek, S. E. 1987. A Hopewellian Homestead in the Ohio River Valley. M.A. thesis, Department of Anthropology, University of Cincinnati, Ohio.

———. 1997. Determining Sedentism in the Archaeological Record. In *Ohio Hopewell Community Organization*. Edited by W. S. Dancey and P. J. Pacheco, 131–152. Kent, Ohio: Kent State University Press.

Kraft, H. C. 1995. Review of D. McCutchen's *The Red Record*. *Pennsylvania Archaeologist* 65:49–51.

Kreinbrink, J. 1992. The Rogers Site Complex in Boone County, Kentucky. In *Current Archaeological Research in Kentucky*, Vol. 2. Edited by D. Pollack and A. G. Henderson, 79–102. Frankfort: Kentucky Heritage Council.

Krupp, E. C. 1997. *Skywatchers, Shamans, and Kings: Astronomy and the Archaeology of Power*. New York: John Wiley and Sons.

Kuchler, A. W. 1974. A New Vegetation Map of Kansas. *Ecology* 55:586–604.

Kuznar, L. A. 1999. The Inca Empire: Detailing the Complexities of Core/Periphery Interactions. In *World-Systems Theory in Practice: Leadership, Production, and Exchange*. Edited by P. N. Kardulias, 223–241. Lanham, Md.: Rowman and Littlefield.

Kwas, M. L., and R. C. Mainfort Jr. 1986. The Johnston Site: Precursor to Pinson Mounds? *Tennessee Anthropologist* 11:29–41.

Lacer, C., Jr. n.d. The Mann Site. Manuscript on file, Glenn A. Black Laboratory of Archaeology, Indiana University. Bloomington.

Lapham, I. A. 1855. *The Antiquities of Wisconsin*. Contributions to Knowledge 7. Washington, D.C.: Smithsonian Institution Press.

Larsen, C. S., and P. J. O'Brien. 1973. The Cochran Mound, 23PL86, Platte County, Missouri. *Missouri Archaeological Society Newsletter* No. 267.

Lathrap, D. W. 1973. Gifts of the Cayman: Some Thoughts on the Subsistence Basis of

Chavín. In *Variation in Anthropology: Essays in Honor of John C. McGregor*. Edited by D. W. Lathrap and J. Douglas, 91–105. Urbana: Illinois Archaeological Survey.

Lax, E. 1982. The Pitzner Site Fauna. In *Archaeology in the Southeastern Wisconsin Glaciated Region: Phase I*. Archaeological Research Laboratory, Report of Investigations 64. Edited by L. G. Goldstein, 218–240. Milwaukee: University of Wisconsin–Milwaukee.

Lazazzera, A. 2000. Hopewell Community Evolution: Evidence from the Fort Ancient Site. Paper presented at the Perspectives on Middle Woodland at the Millennium conference, Grafton, Illinois.

LCAALS (Licking County Archaeology and Landmarks Society). 1985. *Discovering the Prehistoric Mound Builders of Licking County, Ohio*. Newark, Ohio: Licking County Archaeology and Landmarks Society.

Leeming, D. A., and J. Page. 1998. *The Mythology of Native North America*. Norman: University of Oklahoma Press.

Leigh, D. S. 1992. Geomorphology. In *Early Woodland Occupations at the Ambrose Flick Site in the Sny Bottom of West-Central Illinois*. Research Series, Vol. 10. Edited by C. R. Stafford, 21–57. Kampsville, Ill.: Center for American Archeology.

Leigh, S. R. 1988. Comparative Analysis of the Elizabeth Middle Woodland Artifact Assemblage. In *The Archaic and Woodland Cemeteries at the Elizabeth Site in the Lower Illinois Valley*. Research Series, Vol. 7. Edited by D. K. Charles, S. R. Leigh, and J. E. Buikstra, 191–217. Kampsville, Ill.: Center for American Archeology.

Leigh, S. R., D. K. Charles, and D. G. Albertson. 1988. Middle Woodland Component. In *The Archaic and Woodland Cemeteries at the Elizabeth Site in the Lower Illinois Valley*. Research Series, Vol. 7. Edited by D. K. Charles, S. R. Leigh, and J. E. Buikstra, 41–84. Kampsville, Ill.: Center for American Archeology.

Leighton, M. M. 1928. Field Notes 5006, "Notes and Diagrams of Explorations Made in the Dickson-Ogden Mound in the Se. Part of Sepo, December 22, 1928, Explorations Under the Auspices of the State University and Under the Direction of Mr. J. L. B. Taylor." Urbana: Illinois State Geological Survey, Geological Records Section, Field Notebook "M. M. Leighton #828."

———. 1930. Geology of the Indian Mounds. *Transactions of the Illinois State Academy of Science* 22:65–71.

———. 1932. Field Notes 5006. "Aug. 5, 1932: Examined New Section F. 78 in Liverpool Mound with E.A. Norton of Soil Survey, and Deuel of Univ. of Chicago, Archaeology Party, to Supplement Data Obtained Last Year in F 77." Urbana: Illinois State Geological Survey, Geological Records Section, Field Notebook "M. M. Leighton #828."

Lekson, S. H. 1999. *The Chaco Meridian: Centers of Political Power in the Ancient Southwest*. Walnut Creek, Calif.: Altamira Press.

Lemons, R., and F. Church. 1998. A Use Wear Analysis of Hopewell Bladelets from Paint Creek Lake Site #5, Ross County, Ohio. *North American Archaeology* 19:269–277.

Lepper, B. T. 1988. An Historical Review of Archaeological Research at the Newark Earthworks. *Journal of the Steward Anthropological Society* 18:118–140.

———. 1989. An Historical Review of Archaeological Research at the Newark Earthworks. *Journal of the Steward Anthropological Society* 18(1/2):118–140.

———. 1995. Tracking Ohio's Great Hopewell Road. *Archaeology* 48:52–56.

———. 1996. The Newark Earthworks and the Geometric Enclosures of the Scioto Valley: Connections and Conjectures. In *A View from the Core: A Synthesis of Ohio Hopewell Archaeology*. Edited by P. J. Pacheco, 224–241. Columbus: Ohio Archaeological Council.

———. 1998a. Ancient Astronomers of the Ohio Valley. *Timeline* 15:2–11.

———. 1998b. The Archaeology of the Newark Earthworks. In *Ancient Earthen Enclosures of the Eastern Woodlands*. Edited by R. C. Mainfort Jr. and L. P. Sullivan, 114–134. Gainesville: University Press of Florida.

Lepper, B. T., and R. W. Yerkes. 1997. Hopewellian Occupations at the Northern Periphery of the Newark Earthworks: The Newark Expressway Revisited. In *Ohio Hopewell Community Organization*. Edited by W. S. Dancey and P. J. Pacheco, 175–206. Kent, Ohio: Kent State University Press.

Lepper, B. T., R. W. Yerkes, and W. H. Pickard. 2001. Prehistoric Flint Procurement Strategies at Flint Ridge, Licking County, Ohio. *Midcontinental Journal of Archaeology* 26:53–78.

Levinson, S. C. 1983. *Pragmatics*. Cambridge: Cambridge University Press.

Lewis, T. M. N., and M. Kneberg. 1946. *Hiwassee Island*. Knoxville: University of Tennessee Press.

———. 1957. The Camp Creek Site. *Tennessee Archaeologist* 14:60–79.

Lewis-Williams, D. 2002. *The Mind in the Cave*. London: Thames and Hudson.

———. 2004. Constructing a Cosmos: Architecture, Power, and Domestication at Çatalhöyük. *Journal of Social Archaeology* 4:28–59.

Lilly, E. 1937. *Prehistoric Antiquities of Indiana*. Indianapolis: Indiana Historical Society.

Limp, W. F. 1983. Rational Location Choice and Prehistoric Settlement Analysis. Ph.D. dissertation, Department of Anthropology, Indiana University, Bloomington.

Lippold, L. K. 1973. Animal Resource Utilization at the Cooper's Shore Site [47R02], Rock County, Wisconsin. *Wisconsin Archaeologist* 54:36–62.

Lloyd, T. C. 1999. A Comparison of the Two Large Oblong Mounds at the Hopewell Site. Paper presented at the 64th annual meeting of the Society for American Archaeology, Chicago.

Logan, B. 1981. *An Archaeological Survey of the Stranger Creek Drainage System, Northeast Kansas*. Museum of Anthropology, Project Report Series, No. 48. Lawrence: University of Kansas.

———. 1985. O-Keet-Sha: Culture History and Its Environmental Context—the Archaeology of Stranger Creek Basin, Northeastern Kansas. Ph.D. dissertation, Department of Anthropology, University of Kansas, Lawrence.

———, ed. 1987. *Archaeological Investigations in the Clinton Lake Project Area, Northeastern Kansas: National Register Evaluation of 27 Prehistoric Sites*. Report submitted to the Kansas City District, U.S. Army Corps of Engineers by Kaw Valley Engineering and Development, Junction City, Kansas.

———, ed. 1990. *Archaeological Investigations in the Plains Village Frontier, Northeastern Kansas*. Museum of Anthropology, Project Report Series, No. 70. Lawrence: University of Kansas.

———, ed. 1993. *Quarry Creek: Excavation, Analysis, and Prospect of a Kansas City Hopewell Site, Fort Leavenworth, Kansas*. Museum of Anthropology, Project Report Series, No. 80. Lawrence: University of Kansas.

———. 1998a. Oneota Far West: The White Rock Phase. *Wisconsin Archaeologist* 79:248–267.

———. 1998b. Synthesis and Interpretations. In *The View from DB Ridge, Fort Leavenworth, Kansas*. Museum of Anthropology, Project Report Series, No. 98. Edited by B. Logan, 301–332. Lawrence: University of Kansas.

———. 2004. Archaeological Investigations at the Evans Locality, Stranger Creek Valley,

Northeastern Kansas—2003. Report submitted to the Historic Preservation Office, Cultural Resources Division, Kansas State Historical Society by Department of Sociology, Anthropology, and Social Work, Kansas State University.

———. n.d. A Brief Survey of 14LV1079, 14LV1080, and 14LV1081, Lower Stranger Creek, Leavenworth County, Kansas. Manuscript on file, Office of Archaeological Research, Museum of Anthropology, University of Kansas, Lawrence.

Logan, B., and W. E. Banks. 1993. Faunal Remains. In *Quarry Creek: Excavation, Analysis, and Prospect of a Kansas City Hopewell Site, Fort Leavenworth, Kansas.* Museum of Anthropology, Project Report Series, No. 80. Edited by B. Logan. Lawrence: University of Kansas.

Logan, W. D. 1976. *Woodland Complexes in Northeastern Iowa.* Publications in Archeology 15. Washington, D.C.: National Park Service.

Lopinot, N. H. 1992. Spatial and Temporal Variability in Mississippian Subsistence: The Archaeological Record. In *Late Prehistoric Agriculture: Observations from the Midwest.* Edited by W. I. Woods, 44–94. Springfield: Illinois Preservation Agency.

———. 1997. Cahokian Food Production Reconsidered. In *Cahokia: Domination and Ideology in the Mississippian World.* Edited by T. K. Pauketat and T. E. Emerson, 52–68. Lincoln: University of Nebraska Press.

Losey, T. C. 1967. Toft Lake Village Site. *Michigan Archaeologist* 13:129–134.

Lothrop, S. K. 1937. *Coclé: An Archaeological Study of Central Panama,* Part 1. Memoirs of the Peabody Museum of Archaeology and Ethnology 7. Cambridge, Mass.: Harvard University.

Lovis, W. A. 1990. Accelerator Dating the Ceramic Assemblage from the Fletcher Site: Implications of a Pilot Study for Interpretation of the Wayne Period. *Midcontinental Journal of Archaeology* 15:37-50.

Lovis, W. A., K. Egan, B. A. Smith, and G. W. Monaghan. 1994. Origins of Horticulture in the Saginaw Valley: A New View from the Schultz Site. Paper presented at the Southeastern Archaeological Conference, Lexington, Kentucky.

Lowie, R. H. 1913. *Societies of the Crow, Hidatsa, and Mandan Indians.* Anthropological Papers 11. New York: American Museum of Natural History.

———. 1920. *The Tobacco Society of the Crow Indians.* Anthropological Papers, Vol. 21, No. 2. New York: American Museum of Natural History

———. 1956. *The Crow Indians.* New York: Rinehart and Company.

Loy, J. A. 1968. A Comparative Style Analysis of Havana Series Pottery from Two Illinois Valley Sites. In *Hopewell and Woodland Site Archaeology in Illinois.* Bulletin No. 6, 129–200. Urbana: Illinois Archaeological Survey.

Luxenberg, B. 1972. Faunal Remains. In *The Schultz Site at Green Point: A Stratified Occupation Area in the Saginaw Valley of Michigan.* Museum of Anthropology, Memoir No. 4. Edited by J. E. Fitting, 91–115. Ann Arbor: University of Michigan.

Lyman, R. L. 1994. *Vertebrate Taphonomy.* Cambridge: Cambridge University Press.

Lynott, M. J. 2000. Recent Research at the Hopeton Earthworks, Ross County, Ohio. Paper presented at the Joint Midwest Archaeological and Plains Conference, St. Paul.

———. 2001. The Hopeton Earthworks: An Interim Report. *Hopewell Archaeology: The Newsletter of Hopewell Archaeology in the Ohio River Valley* 4:1–5.

———. 2002. Archeological Research at the Hopeton Earthworks, Ross County, Ohio. Paper presented at the Midwest Archaeological Conference, Columbus, Ohio.

———. 2004. Earthwork Construction and the Organization of Hopewell Society. Paper presented at the 69th annual meeting of the Society for American Archaeology, Montreal.

Lynott, M. J., and S. M. Monk. 1985. *Mound City, Ohio, Archeological Investigations.* Occasional Studies in Anthropology No. 12. Lincoln, Nebr.: Midwest Archeological Center.

Lynott, M. J., and J. Weymouth. 2002. Preliminary Report, 2001 Investigations, Hopeton Earthworks. *Hopewell Archaeology: The Newsletter of Hopewell Archaeology in the Ohio River Valley* 5:1–7.

MacArthur, R. H., and E. R. Pianka. 1966. On the Optimal Use of a Patchy Environment. *American Naturalist* 100:603–610.

MacNeish, R. S. 1991. *The Origins of Agriculture and Settled Life.* Norman: University of Oklahoma Press.

Madrigal, T. C., and J. Z. Holt. 2002. White-Tailed Deer Meat and Marrow Return Rates and Their Application to Eastern Woodlands Archaeology. *American Antiquity* 67:745–759.

Magne, M., and D. Pokotylo. 1981. A Pilot Study in Bifacial Lithic Reduction Sequences. *Lithic Technology* 10:47.

Magurran, A. E. 1988. *Ecological Diversity and Its Measurement.* Princeton, N.J.: Princeton University Press.

Maher, T. O. 1989. The Middle Woodland Ceramic Assemblage. In *The Holding Site: A Hopewell Community in the American Bottom.* American Bottom Archaeology FAI-270 Site Reports, Vol. 19. Edited by A. C. Fortier, T. O. Maher, J. A. Williams, M. C. Meinkoth, K. E. Parker, and L. S. Kelly, 125–318. Urbana: University of Illinois Press.

———. 1996. Time, Space, and Social Dynamics during the Hopewell Occupation of the American Bottom. Ph.D. dissertation, Department of Anthropology, University of North Carolina, Chapel Hill.

Mainfort, R. C., Jr. 1982. *Pinson Mound: A Middle Woodland Ceremonial Center.* Research Series 7. Nashville: Tennessee Department of Conservation, Division of Archaeology.

———. 1986. *Pinson Mound: A Middle Woodland Ceremonial Center.* Research Series 7. Tennessee Department of Conservation, Division of Archaeology, Nashville.

———. 1989. Adena Chiefdoms? Evidence from the Wright Mounds. *Midcontinental Journal of Archaeology* 14:164–178.

———. 1996. Pinson Mounds and the Middle Woodland in the Midsouth and Lower Mississippi Valley. In *A View from the Core: A Synthesis of Ohio Hopewell Archaeology.* Edited by P. J. Pacheco, 370–391. Columbus: Ohio Archaeological Council.

Mainfort, R. C., Jr., J. B. Broster, and K. M. Johnson. 1982. Recent Radiocarbon Determinations for the Pinson Mounds Site. *Tennessee Anthropologist* 7(1):14–19.

Mainfort, R. C., Jr., J. W. Cogswell, M. J. O'Brien, H. Neff, and M. D. Glascock. 1997. Neutron Activation Analysis from Pinson Mounds and Nearby Sites in Western Kentucky: Local Production vs. Long-Distance Importation. *Midcontinental Journal of Archaeology* 22:43–68.

Mainfort, R. C., Jr., and L. P. Sullivan. 1998a. Explaining Earthen Enclosures. In *Ancient Earthen Enclosures of the Eastern Woodlands.* Edited by R. C. Mainfort Jr. and L. P. Sullivan, 1–16. Gainesville: University Press of Florida.

———, eds. 1998b. *Ancient Earthen Enclosures of the Eastern Woodlands.* Gainesville: University Press of Florida.

Mainfort, R. C., Jr., and R. Walling. 1992. Excavations at Pinson Mounds: Ozier Mound. *Midcontinental Journal of Archaeology* 17:112–135.

Mallouf, R. 1982. An Analysis of Plow-Damaged Chert Artifacts: The Brookeen Creek Cache (41HI86). *Journal of Field Archaeology* 9:79–98.

Malville, J. M., and N. J. Malville. 2001. Pilgrimage and Periodic Festivals as Processes of Social Integration at Chaco Canyon. *Kiva* 66:327–344.

Mangold, W. M. 1973. Birdstone or Dog Effigy? *Central States Archaeological Journal* 20:146–148.

———. 1981a. An Archaeological Survey of the Galien River Basin. *Michigan Archaeologist* 27:31–51.

———. 1981b. Middle Woodland Ceramics in Northwestern Indiana and Western Michigan. M.A. thesis, Department of Anthropology, Western Michigan University, Kalamazoo.

———. 1997. An Archaeological Reconnaissance of Sites Associated with the Goodall Mounds, Laporte County, Indiana. Manuscript on file, Archaeology Laboratory, University of Notre Dame, Notre Dame, Indiana.

———. 1998. Ernest W. Young and the Goodall Site (12 Le 9), Laporte County, Indiana. Paper presented at the Midwest Archaeological Conference, Muncie, Indiana.

Margry, P., ed. 1886. *Découvertes et éstablissements des Francais dans l'ouest et dans le sud de l'Amérique septentrionale (1614–1754).* 6. partie, Exploration des affluents du Mississipi et découverte des Montagnes Rocheuses (1679–1754), Sixie. Paris: D. Jouaust.

Marquardt, W. H., and C. L. Crumley. 1987. Theoretical Issues in the Analysis of Spatial Patterning. In *Regional Dynamics: Burgundian Landscapes in Historical Perspective.* Edited by C. L. Crumley and W. H. Marquardt, 1–39. San Diego: Academic Press.

Marriott, A., and C. K. Rachlin. 1968. *North American Indian Mythology.* New York: Thomas Y. Crowell.

Marshall, J. A. 1996. Towards a Definition of the Ohio Hopewell Core and Periphery Utilizing the Geometric Earthworks. In *A View from the Core: A Synthesis of Ohio Hopewell Archaeology.* Edited by P. J. Pacheco, 210–220. Columbus: Ohio Archaeological Council.

Martin, F. P. 1958. Southern Affinities of the Ellerbusch Site, Warrick County, Indiana. *Proceedings of the Indiana Academy of Science* 67:90.

Martin, P. S., G. I. Quimby Jr., and D. Collier. 1947. *Indians Before Columbus.* Chicago: University of Chicago Press.

Martin, T. J. 1975. Animal Remains from the Spoonville Site, 20–OT-1, Ottawa County, Michigan. *Michigan Archaeologist* 21:1–8.

———. 1976. A Faunal Analysis of Five Woodland Period Archaeological Sites in Southwestern Michigan. M.A. thesis, Department of Anthropology, Western Michigan University, Kalamazoo.

———. 1993. *Animal Remains from the Arthursburg Hill Earthwork (20IA37) and Campsite (20IA48) in Ionia County, Michigan.* Technical Report 93–000–27. Springfield: Quaternary Studies Program, Illinois State Museum Society.

———. 2002. Woodland Period Animal Exploitation in the Valley of the Grand: Perspectives from the Converse Site. Paper presented at the 67th annual meeting of the Society for American Archaeology, Denver.

———. 2003. Faunal Analysis. In *Phase III Archaeological Data Recovery for the U.S. 131 S-Curve Realignment Project, Grand Rapids, Michigan.* Report No. R-0446. Edited by M. J. Hambacher, J. G. Brashler, K. C. Egan-Bruhy, D. R. Hayes, B. Hardy, D. G. Landis, T. J. Martin, G. W. Monaghan, K. Murphy, J. A. Robertson, and D. L. Seltz, section 8.0. Report submitted to the Michigan Department of Transportation, Lansing, by Commonwealth Cultural Resources Group, Jackson, Michigan.

Martin, T. J., and M. C. Masulis. 1993. Faunal Remains from the Weaver Component. In

Rench: A Stratified Site in the Central Illinois River Valley. Reports of Investigations No. 49. Edited by M. A. McConaughy, 274–307. Springfield: Illinois State Museum.

Maslowski, R. F., C. M. Niquette, and D. M. Wingfield. 1995. The Kentucky, Ohio, and West Virginia Radiocarbon Database. *West Virginia Archaeologist* 47[1-2].

Maslowski, R. F., and M. F. Seeman. 1992. Woodland Archaeology in the Mid-Ohio Valley: Setting the Parameters of Ohio Main Stem/Tributary Comparison. In *Cultural Variability in Context: Woodland Settlements of the Mid-Ohio Valley.* Midcontinental Journal of Archaeology Special Papers No. 7. Edited by M. F. Seeman, 10–14. Kent, Ohio: Kent State University Press.

Mason, R. J. 1966. *Two Stratified Sites on the Door Peninsula of Wisconsin.* Museum of Anthropology, Anthropological Papers 26. Ann Arbor: University of Michigan.

———. 1981. *Great Lakes Archaeology.* New York: Academic Press.

———. 2000. Archaeology and Native American Oral Traditions. *American Antiquity* 65:239–266.

Mathews, A. 1882. *History of Cass County, Michigan.* Chicago: Waterman, Watkins.

Mauldin, R. P., and D. S. Amick. 1989. Investigating Patterning in Debitage from Experimental Bifacial Core Reduction. In *Experiments in Lithic Technology.* BAR International Series 528. Edited by D. S. Amick and R. P. Mauldin, 67–88. Oxford: Oxford University Press.

Maxwell, M. S. 1951. *Woodland Cultures of Southern Illinois: Archaeological Investigations of the Carbondale Area.* Logan Museum Publications in Anthropology Bulletin 7. Beloit, Wisc.: Beloit College.

McAdams, W. C. 1881. Ancient Mounds of Illinois. *Proceedings of the American Association for the Advancement of Science* 29:710–718.

McAllister, J. G. 1932. The Archaeology of Porter County. *Indiana History Bulletin* 10.

McElrath, D. L., T. E. Emerson, A. C. Fortier, and J. L. Phillips. 1984. Late Archaic Period. In *American Bottom Archaeology.* Edited by C. J. Bareis and J. W. Porter, 34–58. Urbana: University of Illinois Press.

McElrath, D. L., and A. C. Fortier. 2000. The Early Late Woodland Occupation of the American Bottom. In *Late Woodland Societies: Tradition and Transformation Across the Midcontinent.* Edited by T. E. Emerson, D. L. McElrath, and A. C. Fortier, 97–121. Lincoln: University of Nebraska Press.

McGimsey, C. R. 1988. *The Haw Creek Site (11–Kx-3), Knox County, Illinois: A Middle Woodland Occupation in the Upper Spoon River Valley.* Archaeological Research Program, Technical Report 88–257–7. Springfield: Illinois State Museum.

McGimsey, C. R., M. A. McConaughy, J. R. Purdue, B. W. Styles, F. B. King, and M. B. Schroeder. 1985. *Investigations at Two Central Illinois Sites: The Guard Site (11 SG 262), an Early Late Woodland Weaver Phase Occupation and the McGill Site (11 SG 259), a Multicomponent Lithic Scatter.* Archaeological Program Technical Report 85–30–12. Illinois State Museum.

McGimsey, C. R., and M. D. Wiant. 1986. The Woodland Occupations: Summary and Conclusions. In *Woodland Period Occupations of the Napoleon Hollow Site in the Lower Illinois Valley.* Research Series, Vol. 6. Edited by M. D. Wiant and C. R. McGimsey, 527–541. Kampsville, Ill.: Center for American Archeology.

McGregor, J. C. 1952. The Havana Site. In *Hopewellian Communities in Illinois.* Scientific Papers 5. Edited by T. Deuel, 43–91. Springfield: Illinois State Museum.

———. 1958. *The Pool and Irving Villages.* Urbana: University of Illinois Press.

McKern, W. C. 1929. Ohio Type of Mounds in Wisconsin. *Year Book of the Public Museum of the City of Milwaukee* 8:7–21.

———. 1931. A Wisconsin Variant of the Hopewell Culture. *Bulletin of the Public Museum of the City of Milwaukee* 10:185–328.

———. 1932. New Excavations in Wisconsin Hopewell Mounds. *Year Book of the Public Museum of the City of Milwaukee* 10:9–27.

———. 1942. The First Settlers of Wisconsin. *Wisconsin Magazine of History* 26:153–169.

McKinley, W. 1873. *Mounds in Georgia.* Annual Report for 1872. Washington, D.C.: Smithsonian Institution.

McLaughlan, K. 2000a. Plant Cultivation and Forest Clearance by Prehistoric North Americans: Pollen Evidence from Fort Ancient, Ohio, USA. M.A. thesis, Department of Ecology, Evolution, and Behavior, University of Minnesota, St. Paul.

———. 2000b. Pollen Evidence of Open Landscape and Plant Cultivation Contemporaneous with Hopewell Occupation within the Fort Ancient Site. Paper presented at the Perspectives on Middle Woodland at the Millennium conference, Grafton, Illinois.

McNerney, M. J. 1987. Crab Orchard Core Technology at the Consol Site, Jackson County, Illinois. In *The Organization of Core Technology.* Edited by J. K. Johnson and C. A. Morrow, 63–85. Boulder, Colo.: Westview Press.

Meekhof, E., and T. J. Martin. 1998. Middle Woodland Animal Exploitation in the Middle Grand River Valley, Michigan: Impressions from the Prison Farm Site (20IA58). Paper presented at the Midwest Archaeological Conference, Muncie, Indiana.

Megapolensis, J., Jr. [1644] 1996. A Short Account of the Mohawk Indians. In *In Mohawk Country: Early Narratives about a Native People.* Edited by D. R. Snow, C. T. Gehring, and W. Starna, 38–46. Syracuse, N.Y.: Syracuse University Press.

Meinkoth, M. C., K. Hedman, M. Simon, T. E. Berres, and D. Brewer. 1995. *The Sister Creeks Site Mounds: Middle Woodland Mortuary Practices in the Illinois River Valley.* Report No. 2. Urbana: Illinois Transportation Archaeological Research Program.

Metcalf, D., and K. T. Jones. 1988. A Reconsideration of Animal Body-Part Utility Indices. *American Antiquity* 53:486–504.

Mikulic, D. G., and J. Kluessendorf. 1982. *Preservation of Scientifically and Historically Important Geologic Sites in Milwaukee County, Wisconsin.* Technical Record 4 (3). Milwaukee: Southeastern Wisconsin Planning Commission.

Milanich, J. T. 2002. Weeden Island Cultures. In *The Woodland Southeast.* Edited by D. G. Anderson and R. C. Mainfort Jr., 352–372. Tuscaloosa: University of Alabama Press.

Milanich, J. T., A. S. Cordell, V. J. Knight Jr., T. A. Kohler, and B. Siegler-Lavelle. 1984. *McKeithen Weeden Island: The Culture of Northern Florida, A.D. 200–900.* Orlando: Academic Press.

Mills, W. C. 1900. Report of Field Work. *Ohio Archaeological and Historical Society Publications* 8:309–345.

———. 1902. Excavations of the Adena Mound. *Ohio Archaeological and Historical Quarterly* 10:452–479.

———. 1906. Baum Prehistoric Village. *Ohio Archaeological and Historical Quarterly* 15:45–136.

———. 1907. The Exploration of the Edwin Harness Mound. *Ohio Archaeological and Historical Quarterly* 16:113–193.

———. 1908. *Field Notes from the 1908 Excavations at Fort Ancient.* Columbus: Ohio Historical Society.

———. 1909. Explorations of the Seip Mound. *Ohio Archaeological and Historical Quarterly* 18:269–321.

———. 1914. *Archaeological Atlas of Ohio*. Columbus: Ohio State Archaeological and Historical Society.

———. 1916. Exploration of the Tremper Mound. *Ohio Archaeological and Historical Quarterly* 25:262–398.

———. 1922. Exploration of the Mound City Group, Ross County. *Ohio Archaeological and Historical Quarterly* 31:423–584.

Milner, G. R. 1995. An Osteological Perspective on Prehistoric Warfare. In *Regional Approaches to Mortuary Analysis*. Edited by L. A. Beck, 221–247. New York: Plenum Press.

———. 1998. *The Cahokia Chiefdom: The Archaeology of a Mississippian Society*. Washington, D.C.: Smithsonian Institution Press.

Monks, G. 1981. Seasonality Studies. In *Advances in Archaeological Method and Theory*, Vol. 4. Edited by M. B. Schiffer, 177–240. San Diego: Academic Press.

Montet-White, A. M. 1965. Typology of Some Middle Woodland Projectile Points from Illinois and Michigan. In *Papers of the Michigan Academy of Science, Arts, and Letters* 50:355–364.

———. 1968. *The Lithic Industries of the Illinois Valley in the Early and Middle Woodland Period*. Museum of Anthropology, Anthropological Papers 35. Ann Arbor: University of Michigan.

Montgomery, M. W., J. N. Gundersen, and F. J. Mathien. 2001. Meta-Argillites: Raw Materials of the Chaco Canyon Area. Poster presented at the Pecos Conference, Chaco Canyon, New Mexico.

Moore, R. 1980. Salisbury Steak. *Albany Medical Nexus* 24 November 1980, p. 6.

Moorehead, W. K. 1890. *Fort Ancient the Great Prehistoric Earthwork of Warren County, Ohio Compiled from a Careful Survey with an Account of Its Mounds and Graves*. Cincinnati, Ohio: Robert Clarke.

———. 1892. *Primitive Man in Ohio*. New York: Putnam, Knickerbocker Press.

———. 1895. A Description of Fort Ancient. In *Ohio Archaeological and Historical Publications*, Vol. 4, 313–315. Columbus, Ohio: Fred J. Heer.

———. 1922. The Hopewell Mound Group of Ohio. *Field Museum of Natural History Anthropological Series* 6:73–184.

———. 1929. Appendix C: The Dickson Mound and Log Tomb Burials at Liverpool. In *The Cahokia Mounds, Part I: Explorations of 1922, 1923, 1924, and 1927*. University of Illinois Bulletin 26, 167–170. Urbana, Ill.

Moran, E. F. 1990. Levels of Analysis and Analytical Level Shifting: Examples from Amazonian Ecosystem Research. In *The Ecosystem Approach in Anthropology: From Concept to Practice*. Edited by E. F. Moran, 279–308. Ann Arbor: University of Michigan Press.

Morgan, D. L., and C. I. Wheat. 1954. *Jedediah Smith and His Maps of the American West*. San Francisco: California Historical Society.

Morgan, D. T. 1985. Ceramic Analysis. In *Smiling Dan: Structure and Function at a Middle Woodland Settlement in the Illinois Valley*. Research Series, Vol. 2. Edited by B. D. Stafford and M. B. Sant, 183–257. Kampsville, Ill.: Center for American Archeology.

———. 1986. Ceramics. In *Woodland Period Occupations of the Napoleon Hollow Site in the Lower Illinois Valley*. Research Series, Vol. 6. Edited by M. D. Wiant and C. R. McGimsey, 364–426. Kampsville, Ill.: Center for American Archeology.

Morgan, L. H. 1851. *Report on the Fabrics, Inventions, Implements and Utensils of the Iroquois, Made to the Regents of the University, Jan. 22, 1851.* Albany, N.Y.: Richard H. Pease.

———. 1876. Houses of the Mound-Builders. *North American Review* 124:60–85.

———. 1881. *Houses and House-Life of the American Aborigines.* Contributions to North American Ethnology, Vol. 4. Washington, D.C.: Government Printing Office.

Morgan, R. G. 1946. *Fort Ancient.* Columbus: Ohio State Archaeological and Historical Society.

———. 1952. Outline of Cultures in the Ohio Region. In *Archeology of Eastern United States.* Edited by J. B. Griffin, 83–98. Chicago: University of Chicago Press.

Morinis, A. 1992. Introduction: The Territory of the Anthropology of Pilgrimage. In *Sacred Journeys: The Anthropology of Pilgrimage.* Edited by A. Morinis, 1–28. Westport, Conn.: Greenwood Press.

Morrissey, E., J. G. Brashler, and A. Detz. 1998. Ceramics from the 1996 Excavations at the Prison Farm Site. Paper presented at the annual meeting of the Michigan Academy of Science, Arts and Letters, Alma.

Morrow, C. A. 1987. Blades and Cobden Chert: A Technological Argument for Their Role as Markers of Regional Identification during the Hopewell Period in Illinois. In *The Organization of Core Technology.* Edited by J. K. Johnson and C. A. Morrow, 119–149. Boulder, Colo.: Westview Press.

———. 1988. Middle Woodland Chert Exchange at Macoupin: Multiple Levels of Interaction in the Lower Illinois River Valley. *Journal of the Steward Anthropological Society* 18:72–86.

———. 1991. Observations on the Baehr Mound Chert Disks. *Illinois Archaeology* 3:77–92.

Morrow, C. A., J. M. Elam, and M. D. Glascock. 1992. The Use of Blue-Gray Chert in Midwestern Prehistory. *Midcontinental Journal of Archaeology* 17:166–197.

Morse, D., and P. Morse. 1983. *Archaeology of the Central Mississippi Valley.* Orlando, Fla.: Academic Press.

Morse, D. F. 1963. *The Steuben Village and Mounds: A Multicomponent Late Hopewell Site in Illinois.* Museum of Anthropology, Anthropological Papers 21. Ann Arbor: University of Michigan.

Moulton, G. E., ed. 1983. *The Journals of the Lewis and Clark Expedition,* Vol. 1, *Atlas of the Lewis and Clark Expedition.* Lincoln: University of Nebraska Press.

———, ed. 1986. *The Journals of the Lewis and Clark Expedition,* Vol. 2, *August 30, 1803–August 24, 1804.* Lincoln: University of Nebraska Press.

Muller, J. 1986. *Archaeology of the Lower Ohio River Valley.* New York: Academic Press.

———. 1997. *Mississippian Political Economy.* New York: Plenum Press.

Munson, C. A. n.d. Hovey Lake. Manuscript on file, Glenn A. Black Laboratory of Archaeology, Indiana University. Bloomington.

Munson, P. J. 1967. A Hopewellian Enclosure Earthwork in the Illinois River Valley. *American Antiquity* 32:391–393.

———. 1971. *An Archaeological Survey of the Wood River Terrace and Adjacent Bottoms and Bluffs in Madison County, Illinois.* Reports of Investigations, No. 21. Springfield: Illinois State Museum.

———. 1986. Black Sand and Havana Tradition Ceramic Assemblages and Culture History in the Central Illinois River Valley. In *Early Woodland Archaeology.* Seminars in

Archeology, No. 2. Edited by K. B. Farnsworth and T. E. Emerson, 280–300. Kampsville, Ill.: Center for American Archeology.

Munson, P. J., P. W. Parmalee, and R. A. Yarnell. 1971. Subsistence Ecology of Scovill, a Terminal Middle Woodland Village. *American Antiquity* 36:410–436.

Murdock, G. P. 1967. Ethnographic Atlas: A Summary. *Ethnology* 6:109–236.

Murphy, J. L. 1989. *An Archaeological History of the Hocking Valley.* 2nd edition. Athens: Ohio University Press.

Murphy, M. L. 1986. A Statistical Analysis of the Lithic Material from the Zemaitis Site (20OT68), Ottawa County Michigan. M.A. thesis, Department of Anthropology Western Michigan University, Kalamazoo.

Murray, P. 1980. Discard Location: The Ethnographic Data. *American Antiquity* 45:490–502.

Myers, T. P. 1978. Formative-Period Interaction Spheres in the Intermediate Area: Archaeology of Central America and Adjacent South America. In *Advances in Andean Archaeology.* Edited by D. L. Browman, 203–234. The Hague: Mouton.

———. 1981. Aboriginal Trade Networks in Amazonia. In *Networks of the Past: Regional Interaction in Archaeology.* Edited by P. D. Francis, F. J. Kense, and P. G. Duke. Calgary: Archaeological Association, University of Calgary.

Nabokov, P. 1996. Native Views of History. In *The Cambridge History of the Native Peoples of the Americas,* Vol. 1, *North America, Part 1.* Edited by B. G. Trigger and W. E. Washburn, 1–59. Cambridge: Cambridge University Press.

Naroll, R., and E. Margolis. 1974. Maximum Settlement Size: A Compilation. *Behavior Science Research* 9:319–326.

Nass, J. P., Jr. 1987. Use-Wear Analysis and Household Archaeology: A Study of the Activity Structure of the Incinerator Site, an Anderson Phase Fort Ancient Community in Southwestern Ohio. Ph.D. dissertation, Department of Anthropology, Ohio State University, Columbus.

———. 1988. Fort Ancient Agricultural Systems and Settlement: A View from Southwestern Ohio. *North American Archaeologist* 9:319–347.

Nass, J. P., Jr., and R. W. Yerkes. 1995. Social Differentiation in Mississippian and Fort Ancient Societies. In *Mississippian Communities and Households.* Edited by J. D. Rogers and B. D. Smith, 58–80. Tuscaloosa: University of Alabama Press.

Neff, H., F. J. Bove, B. Lou, and M. F. Piechowski. 1992. Ceramic Raw Material Survey in Pacific Coastal Guatemala. In *Chemical Characterization of Ceramic Pastes in Archaeology.* Monographs in World Archaeology, No. 7. Edited by H. Neff, 59–84. Madison, Wisc.: Prehistory Press.

Neill, W. T. 1971. *The Last of the Ruling Reptiles: Alligators, Crocodiles, and Their Kin.* New York: Columbia University Press.

Nelson, S. 1952. *History of Pleasant Plain, Ohio (Formerly New Columbia).* Privately printed.

Neuman, R. W. 1975. *The Sonota Complex and Associated Sites on the Northern Great Plains.* Publications in Anthropology 6. Lincoln: Nebraska State Historical Society.

Neumann, G. K., and M. L. Fowler. 1952. Hopewellian Sites in the Wabash Valley. In *Hopewellian Communities in Illinois.* Scientific Papers 5. Edited by T. Deuel, 175–248. Springfield: Illinois State Museum.

Nials, F., J. Stein, and J. Roney. 1987. Chacoan Roads in the Southern Periphery: Results of Phase II of the BLM Chaco Roads Project. Cultural Resources Series No. 1. U.S. Department of the Interior, Bureau of Land Management, Albuquerque.

Nicollet, J. N. 1976. *Hydrographical Basin of the Upper Mississippi River (Print from the Original 1843 Map)*. St. Paul: Minnesota Historical Society.

O'Brien, M. J. 1987. Sedentism, Population Growth, and Resource Selection in the Woodland Midwest. *Current Anthropology* 28:177–198.

O'Brien, M. J., and R. L. Lyman. 2000. *Applying Evolutionary Archaeology: A Systematic Approach*. Norwell, Mass.: Kluwer.

O'Brien, M. J., and W. R. Wood. 1998. *The Prehistory of Missouri*. Columbia: University of Missouri Press.

O'Brien, P. J. 1972. The Don Wells Site (14RY404), a Hopewellian Site near Manhattan, Kansas, and Its Implications. *Kansas Anthropological Association Newsletter* 17:1–11.

O'Brien, P. J., M. Caldwell, J. Jilka, L. Toburen, and B. Yeo. 1979. The Ashland Bottoms Site (14RY603): A Kansas City Hopewell Site in North-Central Kansas. *Plains Anthropologist* 24:1–20.

O'Brien, P. J., C. S. Larsen, J. Organdy, B. O'Neill, and A. S. Stirland. 1973. The Elliott Site (14GE303): A Preliminary Report. *Plains Anthropologist* 18:54–72.

O'Connor, M. I. 1997. The Pilgrimage to Magdalena. In *Anthropology of Religion: A Handbook*. Edited by S. D. Glazier, 369–389. Westport, Conn.: Greenwood Press.

Odell, G. H. 1985a. Small Sites Archaeology and Use-Wear on Surface-Collected Artifacts. *Midcontinental Journal of Archaeology* 10:21–48.

———. 1985b. Microwear Analysis of Middle Woodland Lithics. In *Smiling Dan: Structure and Function at a Middle Woodland Settlement in the Illinois Valley*. Research Series, Vol. 2. Edited by B. D. Stafford and M. B. Sant, 298–326. Kampsville, Ill.: Center for American Archeology.

———. 1994. The Role of Stone Bladelets in Middle Woodland Society. *American Antiquity* 59:102–120.

———. 1998. Investigating Correlates of Sedentism and Domestication in Prehistoric North America. *American Antiquity* 63:553–571.

Oestreicher, D. M. 1994. Unmasking the Walam Olum: A 19th Century Hoax. *Bulletin of the Archaeological Society of New Jersey* 49:1–44.

———. 1995. Text Out of Context: The Arguments That Created and Sustained the Walam Olum. *Bulletin of the Archaeological Society of New Jersey* 50:31–52.

O'Gorman, J., ed. 2003. *Middle Woodland Archeology of the Hannibal Bridge Project C House Site*. Center for American Archeology Contract Completion Report submitted to the Illinois Department of Transportation, Springfield.

Owens, J. D. 1994. Activity Organization and Site Function at a Late Middle Woodland Regional Center in the Lower Illinois River Valley: Preliminary Investigations of Variability in Surface Scatters at the Baehr-Gust Site. M.A. thesis, Department of Anthropology, New York University.

Oyuela-Caycedo, A. 2001. The Rise of Religious Routinization: The Study of Changes from Shaman to Priestly Elite. In *Mortuary Practices and Ritual Associations: Shamanic Elements in Prehistoric Funerary Contexts in South America*. BAR International Series 982. Edited by J. E. Staller and E. J. Currie, 5–17. Oxford: Oxford University Press.

Ozker, D. 1982. *An Early Woodland at the Schultz Site (20SA2) in the Saginaw Valley and the Nature of the Early Woodland Adaptation in the Great Lakes Region*. Museum of Anthropology, Anthropological Papers 70. Ann Arbor: University of Michigan.

Pacheco, P. J. 1988. Ohio Middle Woodland Settlement Variability in the Upper Licking River Drainage. *Journal of the Steward Anthropological Society* 18:87–117.

———. 1989. Spatial Distribution of Ohio Woodland Period Mounds in the Lower Muskingum River Drainage. In *Anthropology: Unity in Diversity*. Department of Anthropology, Occasional Papers No. 4. Edited by M. Sidky, J. Foradas, and P. J. Pacheco, 20–33. Columbus: Ohio State University.

———. 1993. Ohio Hopewell Settlement Patterns: An Application of the Vacant Center Model to Middle Woodland Period Intracommunity Settlement Variability in the Upper Licking River Valley. Ph.D. dissertation, Department of Anthropology, Ohio State University, Columbus.

———. 1996a. Ohio Hopewell Regional Settlement Patterns. In *A View from the Core: A Synthesis of Ohio Hopewell Archaeology*. Edited by P. J. Pacheco, 16–35. Columbus: Ohio Archaeological Council.

———, ed. 1996b. *A View from the Core: A Synthesis of Ohio Hopewell Archaeology.* Columbus: Ohio Archaeological Council.

———. 1997. Ohio Middle Woodland Intracommunity Settlement Variability: A Case Study from the Licking Valley. In *Ohio Hopewell Community Organization*. Edited by W. S. Dancey and P. J. Pacheco, 41–84. Kent, Ohio: Kent State University Press.

Palmer, E. 1884. Mercier Mounds, Early County, Georgia. Report on file, National Anthropology Archives, American Museum of Natural History, Smithsonian Institution, Washington, D.C.

Paper, J. 1988. *Offering Smoke: The Sacred Pipe and Native American Religion.* Moscow: University of Idaho Press.

Park, S. 1870. *Notes of the Early History of Union Township.* Terre Haute, Ind.: O. J. Smith.

Parker, A. C. 1923. *Seneca Myths and Folktales.* Buffalo, N.Y.: Buffalo Historical Society.

Parker, J. 1976. *The Journals of Jonathan Carver and Related Documents 1766–1770.* St. Paul: Minnesota Historical Society Press.

Parker, K. E. 1989. Archaeobotanical Assemblage. In *The Holding Site: A Hopewell Community in the American Bottom (11–Ms-118)*. American Bottom Archaeology, FAI-270 Site Reports. Edited by A. C. Fortier, T. O. Maher, J. A. Williams, M. C. Meinkoth, K. E. Parker, and L. S. Kelly, 429–464. Urbana: University of Illinois Press.

———. 1990. Botanical Remains. In *Late Archaic and Early Woodland Adaptation in the Lower St. Joseph River Valley, Berrien County, Michigan: The US-31 Berrien County Freeway Project*. Michigan Cultural Resource Investigation Series, Vol. 2. Edited by E. B. Garland, 396–411. Lansing: Michigan Department of Transportation.

———. 1996. Three Corn Kernels and a Hill of Beans. In *Investigating the Archaeological Record of the Great Lake State: Essays in Honor of Elizabeth Baldwin Garland*. Edited by M. B. Holman, J. G. Brashler, and K. Parker, 307–339. Kalamazoo, Mich.: New Issues Press.

Parkman, F. 1946. *The Oregon Trail.* Garden City, N.Y.: Doubleday.

Parks, S. G. 1978. *Test Excavations at 14GE1: A Schultz Focus Habitation Site, at Milford Lake, Kansas*. Report submitted to the Kansas City District, U.S. Army Corps of Engineers by Department of Sociology, Anthropology, and Social Work, Kansas State University.

Parmalee, P. W., A. A. Paloumpis, and N. Wilson. 1972. *Animals Utilized by Woodland Peoples Occupying the Apple Creek Site, Illinois*. Reports of Investigations No. 23. Springfield: Illinois State Museum.

Parmalee, P. W., and G. H. Perino. 1971. A Prehistoric Record of the Roseate Spoonbill in Illinois. *Central States Archaeological Journal* 18:80–85.

Parry, W. J. 1994. Prismatic Blade Technologies in North America. In *The Organization of North American Prehistoric Chipped Stone Tool Technologies.* Museum of Anthropology, International Monographs in Prehistory 7. Edited by P. J. Carr, 87–98. Ann Arbor: University of Michigan.

Parry, W. J., and R. L. Kelly. 1987. Expedient Core Technology and Sedentism. In *The Organization of Core Technology.* Edited by J. K. Johnson and C. A. Morrow, 285–304. Boulder, Colo.: Westview Press.

Pauketat, T. K. 1989. Monitoring Mississippian Homestead Occupation Span and Economy Using Ceramic Refuse. *American Antiquity* 54:288–310.

———. 2001. Practice and History in Archaeology: An Emerging Paradigm. *Anthropological Theory* 1:73–98.

Pauketat, T. K., and T. E. Emerson, eds. 1997. *Cahokia: Domination and Ideology in the Mississippian World.* Lincoln: University of Nebraska Press.

Pauketat, T. K., L. S. Kelly, G. J. Fritz, N. H. Lopinot, S. Elias, and E. Hargrave. 2002. The Residues of Feasting and Public Ritual at Early Cahokia. *American Antiquity* 67:257–279.

Pauketat, T. K., M. A. Rees, and S. L. Pauketat. 1998. *An Archaeological Survey of the Horseshoe Lake State Park, Madison County, Illinois.* Reports of Investigations, No. 55. Springfield: Illinois State Museum.

Paynter, R. W. 1983. Expanding the Scope of Settlement Analysis. In *Archaeological Hammers and Theories.* Edited by J. A. Moore and A. S. Keene, 234–277. New York: Academic Press.

Pederson, J., and J. J. Burks. 2000. *Hopewell Mound Group, Magnetic Survey along the Eastern Edge of the Main Embankment.* Report on file, Hopewell Culture National Historical Park, Chillicothe, Ohio.

———. 2001. Recent Remote Sensing at the Hopewell Mound Group (33Ro27), Ross County, Ohio. Paper presented at the 66th annual meeting of the Society for American Archaeology, New Orleans.

———. 2002. Detecting the Shriver Circle Earthwork, Ross County, Ohio. *Hopewell Archaeology: The Newsletter of Hopewell Archaeology in the Ohio River Valley* 5:10–11.

Pederson, J., J. J. Burks, and W. S. Dancey. 2002. Hopewell Mound Group: Data Collection in 2001. *Ohio Archaeological Council Newsletter* 14:17–19.

Percy, G. W., and D. S. Brose. 1974. Weeden Island Ecology, Subsistence and Village Life in Northwest Florida. Paper presented at the 39th annual meeting of the Society for American Archaeology, Washington, D.C.

Peregrine, P. N. 1991. *The Evolution of Mississippian Society: A World System Perspective.* Madison, Wisc.: Prehistory Press.

———. 1995. Networks of Power: The Mississippian World-System. In *Native American Interactions.* Edited by M. S. Nassaney and K. E. Sassaman, 247–265. Knoxville: University of Tennessee Press.

Perino, G. H. 1961. The Pete Klunk Mound Group, Calhoun County, Illinois: The Archaic and Hopewell Occupations (with an Appendix on the Gibson Mound Group). In *Hopewell and Woodland Site Archaeology in Illinois.* Bulletin 6. Edited by J. A. Brown, 9–124. Springfield: Illinois Archaeological Survey.

———. 1968a. The Pete Klunk Mound Group, Calhoun County, Illinois: The Archaic and Hopewell Occupations. In *Hopewell and Woodland Site Archaeology in Illinois*. Bulletin 6. Edited by J. A. Brown, 9–124. Urbana: Illinois Archaeological Survey.

———. 1968b. The Shiny "Red Stone" That Wouldn't Break. *Central States Archaeological Journal* 15:98–108.

———. n.d. The Bedford Mound Group, Pike County, Illinois. Manuscript on file at the Center for American Archeology, Kampsville, Ill.

Perlès, C. 1992. Systems of Exchange and Organization of Production in Neolithic Greece. *Journal of Mediterranean Archaeology* 5:115–164.

Persson, P., and K.-G. Sjögren. 1995. Radiocarbon and the Chronology of Scandinavian Megalithic Graves. *European Journal of Archaeology* 3:59–88.

Petro, J. H., W. H. Shumate, and M. F. Tabb. 1967. *Soil Survey of Ross County, Ohio*. Washington, D.C.: U.S. Department of Agriculture, Soil Conservation Service.

Phagan, C.J. 1977. Intensive Archaeological Survey of the S.R. 315 Wastewater Treatment Facility Location Known as the DECCO-1 Site (33Dl28). Progress Report submitted to the Board of County Commissioners, Delaware County, Ohio. Report on file, Ohio Historic Preservation Office, Columbus.

Phillips, J. L. 1998. Remarks on Seasonality and Sedentism: Archaeological Perspectives from Old and New World Sites. In *Seasonality and Sedentism: Archaeological Perspectives from Old and New World Sites*. Peabody Museum of Archaeology and Ethnography Bulletin 6. Edited by T. R. Rocek and O. Bar-Yosef, 217–221. Cambridge, Mass.: Harvard University Press.

Phillips, P. 1970. *Archaeological Survey in the Lower Yazoo Basin, Mississippi, 1949–1955*. Papers of the Peabody Museum of Archaeology and Ethnology 60. Cambridge, Mass.: Harvard University Press.

Phillips, P., and J. A. Brown. 1978. *Pre-Columbian Shell Engravings from the Craig Mound at Spiro, Oklahoma*, Part 1. Cambridge, Mass.: Peabody Museum of Archaeology and Ethnology, Harvard University.

Pickard, W. H. 1996. Excavations at Capitolium Mound (33Wn13) Marietta, Washington County, Ohio: A Working Evaluation. In *A View from the Core: A Synthesis of Ohio Hopewell Archaeology*. Edited by P. J. Pacheco, 274–285. Columbus: Ohio Archaeological Council.

Pickard, W. H., and L. Pahdopony. 1995. Paradise Regained and Lost Again: The Anderson Earthwork, Ross County, Ohio (33Ro551). *Hopewell Archaeology: The Newsletter of Hopewell Archaeology in the Ohio River Valley* 1:3–6.

Pickett, A. J. 1851. *History of Alabama and Incidentally, Georgia and Mississippi*. Birmingham, Ala.: Birmingham Magazine Company.

Plog, F. 1974. *The Study of Prehistoric Change*. New York: Academic Press.

Plog, S. E. 1990. Sociopolitical Implications of Stylistic Variation in the American Southwest. In *The Use of Style in Archaeology*. Edited by M. W. Conkey and C. A. Hastorf, 61–72. Cambridge: Cambridge University Press.

Plog, S. E., and M. Hegmon. 1993. The Sample Size-Richness Relation: The Relevance of Research Questions, Sampling Strategies, and Behavioral Variation. *American Antiquity* 58:489-496.

Pluckhahn, T. J. 1998. *Kolomoki Revisited: The 1998 Field Season*. Publication 46. Watkinsville, Ga.: Lamar Institute.

———. 2000. Fifty Years since Sears: Deconstructing the Domestic Sphere at Kolomoki. *Southeastern Archaeology* 19:145–155.

———. 2002. Kolomoki: Settlement, Ceremony and Status in the Deep South, AD 350 to 750. Ph.D. dissertation, Department of Anthropology, University of Georgia, Athens.

———. 2003. *Kolomoki: Settlement, Ceremony, and Status in the Deep South, A.D. 350 to 750.* Tuscaloosa: University of Alabama Press.

Politis, G. 2003. The Theoretical Landscape and the Methodological Development of Archaeology in Latin America. *American Antiquity* 68:245–272.

Poolaw, L. 1993. Foreword. In *The Red Record, the Wallam Olum: The Oldest Native American History.* Edited by D. McCutchen, ix–x. Garden City Park, N.Y.: Avery Publishing Group.

Prahl, E. J. 1970. The Middle Woodland Period of the Lower Muskegon Valley and the Northern Hopewellian Frontier. Ph.D. dissertation, Department of Anthropology, University of Michigan, Ann Arbor.

———. 1991. The Mounds of the Muskegon. In *Pilot of the Grand: Papers in Tribute to Richard E. Flanders,* Part 2. Edited by T. J. Martin and C. E. Cleland. *Michigan Archaeologist* 37(2):59–125.

Preucel, R. W. 1991. Introduction. In *Processual and Postprocessual Archaeologies: Multiple Ways of Knowing the Past.* Center for Archaeological Investigations, Occasional Paper No. 10. Edited by R. W. Preucel, 1–14. Carbondale: Southern Illinois University at Carbondale.

———. 1995. The Postprocessual Condition. *Journal of Archaeological Research* 3: 147–175.

Preucel, R. W., and I. Hodder. 1996. Nature and Culture. In *Contemporary Archaeology in Theory: A Reader.* Edited by R. W. Preucel and I. Hodder, 23–38. Oxford: Blackwell.

Price, T. D., ed. 2000. *Europe's First Farmers.* Cambridge: Cambridge University Press.

Price, T. D., and A. B. Gebauer, eds. 1995. *Last Hunters—First Farmers.* Santa Fe: SAR Press.

Prufer, O. H. 1964a. The Hopewell Complex of Ohio. In *Hopewellian Studies.* Scientific Papers 12. Edited by J. R. Caldwell and R. L. Hall, 35–83. Springfield: Illinois State Museum.

———. 1964b. The Hopewell Cult. *Scientific American* 211:90–102.

———. 1965. *The McGraw Site: A Study in Hopewellian Dynamics.* Scientific Publications 4 (1). Cleveland: Cleveland Museum of Natural History.

———. 1967. The Scioto Valley Archaeological Survey. In *Studies in Ohio Archaeology.* Edited by O. H. Prufer and D. H. McKenzie, 267–328. Cleveland: The Press of Western Reserve University.

———. 1968. *Ohio Hopewell Ceramics: An Analysis of the Extant Collections.* Museum of Anthropology, Anthropology Papers 33. Ann Arbor: University of Michigan.

———. 1996. Core and Periphery: The Final Chapter on Ohio Hopewell. In *A View from the Core: A Synthesis of Ohio Hopewell Archaeology.* Edited by P. J. Pacheco, 408–425. Columbus: Ohio Archaeological Council.

———. 1997a. Fort Hill, 1964: New Data and Reflections on Hopewell Hilltop Enclosures in Southern Ohio. In *Ohio Hopewell Community Organization.* Edited by W. S. Dancey and P. J. Pacheco, 311–330. Kent, Ohio: Kent State University Press.

———. 1997b. How to Construct a Model: A Personal Memoir. In *Ohio Hopewell Community Organization.* Edited by W. S. Dancey and P. J. Pacheco, 105–128. Kent, Ohio: Kent State University Press.

Prufer, O. H., and D. H. McKenzie, eds. 1967. *Studies in Ohio Archaeology.* Kent, Ohio: Kent State University Press.

Prufer, O. H., and O. C. Shane III. 1970. *Blain Village and the Fort Ancient Tradition of Ohio.* Kent, Ohio: Kent State University Press.

Pulszky, F. A., and T. Pulszky. 1853. *White, Red, Black: Sketches of American Society in the United States During the Visit of Their Guests [Louis Kossuth].* New York: Redfield.

Purdy, B. A. 1991. *The Art and Archaeology of Florida's Wetlands.* Boca Raton, Fla.: CRC Press.

Putnam, F. W. 1884. Field Notes on Excavations of the Liberty Group, Ross County, Ohio. Manuscript on file, Peabody Museum of Archaeology and Ethnology, Harvard University, Cambridge, Mass.

———. 1885. Explorations of the Harness Mounds in the Scioto Valley, Ohio. *Peabody Museum 18th and 19th Annual Reports* (1884–1885). Cambridge, Mass.: Harvard University.

———. 1886. Report of the Curator. In *Peabody Museum, Eighteenth and Nineteenth Annual Reports, 1884, 1885.* [*Reports 3 (5–6):401–418.*] Cambridge, Mass.: Harvard University.

Quimby, G. I. 1941a. Hopewell Pottery Types in Michigan. *Papers of the Michigan Academy of Science, Arts, and Letters* 26:489–494.

———. 1941b. The Goodall Focus: An Analysis of Ten Hopewellian Components in Michigan and Indiana. *Indiana Historical Society, Prehistoric Research Series* 2:61–161.

———. 1943. The Ceramic Sequence within the Goodall Focus. *Papers of the Michigan Academy of Science, Arts, and Letters* 28:543–548.

———. 1944. Some New Data on the Goodall Focus. *Papers of the Michigan Academy of Science, Arts, and Letters* 29:419–423.

Rackerby, F. 1983. Some Subsistence Settlement Insight from Macoupin: An Havana Hopewell Site in Jersey County, Illinois. Paper presented at the annual meeting of the Midwest Archaeological Conference, Cleveland.

Rafferty, J. 1983. A New Map of the Ingomar Mounds Site. *Mississippi Archaeology* 18:18–27.

———. 1985. The Archaeological Record on Sedentariness: Recognition, Development, and Implications. In *Advances in Archaeological Method and Theory,* Vol. 8. Edited by M. B. Schiffer, 113-156. New York: Academic Press.

———. 1987. The Ingomar Mounds Site: Internal Structure and Chronology. *Midcontinental Journal of Archaeology* 12:147–173.

Railey, J., ed. 1984. *The Pyles Site (15MS28), a Newtown Village in Mason County, Kentucky.* Occasional Paper No. 1. Lexington, Ky.: William S. Webb Archaeological Society.

———. 1991. Woodland Settlement Trends and Symbolic Architecture in the Kentucky Bluegrass. In *The Human Landscape in Kentucky's Past.* Edited by C. Stout and C. K. Hensley, 56–77. Frankfort: Kentucky Heritage Council.

Rau, C. E. 1873. Ancient Aboriginal Trade in North America. In *Smithsonian Institution Annual Report for 1872,* 348–394. Washington, D.C.: Smithsonian Institution.

Raymond, C. B., R. A. Rothman, and B. Logan. 1993. Formal Chipped Stone Tool Analysis. In *Quarry Creek: Excavation, Analysis and Prospect of a Kansas City Hopewell Site, Fort Leavenworth, Kansas.* Museum of Anthropology, Project Report Series No. 80. Edited by B. Logan, 133–145. Lawrence: University of Kansas.

Redfield, R. 1953. *The Primitive World and Its Transformations.* Ithaca, N.Y.: Cornell University Press.

Redmond, B. G. 1990. The Yankeetown Phase: Emergent Mississippian Cultural Adaptation in the Lower Ohio River Valley. Ph.D. dissertation, Department of Anthropology, Indiana University, Bloomington.

Reed, M. 1990. *The Landscapes of Britain: From the Beginnings to 1914*. London: Routledge.

Reeves, D. M. 1936. A New Discovered Extension of the Newark Works. *Ohio Archaeological and Historical Quarterly* 45:187–193.

Reichel-Dolmatoff, G. 1971. *Amazonian Cosmos: The Sexual and Religious Symbolism of the Tukano Indians*. Chicago: University of Chicago Press.

Reid, K. C. 1976. Prehistoric Trade in the Lower Missouri River Valley: An Analysis of Middle Woodland Bladelets. In *Hopewellian Archaeology in the Lower Missouri River Valley*. Publications in Anthropology 8. Edited by A. E. Johnson, 63–99. Lawrence: University of Kansas.

———. 1980. The Achievement of Sedentism in the Kansas City Region. In *Archaic Prehistory on the Prairie Plains Border*. Publications in Anthropology 12. Edited by A. E. Johnson, 29–42. Lawrence: University of Kansas.

Reidhead, V. A. 1981. *A Linear Programming Model of Prehistoric Subsistence Optimization: A Southern Indiana Example*. Prehistoric Research Series 6 (1). Indianapolis: Indiana Historical Society.

Rein, J. S. 1974. The Complicated Stamped Pottery of the Mann Site, Posey County, Indiana. M.A. thesis, Department of Anthropology, Indiana University, Bloomington.

Renfrew, C. 1973a. *Before Civilisation: The Radiocarbon Revolution and Prehistoric Europe*. London: Jonathan Cape.

———. 1973b. Monuments, Mobilization, and Social Organization in Neolithic Wessex. In *The Explanation of Culture Change: Models in Prehistory*. Edited by C. Renfrew, 539–558. London: Duckworth.

———. 1975. Trade as an Action at a Distance: Questions of Integration and Communication. In *Ancient Civilization and Trade*. Edited by J. A. Sabloff and C. C. Lamberg-Karlovsky, 3–59. Albuquerque: University of New Mexico Press.

———. 1976. Megaliths, Territories, and Populations. In *Acculturation and Continuity in Atlantic Europe*. Edited by S. J. De Laet, 198–220. Brugge: De Tempel.

———. 1977. Alternative Models for Exchange and Spatial Distribution. In *Exchange Systems in Prehistory*. Edited by T. K. Earle and J. E. Ericson, 71–90. New York: Academic Press.

Renfrew, C., and J. F. Cherry, eds. 1986. *Peer Polity Interaction and Socio-political Change*. Cambridge: Cambridge University Press.

Rice, P. M. 1987. *Pottery Analysis: A Sourcebook*. Chicago: University of Chicago Press.

Richards, C. 1996. Monuments as Landscape: Creating the Centre of the World in Late Neolithic Orkney. *World Archaeology* 28:190–208.

Richards, J. D., and R. J. Jeske. 2002. Location, Location, Location: The Temoral and Cultural Context of Late Prehistoric Settlement in Southeast Wisconsin. *Wisconsin Archeologist* 83:32–54.

Rick, J. W. 1978. *Heat Altered Cherts of the Lower Illinois Valley: An Experimental Study in Prehistoric Technology*. Prehistoric Records 2. Evanston, Ill.: Northwestern University Archeological Program.

Riggs, R. 1998. Ceramics, Chronology, and Cultural Change in the Lower Miami River Valley, Southwestern Ohio, circa 100 B.C. to circa A.D. 1650. Ph.D. dissertation, Department of Anthropology, University of Wisconsin, Madison.

Riley, T. J. 1987. Ridged-Field Agriculture and the Mississippian Economic Pattern. In *Emergent Horticultural Economies of the Eastern Woodlands*. Center for Archaeological Investigations, Occasional Paper No. 7. Edited by W. F. Keegan, 295–304. Carbondale: Southern Illinois University at Carbondale.

Riley, T. J., R. Edging, and J. Rossen. 1990. Cultigens in Prehistoric Eastern North America. *Current Anthropology* 31:525–541.

Riley, T. J., G. R. Waltz, C. J. Bareis, A. C. Fortier, and K. E. Parker. 1994. Accelerator Mass Spectrometry (AMS) Dates Confirm Early Zea Mays in the Mississippi River Valley. *American Antiquity* 59:490–497.

Rindos, D. 1980. Symbiosis, Instability, and the Origins and Spread of Agriculture. *Current Anthropology* 21:751–772.

———. 1984. *The Origins of Agriculture: An Evolutionary Perspective.* New York: Academic Press.

Riordan, R. V. 1995. A Construction Sequence for a Middle Woodland Hilltop Enclosure. *Midcontinental Journal of Archaeology* 20:62–104.

———. 1996. The Enclosed Hilltops of Southern Ohio. In *A View from the Core: A Synthesis of Ohio Hopewell Archaeology.* Edited by P. J. Pacheco, 242–257. Columbus: Ohio Archaeological Council.

Ripinsky-Naxon, M. 1993. *The Nature of Shamanism: The Substance and Function of a Religious Metaphor.* Albany: State University of New York Press.

Ritterbush, L. W., and B. Logan. 2000. Late Prehistoric Oneota Population Migration into the Central Plains. *Plains Anthropologist* 45:257–272.

Robertson, J. A., and M. J. Hambacher. 2002. Some New Insights on Michigan Hopewell as Seen from the Converse Site (20KT2), Grand Rapids, Michigan. Symposium Organized for the Midwest Archaeological Conference, Columbus, Ohio.

Robicsek, F. 1978. *The Smoking Gods: Tobacco in Maya Art, History, and Religion.* Norman: University of Oklahoma Press.

Rocek, T. R., and O. Bar-Yosef. 1998. *Seasonality and Sedentism: Archaeological Perspectives from Old and New World Sites.* Peabody Museum of Archaeology and Ethnography, Peabody Museum Bulletin 6. Cambridge, Mass.: Harvard University Press.

Rogers, M. B. 1972. The 46th Street Site and the Occurrence of Allegan Ware in Southwestern Michigan. *Michigan Archaeologist* 18:47–108.

Romain, W. F. 1994. Hopewell Geometric Enclosures: Symbols of an Ancient World View. *Ohio Archaeologist* 44:37–43.

———. 1996. Hopewellian Geometry: Forms at the Interface of Time and Eternity. In *A View from the Core: A Synthesis of Ohio Hopewell Archaeology.* Edited by P. J. Pacheco, 194–209. Columbus: Ohio Archaeological Council.

———. 2000. *Mysteries of the Hopewell Astronomers, Geometers, and Magicians of the Eastern Woodlands.* Akron: Ohio University of Akron Press.

Root, D. 1983. Information Exchange and the Spatial Configurations of Egalitarian Societies. In *Archaeological Hammers and Theories.* Edited by J. A. Moore and A. S. Keene, 193–219. New York: Academic Press.

Roper, D. C. 1979. *Archaeological Survey and Settlement Pattern Models in Central Illinois.* Midcontinental Journal of Archaeology Special Paper No. 2. Kent, Ohio: Kent State University Press.

Roundtree, H. C. 1989. *The Powhatan Indians of Virginia: Their Traditional Culture.* Norman: University of Oklahoma Press.

Rubey, W. W. 1952. *Geology and Mineral Resources of the Hardin and Brussels Quadrangles (In Illinois).* United States Geological Survey Professional Paper 218. Washington, D.C.: Government Printing Office.

Ruby, B. J. 1993. *An Archaeological Investigation of Mann Phase Settlement Patterns in Southwestern Indiana.* Glenn A. Black Laboratory of Archaeology, Reports of Investigations 93–18. Bloomington: Indiana University.

———. 1997a. Research at the Hopeton Earthworks. *Hopewell Archaeology: The Newsletter of Hopewell Archaeology in the Ohio River Valley* 2:2–5.

———. 1997b. The Mann Phase: Hopewellian Subsistence and Settlement Adaptations in the Wabash Lowlands of Southwestern Indiana. Ph.D. dissertation, Department of Anthropology, Indiana University, Bloomington.

———. 1998. *An Archaeological and Historical Investigation of the Nature, Integrity, and Significance of the Spruce Hill Works, Ross County, Ohio.* Reports of Investigations 98–1. Chillicothe: Hopewell Culture National Historical Park.

Ruby, B. J., C. Carr, and D. K. Charles. 2005. Community Organizations in the Scioto, Mann, and Havana Hopewellian Regions: A Comparative Perspective. In *Gathering Hopewell: Society, Ritual, and Ritual Interaction.* Edited by C. Carr and D. Troy Case, 119–176. New York: Kluwer Academic/Plenum Publishing.

Ruby, B. J., J. K. Kearney, and W. R. Adams. 1993. Faunal Remains from the Grabert Site (12 Po 248): A Middle Woodland Occupation in Posey County, Indiana. In *Current Research in Indiana Archaeology and Prehistory, 1991–1992.* Glenn A. Black Laboratory of Archaeology, Research Reports 14. Edited by B. G. Redmond, 46–48. Bloomington: Indiana University.

Ruby, B. J., and C. M. Shriner. 2000. Ceramic Composition and Hopewellian Interactions at the Mann Site, Southwestern Indiana. Paper presented at the Perspectives on Middle Woodland at the Millennium conference, Grafton, Illinois.

Ruhl, K. C. 1992. Copper Earspools from Ohio Hopewell Sites. *Midcontinental Journal of Archaeology* 17:46–79.

———. 1996. Copper Ear Spools in the Hopewell Interaction Sphere: The Temporal and Social Implications. M.A. thesis, Department of Anthropology, Kent State University, Kent, Ohio.

———. 2002. Hopewell Copper Ear Spools. Poster presented at the Midwest Archaeological Conference, Columbus, Ohio.

Ruhl, K. C., and M. F. Seeman. 1998. The Temporal and Social Implications of Ohio Hopewell Ear Spool Design. *American Antiquity* 63:651–662.

Sackett, J. R. 1985. Style and Ethnicity in the Kalahari: A Reply to Wiessner. *American Antiquity* 50:154–159.

Sahlins, M. D. 1968. *Tribesmen.* Englewood Cliffs, N.J.: Prentice-Hall.

———. 1994. Cosmologies of Capitalism: The Trans-Pacific Sector of "The World-System." In *Culture/Power/History.* Edited by N. B. Dirks, G. Eley, and S. B. Ortner, 412–455. Princeton, N.J.: Princeton University Press.

Salisbury, J. H., and C. B. Salisbury. 1862. *Accurate Surveys & Descriptions of the Ancient Earthworks at Newark, Ohio.* Worcester, Mass.: American Antiquarian Society.

Sallnow, M. J. 1981. Communitas Reconsidered: The Sociology of Andean Pilgrimage. *Man* 16:163–182.

Salzer, R. J. 1986a. The Middle Woodland Stage. *Wisconsin Archaeologist* 42:263–282.

———. 1986b. The Woodland Tradition—An Introduction. *Wisconsin Archaeologist* 42:239–242.

———. 1987. Preliminary Report on the Gottschall Site (47Ia80). *Wisconsin Archaeologist* 68:419–472.

———. n.d. The Waukesha Focus: Hopewell in Southeastern Wisconsin. Manuscript on file, Logan Museum of Anthropology, Beloit College, Beloit, Wis.

Salzer, R. J., and M. Stock. 1974. The Wisconsin North Lakes Project: A Preliminary Report. In *Aspects of Upper Great Lakes Anthropology.* Minnesota Prehistoric Archaeology Series, Vol. 11. Edited by E. Johnsen, 40–54. St. Paul: Minnesota Historical Society.

Sanders, D. 1990. Behavioral Conventions and Archaeology: Methods for the Analysis of Ancient Architecture. In *Domestic Architecture and the Use of Space: An Interdisciplinary Cross-Cultural Study.* Edited by S. Kent, 43–72. Cambridge: Cambridge University Press.

Sank, K., and K. Sampson. 1994. A Falcon from the Depths. *Illinois Antiquity* 29:4–8.

Saunders, J. W., R. D. Mandel, R. T. Saucier, E. T. Allen, C. T. Hallmark, J. K. Johnson, E. H. Jackson, C. M. Allen, G. L. Stringer, D. S. Frink, J. K. Feathers, S. Williams, K. J. Gremillion, M. F. Vidrine, and R. Jones. 1997. A Mound Complex in Louisiana at 5400–5000 Years before Present. *Science* 277:1796.

Saville, M. H. 1935. The Ancient Maya Causeways of Yucatan. *Antiquity* 9:67–73.

Scarry, C. M., ed. 1993. *Foraging and Farming in the Eastern Woodlands.* Gainesville: University Press of Florida.

Scheele, W. E. 1960. *The Mound Builders.* Cleveland: World Publishing.

Schele, L., and D. A. Freidel. 1990. *A Forest of Kings: The Untold Story of the Ancient Mayas.* New York: William Morrow.

Schlesier, K. H. 1987. *The Wolves of Heaven: Cheyenne Shamanism, Ceremonies, and Prehistoric Origins.* Norman: University of Oklahoma Press.

———. 1990. Rethinking the Midewiwin and the Plains Ceremonial Called the Sun Dance. *Plains Anthropologist* 35:1–28.

Schmits, L. J. 1987. *Archaeological Survey and Testing at Perry Lake, Jefferson County, Kansas.* Publications in Archaeology No. 2. Shawnee Mission, Kans.: Environmental Systems Analysis.

———. 1989. *Prehistory of the Little Blue River Valley, Western Missouri: Archaeological Investigations at Blue Springs Lake.* Report submitted to the Kansas City District, U.S. Army Corps of Engineers by Environmental Systems Analysis.

Schneider, J. 1991. Was There a Precapitalist World-System? In *Core/Periphery Relations in Precapitalist Worlds.* Edited by C. Chase-Dunn and T. D. Hall, 45–66. Boulder, Colo.: Westview Press.

Schnell, F., V. J. Knight Jr., and G. Schnell. 1981. *Cemochechobee: Archaeology of a Mississippian Ceremonial Center on the Chattahoochee River.* Ripley P. Bullen Monographs in Anthropology and History 3. Gainesville: University of Florida Press.

Schoolcraft, H. R. 1847. *Notes on the Iroquois.* Albany, N.Y.: Erastus H. Pease.

Schultes, R. E. 1970. The Botanical and Chemical Distribution of Hallucinogens. *Annual Review of Plant Physiology* 21:571–598.

———. 1972. An Overview of Hallucinogens in the Western Hemisphere. In *Flesh of the Gods: The Ritual Use of Hallucinogens.* Edited by P. T. Furst, 3–54. New York: Praeger.

Schultz, F., and A. Spaulding. 1948. A Hopewellian Burial Site in the Lower Republican Valley, Kansas. *American Antiquity* 13:306–313.

Schurr, M. R. 1992. *An Archaeological Assessment, Field Reconnaissance, and Test Excavation in St. Joseph County, Indiana.* Report of Investigations 92–2. Notre Dame, Ind.: Department of Anthropology, Archaeology Laboratory, University of Notre Dame.

———. 1993. *Woodland and Early Historic Period Settlement Patterns in the Kankakee Drainage of Laporte County, Indiana.* Report of Investigations 93–1. Notre Dame, Ind.: Department of Anthropology, Archaeology Laboratory, University of Notre Dame.

———. 1997a. The Bellinger Site (12SJ6) and the Origin of the Goodall Tradition. *Archaeology of Eastern North America* 25:125–142.

———. 1997b. Using the Concept of the Learning Curve to Increase the Productivity of Geophysical Surveys. *Archaeological Prospection* 4:69–83.

———. 1998. *The 1997 Archaeological Investigations at the Goodall Site (12 Le 9): A Middle Woodland Mound Group and Habitation Site in Laporte County, Indiana.* Report of Investigations 98–2. Notre Dame, Ind.: Department of Anthropology, Archaeology Laboratory, University of Notre Dame.

———. 1999. *Geophysical Surveys of Middle Woodland Mounds in Northwestern Indiana.* Report of Investigations 99–1. Notre Dame, Ind.: Department of Anthropology, Archaeology Laboratory, University of Notre Dame.

Sciulli, P. W. 1997. Dental Evolution in Prehistoric Native Americans of the Ohio Valley Area. I. Wear and Pathology. *International Journal of Osteoarchaeology* 7: 507–524.

Searle, J. R. 1979. *Expression and Meaning.* Cambridge: Cambridge University Press.

———. 1983. *Intentionality.* Cambridge: Cambridge University Press.

———. 1995. *The Construction of Social Reality.* New York: Free Press.

Sears, W. H. 1951a. *Excavations at Kolomoki, Season I-1948.* University of Georgia Series in Anthropology No. 2. Athens: University of Georgia Press.

———. 1951b. *Excavations at Kolomoki, Season II: Mound E.* University of Georgia Series in Anthropology No. 3. Athens: University of Georgia Press.

———. 1953. *Excavations at Kolomoki, Seasons III and IV: Mound D.* University of Georgia Series in Anthropology No. 4. Athens: University of Georgia Press.

———. 1956. *Excavations at Kolomoki: Final Report.* University of Georgia Series in Anthropology No. 5. Athens: University of Georgia Press.

———. 1962. The Hopewellian Affiliation of Certain Sites on the Gulf Coast of Florida. *American Antiquity* 28:5–18.

———. 1963. *The Tucker Site on Alligator Harbor, Franklin County, Florida.* Contributions of the Florida State Museum, No. 9. Gainesville: University of Florida Press.

———. 1968. The State and Settlement Patterns in the New World. In *Settlement Archaeology.* Edited by K. C. Chang, 134–153. Palo Alto, Calif.: National Press Books.

———. 1973. The Sacred and Secular in Prehistoric Ceramics. In *Variation in Anthropology: Essays in Honor of John C. McGregor.* Edited by D. Lathrop and J. Douglas, 31–42. Urbana: Illinois Archaeological Survey.

———. 1982. *Fort Center: An Archaeological Site in the Lake Okeechobee Basin.* Gainesville: University Press of Florida.

———. 1992. Mea Culpa. *Southeastern Archaeology* 11:66–71.

Seeman, M. F. 1977. Stylistic Variation in Middle Woodland Pipe Styles: The Chronological Implications. *Midcontinental Journal of Archaeology* 2:47–66.

———. 1979a. Feasting with the Dead: Ohio Hopewell Charnel House Ritual as a Context for Redistribution. In *Hopewell Archaeology: The Chillicothe Conference.* Edited by D. S. Brose and N. B. Greber, 39–46. Kent, Ohio: Kent State University Press.

———. 1979b. *The Hopewell Interaction Sphere: The Evidence for Interregional Trade and Structural Complexity.* Prehistoric Research Series 5 (2). Indianapolis: Indiana Historical Society.

———. 1981a. *An Archaeological Survey of the Hopewell Site (33Ro27) and Vicinity, Ross County, Ohio.* Report submitted to the Ohio Historic Preservation Office in partial fulfillment of a survey and planning grant.

———. 1981b. *Phase I (Literature Search) and Phase II (Locational Survey) Investigations of the Chillicothe Correctional Institute, Chillicothe, Ohio.* Report Prepared for the Bureau of Prisons, United States Department of Justice, in fulfillment of Contract No. J100c-068.

———. 1981c. The Question of "Villages" at the Hopewell Site: An Archaeological Survey of the Hopewell Site (33Ro27) and Vicinity, Ross County, Ohio. Paper presented at the Midwestern Archaeological Conference, Madison, Wisconsin.

———. 1986. Adena "Houses" and the Implications for Early Woodland Settlement Models in the Ohio Valley. In *Early Woodland Archeology*. Seminars in Archeology, No. 2. Edited by K. B. Farnsworth and T. E. Emerson. Kampsville, Ill.: Center for American Archeology.

———. 1988. Ohio Hopewell Trophy-Skull Artifacts as Evidence for Competition in Middle Woodland Societies circa 50 B.C.–A.D. 350. *American Antiquity* 53:565–577.

———. 1992a. *Report on the Age, Affiliation, and Significance of the GE Site (12 Po 885)*. Submitted to the United States Attorney's Office (draft copy).

———. 1992b. Woodland Traditions in the Midcontinent: A Comparison of Three Regional Sequences. *Research in Economic Anthropology, Supplement* 6:3–46.

———. 1995. When Words Are Not Enough: Hopewell Interregionalism and the Use of Material Symbols at the GE Mound. In *Native American Interactions: Multiscalar Analyses and Interpretations in the Eastern Woodlands*. Edited by M. S. Nassaney and K. E. Sassaman, 123–143. Knoxville: University of Tennessee Press.

———. 1996. The Ohio Hopewell Core and Its Many Margins: Deconstructing Upland and Hinterland Relations. In *A View from the Core: A Synthesis of Ohio Hopewell Archaeology*. Edited by P. J. Pacheco, 304–315. Columbus: Ohio Archaeological Council.

———. 1998. *An Archaeological Overview and Assessment of the Harness Group (33Ro22), Ross County, Ohio*. Report submitted to the Hopewell Culture National Historical Park by Research and Sponsored Programs, Kent State University, Kent, Ohio.

———. 2000. The Hopewell Mounds of Ross County, Ohio, and Their Place in a Developing Woodland Landscape. Paper presented at the Woodland Conference, Chillicothe, Ohio.

Seeman, M. F., and F. Soday. 1980. The Russell Brown Mounds: Three Hopewell Mounds in Ross County, Ohio. *Midcontinental Journal of Archaeology* 5:73–116.

Seeman, M. F., and H. D. Wilson. 1984. The Food Potential of Chenopodium for the Prehistoric Midwest. In *Experiments and Observations on Aboriginal Wild Plant Food Utilization in Eastern North America*. Prehistoric Research Series 6 (2). Edited by P. J. Munson, 299–316. Indianapolis: Indiana Historical Society.

Sella, D. 1977. The World System and Its Dangers. *Peasant Studies* 6:29–32.

Service, E. R. 1962. *Primitive Social Organization*. New York: Random House.

Shane, O. C., III. 1971. The Scioto Hopewell. In *Adena: The Seeking of an Identity*. Edited by J. B. K. Swartz, 142–157. Muncie, Ind.: Ball State University.

———. 1973. Report on the Excavation at the High Bank Earthwork, Ross County, Ohio. Paper presented at the annual meeting of the Ohio Academy of Science, Cleveland.

Shelford, V. 1963. *The Ecology of North America*. Urbana: University of Illinois Press.

Shennan, S. 1988. *Quantifying Archaeology*. Edinburgh: Edinburgh University Press.

Shetrone, H. C. 1925. Exploration of the Ginther Mound; the Miesse Mound. *Ohio State Archaeological and Historical Quarterly* 34:154–168.

———. 1926. Explorations of the Hopewell Group of Prehistoric Earthworks. *Ohio Archaeological and Historical Quarterly* 35:1–227.

———. 1930. *The Mound Builders*. New York: Appleton and Company.

———. 1937. Anent the Newark Earthworks. *Museum Echoes* 10:1.

Shetrone, H. C., and E. F. Greenman. 1931. Explorations of the Seip Group of Prehistoric Earthworks. *Ohio Archaeological and Historical Quarterly* 40:343–509.

Shields, W. F. n.d. The Ogden-Fettie Site: An Archaeographic Compendium. Manuscript on file, Illinois State Museum, Springfield.

Shippee, J. M. 1967. *Archaeological Remains in the Area of Kansas City: The Woodland Period, Early, Middle, Late.* Research Series No. 5. Columbia: Missouri Archaeological Society.

Shott, M. J. 1994. Size and Form in the Analysis of Flake Debris: Review and Recent Approaches. *Journal of Archaeological Method and Theory* 1:69–110.

———. 1996. Mortal Pots: On Use Life and Vessel Size in the Formation of Ceramic Assemblages. *American Antiquity* 61:463–482.

Shriver, P. R. 1987. Ohio's White-Tailed Deer and Other Prehistoric and Historic Game and Fur Animals. *Ohio Archaeologist* 37:29–33.

Sieg, L. E., and R. P. Connolly. 1997. 1995 Report of Investigations at Fort Ancient State Memorial, Ohio (33Wa2), Vol. 2, The Gateway 84 Embankment Wall. Manuscript on file, Ohio Historical Society, Columbus.

Siegal, S. 1989. Pharmacological Conditioning and Drug Effects. In *Psychoactive Drugs: Tolerance and Sensitisation.* Edited by M. Emmett-Oglesby, 115–180. Clifton, N.J.: Humana Press.

Silverberg, R. 1968. *Mound Builders of Ancient America.* Greenwich, Conn.: New York Graphic Society.

Silverman, H. 1994. The Archaeological Identification of an Ancient Peruvian Pilgrimage Center. *World Archaeology* 26:1–18.

Skibo, J. M. 1995. The Clay Cooking Pot: An Exploration of Women's Technology. In *Expanding Archaeology.* Edited by J. M. Skibo, W. H. Walker, and A. E. Neilson, 80–91. Salt Lake City: University of Utah Press.

Skibo, J. M., and M. B. Schiffer. 1995. The Clay Cooking Pot: An Exploration of Women's Technology. In *Expanding Archaeology.* Edited by J. M. Skibo, W. H. Walker, and A. E. Neilsen, 80–91. Salt Lake City: University of Utah Press.

Skinner, A. B. 1920. *Medicine Ceremony of the Menomini, Iowa, and Wahpeton Dakota, with Notes on the Ceremony among the Ponca, Bungi, Ojibwa, and Potawatomi.* Indian Notes and Monographs 5. New York: Museum of the American Indian, Heye Foundation.

Slattery, R. n.d. Notes on Excavattions of the Alberts Site. Manuscript on file at the Archaeological Research Laboratory, University of Wisconsin-Milwaukee, Milwaukee.

Smith, B. A. 1975. A Re-analysis of the Mandeville Site, 9 Cla 1, Focusing on Its Internal History and External Relations. Ph.D. dissertation, Department of Anthropology, University of Georgia, Athens.

———. 1979. The Hopewell Connection in Southwest Georgia. In *Hopewell Archaeology: The Chillicothe Conference.* Edited by D. S. Brose and N. B. Greber, 181–187. Kent, Ohio: Kent State University Press.

Smith, B. A., K. C. Egan, W. A. Lovis, and G. W. Monaghan. 1994. Targeting the Marsh: A Reanalysis of Subsistence Patterns and Local Environments at the Schultz Site, Michigan. Paper presented to the Ontario Archaeological Society, Toronto.

Smith, B. D. 1975. *Middle Mississippi Exploitation of Animal Populations.* Museum of Anthropology, Anthropological Papers 57. Ann Arbor: University of Michigan.

———. 1978. *Prehistoric Patterns of Human Behavior.* New York: Academic Press.

———. 1985a. *Chenopodium berlandieri* spp. *jonesianum*: Evidence for a Hopewellian Domesticate from Ash Cave, Ohio. *Southeastern Archaeology* 4:107–133.

———. 1985b. The Role of Chenopodium as a Domesticate in Premaize Garden Systems of the Eastern United States. *Southeastern Archaeology* 4:51–72.

———. 1986. The Archaeology of the Southeastern United States: From Dalton to De Soto, 10,500–500 B.P. In *Advances in World Archaeology,* Vol. 5. Edited by F. Wendorf and A. E. Close, 1–92. New York: Academic Press.

———. 1987. The Independent Domestication of Indigenous Seed-Bearing Plants in Eastern North America. In *Emergent Horticultural Economies of the Eastern Woodlands.* Center for Archaeological Investigations, Occasional Paper No. 7. Edited by W. F. Keegan, 3–47. Carbondale: Southern Illinois University at Carbondale.

———. 1989. Origins of Agriculture in Eastern North America. *Science* 246.

———. 1992a. Hopewellian Farmers of Eastern North America. In *Rivers of Change: Essays on Early Agriculture in Eastern North America.* Edited by B. D. Smith, 201–248. Washington, D.C.: Smithsonian Institution Press.

———, ed. 1992b. *Rivers of Change: Essays on Early Agriculture in Eastern North America.* Washington, D.C.: Smithsonian Institution Press.

———. 1995. *The Emergence of Agriculture.* New York: W. H. Freeman.

———. 2001. Low Level Food Production. *Journal of Archaeological Research* 9:1–43.

———, ed. 2002. *Rivers of Change: Essays on Early Agriculture in Eastern North America.* Paperback edition. Washington D.C.: Smithsonian Institution Press.

———. 2005. Documenting the Transition to Food Production along the Borderlands. In *Current Perspectives on the Late Archaic across the Borderlands.* Edited by R. K. Vierra, 300–317. Austin: University of Texas Press.

Smith, B. D., C. W. Cowan, and M. P. Hoffman. 1992. Is It an Indigene or a Foreigner? In *Rivers of Change: Essays on Early Agriculture in Eastern North America.* Edited by B. D. Smith, 67–100. Washington, D.C.: Smithsonian Institution Press.

Snow, D. R. 1994. *The Iroquois.* Oxford: Blackford Press.

Snow, F. 1998. Swift Creek Design Investigations: The Hartford Case. In *A World Engraved: Archaeology of the Swift Creek Culture.* Edited by J. M. Williams and D. T. Elliott, 61–98. Tuscaloosa: University of Alabama Press.

Snyder, J. F. 1894. Buried Deposits of Hornstone Disks. *Proceedings of the American Association for the Advancement of Science* XLII:318–324.

———. 1895. A Group of Illinois Mounds. *Archaeologist* 3:77–81.

———. 1898. A Group of Illinois Mounds. *The American Archaeologist* 2:16–23.

Snyder, L. M. 1991. Barking Mutton: Ethnohistoric, Ethnographic, Archaeological, and Nutritional Evidence Pertaining to the Dog as a Native American Food Resource on the Plains. In *Beamers, Bobwhites, and Blue-Points: Tributes to the Career of Paul W. Parmalee.* Scientific Papers 23. Edited by J. R. Purdue, W. E. Klippel, and B. W. Styles, 359–378. Springfield: Illinois State Museum.

Speck, F. A. 1915. *Myths and Folk-Lore of the Timiskaming Algonquin and Timagami Ojibwa.* Anthropological Series, No. 9, Geological Survey, Memoir 71. Ottawa: Canada Department of Mines.

———. 1931. *A Study of the Delaware Indian Big House Ceremony.* Harrisburg: Pennsylvania Historical Commission.

Spence, M. W., W. D. Finlayson, and R. H. Pihl. 1979. Hopewellian Influences on Middle Woodland Cultures in Southern Ontario. In *Hopewell Archaeology: The Chillicothe Conference.* Edited by D. S. Brose and N. B. Greber, 115–121. Kent, Ohio: Kent State University Press.

Spero, G. B., M. M. Spero, L. G. Dorothy, and A. C. Noecker. 1991. The Armintrout-

Blackman Site: A Middle Woodland Site in the Kalamazoo River Valley. *Michigan Archaeologist* 37:213–254.

Spielmann, K. A. 2002. Feasting, Craft-Specialization, and the Ritual Mode of Production in Small-Scale Societies. *American Anthropologist* 104:195–207.

Springer, J. W. 1981. An Ethnohistorical Study of the Smoking Complex in Eastern North America. *Ethnohistory* 28:217–235.

Squier, E. G., and E. H. Davis. 1848. *Ancient Monuments of the Mississippi Valley.* Smithsonian Contributions to Knowledge 1. Washington, D.C.: Smithsonian Institution.

Staab, M. L. 1984. Peisker: An Examination of Middle Woodland Site Function in the Lower Illinois Valley. Ph.D. dissertation, Department of Anthropology, University of Iowa, Iowa City.

Stafford, B. D. 1985a. Lithic Analysis. In *Smiling Dan: Structure and Function at a Middle Woodland Settlement in the Lower Illinois Valley.* Research Series, Vol. 2. Edited by B. D. Stafford and M. B. Sant, 258–297. Kampsville, Ill.: Center for American Archeology.

———. 1985b. Overview of Material Remains. In *Smiling Dan: Structure and Function at a Middle Woodland Settlement in the Lower Illinois Valley.* Research Series, Vol. 2. Edited by B. D. Stafford and M. B. Sant, 166–182. Kampsville, Ill.: Center for American Archaeology.

———. 1985c. Summary. In *Smiling Dan: Structure and Function at a Middle Woodland Settlement in the Lower Illinois Valley.* Research Series, Vol. 2. Edited by B. D. Stafford and M. B. Sant, 447–455. Kampsville, Ill.: Center for American Archeology.

Stafford, B. D., and M. B. Sant. 1985a. Smiling Dan Phase III Research Design. In *Smiling Dan: Structure and Function at a Middle Woodland Settlement in the Lower Illinois Valley.* Research Series, Vol. 2. Edited by B. D. Stafford and M. B. Sant, 23–31. Kampsville, Ill.: Center for American Archeology.

———, eds. 1985b. *Smiling Dan: Structure and Function at a Middle Woodland Settlement in the Lower Illinois Valley.* Research Series, Vol. 2. Kampsville, Ill.: Center for American Archeology.

Stahl, A. B. 1993. Concepts of Time and Approaches to Analogical Reasoning in Historical Perspective. *American Antiquity* 58:235–260.

Starna, W. A., and J. Relethford. 1985. Deer Densities and Population Dynamics: A Cautionary Note. *American Antiquity* 50:825–832.

Starr, S. F. 1960. The Archaeology of Hamilton County, Ohio. *Journal of the Cincinnati Museum of Natural History* 23(1).

Steeby, M. A. 1997. A Statistical Analysis of the Ceramics from the Dieffenderfer Site (20SJ179), St. Joseph County, Michigan. M.A. thesis, Department of Anthropology, Western Michigan University, Kalamazoo.

Stein, G. J. 1999. Rethinking World-Systems: Power, Distance, and Diasporas in the Dynamics of Interregional Interaction. In *World-Systems Theory in Practice: Leadership, Production, and Exchange.* Edited by P. N. Kardulias, 153–173. Lanham, Md.: Rowman and Littlefield.

Steinen, K. T. 1976. The Weeden Island Ceramic Complex: An Analysis of Distribution. Ph.D. dissertation, Department of Anthropology, University of Florida, Gainesville.

———. 1987. The Balfour Mound: A Weeden Island Mound in South Georgia. Paper presented at the annual meeting of the Southeastern Archaeological Conference, Charleston, South Carolina.

———. 1998. Kolomoki and the Development of Socio-political Organization on the Gulf Coastal Plain. In *A World Engraved: Archaeology of the Swift Creek Culture.* Edited by J. M. Williams and D. T. Elliott, 181–196. Tuscaloosa: University of Alabama Press.

———. 2002. Kolomoki, Swift Creek, and Weeden Island: 53 Years After Willey. Paper presented to the Society for Georgia Archaeology, Ft. Gaines.

Stephenson, K., J. A. Bense and F. Snow. 2002. Aspects of Deptford and Swift Creek on the South Atlantic and Gulf Coastal Plaines. In *The Woodland Southeast.* Edited by D. G. Anderson and R. C. Mainfort Jr., 318–351. Tuscaloosa: University of Alabama Press.

Stevenson, C. M., I. Abdelrehim, and S. W. Novak. 2004. High Precision Measurement of Obsidian Hydration Layers on Artifacts from the Hopewell Site Using Secondary Ion Mass Spectrometry. *American Antiquity* 69:555–567.

Stevenson, K. P., R. F. Boszhardt, C. R. Moffat, P. H. Salkin, T. C. Pleger, J. L. Theler, and C. M. Arzigian. 1997. The Woodland Tradition. *Wisconsin Archaeologist* 78:140–201.

Steventon, R. L., and J. E. Kutzbach. 1983. University of Wisconsin Radiocarbon Dates XX. *Radiocarbon* 25:152–168.

Steward, J. H. 1938. *Basin-Plateau Aboriginal Sociopolitical Groups.* Bureau of American Ethnology, Bulletin 120. Washington, D.C.: Smithsonian Institution.

Stewart, J. D., P. Fralick, R. G. V. Hancock, J. H. Kelley, and E. M. Garret. 1990. Petrographic Analysis and INAA Geochemistry of Prehistoric Ceramics from Robinson Pueblo, New Mexico. *Journal of Archaeological Science* 17:601–625.

Stewart, O. C. 1956. Fire as the First Great Force Employed by Man. In *Man's Role in Changing the Face of the Earth.* Vol. 1. Edited by W. L. Thomas Jr., 115–133. Chicago: University of Chicago Press.

Stoltman, J. B. 1974. *Groton Plantation, an Archaeological Study of a South Carolina Locality.* Monographs of the Peabody Museum 1. Cambridge, Mass.: Harvard University.

———. 1979. Middle Woodland Stage Communities of Southwestern Wisconsin. In *Hopewell Archaeology: The Chillicothe Conference.* Edited by D. S. Brose and N. B. Greber, 122–139. Kent, Ohio: Kent State University Press.

———. 1986. The Prairie Phase: An Early Woodland Manifestation in the Upper Mississippi Valley. In *Early Woodland Archeology.* Seminars in Archeology, No. 2. Edited by K. B. Farnsworth and T. E. Emerson, 121–136. Kampsville, Ill.: Center for American Archaeology.

———. 1990. The Woodland Tradition in the Prairie du Chien Locality. In *The Woodland Tradition in the Western Great Lakes: Papers Presented to Elden Johnson.* Publications in Anthropology No. 4. Edited by G. E. Gibbon, 239–259. Minneapolis: University of Minnesota.

———. 1991. Ceramic Petrography as a Technique for Documenting Cultural Interaction: An Example from the Upper Mississippi Valley. *American Antiquity* 56:103–120.

Stoltman, J. B., and D. A. Baerreis. 1983. The Evolution of Human Ecosystems in the Eastern United States. In *Late Quaternary Environments of the United States,* Vol. 2. Edited by H. E. Wright Jr., 252–270. Minneapolis: University of Minnesota Press.

Stoltman, J. B., and G. W. Christiansen. 2000. The Late Woodland Stage in the Driftless Area of the Upper Mississippi Valley. In *Late Woodland Societies.* Edited by T. E.

Emerson, D. L. McElrath, and A. C. Fortier, 497–524. Lincoln: University of Nebraska Press.

Stoltman, J. B., and R. E. Hughes. 2004. Obsidian in Early Woodland Contexts in the Upper Mississippi Valley. *American Antiquity* 69:751–759.

Stothers, D. M., and T. J. Abel. 1993. Archaeological Reflections of the Late Archaic and Early Woodland Time Periods in the Western Lake Erie Region. *Archaeology of Eastern North America* 21:25–109.

Stothers, D. M., J. R. Graves, S. K. Bechtel, and T. J. Abel. 1994. Current Perspectives on the Late Prehistory of the Western Lake Erie Region: An Alternative to Murphy and Ferris. *Archaeology of Eastern North America* 22:135–196.

Stretton, S. C., L. A. Chapman, and J. G. Brashler. 2000. Investigations in the Hinterlands: An Analysis of Several Archaeological Sites in the Wabasis Creek Watershed. *Michigan Archaeologist* 46:13–74.

Struever, S. 1960. The Kamp Mound Group and a Hopewell Mortuary Complex in the Lower Illinois Valley. M.A. thesis, Department of Anthropology, Northwestern University, Evanston, Illinois.

———. 1964. The Hopewell Interaction Sphere in Riverine–Western Great Lakes Culture History. In *Hopewellian Studies*. Scientific Papers 12. Edited by J. R. Caldwell and R. L. Hall, 85–106. Springfield: Illinois State Museum.

———. 1965. Middle Woodland Culture History in the Great Lakes Riverine Area. *American Anthropologist* 31:211–223.

———. 1968a. A Re-examination of Hopewell in Eastern North America. Ph.D. dissertation, Department of Anthropology, University of Chicago.

———. 1968b. Woodland Subsistence-Settlement Systems in the Lower Illinois Valley. In *New Perspectives in Archeology*. Edited by S. R. Binford and L. R. Binford, 285–312. Chicago: Aldine.

Struever, S., and G. L. Houart. 1972. An Analysis of the Hopewell Interaction Sphere. In *Social Exchange and Interaction*. Museum of Anthropology, Anthropological Papers 46. Edited by E. N. Wilmsen, 47–79. Ann Arbor: University of Michigan.

Struever, S., and K. D. Vickery. 1973. The Beginnings of Cultivation in the Midwest-Riverine Area of the United States. *American Anthropologist* 75:1197–1220.

Stuiver, M., and P. J. Reimer. 1993. Extended [14]C Database and Revised Calib3.0 [14]C Age Calibration Program. *Radiocarbon* 35:215–230.

Stuiver, M., P. J. Reimer, E. Bard, J. W. Beck, G. S. Burr, K. A. Hughen, B. Kromer, G. McCormac, J. van der Plicht, M. Spurk. 1998. INTCAL98 Radiocarbon Age Calibration, 24,000–0 cal BP. *Radiocarbon* 40:1041–1083.

Styles, B. W. 1981. *Faunal Exploitation and Resource Selection: Early Late Woodland Subsistence in the Lower Illinois Valley*. Scientific Papers No. 3. Evanston, Ill.: Northwestern University Archeology Program.

———. 2000. Late Woodland Faunal Exploitation in the Midwestern United States. In *Late Woodland Societies: Tradition and Transformation across the Midcontinent*. Edited by T. E. Emerson, D. L. McElrath, and A. C. Fortier, 77–94. Lincoln: University of Nebraska Press.

Styles, B. W., and W. E. Klippel. 1996. Mid-Holocene Faunal Exploitation in the Southeastern United States. In *Archaeology of the Mid-Holocene Southeast*. Edited by K. Sassaman and D. G. Anderson, 115–133. Gainesville: University Press of Florida.

Styles, B. W., and J. R. Purdue. 1986. Middle Woodland Faunal Exploitation. In *Woodland Period Occupations of the Napoleon Hollow Site in the Lower Illinois Valley*.

Research Series, Vol. 6. Edited by M. D. Wiant and C. R. McGimsey, 513–526. Kampsville, Ill.: Center for American Archeology.

———. 1991. Ritual and Secular Use of Fauna by Middle Woodland Peoples in Western Illinois. In *Beamers, Bobwhites, and Blue-Points: Tributes to the Career of Paul W. Parmalee*. Research Series 2. Edited by J. R. Purdue, W. E. Klippel, and B. W. Styles, 421–436. Springfield: Illinois State Museum.

Styles, B. W., J. R. Purdue, and M. L. Colburn. 1985. Faunal Exploitation at the Smiling Dan Site. In *Smiling Dan: Structure and Function at a Middle Woodland Settlement in the Lower Illinois Valley*. Research Series, Vol. 2. Edited by B. D. Stafford and M. B. Sant, 402–435. Kampsville, Ill.: Center for American Archeology.

Styles, T. R. 1985. *Holocene and Late Pleistocene Geology of the Napoleon Hollow Site in the Lower Illinois Valley*. Research Series, Vol. 5. Kampsville, Ill.: Center for American Archeology.

Sumner, W. M. 1989. Population and Settlement Area: An Example from Iran. *American Anthropologist* 91:631–641.

Sunderhaus, T. K., and J. K. Blosser. 2001. *Pedestrian Survey, Fort Ancient State Memorial in Warren County, Ohio 33 Wa2, 1996–2000*. Manuscript on file, Ohio Historical Society, Columbus.

Sunderhaus, T. K., R. Riggs, and F. L. Cowan. 2001. The Smith Site: A Small Hopewell Site Overlooking the Stubbs Earthworks. *Ohio Archaeological Council Newsletter* 13:5–12.

Swanton, J. R. 1922. *Early History of the Creek Indians and Their Neighbors*. Bulletin No. 73. Washington, D.C.: Bureau of American Ethnology.

———. 1931. Modern Square Grounds of the Creek Indians. In *Smithsonian Miscellaneous Collections*, 73:1–46. Washington, D.C.: Smithsonian Institution.

———. 1946. *Indians of the Southeastern United States*. Bulletin 137. Washington, D.C.: Bureau of American Ethnology.

Tainter, J. A. 1977. Woodland Social Change in West-Central Illinois. *Midcontinental Journal of Archaeology* 2:67–98.

———. 1978. Mortuary Practices and the Study of Social Systems. In *Advances in Archaeological Method and Theory*, Vol. 1. Edited by M. B. Schiffer, 105–141. New York: Academic Press.

———. 1983. Woodland Social Change in the Central Midwest: A Review and Evaluation of Interpretive Trends. *North American Archaeologist* 4:141–161.

Taylor, W. E., Jr. 1958. Report of Archaeological Survey of the Illinois River Valley. In *The Pool and Irving Villages: A Study of Hopewell Occupation in the Illinois River Valley*. Edited by J. C. McGregor, 193–208. Urbana: University of Illinois Press.

Theler, J. L. 1981. An Archaeological Survey of Mill Coulee and the Adjacent Uplands of Crawford County, Wisconsin—1979. *Wisconsin Archaeologist* 26:168–205.

———. 1986. The Early Woodland Component at the Mill Pond Site, Wisconsin. In *Early Woodland Archeology*. Seminars in Archeology, No. 2. Edited by K. B. Farnsworth and T. E. Emerson, 137–158. Kampsville, Ill.: Center for American Archeology.

———. 1987. *Woodland Tradition Economic Strategies: Animal Resource Utilization in Southwest Wisconsin and Northeastern Iowa*. Report 17. Office of the State Archaeologist, University of Iowa, Iowa City.

Thomas, C. 1894. *Report on the Mound Explorations of the Bureau of Ethnology*. Twelfth Annual Report of the Bureau of Ethnology to the Secretary of the Smithsonian Institution, 1890–91. Washington, D.C.: Smithsonian Institution.

Thomas, J. 1991. *Rethinking the Neolithic.* Cambridge: Cambridge University Press.

———. 1996. *Time, Culture, and Identity.* London: Routledge.

Tilley, C. 1994. *A Phenomenology of Landscape.* Oxford: Berg.

Tixier, J. 1974. *Glossary for the Description of Stone Tools, with Special Emphasis to the Epipaleolithic of the Mahgreb.* Newsletter of Lithic Technology, Special Publication, Vol. 1. (Translated by M. H. Newcomer.)

Tjaden, R. 1974. The Cogan Mounds, 23PL125, Platte County, Missouri. *Missouri Archaeological Society Newsletter* No. 284.

Tomak, C. H. 1990. *The Mount Vernon Site: A Hopewell Ceremonial/Burial Site in Posey County, Indiana.* Report submitted to the Indiana Department of Transportation, Indianapolis.

———. 1994. The Mount Vernon Site: A Remarkable Hopewell Mound in Posey County, Indiana. *Archaeology of Eastern North America* 22:1–46.

Tomka, S. A. 1989. Differentiating Lithic Reduction Techniques: An Experimental Approach. In *Experiments in Lithic Technology.* BAR International Series 528. Edited by D. S. Amick and R. P. Mauldin, 137–161. Oxford: Oxford University Press.

Toth, A. 1974. *Archaeology and Ceramics at the Marksville Site.* Museum of Anthropology, Anthropological Papers 56. Ann Arbor: University of Michigan.

———. 1979. The Marksville Connection. In *Hopewell Archaeology: The Chillicothe Conference.* Edited by D. S. Brose and N. B. Greber, 188–199. Kent, Ohio: Kent State University Press.

Townsend, J. B. 1997. Shamanism. In *The Anthropology of Religion: A Handbook.* Edited by S. D. Glazier, 429–469. Westport, Conn.: Greenwood Press.

Tozzer, A. M., ed. 1941. *Landa's Relacion de Las Cosas de Yucatan, a Translation.* Papers of the Peabody Museum of American Archaeology and Ethnology, Vol. 18. Cambridge, Mass.: Harvard University Press.

Transeau, E. N. 1935. The Prairie Peninsula. *Ecology* 26:423–427.

Trigger, B. G. 1998. Archaeology and Epistemology: Dialoguing across the Darwinian Chasm. *American Journal of Archaeology* 102:1–34.

Trombold, C. D., ed. 1991. *Ancient Road Networks and Settlement Hierarchies in the New World.* Cambridge: Cambridge University Press.

Tschauner, H. 1996. Middle-Range Theory, Behavioral Archaeology, and Postempiricist Philosophy of Science in Archaeology. *Journal of Archaeological Method and Theory* 3:1–30.

Turner, V. 1974. *Dramas, Fields, and Metaphors: Symbolic Action in Human Society.* Ithaca, N.Y.: Cornell University Press.

Tykot, R. 1996. Obsidian Procurement and Distribution in the Central and Western Mediterranean. *Journal of Mediterranean Archaeology* 9:39–82.

USDA (United States Department of Agriculture). 1976. *Ohio Drainage Guide.* Jointly prepared by the U.S. Department of Agriculture, Soil Conservation Service, Ohio State University Cooperative Extension Service, Ohio Department of Natural Resources, Division of Lands and Soil.

USGS (United States Geological Survey). 1916. Morrow, Ohio, Quadrangle. Washington, D.C.: United States Department of the Interior.

Van Gilder, C., and D. K. Charles. 2003. Archaeology as Cultural Encounter: The Legacy of Hopewell. In *Theory, Method, and Practice in Modern Archaeology.* Edited by R. J. Jeske and D. K. Charles, 114–129. Westport, Conn.: Praeger.

Van Langen, H. 1986. The Klug Site, a Middle Woodland Camp and Refuse Site in Ozaukee, County, Wisconsin. *Wisconsin Archaeologist* 67:128–152.

Van Nest, J. 1990. *Archeological Geology in the Sny Bottom of the Mississippi River Valley, Western Illinois.* Report of Investigations 193. Kampsville, Ill.: Center for American Archeology.

———. 1997. Late Quaternary Geology, Archeology, and Vegetation in West-Central Illinois: A Study in Geoarcheology. Ph.D. dissertation, Department of Geology, University of Iowa, Iowa City.

———. 1998. Geological Investigations at the Mound House Site (Appendix 3). In *Staging Ritual: Hopewell Ceremonialism at the Mound House Site, Greene County, Illinois.* Studies in Archeology and History, No. 1. J. E. Buikstra, D. K. Charles, and G. F. M. Rakita, pp. 118–173. Kampsville, Ill.: Center for American Archeology.

———. 2000. Geoarchaeological Reconnaissance of the Baehr-Gust Mound Group, Brown County, Illinois (appendix B, pp. 394–438). In Animal Exploitation and the Middle to Late Woodland Transition: A Comparison of Animal Use at Mound Centers and Hamlets in the Lower and Central Illinois Valleys. Ph.D. dissertation by J. Z. Holt, Department of Anthropology, New York University.

Van Nest, J., and D. L. Asch. 2001. The Illinois Hopewell Mounds at Kamp: Reinterpreting a 40–Year-Old Excavation from a Geoarchaeological Perspective. Paper presented at the 66th annual meeting of the Society for American Archaeology, New Orleans.

Van Nest, J., D. K. Charles, J. E. Buikstra, and D. L. Asch. 2001. Sod Blocks in Illinois Hopewell Mounds. *American Antiquity* 66:633–650.

Van Pool, C. S., and T. L. Van Pool. 1999. The Scientific Nature of Postprocessualism. *American Antiquity* 64:33–53.

Vickery, K. D. 1983. The Flintstone Sources. In *Recent Excavations at the Edwin Harness Mound, Liberty Works, Ross County, Ohio.* Midcontinental Journal of Archaeology Special Paper No. 5. Edited by N. B. Greber, 73–85. Kent, Ohio: Kent State University Press.

———. 1996. Flint Raw Material Use in Ohio Hopewell. In *A View from the Core: A Synthesis of Ohio Hopewell Archaeology.* Edited by P. J. Pacheco, 108–127. Columbus: Ohio Archaeological Council.

Voegelin, C. F. 1954. *Walam Olum; Or, Red Score, the Migration Legend of the Lenni Lenape or Delaware Indians.* Indianapolis: Indiana Historical Society.

von Gernet, A. 1990. Review of "Offering Smoke: The Sacred Pipe and Native American Religion" by Jordan Paper. *American Anthropologist* 92:1040–1041.

———. 1992a. Hallucinogens and the Origins of the Iroquoian Pipe/Tobacco/Smoking Complex. In *Proceedings of the 1989 Smoking Pipe Conference.* Edited by C. F. Hayes, 171–185. Rochester, N.Y.: Rochester Museum and Science Center.

———. 1992b. New Directions in the Construction of Prehistoric Amerindian Belief Systems. In *Ancient Images, Ancient Thought: The Archaeology of Ideology.* Edited by A. S. Goldsmith, S. Garvie, D. Selin, and J. Smith, 133–139. Calgary: University of Calgary Archaeological Association.

———. 1993. The Construction of Prehistoric Ideation: Exploring the Universality-Idiosyncrasy Continuum. *Cambridge Archaeological Journal* 3:67–81.

———. 1995. Nicotian Dreams: The Prehistory and Early History of Tobacco in Eastern North America. In *Consuming Habits.* Edited by J. Goodman, P. E. Lovejoy, and A. Sherratt, 67–87. London: Routledge.

———. 2000. North American Indigenous *Nicotiana* Use and Tobacco Shamanism: The Early Documentary Record, 1520–1660. In *Tobacco Use by Native North Americans.* Edited by J. C. Williams, 59–80. Norman: University of Oklahoma Press.

von Gernet, A., and P. Timmins. 1987. Pipes and Parakeets: Constructing Meaning in an

Early Iroquoian Context. In *Archaeology as Long-Term History.* Edited by I. Hodder, 31–42. Cambridge: Cambridge University Press.

Wagner, G. E. 1996. Feast or Famine? Seasonal Diet at a Fort Ancient Community. In *Case Studies in Environmental Archaeology.* Edited by E. J. Reitz, L. A. Newsom, and S. J. Scudder, 255–271. New York: Plenum Press.

———. 2000. Tobacco in Prehistoric Eastern North America. In *Tobacco Use by Native North Americans.* Edited by J. C. Williams, pp. 185–201. Norman: University of Oklahoma Press.

Wagner, G. E., and G. J. Fritz. 2002. Up in Smoke? Reassessment of Early Eastern Tobacco. Paper presented at the 67th annual meeting of the Society for American Archaeology, Denver.

Wagner, M. J., M. R. McCorvie, B. Koldehoff, T. J. Martin, and K. E. Parker. 1989. *Phase I, II, and III Archaeological Investigations at Fort Leavenworth, Kansas.* Report submitted to the Kansas City District, U.S. Army Corps of Engineers by American Resources Group.

Walker, W. M. 1952. The Dickison Mound Group, Peoria County, Illinois. In *Hopewellian Communities in Illinois.* Scientific Papers 5. Edited by T. Deuel, 13–42. Springfield: Illinois State Museum.

Wallace, A. F. C. 1966. *Religion: An Anthropological View.* New York: Random House.

Wallerstein, I. 1974. *The Modern World System.* New York: Academic Press.

Walthall, J. A. 1973. Copena: A Tennessee Valley Middle Woodland Culture. Ph.D. dissertation, Department of Anthropology, University of North Carolina, Chapel Hill.

———. 1980. *Prehistoric Indians of the Southeast: Archaeology of Alabama and the Middle South.* Tuscaloosa: University of Alabama Press.

———. 1985. Early Hopewellian Ceremonial Encampments in the South Appalachian Highlands. In *Structure and Process in Southeastern Archaeology.* Edited by R. S. Dickens and H. T. Ward, 243–262. Tuscaloosa: University of Alabama Press.

Walthall, J. A., S. H. Stow, and M. J. Karson. 1980. Copena Galena: Source Identification and Analysis. *American Antiquity* 45:21–42.

Walton, C. C., ed. 1962. *John Francis Snyder: Selected Writings.* Springfield: Illinois State Historical Society.

Walz, G. R., K. Hedman, and G. J. Mullen. 1998. *Report on the Recovery and Analysis of Human Skeletal Remains from the Utica Mounds Group, 11Ls1, in La Salle County, Illinois.* Report on file, Illinois Historic Preservation Agency, Springfield.

Waselkov, G. 1989. Indian Maps of the Colonial Southeast. In *Powhatan's Mantle: Indians in the Colonial Southeast.* Edited by P. Wood, G. Waselkov, and M. Hatley, 292–343. Lincoln: University of Nebraska Press.

Watson, A. 2001. Composing Avebury. *World Archaeology* 33:296–314.

Watson, P. J. 1986. Prehistoric Gardening and Agriculture in the Midwest and Midsouth. Paper presented at the Midwest Archaeological Conference, Columbus, Ohio.

———. 1988. Prehistoric Gardening and Agriculture in the Midwest and Midsouth. In *Interpretations of Culture Change in the Eastern Woodlands during the Late Woodland Period.* Department of Anthropology, Occasional Papers in Anthropology 3. Edited by R. W. Yerkes, 39–67. Columbus: Ohio State University.

———. 1989. Early Plant Cultivation in the Eastern Woodlands of North America. In *Foraging and Farming: The Evolution of Plant Exploitation.* Edited by D. R. Harris and G. C. Hillman, 555–571. London: Unwin Hyman.

———. 1996. Of Caves and Shell Mounds in West-Central Kentucky. In *Of Caves and Shell Mounds.* Edited by K. C. Karstens and P. J. Watson, 159–164. Tuscaloosa: University of Alabama Press.

Webb, W. S., and R. S. Baby. 1957. *The Adena People—No. 2.* Columbus: Ohio Historical Society.

Webb, W. S., and C. E. Snow. 1945. *The Adena People.* Reports in Anthropology and Archaeology No. 6. Lexington: University of Kentucky.

Wedel, W. R. 1943a. *An Introduction to Kansas Archeology.* Bureau of American Ethnology, Bulletin 174. Washington, D.C.: Smithsonian Institution.

———. 1943b. *Archaeological Investigations in Platte and Clay Counties, Missouri.* United States National Museum, Bulletin 183. Washington, D.C.: Smithsonian Institution.

———. 1959. *An Introduction to Kansas Archeology.* Bureau of American Ethnology, Bulletin 174. Washington, D.C.: Smithsonian Institution.

Weiant, W. 1931. Correspondence to E. Greenman. On file, Ohio Historical Society, Department of Archaeology, Columbus.

Weller von Molsdorff, R. J., J. J. Burks, and J. B. Burcham. 1999. *Phase II Cultural Resource Management Assessment of Sites 33FR1520 and 33FR1521 in Plain Township, Franklin County, Ohio.* Report submitted to EMH&T by Applied Archaeological Services.

Wesson, C. B. 1998. Mississippian Sacred Landscapes: The View from Alabama. In *Mississippian Towns and Sacred Spaces: Searching for an Architectural Grammar.* Edited by R. B. Lewis and C. Stout, 93–122. Tuscaloosa: University of Alabama Press.

Wheatley, D. 1996. The Use of GIS to Understand Regional Variation in Neolithic Wessex. In *New Methods, Old Problems: Geographic Information Systems in Modern Archaeological Research.* Center for Archaeological Investigations, Occasional Paper No. 15. Edited by D. G. Maschner, 75–103. Carbondale: Southern Illinois University Press.

Whitacre, D., and B. Whitacre. 1986. The Whitacre Site (12D246). *Ohio Archaeologist* 36:24–36.

White, G. 1854. *Historical Collections of Georgia.* New York: Pudney and Russell.

Whittle, A. 1996. *Europe in the Neolithic: The Creation of New Worlds.* Cambridge: Cambridge University Press.

———. 1997. *Sacred Mound, Holy Rings. Silbury Hill and the West Kennet Palisade Enclosures: A Later Neolithic Complex in North Wiltshire.* Oxford: Oxbow Books.

Whittlesey, C. 1836. Unpublished map of the Newark Earthworks. E. Squier and E. Davis Papers, on file in the National Archives, Washington, D.C.

———. 1851. *Descriptions of Ancient Works in Ohio.* Smithsonian Contributions to Knowledge. Washington, D.C.: Smithsonian Institution.

Wiant, M. D., and C. R. McGimsey. 1986a. The Middle Woodland Lithic Assemblage. In *Woodland Period Occupations of the Napoleon Hollow Site in the Lower Illinois Valley.* Research Series, Vol. 6. Edited by M. D. Wiant and C. R. McGimsey, 330–363. Kampsville, Ill.: Center for American Archeology.

———, eds. 1986b. *Woodland Period Occupations of the Napoleon Hollow Site in the Lower Illinois Valley.* Research Series, Vol. 6. Kampsville, Ill.: Center for American Archeology.

Wicklein, J. 1994. Spirit Paths of the Anasazi. *Archaeology* 47:36–41.

Wiersum, W. 1968. The Cooper's Shore Site (47RO2), a Late Havana Hopewell Village Site in South Central Wisconsin. M.A. thesis, Department of Anthropology, University of Wisconsin, Madison.

Wiessner, P. 1985. Style or Isochrestic Variation? A Reply to Sackett. *American Antiquity* 50:160–166.

Wilbert, J. 1987. *Tobacco and Shamanism in South America*. New Haven, Conn.: Yale University Press.

Willey, G. R. 1949. *Archaeology of the Florida Gulf Coast*. Smithsonian Miscellaneous Collections, Volume 113. Washington, D.C.: Smithsonian Institution.

Willey, G. R., C. C. DiPeso, D. W. Lathrap, W. A. Ritchie, I. Rouse, and J. H. Rowe. 1956. An Archaelogical Classification of Culture Contact Situations. In *Seminars in Archaeology: 1955*. Memoir 11. Edited by R. Wauchrope, 1<>30. Washington, D.C.: Society for American Archaeology.

Willey, G. R., and P. Phillips. 1958. *Method and Theory in American Archaeology*. Chicago: University of Chicago Press.

Williams, S. 1958. Review of Excavations at Kolomoki: Final Report by William H. Sears. *American Antiquity* 23:321–323.

Willoughby, C. C. 1935. Michabo, the Great Hare: a Patron of the Hopewell Mound Settlement. *American Anthropologist* 37:280–286.

Willoughby, C. C., and E. A. Hooton. 1922. *The Turner Group of Earthworks, Hamilton County, Ohio*. Papers of the Peabody Museum No. 8 (3). Cambridge, Mass.: Harvard University.

Wills, W. 2000. Political Leadership and the Construction of Chacoan Great Houses, A.D. 1020–1140. In *Alternative Leadership Strategies in the Prehispanic Southwest*. Edited by B. Mills, 19–44. Tucson: University of Arizona Press.

Wilson, M. 1963. *Good Company: A Study of Nyakyusa Age Villages*. Boston: Beacon Press.

Winter, J. C. 2000a. Botanical Description of the North American Tobacco Species. In *Tobacco Use by Native North Americans*. Edited by J. C. Williams, 87–127. Norman: University of Oklahoma Press.

———. 2000b. Food of the Gods: Biochemistry, Addiction, and the Development of Native American Tobacco Use. In *Tobacco Use by Native North Americans*. Edited by J. C. Williams, 305–328. Norman: University of Oklahoma Press.

———. 2000c. From Earth Mother to Snake Woman: The Role of Tobacco in the Evolution of Native American Religious Organization. In *Tobacco Use by Native North Americans*. Edited by J. C. Williams, 265–304. Norman: University of Oklahoma Press.

Winters, H. D. 1961. The Adler Mound Group, Will County, Illinois. In *Chicago Area Archaeology*. Bulletin No. 3. Edited by E. A. Bluhm, 57–88. Urbana: Illinois Archaeological Survey.

———. 1968. Value Systems and Trade Cycles of the Late Archaic in the Midwest. In *New Perspectives in Archeology*. Edited by S. R. Binford and L. R. Binford, 175–221. Chicago: Aldine.

———. 1984. The Significance of Chert Procurement and Exchange in the Middle Woodland Traditions of the Illinois Area. In *Prehistoric Chert Exploitation: Studies from the Midcontinent*. Center for Archaeological Investigations, Occasional Paper No. 2. Edited by B. M. Butler and E. E. May, 3–21. Carbondale: Southern Illinois University at Carbondale.

———. 1993. Background Statement for the 1993 Baehr-Gust Project, Versailles, Brown County, Illinois. Manuscript on file at Department of Anthropology, New York University.

Wittry, W. L. 1959. Archaeological Studies of Four Wisconsin Rockshelters. *Wisconsin Archaeologist* 40:137–267.

Witty, C. O., and J. E. Kelly. 1993. *Summary of Archaeological Investigations of the*

Grassy Lake (11–Ms-4) and South Roxana (11–Ms-66) Sites, South Roxana, Madison County, Illinois. Report submitted to the Illinois Department of Transportation, Springfield, by the Contract Archaeology Program, Southern Illinois University at Edwardsville.

Witty, T. A., Jr. 1983. *Four Archeological Sites of the Perry Lake, Kansas.* Anthropological Series No. 11. Topeka: Kansas State Historical Society.

Witty, T. A., Jr., and J. O. Marshall. 1968. *Archeological Survey of the Lower Salt and Plum Creek Valley, Leavenworth County, Kansas.* Anthropological Series No. 4. Topeka: Kansas State Historical Society.

Wobst, M. H. 1977. Stylistic Behavior and Information Exchange. In *For the Director: Research Essays in Honor of James B. Griffin.* Museum of Anthropology, Anthropological Papers 61. Edited by C. E. Cleland, 317–342. Ann Arbor: University of Michigan.

Wolforth, T. R. 1993. The Stueben Phase: A Late Middle Woodland Phase in the Upper Illinois River Valley. Paper presented at the 48th annual meeting of the Society for America Archaeology, St. Louis.

———. 1995. An Analysis of the Distribution of Steuben Punctated Ceramics. *Wisconsin Archaeologist* 76:27–47.

Woods, W. I. 1987. Maize Agriculture and the Late Prehistoric: A Characterization of Settlement Location Strategies. In *Emergent Horticultural Economies of the Eastern Woodlands.* Center for Archaeological Investigations, Occasional Paper No. 7. Edited by W. F. Keegan, 275–294. Carbondale: Southern Illinois University at Carbondale.

Wray, D. E. 1952. Archaeology of the Illinois Valley, 1950. In *Archaeology of Eastern United States.* Edited by J. B. Griffin, 152–164. Chicago: University of Chicago Press.

Wray, D. E., and R. S. MacNeish. 1961. *The Hopewellian and Weaver Occupations of the Weaver Site, Fulton County, Illinois.* Scientific Papers 7. Springfield: Illinois State Museum.

Wright, G. A. 1972. Ohio Hopewell Trade. *Explorer* 14:4–11.

Wright, G. A., H. Chaya, and J. McDonald. 1990. The Location of the Field Museum Yellowstone (F.M.Y., 90) Group Obsidian Source. *Plains Anthropologist* 35:71–74.

Wright, G. A., J. B. Griffin, and A. A. Gordus. 1969. Preliminary Report on Obsidian Samples from Veratic Rockshelter, Idaho. *Tebiwa* 12:27–30.

Wylie, A. 1985. The Reaction against Analogy. In *Advances in Archaeological Method and Theory,* Vol. 8. Edited by M. B. Schiffer, 63–111. New York: Academic Press.

———. 1992. The Interplay of Evidential Constraints and Political Interests: Recent Archaeological Research on Gender. *American Antiquity* 57:15–35.

Wymer, D. A. 1987a. The Middle Woodland–Late Woodland Interface in Central Ohio: Subsistence Continuity amid Cultural Change. In *Emergent Horticultural Economies of the Eastern Woodlands.* Center for Archaeological Investigations, Occasional Paper No. 7. Edited by W. F. Keegan, 201–216. Carbondale: Southern Illinois University at Carbondale.

———. 1987b. The Paleoethnobotanical Record of Central Ohio—100 B.C. to A.D. 800: Subsistence Continuity and Cultural Change. Ph.D. dissertation, Department of Anthropology, Ohio State University, Columbus.

———. 1992. Trends and Disparities: The Woodland Paleoethnobotanical Record of the Mid-Ohio Valley. In *Cultural Variability in Context: Woodland Settlements of the Mid-Ohio Valley.* Midcontinental Journal of Archaeology Special Paper No. 7. Edited by M. F. Seeman, 65–76. Kent, Ohio: Kent State University Press.

———. 1993. Cultural Change and Subsistence: The Middle and Late Woodland Transition in the Mid-Ohio Valley. In *Foraging and Farming in the Eastern Woodlands*. Edited by C. M. Scarry, 138–156. Gainesville: University Press of Florida.

———. 1996. The Ohio Hopewell Econiche: Human-Land Interaction in the Core Area. In *A View from the Core: A Synthesis of Ohio Hopewell Archaeology*. Edited by P. J. Pacheco, 36–53. Columbus: Ohio Archaeological Council.

———. 1997. Paleoethnobotany in the Licking River Valley, Ohio: Implications for Understanding Ohio Hopewell. In *Ohio Hopewell Community Organization*. Edited by W. S. Dancey and P. J. Pacheco, 153–171. Kent, Ohio: Kent State University Press.

Wymer, D. A., B. T. Lepper, and W. H. Pickard. 1992. Recent Excavations at the Great Circle, Newark, Ohio. Paper presented at the Midwest Archaeological Conference, Grand Rapids, Michigan.

Yarnell, R. A. [1969] 1974. Plant Food and Cultivation of the Salts Cave. In *Archaeology of the Mammoth Cave Area*. Edited by P. J. Watson, 113–122. Orlando, Fla.: Academic Press.

———. 1978. Domestication of Sunflower and Sumpweed in Eastern North America. In *The Nature and Status of Ethnobotany*. Museum of Anthropology, Anthropological Papers 67. Edited by R. I. Ford, 289–300. Ann Arbor: University of Michigan.

———. 1993. The Importance of Native Crops during the Late Archaic and Woodland Periods. In *Foraging and Farming in the Eastern Woodlands*. Edited by C. M. Scarry, 11–26. Gainesville: University Press of Florida.

Yeatts, M. L. 1990. A Chemical Characterization of the Ceramics from the McGraw Site in Ohio with Electron Microprobe. M.A. thesis, Department of Anthropology, Arizona State University, Tempe.

Yerkes, R. W. 1986. Late Archaic Settlement and Subsistence on the American Bottom. In *Foraging, Collecting, and Harvesting: Archaic Period Subsistence in the Eastern Woodlands*. Center for Archaeological Investigations, Occasional Paper No. 6. Edited by S. W. Neusius, 225–245. Carbondale: Southern Illinois University at Carbondale.

———. 1987. Seasonal Patterns in Late Prehistoric Fishing Practices in the North American Midwest. *Archaeozoologia* 1:137–148.

———. 1988. The Woodland and Mississippian Traditions in the Prehistory of Midwestern North America. *Journal of World Prehistory* 2:307–358.

———. 1990. Using Microwear Analysis to Investigate Domestic Activities and Craft Specialization at the Murphy Site, a Small Middle Woodland Settlement in Licking County, Ohio. In *The Interpretive Possibilities of Microwear Studies, Aun 14*. Edited by B. Graslund, H. Knutsson, K. Knutsson, and J. Taffinder, 167–176. Uppsala, Sweden: Societas Archaeologica Upsaliensis.

———. 1994. A Consideration of the Function of Ohio Hopewell Bladelets. *Lithic Technology* 19:109–127.

———. 1997. Using Lithic Artifacts to Study Craft Specialization in Ancient Societies. Paper presented at the 99th annual meeting of the Archaeological Institute of America, Chicago.

———. 2002a. Hopewell Tribes: A Study of Middle Woodland Social Organization in the Ohio Valley. In *The Archaeology of Tribal Societies*. Archaeological Series 15. Edited by W. A. Parkinson, 227–245. Ann Arbor, Mich.: International Monographs in Prehistory.

———. 2002b. Using Lithic Artifacts to Study Craft Specialization in Ancient Societies. In *Written in Stone: The Multiple Dimensions of Lithic Analysis*. Edited by R. W. Yerkes and P. N. Kardulias, 17–34. Boston: Rowman and Littlefield, Lexington Books.

Yingst, J. R. 1990. Introduction: A Historical Perspective on Short-Term Middle Wood-land Site Archaeology in West-Central Illinois. *Illinois Archaeology* 2:5–16.

Young, E. W. 1943. Some Notes on Northwestern Indiana and Southwestern Michigan Hopewell. Manuscript on file, Ernest W. Young Collection, Illinois State Museum, Springfield.

Zeisberger, D. [1780] 1910. A History of the Indians. *Ohio Archaeological and Historical Society Publications* 19:12–189.

Zvelebil, M. 1993. Hunters or Farmers: The Neolithic and Bronze Age Societies of North-East Europe. In *Cultural Transformations and Interactions in Eastern Europe*. Edited by J. Chapman and P. Dolvkhanov, 146–162. Avebury: Aldershot.

———. 1995. Hunting, Gathering, or Husbandry? Management of Food Resources by the Late Mesolithic Communities of Temperate Europe. In *Before Farming: Hunter-Gatherer Society and Subsistence*. Supplement to Vol. 12, MASCA Research Papers in Science and Archaeology. Edited by D. Campana, 79–104. Philadelphia: University of Pennsylvania Museum of Archaeology and Anthropology.

———. 1996. The Agricultural Frontier and the Transition to Farming in the Circum-Baltic Region. In *The Origins and Spread of Agriculture and Pastoralism in Eurasia*. Edited by D. R. Harris, 323–345. Washington, D.C.: Smithsonian Institution Press.

Zvelebil, M., and P. Rowley-Conwy. 1986. Foragers and Farmers in Atlantic Europe. In *Hunters in Transition: Mesolithic Societies of Temperate Eurasia and Their Transition to Farming*. Edited by M. Zvelebil, 67–93. Cambridge: Cambridge University Press.

Contributors

Jack K. Blosser is site manager at the Fort Ancient State Memorial, Ohio Historical Society.

James L. Branch is a Geographic Information System (GIS) administrator for Lake County, Ohio.

Janet G. Brashler is professor and curator of anthropology at Grand Valley State University in Allendale, Michigan.

James A. Brown is professor of anthropology at Northwestern University.

Jane E. Buikstra is professor of bioarchaeology and director of the Center for Bioarchaeological Research, School of Evolution and Social Change, Arizona State University.

Jarrod Burks is director of geophysical survey, Ohio Valley Archaeological Consultants, Worthington, Ohio.

A. Martin Byers is retired from Vanier College, Montreal, and is currently a research affiliate in the Department of Anthropology, McGill University, Montreal, Canada.

Robert Chapman is professor of archaeology at the University of Reading, UK.

Douglas K. Charles is professor of anthropology and archaeology at Wesleyan University.

Frank L. Cowan is a consulting archaeologist based in Cincinnati.

William S. Dancey is associate professor of anthropology at Ohio State University.

Arthur L. DesJardins received his M.A. in anthropology from Western Michigan University.

Shannon M. Fie is assistant professor of anthropology at Beloit College in Wisconsin.

Andrew C. Fortier is a senior cultural resource archaeologist with the Illinois Transportation Archaeological Research Program at the University of Illinois, Champaign-Urbana.

Elizabeth B. Garland is professor emerita of anthropology at Western Michigan University.

N'omi B. Greber is curator of archaeology at the Cleveland Museum of Natural History and adjunct associate professor, Department of Anthropology, Case Western Reserve University.

Robert L. Hall is professor emeritus of anthropology at the University of Illinois at Chicago and adjunct curator of Plains and midwestern archaeology and ethnology with the Field Museum, Chicago.

Michael J. Hambacher is principal investigator and senior analyst for Commonwealth Cultural Resources Group, Jackson, Michigan.

Julie Zimmermann Holt is assistant professor of anthropology at Southern Illinois University–Edwardsville.

Richard E. Hughes is director of geochemical research Laboratory, Portola Valley, California.

Richard W. Jefferies is associate professor of anthropology at the University of Kentucky.

Robert J. Jeske is associate professor of anthropology at the University of Wisconsin–Milwaukee.

Bradley T. Lepper is curator of archaeology for the Ohio Historical Society and occasional visiting professor in the Department of Sociology and Anthropology at Denison University.

Brad Logan is research associate professor of anthropology at Kansas State University.

William L. Mangold is senior archaeologist with the Indiana Department of Natural Resources, Division of Historic Preservation and Archaeology.

Terrance J. Martin is curator of anthropology at the Illinois State Museum, Springfield.

Paul J. Pacheco is assistant professor of anthropology at the State University of New York–Geneseo.

Kathryn E. Parker is a consulting ethnobotanist with Great Lakes Ecosystems, Cheboygan, Michigan.

Jennifer Pederson is park achaeologist at Hopewell Culture National Historical Park in Chillicothe, Ohio.

Robert V. Riordan is professor of anthropology and chair of the Department of sociology and anthropology at Wright State University in Dayton, Ohio.

James A. Robertson is technical vice president at Commonwealth Cultural Resources Group, Jackson, Michigan.

Bret J. Ruby is cultural resource manager at Fort Lewis, Washington.

Mark R. Schurr is associate professor of anthropology at the University of Notre Dame.

Mark F. Seeman is professor of anthropology at Kent State University.

Bruce D. Smith is curator of North American archaeology and senior research scientist at the National Museum of Natural History, Smithsonian Institution, Washington, D.C.

Karl T. Steinen is professor of anthropology at the State University of West Georgia.

James B. Stoltman is professor emeritus in the Department of Anthropology, University of Wisconsin–Madison.

Ted S. Sunderhaus is a research associate in the Department of Anthropology, Cincinnati Museum Center.

Julieann Van Nest is a senior scientist of geology and geoarchaeology at the New York State Museum.

Richard W. Yerkes is associate professor of anthropology at Ohio State University.

Index